Lecture Notes in Computer Science 7537

Commenced Publication in 1973
Founding and Former Series Editors:
Gerhard Goos, Juris Hartmanis, and Jan van]

T0216586

Chuan-Kun Wu   Moti Yung
Dongdai Lin (Eds.)

Information Security and Cryptology

7th International Conference, Inscrypt 2011
Beijing, China, November 30 – December 3, 2011
Revised Selected Papers

 Springer

Volume Editors

Chuan-Kun Wu
Chinese Academy of Sciences
Institute of Information Engineering
Beijing 100093, China
E-mail: ckwu@iie.ac.cn

Moti Yung
Google Inc. and Columbia University
Computer Science Department
S.W. Mudd Building
New York, NY 10027, USA
E-mail: motiyung@gmail.com

Dongdai Lin
Chinese Academy of Sciences
Institute of Information Engineering
Beijing 100093, China
E-mail: ddlin@iie.ac.cn

ISSN 0302-9743   e-ISSN 1611-3349
ISBN 978-3-642-34703-0   e-ISBN 978-3-642-34704-7
DOI 10.1007/978-3-642-34704-7
Springer Heidelberg Dordrecht London New York

Library of Congress Control Number: 2012950703

CR Subject Classification (1998): K.6.5, E.3, E.4, F.2.1, D.4.6, J.1, K.4.4

LNCS Sublibrary: SL 4 – Security and Cryptology

Typesetting: Camera-ready by author, data conversion by Scientific Publishing Services, Chennai, India

Printed on acid-free paper

Springer is part of Springer Science+Business Media (www.springer.com)

Preface

This volume contains the papers presented at Inscrypt 2011, the 7th China International Conference on Information Security and Cryptography, which took place in Beijing during November 30 – December 3, 2011. The conference is a leading international event, which has taken place in China annually since 2005. The conference received 80 submissions and the committee decided to accept 24 of them. The program also included 2 invited talks given by Prof. Moti Yung and Prof. Phong Nguyen.

Inscrypt 2011 was co-organized by the State Key Laboratory of Information Security (SKLOIS), Chinese Academy of Sciences and by the Chinese Association for Cryptologic Research (CACR). Support from these organizations was crucial to the success of the conference and we would like to thank the organizations for their continued help and assistance.

The use of the EasyChair system made the management of the conference very convenient and is highly appreciated. We would also like to thank the organizing committee and the technical program committee as well as the external experts who reviewed papers for their efforts in choosing the program and making the conference a reality. Finally, we would like to thank all authors who submitted papers to the conference and all conference attendees whose continued interest and support assures the continuation of the Inscrypt conference series.

May 2012

Chuan-Kun Wu
Moti Yung
Dongdai Lin

Organization

Program Committee

Frederik Armknecht	University of Mannheim, Germany
Claude Carlet	University of Paris 8, France
Aldar Chan	NUS, Singapore
Donghoon Chang	CIST, Korea University
Kefei Chen	Shanghai Jiaotong University, China
Liqun Chen	Hewlett-Packard Laboratories, Bristol, Uk
Seung-Geol Choi	University of Maryland, College Park, USA
Jintai Ding	University of Cincinnati, USA
Dov Gordon	University of Maryland, College Park, USA
Kishan Chand Gupta	Indian Statistical Institute, Kolkata, India
James Hughes	Huawei
Jiwu Jing	Chinese Academy of Sciences, China
Seny Kamara	Microsoft Research
Brian King	Indiana University-Purdue University Indianapolis, USA
Miroslaw Kutylowski	Wroclaw University of Technology, Poland
Albert Levi	Sabanci University, Istanbul, Turkey
Peng Liu	The Pennsylvania State University, USA
Javier Lopez	University of Malaga, Spain
Subhamony Maitra	Indian Statistical Institute, Kolkata, India
Atsuko Miyaji	School of Information Science, JAIST, Japan
Yi Mu	University of Wollongong, Australia
Peng Ning	North Corolina State University, Raleigh, USA
Miyako Ohkubo	NICT, Japan
Raphael Phan	Loughborough University, UK
Josef Pieprzyk	Macquarie University, Sydney, Australia
Kui Ren	Illinois Institute of Technology, Chicago, USA
Yu Sasaki	NTT Corporation, Japan
Tsuyoshi Takagi	Kyushu University, Japan
Huaxiong Wang	Nanyang Technological University, Singapore
Chuankun Wu	Chinese Academy of Sciences, China
Wenling Wu	Chinese Academy of Sciences, China
Chung-Huang Yang	National Kaohsiung Normal University, Taiwan, China
Moti Yung	Google and Columbia University, New York, USA
Erik Zenner	Technical University of Denmark
Rui Zhang	Chinese Academy of Sciences, China

Table of Contents

Adaptively Secure Forward-Secure Non-interactive Threshold
Cryptosystems.. 1
    Benoît Libert and Moti Yung

Cryptanalysis vs. Provable Security 22
    Phong Q. Nguyen

Boosting Scalability in Anomaly-Based Packed Executable Filtering 24
    Xabier Ugarte-Pedrero, Igor Santos, and Pablo G. Bringas

Searching Short Recurrences of Nonlinear Shift Registers via Directed
Acyclic Graphs 44
    Lin Wang, Bing Shen, and TongXu Qiao

Differential and Linear Cryptanalysis Using Mixed-Integer Linear
Programming... 57
    Nicky Mouha, Qingju Wang, Dawu Gu, and Bart Preneel

Adleman-Manders-Miller Root Extraction Method Revisited 77
    Zhengjun Cao, Qian Sha, and Xiao Fan

Multi-pixel Encryption Visual Cryptography 86
    Teng Guo, Feng Liu, and ChuanKun Wu

An Improved Electronic Voting Scheme without a Trusted Random
Number Generator 93
    Yining Liu, Peiyong Sun, Jihong Yan, Yajun Li, and Jianyu Cao

Fault Attacks against the Miller Algorithm in Hessian Coordinates 102
    Jiang Weng, Yunqi Dou, and Chuangui Ma

Benchmarking for Steganography by Kernel Fisher Discriminant
Criterion... 113
    Wei Huang, Xianfeng Zhao, Dengguo Feng, and Rennong Sheng

Improved Tradeoff between Encapsulation and Decapsulation
of HK09 131
    Xianhui Lu, Bao Li, Qixiang Mei, and Yamin Liu

Non-interactive Deniable Authentication Protocols   142
    Haibo Tian, Xiaofeng Chen, and Zhengtao Jiang

On the Probability Distribution of the Carry Cells of Stream Ciphers
F-FCSR-H v2 and F-FCSR-H v3   160
    Haixin Song, Xiubin Fan, Chuankun Wu, and Dengguo Feng

Efficient Self-certified Signatures with Batch Verification   179
    Nan Li, Yi Mu, and Willy Susilo

A Generic Construction from Selective-IBE to Public-Key Encryption
with Non-interactive Opening   195
    Jiang Zhang, Xiang Xie, Rui Zhang, and Zhenfeng Zhang

Fast Tate Pairing Computation on Twisted Jacobi Intersections
Curves   210
    Xusheng Zhang, Shan Chen, and Dongdai Lin

Weak-Key Class of MISTY1 for Related-Key Differential Attack   227
    Yi-bin Dai and Shao-zhen Chen

Cryptanalysis of Reduced-Round KLEIN Block Cipher   237
    Xiaoli Yu, Wenling Wu, Yanjun Li, and Lei Zhang

An Efficient RSA Implementation without Precomputation   251
    Wuqiong Pan, Jiwu Jing, Luning Xia, Zongbin Liu, and Meng Yu

The Stream Cipher Core of the 3GPP Encryption Standard 128-EEA3:
Timing Attacks and Countermeasures   269
    Gautham Sekar

Batching Multiple Protocols to Improve Efficiency of Multi-Party
Computation   289
    Naoto Kiribuchi, Ryo Kato, Takashi Nishide, and Hiroshi Yoshiura

Towards Attack Resilient Social Network Based Threshold Signing   309
    Jian Zhou, Ji Xiang, and Neng Gao

A Ciphertext Policy Attribute-Based Encryption Scheme without
Pairings   324
    Jiang Zhang and Zhenfeng Zhang

Cryptanalysis of Randomized Arithmetic Codes Based on Markov
Model   341
    Liang Zhao, Takashi Nishide, Avishek Adhikari,
    Kyung-Hyune Rhee, and Kouichi Sakurai

Concurrent Non-Malleable Witness Indistinguishable Argument from
Any One-Way Function   363
    Guifang Huang and Lei Hu

Pseudorandom Generators Based on Subcovers for Finite Groups   379
    Chenggen Song, Maozhi Xu, and Chunming Tang

Author Index   393

Adaptively Secure Forward-Secure Non-interactive Threshold Cryptosystems

Benoît Libert[1,*] and Moti Yung[2]

[1] Université catholique de Louvain, ICTEAM Institute, Belgium
[2] Google Inc. and Columbia University, USA

Abstract. Threshold cryptography aims at enhancing the availability and security of decryption and signature schemes by splitting private keys into several (say n) shares (typically, each of size comparable to the original secret key). In these schemes, a quorum of at least $(d \leq n)$ servers needs to act upon a message to produce the result (decrypted value or signature), while corrupting less than d servers maintains the scheme's security. For about two decades, extensive study was dedicated to this subject, which created a number of notable results. So far, most practical threshold signatures, where servers act non-interactively, were analyzed in the limited static corruption model (where the adversary chooses which servers will be corrupted at the system's initialization stage). Existing threshold encryption schemes that withstand the strongest combination of adaptive malicious corruptions (allowing the adversary to corrupt servers at any time based on its complete view), and chosen-ciphertext attacks (CCA) all require interaction (in the non-idealized model) and attempts to remedy this problem resulted only in relaxed schemes. The same is true for threshold signatures secure under chosen-message attacks (CMA).

It was open (for about 10 years) whether there are non-interactive threshold schemes providing the highest security (namely, CCA-secure encryption and CMA-secure signature) with scalable shares (*i.e.*, as short as the original key) and adaptive security. This paper first surveys our ICALP 2011 work which answers this question affirmatively by presenting such efficient decryption and signature schemes within a unified algebraic framework. The paper then describes how to design on top of the surveyed system the first "forward-secure non-interactive threshold cryptosystem with adaptive security."

Keywords. Threshold cryptography, encryption schemes, digital signatures, adaptive corruptions, non-interactivity, forward security.

1 Introduction

Threshold cryptography [27,28,14] avoids single points of failure by splitting cryptographic keys into $n > 1$ shares which are stored by servers in distinct

---

* This author acknowledges the Belgian National Fund For Scientific Research (F.R.S.-F.N.R.S.) for his "Collaborateur scientifique" fellowship and the BCRYPT Interuniversity Attraction Pole.

C.-K. Wu, M. Yung, and D. Lin (Eds.): Inscrypt 2011, LNCS 7537, pp. 1–21, 2012.

locations. Cryptographic schemes are then designed in such a way that at least d out of n servers should contribute to private key operations in order for these to succeed. In (d, n)-threshold cryptosystems (resp. signature schemes), an adversary breaking into up to $d - 1$ servers should be unable to decrypt ciphertexts (resp. generate signatures) on its own.

1.1   Related Work

Designing secure threshold public key schemes has proved to be a highly non-trivial task. For example, the random oracle model [8] was needed to analyze the first chosen-ciphertext secure (or CCA-secure for short) threshold encryption systems put forth by Shoup and Gennaro [50]. Canetti and Goldwasser [19] gave a standard model implementation based on the Cramer-Shoup encryption scheme [20]. Their scheme, however, eliminates random oracles at the expense of using interaction between decryption servers to obtain robustness (*i.e.*, ensure that no dishonest minority deviating from the protocol can prevent uncorrupted servers from successfully decrypting) and to make sure that invalid ciphertexts do not reveal useful information to the adversary. The approach of [19] consists in randomizing the decryption process in such a way that decryption queries on invalid ciphertexts result in meaningless partial decryptions. To avoid decryption servers to jointly generate random values, they can alternatively store a large number of pre-shared secrets. Other chosen-ciphertext-secure threshold cryptosystems were suggested in [3,45,29,11].

NON-INTERACTIVE SCHEMES. Using the innovative Canetti-Halevi-Katz (CHK) methodology [22], Boneh, Boyen and Halevi [11] showed the first *non-interactive* robust CCA-secure threshold cryptosystem with a security proof in the standard model (*i.e.*, without the random oracle idealization): in their scheme, decryption servers can compute their partial decryption result (termed "decryption share") *without* having to talk to each other and, in groups with a bilinear map, decryption shares contain built-in proofs of their validity, which guarantees robustness. These properties were obtained by notably taking advantage of the fact that, using bilinear maps, valid ciphertexts are publicly recognizable in the Boneh-Boyen identity-based encryption system [9]. Similar applications of the CHK methodology were studied in [15,39].

In the context of digital signatures, Shoup [51] described non-interactive threshold signatures based on RSA and providing robustness.

ADAPTIVE CORRUPTIONS. Historically, threshold primitives (including [50,19,29,33,11]) have been mostly studied in a static corruption model, where the adversary chooses which servers it wants to corrupt *before* the scheme is set up. Unfortunately, adaptive adversaries – who can choose whom to corrupt at any time and depending on the previously collected information – are known (see, e.g., [23]) to be strictly stronger and substantially harder to deal with. As discussed in [19], properly handling them sometimes requires to sacrifice useful properties. For example, the Canetti-Goldwasser system can be proved secure against adaptive corruptions when the threshold d is sufficiently small (typically, when $d = O(n^{1/2})$) but this comes at the expense of a lower resilience and schemes supporting a linear number of faulty servers seem preferable.

To address the above concerns, Canetti et al. [18] proposed a method to cope with adaptive corruptions assuming reliable erasures (i.e., players must be able to safely erase their local data when they no longer need them) and also achieve proactive security [47]. In the case of proactive RSA signatures, this approach requires all servers to refresh their shares (by jointly computing a sharing of zero) after each distributed private key operation (effectively making schemes n-out-of-n rather than d-out-of-n for any $d \leq n$). This limitation was removed in [35] and [6], where simpler adaptively secure proactive RSA signatures are described. In 1999, Frankel, MacKenzie and Yung [34,35] showed different techniques to achieve adaptive security while still using erasures.

Later on, Jarecki and Lysyanskaya [37] eliminated the need for erasures and gave an adaptively secure variant of the Canetti-Goldwasser CCA-secure threshold cryptosystem [19]. Unfortunately, their scheme – which is also designed to remain secure in concurrent environments – requires a lot of interaction between decryption servers. Abe and Fehr [4] showed how to extend Jarecki and Lysyanskaya's threshold version of Cramer-Shoup in the universal composability framework but without completely eliminating interaction from the decryption algorithm.

Recently, Qin et al. [48] suggested a non-interactive threshold cryptosystem (more precisely, a threshold broadcast encryption scheme whose syntax is similar to [24,25]) with adaptive security. Its downside is its lack of scalability since private key shares consist of $O(n)$ elements, where n is the number of servers (while, in prior schemes, the share size only depends on the security parameter). Moreover, the security proof requires the threshold d to be at most poly-logarithmic in the security parameter, even if n is polynomial.

1.2 Our Results

FULLY NON-INTERACTIVE ADAPTIVELY SECURE THRESHOLD CRYPTOSYSTEMS. At ICALP 2011 [42], we gave the first robust threshold cryptosystem which is simultaneously chosen-ciphertext secure under adaptive corruptions and non-interactive while being scalable (i.e., providing short private keys). By "non-interactive", we mean that no on-line conversation is needed among decryption servers during the decryption process: each decryption server only sends one message to the combiner that gathers partial decryption results.

Unlike [48], our scheme [42] features constant-size private key shares (where "constant" means independent of d and n) for public keys of comparable size. In addition, it is conceptually simple and relies on assumptions of constant-size whereas [48] relies on a "q-type" assumption where the input is a sequence of the form $(g, g^\alpha, \ldots, g^{(\alpha^q)})$, for some secret $\alpha \in \mathbb{Z}_p$.

The starting point of our system [42] is the identity-based encryption (IBE) system [12,49] proposed by Lewko and Waters [41] and the elegant dual system approach introduced by Waters [52]. The latter has proved useful to demonstrate full security in identity and attribute-based encryption [52,40,41] but, to the best of our knowledge, it has not been applied to threshold cryptosystems so far. It is worth noting that the security proof of our scheme is not simply a direct consequence of applying the CHK paradigm to the Lewko-Waters results [41] as the treatment of adaptive corruptions does not follow from [22,41]. Like [41], our proof uses a sequence of games. While we also use so-called semi-functional decryption shares and ciphertexts as in the IBE setting [41], we have to consider two distinct kinds of semi-functional ciphertexts and an additional step (which aims at making all private key shares semi-functional) is needed in the proof to end up in a game where proving the security is made simple.

Technically speaking, the encryption scheme can be visualized as a variant of the Boneh-Boyen-Halevi threshold system [11] in groups whose order is a product $N = p_1p_2p_3$ of three primes, which are chosen at key generation. Interestingly, if the factorization of N is somehow leaked, the proof of security under static corruptions implied by [11] still applies and only the proof of adaptive security ceases to go through.

In a follow-up work [43], we also described a more general framework, based on very different techniques, for the construction of threshold cryptosystems featuring the same properties with several advantages in terms of efficiency and concrete security.

In the full version of [42], we also gave a non-interactive threshold signature that follows the same line of development and which can be proven secure in the standard model under adaptive corruptions. This appears to be the first security result under adaptive corruptions for non-interactive threshold signatures in the standard model.

NON-INTERACTIVE FORWARD-SECURE THRESHOLD SYSTEMS WITH ADAPTIVE SECURITY. We also present a completely non-interactive threshold cryptosystem with forward-security. Forward-secure cryptographic primitives [5] have their lifetime divided into discrete time intervals at the beginning of which private keys are updated without changing the public key. Their goal is to mitigate the damages key exposures by confining their effect within a certain time frame: when the adversary obtains full access to the private key at a certain period, the scheme becomes insecure from this point forward but past uses of the private key remain safe. Public-key constructions with forward security received much attention in the literature (see [7,2,36,46,21,16] and references therein).

In the threshold setting, forward security guarantees that, even after having broken into d distinct servers, the adversary can obviously compromise future uses of the system but remains unable to abuse it for past periods: whatever was encrypted during past periods remains computationally hidden to the adversary. The combination of forward-secure and threshold mechanisms was suggested for the first time by Abdalla, Miner and Namprempre [1] who argued that both approaches provide complementary security properties. Indeed, breaking into d distinct servers is only worth the effort when the adversary is able to obtain the d-th share sufficiently early in the history of the system. In [1], Abdalla *et al.* provided a way to obtain forward-security in threshold signatures based on factoring. However, their forward-secure threshold signatures require a significant amount of interaction in the signature generation process, but also in the key update algorithm: at the beginning of each time period, all servers have to run an interactive protocol to move their private key shares forward in time. Our construction completely eliminates the need for interaction in the key update mechanism. At the beginning of each time period, decryption servers can autonomously update their private key shares without any input supplied by other parties.

The paper thus gives a security definition for non-interactive forward-secure threshold cryptosystems in the adaptive corruption setting. We then give a concrete realization meeting our security definition. The construction can be seen as a threshold version of the forward-secure public-key encryption scheme put forth by Boneh, Boyen and Goh [10] using groups of composite order to deal with adaptive corruptions in the threshold setting. Using the same design principle, we can also readily obtain forward-secure threshold signatures that are completely non-interactive as well.

1.3   Organization

Section 2 recalls the definitions of threshold cryptosystems. The scheme and its CCA-security are analyzed in Sections 3.1 and 3.2, respectively. In Section 4, we provide a description of our adaptively secure forward-secure threshold encryption scheme. Our threshold signature is presented in the full version of the paper.

2   Background and Definitions

2.1   Definitions for Threshold Public Key Encryption

Definition 1. *A non-interactive (d, n)-threshold encryption scheme is a set of algorithms with the following specifications.*

Setup(λ, d, n)**:** takes as input a security parameter λ and integers $d, n \in \mathsf{poly}(\lambda)$ (with $1 \leq d \leq n$) denoting the number of decryption servers n and the decryption threshold d. It outputs a triple $(PK, \mathbf{VK}, \mathbf{SK})$, where PK is the public key, $\mathbf{SK} = (SK_1, \ldots, SK_n)$ is a vector of n private-key shares and $\mathbf{VK} = (VK_1, \ldots, VK_n)$ is the corresponding vector of verification keys. Decryption server i is given the share (i, SK_i) that allows deriving decryption shares for any ciphertext. For each $i \in \{1, \ldots, n\}$, the verification key VK_i will be used to check the validity of decryption shares generated using SK_i.

Encrypt(PK, M)**:** is a randomized algorithm that, given a public key PK and a plaintext M, outputs a ciphertext C.

Ciphertext-Verify(PK, C)**:** takes as input a public key PK and a ciphertext C. It outputs 1 if C is deemed valid w.r.t. PK and 0 otherwise.

Share-Decrypt(PK, i, SK_i, C)**:** on input of a public key PK, a ciphertext C and a private-key share (i, SK_i), this (possibly randomized) algorithm outputs a special symbol $(i, \perp)$ if **Ciphertext-Verify**$(PK, C) = 0$. Otherwise, it outputs a decryption share $\mu_i = (i, \hat{\mu}_i)$.

Share-Verify(PK, VK_i, C, μ_i): takes as input PK, the verification key VK_i, a ciphertext C and a purported decryption share $\mu_i = (i, \hat{\mu}_i)$. It outputs either 1 or 0. In the former case, μ_i is said to be a *valid* decryption share. We adopt the convention that $(i, \perp)$ is an invalid decryption share.

Combine$(PK, \mathbf{VK}, C, \{\mu_i\}_{i \in S})$: given $PK, \mathbf{VK}, C$ and a subset $S \subset \{1, \ldots, n\}$ of size $d = |S|$ with decryption shares $\{\mu_i\}_{i \in S}$, this algorithm outputs either a plaintext M or $\perp$ if the set contains invalid decryption shares.

CHOSEN-CIPHERTEXT SECURITY. We use a definition of chosen-ciphertext security which is identical to the one of [50,11] with the difference that the adversary can adaptively choose which parties she wants to corrupt.

Definition 2. *A non-interactive (d, n)-Threshold Public Key Encryption scheme is secure against chosen-ciphertext attacks (or IND-CCA2 secure) and adaptive corruptions if no PPT adversary has non-negligible advantage in this game:*

1. *The challenger runs* **Setup**(λ, d, n) *to obtain* PK, $\mathbf{SK} = (SK_1, \ldots, SK_n)$ *and* $\mathbf{VK} = (VK_1, \ldots, VK_n)$. *It gives* PK *and* $\mathbf{VK}$ *to the adversary* $\mathcal{A}$ *and keeps* $\mathbf{SK}$ *to itself.*

2. *The adversary* $\mathcal{A}$ *adaptively makes the following kinds of queries:*

   - *Corruption query:* $\mathcal{A}$ *chooses* $i \in \{1, \ldots, n\}$ *and obtains* SK_i.
   - *Decryption query:* $\mathcal{A}$ *chooses an index* $i \in \{1, \ldots, n\}$ *and a ciphertext* C. *The challenger replies with* $\mu_i = $ **Share-Decrypt**(PK, i, SK_i, C).

3. *$\mathcal{A}$ chooses two equal-length messages M_0, M_1. The challenger flips a fair coin $\beta \xleftarrow{R} \{0, 1\}$ and computes $C^\star = $ **Encrypt**(PK, M_β).*

4. *$\mathcal{A}$ makes further queries as in step 2 but she is not allowed to make decryption queries on the challenge ciphertext $C^\star$.*

5. *$\mathcal{A}$ outputs a bit β' and is deemed successful if (i) $\beta' = \beta$; (ii) no more than $d - 1$ private key shares were obtained by $\mathcal{A}$ (via corruption queries) in the whole game. As usual, $\mathcal{A}$'s advantage is $Adv(\mathcal{A}) = |\Pr[\mathcal{A} \text{ wins}] - \frac{1}{2}|$.*

CONSISTENCY. A (t, n)-Threshold Encryption scheme provides decryption consistency if no PPT adversary has non-negligible advantage in a three-stage game where stages 1 and 2 are identical to those of definition 2. In stage 3, the adversary outputs a ciphertext C and two d-sets of decryption shares $\Phi = \{\mu_1, \ldots, \mu_d\}$ and $\Phi' = \{\mu'_1, \ldots, \mu'_d\}$. The adversary $\mathcal{A}$ is declared successful if

1. **Ciphertext-Verify**$(PK, C) = 1$.
2. Φ and Φ' only consist of valid decryption shares.
3. **Combine**$(PK, \mathbf{VK}, C, \Phi) \neq $ **Combine**$(PK, \mathbf{VK}, C, \Phi')$.

We note that condition 1 aims at preventing an adversary from trivially winning by outputting an invalid ciphertext, for which distinct sets of key shares may give different results. This definition of consistency is identical to the one of [50,11] with the difference that $\mathcal{A}$ can adaptively corrupt decryption servers.

2.2 Bilinear Maps and Hardness Assumptions

We use groups $(\mathbb{G}, \mathbb{G}_T)$ of composite order $N = p_1 p_2 p_3$ endowed with an efficiently computable map $e : \mathbb{G} \times \mathbb{G} \to \mathbb{G}_T$ such that: (1) $e(g^a, h^b) = e(g, h)^{ab}$ for any $(g, h) \in \mathbb{G} \times \mathbb{G}$ and $a, b \in \mathbb{Z}$; (2) if $e(g, h) = 1_{\mathbb{G}_T}$ for each $h \in \mathbb{G}$, then $g = 1_{\mathbb{G}}$. An important property of composite order groups is that pairing two elements of order p_i and p_j, with $i \neq j$, always gives the identity element $1_{\mathbb{G}_T}$.

In the following, for each $i \in \{1, 2, 3\}$, we denote by $\mathbb{G}_{p_i}$ the subgroup of order p_i. For all distinct $i, j \in \{1, 2, 3\}$, we call $\mathbb{G}_{p_i p_j}$ the subgroup of order $p_i p_j$. In this setting, we rely on the following assumptions introduced in [41].

Assumption 1. Given a description of $(\mathbb{G}, \mathbb{G}_T)$ as well as $g \xleftarrow{R} \mathbb{G}_{p_1}, X_3 \xleftarrow{R} \mathbb{G}_{p_3}$ and $\eta \in \mathbb{G}$, it is infeasible to efficiently decide if $\eta \in \mathbb{G}_{p_1 p_2}$ or $\eta \in \mathbb{G}_{p_1}$.

Assumption 2. Let $g, X_1 \xleftarrow{R} \mathbb{G}_{p_1}, X_2, Y_2 \xleftarrow{R} \mathbb{G}_{p_2}, Y_3, Z_3 \xleftarrow{R} \mathbb{G}_{p_3}$. Given a description of $(\mathbb{G}, \mathbb{G}_T)$, a set of group elements $(g, X_1 X_2, Z_3, Y_2 Y_3)$ and η, it is hard to decide if $\eta \in_R \mathbb{G}_{p_1 p_3}$ or $\eta \in_R \mathbb{G}$.

Assumption 3. Let $g \xleftarrow{R} \mathbb{G}_{p_1}, X_2, Y_2, Z_2 \xleftarrow{R} \mathbb{G}_{p_2}, X_3 \xleftarrow{R} \mathbb{G}_{p_3}$ and $\alpha, s \xleftarrow{R} \mathbb{Z}_N$. Given a description of $(\mathbb{G}, \mathbb{G}_T)$, group elements $(g, g^\alpha X_2, X_3, g^s Y_2, Z_2)$ and η, it is infeasible to decide if $\eta = e(g, g)^{\alpha s}$ or $\eta \in_R \mathbb{G}_T$.

3 A Non-interactive CCA2-Secure Threshold Cryptosystem with Adaptive Corruptions

Our starting point is applying the Canetti-Halevi-Katz [22] transform to a (conceptually equivalent) variant of the Lewko-Waters IBE [41] in the same way as [11] derives a CCA2-secure threshold cryptosystem from the Boneh-Boyen IBE [9]. We show that composite order groups and the techniques of [41] make it possible to handle adaptive corruptions in a relatively simple way and without having to refresh private key shares after each private key operation.

To this end, we apply a modification to the IBE scheme [41][Section 3]. The latter encrypts M under the identity $\mathsf{ID} \in \mathbb{Z}_N$ as $(M \cdot e(g, g)^{\alpha \cdot s}, g^s, (u^{\mathsf{ID}} \cdot v)^s)$ for a random exponent $s \in \mathbb{Z}_N$ and where the public key is $(g, u, v, e(g, g)^\alpha)$, with $g, u, v \in \mathbb{G}_{p_1}$. We implicitly use an IBE scheme where messages are encrypted as $(M \cdot e(g, h)^{\alpha \cdot s}, g^s, (u^{\mathsf{ID}} \cdot v)^s)$, where $h \neq g$ and $e(g, h)^\alpha$ is part of the public key.

Another difference is that, in order to ensure the consistency of these scheme (as defined in section 2.1), the ciphertext validation algorithm has to reject all ciphertexts containing components in the subgroup $\mathbb{G}_{p_3}$.

3.1 Description

In the description hereafter, the verification key of the one-time signature is interpreted as an element of $\mathbb{Z}_N$. In practice, longer keys can be hashed into $\mathbb{Z}_N$ using a collision-resistant hash function.

Setup(λ, d, n): given a security parameter $\lambda \in \mathbb{N}$ and integers $d, n \in \mathsf{poly}(\lambda)$ (with $1 \leq d \leq n$), the algorithm does the following.

1. Choose bilinear groups $(\mathbb{G}, \mathbb{G}_T)$ of order $N = p_1 p_2 p_3$, with $p_1, p_2, p_3 > 2^\lambda$.
2. Choose $\alpha \xleftarrow{R} \mathbb{Z}_N$, $g, h, u, v \xleftarrow{R} \mathbb{G}_{p_1}$, $X_{p_3} \xleftarrow{R} \mathbb{G}_{p_3}$ and compute $e(g, h)^\alpha$.
3. Choose a strongly unforgeable one-time signature $\Sigma = (\mathcal{G}, \mathcal{S}, \mathcal{V})$.
4. Choose a polynomial $P[X] = \alpha + \alpha_1 X + \cdots + \alpha_{d-1} X^{d-1} \in \mathbb{Z}_N[X]$, for random coefficients $\alpha_1, \ldots, \alpha_{d-1} \xleftarrow{R} \mathbb{Z}_N$. Define the public key to be

$$PK = \left((\mathbb{G}, \mathbb{G}_T), \ N, \ g, \ e(g, h)^\alpha, \ u, \ v, \ X_{p_3}, \ \Sigma \right)$$

and set private key shares $\mathbf{SK} = (SK_1, \ldots, SK_n)$ as $SK_i = h^{P(i)} \cdot Z_{3,i}$, for $i = 1$ to n, with $Z_{3,1}, \ldots, Z_{3,n} \xleftarrow{R} \mathbb{G}_{p_3}$. Verification keys are then set as $\mathbf{VK} = (VK_1, \ldots, VK_n)$ with $VK_i = e(g, h)^{P(i)}$ for $i = 1$ to n.

The public key PK and the verification key $\mathbf{VK}$ are made publicly available while, for each $i \in \{1, \ldots, n\}$, SK_i is given to decryption server i.

Encrypt(PK, m): to encrypt $m \in \mathbb{G}_T$, generate a one-time signature key pair $(\mathsf{SSK}, \mathsf{SVK}) \leftarrow \mathcal{G}(\lambda)$. Choose $s \xleftarrow{R} \mathbb{Z}_N$ and compute

$$C = \left(\mathsf{SVK}, C_0, C_1, C_2, \sigma \right) = \left(\mathsf{SVK}, \ m \cdot e(g, h)^{\alpha \cdot s}, \ g^s, \ (u^{\mathsf{SVK}} \cdot v)^s, \ \sigma \right),$$

where $\sigma = \mathcal{S}(\mathsf{SSK}, (C_0, C_1, C_2))$.

Ciphertext-Verify(PK, C): parse the ciphertext C as $(\mathsf{SVK}, C_0, C_1, C_2, \sigma)$. Return 1 if $\mathcal{V}(\mathsf{SVK}, (C_0, C_1, C_2), \sigma) = 1$, $e(C_j, X_{p_3}) = 1_{\mathbb{G}_T}$ for $j \in \{1, 2\}$ and $e(g, C_2) = e(C_1, u^{\mathsf{SVK}} \cdot v)$. Otherwise, return 0.

Share-Decrypt(i, SK_i, C): Parse C as $(\mathsf{SVK}, C_0, C_1, C_2, \sigma)$ and SK_i as an element of $\mathbb{G}$. Return $(i, \bot)$ if **Ciphertext-Verify**$(PK, C) = 0$. Otherwise, choose $r \xleftarrow{R} \mathbb{Z}_N$, $W_3, W_3' \xleftarrow{R} \mathbb{G}_{p_3}$, compute and return $\mu_i = (i, \hat{\mu}_i)$, where

$$\hat{\mu}_i = (D_{i,1}, D_{i,2}) = \left(SK_i \cdot (u^{\mathsf{SVK}} \cdot v)^r \cdot W_3, \ g^r \cdot W_3' \right). \tag{1}$$

Share-Verify$(PK, C, (i, \hat{\mu}_i))$: parse C as $(\mathsf{SVK}, C_0, C_1, C_2, \sigma)$. If $\hat{\mu}_i = \bot$ or $\hat{\mu}_i \notin \mathbb{G}^2$, return 0. Otherwise, parse $\hat{\mu}_i$ as a pair $(D_{i,1}, D_{i,2}) \in \mathbb{G}^2$ and return 1 if $e(D_{i,1}, g) = VK_i \cdot e(u^{\mathsf{SVK}} \cdot v, D_{i,2})$. In any other situation, return 0.

Combine$(PK, C, \{(i, \hat{\mu}_i)\}_{i \in S})$: for each $i \in S$, parse the share $\hat{\mu}_i$ as $(D_{i,1}, D_{i,2})$ and return $\bot$ if **Share-Verify**$(PK, C, (i, \hat{\mu}_i)) = 0$. Otherwise, compute $(D_1, D_2) = \left(\prod_{i \in S} D_{i,1}^{\Delta_{i,S}(0)}, \prod_{i \in S} D_{i,2}^{\Delta_{i,S}(0)} \right)$, which equals

$$(D_1, D_2) = \left(h^\alpha \cdot (u^{\mathsf{SVK}} \cdot v)^{\tilde{r}} \cdot \tilde{W}_3, \ g^{\tilde{r}} \cdot \tilde{W}_3' \right),$$

for some $\tilde{W}_3, \tilde{W}_3' \in \mathbb{G}_{p_3}$ and $\tilde{r} \in \mathbb{Z}_{p_1}$. Using (D_1, D_2), compute and output the plaintext $m = C_0 \cdot e(C_1, D_1)^{-1} \cdot e(C_2, D_2)$.

As far as efficiency goes, the ciphertext-validity check can be optimized by choosing $\omega_1, \omega_2 \xleftarrow{R} \mathbb{Z}_N$ and checking that $e(g \cdot X_{p_3}^{\omega_1}, C_2) = e(C_1, (u^{\mathsf{SVK}} \cdot v) \cdot X_{p_3}^{\omega_2})$, which rejects ill-formed ciphertexts with overwhelming probability and saves two pairing evaluations. Similar batch verification techniques apply to simultaneously test d or more decryption shares using only two pairing evaluations[1].

We observe that, as in [11], decryption shares can be seen as signature shares (for a message consisting of the verification key SVK) calculated by decryption servers. In the full version, we show that the underlying threshold signature is secure against chosen-message attacks in the adaptive corruption scenario.

3.2 Security

The security proof departs from approaches that were previously used in threshold cryptography in that we do not construct an adversary against the centralized version of the scheme out of a CCA2 adversary against its threshold implementation. Instead, we directly prove the security of the latter using the dual encryption paradigm [52,41].

Our proof proceeds with a sequence of games and uses semi-functional ciphertexts as in [41], and decryption shares. Still, there are two differences. First, two kinds of semi-functional ciphertexts (that differ in the presence of a component of order p_2 in the target group $\mathbb{G}_T$) have to be involved. The second difference is that we need to introduce semi-functional private key shares at some step of the proof and argue that they cannot be distinguished from real key shares. The proof takes advantage of the fact that, at each step of the sequence, the simulator knows either the $\mathbb{G}_{p_1}$ components of private key shares $\{h^{P(i)}\}_{i=1}^n$ or a "blinded" version $\{h^{P(i)} \cdot Z_{2,i}\}_{i=1}^n$ of those shares, for some $Z_{2,i} \in_R \mathbb{G}_{p_2}$, which suffices to consistently answer adaptive corruption queries.

Theorem 1. *The scheme is IND-CCA2 against adaptive corruptions assuming that Assumption 1, Assumption 2 and Assumption 3 all hold and that Σ is a strongly unforgeable[2] one-time signature.*

Proof. The proof proceeds using a sequence of games including steps similar to [41] and additional steps. As in [52,41], the proof makes use of semi-functional ciphertexts and decryption shares (which are actually private keys in [41]). In addition, we also have to consider semi-functional private key shares. Another difference is that we need two kinds of semi-functional ciphertexts.

- Semi-functional ciphertexts of Type I are generated from a normal ciphertext (C_0', C_1', C_2') and some $g_2 \in \mathbb{G}_{p_2}$, by choosing random $\tau, z_c \xleftarrow{R} \mathbb{Z}_N$ and setting

$$C_0 = C_0', \qquad C_1 = C_1' \cdot g_2^\tau, \qquad C_2 = C_2' \cdot g_2^{\tau z_c}.$$

- Semi-functional ciphertexts of Type II are generated from a normal ciphertext (C_0', C_1', C_2') by choosing random $\tau, z_c, \theta \xleftarrow{R} \mathbb{Z}_N$ and setting

$$C_0 = C_0' \cdot e(g_2, g_2)^\theta, \qquad C_1 = C_1' \cdot g_2^\tau, \qquad C_2 = C_2' \cdot g_2^{\tau z_c}.$$

---

[1] Namely, d shares $\{\mu_i = (D_{i,1}, D_{i,2})\}_{i=1}^d$ can be batch-verified by drawing $\omega_1, \ldots, \omega_d \xleftarrow{R} \mathbb{Z}_N$ and testing if $e(g, \prod_{i=1}^d D_{i,1}^{\omega_i}) = \prod_{i=1}^d VK_i^{\omega_i} \cdot e(u^{SVK} \cdot v, \prod_{i=1}^d D_{i,2}^{\omega_i})$.

[2] Strong unforgeability refers to the infeasibility, after having obtained a message-signature pair (M, σ), of computing a new pair $(M^\star, \sigma^\star) \neq (M, \sigma)$.

○ Semi-functional decryption shares are obtained from a normal decryption share $(D'_{i,1}, D'_{i,2})$ by picking $\gamma, z_k \xleftarrow{R} \mathbb{Z}_N$, $W_3, W'_3 \xleftarrow{R} \mathbb{G}_{p_3}$ and setting

$$D_{i,1} = D'_{i,1} \cdot g_2^{\gamma z_k} \cdot W_3, \qquad D_{i,2} = D'_{i,2} \cdot g_2^{\gamma} \cdot W'_3.$$

○ Semi-functional private key shares $\{SK_i\}_{i=1}^n$ are obtained from normal shares $\{SK'_i\}_{i=1}^n$ by setting $SK_i = SK'_i \cdot Z_{2,i}$, where $Z_{2,i} \xleftarrow{R} \mathbb{G}_{p_2}$, for $i = 1$ to n.

The proof considers a sequence of $q + 6$ games. It starts with the real game Game_{real} followed by $\mathsf{Game}_{restricted}$, $\mathsf{Game}_{restricted}^*$ Game_0, $\mathsf{Game}_1, \ldots, \mathsf{Game}_q$ and finally Game_q^* and Game_{final}.

$\mathsf{Game}_{restricted}$: is identical to Game_{real} with the difference that the challenger $\mathcal{B}$ rejects all post-challenge decryption queries $(\mathsf{SVK}, C_0, C_1, C_2, \sigma)$ for which $\mathsf{SVK} = \mathsf{SVK}^*$, where SVK^* denotes the one-time verification key included in the challenge ciphertext.

$\mathsf{Game}_{restricted}^*$: is identical to $\mathsf{Game}_{restricted}$ with the difference that the adversary $\mathcal{A}$ is not allowed to make decryption queries $(\mathsf{SVK}, C_0, C_1, C_2, \sigma)$ for which $\mathsf{SVK} = \mathsf{SVK}^* \bmod p_2$.

Game_0: is identical to $\mathsf{Game}_{restricted}^*$ but the normal challenge ciphertext is replaced by a semi-functional ciphertext of Type I.

Game_k $(1 \leq k \leq q)$: in this game, the challenge ciphertext is a semi-functional ciphertext of Type I and the challenger $\mathcal{B}$ answers the first k decryption queries by returning semi-functional decryption shares. As for the last $q - k$ decryption queries, they are answered using normal decryption shares.

Game_q^*: is identical to Game_q with the following two differences.

- All private key shares are made semi-functional and thus contain a random $\mathbb{G}_{p_2}$ component.
- The Type I semi-functional challenge ciphertext is traded for a semi-functional ciphertext of Type II.

Game_{final}: is as Game_q^* but the Type II semi-functional challenge ciphertext is replaced by a semi-functional encryption of a random plaintext (instead of M_β). In this game, $\mathcal{A}$ has no information on the challenger's bit $\beta \in \{0, 1\}$ and cannot guess it with better probability than $1/2$.

As in [41], when a semi-functional decryption share is used (in combination with $d - 1$ normal decryption shares) to decrypt a semi-functional ciphertext, decryption only works when $z_k = z_c$, in which case the decryption share is called *nominally* semi-functional. For each $k \in \{1, \ldots, q\}$, the transitions between Game_{k-1} and Game_k is done in such a way that the distinguisher cannot directly decide (*i.e.*, without interacting with $\mathcal{A}$) whether the kth decryption share is normal or semi-functional by generating this share for the challenge verification key SVK^*. Indeed, in such an attempt, the generated decryption share is necessarily either normal or nominally semi-functional, so that decryption succeeds either way.

Moreover, during the transition between Game_q and Game_q^*, we have to make sure that the distinguisher cannot bypass its interaction with the adversary and try to distinguish the two games by itself either. Should it attempt to decrypt the challenge ciphertext using the private key shares, the transition is organized in such a way that decryption succeeds regardless of whether the private key shares (resp. the challenge ciphertext) are normal or semi-functional (resp. semi-functional of Type I or II).

In the full version of [42], it is shown that all games are computationally indistinguishable as long as the one-time signature is strongly unforgeable and Assumptions 1, 2, 3 hold.   □

Unlike [50,11], where consistency holds statistically, we demonstrate consistency in the computational sense and prove the next result in the full version.

Theorem 2. *The scheme provides consistency if Assumption 1 holds.*

4 Non-interactive Forward-Secure Threshold Cryptosystems with Adaptive Security

In this section, we define the syntax of forward-secure non-interactive threshold encryption schemes and their security in the adaptive corruption scenario. We then explain how to confer forward security to our scheme of Section 3.

4.1 Definitions for Forward-Secure Threshold Public Key Encryption

Definition 3. *A non-interactive (d, n)-forward-secure threshold cryptosystem is a set of algorithms with the following specifications.*

Setup(λ, d, n, T)**:** takes as input a security parameter λ and integers $d, n, T \in$ poly(λ) (with $1 \leq d \leq n$) denoting the number of decryption servers n, the decryption threshold d and the number of time periods T. It outputs a triple $(PK, \mathbf{VK}, \mathbf{SK}^{(0)})$, where PK is the public key, $\mathbf{SK}^{(0)} = (SK_1^{(0)}, \ldots, SK_n^{(0)})$ is an initial vector of private-key shares and $\mathbf{VK} = (VK_1, \ldots, VK_n)$ is the corresponding vector of verification keys. Decryption server i is given the share $(i, SK_i^{(0)})$ that allows computing decryption shares for any ciphertext. For each $i \in \{1, \ldots, n\}$, the verification key VK_i will be used to check the validity of decryption shares generated using $SK_i^{(0)}$.

Update$(i, t, SK_i^{(t)})$**:** is a non-interactive key update algorithm run by decryption server $i \in \{1, \ldots, n\}$ at the end of period $t \in \{0, \ldots, T - 2\}$. On input of a private key share $SK_i^{(t)}$ for period t, it outputs an updated private key share $SK_i^{(t+1)}$ for period $t + 1$ and erases $SK_i^{(t)}$.

Encrypt(PK, t, M)**:** is a probabilistic algorithm that takes as input a public key PK, a period number $t \in \{0, \ldots, T - 1\}$ and a plaintext M. It outputs a ciphertext C.

Ciphertext-Verify(PK, t, C)**:** takes as input a public key PK and a ciphertext C. It outputs 1 if C is deemed valid w.r.t. (PK, t) and 0 otherwise.

Share-Decrypt$(PK, t, i, SK_i^{(t)}, C)$**:** takes as input a public key PK, a period
number $t \in \{0, \ldots, T-1\}$, a ciphertext C and a private-key share $(i, SK_i^{(t)})$.
It outputs a special symbol $(i, \perp)$ if **Ciphertext-Verify**$(PK, t, C) = 0$.
Otherwise, it outputs a decryption share $\mu_i = (i, \hat{\mu}_i)$.

Share-Verify(PK, VK_i, t, C, μ_i)**:** takes as input PK, the verification key VK_i,
a ciphertext C and a purported decryption share $\mu_i = (i, \hat{\mu}_i)$. It outputs
either 1 or 0. In the former case, μ_i is said to be a *valid* decryption share.
We adopt the convention that $(i, \perp)$ is an invalid decryption share.

Combine$(PK, \mathbf{VK}, t, C, \{\mu_i\}_{i \in S})$**:** given $PK, \mathbf{VK}, C$ and a subset $S \subset \{1, \ldots, n\}$
of size $d = |S|$ with decryption shares $\{\mu_i\}_{i \in S}$, this algorithm outputs either
a plaintext M or $\perp$ if the set contains invalid decryption shares.

CHOSEN-CIPHERTEXT SECURITY. We use a definition of chosen-ciphertext security which is identical to the one of [50,11] with the difference that the adversary
can adaptively choose which parties it wants to corrupt.

Definition 4. *A non-interactive (d, n)-Threshold Public Key Encryption scheme
is secure against chosen-ciphertext attacks (or IND-CCA2 secure) and adaptive
corruptions if no PPT adversary has non-negligible advantage in this game:*

1. *The challenger runs* **Setup**(λ, d, n) *to obtain a public key PK, an initial
   vector of private key shares* $\mathbf{SK}^{(0)} = (SK_1^{(0)}, \ldots, SK_n^{(0)})$ *and a vector of
   verification keys* $\mathbf{VK} = (VK_1, \ldots, VK_n)$. *It gives PK and* $\mathbf{VK}$ *to the adversary $\mathcal{A}$ and keeps* $\mathbf{SK}^{(0)}$ *to itself. The initial period number is set to $t = 0$.*

2. *The adversary $\mathcal{A}$ adaptively makes the following kinds of queries:*

   - *Update query: when $\mathcal{A}$ decides to move to the next time period, he notifies
     the challenger. If $t < T - 1$, the challenger increments the period number
     t. Otherwise, it returns $\perp$.*
   - *Corruption query: at any time, $\mathcal{A}$ can choose an index $i \in \{1, \ldots, n\}$
     and obtains the current private key share $SK_i^{(t)}$ of server i.*
   - *Decryption query: $\mathcal{A}$ chooses an index $i \in \{1, \ldots, n\}$ and a period-
     ciphertext pair (t, C). The challenger replies with the partial decryption
     $\mu_i = $ **Share-Decrypt**$(PK, t, i, SK_i^{(t)}, C)$.*

3. *When $\mathcal{A}$ decides to enter the challenge phase, he chooses two equal-length
   messages M_0, M_1. The challenger flips a fair coin $\beta \xleftarrow{R} \{0, 1\}$ and computes
   $C^\star = $ **Encrypt**$(PK, t^\star, M_\beta)$, where $t^\star$ is the index of the current time period
   $t^\star$. It is required that no more than $d - 1$ private key shares $SK_i^{(t)}$ be obtained
   by $\mathcal{A}$ throughout periods $t \le t^\star$.*

4. *$\mathcal{A}$ makes further queries as in step 2 but it is not allowed to make decryption
   queries on the challenge ciphertext $C^\star$ for period $t^\star$.*

5. *$\mathcal{A}$ outputs a bit β' and is deemed successful if $\beta' = \beta$. As usual, $\mathcal{A}$'s advantage
   is measured as the distance* $\mathbf{Adv}(\mathcal{A}) = |\Pr[\beta' = \beta] - \frac{1}{2}|$.

4.2   A Construction with Chosen-Plaintext Security against Passive Adversaries

For simplicity, we do not consider chosen-ciphertext security or robustness in this section. However, both features can be added by simply using the same techniques as in Section 3. For this reason, we do not provide an algorithm for verifying the validity of decryption shares here. Later on, we will outline how chosen-ciphertext security and robustness can both be added.

As in [38], we associate time periods with the leaves of a binary tree. As in all existing forward-secure encryption schemes, we only need a Binary Tree encryption system providing selective-node security [22] (i.e. the adversary has to choose the node to attack ahead of time) if we were only aiming for forward security. However, to achieve adaptive security in the threshold setting, we will start from the Lewko-Waters HIBE system.

In the description below, we imagine binary tree of height ℓ where the root (at depth 0) has label ε. When a node at depth $\leq \ell$ has label w, its children are labeled with $w0$ and $w1$. Besides, $\langle t \rangle$ stands for the ℓ-bit representation of integer t. The leaves of the tree correspond to successive time periods in the obvious way, stage t being associated with the leaf labeled by $\langle t \rangle$. Periods are indexed from 0 to $T - 1$ with $T = 2^\ell$. As in [38], partial decryptions are generated using the private key of node $\langle t \rangle$ at stage t where the full private key also includes node keys for all right siblings for nodes on the path from $\langle t \rangle$ to the root. The latter key material allows for key updates from period t to the next one.

Keygen(λ, d, n, T): given a security parameter $\lambda \in \mathbb{N}$, the desired number of time periods $T = 2^\ell$, the number of servers $n \in \mathsf{poly}(\lambda)$ and a threshold $d \in \{1, \ldots, n\}$, do the following.

1. choose bilinear map groups $(\mathbb{G}, \mathbb{G}_T)$ of order $N = p_1 p_2 p_3$, with $p_i > 2^\lambda$ for each $i \in \{1, 2, 3\}$ and $g, h \in \mathbb{G}_{p_1}$.
2. Compute $e(g, h)^\alpha$ for a random $\alpha \xleftarrow{R} \mathbb{Z}_p^*$. Choose $h_0, h_1, \ldots, h_\ell \xleftarrow{R} \mathbb{G}_{p_1}$ and $X_{p_3} \xleftarrow{R} \mathbb{G}_{p_3}$.
3. Define a function $F : \{0,1\}^{\leq \ell} \to \mathbb{G}_{p_1}$, as

$$F(w) = h_0 \cdot \prod_{j=1}^{l} h_j^{w_j}$$

   where $w = w_1 \ldots w_l$ and $w_\tau \in \{0,1\}$ for all $\tau \in \{1, \ldots, l\}$. The public key is

$$PK = \Big(g,\ e(g,h)^\alpha,\ h_0,\ h_1,\ \ldots,\ h_\ell,\ X_{p_3} \Big).$$

4. Choose a random polynomial $P[X]$ of degree $d - 1$ such that $P(0) = \alpha$.
5. For each $i \in \{1, \ldots, n\}$, choose $r_{i,0}, r_{i,1} \xleftarrow{R} \mathbb{Z}_N$ and, for each $b \in \{0,1\}$, $Y_i^b, Z_i^b, R_{i,2}^b, \ldots, R_{i,\ell}^b \xleftarrow{R} \mathbb{G}_{p_3}$ and set

$$\mathsf{sk}_{i,0} = \big(h^{P(i)} \cdot h_0^{r_{i,0}} \cdot Y_i^0,\ g^{r_{i,0}} \cdot Z_i^0,\ h_2^{r_{i,0}} \cdot R_{i,2}^0, \ldots, h_\ell^{r_{i,0}} \cdot R_{i,\ell}^0 \big),$$

$$\mathsf{sk}_{i,1} = \big(h^{P(i)} \cdot (h_0 \cdot h_1)^{r_{i,1}} \cdot Y_i^1,\ g^{r_{i,1}} \cdot Z_i^1,\ h_2^{r_{i,1}} \cdot R_{i,2}^1, \ldots, h_\ell^{r_{i,1}} \cdot R_{i,\ell}^1 \big).$$

Using $\mathsf{sk}_{i,0}$, recursively apply algorithm Extract (defined below) to obtain node keys $\mathsf{sk}_{i,01}, \mathsf{sk}_{i,001}, \ldots \mathsf{sk}_{i,0^{\ell-1}1}$ and $\mathsf{sk}_{i,0^\ell}$.

6. For each $i \in \{1, \ldots, n\}$, the initial private share of server i is defined as
$$SK_{i,0}^{(0)} = \left(\mathsf{sk}_{i,0^\ell}, \{\mathsf{sk}_{i,1}, \mathsf{sk}_{i,01}, \mathsf{sk}_{i,001}, \ldots, \mathsf{sk}_{i,0^{\ell-1}1}\}\right).$$

Extract$(\mathsf{sk}_{i,w_1\ldots w_{k-1}})$: to generate private keys for its children, a node of label $w = w_1 \ldots w_{l-1}$ at level $l-1$ parses its private key into

$$\mathsf{sk}_{i,w_1\ldots w_{l-1}} = (A_{i,0}, A_{i,1}, B_{i,l}, \ldots, B_{i,\ell})$$
$$= \left(h^{P(i)} \cdot F(w_1 \ldots w_{l-1})^{r'_{i,w}} \cdot Y_{i,w}, \ g^{r'_{i,w}} \cdot Z_{i,w}, \right.$$
$$\left. h_l^{r'_{i,w}} \cdot R_{i,w,l}, \ldots, \ h_\ell^{r'_{i,w}} \cdot R_{i,w,\ell}\right),$$

for some $Y_{i,w}, Z_{i,w}, R_{i,w,l}, \ldots, R_{i,w,\ell} \in_R \mathbb{G}_{p_3}$. For each $j \in \{0,1\}$, it chooses $t_j \xleftarrow{R} \mathbb{Z}_N$ as well as random $Y_i'^j, Z_i'^j \xleftarrow{R} \mathbb{G}_{p_3}$, $R_{i,l+1}'^j, \ldots, R_{i,\ell}'^j \xleftarrow{R} \mathbb{G}_{p_3}$ and computes

$$\mathsf{sk}_{i,w_1\ldots w_{l-1}j} = \left(A_{i,0} \cdot B_{i,l}^j \cdot F(w_1 \ldots w_{l-1}j)^{t_j} \cdot Y_i'^j, \ A_{i,1} \cdot g^{t_j} \cdot Z_i'^j, \right.$$
$$\left. B_{i,l+1} \cdot h_{l+1}^{t_j} \cdot R_{i,l+1}'^j, \ldots, \ B_{i,\ell} \cdot h_\ell^{t_j} \cdot R_{i,\ell}'^j\right)$$
$$= \left(h^{P(i)} \cdot F(w_1 \ldots w_{l-1}j)^{r_{j,w}} \cdot \tilde{Y}_i^j, \ g^{r_{j,w}} \cdot \tilde{Z}_i^j, \right.$$
$$\left. h_{i,l+1}^{r_{j,w}} \cdot \tilde{R}_{i,l+1}^j, \ldots, \ h_{i,\ell}^{r_{j,w}} \cdot \tilde{R}_{i,\ell}^j\right)$$

where $r_{j,w} = r'_{i,w} + t_j$ and for some $\tilde{Y}_i^j, \tilde{Z}_i^j, \tilde{R}_{i,l+1}^j, \ldots, \tilde{R}_{i,\ell}^j \in_R \mathbb{G}_{p_3}$.

Update$(i, t, SK_i^{(t)})$: (where $t < T - 2$)

1. Parse $\langle t \rangle$ as $t_1 \ldots t_\ell \in \{0,1\}^\ell$. Parse $SK_i^{(t)}$ as
$$\left(\mathsf{sk}_{i,\langle t\rangle}, \{\mathsf{sk}_{i,t_1\ldots t_{l-1}1}\}_{l \in \{1,\ldots,\ell\} \text{ s.t. } t_l=0}\right)$$
and erase $\mathsf{sk}_{i,\langle t\rangle}$.

2. If $t_\ell = 0$, $SK_i^{(t+1)}$ simply consists of remaining node keys:
$$SK_i^{(t+1)} = \left(\mathsf{sk}_{i,t_1\ldots t_{\ell-1}1}, \{\mathsf{sk}_{i,t_1\ldots t_{l-1}1}\}_{l \in \{1,\ldots,\ell-1\} \text{ s.t. } t_l=0}\right).$$

Otherwise, let $l' \in \{1, \ldots, \ell\}$ denote the largest index such that $t_{l'} = 0$. Let $w' = t_1 \ldots t_{l'-1}1 \in \{0,1\}^{l'}$. Using the node key $\mathsf{sk}_{i,w'}$ (which is available as part of $SK_i^{(t)}$), recursively apply Extract to obtain node keys $\mathsf{sk}_{i,w'1}, \mathsf{sk}_{i,w'01}, \ldots, \mathsf{sk}_{i,w'0^{\ell-l'-1}1}$ and finally $\mathsf{sk}_{i,\langle t+1\rangle} = \mathsf{sk}_{i,w'0^{\ell-l'}}$. Erase $\mathsf{sk}_{i,w'}$ and return

$$SK_i^{(t+1)} = \left(\mathsf{sk}_{i,\langle t+1\rangle}, \{\mathsf{sk}_{i,t_1\ldots t_{l-1}1}\}_{l \in \{1,\ldots,l'-1\} \text{ s.t. } t_l=0}\right.$$
$$\left. \cup \{\mathsf{sk}_{i,w'1}, \mathsf{sk}_{i,w'01}, \ldots, \mathsf{sk}_{i,w'0^{\ell-l'-1}1}\}\right).$$

Encrypt(M, t, PK) : let $\langle t \rangle = t_1 \ldots t_\ell \in \{0,1\}^\ell$ be the binary expansion of the period number t. To encrypt $M \in \mathbb{G}_T$, choose $s \xleftarrow{R} \mathbb{Z}_N$ and compute
$$C = (t, C_0, C_1, C_2) = \left(t, \ M \cdot e(g,h)^s, \ g^s, \ F(t_1 \ldots t_\ell)^s\right).$$

Share-Decrypt$(i, t, SK_i^{(t)}, C)$: let $\langle t \rangle = t_1 \ldots t_\ell$. Parse $SK_i^{(t)}$ as

$$\left(\mathsf{sk}_{i, \langle t \rangle}, \{ \mathsf{sk}_{i, t_1 \ldots t_{l-1} 1} \}_{l \in \{1, \ldots, \ell\} \text{s.t.} t_l = 0} \right)$$

and the node key $\mathsf{sk}_{i, \langle t \rangle}$ as

$$(A_{i,0}, A_{i,1}) = \left(h^{P(i)} \cdot F(t_1 \ldots t_\ell)^{r_{i, \langle t \rangle}} \cdot Y_{i, \langle t \rangle}, \; g^{r_{i, \langle t \rangle}} \cdot Z_{i, \langle t \rangle} \right),$$

for some $r_{i, \langle t \rangle} \in \mathbb{Z}_N$ and $Y_{i, \langle t \rangle}, Z_{i, \langle t \rangle} \in \mathbb{G}_{p_3}$ (note that $\mathsf{sk}_{i, \langle t \rangle}$ can be seen as a HIBE a key at depth ℓ). Then, compute and return $(i, \hat{\mu}_i)$, where

$$\hat{\mu}_i = e(g, h)^{s \cdot P(i)} = \frac{e(C_1, A_{i,0})}{e(C_2, A_{i,1})}.$$

Combine$(PK, C, \{(i, \hat{\mu}_i)\}_{i \in S})$: for each $i \in S$, return $\perp$ if $\hat{\mu}_i \notin \mathbb{G}_T$. Otherwise, compute and output

$$M = C_0 \cdot \prod_{i \in S} \hat{\mu}_i^{-\Delta_{i,S}(0)}.$$

From an efficiency standpoint, the scheme inherits the efficiency of the underlying HIBE scheme with ciphertexts of constant size as in [10,41]. As in the centralized forward-secure cryptosystem, public keys and private key shares consist of $O(\log T)$ and $O(\log^2 T)$ group elements, respectively.

As established by Theorem 3, the scheme is forward-secure against adaptive corruptions and chosen-plaintext attacks. We note that the proof is not just a matter of adapting the proof of Theorem 1 to the hierarchical setting.

Indeed, in several games, the challenger is forced to reveal node keys for ancestors of the leaf associated with the attacked time period. For these nodes, the reduction has to be careful and refrain from directly inserting semi-functional components in the corresponding keys. Otherwise, an unbounded adversary might be able to detect some correlation between these semi-functional components and those of the challenge ciphertext.

To address this problem, the challenger has to guess upfront which leaf will correspond to the attacked time period. By doing so, if the guess is correct (which occurs with non-negligible probability since the number of leaves is polynomial), the reduction knows which node keys can be safely and gradually augmented with semi-functional components in a first step. In a second step, the reduction has to take care of ancestors of the expected target leaf and turn them into semi-functional keys in the same way as in the proof of Theorem 1.

Theorem 3. *The scheme provides forward security against adaptive corruptions in the threshold setting assuming that Assumption 1, Assumption 2 and Assumption 3 all hold.*

Proof. The proof proceeds using a sequence of games including steps similar to [41] and additional steps. As in [52,41], the proof makes use of semi-functional ciphertexts and decryption shares (which are actually private keys in [41]). In addition, we also have to consider semi-functional private key shares. Another difference is that we need two kinds of semi-functional ciphertexts.

○ Semi-functional ciphertexts of Type I are generated from a normal ciphertext (C_0', C_1', C_2') and some $g_2 \in \mathbb{G}_{p_2}$, by choosing random $\tau, z_c \xleftarrow{R} \mathbb{Z}_N$ and setting

$$C_0 = C_0', \qquad\qquad C_1 = C_1' \cdot g_2^{\tau}, \qquad\qquad C_2 = C_2' \cdot g_2^{\tau z_c}.$$

○ Semi-functional ciphertexts of Type II are generated from a normal ciphertext (C_0', C_1', C_2') by choosing random $\tau, z_c, \theta \xleftarrow{R} \mathbb{Z}_N$ and setting

$$C_0 = C_0' \cdot e(g_2, g_2)^{\theta}, \qquad C_1 = C_1' \cdot g_2^{\tau}, \qquad C_2 = C_2' \cdot g_2^{\tau z_c}.$$

○ For a node of label $w = w_1 \ldots w_l \in \{0,1\}^l$, a Type I semi-functional node key is obtained from normal a node key

$$\begin{aligned}
\mathsf{sk}_{i,w_1 \ldots w_k} &= (A_{i,0}, A_{i,1}, B_{i,l+1}, \ldots, B_{i,\ell}) \\
&= \big(h^{P(i)} \cdot F(w_1 \ldots w_l)^{r_{i,w}} \cdot Y_{i,w}, \; g^{r_{i,w}} \cdot Z_{i,w}, \\
&\qquad\qquad h_{l+1}^{r_{i,w}} \cdot R_{i,w,l+1}, \ldots, h_{\ell}^{r_{i,w}} \cdot R_{i,w,\ell} \big)
\end{aligned}$$

by setting $(A_{i,0}', A_{i,1}', B_{i,l+1}', \ldots, B_{i,\ell}')$ as

$$\begin{aligned}
A_{i,0} &= A_{i,0}' \cdot g_2^{\gamma_{i,w} \cdot z_{i,w}} \cdot Y_{i,w}', \\
A_{i,1} &= A_{i,1}' \cdot g_2^{\gamma_{i,w}} \cdot Z_{i,w}', \\
B_{i,l+1}' &= B_{i,l+1} \cdot g_2^{\gamma_{i,w} \cdot y_{i,w,l+1}} \cdot R_{i,w,l+1}', \\
&\qquad\vdots \\
B_{i,\ell}' &= B_{i,\ell} \cdot g_2^{\gamma_{i,w} \cdot y_{i,w,\ell}} \cdot R_{i,w,\ell}'
\end{aligned} \qquad (2)$$

using random $\gamma_{i,w}, z_{i,w}, y_{i,w,l+1}, \ldots, y_{i,w,\ell} \xleftarrow{R} \mathbb{Z}_N$, $Y_{i,w}', Z_{i,w}' \xleftarrow{R} \mathbb{G}_{p_3}$ and $R_{i,w,l+1}', \ldots, R_{i,w,\ell}' \xleftarrow{R} \mathbb{G}_{p_3}$, where g_2 is a generator of $\mathbb{G}_{p_2}$.

We also make use of Type II semi-functional node keys.

○ Semi-functional node keys of Type II are obtained from a normal node key $(A_{i,0}', A_{i,1}', B_{i,l+1}', \ldots, B_{i,\ell}')$ by setting

$$(A_{i,0}, A_{i,1}, B_{i,l+1}, \ldots, B_{i,\ell}) = (A_{i,0}' \cdot g_2^{z_{i,w}}, \; A_{i,1}, \; B_{i,l+1}', \; \ldots, \; B_{i,\ell}')$$

using a random $z_{i,w} \xleftarrow{R} \mathbb{Z}_N$.

The proof considers a sequence of $n(2T - 1) + 4$ games. It starts with the real game Game_0. For each i, we denote by S_i the probability that the challenger outputs 1 at the end of Game_i. We also define $\mathsf{Adv}_i := |\Pr[S_i] - 1/2|$ for each i.

Game_0: is the real attack game. At the end of Game_0, we call S_0 the event that the attacker $\mathcal{A}$ outputs a bit $\beta' \in \{0,1\}$ and wins if $\beta' = \beta$, where $\beta \in_R \{0,1\}$ is the challenger's bit in the challenge phase. In this game, we have $\mathsf{Adv}_0 = |\Pr[S_0] - 1/2|$.

Game_1: is like Game_0 with the difference that, at the beginning of the game, the challenger chooses an index $t^{\ddagger} \xleftarrow{R} \{0, \ldots, T-1\}$. At the challenge phase, the challenger halts and outputs a random bit if the challenge ciphertext is encrypted for a period $t^{\star}$ such that $t^{\star} \neq t^{\ddagger}$. Since the choice of $t^{\ddagger}$ is independent of $\mathcal{A}$'s view, we have $\Pr[S_1] \geq \Pr[S_0]/T$. Recall that, since $T \in \mathsf{poly}(\lambda)$, the probability to have $t^{\ddagger} = t^{\star}$ is non-negligible and the multiplicative gap between $\Pr[S_1]$ and $\Pr[S_0]$ is thus acceptable. In the following, we denote by $\mathsf{path}^{\ddagger}$ the path from the root to the leaf associated with $t^{\ddagger}$.

Game_2: is identical to Game_1 but the normal challenge ciphertext is replaced by a semi-functional ciphertext of Type I.

$\mathsf{Game}_{2.1.0}$: is like Game_2 with the difference that, for each server $i \in \{1, \ldots, n\}$ and each node w in the tree, the node keys $\{\mathsf{sk}_{i,w}\}_{i=1}^{n}$ are calculated at the outset of the game. The challenger thus pre-computes a polynomial number of $n(2T-1)$ node keys overall.

$\mathsf{Game}_{2.j.\kappa}$ ($1 \leq j \leq n$, $1 \leq \kappa \leq 2T-1$): in this game, the challenge ciphertext is a semi-functional ciphertext of Type I and, in the tree, the generation of node keys depends on indices (j, κ).

- For each server $i \in \{1, \ldots, j-1\}$, all node keys $\mathsf{sk}_{i,w}$ are computed as semi-functional node keys if $w \notin \mathsf{path}^{\ddagger}$. For all labels $w \in \mathsf{path}^{\ddagger}$, $\mathsf{sk}_{i,w}$ is generated as a normal node key.
- For servers $i \in \{j+1, \ldots, n\}$, all node keys $\mathsf{sk}_{i,w}$ are normal keys.
- As for the server j, the distribution of the node key $\mathsf{sk}_{j,w}$ depends on w. If $w \notin \mathsf{path}^{\ddagger}$ and w is the label of one of the first κ node keys (in some order), $\mathcal{B}$ computes $\mathsf{sk}_{j,w}$ as a normal node key. Otherwise, $\mathsf{sk}_{j,w}$ is computed as a normal node key.

Game_3: is identical to $\mathsf{Game}_{2.n.(2T-1)}$ with the following two differences.

- For each server $i \in \{1, \ldots, n\}$, the node keys $\{\mathsf{sk}_{i,w}\}_{w \in \mathsf{path}^{\ddagger}}$ – which still have the normal distribution in $\mathsf{Game}_{2.n.(2T-1)}$ – are now generated as semi-functional node keys of Type II. Namely, their $A_{i,0}$ component now contains a random $\mathbb{G}_{p_2}$ component.
- The Type I semi-functional challenge ciphertext is replaced by a Type II semi-functional ciphertext.

Game_4: is as Game_3 but the Type II semi-functional challenge ciphertext is replaced by a semi-functional encryption of a random plaintext (instead of M_{β}). In this game, $\mathcal{A}$ has no information on the challenger's bit $\beta \in \{0,1\}$ and cannot guess it with better probability than $1/2$.

When counting probabilities, we first note that the transition from Game_0 to Game_1 is a transition based on a failure event of large probability, according to the terminology of [26]. As shown in [26], we thus have $\mathsf{Adv}_1 = |\Pr[S_1] - 1/2| = \mathsf{Adv}_0/T$. In the full version of [42], it is shown that $|\Pr[S_1] - \Pr[S_2]| \leq \mathbf{Adv}^1(\mathcal{B}_1)$, where the latter function is an upper bound on the advantage of any PPT distinguisher $\mathcal{B}_1$ for Assumption 1. It is straightforward that moving from Game_2 to $\mathsf{Game}_{2.1.0}$ is just a conceptual change since $\mathcal{A}$'s view is the same in both games. Then, for each $j \in \{1, \ldots, n\}$ and $\kappa \in \{1, \ldots, 2T-1\}$, the full version of [42] demonstrates the existence of a PPT distinguisher $\mathcal{B}_2$ against Assumption 2 such that $|\Pr[S_{2.j.\kappa}] - \Pr[S_{2.j.(\kappa-1)}]| \leq \mathbf{Adv}^1(\mathcal{B}_2)$. As for the transition from $\mathsf{Game}_{2.n.(2T-1)}$ to Game_3, the full version of [42] constructs a distinguisher $\mathcal{B}_2'$ for Assumption 2 such that $|\Pr[S_{2.n.(2T-1)}] - \Pr[S_3]| \leq \mathbf{Adv}^1(\mathcal{B}_2')$. Finally, it is established in [42] that $|\Pr[S_3] - \Pr[S_4]| \leq \mathbf{Adv}^3(\mathcal{B}_3)$, for some distinguisher against Assumption 3. Since $\Pr[S_3] = 1/2$, by combining the above, we can write.

$$\mathrm{Adv}_0 \leq T \cdot \Big(\mathrm{Adv}^1(\mathcal{B}_1) + \big(n \cdot (2T-1) + 1\big) \cdot \mathrm{Adv}^2(\mathcal{B}_2) + \mathrm{Adv}^3(\mathcal{B}_3) \Big),$$

where, for each $i \in \{1, 2, 3\}$, $\mathrm{Adv}^i(\mathcal{B}_i)$ denotes the maximal advantage of any PPT adversary $\mathcal{B}_i$ against Assumption i. □

5 Conclusion

This paper reviewed our results regarding the first fully non-interactive robust threshold cryptosystems with chosen-ciphertext security against adaptive adversaries. Our results are proved in the sense of a game-based security definition akin to the one of Shoup and Gennaro [50], but with adaptive corruptions.

Using the same techniques, we also gave an adaptively secure non-interactive threshold signatures in the standard model. Motivated by the work of Abdalla, Miner and Namprempre [1], here we gave formal definitions for robust non-interactive forward-secure threshold public-key encryption, as well as the first completely non-interactive construction with adaptive security. In a follow-up work [43], we recently defined a more general framework for constructing threshold public-key encryption schemes with similar properties.

References

1. Abdalla, M., Miner, S.K., Namprempre, C.: Forward-Secure Threshold Signature Schemes. In: Naccache, D. (ed.) CT-RSA 2001. LNCS, vol. 2020, pp. 441–456. Springer, Heidelberg (2001)
2. Abdalla, M., Reyzin, L.: A New Forward-Secure Digital Signature Scheme. In: Okamoto, T. (ed.) ASIACRYPT 2000. LNCS, vol. 1976, pp. 116–129. Springer, Heidelberg (2000)
3. Abe, M.: Robust Distributed Multiplication without Interaction. In: Wiener, M. (ed.) CRYPTO 1999. LNCS, vol. 1666, pp. 130–147. Springer, Heidelberg (1999)
4. Abe, M., Fehr, S.: Adaptively Secure Feldman VSS and Applications to Universally-Composable Threshold Cryptography. In: Franklin, M. (ed.) CRYPTO 2004. LNCS, vol. 3152, pp. 317–334. Springer, Heidelberg (2004)
5. Anderson, R.: Two Remarks on Public Key Cryptology. Invited lecture. In: ACM Conference on Computer and Communications Security (1997)
6. Almansa, J.F., Damgård, I., Nielsen, J.B.: Simplified Threshold RSA with Adaptive and Proactive Security. In: Vaudenay, S. (ed.) EUROCRYPT 2006. LNCS, vol. 4004, pp. 593–611. Springer, Heidelberg (2006)
7. Bellare, M., Miner, S.: A Forward-Secure Digital Signature Scheme. In: Wiener, M. (ed.) CRYPTO 1999. LNCS, vol. 1666, pp. 431–448. Springer, Heidelberg (1999)

8. Bellare, M., Rogaway, P.: Random oracles are practical: A paradigm for designing efficient protocols. In: ACM CCS (1993)
9. Boneh, D., Boyen, X.: Efficient Selective-ID Secure Identity-Based Encryption Without Random Oracles. In: Cachin, C., Camenisch, J.L. (eds.) EUROCRYPT 2004. LNCS, vol. 3027, pp. 223–238. Springer, Heidelberg (2004)
10. Boneh, D., Boyen, X., Goh, E.-J.: Hierarchical Identity Based Encryption with Constant Size Ciphertext. In: Cramer, R. (ed.) EUROCRYPT 2005. LNCS, vol. 3494, pp. 440–456. Springer, Heidelberg (2005)
11. Boneh, D., Boyen, X., Halevi, S.: Chosen Ciphertext Secure Public Key Threshold Encryption Without Random Oracles. In: Pointcheval, D. (ed.) CT-RSA 2006. LNCS, vol. 3860, pp. 226–243. Springer, Heidelberg (2006)
12. Boneh, D., Franklin, M.: Identity-Based Encryption from the Weil Pairing. SIAM J. of Computing 32(3), 586–615 (2003); Earlier version in Kilian, J. (ed.) CRYPTO 2001. LNCS, vol. 2139, pp. 213–229. Springer, Heidelberg (2001)
13. Boneh, D., Franklin, M.: Efficient Generation of Shared RSA Keys. In: Kaliski Jr., B.S. (ed.) CRYPTO 1997. LNCS, vol. 1294, pp. 425–439. Springer, Heidelberg (1997)
14. Boyd, C.: Digital Multisignatures. In: Beker, H.J., Piper, F.C. (eds.) Cryptography and Coding, pp. 241–246. Oxford University Press (1989)
15. Boyen, X., Mei, Q., Waters, B.: Direct Chosen Ciphertext Security from Identity-Based Techniques. In: ACM CCS 2005 (2005)
16. Boyen, X., Shacham, H., Shen, E., Waters, B.: Forward-Secure Signatures with Untrusted Update. In: ACM CCS 2006. ACM Press (2006)
17. Canetti, R., Goldreich, O., Halevi, S.: The random oracle methodology, revisited. Journal of the ACM 51(4), 557–594 (2004); Earlier version in STOC 1998 (1998)
18. Canetti, R., Gennaro, R., Jarecki, S., Krawczyk, H., Rabin, T.: Adaptive Security for Threshold Cryptosystems. In: Wiener, M. (ed.) CRYPTO 1999. LNCS, vol. 1666, pp. 98–116. Springer, Heidelberg (1999)
19. Canetti, R., Goldwasser, S.: An Efficient *Threshold* Public Key Cryptosystem Secure against Adaptive Chosen Ciphertext Attack. In: Stern, J. (ed.) EUROCRYPT 1999. LNCS, vol. 1592, pp. 90–106. Springer, Heidelberg (1999)
20. Cramer, R., Shoup, V.: A Practical Public Key Cryptosystem Provably Secure against Adaptive Chosen Ciphertext Attack. In: Krawczyk, H. (ed.) CRYPTO 1998. LNCS, vol. 1462, pp. 13–25. Springer, Heidelberg (1998)
21. Canetti, R., Halevi, S., Katz, J.: A Forward-Secure Public-Key Encryption Scheme. In: Biham, E. (ed.) EUROCRYPT 2003. LNCS, vol. 2656, pp. 255–271. Springer, Heidelberg (2003)
22. Canetti, R., Halevi, S., Katz, J.: Chosen-Ciphertext Security from Identity-Based Encryption. In: Cachin, C., Camenisch, J.L. (eds.) EUROCRYPT 2004. LNCS, vol. 3027, pp. 207–222. Springer, Heidelberg (2004)
23. Cramer, R., Damgård, I., Dziembowski, S., Hirt, M., Rabin, T.: Efficient Multiparty Computations Secure against an Adaptive Adversary. In: Stern, J. (ed.) EUROCRYPT 1999. LNCS, vol. 1592, pp. 311–326. Springer, Heidelberg (1999)
24. Daza, V., Herranz, J., Morillo, P., Ràfols, C.: CCA2-Secure Threshold Broadcast Encryption with Shorter Ciphertexts. In: Susilo, W., Liu, J.K., Mu, Y. (eds.) ProvSec 2007. LNCS, vol. 4784, pp. 35–50. Springer, Heidelberg (2007)
25. Delerablée, C., Pointcheval, D.: Dynamic Threshold Public-Key Encryption. In: Wagner, D. (ed.) CRYPTO 2008. LNCS, vol. 5157, pp. 317–334. Springer, Heidelberg (2008)
26. Dent, A.-W.: A Note On Game-Hopping Proofs. Cryptology ePrint Archive: Report 2006/260

27. Desmedt, Y.: Society and Group Oriented Cryptography: A New Concept. In: Pomerance, C. (ed.) CRYPTO 1987. LNCS, vol. 293, pp. 120–127. Springer, Heidelberg (1988)

28. Desmedt, Y., Frankel, Y.: Threshold Cryptosystems. In: Brassard, G. (ed.) CRYPTO 1989. LNCS, vol. 435, pp. 307–315. Springer, Heidelberg (1990)

29. Dodis, Y., Katz, J.: Chosen-Ciphertext Security of Multiple Encryption. In: Kilian, J. (ed.) TCC 2005. LNCS, vol. 3378, pp. 188–209. Springer, Heidelberg (2005)

30. El Gamal, T.: A Public Key Cryptosystem and a Signature Scheme Based on Discrete Logarithms. In: Blakely, G.R., Chaum, D. (eds.) CRYPTO 1984. LNCS, vol. 196, pp. 10–18. Springer, Heidelberg (1985)

31. Goldwasser, S., Micali, S., Rivest, R.: A Digital Signature Scheme Secure Against Adaptive Chosen-Message Attacks. SIAM J. Comput. 17(2), 281–308 (1988)

32. Gennaro, R., Jarecki, S., Krawczyk, H., Rabin, T.: Secure Distributed Key Generation for Discrete-Log Based Cryptosystems. In: Stern, J. (ed.) EUROCRYPT 1999. LNCS, vol. 1592, pp. 295–310. Springer, Heidelberg (1999)

33. Fouque, P.-A., Pointcheval, D.: Threshold Cryptosystems Secure against Chosen-Ciphertext Attacks. In: Boyd, C. (ed.) ASIACRYPT 2001. LNCS, vol. 2248, pp. 351–368. Springer, Heidelberg (2001)

34. Frankel, Y., MacKenzie, P., Yung, M.: Adaptively-Secure Distributed Public-Key Systems. In: Nešetřil, J. (ed.) ESA 1999. LNCS, vol. 1643, pp. 4–27. Springer, Heidelberg (1999)

35. Frankel, Y., MacKenzie, P., Yung, M.: Adaptively-Secure Optimal-Resilience Proactive RSA. In: Lam, K.-Y., Okamoto, E., Xing, C. (eds.) ASIACRYPT 1999. LNCS, vol. 1716, pp. 180–195. Springer, Heidelberg (1999)

36. Itkis, G., Reyzin, L.: Forward-Secure Signatures with Optimal Signing and Verifying. In: Kilian, J. (ed.) CRYPTO 2001. LNCS, vol. 2139, pp. 332–354. Springer, Heidelberg (2001)

37. Jarecki, S., Lysyanskaya, A.: Adaptively Secure Threshold Cryptography: Introducing Concurrency, Removing Erasures (Extended Abstract). In: Preneel, B. (ed.) EUROCRYPT 2000. LNCS, vol. 1807, pp. 221–242. Springer, Heidelberg (2000)

38. Katz, J.: A Forward-Secure Public-Key Encryption Scheme. Cryptology ePrint Archive: Report 2002/060 (2002)

39. Kiltz, E.: Chosen-Ciphertext Security from Tag-Based Encryption. In: Halevi, S., Rabin, T. (eds.) TCC 2006. LNCS, vol. 3876, pp. 581–600. Springer, Heidelberg (2006)

40. Lewko, A., Okamoto, T., Sahai, A., Takashima, K., Waters, B.: Fully Secure Functional Encryption: Attribute-Based Encryption and (Hierarchical) Inner Product Encryption. In: Gilbert, H. (ed.) EUROCRYPT 2010. LNCS, vol. 6110, pp. 62–91. Springer, Heidelberg (2010)

41. Lewko, A., Waters, B.: New Techniques for Dual System Encryption and Fully Secure HIBE with Short Ciphertexts. In: Micciancio, D. (ed.) TCC 2010. LNCS, vol. 5978, pp. 455–479. Springer, Heidelberg (2010)

42. Libert, B., Yung, M.: Adaptively Secure Non-Interactive Threshold Cryptosystems. In: Aceto, L., Henzinger, M., Sgall, J. (eds.) ICALP 2011, Part II. LNCS, vol. 6756, pp. 588–600. Springer, Heidelberg (2011)

43. Libert, B., Yung, M.: Non-interactive CCA-Secure Threshold Cryptosystems with Adaptive Security: New Framework and Constructions. In: Cramer, R. (ed.) TCC 2012. LNCS, vol. 7194, pp. 75–93. Springer, Heidelberg (2012)

44. Lysyanskaya, A., Peikert, C.: Adaptive Security in the Threshold Setting: From Cryptosystems to Signature Schemes. In: Boyd, C. (ed.) ASIACRYPT 2001. LNCS, vol. 2248, pp. 331–350. Springer, Heidelberg (2001)
45. MacKenzie, P.: An Efficient Two-Party Public Key Cryptosystem Secure against Adaptive Chosen Ciphertext Attack. In: Desmedt, Y.G. (ed.) PKC 2003. LNCS, vol. 2567, pp. 47–61. Springer, Heidelberg (2003)
46. Malkin, T., Micciancio, D., Miner, S.K.: Efficient Generic Forward-Secure Signatures with an Unbounded Number of Time Periods. In: Knudsen, L.R. (ed.) EUROCRYPT 2002. LNCS, vol. 2332, pp. 400–417. Springer, Heidelberg (2002)
47. Ostrovsky, R., Yung, M.: How to Withstand Mobile Virus Attacks. In: 10th ACM Symp. on Principles of Distributed Computing, PODC 1991 (1991)
48. Qin, B., Wu, Q., Zhang, L., Domingo-Ferrer, J.: Threshold Public-Key Encryption with Adaptive Security and Short Ciphertexts. In: Soriano, M., Qing, S., López, J. (eds.) ICICS 2010. LNCS, vol. 6476, pp. 62–76. Springer, Heidelberg (2010)
49. Shamir, A.: Identity-Based Cryptosystems and Signature Schemes. In: Blakely, G.R., Chaum, D. (eds.) CRYPTO 1984. LNCS, vol. 196, pp. 47–53. Springer, Heidelberg (1985)
50. Shoup, V., Gennaro, R.: Securing Threshold Cryptosystems against Chosen Ciphertext Attack. In: Nyberg, K. (ed.) EUROCRYPT 1998. LNCS, vol. 1403, pp. 1–16. Springer, Heidelberg (1998)
51. Shoup, V.: Practical Threshold Signatures. In: Preneel, B. (ed.) EUROCRYPT 2000. LNCS, vol. 1807, pp. 207–220. Springer, Heidelberg (2000)
52. Waters, B.: Dual System Encryption: Realizing Fully Secure IBE and HIBE under Simple Assumptions. In: Halevi, S. (ed.) CRYPTO 2009. LNCS, vol. 5677, pp. 619–636. Springer, Heidelberg (2009)

Cryptanalysis vs. Provable Security

Phong Q. Nguyen

INRIA, France and Tsinghua University, China
http://www.di.ens.fr/~pnguyen/

Abstract. In 2004, Koblitz and Menezes started [2] a series of papers questioning the methodology and impact of provable security. We take another look, by comparing cryptanalysis results and provable security results on a variety of topics. We argue that security is complex, and that there is much to gain from better interaction between cryptanalysis and provable security.

Security evaluations of cryptographic schemes or protocols used to be exclusively based on cryptanalysis. A cryptosystem was deemed secure if no efficient attack was known. This traditional approach has obvious limitations: if there is no attack today, it does not imply that there will not be an attack tomorrow, as the history of cryptography has shown repeatedly. Nevertheless, cryptographic key sizes and parameters are still routinely selected based on the state-of-the-art in cryptanalysis.

The field of provable security was developed to provide a new kind of insurance. Its goal is to mathematically prove security properties: a typical provable security result states that a cryptographic scheme A is secure in the security model B, provided that a set C of assumptions hold. Here, an element of C could be a computational assumption – *e.g.* factoring is hard, or a security assumption on a given primitive or protocol – *e.g.* AES is a pseudo-random permutation. That such kinds of statements can be proved is fascinating, and represents a major achievement of theoretical cryptography. Yet, this approach also has well-known limitations, see for instance [2,1,4,5]. In particular, there are provably-secure cryptosystems which were later shown to be insecure, in practice and/or in theory, for various reasons.

These limitations do not mean that one should/could ignore cryptanalysis or provable security. On the contrary, it serves as a reminder that cryptographic security is complex, and that if one is interested in actual security, one should gather as much information as possible, from both cryptanalysis and provable security, without ignoring one or the other. We illustrate this point with several examples from the past thirty years.

We argue that there are a lot of similarities between cryptology and physics. Both use a lot of mathematics, but neither is part of mathematics. Physics aims at discovering the laws of nature and understanding how the physical world works, but we can never know for sure if our theories are correct: we can only tell if our theories are consistent with state-of-the-art experiments. We invent theoretical models to capture reality better and better, but this might be a

C.-K. Wu, M. Yung, and D. Lin (Eds.): Inscrypt 2011, LNCS 7537, pp. 22–23, 2012.

never-ending work in progress: even if we find the right theory of everything in theoretical physics, we will never know for sure if it is the right one. Similarly, cryptology aims at achieving security, but in some sense, we never know if something is really secure in the real world, especially in the long term. We keep refining our security models, *e.g.* to take into account side-channel attacks. At best, we can say that something is theoretically secure within a certain security model, or that something seems to be secure in practice for now.

Finally, we argue that there is much to gain from better interaction/dialogue between cryptanalysis and provable security. A security proof can help cryptanalysts to identify weak points: for instance, if the security model or the assumption seems to be unreasonable in practice, this could be the starting point for an attack. Reciprocally, cryptanalysis can help provable security by playing a rôle similar to experiments in physics.

References

1. Chatterjee, S., Menezes, A., Sarkar, P.: Another Look at Tightness. In: Miri, A., Vaudenay, S. (eds.) SAC 2011. LNCS, vol. 7118, pp. 293–319. Springer, Heidelberg (2012)
2. Koblitz, N., Menezes, A.: Another look at "provable security". IACR Cryptology ePrint Archive, 2004:152 (2004); Published in [3], All papers available at http://anotherlook.ca/, the most recent ones being [1,4]
3. Koblitz, N., Menezes, A.: Another look at "provable security". J. Cryptology 20(1), 3–37 (2007)
4. Koblitz, N., Menezes, A.: Another look at HMAC. IACR Cryptology ePrint Archive, 2012:74 (2012)
5. Leurent, G., Nguyen, P.Q.: How Risky Is the Random-Oracle Model? In: Halevi, S. (ed.) CRYPTO 2009. LNCS, vol. 5677, pp. 445–464. Springer, Heidelberg (2009)

Boosting Scalability in Anomaly-Based Packed Executable Filtering

Xabier Ugarte-Pedrero, Igor Santos, and Pablo G. Bringas

S^{3}Lab, DeustoTech - Computing, Deusto Institute of Technology
University of Deusto,
Avenida de las Universidades 24, 48007
Bilbao, Spain
{xabier.ugarte,isantos,pablo.garcia.bringas}@deusto.es

Abstract. During the last years, malware writers have been using several techniques to evade detection. One of the most common techniques employed by the anti-virus industry is signature scanning. This method requires the end-host to compare files against a database that should contain signatures for each malware sample. In order to allow their creations to bypass these protection systems, programmers use software encryption tools and code obfuscation techniques to hide the actual behaviour of their malicious programs. One of these techniques is packing, a method that encrypts the real code of the executable and places it as data in a new executable that contains an unpacking routine. In previous work, we designed and implemented an anomaly detector based on PE structural characteristics and heuristic values, and we were able to decide whether an executable was packed or not. We stated that this detection system could serve as a filtering step for a generic and time consuming unpacking phase. In this paper, we improve that system applying a data reduction algorithm to our representation of normality (i.e., not packed executables), finding similarities among executables and grouping them to form consistent clusters that reduce the amount of comparisons needed. We show that this improvement reduces drastically the processing time, while maintaining detection and false positive rates stable.

Keywords: malware, packer, anomaly detection, dataset clustering, computer security.

1 Introduction

Malware (or malicious software) is the term used to define any software that has been written with malicious intentions to harm computers or networks and usually to obtain personal benefits in an illegitimate way. Malware authors' intentions have evolved in the last years. In the past, the intentions behind malware were fame and self-pride, but nowadays money is the main motivation. For this reason, efforts to bypass anti-virus tools have increased and thus, the power and variety of malware programs, together with their ability to overcome all kinds of security barriers [1]. One of the most commonly used techniques

C.-K. Wu, M. Yung, and D. Lin (Eds.): Inscrypt 2011, LNCS 7537, pp. 24–43, 2012.

is executable packing, which consists of cyphering or compressing the actual malicious code in order to hide it and evade signature scanning methods. Packed programs include a decryption routine that is first executed. This code extracts the real payload from memory and executes it. Some reports claim that up to an 80% of the malware analysed is packed [2].

Traditional anti-virus systems apply signature scanning to identify malicious code. This technique has been also applied to detect executables protected with well known packers by scanning for certain byte sequences. PEID [3] is able to detect a wide range of well-known packers. Besides, Faster Universal Unpacker (FUU) [4] tries to identify the packer utilised to hide the original code and then applies custom unpacking routines designed and written for each packer. However, this approach has the same shortcoming as signatures for malware detection: it is not effective with unknown obfuscation techniques, nor with custom packers (i.e.,executable packing-unpacking algorithms exclusively designed for a certain malicious program). Actually, according to Morgenstern and Pilz [5], 35% of malware is packed by a custom packer. This fact makes custom packers an important issue to consider.

Several approaches have been proposed to overcome this evasion technique. We can divide these approaches into static and dynamic approaches. Static approaches gather information about the employed packer without executing the sample, while dynamic unpacking approaches trace the execution of an executable and extract its protected code once unpacked. Normally, the samples are run inside an isolated environment like a virtual machine or an emulator [6].

Numerous dynamic unpackers try to identify the original entry point (i.e., where the execution jumps from the unpacking routine to the original code) by using heuristics. Once the execution flow reaches that point, the memory content is dumped to disk in order to obtain an unpacked version of the malicious code (e.g., Universal PE Unpacker [7] and OllyBonE [8]). Nevertheless, specific heuristics cannot be universalised to all the packers in the wild, since all of them work in very different manners. For instance, some packers use virtual instruction sets and attach an interpreter to the executable in such a way that the original code is never present in memory [9]. Other approaches decrypt frames of code before they are executed and once executed they encode them again. In this way, the whole malicious code is never loaded in memory at the same time [10].

In contrast, not so highly heuristic-dependent approaches have been proposed for generic dynamic unpacking (e.g., PolyUnpack [11], Renovo [12], OmniUnpack [13] and Eureka [14]). Nonetheless, these methods are time-consuming and cannot counter conditional execution of unpacking routines, a technique used for anti-debugging and anti-monitoring defense [15–17].

PE-Miner [18] extracts characteristics from the PE file header and builds classifiers that determine if an executable is malicious or not. PE-Probe [19], an improvement of PE-Miner, previously determines if the executable is packed and then applies a different classifier in each case. Perdisci et al. proposed in [20] a method for the classification of packed executables using certain heuristics extracted from the PE structural data, as a previous step to the actual unpacking process.

In previous work [21], we proposed a method based on anomaly detection to filter executables that are not packed in order to avoid the processing overhead caused by generic unpackers. Our system calculated vectors composed of certain structural and heuristic features and compared the samples against a set of vectors representing not packed executables. If the sample was different enough, then it was considered as packed. Although the results obtained were significant enough to validate our method, the number of comparisons needed to analyse each sample was considerably high and consequently, it presented a high processing overhead.

In consideration of this background, we propose here an enhancement of our previous method [21], that applies partitional clustering to the dataset in order to reduce the number of vectors in the knowledge base. This improvement boosts the scalability of the system, reducing the processing time. The results obtained for the reduced dataset and the time saved by this technique reaffirms our initial hypothesis: A fast and efficient initial filtering step can improve generic and dynamic unpacking systems' performance by reducing the amount of executables to be analysed.

Summarising, our main contributions are:

- We propose a method for dataset reduction based on the partitional clustering algorithm Quality Threshold (QT) clustering, and generate reduced datasets of different sizes.
- We evaluate our system for different reduction rates, testing its accuracy results and comparing them to previous work.
- We prove that a unique sample synthetically generated from not-packed executables is sufficiently representative to implement an anomaly detection system without compromising accuracy results.

The remainder of this paper is organised as follows. Section 2 details our anomaly-based method. Section 3 describes the experiments and presents results. Section 4 discusses the obtained results and their implications, and outlines avenues for future work.

2   Method Description

The method described in this paper is based on our previous work, a packed executable detector based on an anomaly detection system [21]. Our approach consisted in the measurement of the distance from binary files to a set of binaries not packed. Any sample that deviates sufficiently from a representation of normality (not packed executables) is classified as packed. Contrary to supervised learning approaches, this method does not need a model training phase, and thus it does not require labelled packed executables, reducing the efforts needed to find and label a set of packed binaries. Nevertheless, it is necessary to compute as many distance values as executables in the not packed set.

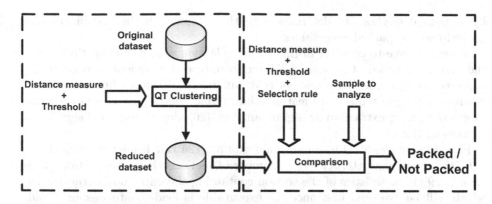

Fig. 1. Architecture of the proposed system. The QT clustering algorithm transforms the original dataset into a new reduced synthetic dataset. It requires 2 parameters: the distance measure and the threshold. The comparison system compares samples against the reduced dataset obtained, applying a distance measure, a distance threshold, and a selection rule. Finally the system is classifies the sample as packed or not packed.

In this paper, we improve the efficiency of our system by designing a data reduction phase capable of boosting the detector's scalability. Fig. 1 shows the architecture of our proposed system. The first objective of our method is to improve its efficiency by applying data reduction. The data reduction phase consists in the application of the QT clustering algorithm to the original dataset to obtain a reduced version that conserves the original dataset's features. In this way, the number of comparisons performed, and thus, the comparison time required for the analysis of each sample are much lower.

The second objective is to measure the precision of our system when the training set is incrementally reduced, in order to evaluate the trade-off between efficiency and accuracy. In addition, this data reduction approach enables us to test the performance of the system when a unique representation of a 'normal' executable is used, and to determine if it can to correctly classify packed and not packed executables.

2.1   Structural Features

In previous work [21], we selected a set of 211 structural features of the PE executables from the conclusions obtained in previous research in the area [18–20]. Some features are extracted directly from the PE file header, while others are calculated values based on heuristics commonly used for detecting packers. Farooq et al. [18] and Perdisci et al. [20] used PE executable structural features, as well as heuristics like entropy analysis or certain section characteristics to determine if an executable is packed or not, as a previous step to a second analysis phase. To select the set of features we combined both points of view, structural characteristics and heuristics, and analysed their individual relevance by statistical methods to determine how they impact on the classification of packed and not packed executables.

A second issue to consider in the feature selection was extraction time, since the system is aimed at becoming a filter to reduce the amount of executables analysed in dynamic environments that can be much more time consuming. Therefore, we selected a set of features that, unlike techniques such as code dissassembly, string extraction or n-gram analysis [20], do not require a significant processing time.

Features are classified into four main groups: 125 raw header characteristics [19], 33 section characteristics (i.e., number of sections that meet certain properties), 29 characteristics of the section containing the entry point (the section which will be executed first once the executable is loaded into memory) and, finally, 24 entropy values. For each feature, we calculated the Information Gain (IG) value [22]. IG provides a ratio for each feature that outlines its importance in order to classify a sample as packed or not packed. To calculate these weight values, we used a dataset comprised of 1,000 packed and 1,000 not packed executables.

- **DOS header characteristics (31).** The first bytes of the PE file header correspond to the DOS executable header fields. IG results showed that these characteristics are not specially relevant, having a maximum IG value of 0.23, corresponding to a reserved field, which intuitively may not be a relevant field. 15 values range from 0.10 to 0.16, and the rest present a relevance bellow 0.10.
- **File header block (23).** This header block (also named COFF header) is present in both image files (executable files), and object files. From a total of 23 characteristics, 14 have an IG value greater than 0, and only 2 of them have an IG value greater than 0.01: the number of sections (0.3112) and the time stamp (0.1618).
- **Optional Header Block (71).** This block is present in image files but not in object files, and contains data about how the executable must be loaded into memory. The data directory is located at the end of this structure and provides the address and size for very useful data structures. 37 features have an IG value over 0, but the most relevant ones are: the address of entry point (0.5111), the Import Address Table (IAT) size (0.3832) and address (0.3733) (relative to the number of imported DLLs), the size of the code (0.3011), the base of the data (0.2817), the base of the code (0.2213),the major linker version (0.1996), checksum (0.1736), the size of initialised data (0.1661), the size of headers (0.1600), the size of relocation table (0.1283) and the size of image (0.1243).
- **Section characteristics (33).** From the 33 characteristics that conform this group, 22 have an IG value greater than 0. The most significant ones are: the number of non-standard sections (0.7606), the number of executable sections (0.7127); the maximum raw data per virtual size ratio (0.5755) ($rawSize/virtualSize$, where $rawSize$ is defined as the section raw data

size and *virtualSize* is the section virtual size, both expressed in bytes), the number of readable and executable sections (0.5725) and the number of sections with a raw data per virtual size ratio lower than 1 (0.4842).

- **Section of entry point characteristics (29).** This group contains characteristics relative to the section which will be executed once the executable is loaded into memory. 26 characteristics have an IG value greater than 0, from which 11 have a significant relevance: the characteristics field in its raw state (0.9757), its availability to be written (0.9715), the raw data per virtual size ratio (0.9244), the virtual address (0.7386), whether is a pointer to raw data or not (0.6064), whether is a standard section or not (0.5203), the virtual size (0.4056), whether it contains initialised data (0.3721), the size of raw data (0.2958) and its availability to be executed (0.1575).

- **Entropy values (24).** We have selected 24 entropy values, commonly used in previous works [20], from which 22 have an IG value greater than 0, and 9 have a relevant IG value: max section entropy (0.8375), mean code section entropy (0.7656), mean section entropy (0.7359), file entropy (0.6955), entropy of the section of entry point (0.6756), mean data section entropy (0.5637), header entropy (0.1680), number of sections with an entropy value greater than 7.5 (0.7445), and number of sections with an entropy value between 7 and 7.5 (0.1059).

After the extraction, every feature has to be normalised: each value is divided by the maximum value for that feature in the whole dataset. In this way, each executable is represented as a vector of decimal values that range from 0 to 1. Finally, each feature value is multiplied by its relevance IG value to obtain the final vector that will be used in the next steps. These weights are used to compute a better distance measure among samples and to reduce the amount of features selected, given that only 151 of them have an IG value greater than 0.

2.2   Data Reduction

Dataset reduction is a step that has to be faced in very different problems that have to work with large datasets. In our work [21], the experiments were performed with a base of 900 not packed executables, which means that every sample analysed had to be compared 900 times to classify it as packed or not. Now, we propose a data reduction algorithm based on partitional clustering. Cluster analysis divides data into meaningful groups [23]. These techniques usually employ distance measures to compare instances in datasets to make groups with those which appear to be similar. We can identify several types of clustering, but most common ones are hierarchical clustering and partitional clustering. The first approach generates clusters in a nested style, which means that the clusters generated from the dataset are related hierarchically. In contrast, partional clustering techniques create a one-level (unnested) partitioning of the data points [23]. We are interested in this last technique to validate our initial hypothesis: it is possible to divide a big set of executables that represent normality (i.e., not packed executables) into a reduced set of representations.

input : The original dataset $\mathcal{V}$, the distance threshold for each cluster
threshold, and the minimum number of vectors in each cluster
minimumvectors
output: The reduced dataset $\mathcal{R}$

```
// Calculate the distance from each vector (set of executable
   features) to the rest of vectors in the dataset.
```
foreach $\{v_i | v_i \in \mathcal{V}\}$ **do**
    foreach $\{v_j | v_j \in \mathcal{V}\}$ **do**
```
      // If a vector vj's distance to vi is lower than the specified
         threshold, then vj is added to the potential cluster Ai,
         associated to the vi vector
```
        if distance(v_i, v_j) $\geq$ *threshold* **then**
            $\mathcal{A}_i$.add(v_j)

```
// In each loop, select the potential cluster with the highest
   number of vectors
```
while $\exists \mathcal{A}_i \in \mathcal{A} : |\mathcal{A}_i| \geq$ *minimumvectors and* $\forall \mathcal{A}_j \in \mathcal{A} : |\mathcal{A}_i| \geq |\mathcal{A}_j|$ *and* $i \neq j$
do
```
   // Add the centroid vector for the cluster to the result set
```
    $\mathcal{R}$.add(centroid($\mathcal{A}_i$))
```
   // Discard potential clusters associated to vectors vj ∈ Ai
```
    foreach $\{v_j | v_j \in \mathcal{A}_i\}$ **do**
        $\mathcal{A}$.remove($\mathcal{A}_j$)
        $\mathcal{V}$.remove(v_j)
```
   // Remove vectors vj ∈ Ai from the clusters Ak remaining in A
```
    foreach $\{\mathcal{A}_k | \mathcal{A}_k \in \mathcal{A}\}$ **do**
        foreach $\{v_j | v_j \in \mathcal{A}_k \text{ and } v_j \in \mathcal{A}_i\}$ **do**
            $\mathcal{A}_k$.remove(v_j)

```
// Add the remaining vectors to the final reduced dataset
```
foreach $\{v_j | v_j \in \mathcal{V}\}$ **do**
    $\mathcal{R}$.add(v_j)

Fig. 2. QT Clustering based dataset reduction algorithm

Quality Threshold (QT) clustering algorithm was proposed by Heyer et al. [24] to extract useful information from large amounts of gene expression data. K-means is a classic algorithm for partitional clustering, but it requires to specify the number of clusters desired. In contrast, QT clustering algorithm does not need this specification. Concretely, it uses a similarity threshold value to determine the maximum radial distance of any cluster. This way, it generates a variable number of clusters that meet a quality threshold. Its main disadvantage is the high number of distance calculations needed. Nevertheless, in our case, this computational overhead is admissible because we only have to reduce the dataset once, (we employ an static representation of normality that only varies from platform to platform).

Our algorithm, shown in Fig. 2, is based on the concepts proposed by Heyer et al. [24], but it is adapted to our data reduction problem and it is implemented iteratively, instead of recursively.

Let $\mathcal{A} = \{\mathcal{A}_0, \mathcal{A}_1, ..., \mathcal{A}_n\}$ be the set of potential clusters. For each vector v_i in the dataset $\mathcal{V}$, there is potential cluster $\mathcal{A}_i \in \mathcal{A}$. A potential cluster $\mathcal{A}_i$ is composed of the set of vectors at a distance respect to v_i not higher than the *threshold* previously specified.

Once the potential clusters are calculated, we select the cluster with the highest number of vectors as a final cluster. Then, we calculate its centroid, defined as $c = x_1 + x_2 + \cdots + x_k/k$ where $x_1, x_2, \cdots, x_k$ are points in the feature space. The resultant centroid is added to the final reduced dataset. Afterwards, each vector v_j present in the selected cluster $\mathcal{A}_i$ is removed from the original dataset $\mathcal{V}$ (as they will be represented by the previously calculated centroid). Moreover, the potential clusters $\mathcal{A}_j \in \mathcal{A}$ associated to each vector v_j previously removed are also discarded. When there are not more clusters available with a number of vectors higher than the parameter *minimumvectors*, the remaining vectors in $\mathcal{V}$ are added to the final reduced dataset and the algorithm finishes and returns the resulting reduced dataset. The final result is a dataset composed of one centroid representing each cluster and all the vectors that were not associated to any cluster by the QT clustering algorithm (i.e., outliers).

2.3   Anomaly Detection

The features described represent each executable as a point in the feature space. Our anomaly detection system analyses points in the feature space and classifies executables based on their similarity. The analysis of an executable consists of 3 different phases:

- Extraction of the features from the executable file.
- Computation of calculated values.
- Measurement of the distance from the point representing the executable file to the points that symbolise normality (i.e., not packed executables) that conform the knowledge base.

As a result, any point at a distance from normality that surpasses an established threshold is considered to be an anomaly and thus, a packed executable. In this study, we have considered 2 different distance measures:

- **Manhattan Distance.** This distance between two points x and y is the sum of the lengths of the projections of the line segment between the points onto the coordinate axes:

$$d(x, y) = \sum_{i=0}^{n} |x_i - y_i|$$

where x is the first point; y is the second point; and x_i and y_i are the ith component of first and second point, respectively.

– **Euclidean Distance.** This distance is the length of the line segment connecting two points. It is calculated as:

$$d(x, y) = \sum_{i=0}^{n} \sqrt{x_i^2 - y_i^2}$$

where x is the first point; y is the second point; and x_i and y_i are the ith component of first and second point, respectively.

In previous work [21] we noticed that the cosine similarity measure, (i.e., a distance measure computationally more expensive), does not produce better results.

Since we have to compute this measure with a variable number of points representing not packed executables, a combination metric is required in order to obtain a final distance value which considers every measure performed. To this end, we employ 3 simple rules:

– **Mean rule.** Select the average distance value.
– **Max rule.** Select the highest distance value.
– **Min rule.** Select the lowest distance value.

In this way, when an executable is analysed, the final distance value calculated depends on the distance measure and the combination rule selected.

3   Empirical Validation

To evaluate the performance of our method, we have conducted an experiment consisting of 2 phases: firstly, we reduce the set of vectors corresponding to not packed executables that represent normality, and secondly we start the anomaly detection step to measure accuracy and efficiency.

3.1   Experimental Configuration

The experiment designed to evaluate this system was performed using an executable collection comprising 1,000 packed and 1,000 not packed executables. Initially, 1,000 goodware executables were extracted from a common Microsoft Windows XP installation, and 1,000 malicious executables were gathered from the website VxHeavens [25]. All the executables where analysed with PEiD to assure that they were not packed. To generate the packed dataset, we employed 1,000 not packed executables (500 benign and 500 malicious) and we packed them using 10 different packing tools with different configurations: Armadillo, ASProtect, FSG, MEW, PackMan, RLPack, SLV, Telock, Themida and UPX. The not packed dataset was comprised of the remaining 1,000 executables.

The experimental method used was 10-fold cross validation [26], dividing the whole dataset into 10 different divisions. In this way, each fold is composed of 900 not packed executables as knowledge base and 1,100 testing executables, from which 100 are not packed and 1,000 are packed executables.

In order to test the dataset reduction algorithm proposed, 4 experimental configurations were selected for each distance measure. The threshold parameter values for our QT clustering based algorithm were selected by empirical observation. In particular, the thresholds for Manhattan distance were set as the double of the thresholds selected for Euclidean distance. While Manhattan distance sums the lengths of the projections of the line segment between the points onto the different coordinate axes, the Euclidean distance measures the line between two points, that is always shorter. Table 1 shows the results obtained in the process. Reduction ratio varies from 76.12% for Euclidean distance and threshold 0.25 to 99.88% for both Euclidean and Manhattan distance and an infinite threshold (in practice, this threshold is set to the maximum value allowed for a 64-bit double variable). The result obtained for this configuration is a unique centroid of the whole dataset that represents the arithmetic mean vector, or a single representation of normality. In this case, selection rules do not influence the final result because it is only performed one single comparison for each sample.

Table 1. Number of vectors that conform the reduced dataset for the different reduction parameters. The initial dataset is in all cases comprised of 900 not packed vectors.

Distance measure	Quality threshold	% Average reduction	Number of vectors in each fold									
			1	2	3	4	5	6	7	8	9	10
Euclidean	0.25	76.12%	217	215	214	218	216	208	216	219	206	220
	0.50	95.35%	44	42	39	44	41	44	42	42	39	41
	1.00	99.12%	7	8	8	8	8	8	8	8	8	8
	∞	99.88%	1	1	1	1	1	1	1	1	1	1
Manhattan	0.50	83.63%	153	148	150	149	151	145	147	143	141	146
	1.00	95.42%	41	41	41	43	40	42	40	43	38	43
	2.00	98.98%	7	10	11	10	8	10	9	10	8	8
	∞	99.88%	1	1	1	1	1	1	1	1	1	1

3.2 Efficiency Results

During our experimental evaluation, we measured the times employed in each different phase. In this way, we can distinguish 3 different phases in the experiment:

- **Feature Extraction and Normalization.** The first step in the experiment was to extract the characteristics from the executables and to calculate values such as entropy or size ratios. Once extracted, these features were normalised to obtain a value ranging from 0 to 1 for each point in the feature space. This stage was performed in a virtual machine to keep all malware samples isolated from the host system and to prevent any possible infection. The virtual machine used was VMWare[27], hosted in an Intel Core i5 650 clocked at 3.20 GHz and 16 GB of RAM memory. The guest machine specification was the following: 1 processor, 1 GB of RAM memory and Windows XP SP3 as operative system. Fig. 3 shows the time required by the feature extraction and normalization process for each file. This step took an average time of 28.57 milliseconds for each file analysed (93.66 μseconds/KB). Although the extraction of certain features such as PE executable header fields should require a similar amount of time for all the executables, some other values such as entropy are calculated using all the bytes present in the file: the higher the file size, the higher the time it takes to analyse it. Once extracted, feature vectors were saved into CSV files for further use.

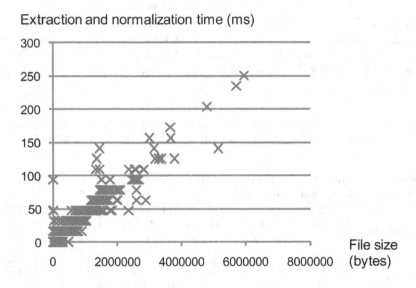

Fig. 3. Time required to extract and normalize the selected features from each executable file. The X axis represents the file size, expressed in bytes, while the Y axis shows the time taken by the extraction process, expressed in milliseconds.

- **Data Reduction.** The second step was data reduction. In this phase, we reduced the original datasets, composed of 900 vectors for each fold, which were previously saved into CSV files. In this way, we used 8 different configurations to reduce each different dataset: Euclidean distance (0.25, 0.50, 1, and ∞) and Manhattan distance (0.50, 1, 2, and ∞). This stage was conducted directly in the host machine. Fig. 4 shows the time employed in the data reduction phase. It can be observed that times do not vary considerably for the different thresholds used for each distance measure. This occurs because the operations that take a higher processing overhead are the distance measure calculations, and the algorithm proposed in Fig. 2 calculates all the distances between points before starting the clustering step. Consequently, the data reduction algorithm performs the same heavy calculations independently of the threshold specified. The average processing time consumed to reduce each fold is 97.83 seconds for Euclidean distance and 65.05 seconds for Manhattan distance. Note that this process, in spite of being very time consuming, is executed only once and does not interfere in the performance of the system.

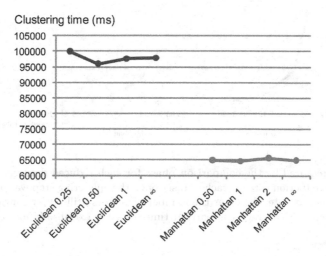

Fig. 4. Time required to reduce the original dataset composed of 900 not packed executables. The X axis shows the different experimental configurations selected for the data reduction step. The Y axis shows the time required by each clustering process performed, expressed in milliseconds.

- **Sample comparison.** Finally, the last step was the comparison of samples. For each experimental configuration employed in the data reduction stage, the samples under test (1,000 packed samples and 100 not packed samples) were compared against the reduced dataset. The total number of comparisons depends exclusively on the number of vectors present in the reduced datasets, so it is straightforward that the time employed in this step is inversely proportional to the threshold value used in the clustering process. As the previous phase, the sample comparison process was performed in the host machine. Fig. 5 shows the average time employed by the comparison step for each executable file. It can be noticed that the time required for comparison is lower when fewer vectors are utilised. For Euclidean distance the average comparison time varies from 25.62 ms for a 0.25 clustering threshold value, to 0.13 ms for an ∞ threshold (single vector representation). In the case of Manhattan distance, performance overhead is lower due to the simplicity of the calculations, and varies from 11.62 ms for a 0.50 clustering threshold value, to 0.08 ms for an ∞ threshold.

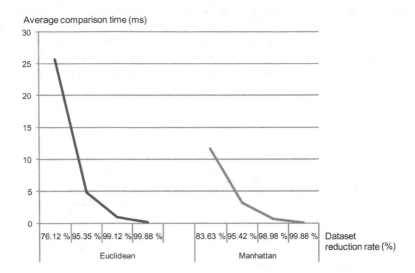

Fig. 5. Time required by the comparison phase for each reduced dataset. The X axis represents the reduction rate for each dataset once the clustering step was applied. The higher the reduction rate, the lower the number of vectors utilised for comparison. The Y axis represents the average comparison time for each executable file, expressed in milliseconds.

Subsequently, once the reduced datasets are obtained, the analysis of an executable file depends on extraction, normalization and comparison time. The times obtained highlight the conclusion that our system is able to compute between 1,000 and 2,000 executables in a minute.

3.3   Efficacy Results

Hereafter, we extracted the selected features from the executables and reduced the dataset using the 2 different distance measures and 4 different threshold values (resulting into 8 different reduced datasets). Afterwards, we employed the same 2 distance measures and the 3 combination rules described in Section 2.3 to test the datasets and obtain a final measure of deviation for each testing executable. For each measure and combination rule, we established 10 different thresholds to determine whether an executable is packed or not, and selected the one which conducted to the best results in each case in terms of False Negative Rate and False Positive Rate.

We evaluated accuracy by measuring False Negative Rate (FNR), False Positive Rate (FPR), and the Area Under the ROC Curve (AUC).

In particular, FNR is defined as:

$$FNR(\beta) = \frac{FN}{FN + TP}$$

where TP is the number of packed executable cases correctly classified (true positives) and FN is the number of packed executable cases misclassified as not packed software (false negatives).

As well, FPR is defined as:

$$FPR(\alpha) = \frac{FP}{FP + TN}$$

where FP is the number of not packed executables incorrectly detected as packed while TN is the number of not packed executables correctly classified.

Finally, the AUC is defined as the area under the curve formed by the union of the points representing FPR and TPR for each possible threshold in a plot where the X axis represents the FPR and the Y axis represents the TPR. To calculate the AUC we used the points corresponding to the 10 thresholds selected. The lowest and the highest thresholds were selected in such a way that they produced a 0% FNR and a 0% FPR respectively. The rest of thresholds were selected by equally dividing the range between the first and the last threshold. The area under the curve formed by that points was calculated dividing it into 9 trapezoidal subareas and computing them independently:

$$AUC = \sum_{i=0}^{i=9} \left((x_{i+1} - x_i) \cdot y_i + \frac{(x_{i+1} - x_i) \cdot (y_{i+1} - y_i)}{2} \right)$$

Table 2 shows the obtained results. To simplify the results presented, we only show the performance that corresponds to the best possible threshold for each configuration. Despite Euclidean distance is more time consuming than Manhattan distance, both distance measures achieve similar results for each dataset configuration. In particular, our anomaly-based packed executable detector is able to correctly detect more than 99% of packed executables while maintaining the rate of misclassified not packed executables lower than 1%. As it can be observed, mean combination rule presents slightly better results both for FNR and FPR.

Nevertheless the most important issue to consider is data reduction. We propose 4 different data reduction configurations for each distance measure. We can observe in Table 2 that results slightly get worse when a higher threshold is applied (higher reduction rate). Fig. 6 shows 6 different plots for each distance measure and selection rule. Each plot shows 4 ROC curves corresponding to the 4 different reduced datasets. We can observe that in most of the cases the ROC curves show inferior results as the threshold increases (and thus, the number of vectors to compare with, decreases). Fig. 8 represents this evolution. In each case, as the number of vectors is reduced, the system looses accuracy. Nevertheless, when the executables are compared against the mean vector, the results obtained improve and in some occasions are even better than the ones achieved for the less reduced dataset (Euclidean distance with Max selector, in Fig. 6(c), and Manhattan distance with Max and Min selectors in Fig. 6(d) and Fig. 6(f)). This behaviour is more noticeable for Max and Min selectors, owing to the fact that this selectors are more sensitive to outlier vectors (i.e., vectors

Table 2. Results for the different reduced datasets, combination rules and distance measures. Our method is able to detect more than 99% of the packed executables while maintaining FPR lower than 1%.

Dataset		Selection rule	Threshold	FNR	FPR	AUC
	Prev. work	Mean	1.54000	0.00200	0.00800	0.99676
		Max	2,20000	0,00200	0,01400	0.99887
		Min	0.62000	0.00180	0.01400	0.99815
	0.25	Mean	1.36667	0.00100	0.00500	0.99820
		Max	2.06667	0.01860	0.01000	0.99874
		Min	0.58889	0.00370	0.00700	0.99845
Euclidean	0.50	Mean	1.46667	0.00100	0.00400	0.99821
		Max	2.02222	0.01720	0.02100	0.99784
		Min	0.64444	0.00560	0.00800	0.99808
	1	Mean	1.42222	0.01170	0.01300	0.99786
		Max	1.97778	0.03420	0.02200	0.99383
		Min	0.70000	0.01090	0.03800	0.99448
	∞	-	1.33333	0.00100	0.00400	**0.99830**
	Prev. work	Mean	4.05000	0.00160	0.01000	0.99819
		Max	7.40000	0.00820	0.01800	0.99808
		Min	1.55000	0.00180	0.00800	0.99914
	0.50	Mean	3.75556	0.00110	0.00500	0.99898
		Max	6.33333	0.00780	0.01900	0.99829
		Min	1.22222	0.00100	0.00400	0.99925
Manhattan	1	Mean	3.87778	0.00110	0.00500	0.99921
		Max	6.33333	0.00890	0.01500	0.99850
		Min	1.36667	0.00200	0.00800	0.99858
	2	Mean	3.84444	0.00740	0.01700	0.99853
		Max	5.94444	0.06440	0.04700	0.98612
		Min	1.60000	0.01220	0.02300	0.99782
	∞	-	3.47778	0.00200	0.00500	**0.99901**

distant from the normality representation) and can affect in a negative way as they alter the distance value obtained. Fig. 7 visually represents this effect. In the clustering process, 3 clusters are generated. Unfortunately, 2 clusters correspond to 2 outlier vectors that do not match with the majority of the not packed vectors. Arrows in Fig.7(b) show how the final distance value is very high for the not packed sample under analysis when Max selector is chosen. At the same time, the packed sample is misclassified if the Min selector is applied, due to the proximity of a not packed sample. In contrast, as Fig. 7(c) shows, mean vector is the representation of the whole dataset and the negative effects caused by distant vectors over the single centroid are smoothed by the rest of the vectors in the group.

The results obtained indicate that it is not necessary to renounce to accuracy in order to improve the efficiency of our anomaly detection approach. Although

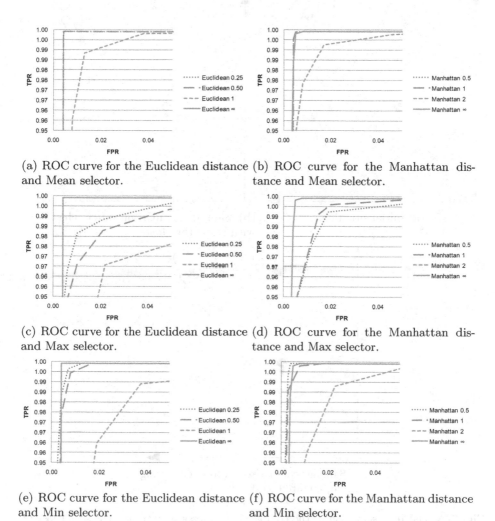

(a) ROC curve for the Euclidean distance and Mean selector.

(b) ROC curve for the Manhattan distance and Mean selector.

(c) ROC curve for the Euclidean distance and Max selector.

(d) ROC curve for the Manhattan distance and Max selector.

(e) ROC curve for the Euclidean distance and Min selector.

(f) ROC curve for the Manhattan distance and Min selector.

Fig. 6. ROC curves for the different experimental configurations. Each figure shows 4 ROC curves corresponding to the different reduced datasets. The scale selected for the X and Y axes has been reduced to 0.00 to 0.04 for X axis (false positive rate) and 0.95 to 1.00 for Y axis (true positive rate), to facilitate legibility and to represent precisely the differences among the different datasets tested. Unfortunately, the curve for Manhattan reduction with a threshold of 2 is out of the scope of the scale shown in the plot in 6(d). Note that in 6(a) and 6(b), some of the curves represented slightly overlap.

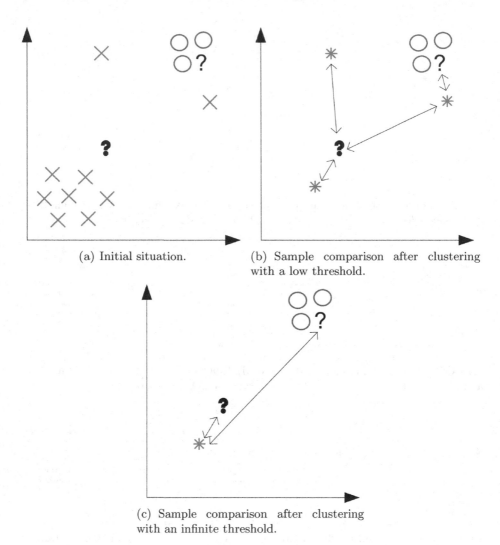

(a) Initial situation.

(b) Sample comparison after clustering with a low threshold.

(c) Sample comparison after clustering with an infinite threshold.

Fig. 7. Visual representation of the comparison process in two different scenarios. In 7(a) it is shown the initial situation. Crosses represent not packed executables, circles are packed files and question marks stand for samples to classify. In particular, bold question marks symbolise not packed vectors whereas flat ones are packed vectors. Finally, asterisks represent the centroid vectors generated for each cluster after the clustering process is performed. In 7(b) we show the vectors generated in the clustering process for a low threshold, and the effects over the distance measures obtained in the comparison phase. Similarly, 7(b) shows the unique centroid generated for the clustering with infinite threshold, and the distance measures obtained with this configuration.

accuracy is reduced when a higher reduction rate is applied, when the samples are compared to a single representation (centroid of the group), results improve. This is the configuration that should be considered to implement an efficient and accurate packed executable filter.

Empieza la figura EFFICIENCY ACCURACY

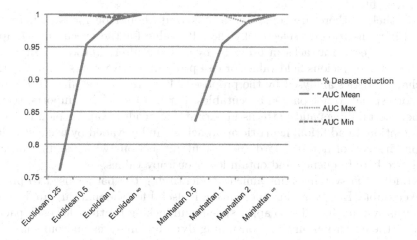

Fig. 8. Dataset reduction rate and accuracy achieved with each reduced dataset. The continuous line represents the increasing reduction rate (the higher the rate, the lower the number of samples in the reduced dataset), while the dotted lines represent the area under the ROC curve (AUC) obtained with each reduced dataset.

4   Discussion and Conclusions

The method proposed in this paper was focused on executable pre-filtering, in order to distinguish between packed and not packed executables. More specifically, it improves our previous work [21] by providing a new method for data reduction that boosts scalability in the anomaly detection process, enabling a much more efficient comparison of executable characteristics. As opposite to other approaches, anomaly detection systems do not need previously labelled data about packed executables or specific packers, as they measure the deviation of executables respect to normality (not packed executables). In contrast to signature scanning methods, this approach is packer independent.

Furthermore, accuracy results are not compromised by the dataset reduction process. It can be observed that the AUC varies slightly as the number of vectors in the dataset decreases. Nonetheless, when a single centroid vector is used, results are still sound, or even better than the ones obtained with no reduction. This fact brings us to the conclusion that it is possible to determine a single representation for not-packed executables, and that this single point is sufficiently representative to correctly classify executables as packed or not packed. Although anomaly detection systems tend to produce high false positive rates, our experimental results show very low values in all cases. These results, in addition to the time results presented in section 3.2 show that this method is a valid pre-process step for a generic unpacking schema. Since the main limitation of these unpackers is their performance overhead, a packed executable detector like our anomaly-based method with data reduction can improve their workload, acting as a filter.

Nevertheless, there are some limitations that should be focused in further work. First, the features selected by their IG value for the executable comparison are subject to attacks in order to bypass the filter. Malware writers can avoid certain suspicious field values or can program malware in such a way that the characteristics analysed by the proposed filter are more similar to the ones that correspond to not packed executables. For instance, DLL imports, section number, certain flags and patterns in executable headers can be modified with this intention. In addition, heuristic approaches can be evaded by using standard sections instead of not standard ones, or filling sections with padding data to unbalance byte frequency and obtain lower entropy values.

Secondly, the system is not aimed at identifying the packer used to protect the executable. However, this information is useful for the malware analyst and anti-virus systems in order to apply specific unpacking routines for each packer, avoiding the execution on time consuming dynamic analysis environments.

Finally, the dataset we employed was composed of executables protected with only 10 known packers. Some other packers, as well as custom packers, may implement some of the mentioned evasion techniques to bypass our filter.

In further work we will study different characteristics and alternative representations of executables to obtain an static detection system capable of providing more information about the packer used, if any. In addition, characteristics subject to attacks should be considered, in order to make the system resilient to new techniques employed by malware writers.

Acknowledgements. This research was partially supported by the Basque Government under a pre-doctoral grant given to Xabier Ugarte-Pedrero.

References

1. Kaspersky: Kaspersky security bulletin: Statistics 2008 (2008),
   http://www.viruslist.com/en/analysis?pubid=204792052
2. McAfee Labs: Mcafee whitepaper: The good, the bad, and the unknown (2011),
   http://www.mcafee.com/us/resources/white-papers/
   wp-good-bad-unknown.pdf
3. PEiD: PEiD webpage (2010), http://www.peid.info/
4. Faster Universal Unpacker: (1999), http://code.google.com/p/fuu/
5. Morgenstern, M., Pilz, H.: Useful and useless statistics about viruses and anti-virus programs. In: Proceedings of the CARO Workshop (2010),
   http://www.f-secure.com/weblog/archives/
   Maik_Morgenstern_Statistics.pdf
6. Babar, K., Khalid, F.: Generic unpacking techniques. In: Proceedings of the 2nd International Conference on Computer, Control and Communication (IC4), pp. 1–6. IEEE (2009)
7. Data Rescue: Universal PE Unpacker plug-in,
   http://www.datarescue.com/idabase/unpack_pe

8. Stewart, J.: Ollybone: Semi-automatic unpacking on ia-32. In: Proceedings of the 14th DEF CON Hacking Conference (2006)
9. Rolles, R.: Unpacking virtualization obfuscators. In: Proceedings of the 3rd USENIX Workshop on Offensive Technologies (WOOT) (2009)
10. Böhne, L.: Pandora's bochs: Automatic unpacking of malware. PhD thesis (2008)
11. Royal, P., Halpin, M., Dagon, D., Edmonds, R., Lee, W.: Polyunpack: Automating the hidden-code extraction of unpack-executing malware. In: Proceedings of the 2006 Annual Computer Security Applications Conference (ACSAC), pp. 289–300 (2006)
12. Kang, M., Poosankam, P., Yin, H.: Renovo: A hidden code extractor for packed executables. In: Proceedings of the 2007 ACM Workshop on Recurring Malcode, pp. 46–53 (2007)
13. Martignoni, L., Christodorescu, M., Jha, S.: Omniunpack: Fast, generic, and safe unpacking of malware. In: Proceedings of the 2007 Annual Computer Security Applications Conference (ACSAC), pp. 431–441 (2007)
14. Sharif, M., Yegneswaran, V., Saidi, H., Porras, P., Lee, W.: Eureka: A Framework for Enabling Static Malware Analysis. In: Jajodia, S., Lopez, J. (eds.) ESORICS 2008. LNCS, vol. 5283, pp. 481–500. Springer, Heidelberg (2008)
15. Danielescu, A.: Anti-debugging and anti-emulation techniques. CodeBreakers Journal 5(1) (2008), http://www.codebreakers-journal.com/
16. Cesare, S.: Linux anti-debugging techniques, fooling the debugger (1999), http://vx.netlux.org/lib/vsc04.html
17. Julus, L.: Anti-debugging in WIN32 (1999), http://vx.netlux.org/lib/vlj05.html
18. Shafiq, M.Z., Tabish, S.M., Mirza, F., Farooq, M.: PE-Miner: Mining Structural Information to Detect Malicious Executables in Realtime. In: Kirda, E., Jha, S., Balzarotti, D. (eds.) RAID 2009. LNCS, vol. 5758, pp. 121–141. Springer, Heidelberg (2009)
19. Shafiq, M., Tabish, S., Farooq, M.: PE-Probe: Leveraging Packer Detection and Structural Information to Detect Malicious Portable Executables. In: Proceedings of the 2009 Virus Bulletin Conference (VB), pp. 1–10 (2009)
20. Perdisci, R., Lanzi, A., Lee, W.: McBoost: Boosting scalability in malware collection and analysis using statistical classification of executables. In: Proceedings of the 2008 Annual Computer Security Applications Conference (ACSAC), pp. 301–310 (2008)
21. Ugarte-Pedrero, X., Santos, I., Bringas, P.G.: Structural Feature Based Anomaly Detection for Packed Executable Identification. In: Herrero, Á., Corchado, E. (eds.) CISIS 2011. LNCS, vol. 6694, pp. 230–237. Springer, Heidelberg (2011)
22. Kent, J.: Information gain and a general measure of correlation. Biometrika 70(1), 163–173 (1983)
23. Kumar, V.: An introduction to cluster analysis for data mining. Computer Science Department, University of Minnesota, USA (2000)
24. Heyer, L., Kruglyak, S., Yooseph, S.: Exploring expression data: identification and analysis of coexpressed genes. Genome Research 9(11), 1106–1115 (1999)
25. VX Heavens, http://vx.netlux.org/
26. Kohavi, R.: A study of cross-validation and bootstrap for accuracy estimation and model selection. In: Proceedings of the International Joint Conference on Artificial Intelligence, vol. 14, pp. 1137–1145 (1995)
27. VMware: (2011), http://www.vmware.com

Searching Short Recurrences of Nonlinear Shift Registers via Directed Acyclic Graphs

Lin Wang[1], Bing Shen[1], and TongXu Qiao[2]

[1] Science and Technology on Communication Security Laboratory,
Chengdu 610041, Sichuan, P.R. China
linwang@math.pku.edu.cn, shenbing1115@gmail.com
[2] No.30 Institute of CETC,
Chengdu 610041, Sichuan, P.R. China
qiaotx@yahoo.com

Abstract. Finding a recurrence of a shift register gives its equivalent shift register in Fibonacci configuration and hence helps to decide whether different nonlinear shift registers are equivalent, i.e., whether they generate the same set of output sequences. We define a dependence graph of a shift register and it is a directed acyclic graph related to the shift register. We show that existence of a dependence graph with a special property of a nonlinear shift register ensures existence of a short recurrence of the sequence generated by the nonlinear shift register. We also present an algorithm to search dependence graphs of a nonlinear shift register.

Keywords: nonlinear feedback shift register, directed acyclic graph, topological ordering, dependence graph, feedback graph.

1 Introduction

Stream ciphers are an important method to protect confidential data in modern communication. Though block ciphers have attracted more and more research interests, particularly after the birth of the Advanced Encryption Standard[7], stream ciphers remain interesting especially due to their comparatively higher efficiency in hardware implementation. Moreover, the design philosophy of block ciphers and stream ciphers exert mutual influence [4,5,10,15].

Feedback shift registers are a primitive unit to design stream ciphers. Much work was devoted to linear feedback shift registers (abbr. LFSR)[14] and cryptosystems based on them. However, generally it is much more difficult and hence challenging to analyze nonlinear feedback shift registers (abbr. NLFSR). Recently, using NLFSRs as pseudo-random generators has turned out to be a new trend, e.g. Trivium, a finalist of eSTREAM[5]. Thus, better analysis of NLFSRs is highly desirable.

NLFSRs have two special types: the Fibonacci configuration and the Galois configuration. The former is clearly characterized by a recurrence equation and was paid much attention[11,13]; the latter probably can be more efficiently implemented because of potentially less circuit depth. However, so far the theoretical

C.-K. Wu, M. Yung, and D. Lin (Eds.): Inscrypt 2011, LNCS 7537, pp. 44–56, 2012.

analysis of NLFSRs is not as mature as that of LFSRs, which is an obstacle to applying Galois NLFSRs in practical stream ciphers on a reliable basis. Two approaches are possible choices. One approach is to construct Galois NLFSRs from Fibonacci NLFSRs. Dubrova [8] gave a sufficient condition on which two NLFSRs generate the same set of sequences, and also presented an algorithm to transform a Fibonacci NLFSR to its equivalent NLFSR in a special Galois configuration. Thereafter efficiency of Galois configuration was improved at circuit level[6]. The other is to characterize Galois NLFSRs by their equivalent Fibonacci NLFSRs, which is nonetheless challenging.

Our contribution is a sufficient condition in the language of graph theory to ensure existence of a short (nonlinear) recurrence of an NLFSR. This condition is tested algorithmically and an algorithm is presented to generate the recurrence if this sufficient condition holds. This result partially helps to decide whether different NLFSRs are equivalent and whether a Galois NLFSR can be transformed to a short Fibonacci NLFSR.

The rest of this paper is organized as follows. Section 2 defines dependence graphs of an NLFSR and explains that a special type of dependence graphs generate recurrences of the NLFSR. Section 3 describes an algorithm to search dependence graphs of an NLFSR. In Section 4 we show that our method extends the previous result by Dubrova[8]. Section 5 presents a vivid toy example. In the last section, we conclude by leaving some problems in future.

2   A Sufficient Condition for Existence of Short Recurrences

An NLFSR of order n has n bits and its state at clock cycle t is represented by the vector

$$s(t) = (s_0(t), s_1(t), \cdots, s_{n-1}(t)).$$

Then $(s_i(t))_{t=0}^{\infty}$ is the sequence of values of the i-th bit.

A general NLFSR of order n is characterized by the state transition equations below

$$\left\{ \begin{array}{ll} s_0(t) &= f_0(s_0(t-1), s_1(t-1), \cdots, s_{n-1}(t-1)), \\ s_1(t) &= f_1(s_0(t-1), s_1(t-1), \cdots, s_{n-1}(t-1)), \\ \vdots \\ s_{n-1}(t) &= f_{n-1}(s_0(t-1), s_1(t-1), \cdots, s_{n-1}(t-1)), \end{array} \right. \tag{1}$$

where $f_0, f_1, \cdots, f_{n-1}$ are boolean functions of n variables. The output sequence of this NLFSR is determined by Eqs.(1) and its initial state $s(0)$.

Definition 1. [8] For the NLFSR defined by Eqs.(1), the nonlinear recurrence of order m describing the sequence of values of the i-th bit is the expression of type

$$s_i(t) = \bigoplus_{j=0}^{2^m-1} \left(a_j \prod_{k=0}^{m-1} (s_i(t-m+k))^{j_k} \right),$$

where $a_j \in \{0, 1\}$, $\oplus$ is addition modulo 2, $(j_{m-1} \cdots j_1 j_0)$ is the binary expansion of j with j_0 being the least significant bit, and $(s_i(t - m + k))^{j_k}$ is defined as follows:

$$(s_i(t - m + k))^{j_k} = \begin{cases} s_i(t - m + k), & \text{for } j_k = 1; \\ 1, & \text{for } j_k = 0. \end{cases}$$

Definition 2. For the NLFSR defined by Eqs.(1), let $s_\ell(t)$ be expressed by a boolean function f defined on

$$\{s_i(t_j) : i = 0, 1, \cdots, n - 1; 0 \leqslant t_j < \infty\}.$$

The pair (ℓ, f) is called to be a *representative* of the ℓ-th bit. The *dependence set* of the ℓ-th bit with respect to f, denoted by $\mathrm{dep}_f(\ell)$, is the set of bits i such that $s_i(t')$ at some clock cycle t' occurs in the algebraic normal form of f, i.e.,

$$\mathrm{dep}_f(\ell) = \{i : f|_{s_i(t')=0} \neq f|_{s_i(t')=1} \text{ for some clock cycle } t'\},$$

where $f|_{s_i(t')=b}$ is the boolean function obtained by replacing each occurrence of $s_i(t')$ by b in f. Let

$$S = \{k : f|_{s_i(t+k)=0}(t) \neq f|_{s_i(t+k)=1}(t) \text{ for some } i \in \{0, 1, \cdots, n - 1\}\}.$$

We call the greatest integer in S to be the *upper time* of the representative (ℓ, f), denoted by $u_t((\ell, f))$, and also the least integer in S as the *lower time* of the representative (ℓ, f), denoted by $l_t((\ell, f))$. If the k-th bit $s_k(t')$ occurs as a linear term in the algebraic normal form of f, then the k-th bit is expressed by a boolean function $f^{(k)}$ as

$$s_k(t') = s_\ell(t) \oplus s_k(t') \oplus f = f^{(k)}. \tag{2}$$

The two representatives (ℓ, f) and $(k, f^{(k)})$ are said to be *associated* to each other. A representative can also be said to be *associated* to itself.

Remark 1. The dependence set $\mathrm{dep}_f(\ell)$ tells exactly which bits determine the value of the ℓ-th bit by the boolean function f. The upper and lower times indicate the range of clock cycles to determine the present value of the ℓ-th bit by the boolean function f. The term *dependence set* occurred in [8].

If f_i is an equation in Eqs.(1) and $(k, f_i^{(k)})$ is an associated representative of (i, f_i) defined by Eq.(2), one sees that $u_t((i, f_i)) = l_t((i, f_i)) = -1$, $u_t((k, f_i^{(k)})) = 1$ and $l_t((k, f_i^{(k)})) = 0$. Actually, the association in Definition 2 defines an equivalence relation of representatives.

Example 1. An NLFSR consisting of four bits satisfies

$$\begin{aligned} s_0(t) &= f_0(s_0(t - 2), s_1(t - 1), s_2(t - 1), s_3(t - 2)) \\ &= s_1(t - 1) \oplus s_0(t - 2)s_2(t - 1)s_3(t - 2). \end{aligned}$$

Then $(0, f_0)$ is a representative of the 0 bit and $\mathrm{dep}_{f_0}(0) = \{0, 1, 2, 3\}$. Besides, $u_t((0, f_0)) = -1$ and $l_t((0, f_0)) = -2$. Moving linear terms yields

$$s_1(t) = f_0^{(1)}(s_0(t-1), s_0(t+1), s_2(t), s_3(t-1))$$
$$= s_0(t+1) \oplus s_0(t-1)s_2(t)s_3(t-1).$$

Hence, $(1, f_0^{(1)})$ is a representative of the 1st bit associated to $(0, f_0)$ and $\mathrm{dep}_{f_0^{(1)}}(1) = \{0, 2, 3\}$. Besides, $u_t((1, f_0^{(1)})) = 1$ and $l_t((1, f_0^{(1)})) = -1$.

If the NLFSR defined by Eqs.(1) satisfies $\mathrm{dep}_{f_i}(i) \subset \{0, 1, \cdots, i, i+1\}$ for each $i = 0, 1, \cdots, n-1$, then it is said to be in a Galois configuration.

While readers are referred to [1,2,3,9] for involved graph theory, some terms are exactly defined below because in the literature there appear quite a few terms concerning the same (or similar) meanings. A *digraph* G is a pair (V, E), where V is the set of nodes and $E \subset V \times V$. The ordered pair $(u, v) \in E$ is called an *edge* of G. If $(u, v) \in E$, u is said to be a *predecessor* of v and v is said to be a *successor* of u. We call $\langle v_0, v_1, \cdots, v_n \rangle$ to be a *path* of *length* n in G if $(v_i, v_{i+1}) \in E$ for $i = 0, 1, \cdots, n-1$. If $v_n = v_0$, this path is called a *cycle*. We call a digraph with no cycle to be a *directed acyclic graph*(abbr.DAG). A node with no predecessors(successors) is called a *source*(*sink*). A *topological ordering* of the digraph G is a linear ordering of its nodes such that u precedes v in the ordering for each $(u, v) \in E$. For a digraph G and its node v, we denote $\mathbf{Pred}_G(v)$ as the set of predecessors of v and $\mathbf{Succ}_G(v)$ as the set of successors of v. If G has a unique source, we write $\mathbf{Depth}_G(v)$ as the *distance* from the source to v, i.e., the length of the shortest path from the source to v. When G is given without ambiguity, we also write respectively $\mathbf{Pred}(v)$, $\mathbf{Succ}(v)$ and $\mathbf{Depth}(v)$ for convenience.

Definition 3. A *dependence graph* for the ℓ-th bit of the NLFSR defined by Eqs.(1) is a DAG G satisfying the following conditions:

1. There exists a unique source node v_σ.
2. Denote V to be the set of nodes of G, and denote B to be the set of boolean functions defined on $s_i(t_l)$ for $i = 0, 1, 2, \cdots, n-1$ and $0 \leqslant t_l < \infty$. The mapping $\theta : V \to \{0, 1, 2, \cdots, n-1\}$ attaches to each node an integer. Particularly, we define $\theta(v_\sigma) = \ell$. There also exists only one sink node v_τ such that $\theta(v_\tau) = \ell$. Besides, the mapping $\lambda : V \backslash \{v_\sigma\} \to B$ attaches to each non-source node a boolean function. Furthermore, for each non-source node v of G, $(\theta(v), \lambda(v))$ is a representative of the $\theta(v)$-th bit of this NLFSR.
3. Let v be a non-source node of G. For $v_1 \neq v_2$, where $v_1, v_2 \in \mathbf{Pred}(v)$, it holds that $\theta(v_1) \neq \theta(v_2)$. Besides,

$$\mathrm{dep}_{\lambda(v)}(\theta(v)) = \{\theta(v') : v' \in \mathbf{Pred}(v)\}.$$

4. For a node v with $\mathbf{Depth}(v) \geqslant 2$, the attached representative $(\theta(v), \lambda(v))$ is not associated to $(\theta(v'), \lambda(v'))$ for any $v' \in \mathbf{Pred}(v)$.

5. No representative is attached more than once, i.e., for any two distinct non-source nodes v_1 and v_2 of G,

$$(\theta(v_1), \lambda(v_1)) \neq (\theta(v_2), \lambda(v_2)).$$

Remark 2. Restrictive conditions 4 and 5 in Definition 3 are not essential but used to reduce redundancy. See Prop.1 below.

Proposition 1. *Let G be a DAG satisfying Conditions 1-3 in Definition 3 but not Condition 4 or 5. Let $R = \{(\theta(v), \lambda(v)) : v$ is a non-source node of $G\}$. Then there exists a dependence graph G' for the ℓ-th bit such that for each non-source node v' of G',*

$$(\theta(v'), \lambda(v')) \in R.$$

Proof. Assume that there exist a pair of nodes v and w such that w is a successor of v and $(\theta(v), \lambda(v))$ is associated to $(\theta(w), \lambda(w))$. By Definition 2, there exists a node u as a predecessor of v such that $\theta(u) = \theta(w)$. For each $v' \in \mathbf{Succ}_G(w)$ add an edge from u to v'. Now remove w and delete all edges starting from w or heading to w. Notice that newly added edges admit any topological ordering of G and hence no cycle is added. However, new incompatibility of Condition 4 is possibly introduced, say, $(\theta(u), \lambda(u))$ is associated to $(\theta(v'), \lambda(v'))$ where $v' \in \mathbf{Succ}_G(w)$ is a successor of w in the original G. Anyhow, since

$$\min\{\mathbf{Depth}_G(u), \mathbf{Depth}_G(v')\} < \min\{\mathbf{Depth}_G(v), \mathbf{Depth}_G(w)\},$$

applying this process recursively for finitely many times finally yields a DAG G_1 admitting Conditions 1-4.

Assume that nodes $v_1, v_2, \cdots, v_i$ exactly share the same representative (k, f), i.e.,

$$\{v_1, v_2, \cdots, v_i\} = \{v : (\theta(v), \lambda(v)) = (k, f)\}.$$

Without loss of generality, suppose that $\mathbf{Depth}_{G_1}(v_1) \leqslant \mathbf{Depth}_{G_1}(v_j)$ for $j = 2, 3, \cdots, i$. That is, there exists a topological ordering of G in which v_1 occurs before $v_2, v_3, \cdots, v_i$. Let $S = \mathbf{Succ}_{G_1}(v_2) \cup \mathbf{Succ}_{G_1}(v_3) \cup \cdots \cup \mathbf{Succ}_{G_1}(v_i)$. For each $w \in S$, add a new edge from v_1 to w. Since there is no path from w to v_1, no cycle appears. Then remove nodes $v_2, v_3, \cdots, v_i$ and delete all edges starting from them or heading to them. This process does not contradict Conditions 1-4 in Definition 3, but reduces at least one representative incompatible with Condition 5. Inductively, a dependence graph G' can be constructed such that G' satisfies Conditions 1-5 in Definition 3. Through our construction above, no representatives are attached to nodes of G' other than those attached to nodes of G. □

Definition 4. Let G be a dependence graph for the ℓ-th bit of an NLFSR. For the source v_σ of G we define the *upper time* $U(v_\sigma) = 0$ and iteratively $U(v) = \max\{U(v') : v' \in \mathbf{Pred}(v)\} + u_t((\theta(v), \lambda(v)))$ as the *upper time* of a non-source node v. Similarly, we define the *lower time* $L(v_\sigma) = 0$ and iteratively $L(v) = \min\{L(v') : v' \in \mathbf{Pred}(v)\} + l_t((\theta(v), \lambda(v)))$ as the *lower time* of a non-source node v.

Proposition 2. *If there exists a dependence graph G for the ℓ-th bit of an NLFSR, then there exists an algebraic equation in values of the ℓ-th bit at most $U(v_\tau) - L(v_\tau) + 1$ clock cycles, where v_τ is the sink of G such that $\theta(v_\tau) = \ell$.*

Proof. Below we present Algorithm 1 to obtain an algebraic equation involving values of the ℓ-th bit from a given dependence graph for the ℓ-th bit.

Algorithm 1. Find an equation from a dependence graph

Input: a dependence graph G for the ℓ-th bit
Output: an equation involving values of the ℓ-th bit
1: compute a topological ordering of G from v_σ until v_τ: $v_0, v_1, \cdots, v_k$, where $v_0 = v_\sigma$, $v_k = v_\tau$.
2: let g_0 be the identity mapping.
3: **for** $i = 1$ to k **do**
4:    **for each** $v_j \in \mathbf{Pred}(v_i)$ **do**
5:       replace each occurrence of $s_{\theta(v_j)}(t)$ in $\lambda(v_i)$ by g_j, where g_j is an expression of $s_{\theta(v_j)}(t)$ in $s_\ell(t_l)$ at some clock cycles t_l. {substitute for variables involving non-ℓ bits}
6:    **end for**
7:    get the expression g_i of $s_{\theta(v_i)}(t)$ in $s_\ell(t_l)$ at some clock cycles t_l.
8: **end for**
9: **return** the expression $s_\ell(t) = g_k$.

Existence of a topological ordering ensures correctness of this algorithm.

For each $j \in \{1, 2, \cdots, k\}$, Algorithm 1 gives an expression of $s_{\theta(v_j)}(t)$ by g_j. Then $(\theta(v_j), g_j)$ is an representative of the $\theta(v_j)$-th bit of this NLFSR. Moreover, notice that

$$L(v_j) \leqslant l_t((\theta(v_j), g_j)) \leqslant u_t((\theta(v_j), g_j)) \leqslant U(v_j).$$

Thus, $s_\ell(t) = g_k$ involves at most $U(v_\tau) - L(v_\tau) + 1$ clock cycles.   □

Note that (ℓ, g_k) obtained by Algorithm 1 is a representative. Thus, if $U(v_\tau) = U(v_k) < 0$, then $s_\ell(t) = g_k$ is a recurrence. Since $l_t((\ell, g_k)) \geqslant L(v_k)$, $-L(v_\tau)$ is an upper bound of the order of this recurrence, i.e., to determine $s_\ell(t)$ we need at most the values of $-L(v_\tau)$ previous clock cycles. Therefore, we conclude that

Proposition 3. *Use conditions in Prop.2. If $U(v_\tau) < 0$, then the expression of $s_\ell(t)$ obtained by Algorithm 1 gives a recurrence describing the sequence of values of the ℓ-th bit whose order is less than or equal to $-L(v_\tau)$.*

Remark 3. Let G be a dependence graph of the NLFSR defined by Eqs.(1) such that each $(\theta(v), \lambda(v))$ attached to one of its nodes is (associated to) a representative generated by Eqs.(1), i.e. (i, f_i), $i = 0, 1, \cdots, n - 1$ and their associated representatives. (Algorithm 2 in Section 3 seeks such a dependence graph.) Then we have $U(v_\tau) \leqslant \mathbf{Depth}(v_\tau)$, $L(v_\tau) \geqslant -\mathbf{Depth}(v_\tau)$ and $U(v_\tau) - L(v_\tau) \leqslant \mathbf{Depth}(v_\tau)$. Since $-L(v_\tau) \leqslant \mathbf{Depth}(v_\tau) \leqslant n^2$, the recurrence by Algorithm 1 involves at most n^2 clock cycles, not too large compared with the number of bits of the NLFSR. In this sense, we roughly call the recurrence generated from a dependence graph to be *short*. (This is not a definition.)

Complexity of Algorithm 1. We estimate the running time of Algorithm 1 for a dependence graph as in Remark 3. Recall big Oh notations to describe the asymptotic behavior of an algorithm. An algorithm is said to be of complexity $O(f(n))$ if it can be completed by $cf(n)$ basic operations for some constant c when the problem size n approaches to infinity. Let n be the number of bits of the NLFSR defined by Eqs.(1), and let m be the greatest number of terms of algebraic normal forms of f_i in Eqs.(1), $i = 0, 1, \cdots, n - 1$. For an LFSR, $m \leqslant n$. For general NLFSRs, $1 \leqslant m \leqslant 2^n$ and we use both n and m to describe the problem size. When the system of equations (1) is sparse, m is possibly of size $O(n)$; When the system of equations (1) is dense, m is possibly of size $O(2^n)$. Let G be a dependence graph of the NLFSR given by Eqs.(1) with r nodes and e edges. See $r \leqslant n^2$ and $e \leqslant n(r - 1) \leqslant n^3$. Note that the topological ordering of G can be computed in linear time with respect to $r + e$[3], in time $O(n^3)$. Besides, replacing a variable in $\lambda(v_i)$ is computationally equivalent to a polynomial multiplication. Thus, Algorithm 1 requires at most $O(n^3)$ polynomial multiplications. More precise estimation on the complexity of Algorithm 1 in bit operations depends also on the number of terms of Eqs.(1). Below we give a rough estimation of bit operations of the prototype Algorithm 1. For polynomials p of a terms and q of b terms, multiplication for pq can be implemented by ab bit operations. Denote $T(v_i)$ to be the number of terms of g_i in Algorithm 1, i.e. the number of bit operations in Line 5 of Algorithm 1. For $w \in G$, we have

$$T(w) \leqslant m \prod_{v \in \mathbf{Pred}(w)} T(v).$$

Hence, $\log_m T(v_i) \leqslant 1 + \sum_{j=0}^{i-1} \log_m T(v_j) \leqslant 2^{i-1}$, i.e. $T(v_i) \leqslant m^{2^{i-1}}$. Since $\sum_{i=0}^k m^{2^i} \leqslant 2m^{2^k}$, seeing $k < n^2$, we have

$$\sum_{i=0}^k T(v_i) \leqslant m^{2^{n^2}}.$$

Therefore, Algorithm 1 has bit complexity $O(m^{2^{n^2}})$. It is desirable to improve efficiency of the raw Algorithm 1.

Remark 4. Prop.2 and Prop.3 together only give a sufficient condition to ensure existence of recurrences of lower order. On one hand, generally it is difficult to decide whether the algebraic expression obtained by Algorithm 1 implies a recurrence. Prop.3 gives only a sufficient condition to ensure existence of a recurrence, and it is possible that a dependence graph with $U(v_\tau) > 0$ also generates a recurrence through Algorithm 1. See the example in Section 5. On the other hand, the converse statement of Prop.2 is not necessarily true. For example, an NLFSR of order three defined by

$$\begin{cases} s_0(t) = s_0(t-1)s_1(t-1) \oplus s_1(t-1), \\ s_1(t) = s_0(t-1)s_1(t-1)s_2(t-1), \\ s_2(t) = s_0(t-1) \oplus s_0(t-1)s_2(t-1), \end{cases}$$

has no dependence graph. Anyhow, the sequence of values of the 1st bit is described by

$$s_1(t) = s_1(t-1) \oplus s_1(t-1)s_1(t-2), t \geqslant 2.$$

3   Search Dependence Graphs of an NLFSR

In this section we give an algorithm to search possible dependence graphs of an NLFSR.

Given a list of all representatives computed by Eqs.(1), i.e. (i, f_i), $i = 0, 1,$ $\cdots, n-1$ and their associated representatives, Algorithm 2 below generates a dependence graph for the ℓ-th bit of this NLFSR if there exists one.

Algorithm 2. Search a dependence graph of an NLFSR

Input: all representatives computed from Eqs.(1)
Output: a dependence graph for the ℓ-th bit if there exists one, or failure
1: Add v_σ in G and set $\theta(v_\sigma) = \ell$. {initialize the source node}
2: **for each unused** representative (k, f) **do**
3:      **if** there exists nodes $v_1, v_2, \cdots, v_l$ in G such that $\theta(v_i) \neq \theta(v_j), i, j \in \{1, 2, \cdots, l\}$,

$$\mathrm{dep}_f(k) = \{\theta(v_i) : i = 1, 2, \cdots, l\}$$

and (k, f) is not associated to $(\theta(v_i), \lambda(v_i))$, $i = 1, 2, \cdots, l$ **then**
4:          add a node v to G, set $(\theta(v), \lambda(v)) = (k, f)$ and append new edges from v_i to v, $i = 1, 2, \cdots, l$.
5:          **if** $\theta(v) = \ell$ **then**
6:              **return** G
7:          **end if**
8:          tag the representative (k, f) to be **used**
9:      **else**
10:          **return failure**
11:      **end if**
12: **end for**

Correctness of Algorithm 2. It is tedious but not difficult to check that a graph constructed by Algorithm 2 is a DAG complying with conditions in Definition 3.

Completeness of Algorithm 2. We have to show that there exists no dependence graph for the ℓ-th bit of the NLFSR if Algorithm 2 returns **failure**. Assume that Algorithm 2 constructs a graph G_b and stops at Line 10, but nevertheless assume that there exists a dependence graph G for the ℓ-th bit of the NLFSR. Let $v_\sigma, v_1, v_2, \cdots, v_l, v_\tau$ be (part of) a topological ordering of G, where v_σ is the source and v_τ is the sink satisfying $\theta(v_\tau) = \ell$. Notice that v_σ is also the source of G_b but v_τ is not a node of G_b(Otherwise, Algorithm 2 stops at Line 6). Then suppose v_k to be the first node not appearing in G_b by the topological ordering. More precisely, in the topological ordering above each representative $(\theta(v_i), \lambda(v_i))$ is attached to some node in G_b for $i = 1, 2, \cdots, k - 1$ but the representative $(\theta(v_k), \lambda(v_k))$ is attached to no node of G_b. However, by Definition 3 and the supposition above, there exists nodes $v'_1, v'_2, \cdots, v'_j$ in G_b such that

$$\text{dep}_{\lambda(v_k)}(\theta(v_k)) = \{\theta(v'_i) : i = 1, 2, \cdots, j\}$$

and $(\theta(v_k), \lambda(v_k))$ is not associated to $(\theta(v'_i), \lambda(v'_i))$, $i = 1, 2, \cdots, j$. Hence we can append v_k into G_b, contradictory to our assumptions above. Moreover, since there exists at least one representative of the ℓ-th bit, Algorithm 2 stops either at Line 6 or at Line 10.

Complexity of Algorithm 2. Use the same notation as in Setion 2. We denote m as the greatest number of terms of equations in Eqs.(1). Main computation of Algorithm 2 is implicit search in Line 3. It scans an equation f to find $\text{dep}_f(k)$, taking $O(m)$ bit operations. Decision in Line 3 also requires searching G once, with complexity $O(e)$, where e is the number of edges of G. Since $e < n^3$, a search of G takes $O(n^3)$ bit operations. Furthermore, we have at most n^2 representatives from Eqs.(1). Thus, the complexity of Algorithm 2 is $O(n^2(m + n^3))$. Here is only a prototype algorithm. Heuristic search algorithms[3], robotic learning or other maneuvers of artificial intelligence[12] are possible candidates to improve efficiency of this algorithm .

Non-unique outputs of Algorithm 2. An NLFSR possibly has more than one dependence graphs. See the example in Section 5.

4   The Relation with the Previous Result

In the language of graph reduction, Dubrova [8, III] gave a sufficient condition for existence of a recurrence.

A *feedback graph* of the NLFSR defined by Eqs.(1) consists of nodes 0, 1, $\cdots$, $n - 1$ which represent corresponding bits, and a directed edge (i, j) is defined if and only if $i \in \text{dep}_{f_j}(j)$. Provided that j is the unique predecessor of i, the *substitution* $\text{sub}(i, j)$ removes the node i and replaces any edge (i, k) by (j, k) for $k \neq i$.

Proposition 4. *[8, Lemma 1] If the feedback graph of an n-bit NLFSR can be reduced to a single node ℓ by substitutions, then there exists a nonlinear recurrence of order n describing the sequence of values of the bit ℓ.*

As explained below, Prop.2 and Prop.3 together extend Prop.4.

Proposition 5. *If the feedback graph of the NLFSR defined by Eqs.(1) is reduced to a single node ℓ by substitutions, then there exists a dependence graph for the ℓ-th bit such that $U(v_\tau) < 0$ and $L(v_\tau) \geqslant -n$, where v_τ is the sink of this dependence graph satisfying $\theta(v_\tau) = \ell$.*

Proof. Without loss of generality, suppose that the feedback graph G is reduced to a single node 0 through a sequence of substitutions.

We define a new digraph G' as follows: the nodes of G' is $\{v_0, v_1, \cdots, v_{n-1}, v_\tau\}$; (v_i, v_j), where $v_j \neq v_0$, is an edge of G' if and only if (i, j) is an edge of G; (v_i, v_τ) is an edge of G' if and only if $(i, 0)$ is an edge of G. Let $v_\sigma = v_0$. Define $\theta(v_\sigma) = 0$, $(\theta(v_\tau), \lambda(v_\tau)) = (0, f_0)$, and $(\theta(v_i), \lambda(v_i)) = (i, f_i)$ for $i = 1, 2, \cdots, n-1$.

On one hand, notice that a substitution does not eliminate any cycle in a feedback graph. On the other hand, G' is a DAG if and only if each cycle in G passes through the node 0. Since G collapses to the node 0 via substitutions, G' is therefore a DAG with a unique source v_σ and a sink v_τ.

Moreover, since G' has exactly $n + 1$ nodes and all attached representatives are distinct, Conditions 4 and 5 in Definition 3 also hold. Therefore, G' is a dependence graph of this NLFSR.

Furthermore, since $u_t((\theta(v), \lambda(v))) = -1$ for any non-source node v, we have $U(v) < 0$. Particularly, $U(v_\tau) < 0$. Since $l_t((\theta(v), \lambda(v))) = -1$ and $\mathbf{Depth}_{G'}(v_\tau) \leqslant n$, $L(v_\tau) \geqslant -n$. $\qquad \square$

Remark 5. The inverse of Prop.5 is not necessarily true. It is possible that an NLFSR has a dependence graph but its feedback graph does not reduce to a single node through substitutions. See the example in Section 5.

5   A Toy Example

An NLFSR is given by state transition equations (3) as below [8, III]:

$$
\begin{cases}
s_0(t) = f_0(s_0(t-1), s_1(t-1), s_2(t-1), s_3(t-1)) \\
\quad\quad = s_0(t-1) \oplus s_1(t-1), \\
s_1(t) = f_1(s_0(t-1), s_1(t-1), s_2(t-1), s_3(t-1)) \\
\quad\quad = s_2(t-1), \\
s_2(t) = f_2(s_0(t-1), s_1(t-1), s_2(t-1), s_3(t-1)) \\
\quad\quad = s_3(t-1), \\
s_3(t) = f_3(s_0(t-1), s_1(t-1), s_2(t-1), s_3(t-1)) \\
\quad\quad = s_0(t-1) \oplus s_2(t-1)s_3(t-1).
\end{cases}
\tag{3}
$$

We can no more use Prop.4 to get a recurrence describing the sequence of values of some bit of the NLFSR (3), since the feedback graph of Eqs.(3), Fig.1, cannot reduce to a single node through substitutions. However, below we use our method to give such a recurrence.

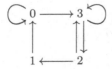

Fig. 1. Feedback graph

First, possible representatives are listed in Table 1. Each column contains a representative, its dependence set and its associated representative(s).

Table 1. Representatives by Eqs.(3)

representative	$(0, f_0)$	$(0, f_3^{(0)})$	$(1, f_0^{(1)})$	$(1, f_1)$	$(2, f_2)$	$(2, f_1^{(2)})$	$(3, f_3)$	$(3, f_2^{(3)})$
dependence set	$\{0,1\}$	$\{2,3\}$	$\{0\}$	$\{2\}$	$\{3\}$	$\{1\}$	$\{0,2,3\}$	$\{2\}$
associated reps.	$(1, f_0^{(1)})$	$(3, f_3)$	$(0, f_0)$	$(2, f_1^{(2)})$	$(3, f_2^{(3)})$	$(1, f_1)$	$(0, f_3^{(0)})$	$(2, f_2)$

Fig.2 and Fig.3 are two dependence graphs for the 0 bit of this NLFSR.

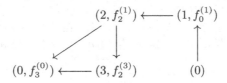

Fig. 2. Dependence graph 1

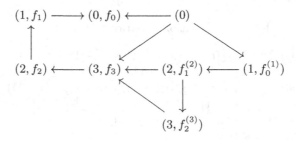

Fig. 3. Dependence graph 2

For the dependence graph Fig.3, we have $U(v_\tau) = -1$ and there exists a recurrence of order not larger than $-L(v_\tau) = 4$ describing the sequence of values of the 0 bit. For the dependence graph Fig.2, we have $U(v_\tau) = 4$ and $L(v_\tau) = 0$. Anyhow, running Algorithm 1 on the dependence graph Fig.2 gives expressions involving the 0 bit:

$$s_1(t) = s_0(t+1) \oplus s_0(t),$$
$$s_2(t) = s_0(t+2) \oplus s_0(t+1),$$
$$s_3(t) = s_0(t+3) \oplus s_0(t+2),$$
$$s_0(t) = s_0(t+2) \oplus s_0(t+3) \oplus s_0(t+4) \oplus s_0(t+2)s_0(t+3)$$
$$\oplus s_0(t+1)s_0(t+3) \oplus s_0(t+1)s_0(t+2).$$

Equivalently, we get the recurrence of the sequence of values of the 0 bit as below

$$s_0(t) = s_0(t-4) \oplus s_0(t-1) \oplus s_0(t-2) \oplus s_0(t-2)s_0(t-3)$$
$$\oplus s_0(t-1)s_0(t-3) \oplus s_0(t-1)s_0(t-2).$$

6   Conclusion and Future Work

We give a sufficient condition, existence of a dependence graph with $U(v_\tau) < 0$, to ensure existence of a recurrence describing the sequence of values of a bit of a general NLFSR. We also present an algorithm to find such dependence graphs based on state transition equations and also an algorithm to construct a recurrence from such a dependence graph. As Remark 4 shows, our method is restricted. Thus, it is natural to ask what percentage of NLFSRs have a dependence graph. Besides, since an NLFSR possibly has more than one dependence graphs, it is desirable to give an algorithm to find the dependence graph of small size. Furthermore, it also remains interesting to optimize Algorithm 1 for better performance.

Acknowledgments. The authors would like to express their sincere gratitude to the anonymous referees who made a number of valuable comments to improve the manuscript.

References

1. Adriansyah, A., van Dongen, B.F., van der Aalst, W.M.P.: Towards Robust Conformance Checking. In: zur Muehlen, M., Su, J. (eds.) BPM 2010 Workshops. LNBIP, vol. 66, pp. 122–133. Springer, Heidelberg (2011)
2. Bondy, J.A., Murty, U.S.R.: Graph Theory. Springer (2008)
3. Cormen, T.H., Leiserson, C.E., Rivest, R.L., Stein, C.: Introduction to Algorithms, 2nd edn. The MIT Press, Cambridge (2001)
4. De Cannière, C., Preneel, B.: Trivium: a Stream Cipher Construction Inspired by Block Cipher Design Principles. eSTREAM, ECRYPT Stream Cipher Project, Report 2006/021, http://www.ecrypt.eu.org/stream/papersdir/2006/021
5. De Cannière, C., Preneel, B.: TRIVIUM. In: Robshaw, M., Billet, O. (eds.) New Stream Cipher Designs. LNCS, vol. 4986, pp. 244–266. Springer, Heidelberg (2008)
6. Chabloz, J., Mansouri, S.S., Dubrova, E.: An Algorithm for Constructing a Fastest Galois NLFSR Generating a Given Sequence. In: Carlet, C., Pott, A. (eds.) SETA 2010. LNCS, vol. 6338, pp. 41–54. Springer, Heidelberg (2010)
7. Daemen, J., Rijmen, V.: The Design of Rijndael: AES - the Advanced Encryption Standard. Springer (2001)
8. Dubrova, E.: A Transformation from the Fibonacci to the Galois NLFSRs. IEEE Transactions on Information Theory 55(11), 5263–5271 (2009)
9. Foulds, L.R.: Graph Theory Applications. Springer (1992)
10. Golić, J.D.: Modes of Operation of Stream Ciphers. In: Stinson, D.R., Tavares, S. (eds.) SAC 2000. LNCS, vol. 2012, pp. 233–247. Springer, Heidelberg (2001)
11. Golomb, S.: Shift Register Sequences. Aegean Park Press, Walnut Creek (1982)

12. Russell, S.J., Norvis, P.: Artificial Intelligence: a Modern Approach. Prentice Hall, Inc. (1995)
13. Wan, Z.X., Dai, Z.D., Liu, M.L., Feng, X.N.: Nonlinear Shift Registers. Science Press (1978) (in Chinese)
14. Wan, Z.X.: Algebra and Codes. Science Press (1980) (in Chinese)
15. Data Assurance & Communication Security Center, Chinese Science Academy, 3GPP Confidentiality and Integrity Algorithms 128-EEA3 & 128-EIA3, http://zucalg.forumotion.net/

Differential and Linear Cryptanalysis Using Mixed-Integer Linear Programming[*]

Nicky Mouha[1,3,**], Qingju Wang[1,2,3], Dawu Gu[2], and Bart Preneel[1,3]

[1] Department of Electrical Engineering ESAT/SCD-COSIC,
Katholieke Universiteit Leuven. Kasteelpark Arenberg 10, B-3001 Heverlee, Belgium
[2] Department of Computer Science and Engineering, Shanghai Jiao Tong University,
Shanghai, China
[3] Interdisciplinary Institute for BroadBand Technology (IBBT), Belgium
{Nicky.Mouha,Qingju.Wang}@esat.kuleuven.be

Abstract. Differential and linear cryptanalysis are two of the most powerful techniques to analyze symmetric-key primitives. For modern ciphers, resistance against these attacks is therefore a mandatory design criterion. In this paper, we propose a novel technique to prove security bounds against both differential and linear cryptanalysis. We use mixed-integer linear programming (MILP), a method that is frequently used in business and economics to solve optimization problems. Our technique significantly reduces the workload of designers and cryptanalysts, because it only involves writing out simple equations that are input into an MILP solver. As very little programming is required, both the time spent on cryptanalysis and the possibility of human errors are greatly reduced. Our method is used to analyze Enocoro-128v2, a stream cipher that consists of 96 rounds. We prove that 38 rounds are sufficient for security against differential cryptanalysis, and 61 rounds for security against linear cryptanalysis. We also illustrate our technique by calculating the number of active S-boxes for AES.

Keywords: Differential cryptanalysis, Linear Cryptanalysis, Mixed-Integer Linear Programming, MILP, Enocoro, AES, CPLEX.

1 Introduction

Differential cryptanalysis [1] and linear cryptanalysis [19] have shown to be two of the most important techniques in the analysis of symmetric-key cryptographic

---

[*] This work was supported in part by the Research Council K.U.Leuven: GOA TENSE, the IAP Program P6/26 BCRYPT of the Belgian State (Belgian Science Policy), and in part by the European Commission through the ICT program under contract ICT-2007-216676 ECRYPT II, and is funded by the National Natural Science Foundation of China (No. 61073150).

[**] This author is funded by a research grant of the Institute for the Promotion of Innovation through Science and Technology in Flanders (IWT-Vlaanderen).

C.-K. Wu, M. Yung, and D. Lin (Eds.): Inscrypt 2011, LNCS 7537, pp. 57–76, 2012.
© Springer-Verlag Berlin Heidelberg 2012

primitives. For block ciphers, differential cryptanalysis analyzes how input differences in the plaintext lead to output differences in the ciphertext. Linear cryptanalysis studies probabilistic linear relations between plaintext, ciphertext and key. If a cipher behaves differently from a random cipher for differential or linear cryptanalysis, this can be used to build a distinguisher or even a key-recovery attack.

For stream ciphers, differential cryptanalysis can be used in the context of a resynchronization attack [11]. In one possible setting, the same data is encrypted several times with the same key, but using a different initial value (IV). This is referred to as the standard (non-related-key) model, where the IV value is assumed to be under control of the attacker. An even stronger attack model is the related-key setting, where the same data is encrypted with different IVs *and* different keys. Not only the IV values, but also the differences between the keys are assumed to be under control of the attacker. Similar to differential cryptanalysis, linear cryptanalysis can also be used to attack stream ciphers in both the standard and related-key model. In the case of stream ciphers, linear cryptanalysis amounts to a known-IV attack instead of a chosen-IV attack.

Resistance against linear and differential cryptanalysis is a standard design criterion for new ciphers. For the block cipher AES [13], provable security against linear and differential cryptanalysis follows from the wide trail design strategy [12]. In this work, we apply a similar strategy. After proving a lower bound on the number of active S-boxes for both differential and linear cryptanalysis, we use the maximum differential probability (MDP) of the S-boxes to derive an upper bound for the probability of the best characteristic. We assume (as is commonly done) that the probability of the differential can accurately be estimated by the probability of the best characteristic. Several works focus on calculating the minimum number of active S-boxes for both Substitution-Permutation Networks (SPNs) [12] and (Generalized) Feistel Structures (GFSs) [5, 6, 16, 24]. Unfortunately, it seems that a lot of time and effort in programming is required to apply those techniques. This may explain why many related constructions have not yet been thoroughly analyzed. In this paper, we introduce a novel technique using mixed-integer linear programming in order to overcome these problems.

Linear programming (LP) is the study of optimizing (minimizing or maximizing) a linear objective function $f(x_1, x_2, \ldots, x_n)$, subject to linear inequalities involving decision variables x_i, $1 \leq i \leq n$. For many such optimization problems, it is necessary to restrict certain decision variables to integer values, i.e. for some values of i, we require $x_i \in \mathbb{Z}$. Methods to formulate and solve such programs are called mixed-integer linear programming (MILP). If all decision variables x_i must be integer, the term (pure) integer linear programming (ILP) is used. MILP techniques have found many practical applications in the fields of economy and business, but their application in cryptography has so far been limited. For a good introductory level text on LP and (M)ILP, we refer to Schrage [23].

In [7], Borghoff *et al.* transformed the quadratic equations describing the stream cipher Bivium into a MILP problem. The IBM ILOG CPLEX Optimizer[1] was then used to solve the resulting MILP problem, which corresponds to recovering the internal state of Bivium. In the case of Bivium A, solving this MILP problem takes less than 4.5 hours, which is faster than Raddum's approach (about a day) [22], but much slower than using MiniSAT (21 seconds) [9].

For the hash function SIMD, Bouillaguet *et al.* [8] used an ILP solver to find a differential characteristic based on local collisions. Using the SYMPHONY solver[2], they could not find the optimal solution, but found lower bounds for both SIMD-256 and SIMD-512. The computation for SIMD-512 took one month on a dual quad-core computer.

In [5, 6], Bogdanov calculated the minimum number of linearly and differentially active S-boxes of unbalanced Feistel networks with contracting MDS diffusion. He proved that some truncated difference weight distributions are impossible or equivalent to others. For the remaining truncated difference weight distributions, he constructed an ILP program which he then solved using the MAGMA[3] Computational Algebra System [4]. Compared to Bogdanov's technique, the fully automated method in this paper is much simpler to apply: Bogdanov's approach requires a significant amount of manual work, and the construction of not one but several ILP programs. We will show how this can be avoided by introducing extra dummy variables into the MILP program.

While this paper was under submission, Wu and Wang released a paper on ePrint [28] that also uses integer linear programming to count the number of active S-boxes for both linear and differential cryptanalysis. Just as in Bogdanov's approach, their algorithms require a large number of ILP programs to be solved, instead of only one as in the technique of this paper.

We apply our technique to the stream cipher Enocoro-128v2 [26, 27], in order to obtain bounds against differential and linear cryptanalysis. We consider both the standard and related-key model. All MILP programs are solved using CPLEX. There are 96 initialization rounds in Enocoro-128v2. We prove that 38 rounds are sufficient for security against differential cryptanalysis, and 61 rounds against linear cryptanalysis. These security bounds are obtained after 52.68 and 228.94 seconds respectively. We also calculate the minimum number of active S-boxes for up to 14 rounds of AES, which takes at most 0.40 seconds for each optimization program. Our experiments are performed on a 24-core Intel Xeon X5670 Processor, with 16 GB of RAM.

This paper is organized as follows. Sect. 2 explains how to find the minimum number of active S-boxes for a cryptographic primitive by solving an MILP program. A brief description of Enocoro-128v2 is given in Sect. 3. In Sect. 4 and Sect. 5, we construct an MILP program to prove that Enocoro-128v2 is secure against differential cryptanalysis and linear cryptanalysis respectively. We provide some ideas for future work in Sect. 6, and conclude the paper in

---

[1] http://www.ibm.com/software/integration/optimization/cplex-optimizer/

[2] http://projects.coin-or.org/SYMPHONY

[3] http://magma.maths.usyd.edu.au/

Sect. 7. In App. A, we calculate the minimum number of active S-boxes for AES using our technique, and provide the full source code of our program.

2 Constructing an MILP Program to Calculate the Minimum Number of Active S-Boxes

We now explain a technique to easily prove the security of many ciphers against differential and linear cryptanalysis. Our method is based on counting the minimum number of active S-boxes. To illustrate our technique, we use Enocoro-128v2 and AES as test cases in this paper. The equations we describe are not specific to these ciphers, but can easily be applied to any cipher constructed using S-box operations, linear permutation layers, three-forked branches and/or XOR operations.

2.1 Differential Cryptanalysis

We consider truncated differences, that is, every byte in our analysis can have either a zero or a non-zero difference. More formally, we define the following difference vector:

Definition 1 *Consider a string Δ consisting of n bytes $\Delta = (\Delta_0, \Delta_1, \ldots, \Delta_{n-1})$. Then, the difference vector $x = (x_0, x_1, \ldots, x_{n-1})$ corresponding to Δ is defined as*

$$x_i = \begin{cases} 0 & \text{if } \Delta_i = 0 \ , \\ 1 & \text{otherwise} \ . \end{cases}$$

Equations Describing the XOR Operation. Let the input difference vector for the XOR operation be $(x_{in_1}^{\oplus}, x_{in_2}^{\oplus})$ and the corresponding output difference vector be $x_{out}^{\oplus}$. The differential branch number is defined as the minimum number of input and output bytes that contain differences, excluding the case where there are no differences in inputs nor outputs. For XOR, the differential branch number is 2. In order to express this branch number in equations, we need to introduce a new binary dummy variable $d^{\oplus}$.[4] If and only if all of the three variables $x_{in_1}^{\oplus}, x_{in_2}^{\oplus}$ and $x_{out}^{\oplus}$ are zero, $d^{\oplus}$ is zero, otherwise it should be one. Therefore we obtain the following linear equations (in binary variables) to describe the relation between the input and output difference vectors:

$$x_{in_1}^{\oplus} + x_{in_2}^{\oplus} + x_{out}^{\oplus} \geq 2d^{\oplus} \ ,$$
$$d^{\oplus} \geq x_{in_1}^{\oplus} \ ,$$
$$d^{\oplus} \geq x_{in_2}^{\oplus} \ ,$$
$$d^{\oplus} \geq x_{out}^{\oplus} \ .$$

---

[4] Note that this extra variable was not added in [5,6], which is why Bogdanov had to solve several ILP programs instead of only one.

Equations Describing the Linear Transformation. The equations for a linear transformation L can be described as follows. Assume L transforms the input difference vector $(x^L_{in_1}, x^L_{in_2}, \cdots, x^L_{in_\mathcal{M}})$ to the output difference vector $(x^L_{out_1}, x^L_{out_2}, \cdots, x^L_{out_\mathcal{M}})$. Given the differential branch number $\mathcal{B}_D$, a binary dummy variable d^L is again needed to describe the relation between the input and output difference vectors. The variable d^L is equal to 0 if all variables $x^L_{in_1}, x^L_{in_2}, \cdots, x^L_{in_\mathcal{M}}, x^L_{out_1}, x^L_{out_2}, \cdots, x^L_{out_\mathcal{M}}$ are 0, and 1 otherwise. Therefore the linear transformation L can be constrained by the following linear equations:

$$x^L_{in_1} + x^L_{in_2} + \cdots + x^L_{in_\mathcal{M}} + x^L_{out_1} + x^L_{out_2} + \cdots + x^L_{out_\mathcal{M}} \geq \mathcal{B}_D d^L ,$$
$$d^L \geq x^L_{in_1} ,$$
$$d^L \geq x^L_{in_2} ,$$
$$\cdots \cdots$$
$$d^L \geq x^L_{in_\mathcal{M}} ,$$
$$d^L \geq x^L_{out_1} ,$$
$$d^L \geq x^L_{out_2} ,$$
$$\cdots \cdots$$
$$d^L \geq x^L_{out_\mathcal{M}} .$$

The Objective Function. The objective function that has to be minimized, is the number of active S-boxes. This function is equal to the sum of all variables that correspond to the S-box inputs.

Additional Constraints. An extra linear equation is added to ensure that at least one S-box is active: this avoids the trivial solution where the minimum active S-boxes is zero. If all d-variables and all x-variables are restricted to be binary, the resulting program is a pure ILP (Integer Linear Programming) problem. If all d-variables are restricted to be binary, but only the x-variables corresponding to the input (plaintext), the equations ensure that the optimal solution for all other x-variables will be binary as well. This is similar to Borghoff's suggestion in [7], and results in an MILP (Mixed-Integer Linear Programming) problem that may be solved faster.

2.2   Linear Cryptanalysis

For linear cryptanalysis, we define a linear mask vector as follows:

Definition 2 *Given a set of linear masks* $\Gamma = (\Gamma_0, \Gamma_1, \ldots, \Gamma_{n-1})$*, the linear mask vector* $y = (y_0, y_1, \ldots, y_{n-1})$ *corresponding to* Γ *is defined as*

$$y_i = \begin{cases} 0 & \text{if } \Gamma_i = 0 , \\ 1 & \text{otherwise} . \end{cases}$$

The duality between differential and linear cryptanalysis was already pointed out by Matsui [20]. The equations describing a linear function are the same as in the case for differential cryptanalysis, however the differential branch number $\mathcal{B}_D$ is replaced by the linear branch number $\mathcal{B}_L$. The linear branch number is the minimum number of non-zero linear masks for the input and output of a function, excluding the all-zero case. No extra equations are introduced for the XOR operations, because the input and output linear masks are the same.

For a three-forked branch, we proceed as follows. Let the input linear mask vector for the three-forked branch be $y_{in}^{\vdash}$, and the corresponding output linear mask vector be $(y_{out_1}^{\vdash}, y_{out_2}^{\vdash})$. We introduce a binary dummy variable $l^{\vdash}$ to generate the following linear equations for the three-forked branch:

$$y_{in}^{\vdash} + y_{out_1}^{\vdash} + y_{out_2}^{\vdash} \geq 2l^{\vdash} \ ,$$
$$l^{\vdash} \geq y_{in}^{\vdash} \ ,$$
$$l^{\vdash} \geq y_{out_1}^{\vdash} \ ,$$
$$l^{\vdash} \geq y_{out_2}^{\vdash} \ .$$

3   Description of Enocoro-128v2

The first Enocoro specification was given in [25]. Enocoro is a stream cipher, inspired by the PANAMA construction [10]. Two versions of Enocoro were specified: Enocoro-80v1 with a key size of 80 bits, and Enocoro-128v1 with a key size of 128 bits. Later, a new version for the 128-bit key size appeared in [15]. It is referred to as Enocoro-128v1.1. We now give a short description of Enocoro-128v2. For more details, we refer to the design document [26, 27].

Internal State. The internal state of Enocoro-128v2 is composed of a buffer b consisting of 32 bytes $(b_0, b_1, \ldots, b_{31})$ and a state a consisting of two bytes (a_0, a_1). The initial state is loaded with a 128-bit key K and a 64-bit IV I as follows:

$$b_i^{(-96)} = K_i, \qquad 0 \leq i < 16 \ ,$$
$$b_{i+16}^{(-96)} = I_i, \qquad 0 \leq i < 8 \ .$$

All other internal state bytes are loaded with predefined constants.

Update Function. The update function $Next$ uses functions ρ and λ to update the internal state as follows:

$$(a^{(t+1)}, b^{(t+1)}) = Next(S^{(t)}) = (\rho(a^{(t)}, b^{(t)}), \lambda(a^{(t)}, b^{(t)})) \ .$$

An schematic overview of this function is given in Fig. 1.

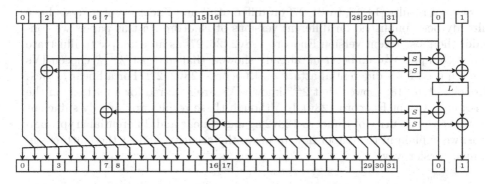

Fig. 1. State Update during the Initialization of Enocoro-128v2. Indices of buffer (on the left) refer to b-variables, indices of the state (on the right) refer to a-variables.

Function ρ. The function ρ updates the state a. It consists of an 8-bit S-box operation, a linear transformation L and XORs. The transformation L is defined as a linear transformation with a 2-by-2 matrix over $\mathrm{GF}(2^8)$:

$$\begin{pmatrix} v_0 \\ v_1 \end{pmatrix} = L(u_0, u_1) = \begin{pmatrix} 1 & 1 \\ 1 & d \end{pmatrix} \begin{pmatrix} u_0 \\ u_1 \end{pmatrix} , \qquad d \in \mathrm{GF}(2^8) ,$$

where $d = \mathtt{0x02}$, $u_0 = a_0^{(t)} \oplus S[b_2^{(t)}]$ and $u_1 = a_1^{(t)} \oplus S[b_7^{(t)}]$. The updated state $(a_0^{(t+1)}, a_1^{(t+1)})$ is then calculated as follows:

$$a_0^{(t+1)} = v_0 \oplus S[b_{16}^{(t)}] ,$$
$$a_1^{(t+1)} = v_1 \oplus S[b_{29}^{(t)}] .$$

Function λ. The λ function of Enocoro-128v2 consists of XOR operations and a byte-wise rotation of the buffer b. It is defined as follows:

$$b_i^{(t+1)} = \begin{cases} b_{31}^{(t)} \oplus a_0^{(t)}, & \text{if } i = 0 , \\ b_2^{(t)} \oplus b_6^{(t)}, & \text{if } i = 3 , \\ b_7^{(t)} \oplus b_{15}^{(t)}, & \text{if } i = 8 , \\ b_{16}^{(t)} \oplus b_{28}^{(t)}, & \text{if } i = 17 , \\ b_{i-1}^{(t)} & \text{otherwise} . \end{cases}$$

Output Function _Out_. After 96 initialization rounds, the Enocoro-128v2 output function outputs the lower byte of the state.

$$Out(S^{(t)}) = a_1^{(t)} .$$

Several results [14, 17, 18, 21, 27] on differential and linear cryptanalysis have already been published for different versions of Enocoro. In this paper, we consider the most recent version Enocoro-128v2 [26, 27] as an example to illustrate our technique. Watanabe *et al.* already showed that at least $2^{177.8}$ chosen IVs are required for a differential attack on Enocoro-128v2 [27]. For a linear attack, Konosu *et al.* [18] showed that 2^{216} known IVs are required for an attack on the 64-round variant Enocoro-128v1.1. Although these results are already sufficient to prove the security of Enocoro-128v2 against linear and differential cryptanalysis, we explain in this paper how to prove the security against these attacks in a much easier way.

4   Differential Cryptanalysis of Enocoro-128v2

Our technique is now used to find the minimum number of active S-boxes for the stream cipher Enocoro-128v2. We will consider an idealized variant of Enocoro-128v2, for which the minimum number of active S-boxes is a lower bound for the real Enocoro-128v2. In this idealized variant of Enocoro-128v2, the S-boxes can map any non-zero input difference to any non-zero output difference. The same holds for the L-function, with the restriction that the branch number is 3.

For this idealized variant of Enocoro-128v2, we have written a program to calculate the minimum number of active S-boxes. We present our problem as a mixed-integer linear programming (MILP) problem, and use CPLEX to solve it. The solution corresponds to the minimum number of differentially active S-boxes for Enocoro-128v2. It is used to prove the security of the cipher against differential cryptanalysis, using a similar proof as for the block cipher AES [12, 13]. Note that an actual characteristic with the given number of active S-boxes may or may not exist, depending on the specific S-box and L-function that is used. This is not a concern for us, as our goal is to prove a security bound against differential cryptanalysis.

4.1   Constructing the MILP Program

Enocoro-128v2 has eight XOR operations and one linear transformation L in each round. We represent the differential behavior of each of these operations by a set of linear equations, as described in Sect. 2. Let us take the first round of Enocoro-128v2 as an example. The initial difference vector in the buffer and states is represented by the binary variables $(x_0, x_1, \ldots, x_{31})$ and (x_{32}, x_{33}) respectively. Let us consider the XOR operation which has the rightmost byte of buffer b, i.e. b_{31}, and state byte a_0 as inputs. These correspond to binary variables x_{31} and x_{32} respectively, the input difference vector for this XOR operation. From the update function, we can obtain the corresponding value of the leftmost byte of buffer b, i.e. b_0, after the first round. Let the corresponding output difference vector be x_{34}, which is the first new binary variable that we

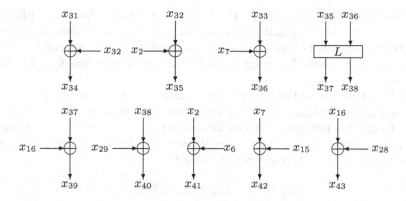

Fig. 2. Difference Vectors for Nine Operations in the First Round

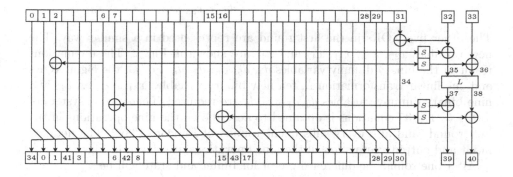

Fig. 3. Differential State Update during the Initialization of Enocoro-128v2. The indices refer to x-variables.

introduce. After introducing a binary dummy variable d_0, this XOR operation can be described by the equations:

$$x_{31} + x_{32} + x_{34} \geq 2d_0 ,$$
$$d_0 \geq x_{31} ,$$
$$d_0 \geq x_{32} ,$$
$$d_0 \geq x_{34} .$$

We now consider the second XOR operation, for which buffer b_2 (input to the first S-box) and the state a_0 are the inputs. Because the S-box is bijective, it is not only the case that the zero input difference results in a zero output difference, but also that a non-zero input difference results in a non-zero output difference. We find that (x_2, x_{32}) is the difference vector of the second XOR operation. The second new variable, x_{35}, will be the output difference vector for this second

XOR operation. Similarly, for the third XOR operation, the input difference vector is (x_7, x_{33}) (corresponding to (b_7, a_1)), and the output difference vector is x_{36}. Given two binary dummy variables d_1 and d_2 for the second and third XOR operation respectively, we again obtain four linear equations for every XOR operation.

From the structure of the linear transformation of Enocoro-128v2, we know that (x_{35}, x_{36}) is the input difference vector for the linear transformation L in the first round. By introducing a new binary variable d_3, the relations between the output difference vector (x_{37}, x_{38}) and the input difference vector (x_{35}, x_{36}) are easily described by the following equations:

$$x_{35} + x_{36} + x_{37} + x_{38} \geq 3d_3 \; ,$$
$$d_3 \geq x_{35} \; ,$$
$$d_3 \geq x_{36} \; ,$$
$$d_3 \geq x_{37} \; ,$$
$$d_3 \geq x_{38} \; .$$

The other five XORs in the first round are represented in a similar way. The new variables x_{39}, x_{40}, x_{41}, x_{42} and x_{43} are shown in Fig. 2. These equations result in the binary dummy variables d_4, d_5, d_6, d_7, d_8. For all the eight XORs and one linear transformation L, ten new binary variables $x_{34}, x_{35}, \ldots, x_{43}$ and nine binary dummy variables $d_0, d_1, \ldots, d_8$ are required. Therefore, a system of $4 \cdot 8 + 5 \cdot 1 = 37$ equations is obtained to describe all the nine operations in the first round (and also every subsequent round) of Enocoro-128v2. The detailed input and output vectors for all the nine operations are shown in Fig. 2.

After one round the difference vector for buffer and state will be

$$(x_{34}, x_0, x_1, x_{41}, x_3, \ldots, x_6, x_{42}, x_8, \ldots, x_{15}, x_{43}, x_{17}, \ldots, x_{30})$$

and (x_{39}, x_{40}) respectively. All binary x_i-variables obtained for the first round are illustrated in Fig. 3. Therefore, using this technique we can represent the differential update of Enocoro-128v2 for any round with a system of linear equations.

4.2   The Minimum Number of Active S-Boxes for Differential Cryptanalysis

We now focus on the variables that represent the S-box inputs in every round. Note that x_2, x_7, x_{16}, and x_{29} correspond to the input differences of the S-boxes, and therefore determine if the S-box is active or not. Let D_i include the four indices of variables that represent the four S-box inputs in the i-th round $(1 \leq i \leq 96)$. The 96 sets include the indices for variables that represent the four S-box inputs in each round. They can easily be obtained from Sect. 4.1, and are as follows:

$$D_1 = \{2, 7, 16, 29\} \ ,$$
$$D_2 = \{1, 6, 15, 28\} \ ,$$
$$D_3 = \{0, 5, 14, 27\} \ ,$$
$$D_4 = \{34, 4, 13, 26\} \ ,$$
$$D_5 = \{44, 3, 12, 25\} \ ,$$

$$\vdots$$

$$D_{96} = \{954, 941, 902, 863\} \ .$$

Let k_N be the number of active S-boxes for N rounds of Enocoro-128v2. If

$$I_N = \bigcup_{1 \le i \le N} D_i \ ,$$

then

$$k_N = \sum_{i \in I_N} x_i$$

will be the number of active S-boxes in N rounds of Enocoro-128v2. To avoid the trivial case where no S-boxes are active, we add an extra linear constraint to specify that least one S-box is active. If we can minimize the linear function $k_N = \sum_{i \in I_N} x_i$, it will give us the minimum number of active S-boxes for N rounds of Enocoro-128v2. This will provide a security bound for Enocoro-128v2 against differential cryptanalysis. The objective function $k_N = \sum_{i \in I_N} x_i$ is a linear function, constrained by a system of $37N$ linear equations. If all variables must be binary variables, this corresponds to an ILP program.

It is easy to verify that the maximum differential probability for the 8-bit S-box of Enocoro-128v2 is $2^{-4.678}$. As the IV is limited to 64 bits, there are at most 2^{64} IV pairs for any given difference (if the key is fixed). Because there exists a generic attack with a data complexity of 2^{64} IVs (obtaining the entire codebook under one key), attacks requiring 2^{64} IVs or more should not be feasible. Therefore, we do not consider attacks using more than 2^{64} IVs, even in the related-key setting. If the number of active S-boxes in the initialization rounds is at least $14 > 64/4.678$, we consider the cipher to be resistant against differential cryptanalysis. Because we allow differences in both the key and the IV, our results hold both in the single-key and in the related-key setting. We note that typically, differential and linear cryptanalysis are used to attack a few more rounds than the number of rounds of the characteristic. The cipher must also be resistant against other types of attacks and add extra rounds to provide a security margin. For these reasons, more rounds should be used than suggested by our analysis.

In order to optimize the MILP program, we use CPLEX. The experiments are implemented on a 24-core Intel Xeon X5670 @ 2.93 GHz, with 16 GB of RAM. Because this computer is shared with other users, execution times may be longer than necessary, which is why we do not give timing information for all problem instances. We found that it takes about 52.68 seconds to show that the minimum number of active S-boxes for 38 rounds of Enocoro-128v2 is 14. Therefore, 38 rounds of Enocoro-128v2 or more are secure against differential cryptanalysis. The minimum number of active S-boxes for each round of Enocoro-128v2 are listed in Table 1.

We would like to point out to the reader, that the seemingly complex book-keeping of variable indices should not be a concern for the cryptanalyst who wishes to use this technique. The MILP linear equations can be generated by a small computer program. This program keeps track of the next unused x- and d-variables. It is then easy to replace every XOR and L function operation in the reference implementation of the cipher by a function to generate the corresponding equations, and every S-box application by a function that constructs the objective function. For a typical cipher, this should not require more than half an hour of work for a minimally experienced programmer.

If all d-variables are restricted to binary variables, as well as variables x_0 up to x_{33}, the equations ensure that the optimal solution for all other x_i-variables will be binary as well. Therefore, similar to Borghoff's suggestion in [7], we might solve an MILP program where only the d-variables and x_0 up to x_{33} are binary variables, instead of a pure ILP program. We find that Borghoff's observation can give dramatic speed-ups in some cases: for 72 rounds, it takes 5,808.15 seconds using an MILP, compared 342,747.78 seconds using a pure ILP. However, our MILP program for 38 rounds takes longer: 75.68 seconds instead of 52.68 seconds. Explaining this phenomenon seems to be a useful direction for future work.

5 Linear Cryptanalysis of Enocoro-128v2

We will use our technique to analyze an ideal variant of Enocoro-128v2 for linear cryptanalysis. Similarly as for differential cryptanalysis, the real Enocoro-128v2 will have at least as many linearly active S-boxes as the idealized one, and therefore can be used to prove a security bound.

5.1 Constructing the MILP Program

We now illustrate our technique by presenting the equations for the first round of the stream cipher Enocoro-128v2 for linear cryptanalysis. For the initial state, let the linear mask vector for the buffer be $(y_0, y_1, \ldots, y_{31})$, and for the state be (y_{32}, y_{33}). Consider the three-forked branch, which has the state byte a_0 as the input linear mask and buffer byte b_{31} as one output linear mask. We obtain the first new binary variable y_{34} as the other output vector. The input and output linear mask vector for this three-forked branch are then y_{32} and (y_{31}, y_{34}) respectively. By introducing the binary dummy variable l_0, the four equations describing the three-forked branch can be described as follows:

Table 1. Minimum Number of Differentially Active S-boxes $\min(k_N)$ for N rounds of Enocoro-128v2

N	$\min(k_N)$	N	$\min(k_N)$	N	$\min(k_N)$	N	$\min(k_N)$	N	$\min(k_N)$
1	0	21	2	41	16	61	25	81	39
2	0	22	3	42	17	62	26	82	39
3	0	23	3	43	18	63	27	83	40
4	0	24	3	44	18	64	27	84	40
5	0	25	4	45	18	65	28	85	40
6	0	26	5	46	19	66	29	86	41
7	0	27	7	47	20	67	30	87	42
8	0	28	8	48	20	68	30	88	43
9	0	29	8	49	21	69	30	89	43
10	0	30	8	50	22	70	31	90	44
11	0	31	8	51	22	71	32	91	44
12	0	32	9	52	22	72	34	92	45
13	1	33	9	53	22	73	35	93	45
14	1	34	10	54	22	74	35	94	46
15	1	35	11	55	22	75	36	95	47
16	1	36	12	56	22	76	37	96	47
17	1	37	13	57	23	77	37		
18	1	38	14	58	23	78	38		
19	1	39	15	59	24	79	38		
20	2	40	15	60	24	80	38		

$$y_{31} + y_{32} + y_{34} \geq 2l_0 \ ,$$
$$l_0 \geq y_{31} \ ,$$
$$l_0 \geq y_{32} \ ,$$
$$l_0 \geq y_{34} \ .$$

For the XOR operation, the two inputs and the output all have the same linear mask. The bijectiveness of the S-box implies the linear mask at the output will be non-zero if and only if the input mask is non-zero. Therefore, the linear transformation L has an input linear mask vector of (y_{34}, y_{33}), and an output linear mask vector of (y_{35}, y_{36}). Using a new binary dummy variable l_1, the equations describing the L transformation are:

$$y_{34} + y_{33} + y_{35} + y_{36} \geq 3l_1 \ ,$$
$$l_1 \geq y_{34} \ ,$$
$$l_1 \geq y_{33} \ ,$$
$$l_1 \geq y_{35} \ ,$$
$$l_1 \geq y_{36} \ .$$

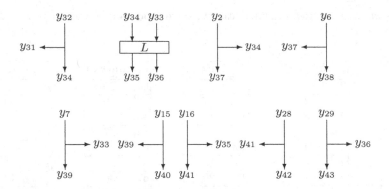

Fig. 4. Linear Mask Vectors for Nine Operations in the First Round

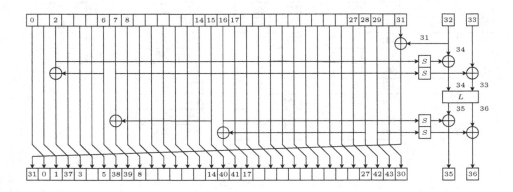

Fig. 5. Linear Mask Vectors Update during the Initialization of Enocoro-128v2. The indices refer to y-variables.

As an Enocoro-128v2 round contains eight three-forked branch operations and one linear transformation L, ten new binary variables $y_{34}, y_{35}, \ldots, y_{43}$, as well as nine binary dummy variables $l_0, l_1, \ldots, l_8$ are introduced. Therefore, $4 \cdot 8 + 5 \cdot 1 = 37$ equations are required to describe the propagation of linear masks for the first round (as well as any subsequent round) of Enocoro-128v2. The input and output linear mask vectors for all nine operations in the first round are shown in Fig. 4. The linear mask vector for the buffer and state after one round are

$$(y_{31}, y_0, y_1, y_{37}, y_3, \cdots, y_5, y_{38}, y_{39}, y_8, \cdots, y_{14}, y_{40}, y_{41}, y_{17}, \cdots, y_{27}, y_{42}, y_{43}, y_{30})$$

and (y_{35}, y_{36}) respectively. They are shown in Fig. 5.

5.2   The Minimum Number of Active S-Boxes for Linear Cryptanalysis

Using the technique in the previous section, we can represent any number of rounds of Enocoro-128v2. We now explain how to calculate the number of active S-boxes. Let L_i include all indices of the four variables representing the input linear mask vector of S-boxes in the i-th round ($1 \leq i \leq 96$). We then obtain the following 96 sets:

$$L_1 = \{34, 33, 35, 36\} ,$$
$$L_2 = \{44, 36, 45, 46\} ,$$
$$L_3 = \{54, 46, 55, 56\} ,$$
$$L_4 = \{64, 56, 65, 66\} ,$$
$$L_5 = \{74, 66, 75, 76\} ,$$

$$\vdots$$

$$L_{96} = \{984, 976, 985, 986\} .$$

Let m_N be the number of active S-boxes for N rounds of Enocoro-128v2. If

$$J_N = \bigcup_{1 \leq j \leq N} L_j ,$$

then

$$m_N = \sum_{j \in J_N} y_j$$

will be the number of active S-boxes for N rounds of Enocoro-128v2. By minimizing the linear objective function m_N, we obtain the minimum number of linearly active S-boxes for N rounds of Enocoro-128v2.

The maximum correlation amplitude of the 8-bit S-box of Enocoro-128v2 is $C_{\max} = 2^{-2}$. For the same reasons as for differential cryptanalysis, we limit the number of IVs to 2^{64}. Let us denote the minimum number of active S-boxes by a. From the limit on the number of IVs, we then find that resistance against linear cryptanalysis requires [13, pp. 142–143]:

$$C_{\max}^a = (2^{-2})^a \leq 2^{-64/2} .$$

This inequality is satisfied for $a \geq 16$. Therefore, if the number of linearly active S-boxes is at least 16, Enocoro-128v2 can be considered to be resistant against linear cryptanalysis (in both the single-key and related-key setting).

If we solve the resulting MILP problem using CPLEX, we find that the minimum number of active S-boxes is 18 for 61 rounds of Enocoro-128v2. This result was obtained after 227.38 seconds. Therefore, we conclude that Enocoro-128v2 with 96 initialization rounds is secure against linear cryptanalysis (in both the single-key and related-key setting). The minimum number of active S-boxes for Enocoro-128v2 are listed in Table 2.

Table 2. Minimum Number of Linearly Active S-boxes min(m_N) for Enocoro-128v2

N	min(m_N)	N	min(m_N)	N	min(m_N)	N	min(m_N)	N	min(m_N)
1	0	21	0	41	6	61	18	81	24
2	0	22	0	42	9	62	18	82	27
3	0	23	0	43	9	63	18	83	27
4	0	24	0	44	9	64	18	84	27
5	0	25	0	45	12	65	18	85	27
6	0	26	0	46	12	66	18	86	27
7	0	27	0	47	12	67	18	87	27
8	0	28	0	48	12	68	21	88	27
9	0	29	0	49	12	69	21	89	27
10	0	30	0	50	12	70	21	90	27
11	0	31	0	51	12	71	21	91	27
12	0	32	0	52	15	72	21	92	27
13	0	33	3	53	15	73	21	93	30
14	0	34	6	54	15	74	21	94	30
15	0	35	6	55	15	75	21	95	33
16	0	36	6	56	15	76	24	96	33
17	0	37	6	57	15	77	24		
18	0	38	6	58	15	78	24		
19	0	39	6	59	15	79	24		
20	0	40	6	60	15	80	24		

6   Future Work

It is interesting to investigate how the internal parameters of CPLEX can be fine-tuned to calculate bounds against linear and differential cryptanalysis in the fastest possible time. If there are symmetries in the round function, these may be used to speed up the search as well. Similarly, the attacker may improve a given (suboptimal) lower bound for a particular cipher by clocking the round functions forward or backward in order to obtain a lower number of S-boxes. To obtain a rough lower bound for a large number of rounds, the "split approach" (see for example [3]) may be used. For example, if r rounds of a cipher contain at least a active S-boxes, then kr rounds of a cipher must contain at least ka active S-boxes. It is useful to explore how these observations can be applied when CPLEX takes a very long time to execute. Otherwise, the shorter solving time does not compensate for the additional time to construct the program. For ILP programs with a very long execution time, it may be better to calculate the minimum number of active S-boxes using a different technique (e.g. [3]).

The technique in this paper is quite general, and may also be used for truncated differentials, higher-order differentials, impossible differentials, saturation attacks,... It can also be applied to other ciphers constructed using S-box operations, linear permutation layers, three-forked branches and/or XOR operations. We leave the exploration of these topics to future work as well.

7   Conclusion

In this paper, we introduced a simple technique to calculate the security of many ciphers against linear and differential cryptanalysis. The only requirement is that the cipher is composed of a combination of S-box operations, linear permutation layers and/or XOR operations. Our technique involves writing a simple program to generate a mixed-integer linear programming (MILP) problem. The objective function of the MILP program is the number of linearly or differentially active S-boxes, which we want to minimize. This MILP problem can then easily be solved using an off-the-shelf optimization package, for example CPLEX. The result can be used to prove the security of a cryptosystem against linear and differential cryptanalysis.

Our technique can be applied to a wide variety of cipher constructions. As an example, we apply the technique in this paper to the stream cipher Enocoro-128v2. We prove that for Enocoro-128v2 38 rounds are sufficient for security against differential cryptanalysis, and 61 rounds against linear cryptanalysis. These results are valid both in the single-key and related-key models. As Enocoro-128v2 consists of 96 initialization rounds, this proves the security of Enocoro-128v2 against linear and differential cryptanalysis.

We would like to point out that only little programming is required to obtain this result. A minimally experienced programmer can modify the reference implementation of a cipher, in order to generate the required MILP program in about half an hour. In the case of Enocoro-128v2, it takes CPLEX less than one minute on a 24-core Intel Xeon X5670 processor to prove security against differential cryptanalysis, and less than four minutes to prove security against linear cryptanalysis. We note that because very little programming is required, both the time spent on cryptanalysis and the possibility of making errors are greatly reduced.

Acknowledgments. The authors would like to thank their colleagues at COSIC, as well as the anonymous reviewers for their detailed comments and suggestions. Special thanks to Hirotaka Yoshida for reviewing an earlier draft of this paper.

References

1. Biham, E., Shamir, A.: Differential Cryptanalysis of DES-like Cryptosystems. J. Cryptology 4(1), 3–72 (1991)
2. Biryukov, A., Gong, G., Stinson, D.R. (eds.): SAC 2010. LNCS, vol. 6544. Springer, Heidelberg (2011)
3. Biryukov, A., Nikolić, I.: Search for Related-Key Differential Characteristics in DES-Like Ciphers. In: Joux, A. (ed.) FSE 2011. LNCS, vol. 6733, pp. 18–34. Springer, Heidelberg (2011)
4. Bodganov, A.: Personal Communication (2011)
5. Bogdanov, A.: Analysis and Design of Block Cipher Constructions. Ph.D. thesis, Ruhr University Bochum (2009)
6. Bogdanov, A.: On unbalanced Feistel networks with contracting MDS diffusion. Des. Codes Cryptography 59(1-3), 35–58 (2011)

7. Borghoff, J., Knudsen, L.R., Stolpe, M.: Bivium as a Mixed-Integer Linear Programming Problem. In: Parker, M.G. (ed.) Cryptography and Coding 2009. LNCS, vol. 5921, pp. 133–152. Springer, Heidelberg (2009)
8. Bouillaguet, C., Fouque, P.A., Leurent, G.: Security Analysis of SIMD. In: Biryukov, et al. (eds.) [2], pp. 351–368
9. McDonald, C., Charnes, C., Pieprzyk, J.: An Algebraic Analysis of Trivium Ciphers based on the Boolean Satisfiability Problem. Cryptology ePrint Archive, Report 2007/129 (2007), http://eprint.iacr.org/
10. Daemen, J., Clapp, C.S.K.: Fast Hashing and Stream Encryption with PANAMA. In: Vaudenay, S. (ed.) FSE 1998. LNCS, vol. 1372, pp. 60–74. Springer, Heidelberg (1998)
11. Daemen, J., Govaerts, R., Vandewalle, J.: Resynchronization Weaknesses in Synchronous Stream Ciphers. In: Helleseth, T. (ed.) EUROCRYPT 1993. LNCS, vol. 765, pp. 159–167. Springer, Heidelberg (1994)
12. Daemen, J., Rijmen, V.: The Wide Trail Design Strategy. In: Honary, B. (ed.) Cryptography and Coding 2001. LNCS, vol. 2260, pp. 222–238. Springer, Heidelberg (2001)
13. Daemen, J., Rijmen, V.: The Design of Rijndael: AES - The Advanced Encryption Standard. Springer (2002)
14. Hell, M., Johansson, T.: Security Evaluation of Stream Cipher Enocoro-128v2. CRYPTREC Technical Report (2010)
15. Muto, K., Watanabe, D., Kaneko, T.: Strength evaluation of Enocoro-128 against LDA and its Improvement. In: Symposium on Cryptography and Information Security, pp. 4A1–1 (2008) (in Japanese)
16. Kanda, M.: Practical Security Evaluation against Differential and Linear Cryptanalyses for Feistel Ciphers with SPN Round Function. In: Stinson, D.R., Tavares, S. (eds.) SAC 2000. LNCS, vol. 2012, pp. 324–338. Springer, Heidelberg (2001)
17. Okamoto, K., Muto, K., Kaneko, T.: Security evaluation of Pseudorandom Number Generator Enocoro-80 against Differential/Linear Cryptanalysis (II). In: Symposium on Cryptography and Information Security, pp. 20–23 (2009) (in Japanese)
18. Konosu, K., Muto, K., Furuichi, H., Watanabe, D., Kaneko, T.: Security evaluation of Enocoro-128 ver.1.1 against resynchronization attack. IEICE Technical Report, ISEC2007-147 (2008) (in Japanese)
19. Matsui, M.: Linear Cryptanalysis Method for DES Cipher. In: Helleseth, T. (ed.) EUROCRYPT 1993. LNCS, vol. 765, pp. 386–397. Springer, Heidelberg (1994)
20. Matsui, M.: On Correlation between the Order of S-Boxes and the Strength of DES. In: De Santis, A. (ed.) EUROCRYPT 1994. LNCS, vol. 950, pp. 366–375. Springer, Heidelberg (1995)
21. Muto, K., Watanabe, D., Kaneko, T.: Security evaluation of Enocoro-80 against linear resynchronization attack. In: Symposium on Cryptography and Information Security (2008) (in Japanese)
22. Raddum, H.: Cryptanalytic Results on Trivium. eSTREAM report 2006/039 (2006), http://www.ecrypt.eu.org/stream/triviump3.html
23. Schrage, L.: Optimization Modeling with LINGO. Lindo Systems (1999), http://www.lindo.com
24. Shibutani, K.: On the Diffusion of Generalized Feistel Structures Regarding Differential and Linear Cryptanalysis. In: Biryukov, et al. (eds.) [2], pp. 211–228
25. Watanabe, D., Kaneko, T.: A construction of light weight Panama-like keystream generator. IEICE Technical Report, ISEC2007-78 (2007) (in Japanese)
26. Watanabe, D., Okamoto, K., Kaneko, T.: A Hardware-Oriented Light Weight Pseudo-Random Number Generator Enocoro-128v2. In: The Symposium on Cryptography and Information Security, pp. 3D1–3 (2010) (in Japanese)

27. Watanabe, D., Owada, T., Okamoto, K., Igarashi, Y., Kaneko, T.: Update on Enocoro Stream Cipher. In: ISITA, pp. 778–783. IEEE (2010)

28. Wu, S., Wang, M.: Security evaluation against differential cryptanalysis for block cipher structures. Cryptology ePrint Archive, Report 2011/551 (2011), http://eprint.iacr.org/

A   Number of Active S-Boxes for AES

The four-round propagation theorem of AES [13] proves that the number of active S-boxes in a differential or linear characteristic of four AES rounds is at least 25. Combined with the properties of the AES S-box, this result was used in the AES design document to prove the resistance against linear and differential attacks. In this section, we illustrate our technique by applying it to the block cipher AES. We not only confirm the four-round propagation theorem, but also determine the minimum number of active S-boxes for up to 14 rounds in Table 4.

An AES round update consists of four operations: AddRoundKey (AR), Sub-Bytes (SB), ShiftRows (SR) and MixColumns (MC). The update of the first AES round is shown in Table 3. Every variable corresponds to a byte of the AES state. The variable is 1 if the difference is non-zero, and 0 if the difference is zero. All variables corresponding to the inputs of the SubByte operations are summed in the objective function, this corresponds to the number of active S-boxes. The linear function used in the MixColumns operation has a differential as well as a linear branch number of 5.

A program was written in C to generate the equations for this optimization problem in the CPLEX LP format. To illustrate the simplicity of our technique, we provide this program (including source code comments) below in full. None of the optimization problems in Table 4 took longer than 0.40 seconds to solve, using only a single core of our 24-core Intel Xeon X5670 processor.

Table 3. The Variables in the First Round Update of AES

$$
\begin{bmatrix} x_0 & x_4 & x_8 & x_{12} \\ x_1 & x_5 & x_9 & x_{13} \\ x_2 & x_6 & x_{10} & x_{14} \\ x_3 & x_7 & x_{11} & x_{15} \end{bmatrix} \xrightarrow{\text{SB}} \begin{bmatrix} x_0 & x_4 & x_8 & x_{12} \\ x_1 & x_5 & x_9 & x_{13} \\ x_2 & x_6 & x_{10} & x_{14} \\ x_3 & x_7 & x_{11} & x_{15} \end{bmatrix} \xrightarrow{\text{SR}} \begin{bmatrix} x_0 & x_4 & x_8 & x_{12} \\ x_5 & x_9 & x_{13} & x_1 \\ x_{10} & x_{14} & x_2 & x_6 \\ x_{15} & x_3 & x_7 & x_{11} \end{bmatrix} \xrightarrow{\text{MC}} \begin{bmatrix} x_{16} & x_{20} & x_{24} & x_{28} \\ x_{17} & x_{21} & x_{25} & x_{29} \\ x_{18} & x_{22} & x_{26} & x_{30} \\ x_{19} & x_{23} & x_{27} & x_{31} \end{bmatrix}
$$

Table 4. Minimum Number of Differentially or Linearly Active S-boxes $\min(k_N)$ for N rounds of AES

N	1	2	3	4	5	6	7	8	9	10	11	12	13	14
$\min(k_N)$	1	5	9	25	26	30	34	50	51	55	59	75	76	80

```c
#include <stdio.h>
int i,j,r;
const int ROUNDS = 4; /* number of rounds */
int next = 0; /* next unused state variable index */
int dummy = 0; /* next unused dummy variable index */

void ShiftRows(int a[4][4]) {
  int tmp[4];
  for(i = 1; i < 4; i++) {
    for(j = 0; j < 4; j++) tmp[j] = a[i][(j + i) % 4];
    for(j = 0; j < 4; j++) a[i][j] = tmp[j];
  }
}
void MixColumn(int a[4][4]) {
  for(j = 0; j < 4; j++) {
    for (i = 0; i < 4; i++) printf("x%i + ",a[i][j]);
    for (i = 0; i < 3; i++) printf("x%i + ",next+i);
    printf("x%i - 5 d%i >= 0\n",next+3,dummy);

    for(i = 0; i < 4; i++)
      printf("d%i - x%i >= 0\n",dummy,a[i][j]);
    for(i = 0; i < 4; i++)
      printf("d%i - x%i >= 0\n",dummy,a[i][j]=next++);
    dummy++;
  }
}
int main() {
  int a[4][4]; /* the bytes of the AES state */
  for (i = 0; i < 4; i++)
    for (j = 0; j < 4; j++)
      a[i][j] = next++; /* initialize variable indices */

  printf("Minimize\n"); /* print objective function */
  for (i = 0; i < ROUNDS*16-1; i++) printf("x%i + ",i);
  printf("x%i\n\n",ROUNDS*16-1);

  printf("Subject To\n"); /* round function constraints */
  for (r = 0; r<ROUNDS; r++) { ShiftRows(a); MixColumn(a); }

  /* at least one S-box must be active */
  for (i = 0; i < ROUNDS*16-1; i++) printf("x%i + ",i);
  printf("x%i >= 1\n\n",ROUNDS*16-1);

  printf("Binary\n"); /* binary constraints */
  for (i = 0; i < 16; i++) printf("x%i\n",i);
  for (i = 0; i < dummy; i++) printf("d%i\n",i);
  printf ("End\n");
  return 0;
}
```

Adleman-Manders-Miller Root Extraction Method Revisited

Zhengjun Cao*, Qian Sha, and Xiao Fan

Department of Mathematics, Shanghai University, Shanghai, China
caozhj@yahoo.cn

Abstract. Adleman, Manders and Miller had mentioned how to extend their square root extraction method to the general rth root extraction over finite fields, but not shown enough details. Actually, there is a dramatic difference between the square root extraction and the general rth root extraction because one has to solve discrete logarithms for rth root extraction. In this paper, we clarify their method and analyze its complexity. Our heuristic presentation is helpful to grasp the method entirely and deeply.

Keywords: square root extraction, rth root extraction.

1 Introduction

Root extraction is a classical problem in computers algebra. It plays an essential role in cryptosystems based on elliptic curves [2]. There are several efficient probabilistic algorithms for square root extraction in finite fields, such as Cipolla-Lehmer [6,7], Tonelli-Shanks [10,12] and Adleman-Manders-Miller [1]. All of them require a quadratic nonresidue as an additional input. In 2004, Müller investigated this topic in Ref.[8]. In 2011, Sze [11] presented a novel idea to compute square roots over finite fields, without being given any quadratic nonresidue, and without assuming any unproven hypothesis.

Adleman-Manders-Miller square root extraction method can be extended to solve the general rth root extraction problem. In recent, Nishihara et al. [9] have specified the Adleman-Manders-Miller method for cube root extraction. Barreto and Voloch [2] proposed an efficient algorithm to compute rth roots in $\mathbb{F}_{p^m}$ for certain choices of m and p. Besides, it requires that $r \,||\, p - 1$ and $(m, r) = 1$, where the notation $a^b||c$ means that a^b is the highest power of a dividing c.

The basic idea of Adleman-Manders-Miller square root extraction in $\mathbb{F}_p$ can be described as follows. Write $p - 1$ in the form $2^t \cdot s$, where s is odd. Given a quadratic residue δ and a quadratic nonresidue ρ, we have

$$(\delta^s)^{2^{t-1}} \equiv 1 \pmod{p}, \quad (\rho^s)^{2^{t-1}} \equiv -1 \pmod{p}$$

If $t \geq 2$, then $(\delta^s)^{2^{t-2}} \pmod{p} \in \{1, -1\}$. Take $k_1 = 0$ or 1 such that

$$(\delta^s)^{2^{t-2}} (\rho^s)^{2^{t-1} \cdot k_1} \equiv 1 \pmod{p}$$

---

* Corresponding author.

C.-K. Wu, M. Yung, and D. Lin (Eds.): Inscrypt 2011, LNCS 7537, pp. 77–85, 2012.

Since $(\delta^s)^{2^{t-3}} (\rho^s)^{2^{t-2} \cdot k_1} \pmod{p} \in \{1, -1\}$, take $k_2 = 0$ or 1 such that

$$(\delta^s)^{2^{t-3}} (\rho^s)^{2^{t-2} \cdot k_1} (\rho^s)^{2^{t-1} \cdot k_2} \equiv 1 \pmod{p}$$

Likewise, we can obtain $k_3, \cdots, k_{t-1} \in \{0, 1\}$ such that

$$(\delta^s) (\rho^s)^{2 \cdot k_1 + 2^2 \cdot k_2 + \cdots + 2^{t-1} \cdot k_{t-1}} \equiv 1 \pmod{p}$$

Thus, we have

$$\left(\delta^{\frac{s+1}{2}} \right)^2 \left((\rho^s)^{k_1 + 2 \cdot k_2 + \cdots + 2^{t-2} \cdot k_{t-1}} \right)^2 \equiv \delta \pmod{p}$$

It should be stressed, however, that there is a dramatic difference between the square root extraction and the general rth root extraction. Write $p - 1$ in the form $r^t \cdot s$, where $(r, s) = 1$. Given a rth residue δ and a rth nonresidue ρ, we have

$$(\delta^s)^{r^{t-1}} \equiv 1 \pmod{p}, \quad (\rho^s)^{r^{t-1}} \not\equiv 1 \pmod{p}$$

Since $(\delta^s)^{r^{t-2}} \pmod{p}$ is a root of the equation $X^r \equiv 1 \pmod{p}$ and the equation has r different roots (these roots can be represented by $(\rho^s)^{k_i \cdot r^{t-1}}$, $k_i \in \{0, 1, \cdots, r-1\}$), it becomes difficult to find k_1 such that

$$(\delta^s)^{r^{t-2}} (\rho^s)^{r^{t-1} \cdot k_1} \equiv 1 \pmod{p}$$

In 1977, Adleman, Manders and Miller [1] had presented a brief description on how to extend their square root extraction method to the general rth root extraction over finite fields, but not shown enough details. By the way, it is the only known method for the general rth root extraction over finite fields. In this paper, we clarify their method and analyze its complexity.

2   Preliminary

Let $\mathbb{Z}_n = \{0, 1, \cdots, n-1\}$ be the set of all numbers smaller than n, $\mathbb{Z}_n^* = \{x \mid 1 \leq x \leq n$ and $\gcd(x, n) = 1\}$ be the set of numbers in $\mathbb{Z}_n$ that are coprime to n. The following definitions and results can be found in Ref.[4].

Definition 1. *A residue $a \in \mathbb{Z}_n^*$ is said to be a quadratic residue if there exists some $x \in \mathbb{Z}_n^*$ such that $x^2 \equiv a \pmod{n}$. If a is not a quadratic residue, then it is referred to as a quadratic non-residue.*

Theorem 2. (Euler's Criterion) *For prime p, an element $a \in \mathbb{Z}_p^*$ is a quadratic residue if and only if $a^{\frac{p-1}{2}} \equiv 1 \pmod{p}$.*

Definition 3. (Legendre Symbol) *For any prime p and $a \in \mathbb{Z}_p^*$, we define the Legendre symbol*

$$\left[\frac{a}{p} \right] = \begin{cases} 1 & \text{if } a \text{ is a quadratic residue (mod } p) \\ -1 & \text{if } a \text{ is a quadratic non-residue (mod } p) \end{cases}$$

For an integer a, we define $\log(a)$ to be the number of bits in the binary representation of $|a|$; more precisely,

$$\log(a) = \begin{cases} \lfloor \log_2 |a| \rfloor + 1 & \text{if } a \neq 0 \\ 1 & \text{if } a = 0 \end{cases}$$

Given $a \in \mathbb{Z}_n$ and a non-negative integer e, the repeated-squaring algorithm computes a^e (mod n) using just $\mathcal{O}(\log(e))$ multiplications in $\mathbb{Z}_n$, thus taking time $\mathcal{O}(\log(e)\log^2 n)$. Therefore, we have the following result:

Proposition 4. *For an odd prime p, we can test whether an integer a is a quadratic residue modulo p by either performing the exponentiation $a^{\frac{(p-1)}{2}}$ (mod p) or by computing the Legendre symbol $\left[\frac{a}{p}\right]$. Assume that $0 < a < p$. Using a standard repeated squaring algorithm, the former method takes time $\mathcal{O}(\log^3 p)$, while using Euclidean-like algorithm, the latter method takes time $\mathcal{O}(\log^2 p)$.*

Proof. See [5].

Let R be a ring. Let us define the length of a polynomial $f(X) \in R[X]$, denoted by $\log(f)$, to be the length of its coefficient vector; more precisely, we define

$$\log(f) = \begin{cases} \deg(f) + 1 & \text{if } f \neq 0 \\ 1 & \text{if } f = 0 \end{cases}$$

Analogous to algorithms for modular integer arithmetic, we can also do arithmetic in the residue class ring $R[X]/(f)$, where $f \in R[X]$ is a polynomial of $\deg(f) > 0$ whose leading coefficient $\mathrm{lc}(f)$ is a unit.

Proposition 5. *Let $R[X]/(f)$ be a residue class ring, where $f \in R[X]$ is a polynomial of $\deg(f) > 0$ whose leading coefficient $\mathrm{lc}(f)$ is a unit. Given $g \in R[X]/(f)$ and a non-negative exponent e, using repeated-squaring algorithm we can compute g^e taking $\mathcal{O}(\log(e) \deg(f)^2)$ operations in R.*

Proof. See [3].

Notice that using a standard representation for $\mathbb{F}_p$, each operation in $\mathbb{F}_p$ takes time $\mathcal{O}(log^2 p)$.

3 Adleman-Manders-Miller Square Root Extraction Method

The Adleman-Manders-Miller square root extraction method requires a quadratic non-residue as an additional input. We classify the method into two kinds because there is a gap between the base field $\mathbb{F}_p$ and the extension $\mathbb{F}_{p^m}$ to test whether an element is a quadratic non-residue.

3.1 Adleman-Manders-Miller Square Root Extraction Method in $\mathbb{F}_p$

Consider the problem to find a solution to the congruence $X^2 \equiv \delta$ (mod p) over finite field $\mathbb{F}_p$, where p is an odd prime.

Adleman, Manders and Miller [1] proposed an algorithm to solve the problem. Their square root extraction method is based on the following facts. Write $p - 1$ in the form $2^t \cdot s$, where s is odd. Given a quadratic residue δ and a quadratic nonresidue ρ, we have

$$(\delta^s)^{2^{t-1}} \equiv 1 \pmod{p}, \quad (\rho^s)^{2^{t-1}} \equiv -1 \pmod{p}$$

If $t = 1$, then $\delta^s \equiv 1 \pmod{p}$. Hence, we have $\left(\delta^{\frac{s+1}{2}}\right)^2 \equiv \delta \pmod{p}$. It means that $\delta^{\frac{s+1}{2}}$ is a square root of δ. In this case, it only takes time $\mathcal{O}(\log(s)\log^2 p)$.

If $t \geq 2$, then $(\delta^s)^{2^{t-2}} \pmod{p} \in \{1, -1\}$. Take $k_1 = 0$ or 1 such that

$$(\delta^s)^{2^{t-2}} (\rho^s)^{2^{t-1} \cdot k_1} \equiv 1 \pmod{p}$$

Take $k_2 = 0$ or 1 such that

$$(\delta^s)^{2^{t-3}} (\rho^s)^{2^{t-2} \cdot k_1} (\rho^s)^{2^{t-1} \cdot k_2} \equiv 1 \pmod{p}$$

Likewise, we obtain $k_3, \cdots, k_{t-1} \in \{0, 1\}$ such that

$$(\delta^s) (\rho^s)^{2 \cdot k_1 + 2^2 \cdot k_2 + \cdots + 2^{t-1} \cdot k_{t-1}} \equiv 1 \pmod{p}$$

Finally, we have

$$\left(\delta^{\frac{s+1}{2}}\right)^2 \left((\rho^s)^{k_1 + 2 \cdot k_2 + \cdots + 2^{t-2} \cdot k_{t-1}}\right)^2 \equiv \delta \pmod{p}$$

Table 1. Adleman-Manders-Miller square root extraction algorithm in $\mathbb{F}_p$

Input: Odd prime p and a quadratic residue δ.
Output: A square root of δ.

Step 1: Choose ρ uniformly at random from $\mathbb{F}_p^*$.
　　　　Compute $\left[\frac{\rho}{p}\right]$ using Euclidean-like algorithm.
Step 2: **if** $\left[\frac{\rho}{p}\right] = 1$, **go to** Step 1.
Step 3: Compute t, s such that $p - 1 = 2^t s$, where s is odd.
　　　　Compute $a \leftarrow \rho^s, b \leftarrow \delta^s, h \leftarrow 1$.
Step 4: **for** $i = 1$ **to** $t - 1$
　　　　　　compute $d = b^{2^{t-1-i}}$
　　　　　　if $d = 1$, $k \leftarrow 0$
　　　　　　else $k \leftarrow 1$
　　　　　　$b \leftarrow b \cdot (a^2)^k, h \leftarrow h \cdot a^k$
　　　　　　$a \leftarrow a^2$
　　　　end for
Step 5: **return** $\delta^{\frac{s+1}{2}} \cdot h$

To find a quadratic non-residue ρ, it requires to check that $[\frac{\rho}{p}] \neq 1$. The computation takes time $\mathcal{O}(\log^2 p)$. If we do this for more than $\mathcal{O}(1)\log p$ different randomly chosen ρ, then with probability $> 1 - (\frac{1}{p})^{\mathcal{O}(1)}$ at least one of them will give a quadratic non-residue. Thus, to find a quadratic nonresidue ρ, it takes expected time $\mathcal{O}(\log^3 p)$. To compute $b^{2^{t-i-1}}$ (mod p), it takes time $\mathcal{O}((t - i - 1)\log^2 p)$. Since there are $1 + 2 + \cdots + (t - 1) = \frac{t(t-1)}{2}$ steps, the loop takes time $\mathcal{O}(t^2 \log^2 p)$. Thus, the total estimate is $\mathcal{O}(\log^3 p + t^2 \log^2 p)$. At worst (if almost all of $p - 1$ is a power of 2), this is $\mathcal{O}(\log^4 p)$.

3.2 Adleman-Manders-Miller Square Root Extraction Method in $\mathbb{F}_{p^m}$

As we mentioned before, the Adleman-Manders-Miller method in the extension field $\mathbb{F}_{p^m}$ differs from the method in the base field $\mathbb{F}_p$ because one can not determine a quadratic non-residue by computing the Legendre Symbol.

Set $q = p^m$. To find a quadratic non-residue ρ, it requires to check that $\rho^{\frac{q-1}{2}} \neq 1$. The computation takes time $\mathcal{O}(\log^3 q)$. If we do this for more than $\mathcal{O}(1)\log q$ different randomly chosen ρ, then with probability $> 1 - (\frac{1}{q})^{\mathcal{O}(1)}$ at least one of them will give a quadratic non-residue. Thus, to find a quadratic nonresidue ρ, it takes expected time $\mathcal{O}(\log^4 q)$.

To compute $b^{2^{t-i-1}}$, it takes time $\mathcal{O}((t - i - 1)\log^2 q)$. Since there are $1 + 2 + \cdots + (t - 1)$ steps, the loop takes time $\mathcal{O}(t^2 \log^2 q)$. Thus, the final estimate is $\mathcal{O}(\log^4 q + t^2 \log^2 q)$.

Table 2. Adleman-Manders-Miller square root extraction algorithm in $\mathbb{F}_{p^m}$

Input: Odd prime p, a positive integer m and a quadratic residue δ.
Output: A square root of δ.

Step 1: Choose ρ uniformly at random from $\mathbb{F}_{p^m}^*$.
Step 2: **if** $\rho^{\frac{p^m-1}{2}} = 1$, **go to** Step 1.
Step 3: Compute t, s such that $p^m - 1 = 2^t s$, where s is odd.
       Compute $a \leftarrow \rho^s, b \leftarrow \delta^s, h \leftarrow 1$.
Step 4: **for** $i = 1$ **to** $t - 1$
       compute $d = b^{2^{t-1-i}}$
       if $d = 1, k \leftarrow 0$
       else $k \leftarrow 1$
       $b \leftarrow b \cdot (a^2)^k, h \leftarrow h \cdot a^k$
       $a \leftarrow a^2$
       end for
Step 5: **return** $\delta^{\frac{s+1}{2}} \cdot h$

---

4   Adleman-Manders-Miller Cubic Root Extraction Method

In 2009, Nishihara et al. [9] specified the Adleman-Manders-Miller method for cube root extraction. See the following description.

Table 3. Adleman-Manders-Miller cubic root extraction algorithm in $\mathbb{F}_{p^m}$

Input: Odd prime p, a positive integer m and a cubic residue δ.
Output: A cubi root of δ.

Step 1: Choose ρ uniformly at random from $\mathbb{F}_{p^m}^*$.
Step 2: **if** $\rho^{\frac{p^m-1}{3}} = 1$, **go to** Step 1.
Step 3: Compute t, s such that $p^m - 1 = 3^t s$, where $s = 3l \pm 1$.
        Compute $a \leftarrow \rho^s, a' \leftarrow \rho^{3^{t-1} \cdot s}, b \leftarrow \delta^s, h \leftarrow 1$.
Step 4: **for** $i = 1$ **to** $t - 1$
            compute $d = b^{3^{t-1-i}}$
            if $d = 1$, $k \leftarrow 0$,
            else if $d = a'$, $k \leftarrow 2$
            else $k \leftarrow 1$
            $b \leftarrow b \cdot (a^3)^k, h \leftarrow h \cdot a^k$
            $a \leftarrow a^3$
        end for
Step 5: $r \leftarrow \delta^l h$
          if $s = 3l + 1$, $r \leftarrow r^{-1}$
          return r

Set $q = p^m$. The cubic root extraction algorithm takes time $\mathcal{O}(\log^4 q + t^2 \log^2 q)$. As for this claim, we refer to the complexity analysis of Adleman-Manders-Miller square root extraction algorithm in Section 3.2.

5   Specification of Adleman-Manders-Miller rth Root Extraction Method

Consider the general problem to find a solution to $X^r = \delta$ in $\mathbb{F}_q$. Clearly, it suffices to consider the following two cases:

$$(1) \ (r, q - 1) = 1; \qquad (2) \ r | q - 1.$$

If $(r, q - 1) = 1$, then $\delta^{r^{-1}}$ is a rth root of δ. Therefore, it suffices to consider the case that $r | q - 1$.

Adleman, Manders and Miller [1] had mentioned how to extend their square root extraction method to rth root extraction, but not specified it. We now clarify it as follows.

If $r | q - 1$, we write $p - 1$ in the form $r^t \cdot s$, where $(s, r) = 1$. Given a rth residue δ, we have $(\delta^s)^{r^{t-1}} = 1$. Since $(s, r) = 1$, it is easy to find the least nonnegative integer α such that $s | r\alpha - 1$. Hence,

$$\left(\delta^{r\alpha-1}\right)^{r^{t-1}} = 1 \tag{1}$$

If $t - 1 = 0$, then δ^α is a rth root of δ. From now on, we assume that $t \geq 2$. Given a rth non-residue $\rho \in \mathbb{F}_q$, we have

$$(\rho^s)^{i \cdot r^{t-1}} \neq (\rho^s)^{j \cdot r^{t-1}} \quad \text{where } i \neq j, \ i, j \in \{0, 1, \cdots, r-1\}$$

Set

$$K_i = (\rho^s)^{i \cdot r^{t-1}} \quad \text{and } \mathbb{K} = \{K_0, K_1, \cdots, K_{r-1}\}$$

It is easy to find that all K_i satisfy $X^r = 1$. Since

$$\left(\left(\delta^{r\alpha-1}\right)^{r^{t-2}}\right)^r = 1$$

there is a unique $j_1 \in \{0, 1, \cdots, r-1\}$ such that

$$\left(\delta^{r\alpha-1}\right)^{r^{t-2}} = K_{r-j_1}$$

where $K_r = K_0$. Hence,

$$\left(\delta^{r\alpha-1}\right)^{r^{t-2}} K_{j_1} = 1$$

That is

$$\left(\delta^{r\alpha-1}\right)^{r^{t-2}} (\rho^s)^{j_1 \cdot r^{t-1}} = 1 \tag{2}$$

By the way, to obtain j_1 one has to solve a discrete logarithm.

Likewise, there is a unique $j_2 \in \{0, 1, \cdots, r-1\}$ such that

$$\left(\delta^{r\alpha-1}\right)^{r^{t-3}} (\rho^s)^{j_1 \cdot r^{t-2}} (\rho^s)^{j_2 \cdot r^{t-1}} = 1 \tag{3}$$

Consequently, we can obtain $j_1, \cdots, j_{t-1}$ such that

$$\left(\delta^{r\alpha-1}\right) (\rho^s)^{j_1 \cdot r} (\rho^s)^{j_2 \cdot r^2} \cdots (\rho^s)^{j_{t-1} \cdot r^{t-1}} = 1 \tag{4}$$

Thus, we have

$$(\delta^\alpha)^r \left((\rho^s)^{j_1 + j_2 \cdot r + \cdots j_{t-1} \cdot r^{t-2}}\right)^r = \delta \tag{5}$$

It means that

$$\delta^\alpha (\rho^s)^{j_1 + j_2 \cdot r + \cdots j_{t-1} \cdot r^{t-2}}$$

is a rth root of δ.

Table 4. Adleman-Manders-Miller rth root extraction algorithm in $\mathbb{F}_q$

Input: $\mathbb{F}_q$ and a rth residue δ, $r|q-1$.
Output: A rth root of δ.

Step 1: Choose ρ uniformly at random from $\mathbb{F}_q^*$.
Step 2: **if** $\rho^{\frac{q-1}{r}} = 1$, **go to** Step 1.
Step 3: Compute t, s such that $q - 1 = r^t s$, where $(r, s) = 1$.
　　　　Compute the least nonnegative integer α such that $s|r\alpha - 1$.
　　　　Compute $a \leftarrow \rho^{r^{t-1}s}, b \leftarrow \delta^{r\alpha-1}, c \leftarrow \rho^s, h \leftarrow 1$
Step 4: **for** $i = 1$ **to** $t - 1$
　　　　　　compute $d = b^{r^{t-1-i}}$
　　　　　　if $d = 1$, $j \leftarrow 0$,
　　　　　　else $j \leftarrow -\log_a d$ (compute the discrete logarithm)
　　　　　　$b \leftarrow b(c^r)^j, h \leftarrow h c^j$
　　　　　　$c \leftarrow c^r$
　　　　end for
Step 5: **return** $\delta^\alpha \cdot h$

6　Complexity Analysis of Adleman-Manders-Miller rth Root Extraction Method

We now discuss the time estimate for this rth root extraction algorithm.

To find a rth non-residue ρ, it requires to check that $\rho^{\frac{q-1}{r}} \neq 1$. The computation takes time $\mathcal{O}(\log^3 q)$. If we do this for more than $\mathcal{O}(1)\log q$ different randomly chosen ρ, then with probability $> 1 - (\frac{1}{q})^{\mathcal{O}(1)}$ at least one of them will give a rth non-residue. Therefore, the expected time of finding a rth non-residue is $\mathcal{O}(\log^4 q)$.

The work done outside the loop amounts to just a handful of exponentiations. Hence, it takes time $\mathcal{O}(\log^3 q)$. To compute $b^{r^{t-i-1}}$, it takes time $\mathcal{O}((t - i - 1)\log r\log^2 q)$. Since there are $1+2+\cdots+(t-1)$ steps, it takes time $\mathcal{O}(t^2\log r\log^2 q)$.

To compute the discrete logarithm $\log_a d$, it takes time $\mathcal{O}(r\log^2 q)$ using brute-force search. Since there are $t - 1$ discrete logarithms at worst, it takes time $\mathcal{O}(tr\log^2 q)$.

Thus, the final estimate is $\mathcal{O}(\log^4 q + r\log^3 q)$. Notice that the algorithm can not run in polynomial time if r is sufficiently large.

7　Conclusion

The basic idea of Adleman-Manders-Miller root extraction method and its complexity analysis have not specified in the past decades. In this paper, we clarify the method and analyze its complexity. We think our heuristic presentation is helpful to grasp the method entirely and deeply.

Acknowledgements. We thank the anonymous referees' for their detailed suggestions. This work is supported by the National Natural Science Foundation of China (Project 60873227, 11171205), and the Key Disciplines of Shanghai Municipality (S30104).

References

1. Adleman, L., Manders, K., Miller, G.: On Taking Roots in Finite Fields. In: Proceedings of the 18th IEEE Symposium on Foundations of Computer Science, pp. 175–177. IEEE Press, New York (1977)
2. Barreto, P., Voloch, J.: Efficient Computation of Roots in Finite Fields. Designs, Codes and Cryptography 39, 275–280 (2006)
3. Gathen, J., Gerhard, J.: Modern Computer Algebra, 2nd edn. Cambridge University Press (2003)
4. Lidl, R., Niederreiter, H.: Introduction to finite fields and their applications. Cambridge University Press (1986)
5. Shoup, V.: A Computational Introduction to Number Theory and Algebra. Cambridge University Press (2005)
6. Cipolla, M.: Un metodo per la risoluzione della congruenza di secondo grado. In: Rendiconto dell'Accademia Scienze Fisiche e Matematiche, Napoli, Ser. 3, vol. IX, pp. 154–163 (1903)
7. Lehmer, D.: Computer technology applied to the theory of numbers. Studies in Number Theory, pp. 117–151. Pretice-Hall, Englewood Cliffs (1969)
8. Müller, S.: On the computation of square roots in finite fields. Designs, Codes and Cryptography 31, 301–312 (2004)
9. Nishihara, N., Harasawa, R., Sueyoshi, Y., Kudo, A.: A remark on the computation of cube roots in finite fields, eprint.iacr.org/2009/457
10. Shanks, D.: Five Number-theoretic Algorithms. In: Proc. 2nd Manitoba Conf., pp. 51–70. Numer. Math. (1972)
11. Sze, T.: On taking square roots without quadratic nonresidues over finite fields. Mathematics of Computation 80, 1797–1811 (2011)
12. Tonelli, A.: Bemerkungüber die Auflösung quadratischer Congruenzen. Nachrichten der Akademie der Wissenschaften in Göttingen, 344–346 (1891)

Multi-pixel Encryption Visual Cryptography*

Teng Guo[1,2], Feng Liu[1], and ChuanKun Wu[1]

[1] State Key Laboratory of Information Security
Institute of Software, Chinese Academy of Sciences, Beijing 100190, China
[2] Graduate University of Chinese Academy of Sciences, Beijing 100190, China
{guoteng,liufeng,ckwu}@is.iscas.ac.cn

Abstract. A visual cryptography scheme (VCS) is a secret sharing method, for which the secret can be decoded by human eyes without needing any cryptography knowledge nor any computation. In their pioneer work, Naor and Shamir mentioned that encrypting a block of pixels simultaneously may result in better result. Inspired by that idea, we first define multi-pixel encryption visual cryptography scheme (ME-VCS), which encrypts a block of t $(1 \leq t)$ pixels at a time. Then we give an upper bound of the overall contrast of ME-VCS. We also give a lower bound of the pixel expansion of (n, n, t)-ME-VCS. At last, we built a contrast-optimal ME-VCS from a contrast-optimal VCS and built an optimal (n, n, t)-ME-VCS from an optimal (n, n)-VCS.

Keywords: Visual cryptography, Multi-pixel encryption, Contrast-optimal, ME-VCS.

1 Introduction

In [13], Naor and Shamir first presented a formal definition of k out of n threshold visual cryptography scheme, denoted as (k, n)-VCS for short. In a (k, n)-VCS, the original secret image is split into n shares, where the stacking of any k shares can reveal the content of the secret image but any less than k shares should provide no information about the secret image, except the size of it. In [1], Ateniese et al. extended the model of Naor and Shamir to general access structure. A general access structure is a specification of qualified participant sets Γ_{Qual} and forbidden participant sets Γ_{Forb}. Any participant set $X \in \Gamma_{Qual}$ can reveal the secret by stacking their shares, but any participant set $Y \in \Gamma_{Forb}$ cannot obtain any information of the secret image, except the size of it.

In [13], Naor and Shamir also mentioned in the footnote that encrypting a block of pixels simultaneously may result in better result. Afterwards, many studies have been spent to multi-pixel encryption. In [9], Hou proposed a method, which encrypts a block of two pixels at a time. However, this method is probabilistic and it is for 2 out of 2 threshold structure only. In [14], Du extended Hou's method to general access structure, but the proposed method is still probabilistic. In [3], Chen proposed a multiple-level (k, k) secret sharing scheme, which

---

* This work was supported by NSFC No.60903210.

C.-K. Wu, M. Yung, and D. Lin (Eds.): Inscrypt 2011, LNCS 7537, pp. 86–92, 2012.
© Springer-Verlag Berlin Heidelberg 2012

encrypts a block of pixels at a time. This method combined with two techniques (histogram width-equalization and histogram depth-equalization) can deal with gray-level images, however it is not perfect secure (in an information-theoretic sense). Other studies on multi-pixel encryption can be found in [2,11,12]. However, they are all probabilistic and not proved to be optimal.

In the model of Naor and Shamir, we encode a pixel at a time, and we can recover the original secret image exactly (recover every pixel of the original secret image). In this sense, the model of Naor and Shamir is also known as deterministic VCS. In this paper, we refer deterministic VCS encoding a pixel at a time (the model of Naor and Shamir) as VCS. We first extend the model of Naor and Shamir (denoted as VCS) to the multi-pixel encryption model (denoted as ME-VCS), for which the model of Naor and Shamir is a special case of the proposed multi-pixel encryption model. Then we give an upper bound of the overall contrast of ME-VCS. For (n, n, t)-ME-VCS, we also give a lower bound of the pixel expansion. At last, we build a contrast-optimal ME-VCS from a contrast-optimal VCS and build an optimal (n, n, t)-ME-VCS from an optimal (n, n)-VCS.

This paper is organized as follows. In Section 2, we give some preliminaries of VCS and ME-VCS. In Section 3, we give an upper bound of the overall contrast of ME-VCS and a lower bound of the pixel expansion of (n, n, t)-ME-VCS. The paper is concluded in Section 4.

2   The Multi-pixel Encryption Model

In this section, we first give the definition of VCS. Then we give the definition of ME-VCS.

Let X be a subset of $\{1, 2, \cdots, n\}$ and let $|X|$ be the cardinality of X. For any $n \times m$ Boolean matrix M, let $M[X]$ denote the matrix M constrained to rows in X, then $M[X]$ is a $|X| \times m$ matrix. We denote by $H(M[X])$ the Hamming weight of the OR result of rows of $M[X]$. Let C_0 and C_1 be two collections of $n \times m$ Boolean matrices, we define $C_0[X] = \{M[X] : M \in C_0\}$, $C_1[X] = \{M[X] : M \in C_1\}$.

In a VCS with n participants, we share one pixel at a time. The pixel is either white or black. If the pixel to be shared is white (resp. black), we randomly choose a share matrix from C_0 (resp. C_1) and distribute its j-th $(0 \le j \le n)$ row to share j. Let $'0'$ denote a white pixel and let $'1'$ denote a black pixel. A VCS for an access structure Γ is defined as follows:

Definition 1 (VCS [13,1,7,8,10]). *Let $(\Gamma_{Qual}, \Gamma_{Forb}, n)$ be an access structure on a set of n participants. The two collections of $n \times m$ Boolean matrices (C_0, C_1) constitute a visual cryptography scheme $(\{\Gamma_{Qual}, \Gamma_{Forb}\}, n)$-VCS if the following conditions are satisfied:*

1. *(Contrast) For any participant set $X \in \Gamma_{Qual}$, we denote $l_X = \max\limits_{M \in C_0[X]} H(M)$, and denote $h_X = \min\limits_{M \in C_1[X]} H(M)$. It holds that $0 \le l_X < h_X \le m$.*

2. *(Security) For any participant set $Y \in \Gamma_{Forb}$, $C_0[Y]$ and $C_1[Y]$ contain the same matrices with the same frequencies.*

h_X (resp. l_X) is the minimum (resp. maximum) Hamming weight of the stacked patterns of a black (resp. white) pixel restricted to qualified set X. The contrast of qualified set X is defined as $\alpha_X = \frac{h_X - l_X}{m}$, and the contrast of the scheme is defined as $\alpha = \min_{X \in \Gamma_{Qual}} \{\alpha_X\}$. The pixel expansion of the scheme is m. The contrast is expected to be as large as possible. The pixel expansion is expected to be as small as possible. When the contrast reaches its maximum, the VCS is contrast-optimal. When the pixel expansion reaches its minimum, the VCS is pixel-expansion-optimal. When the VCS is both contrast-optimal and pixel-expansion-optimal, we say that the VCS is optimal.

Remark: In this paper, VCS means deterministic VCS encoding a pixel at a time, for which the original secret image can be reconstructed exactly. All the results are for deterministic VCS too.

If the two collections of $n \times m$ Boolean matrices (C_0, C_1) can be obtained by permuting the columns of the corresponding $n \times m$ matrix (S_0 for C_0, and S_1 for C_1) in all possible ways, we will call the two $n \times m$ matrices the basis matrices [1]. In this case, the size of the collections (C_0, C_1) is the same (both equal to $m!$). The algorithm for the VCS based on basis matrices has small memory requirement (it keeps only the basis matrices S_0 and S_1, instead of two collections of matrices (C_0, C_1)), and it is efficient (to choose a matrix in C_0 (resp. C_1), it only generate a permutation of the columns of S_0 (resp. S_1)).

In multi-pixel encryption visual cryptography scheme (ME-VCS) with n participants, we share a block of t ($t \geq 1$) pixels at a time. We denote the t pixels as an encryption block. Obviously, the Hamming weights of all possible encryption blocks may be $0, 1, \ldots, t$. There are $t+1$ encryption collections $(C_0, C_1, \ldots, C_t)$, for which C_i ($0 \leq i \leq t$) is for encryption blocks of Hamming weight i. To share an encryption block of Hamming weight i ($0 \leq i \leq t$), we randomly choose a share matrix from C_i, and distribute the j-th ($0 \leq j \leq n$) row to share j. A ME-VCS for an access structure Γ is defined as follows:

Definition 2 (ME-VCS). *Let $(\Gamma_{Qual}, \Gamma_{Forb}, n)$ be an access structure on a set of n participants. The $t+1$ collections of $n \times m$ Boolean matrices $(C_0, C_1, \ldots, C_t)$ constitute a multi-pixel encryption visual cryptography scheme $(\{\Gamma_{Qual}, \Gamma_{Forb}\}, n, t)$-ME-VCS if the following conditions are satisfied:*

1. *(Contrast) For any participant set $X \in \Gamma_{Qual}$, we denote $l_i^X = \min_{M \in C_i[X]} H(M)$ $(0 \leq i \leq t)$, and denote $h_i^X = \max_{M \in C_i[X]} H(M)$. It holds that $0 \leq h_0^X < l_1^X \leq h_1^X < l_2^X \leq h_2^X < l_3^X \leq \ldots \leq h_{t-1}^X < l_t^X \leq m$.*
2. *(Security) For any participant set $Y \in \Gamma_{Forb}$, $C_0[Y]$, $C_1[Y]$, $\ldots$, and $C_t[Y]$ contain the same matrices with the same frequencies.*

l_i^X ($0 \leq i \leq t$) is the minimum Hamming weight of the stacked patterns of encryption blocks of Hamming weight i restricted to qualified set X. h_i^X

$(0 \leq i \leq t)$ is the maximum Hamming weight of the stacked patterns of an encryption block of Hamming weight i restricted to qualified set X. The contrast of qualified set X between encryption blocks of Hamming weight i $(0 \leq i \leq t-1)$ and those of Hamming weight $i + 1$ is defined as $\alpha_i^X = \frac{l_{i+1}^X - h_i^X}{m}$, and the overall contrast of qualified set X is defined as $\alpha_X = \sum_{i=0}^{t-1} \alpha_i^X$. The overall contrast of the scheme is defined as $\alpha = \min_{X \in \Gamma_{Qual}} \alpha_X$. The pixel expansion of the scheme is m. The overall contrast is expected to be as large as possible. Because all possible Hamming weights of encryption blocks are evenly ranging from 0 to t, $\forall\, X \in \Gamma_{Qual}$, the contrasts α_i^X $(0 \leq i \leq t-1)$ are expected to be equal. When the overall contrast reaches its maximum, and $\forall\, X \in \Gamma_{Qual}$, the contrasts α_i^X $(0 \leq i \leq t-1)$ are equal, the ME-VCS is contrast-optimal. The pixel expansion is expected to be as small as possible. When the pixel expansion reaches its minimum, the ME-VCS is pixel-expansion-optimal. When a ME-VCS is both contrast-optimal and pixel-expansion-optimal, we say that the ME-VCS is optimal.

Remark: If the size of encryption blocks is one, the definition of ME-VCS coincides with that of VCS. In other words, a $(\{\Gamma_{Qual}, \Gamma_{Forb}\}, n, 1)$-ME-VCS is the same as a $(\{\Gamma_{Qual}, \Gamma_{Forb}\}, n)$-VCS. The model of Naor and Shamir is a special case of the proposed ME-VCS. The concept of basis matrices in VCS can easily be applied to ME-VCS. When $(\Gamma_{Qual}, \Gamma_{Forb})$ represents a (k, n) threshold structure, for convenience, we can simply write $(\{\Gamma_{Qual}, \Gamma_{Forb}\}, n, t)$-ME-VCS as (k, n, t)-ME-VCS.

3   Multi-pixel Encryption Visual Cryptography Scheme

In this section, we first give an upper bound of the overall contrast of ME-VCS. Then we give a lower bound of the pixel expansion of (n, n, t)-ME-VCS. At last, we build a contrast-optimal ME-VCS from a contrast-optimal VCS and build an optimal (n, n, t)-ME-VCS from an optimal (n, n)-VCS.

Theorem 1. *We denote the contrast of a contrast-optimal $(\{\Gamma_{Qual}, \Gamma_{Forb}\}, n)$-VCS as α^*. We denote the overall contrast of a contrast-optimal $(\{\Gamma_{Qual}, \Gamma_{Forb}\}, n, t)$-ME-VCS as α_{me}. Then we must have that $\alpha_{me} \leq \alpha^*$.*

Proof: Let $(C_0, C_1, \ldots, C_t)$ be the $t + 1$ collections of Boolean matrices of a contrast-optimal $(\{\Gamma_{Qual}, \Gamma_{Forb}\}, n, t)$-ME-VCS. It is easy to see that C_0 and C_t constitute a $(\{\Gamma_{Qual}, \Gamma_{Forb}\}, n)$-VCS.

In the following, we calculate the contrast of the $(\{\Gamma_{Qual}, \Gamma_{Forb}\}, n)$-VCS constructed from C_0 and C_t. Let l_i^X $(0 \leq i \leq t)$ be the minimum Hamming weights of the stacked patterns of a share matrix from C_i restricted to qualified set X. Let h_i^X $(0 \leq i \leq t)$ be the maximum Hamming weights of the stacked patterns of a share matrix from C_i restricted to qualified set X. The contrasts of the $(\{\Gamma_{Qual}, \Gamma_{Forb}\}, n, t)$-ME-VCS restricted to qualified set X are $\alpha_i^X = \frac{l_{i+1}^X - h_i^X}{m}$

$(0 \leq i \leq t-1)$. The contrast of the above $(\{\Gamma_{Qual}, \Gamma_{Forb}\}, n)$-VCS restricted to qualified set X is $\alpha_X = \frac{l_t^X - h_0^X}{m}$. Since $l_i^X \leq h_i^X$ $(0 \leq i \leq t)$, we get that $\sum_{i=0}^{t-1} \alpha_i^X \leq \alpha_X$. From the definition of overall contrast of ME-VCS, we get that

$\alpha_{me} = \min_{X \in \Gamma_{Qual}} \sum_{i=0}^{t-1} \alpha_i^X$. The contrast of the above $(\{\Gamma_{Qual}, \Gamma_{Forb}\}, n)$-VCS constructed from C_0 and C_t is $\alpha = \min_{X \in \Gamma_{Qual}} \alpha_X$. Thus it holds that $\alpha_{me} \leq \alpha$. Since α^* is the optimal (maximal) contrast for $(\{\Gamma_{Qual}, \Gamma_{Forb}\}, n)$-VCS, it results that $\alpha_{me} \leq \alpha \leq \alpha^*$. □

In the following, we give a lower bound of the pixel expansion of (n, n, t)-ME-VCS as follows.

Theorem 2. *In an (n, n, t)-ME-VCS, we denote its pixel expansion as m, then we have that $m \geq t \times 2^{n-1}$.*

Proof: It is known that the contrast of (n, n)-VCS is upper bounded by $\frac{1}{2^{n-1}}$ (see [13]). In an (n, n, t)-ME-VCS, we denote its overall contrast as α_{me}. Because there is only one qualified set in (n, n, t)-ME-VCS, the overall contrast of the scheme equals to the overall contrast restricted to the qualified set. We will not distinguish them in the following discussion. We denote the contrast of the scheme between encryption blocks of Hamming weight i $(0 \leq i \leq t-1)$ and those of Hamming weight $i+1$ as α_i. From the definition of overall contrast, we know that $\alpha_{me} = \sum_{i=0}^{t-1} \alpha_i$. From Theorem 1, we know that $\alpha_{me} \leq \frac{1}{2^{n-1}}$. Thus it holds that $\sum_{i=0}^{t-1} \alpha_i \leq \frac{1}{2^{n-1}}$. Let $\alpha = \min\{\alpha_i\}$. Since $\alpha \leq \frac{1}{t} \times \sum_{i=0}^{t-1} \alpha_i \leq \frac{1}{t \times 2^{n-1}}$, we have that $\frac{1}{\alpha} \geq t \times 2^{n-1}$. Since the difference between the minimal Hamming weight of recovered patterns of encryption blocks of Hamming weight $i+1$ $(0 \leq i \leq t-1)$ and the maximal Hamming weight of those of Hamming weight i is at least one, we have that $\alpha \times m \geq 1$. Thus it holds that $m \geq \frac{1}{\alpha} \geq t \times 2^{n-1}$. □

In the following, we will build a contrast-optimal ME-VCS from a contrast-optimal VCS. Our method is similar to the hybrid technique widely used in complexity theory and theoretical cryptography, see chap. 3 in [5], chap. 2 in [6] and [4]. Let M_0 and M_1 be the basis matrices of a contrast-optimal $(\{\Gamma_{Qual}, \Gamma_{Forb}\}, n)$-VCS with contrast α^* and pixel expansion m. The following $t+1$ basis matrices G_i $(0 \leq i \leq t)$ define a contrast-optimal $(\{\Gamma_{Qual}, \Gamma_{Forb}\}, n, t)$-ME-VCS.

$$G_i = \underbrace{M_0 \circ \ldots \circ M_0}_{t-i} \circ \underbrace{M_1 \circ \ldots \circ M_1}_{i} \qquad (0 \leq i \leq t).$$

Theorem 3. *The above G_i $(0 \le i \le t)$ define a contrast-optimal $(\{\Gamma_{Qual}, \Gamma_{Forb}\},$ $n, t)$-ME-VCS.*

Proof: The Hamming weight of the stacked pattern of M_0 restricted to qualified set X is denoted as w_0^X. The Hamming weight of the stacked pattern of M_1 restricted to qualified set X is denoted as w_1^X. The contrast of the $(\{\Gamma_{Qual}, \Gamma_{Forb}\}, n)$-VCS restricted to qualified set X is $\alpha_X = \dfrac{w_1^X - w_0^X}{m}$. The contrast of the $(\{\Gamma_{Qual}, \Gamma_{Forb}\}, n)$-VCS is $\alpha^* = \min\limits_{X \in \Gamma_{Qual}} \alpha_X$.

The Hamming weight of the stacked pattern of G_i restricted to qualified set X is denoted as l_i^X $(0 \le i \le t)$. From the construction of G_i, we know that $l_i^X = w_0^X \times (t - i) + w_1^X \times i$ $(0 \le i \le t)$. So the contrast of qualified set X between encryption blocks of Hamming weight i $(0 \le i \le t - 1)$ and those of Hamming weight $i + 1$ is $\alpha_i^X = \dfrac{l_{i+1}^X - l_i^X}{m \times t} = \dfrac{w_1^X - w_0^X}{m \times t} = \dfrac{\alpha_X}{t} > 0$. The contrast condition of the ME-VCS is satisfied. The overall contrast of qualified set X is $\alpha_X^{me} = \sum\limits_{i=0}^{t-1} \alpha_i^X = t \times (\dfrac{\alpha_X}{t}) = \alpha_X$. The overall contrast of the scheme is $\alpha = \min\limits_{X \in \Gamma_{Qual}} \alpha_X^{me} = \min\limits_{X \in \Gamma_{Qual}} \alpha_X = \alpha^*$. From Theorem 1, we know that the overall contrast reaches its maximum value. Besides, $\forall\ X \in \Gamma_{Qual}$, the contrasts α_i^X $(0 \le i \le t - 1)$ are equal up. Thus the $(\{\Gamma_{Qual}, \Gamma_{Forb}\}, n, t)$-ME-VCS is contrast-optimal. The security condition follows from the security of the $(\{\Gamma_{Qual}, \Gamma_{Forb}\}, n)$-VCS. Thus the conclusion holds.   □

The construction of an optimal (n, n)-VCS can be found in [13]. In the following, we prove that the above construction builds an optimal (n, n, t)-ME-VCS from an optimal (n, n)-VCS.

Theorem 4. *Let M_0 and M_1 be the basis matrices of an optimal (n, n)-VCS, then the above G_i $(0 \le i \le t)$ define an optimal (n, n, t)-ME-VCS.*

Proof: From Theorem 3, we know that the above (n, n, t)-ME-VCS is contrast-optimal. From the construction of G_i $(0 \le i \le t)$, we know that the pixel expansion of the above (n, n, t)-ME-VCS is $t \times 2^{n-1}$. From Theorem 2, we know that the above (n, n, t)-ME-VCS is pixel-expansion-optimal. Thus the conclusion holds.   □

4   Conclusions

We first extended the model of Naor and Shamir (denoted as VCS) to the multi-pixel encryption model (denoted as ME-VCS), for which the model of Naor and Shamir is a special case of the proposed multi-pixel encryption model. Then we give an upper bound of the overall contrast of ME-VCS. We also give a lower bound of the pixel expansion of (n, n, t)-ME-VCS. At last, we built a contrast-optimal ME-VCS from a contrast-optimal VCS and built an optimal (n, n, t)-ME-VCS from an optimal (n, n)-VCS.

Acknowledgements. This work was supported by NSFC No.60903210.

References

1. Ateniese, G., Blundo, C., De Santis, A., Stinson, D.R.: Visual cryptography for general access structures. Information and Computation 129, 86–106 (1996)
2. Chang, C.Y.: Visual cryptography for color images. MS thesis, National Central University, Taiwan (2000)
3. Chen, Y.F., Chan, Y.K., Huang, C.C., Tsai, M.H., Chu, Y.P.: A multiple-level visual secret-sharing scheme without image size expansion. Information Sciences 177, 4696–4710 (2007)
4. Goldreich, O.: A note on computational indistinguishability (1989), http://www.wisdom.weizmann.ac.il/~oded/PS/iplnote.ps
5. Goldreich, O.: Foundations of cryptography: Basic tools, vol. 1, p. 392. Cambridge University Press (2001)
6. Goldwasser, S., Bellare, M.: Lecture notes on cryptography, (2008), http://cseweb.ucsd.edu/~mihir/papers/gb.pdf
7. Hofmeister, T., Krause, M., Simon, H.U.: Contrast-Optimal k Out of n Secret Sharing Schemes in Visual Cryptography. In: Jiang, T., Lee, D.T. (eds.) COCOON 1997. LNCS, vol. 1276, pp. 176–185. Springer, Heidelberg (1997)
8. Hofmeister, T., Krause, M., Simon, H.U.: Contrast-optimal k out of n secret sharing schemes in visual cryptography. Theoretical Computer Science 240(2), 471–485 (2000)
9. Hou, Y.C., Tu, C.F.: Visual cryptography techniques for color images without pixel expansion. Journal of Information, Technology and Society 1, 95–110 (2004) (in Chinese)
10. Krause, M., Simon, H.U.: Determining the optimal contrast for secret sharing schemes in visual cryptography. Combinatorics, Probability & Computing 12(3), 285–299 (2003)
11. Lin, C.H.: Visual cryptography for color images with image size invariable shares. MS thesis, National Central University, Taiwan (2002)
12. Liu, F., Wu, C.K., Lin, X.J.: Color visual cryptography schemes. IET Information Security 2(4), 151–165 (2008)
13. Naor, M., Shamir, A.: Visual Cryptography. In: De Santis, A. (ed.) EUROCRYPT 1994. LNCS, vol. 950, pp. 1–12. Springer, Heidelberg (1995)
14. Tu, S.F.: On the design of protection scheme for digital images and documents based on visual secret sharing and steganography. PhD thesis, National Central University, Taiwan (2005)

An Improved Electronic Voting Scheme
without a Trusted Random Number Generator

Yining Liu, Peiyong Sun, Jihong Yan, Yajun Li, and Jianyu Cao

School of Mathematics and Computational Science
Guilin University of Electronic Technology
Guilin, China, 541004
ynliu@guet.edu.cn

Abstract. Bingo Voting uses trusted random number generator to realize the correctness and coercion-free. If the trusted random number generator is corrupted, the whole scheme is dangerous, which make it a security bottleneck. With the method of verifiable random number based on interpolating polynomial over F_p, an improved electronic voting scheme is proposed, which not only inherits the good properties of Bingo Voting, but also eliminates the dependence of the trusted random number generator. With the receipt, voter can verify whether the content of vote meets his aspiration or not, but he can not prove to others whom he has vote. The improved e-voting scheme based on verifiable random number that is fair, verifiable, and untraceable can efficiently prevent from colluding and buying vote.

Keywords: E-voting, verifiable random number, finite field, interpolating polynomial, coercion-free, verifiability.

1   Introduction

Election is a very common phenomenon in many countries to assure the legitimacy of the regime, which should meet a lot of requirements, such as directness, freedom, equality, and security. A secure e-voting scheme should satisfy at least three properties: an election should be free, i.e., nobody can be coerced to cast a certain vote, it should be equal, i.e., nobody can influence the result more than with her own vote, and it should be secret: no one can learn the votes of other people.

Proposals for secure electronic voting systems have been emerging over the past 20 years. The basis for security, both in terms of vote privacy, and in terms of preventing from fraud, is provided with the use of cryptography such as blind signature[1,2], mixnets[3,4] and homomorphic encryption[5,6].

The e-voting scheme usually consists of four roles:

1. Votes: the normal requirement of a voter is to cast a vote.
2. Election authority: the deputy of the election authority includes: distribution of ballot forms, recruitment of officials, aggregation of votes, publishing information, announcing the result and so forth.

C.-K. Wu, M. Yung, and D. Lin (Eds.): Inscrypt 2011, LNCS 7537, pp. 93–101, 2012.
© Springer-Verlag Berlin Heidelberg 2012

3. Auditors: auditor provides an expert opinion on evidence of proper function published by the e-voting system, by checking or auditing the published information.
4. Help Organizations.

In recent years, a lot of progress has been achieved in the area of verifiable elections, such as Punchscan[7,8], Prêt à Voter[9] and Scantegrity II [10]. Examples for DRE based schemes are the voting scheme of Moran and Naor[11], and Bingo Voting[12,13].

Bingo Voting is an interesting scheme that uses a random number for each candidate on the receipt which is ingenious but does rely on trust in the random number generation. If the random number generation is corrupted, the privacy of vote should be destroyed.

In the next section, we will introduce Bingo Voting and analyze its security flaw, we present a method of verifiable random number in section 3, give the improved e-voting scheme in section 4, and the paper conclusion is in section 5.

2   Review of Bingo Voting

Bingo Voting consists of three phases: pre-voting, voting, and post-voting, which is for a simple election with a single voting machine and the option to choose one out of n candidates.

- Pre-voting Phase

In the pre-voting phase, $r_1^i, \cdots, r_l^i$ for each candidate P_i are created by voting machine or authority, which is used to yield a commitment to (P_i, r_j^i) called a " dummy vote" for P_i, where l is the number of eligible voters. The dummy votes are shuffled and published. A public proof that there are exactly l dummy votes for each candidate is added. These preparations can be made by the voting authority which must be trusted to ensure ballot secrecy.

- Voting Phase

After the voter has chosen a candidate, a fresh random number is generated by the trusted random number generator and is transferred to the voting machine.

The voting machine creates and prints a receipt that contains a list of candidates with a random number associated to each candidate. The number for the selected candidate must match the number which is displayed by the trusted random number generator; this can be checked by the voter. The other numbers are the random numbers of dummy votes generated during the pre-voting phase. Dummy votes which were printed on a receipt are marked as "used" and will not be selected for further receipts. For simplicity, we denote the receipt $\{(P_1, R_1), (P_2, R_2), \cdots, (P_n, R_n)\}$. This phase is shown in Fig.1.

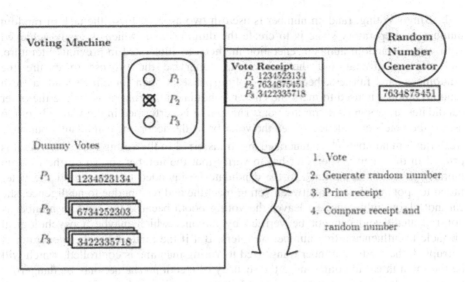

Fig. 1. The voting receipt generation

• Post-voting Phase

After the election, the voting machine calculates the result and sends it together with a proof of correctness to a public bulletin board. The published data consists of :

1. The number of votes of each candidate;
2. The receipts issued by the voting machine;
3. A list of the "unused" pairs (P_i, r_j^i), i.e., dummy votes that are not used on any receipt, together with the unveil information for the corresponding commitment;
4. A proof of the correctness of the result.

In the phase, each voter can check whether her receipt was published correctly, and the tally result is true or false. And the proof of correctness together with the comparisons by the voters guarantees correction of the election result.

• Analysis of Bingo Voting

Many recent secure e-voting schemes guarantee the correctness of the election result with special properties of paper or printers. In contrast to these schemes Bingo Voting uses a random number generator with display as a trust anchor which makes the voter to check her vote without being subject to secrecy/coercion attacks if the voting machine is uncorrupted. In addition to provide correctness and coercion protection, the implementation of Bingo Voting is also efficient which is described in [12].

From the above analysis, we know the secure basis of Bingo Voting is the honest random number generator, which produces genuine random number for the receipt. If the generation of random number is colluded, the scheme is dangerous for voters because their privacy is disclosed.

In Bingo Voting, random number is used in two aspects. First, the task of random number in preparatory stage is to create the dummy vote, which is easily achieved with various random number generation methods as illustrated in previous literature, and election official and the public can supervise the process to ensure the randomness and fairness, because pre-voting phase is open for all. Second, a fresh random number is used to mark the chosen candidate in voting phase while the other candidates are assigned a dummy vote. This phase is performed in the voting booth to assure the vote's confidence. When the voter press the according candidate's button, a fresh random number R is generated and transferred to the voting machine, which is printed in the receipt. The voter has to verify that the number shown on the random number generator is assigned to the candidate he intended to vote for. If the voter failed to spot that the error between voting machine and receipt due to negligence, she can not claim rights once he leaves the voting booth because the random number is non-repeatedly and can not be verified by anyone, which maybe a psychological obstacle to influence a tiny number of voters. But if the random number generator is corrupted, the random number transferred to voting machine is controlled, which will be the main threat to compromise the security of election scheme, may be dangerous to voter and society. The operation and data transmission in voting phase are all performed in closed environment, which make nobody can check whether the random number according to the chosen candidate is genuine random or not. The feasible way is to involve voter's participation in generating random number, and enable voters to verify whether her involvement has played a role.

In this paper, based on verifiable random number, an improved e-voting scheme is proposed, which not only inherits the advantages of Bingo Voting, but no longer requires the trusted random generator, eliminates the security bottleneck.

3   Verifiable Random Number Based on Interpolating Polynomial

3.1   Polynomial Generation over F_p

For simplicity, we assume there are n users and a computing center to generating verifiable random number together. The step is as follows:

1. $U_i (1 \le i \le n)$ selects a pair of number $r_i = (x_i, y_i)$ randomly, and sends it to Computing Center(CC).

2. CC selects a pair of number $r_0 = (x_0, y_0)$ randomly;

3. CC constructs a polynomial $A(x) = a_0 + a_1 x + \cdots + a_n x^n$ using $n+1$ points $(x_0, y_0), (x_1, y_1), \cdots, (x_n, y_n)$ by adopting Lagrange polynomial Interpolation as in [14, 15]. We know it is easy to calculate the corresponding coefficients $(a_0, a_1, \cdots, a_n)$ of interpolated polynomial which satisfies the equation $y_i = A(x_i)$ $(0 \le i \le n)$.

We give two examples for illustrating the interpolated polynomial over F_7.

If there are three points $(x_0, y_0) = (1,2)$, $(x_1, y_1) = (2,6)$, $(x_2, y_2) = (4,5)$, the corresponding Interpolating polynomial is $A(x) = a_0 + a_1 x + \cdots + a_n x^n = 2 + 5x + 2x^2 \in F_7[x]$.

If there are five ordered pairs over F_7, $(x_0, y_0) = (1,5)$, $(x_1, y_1) = (2,3)$, $(x_2, y_2) = (3,1)$, $(x_3, y_3) = (4,6)$, $(x_4, y_4) = (5,2)$, the corresponding polynomial is $A(x) = 5 + x + 2x^3 + 4x^4$.

3.2   Verifiable Random Numbers

There are n candidates; we propose a method of constructing verifiable random number:

1. voter choose his favorite candidate, and cast his ballot to him, nobody knows whom voter has voted for except himself, we assume P_i is selected by voter;
2. every failed candidate is assigned a dummy vote, the corresponding pairs are listed as $(P_1, R_1), \cdots, (P_{i-1}, R_{i-1}), (P_{i+1}, R_{i+1}), \cdots, (P_n, R_n)$;
3. $A(x) = a_{n-2} x^{n-2} + \cdots + a_1 x + a_0 \in F_p[x]$ is generated with $n-1$ pairs by voting machine, P_i is substituted to $A(x)$, $A(P_i)$ is used as verifiable random number for voter, and $(P_1, R_1), \cdots, (P_{i-1}, R_{i-1}), (P_i, A(P_i)), (P_{i+1}, R_{i+1}), \cdots, (P_n, R_n)$ is printed in receipt.
4. If voter doubt that voting machine is corrupted, he can check whether the verifiable random number $A(P_i)$ is generated according his selection. If the verification is true, voter convinces his participant involved in generating polynomial $A(x)$, so the receipt reflects his wish.

4   An Improved E-voting Scheme

4.1   Introduction of Improved Scheme

Based on the method of verifiable random number, an improved e-voting scheme is proposed without a trusted random number generator. The phase of pre-voting and post-voting is same as Bingo Voting, we only add a task of initializing a prime p which should larger than all dummy vote in the phase of pre-voting. We omit the description of these two stages, mainly focus the second phase. The improved voting phase is described as follows:

1.   voter presses the button according his favorite candidate;

2. the other candidates is assigned a dummy vote randomly;
3. the voting machine calculates the verifiable random number and distributes it to the chosen candidate;
4. the voting machine prints the receipt, in which every candidate is attached the corresponding number;
5. Voter leaves the voting booth.

In order to illustrate the process, we simplify the dummy vote and give a example over F_7. First we assume the identifications of P_1, P_2, P_3 are $1, 2, 3$ and the selected candidate is P_2, and the two dummy votes are assigned to P_1, P_3, their according commitment number is $(P_1, 1), (P_3, 6)$, we transform them to $(1,1), (3,6)$. Now voting machine computes the interpolating polynomial $A(x) = 6x + 2 \in F_7[x]$ which passes through two points $(1,1), (3,6)$, then voting machine substitutes P_2 to the polynomial $A(x)$, $A(2) = 0$ that is verifiable random number is assigned to P_2, which is same as fresh random number in Bingo Voting. The voting process is shown as Fig2.

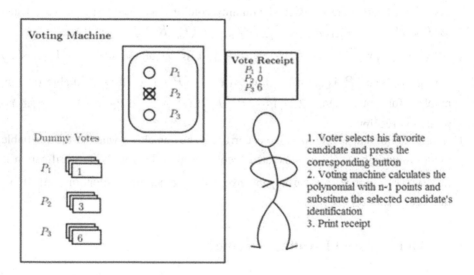

Fig. 2. The improved voting receipt generation

4.2   Analysis

The improved scheme doesn't rely on the trusted random number generator, which eliminates the security bottleneck. From the introduction of the improved scheme, we know the previous properties are all inherited. Now we only analyze the good characteristic derived from the above process.

1. random

In the above proposal, voter chooses his favorite candidate freely in the voting booth, no others can interference him. Once voter presses the button, every failed candidate is distributed a dummy vote randomly by the voting machine, the according interpolating polynomial $A(x)$ is generated with the identification of these failed candidates and their dummy vote. Then the selected candidate is substituted to $A(x)$ to get the verifiable random number for voter, which is assigned to the selected candidate and printed in the receipt. The verifiable random number based on Lagrange interpolating polynomial has the same effect with the trusted random number generator in Bingo Voting, but also the random number is involved every voter's influence including the voter's selection and other's dummy vote, nobody has the controlling role in the scheme, which eliminate the bottleneck of trust.

2. verifiability

Assuming the selected candidate is P_i, $A(x) = a_{n-2}x^{n-2} + \cdots + a_1 x + a_0$ over a finite field is generated with $n-1$ dummy votes ,then substituting P_i for x in $A(x)$, $A(P_i)$ is attached to P_i. The candidates and their number are printed in the receipt, which make voter verify whether the receipt reflects his wish even if he leaves the voting booth. In Bingo Voting, the voter must site inspection the receipt and random number generator. If he leaves the voting booth, he has no evidence to question the fairness.

3. coercion-free

The vote receipt can not be used to prove anything about the contents of a vote to others. In the receipt, every candidate is attached a random number, the failed candidate is distributed from dummy vote pool and the selected candidate is assigned the verifiable random number. $A(x)$ is constructed with arbitrary $n-1$ pairs and the remaining point satisfies $A(x)$. So voter has no idea to prove to others that he has vote the specific candidate, for example, his favorite candidate is P_i, $A(x)$ is generated from $(P_1, R_1), \cdots, (P_{i-1}, R_{i-1}), (P_{i+1}, R_{i+1}), \cdots, (P_n, R_n)$,and $R_i = A(P_i)$,which are all printed in the receipt. But if we replace P_i with P_j, i.e., $(P_1, R_1), \cdots, (P_{j-1}, R_{j-1}), (P_{j+1}, R_{j+1}), \cdots, (P_n, R_n)$ $(j \neq i)$ can retrieve the same $A(x)$, and $R_j = A(P_j)$ is also hold. Voter has not evidence that $A(x)$ is only constructed by $(P_1, R_1), \cdots, (P_{i-1}, R_{i-1}), (P_{i+1}, R_{i+1}), \cdots, (P_n, R_n)$ to prove his selected candidate P_i, which is important to avoid vote selling.

4.3   The Case of 1 Out of 2

In case of 1 out 2 candidates, the polynomial can not be generated with the above method because there is no unique polynomial which passes through one point.

In order to construct verifiable random number, we give a modification to make it available.

In pre-voting phase, voting machine selects a constant C and publishes it. In voting phase, we assume that the favorite candidate of voter is P_2, there is unique polynomial $A(x) = ax + C$ which passes through (P_1, R_1). Then P_2 is substituted to $A(x) = ax + C$ and the verifiable random number is generated and attached to P_2 in the receipt. For example, we set $C = 4 \in F_7$, and $P_1 = 1; P_2 = 2$, and voting machine distributes P_1 a dummy vote $R_1 = 6$. It is easy to know $A(x) = 2x + 4$, and $A(P_2 = 2) = 1$ is verifiable random number for P_2. $(P_1, 6), (P_2, 1)$ are printed in the receipt. The properties in the above analysis is also satisfied in the case of 1 out 2 candidates.

5   Conclusion

In this paper, an improved e-voting scheme based on interpolating polynomial is proposed, which eliminate the security bottleneck to make every voter to authenticate the random number. There are no privacy disclosure in the receipt and nobody can deduce who has been voted, which protect the content of vote and prevent from buying vote. As for calculation cost, a little burden is increased for polynomial construction contrast with Bingo Voting. The construction of verifiable random number based on interpolating polynomial over F_p is efficient. The other phase is same as Bingo Voting, which make the improved scheme inherit all the properties.

References

1. Fujioka, A., Okamoto, T., Ohta, K.: A Practical Secret Voting Scheme for Large Scale Elections. In: Zheng, Y., Seberry, J. (eds.) AUSCRYPT 1992. LNCS, vol. 718, pp. 244–251. Springer, Heidelberg (1993)
2. Okamoto, T.: An electronic voting scheme. In: Proc. IFIP 1996, pp. 21–30 (1996)
3. Chaum, D.: Untraceable electronic mail, return addresses, and digital pseudonyms. Commun. ACM 24(2), 84–88 (1981)
4. Jakobsson, M., Juels, A., Rivest, R.L.: Making mix nets robust for electronic voting by randomized partial checking. In: Proc. 11th USENIX Security Symp., pp. 339–353 (2002)
5. Baudron, O., Fouque, P.A., Pointcheval, D., Stern, J., Poupard, G.: Practical multi-candidate election system. In: Proc. 20th ACM Symp. Principles of Disrib. Computing, New York, pp. 274–283 (2001)
6. Cramer, R., Franklin, M., Schoenmakers, B., Yung, M.: Multi-authority Secret-Ballot Elections with Linear Work. In: Maurer, U. (ed.) EUROCRYPT 1996. LNCS, vol. 1070, pp. 72–83. Springer, Heidelberg (1996)
7. Chaum, D.: Punchscan (2006), http://punchscan.org/

8. Popoveniuc, S., Hosp, B.: An introduction to Punchscan. In: IAVoSS Workshop On Trustworthy Elections (WOTE 2006) (October 15, 2006),
http://punchscan.org/papers/
popoveniuc_hosp_punchscan_introduction.pdf
9. Chaum, D., Ryan, P.Y.A., Schneider, S.: A Practical Voter-Verifiable Election Scheme. In: De Capitani di Vimercati, S., Syverson, P., Gollmann, D. (eds.) ESORICS 2005. LNCS, vol. 3679, pp. 118–139. Springer, Heidelberg (2005)
10. Chaum, D., Carback, R., Clark, J., Essex, A., Popoveniuc, S., Rivest, R.L., Ryan, P.Y.A., Shen, E., Sherman, A.T.: Scantegrity II: Endto-End Verifiability for Optical Scan Election Systems Using Invisible Ink Confirmation (2008),
http://www.usenix.org/event/evt08/tech/full_papers/
chaum/chaum.pdf
11. Moran, T., Naor, M.: Receipt-Free Universally-Verifiable Voting with Everlasting Privacy. In: Dwork, C. (ed.) CRYPTO 2006. LNCS, vol. 4117, pp. 373–392. Springer, Heidelberg (2006)
12. Bohli, J.-M., Müller-Quade, J., Röhrich, S.: Bingo Voting: Secure and Coercion-Free Voting Using a Trusted Random Number Generator. In: Alkassar, A., Volkamer, M. (eds.) VOTE-ID 2007. LNCS, vol. 4896, pp. 111–124. Springer, Heidelberg (2007)
13. Bohli, J.-M., Henrich, C., Kempka, C., Müller-Quade, J.: Enhancing Electronic Voting Machines on the Example of Bingo Voting. IEEE Transactions on Information Forensics and Security 4, 745–750 (2009)
14. Kim, W.H., Ryu, E.K., Im, J.Y., Yoo, K.Y.: New conference key agreement protocol with user anonymity. Computer Standards & Interfaces 27, 185–190 (2005)
15. Shamir, A.: How to Share a Secret. Comm. ACM 22(11), 612–613 (1979)

Fault Attacks against the Miller Algorithm in Hessian Coordinates

Jiang Weng*, Yunqi Dou, and Chuangui Ma

Zhengzhou Information Science and Technology Institute,
Zhengzhou, Henan Province, 450002, China
wengjiang858@163.com, douyunqi@126.com, chuanguima@sina.com

Abstract. In recent years, fault attacks have been developed to be very
powerful tools in the field of attack against crypto-algorithm. The basic
idea of fault attacks is through provoking disturbances, then an adversary is able to recover some secret data from a carelessly implemented
crypto-algorithm. As we known the Miller's algorithm is the critical step
for bilinear pairing calculation. Since the Miller's algorithm is usually
embedded in identity aware devices such as smart card, a lot of attentions are attracted to analyze these devices. In this paper, we investigate
a new approach based on the resolution of a nonlinear system, and this
approach has an advantage that the pairing based cryptography in Hessian coordinates is vulnerable to a fault attack.

Keywords: Hessian   coordinates,   fault   attack,   pairing   based
cryptography.

1 Introduction

In 1984, Shamir [11] challenged that how to find a protocol based on the user's
identity. This challenge was first introduced by Boneh and Franklin [3] in 2001.
They developed an identity-based cryptography (IBC) scheme based on pairings.
The important point is that the decryption operation involves the secret key and
the message in the bilinear pairing calculation, where the secret key is one of the
elliptic curve points input to the pairing. The original algorithm for computing
pairings is due to Miller [8], which is the most widely used technique to compute
the pairings.

Fault attacks against pairing based cryptography [5,12,13] are a recent class
of attacks that have been revealed to be very powerful in practice. By disrupt-
ing the normal execution of an algorithm, an adversary is able to recover some
secret data from the crypto-algorithm. The fault attack consists in modifying
the number of iterations of the algorithm. Page and Vercauteren [5] propose a
fault attack against the pairings for the first time when they demonstrate an attack on the Duursma and Lee algorithm. Then Mrabet further investigates that

* This work was supported in part by the National High Technology Research and
Development Program of China (No. 2009AA01Z417).

C.-K. Wu, M. Yung, and D. Lin (Eds.): Inscrypt 2011, LNCS 7537, pp. 102–112, 2012.

this idea is completed in application to the Miller's algorithm in Weierstrass coordinates. Furthermore, Whelan and Scott [12] conclude that if the secret is used as the first position of the pairing computation, it can not be recovered. More recent studies by Mrabet [6] further examine wherever the position of the secret point is located, the secret key is also recovered. The pairing computation consists of two main parts, the Miller loop and the final exponentiation. Whelan and Scott [13] have given a perfect result about how to dispose the final exponentiation. Therefore we ignore the final exponentiation in the following discussion.

Previous studies only consider under the Weierstrass coordinates. Recently, Hessian coordinates are introduced for computing pairings. However, with further exploration none of these studies mentioned before has been focused on fault attack in the Hessian coordinates. As we known, Hessian curves become interesting for elliptic curve cryptography when it is introduced by Smart in [9], which includes a performance advantage over the standard representation. The advantage of Hessian coordinates is that points are represented with fewer coordinates, which results in substantial memory savings, and a processor can reach around forty percent when it allows the evaluation of a number of field multiplications in parallel. In this context, we investigate the security of pairings in Hessian coordinates.

In this paper, we establish a fault attack against the Miller's algorithm in Hessian coordinates based on hardware error analysis. Moreover, we further investigate how to actively influence the target device and induce faults during the process of computation. Our model is generalize the fault attack to the Miller's algorithm in every possible iteration, not only for the last iteration. Furthermore, no matter where the position of the secret point is located, our model could recover secret, not only for the second position. Our model needs very precise timing, position and an expensive apparatus to be performed. The most attractive point of our model is that we propose the detailed attack process, establish the attack model and analyze the probability of the success. The main contribution is to show that a fault attack against the Miller's algorithm in Hessian coordinates can be done through the resolution of a nonlinear system.

Organization. The remainder of this paper is organized as follows. Firstly we give a short introduction to pairings and to the Miller's algorithm in Section 2. After that the background of Hessian coordinates is presented in Section 3. Section 4 presents our fault attack against pairing based cryptography in Hessian coordinates and gives the method to recover the secret key by solving a nonlinear system. Finally, some remarks are given in section 5.

2 Pairings and the Miller's Algorithm

In this section, we recall a brief overview of the definition and property of pairings. Subsequently, the Miller's algorithm [8] is described in Hessian coordinates.

2.1   A Short Introduction to Pairings

We consider pairings defined over an elliptic curve E over a finite field $\mathbb{F}_q$ with $q = p^n$, where p is a prime number. We describe the attack for pairing calculation in Hessian coordinates.

We consider the elliptic curve in Hessian coordinates: $X^3 + Y^3 + Z^3 = 3aXYZ$, with $a \in \mathbb{F}_q$. Let $l \in \mathbb{N}^*$, and k be the smallest integer such that l divides $(q^k - 1)$, k is called the embedding degree.

Definition 1. *A pairing is a bilinear and non-degenerate function:*

$$e : \begin{cases} G_1 \times G_2 \to G_3 \\ (P, Q) \to e(P, Q). \end{cases}$$

The most useful properties in pairing based cryptography are:

Bilinearity: for any integer m, n, $e([n]P, [m]P) = e(P, Q)^{nm}$ for all $P \in G_1$ and $Q \in G_2$.

Non-degeneracy: for each $P \neq \mathcal{O}$ there exists $Q \in G_2$ such that $e(P, Q) \neq 1$.

2.2   Miller's Algorithm

The Miller's algorithm [8] is the central step for the pairing computation. The goal of Miller's algorithm is to construct a rational function $f_{l,P}$ for $l > 0$, let $P \in G_1, Q \in G_2$, the function $f_{l,P}$ is an $\mathbb{F}_{q^k}$-rational function with divisor:

$$div(f_{l,P}) = l(P) - (lP) - (l - 1)(\mathcal{O}).$$

Miller's algorithm [8] is a double-and-add method to compute $f_{l,P}$ in $\log_2(l)$ operations based on the following observation:

$$f_{i+j,P} = f_{i,P} f_{j,P} \frac{l_{[i]P,[j]P}}{v_{[i+j]P}},$$

where $l_{[i]P,[j]P}$ is the equation of the line through $[i]P$ and $[j]P$ (or the tangent line when $[i]P = [j]P$) and $v_{[i+j]P}$ is the equation of the vertical line through $[i + j]P$.

The Miller's algorithm constructs the rational function $f_{l,P}$ associated to the point P, it evaluates $f_{l,P}(Q)$ for a point Q.

Algorithm 1. Miller' algorithm for elliptic curves

Input: $l = (l_n \cdots l_0)$(binary decomposition), $P \in G_1 \subset E(\mathbb{F}_q)$
and $Q \in G_2 \subset E(\mathbb{F}_{q^k})$;
Output: $f_{l,P} \in G_3 \subset E(\mathbb{F}_{q^k}^*)$;
1 : $T \leftarrow P$
2 : $f \leftarrow 1$
for $i = n - 1$ **to** 0 **do**
$\quad$ 3 : $T \leftarrow [2]T$, where $T = (X, Y, Z)$ and $[2]T = (X_2, Y_2, Z_2)$
$\quad$ 4 : $f \leftarrow f^2 \times h_1(Q)$, h_1 is the equation of the tangent at
$\quad\quad$ the point T
$\quad$ **if** $l_i = 1$ **then**
$\quad\quad$ 5 : $T \leftarrow T + P$
$\quad\quad$ 6 : $f \leftarrow f \times h_2(Q)$, h_2 is the equation of the line (PT)
$\quad$ **end**
end
return $f_{l,P}(Q)$

Algorithm 1 is a simplified version of the Miller's algorithm [8], and without loss of generality we can consider this simplified Miller's algorithm.

3   Background on Hessian Curves

In this section, we briefly introduce the Hessian elliptic curves [9] and the group law.

3.1   Definition and Properties

Definition 2. *An Hessian elliptic curve over* $\mathbb{K}$ *is a plane cubic curve given by an equation of the form*

$$E_{/\mathbb{K}} : x^3 + y^3 + 1 = 3axy,$$

or in projective coordinates,

$$E_{/\mathbb{K}} : X^3 + Y^3 + Z^3 = 3aXYZ,$$

where $a \in \mathbb{K}$ *and* $a^3 \neq 1$.

3.2   The Hessian Group Law

The group law of the Hessian elliptic curve has been introduced in [4,9]. The zero of the group law on E is given by $\mathcal{O} = (1, -1, 0)$. If $T = (X_1, Y_1, Z_1)$, we define $-T = (Y_1, X_1, Z_1)$.

The formulae for point doubling are given by $[2]T = (X_2, Y_2, Z_2)$, where

$$\begin{cases} X_2 = Y_1(Z_1^3 - X_1^3) \\ Y_2 = X_1(Y_1^3 - Z_1^3) \\ Z_2 = Z_1(X_1^3 - Y_1^3). \end{cases}$$

We note $T = (X_1, Y_1, Z_1)$ and $P = (X_2, Y_2, Z_2)$. The addition formulae for point addition are given by $T + P = (X_3, Y_3, Z_3)$, where

$$\begin{cases} X_3 = Y_1^2 X_2 Z_2 - Y_2^2 X_1 Z_1 \\ Y_3 = X_1^2 Y_2 Z_2 - X_2^2 Y_1 Z_1 \\ Z_3 = Z_1^2 Y_2 X_2 - Z_2^2 Y_1 X_1. \end{cases}$$

The doubling formulae operation requires 6 field multiplications and 3 squares, and the addition formulae operation requires 12 field multiplications.

4   Fault Attack against the Miller's Algorithm

We start with the description of a fault attack against the Miller's algorithm, this attack is a type of attacks based on hardware error analysis. For this attack an adversary can actively influence the target device and induce faults during the process of computation. This attack needs very precise timing, position and an expensive apparatus to be performed. However, a new realistic technique [7] is provided for the design of the attack model.

4.1   Description of the Fault Attack

In order to facilitate description the fault attack in the context, we assume that the pairing is used in an identity-based cryptography, in which the secret key is denoted by P as the first position of the pairing and the public parameter is denoted by Q. In contrast, if the secret key is Q as the second position, all the nonlinear system are written in Q coordinates, and the same attack can be applied easily. As a result, no matter where the position of the secret point is located, our fault attack could recover it.

This fault injection attack is to modify the number of iterations in the Miller's algorithm. We complete this process by giving a precise description of the attack, by computing the probability of finding suitable number of iterations and by adapting it to the Miller's algorithm. The fault attack scheme is completely presented in [5].

We assume that the pairing based cryptography is implemented on a smart card, and the secret point P is embedded in this card as the first position of the pairing. The aim of the attack is to find P in the computation of $e(P, Q)$. Suppose as many public data of the point Q as we want can be gained, and for each of them, the pairing between the secret point P and the public point Q can be computed. In order to find the secret P, we modify the number of iterations in algorithm 1. The attack steps are listed as follows:

Step 1. Gain the number of iterations (i.e. l) in the Miller's algorithm.
Step 2. Modify the number of iterations by provoking disturbances.
Step 3. Get the number of Miller loop iterations from counting the clock cycles.
Step 4. Find j from the binary decomposition of l.
Step 5. Show a nonlinear system and resolve it.

Here, we give some detailed explanation of above steps. In the first step, we have to find the flip-flops belonging to the counter of the number of iterations on the smart card. The number of iterations can be gained by using reverse engineering procedures. Once we found it, then modify it in the second step. The disturbance can be induced by a laser [1]. Lasers are nowadays thin enough to make this attack realistic [7]. In the third step, we are able to know how many iterations the Miller loop has done, by counting the number of clock cycles during the pairing calculation. Each time, we record the value of the Miller loop and the number of iterations we made. The aim is to find a couple $(d, d+1)$ of two consecutive values during the Miller's algorithm and the probability of finding such a couple is given in Appendix A. In order to modify the value of l, we execute the Miller algorithm several times and provoke disturbances in every execution, until the output of the dth and $(d+1)^{th}$ iterations of algorithm 1 can be found, and denote the two results by $f_{d,P}(Q)$ and $f_{d+1,P}(Q)$. After d iterations, the algorithm 1 will have calculated $[j]P$. It calculates $[2j]P$ during the $(d+1)^{th}$ iterations. Then considering the value of the $(d+1)^{th}$ bit of l, it either stops at this moment, or it calculates $[2j+1]P$. In the fourth step, we know l from the first step and the number d of iterations from the third step. Furthermore, reading the binary decomposition of l gives us j directly. We consider that at the beginning $j = 1$, if $l_{n-1} = 0$ then $j \leftarrow 2j$, else $j \leftarrow 2j + 1$, and go on, until we arrive at the $(n-1-d)^{th}$ bit of l. For example, let $l = 100001001010$ in basis 2, and $d = 5$, at the first iteration we compute $[2]P$, at the second, as $l_{n-1} = 0$ we only make the doubling, so we calculate $[4]P$, it is the same thing for the second, third and fourth step so we have $[32]P$ in T. At the fifth iteration, $l_{n-6} = 1$, then we make the doubling and the addition, so $j = 2 \times 32 + 1$, i.e. $j = 65$.

To conclude the attack, we consider the ratio $\frac{f_{d+1,P}(Q)}{(f_{d,P}(Q))^2}$, then a nonlinear system can be gained, the secret point P will be revealed in the basis of $\mathbb{F}_{q^k}$ by solving this nonlinear system.

4.2   Curve and Equations

In [2,5,6], only the affine coordinates case is treated and gives a result. Here, we extend to the situation of fault against pairing in Hessian coordinates.

The embedding degree. For simplicity and without loss of generality, in this paper we only consider the embedding degree $k = 4$.

As $k = 4$ is even, we denote $B = \{1, \xi, \sqrt{v}, \xi\sqrt{v}\}$ the basis of $\mathbb{F}_{q^4}$, this basis is constructed by a tower extensions. $P = (X_P, Y_P, Z_P) \in E(\mathbb{F}_q)$ and $Q = (X_Q\sqrt{v}, Y_Q, Z_Q) \in E(\mathbb{F}_{q^4})$ are given in Hessian coordinates, with X_Q, Y_Q, Z_Q and $v \in \mathbb{F}_{q^2}$, $\sqrt{v} \in \mathbb{F}_{q^4}$.

Next, the details of the computation of a Miller iteration are investigated. We take a look into the details of the computation. It is known that the doubling step is required for each iteration of the Miller iteration algorithm, as a result, we consider the following cases.

Case 1: When $l_{d+1} = 0$, we have obtained the results $f_{d,P}(Q)$ and $f_{d+1,P}(Q)$ corresponding to d^{th} and $(d+1)^{th}$ iterations of the Miller's algorithm in Section 4.1. We observe what happens during the $(d+1)^{th}$ iteration.

In the Miller's algorithm, we calculate $[2j]P = (X_{2j}, Y_{2j}, Z_{2j})$ at the step 4 and store the result in the variable T. The coordinate of $[2j]P$ are given by the following formula:

$$\begin{cases} X_{2j} = Y_j(Z_j^3 - X_j^3) \\ Y_{2j} = X_j(Y_j^3 - Z_j^3) \\ Z_{2j} = Z_j(X_j^3 - Y_j^3), \end{cases}$$

where we denote $[j]P = (X_j, Y_j, Z_j)$. The doubling step gives:

$$f_{d+1,P}(Q) = (f_{d,P}(Q))^2 \times h_1(Q),$$

where $h_1(Q) = (3aX_jZ_j^2 - 3Y_j^2Z_j)Y_Q\sqrt{v} + (3aX_jZ_j^2 - 3X_j^2Z_j)X_Q + 3X_j^3 + 3Y_j^3 - 6aX_jY_jZ_j$.

The additional step doesn't need done because of $l_{d+1} = 0$. The return result of the Miller's algorithm is $f_{d+1,P}(Q) = (f_{d,P}(Q))^2 \times h_1(Q)$. We dispose of $f_{d,P}(Q)$, $f_{d+1,P}(Q)$ and the point $Q = (X_Q\sqrt{v}, Y_Q, Z_Q)$, with X_Q, Y_Q and $Z_Q \in \mathbb{F}_{q^2}$.

Recall that the coordinates of Q can be freely chosen, we can calculate the value $R \in \mathbb{F}_{q^4}^*$ of the ratio $\frac{f_{d+1,P}(Q)}{(f_{d,P}(Q))^2}$:

$$R = R_3\xi\sqrt{v} + R_2\sqrt{v} + R_1\xi + R_0,$$

where $R_3, R_2, R_1, R_0 \in \mathbb{F}_q$.

Moreover, we know the expression of R depends on the coordinates of $[j]P$ and Q in the basis $B = \{1, \xi, \sqrt{v}, \xi\sqrt{v}\}$:

$$R = (3aX_jZ_j^2 - 3Y_j^2Z_j)Y_Q\sqrt{v} + (3aX_jZ_j^2 - 3X_j^2Z_j)X_Q + 3X_j^3 + 3Y_j^3 - 6aX_jY_jZ_j.$$

As the point $Q = (X_Q\sqrt{v}, Y_Q, Z_Q)$ is known, we know the decomposition of $X_Q, Y_Q \in \mathbb{F}_{q^2}$ in the basis $(1, \xi)$, $X_Q = x_0 + x_1\xi$, $Y_Q = y_0 + y_1\xi$, and the value of x_0, x_1, y_0, y_1. Furthermore X_j, Y_j, and Z_j are in $\mathbb{F}_q$.

Consequently, with the exact value of R in $\mathbb{F}_{q^4}$, the coordinates of point Q and the expression of R depending on the coordinates of P and Q, we obtain the following system of equations in $\mathbb{F}_q$, by identification in the basis of $\mathbb{F}_{q^4}$,

$$\begin{cases} (3aX_jZ_j^2 - 3Y_j^2Z_j)y_1 = R_3 \\ (3aX_jZ_j^2 - 3Y_j^2Z_j)y_0 = R_2 \\ (3aX_jZ_j^2 - 3X_j^2Z_j)x_1 = R_1 \\ (3aX_jZ_j^2 - 3X_j^2Z_j)x_0 + 3X_j^3 + 3Y_j^3 - 6aX_jY_jZ_j = R_0. \end{cases}$$

Thus this nonlinear system can be rewritten as follows (the value of λ_0, λ_1 and λ_2 are known numbers):

$$\begin{cases} aX_jZ_j^2 - Y_j^2Z_j = \lambda_2 \\ aX_jZ_j^2 - X_j^2Z_j = \lambda_1 \\ X_j^3 + Y_j^3 - 2aX_jY_jZ_j = \lambda_0. \end{cases} \tag{1}$$

After some calculations, this nonlinear system can be regarded as polynomials f and g :

$$\begin{cases} f(X_j, Y_j) = -\lambda_2 X_j^4 + (\lambda_1 + \lambda_2)Y_j^2X_j^2 + a(\lambda_2 - \lambda_1)^2X_j - \lambda_1 Y_j^4 \\ g(X_j, Y_j) = X_j^5 - Y_j^2X_j^3 + (Y_j^3 - \lambda_0)X_j^2 - 2a(\lambda_2 - \lambda_1)Y_jX_j - Y_j^5 - \lambda_0 Y_j^2. \end{cases}$$

At this point we have a system of equations whose solutions are precisely the same as the original system. We calculate the resultant of $f(X_j, Y_j)$ and $g(X_j, Y_j)$ with respect to X_j is:

$$AY_j^2 + BY_j^5 + CY_j^8 + DY_j^{11} + EY_j^{14} = 0, \tag{2}$$

and the values of A, B, C, D and E are given in Appendix B.

Apparently equation (2) contains only one variable Y_j. There are at least 14 solutions in $\mathbb{F}_q$ because of the degree is 14. We use the function `factorff` in *PariGP* [10], a software for mathematical computation, to achieve the factorization of the equation in Y_j, and consequently the solutions of this equation. The equations (1) yields X_j and Z_j, so we construct the point $[j]P$. Moreover we know $[j]P = (X_j, Y_j, Z_j)$, to find the possible points P, we have to compute k the inverse of j modulo l, such that $[j][k]P = [jk]P = P$. The points that do not lie on elliptic curve E can be eliminated by using the elliptic curve equation. Then we perform Miller's algorithm with the remaining points and verify the result. Therefore, we recover the secret point P, in the case $l_{d+1} = 0$.

Case 2: When $l_{d+1} = 1$, in this case, the $(d+1)^{th}$ iteration involves *one* addition in the Miller's algorithm. The doubling step is the same as **Case 1**, for the addition step, we have to calculate $[2j+1]P = (X_{2j+1}, Y_{2j+1}, Z_{2j+1})$, where $[j]P = (X_j, Y_j, Z_j)$, $[2j]P = (X_{2j}, Y_{2j}, Z_{2j})$ and $P = (X_P, Y_P, Z_P)$. We see what happens during the $(d+1)^{th}$ iteration in Miller's algorithm.

At the $(d+1)^{th}$ iteration we have to calculate:

$$f_{d+1,P}(Q) = (f_{d,P}(Q))^2 \times h_1(Q) \times h_2(Q),$$

where $h_2(Q) = (X_PZ_j - X_jZ_P)Y_Q\sqrt{\upsilon} - (Y_PZ_j - Y_jZ_P)X_Q - Y_jX_P + X_jY_P.$

We repeat the scheme of the previous case. The ratio is $R = h_1(Q)h_2(Q)$, with the unknown values X_j, Y_j, Z_j and X_P, Y_P, Z_P. Based on the value of R and Q, as well as the expression of R, we can obtain 4 equations in the 6 unknown values. As the elliptic curve equation provides 2 other equations, through P and $[j]P \in E(\mathbb{F}_q)$.

$$\begin{cases} F_1(X_P, Y_P, Z_P, X_j, Y_j, Z_j) = \lambda_1 \\ F_2(X_P, Y_P, Z_P, X_j, Y_j, Z_j) = \lambda_2 \\ F_3(X_P, Y_P, Z_P, X_j, Y_j, Z_j) = \lambda_3 \\ F_4(X_P, Y_P, Z_P, X_j, Y_j, Z_j) = \lambda_4 \\ X_P^3 + Y_P^3 + Z_P^3 - 3aX_PY_PZ_P = 0 \\ X_j^3 + Y_j^3 + Z_j^3 - 3aX_jY_jZ_j = 0, \end{cases} \tag{3}$$

where, $F_{1,2,3,4}()$ is a polynomial and $\lambda_{1,2,3,4} \in \mathbb{F}_q$. Then we get a more difficult system than **Case 1** to solve, but giving us the coordinates of P directly, because of the coordinates of P are solution of the system. We can also use the resultant method to solve this system. Simplify the form of the above system of expression by substituting multivariate for univariate based on the resultant method, then get a univariate nonlinear equation in finite field. So the secret point P can be recovered based on the resultant method.

5 Conclusion

We have presented the Miller's algorithm in Hessian coordinates which is vulnerable to a fault attack when it is used in pairing based cryptography. This attack consists in modifying the internal counter of a smart card, getting the number of Miller loop and finding j from the binary decomposition of l. In order to realize this fault attack, it is precisely described in this paper. We show the probability of obtaining two consecutive iterations, and find out that a small number of tests are needed to find two consecutive results. We consider the secret point P at the first position of the Miller's algorithm. The result of the fault attack is a nonlinear system. Then we give the method to solve this nonlinear system. Our model is also applicable in the secret point Q at the second position of the Miller's algorithm, all the nonlinear system are written in Q coordinates. Thus, wherever the position of the secret is located, our fault attack will recover it. So we can say that the fault attack is a threat against the Miller's algorithm in Hessian coordinates.

References

1. Anderson, R., Kuhn, M.: Tamper Resistance-a Cautionary Note. In: The Second USENIX Workshop on Electronic Commerce Proceedings, Okland, California, pp. 1–11 (1996)
2. Bajard, J.C., El Mrabet, N.: Pairing in cryptography: an arithmetic point de view. In: Advanced Signal Processing Algorithms, Architectures, and Implementations XVI, part of SPIE (August 2007)

3. Boneh, D., Franklin, M.: Identity-Based Encryption from the Weil Pairing. In: Kilian, J. (ed.) CRYPTO 2001. LNCS, vol. 2139, pp. 213–229. Springer, Heidelberg (2001)

4. Chudnovsky, D.V., Chudnovsky, G.V.: Sequences of numbers generated by addition in formal groups and new primality and factorisation tests. Adv. in Appl. Math. 7, 385–434 (1987)

5. Dan, P., Frederik, V.: Fault and Side Channel Attacks on Pairing based Cryptography. IEEE Transactions on Computers 55(9), 1075–1080 (2006)

6. El Mrabet, N.: What about Vulnerability to a Fault Attack of the Miller's Algorithm During an Identity Based Protocol? In: Park, J.H., Chen, H.-H., Atiquzzaman, M., Lee, C., Kim, T.-H., Yeo, S.-S. (eds.) ISA 2009. LNCS, vol. 5576, pp. 122–134. Springer, Heidelberg (2009)

7. Habing, D.H.: The Use of Lasers to Simulate Radiation-Induced Transients in Semiconductor Devices and Circuits. IEEE Transactions on Nuclear Science 39, 1647–1653 (1992)

8. Miller, V.: The Weil pairing and its efficient calculation. Journal of Cryptology 17, 235–261 (2004)

9. Smart, N.P.: The Hessian Form of an Elliptic Curve. In: Koç, Ç.K., Naccache, D., Paar, C. (eds.) CHES 2001. LNCS, vol. 2162, pp. 118–125. Springer, Heidelberg (2001)

10. PARI/GP, version2.1.7, Bordeaux 2005 (2005), http://pari.math.u-bordeaux.fr/

11. Shamir, A.: Identity-Based Cryptosystems and Signature Schemes. In: Blakely, G.R., Chaum, D. (eds.) CRYPTO 1984. LNCS, vol. 196, pp. 47–53. Springer, Heidelberg (1985)

12. Whelan, C., Scott, M.: Side Channel Analysis of Practical Pairing Implementations: Which Path Is More Secure? In: Nguyên, P.Q. (ed.) VIETCRYPT 2006. LNCS, vol. 4341, pp. 99–114. Springer, Heidelberg (2006)

13. Whelan, C., Scott, M.: The Importance of the Final Exponentiation in Pairings When Considering Fault Attacks. In: Takagi, T., Okamoto, T., Okamoto, E., Okamoto, T. (eds.) Pairing 2007. LNCS, vol. 4575, pp. 225–246. Springer, Heidelberg (2007)

A   Appendix

The Probability for the Fault Attack

The important point of this fault attack is that we can obtain two consecutive couples of iterations, after a realistic number of tests. The number of picks with two consecutive number is the complementary of the number of picks with no consecutive numbers. The number $B(n, N)$ of possible picks of n numbers among N integers with no consecutive number is given by the following recurrence formula:

$$\begin{cases} N \leq 0, n > 0, B(n, N) = 0, \\ \forall N, n = 0, B(n, N) = 1, \\ B(n, N) = \sum_{j=1}^{N} \sum_{k=1}^{n} B(n - k, j - 2). \end{cases}$$

With this formula, we can compute the probability to obtain two consecutive numbers after n picks among N integers. This probability $P(n, N)$ is

$$P(n, N) = 1 - \frac{B(n, N)}{C_{n+N}^n}.$$

The probability for obtaining two consecutive numbers is sufficiently large to make the attack possible. In fact, for an $8 - bits$ architecture only 15 tests are needed to obtain a probability larger than one half, $P(15, 2^8) = 0.56$, and only 28 for a probability larger than 0.9.

B   Appendix

$A = a^5\lambda_2^{10}\lambda_0 - 10a^5\lambda_2^9\lambda_1\lambda_0 + 45a^5\lambda_2^8\lambda_1^2\lambda_0 - 3a^4\lambda_2^9\lambda_0^2 + 24a^4\lambda_2^8\lambda_0^2\lambda_1 - 120a^5\lambda_2^7\lambda_1^3\lambda_0 - 84a^4\lambda_2^7\lambda_1^2\lambda_0^2 + 210a^5\lambda_2^6\lambda_1^4\lambda_0 + 168\lambda_2^6a^4\lambda_1^3\lambda_0^2 - 252\lambda_2^5a^5\lambda_1^5\lambda_0 - 18\lambda_2^7\lambda_0^3a^3\lambda_1 + 3\lambda_2^8\lambda_0^3a^3 + 45\lambda_0^6\lambda_2^3a^3\lambda_1^2 - 210\lambda_2^5\lambda_0^2a^4\lambda_1^4 - 18\lambda_2^3a^3\lambda_1^5\lambda_0^3 + 24\lambda_2^2a^4\lambda_1^7\lambda_0^2 + 210\lambda_2^4a^5\lambda_1^6\lambda_0 - 60\lambda_2^5\lambda_0^3a^3\lambda_1^3 + 168\lambda_2^4\lambda_0^2a^4\lambda_1^5 - 120\lambda_2^3a^5\lambda_1^7\lambda_0 - \lambda_2^7a^2\lambda_0^4 + 4\lambda_2^6a^2\lambda_0^4\lambda_1 + 45\lambda_2^4a^3\lambda_0^3\lambda_1^4 - 84\lambda_2^3a^4\lambda_0^2\lambda_1^6 + 45\lambda_2^2a^5\lambda_1^8\lambda_0 - 6\lambda_2^5a^2\lambda_1^2\lambda_0^4 + 4\lambda_2^4\lambda_0^4a^2\lambda_1^3 - \lambda_2^3\lambda_0^4\lambda_1^4a^2 + 3\lambda_2^2\lambda_0^3a^3\lambda_1^6 - 10\lambda_2a^5\lambda_1^9\lambda_0 - 3\lambda_2\lambda_0^4a^4\lambda_1^8 + a^5\lambda_1^{10}\lambda_0$

$B = 28a^4\lambda_2^8\lambda_1\lambda_0 + 52a^4\lambda_2^6\lambda_1^3\lambda_0 + 64a^3\lambda_2^7\lambda_1\lambda_0^2 - 125a^3\lambda_2^6\lambda_1^2\lambda_0^2 - 40a^4\lambda_2^5\lambda_1^4\lambda_0 + 36a^4\lambda_2^4\lambda_1^5\lambda_0 + 120\lambda_2^5a^3\lambda_1^3\lambda_0^2 - 28\lambda_2^3a^4\lambda_1^6\lambda_0 - 32\lambda_2^6a^2\lambda_1\lambda_0^3 + 36\lambda_2^5\lambda_0^2a^2\lambda_1^2 - 55\lambda_2^4\lambda_0^2a^3\lambda_1^4 + 8\lambda_2^3\lambda_0^2a^3\lambda_1^5 + 12\lambda_2^2a^4\lambda_1^7\lambda_0 - 16\lambda_2^4\lambda_2^3a^2\lambda_1^3 + \lambda_2^2\lambda_0^2a^3\lambda_1^6 - 2\lambda_2a^4\lambda_1^8\lambda_0 + 2\lambda_2^3\lambda_0^3\lambda_1^4a^2 - 52a^4\lambda_2^7\lambda_1^2\lambda_0 + a^5\lambda_2^{10} - a^5\lambda_2^{10} + 48\lambda_2^3a^5\lambda_1^7 - 27\lambda_2^2a^5\lambda_1^8 - 8a^5\lambda_2^9\lambda_1 + 27a^5\lambda_2^8\lambda_1^2 - 48a^5\lambda_2^7\lambda_1^3 + 42a^5\lambda_2^6\lambda_1^4 - 42a^5\lambda_2^4\lambda_1^6 + 8a^5\lambda_2\lambda_1^9 - 6a^4\lambda_2^9\lambda_0 - 13a^3\lambda_2^8\lambda_0^2 + 10a^2\lambda_2^7\lambda_0^3$

$C = 41a^3\lambda_2^7\lambda_1\lambda_0 - 18a^3\lambda_2^6\lambda_1^2\lambda_0 - 45\lambda_2^5a^3\lambda_1^3\lambda_0 - 4\lambda_2^6a^2\lambda_1\lambda_0^2 + 2\lambda_2^5a^2\lambda_1^2\lambda_0^2 + 70\lambda_2^4a^3\lambda_1^4\lambda_0 - 65\lambda_2^3a^3\lambda_1^5\lambda_0 - 3\lambda_2^4\lambda_1^3a^2\lambda_0^2 + 54\lambda_2^3\lambda_1^6a^3\lambda_0 + 16\lambda_2^5\lambda_1a\lambda_0^3 - 37\lambda_2^3\lambda_1^4a^2\lambda_0^2 - 27\lambda_2\lambda_1^7a^3\lambda_0 - 32\lambda_2^4\lambda_1^2a\lambda_0^3 + 54\lambda_2^3\lambda_1^5\lambda_0^2a^2 - 20\lambda_2\lambda_1^6\lambda_0^2a^2 + 12\lambda_1^4\lambda a\lambda_2^3\lambda_0^3 - 4\lambda_2^5\lambda_0^4 - 3\lambda_2^9a^4 - 8\lambda_2^4\lambda_1\lambda_0^4 + 5\lambda_2a^4\lambda_1^8 - 4\lambda_2^3\lambda_0^4\lambda_1^2 + 4a^4\lambda_2^8\lambda_1 + 4a^4\lambda_2^6\lambda_1^3 + 12a^4\lambda_2^4\lambda_1^5 + 4a^4\lambda_2^7\lambda_1^2 - 26a^4\lambda_2^5\lambda_1^4 + 20\lambda_2^3a^4\lambda_1^6 - 20a^4\lambda_2^2\lambda_1^7 - 15a^3\lambda_2^8\lambda_0 + 7a^2\lambda_2^7\lambda_0^2 + 4a\lambda_2^6\lambda_0^3 + 5a^3\lambda_1^8\lambda_0 + a^2\lambda_0^2\lambda_1^7$

$D = 12\lambda_2^3\lambda_0^2a\lambda_1^3 - 28\lambda_2^4\lambda_0^2a\lambda_1^2 + 4\lambda_2^5\lambda_0^2a\lambda_1 - 6a^3\lambda_2^6\lambda_1^2 - a^3\lambda_2^7\lambda_1 - 4a^2\lambda_2^7\lambda_0 + 8\lambda_2^3\lambda_0^3\lambda_1^2 + 16\lambda_2^2a^2\lambda_1^5\lambda_0 - 12\lambda_2^3a^2\lambda_1^4\lambda_0 + 13\lambda_2^3a^3\lambda_1^3 + 4\lambda_2^2\lambda_0^4a\lambda_1^4 - 3\lambda_1^8a^3 + a^3\lambda_2^8 - 8\lambda_2^5\lambda_0^3 - 10\lambda_2^4a^3\lambda_1^4 - 4\lambda_2\lambda_1^6\lambda_0a^2 + 11\lambda_2\lambda_1^7a^3 - 14\lambda_2^2\lambda_1^6a^3 + 8\lambda_2^6\lambda_0^2a + 20a^2\lambda_2^5\lambda_1^2\lambda_0 - 16a^2\lambda_2^4\lambda_1^3\lambda_0 + 9\lambda_2^3a^3\lambda_1^5$

$E = -12\lambda_2\lambda_1^5a\lambda_0 + 12\lambda_2^2\lambda_1^4a\lambda_0 - 8\lambda_2^3a\lambda_1^3\lambda_0 + 12\lambda_2^4a\lambda_1^2\lambda_0 - 12\lambda_2^5\lambda_1a\lambda_0 + 4\lambda_2^6a\lambda_0 - 8\lambda_2\lambda_1^4\lambda_0^2 + 4\lambda_2^2\lambda_1^3\lambda_0^2 - 4\lambda_2^3\lambda_1^2\lambda_0^2 + 8\lambda_2^4\lambda_1\lambda_0^2 - 4\lambda_2^5\lambda_0^2 + 4\lambda_1^6a\lambda_0 + 4\lambda_1^5\lambda_0^2$

Benchmarking for Steganography
by Kernel Fisher Discriminant Criterion

Wei Huang[1,2], Xianfeng Zhao[2], Dengguo Feng[1], and Rennong Sheng[3]

[1] Institute of Software, Chinese Academy of Sciences, Beijing 100190, China
{weihuang,feng}@is.iscas.ac.cn
[2] State Key Laboratory of Information Security, Institute of Information Engineering,
Chinese Academy of Sciences, Beijing 100029, China
xfzhao@is.iscas.ac.cn
[3] Beijing Institute of Electronic Technology and Application, Beijing 100091, China
rennongsheng@vip.sina.com

Abstract. In recent years, there have been many steganographic schemes designed by different technologies to enhance their security. And a benchmarking scheme is needed to measure which one is more detectable. In this paper, we propose a novel approach of benchmarking for steganography via Kernel Fisher Discriminant Criterion (KFDC), independent of the techniques in steganalysis. In KFDC, besides between-class variance resembles what Maximum Mean Discrepancy (MMD) merely concentrated on, within-class variance plays another important role. Experiments show that KFDC is qualified for the indication of the detectability of steganographic algorithms. Then, we use KFDC to illustrate detailed analysis on the security of JPEG and spatial steganographic algorithms.

Keywords: Steganography, benchmarking, kernel Fisher discriminant, between-class variance, within-class variance.

1 Introduction

Steganography [1] is an art and science of hiding information so that its presence cannot be detected, while steganalysis refers to the analysis of intercepted signals to determine whether they contain hidden messages. Steganalytic schemes are special or universal. Universal steganalysis is usually based on universal feature designing. By these features which can be viewed as a low-dimensional model of covers [2], it's much easier to use machine learning engines (MLE) to detect hidden messages.

It's confusing that which steganographic algorithm is more secure since many of them are claimed with "provably" [3], "perfectly secure" [4], "highly undetectable" [5] or "minimal distortion" [6]. Therefore, several researchers have worked on the criteria to compare their undetectability (or security), theoretically or practically. A number of studies and experiments have been published on telling which steganography algorithm is more undetectable. They are mainly in five categories and each has its own advantages and disadvantages.

C.-K. Wu, M. Yung, and D. Lin (Eds.): Inscrypt 2011, LNCS 7537, pp. 113–130, 2012.

1. Information-theoretic based approaches, such as Kullback-Leibler (KL) divergence [1]. Although KL divergence provides fundamental information about the limits of any steganalysis method, it's difficult to estimate accurately from sparse data in high-dimensional spaces [2].

2. Two-sample problem based approaches, such as Maximum Mean Discrepancy (MMD) [2]. MMD needs an acceptable size of samples and lower complexity $O(D^2)$ where D is the sample size, and it's well established theoretically. However, MMD only measures the distance between the centers of two classes. As we know, aggregation of samples in the same class also plays an important part in indicating separability. If two centers of classes are well surrounded by their own samples, they will have better separability.

3. Detecting results from a specific blind detector [7,8]. Up to now, most of blind detectors require a feature set and an MLE. But detecting results are affected by many factors, such as the diversity of the training and testing sets (if the samples are distinct, or if testing samples are similar to training ones), the parameter optimization of MLEs (which MLE is better and which is the best configuration) and the rules of comparison (true rate, Receiver Operating Characteristic curves, and minimum false rate [9]).

4. Embedding efficiency analysis. Many steganographic algorithms have improvements by advanced encoding skills. For instance, F5 [10] utilizes matrix encoding to reduce the payload per coefficient, while Modified Matrix Encoding (MME) [6] enables to modify more than one position to achieve smaller distortion. It's clear that MME is more secure than F5. Considering another approach called Perturbed Quantization (PQ) [7], it only allows distortion on the coefficients whose fractions are close to 0.5. Many efforts help enhance the security, but it's too hard to say which mechanism is more effective, merely their mechanisms given.

5. Multimedia quality based criteria. Audio quality such as basic profile transparency and basic profile robustness [11] can be used to test how the modification distorts the covers and affects human senses. However, qualities of multimedia are different from the statistical characteristics and well-designed features [12,13,14] can detect tiny distortions for human senses.

The contribution of this paper is mainly on proposing a novel benchmarking for steganography considering not only the distance between two classes but also the variance of samples in each class. We aim at providing a fair criterion that eliminates uncertainties in steganalysis techniques as much as possible. Kernel Fisher Discriminant Criterion (KFDC) [15], which is the maximum ratio of variances of between-classes and within-classes in any projection in Reproducing Kernel Hilbert Spaces (RKHS), is a measurement of separability between two classes of samples. Hence, we use KFDC as a criterion to indicate the detectability of steganography.

The rest of this paper is organized as follows: In Section 2, we introduce some existing benchmarking schemes and state the existing problem. Both framework and implementation of our method are described in Section 3. We demonstrate

KFDC benchmarking for public steganographic schemes and compare their security in Section 4. Finally, the paper is concluded in Section 5.

2 Related Work

This section describes the model of steganography and introduces three main benchmarking criteria. Then, the existing problem is stated with a list of conditions for benchmarking criteria.

2.1 Model of Steganography

It's proposed by Cachin [1] that steganography can be viewed as information-theoretic model with passive adversaries. Steganography can be modelled as follows [2]. Let C be the set of all covers c described by a random variable c on C with probability distribution function (pdf) P. A steganographic algorithm S is a mapping $C \times M \times K \to C$. S assigns a new object called stego $s \in C$ with pdf Q to each triple (c, M, K), where $M \in M$ is a secret message selected from the set of communicable messages M and $K \in K$ is the secret key.

2.2 KL Divergence

For the two possible probability distributions, denoted by P and Q, the adversary must decide between cover-text c and stego-text s. The *relative entropy* or *discrimination* between them is defined as

$$D_{\mathrm{KL}}(P\|Q) = \sum_{c \in C} P(c) \log \frac{P(c)}{Q(c)}.$$

For a set of D database images, cover images $X = \{x_1, x_2, \ldots, x_D\}$ and stego images $Y(\alpha) = \{y_1, y_2, \ldots, y_D\}$ explicitly on the relative message length α are generated. It's denoted that $x_i = \psi(c_i)$ and $y_i = \psi(s_i)$ are d-dimensional vectors where $\mathbf{X}$ and $\mathbf{Y}$ are D dependent realizations of the random variables $\psi(c)$ and $\psi(s)$. Then KL divergence can be estimated as

$$D_{\mathrm{KL}}(\psi(c)\|\psi(s)) = \int_{\mathbb{R}^d} p(x) \log \frac{p(x)}{q(x)},$$

where $x, y \in \mathbb{R}^d$.

Although the k-Nearest Neighbour (kNN) estimator can provide accurate results in high dimensional spaces, cross-entropy is more difficult to estimate [2]. After testing on artificial data generated by Gaussian distributions $p = N(-\frac{1}{\sqrt{d}} \cdot \mathbf{1}, \mathbf{I})$ and $q = N(-\frac{1}{\sqrt{d}} \cdot \mathbf{1}, \mathbf{I})$ with $\mathbf{1}$ being the vector of d ones, it is concluded that in many distributions, $D_{\mathrm{KL}}(p\|q)$ is too hard to simply apply existing estimators to data sets because a sample size D much more than 10^5 is required even $d \leq 10$.

2.3 Maximum Mean Discrepancy

Pevný et al. [2] utilized Maximum Mean Discrepancy (MMD) to estimate sparse data in high-dimensional spaces. Assuming the samples $\mathbf{X}$ and $\mathbf{Y}$ are generated from distributions p and q, we need to determine two hypotheses

$$H_0 : p = q$$
$$H_1 : p \neq q.$$

Let $\mathcal{F}$ be a class of functions $f : \mathcal{X} \to \mathbb{R}$. MMD is defined as

$$\text{MMD}[\mathcal{F}, p, q] = \sup_{f \in \mathcal{F}} \left(\mathbf{E}_{x \sim p} f(x) - \mathbf{E}_{y \sim q} f(y) \right).$$

In finite sample setting, we have

$$\text{MMD}[\mathcal{F}, \mathbf{X}, \mathbf{Y}] = \sup_{f \in \mathcal{F}} \left(\frac{1}{D} \sum_{i=1}^{D} f(x) - \frac{1}{D} \sum_{i=1}^{D} f(y) \right).$$

In the Reproducing Kernel Hilbert Spaces (RKHS) $\mathcal{H}$, the supremum is reached for $f = (\mu_p - \mu_q)/\|\mu_p - \mu_q\|_{\mathcal{H}}$. An unbiased estimate based on U-statistics of MMD in an RKHS generated by the Gaussian kernel $k : \mathbb{R} \times \mathbb{R} \to \mathbb{R}$

$$k(x, y) = \exp\left(-\gamma(x - y)^2 \right) \tag{1}$$

is provided as

$$\text{MMD}_u[\mathcal{F}, \mathbf{X}, \mathbf{Y}] = \left[\frac{1}{D(D-1)} \sum_{i \neq j} k(x_i, x_j) + k(y_i, y_j) - k(x_i, y_j) - k(y_i, x_j) \right]^{\frac{1}{2}}$$

when the joint pdfs p and q is factorizable $p(x_1, \ldots, x_n) = p(x_1) \cdot \ldots \cdot p(x_d)$ and $q(y_1, \ldots, y_n) = q(x_1) \cdot \ldots \cdot q(x_d)$. MMD can be shown that

$$\text{MMD}^2[\mathcal{F}, p, q] = \left(\sum_{n=0}^{\infty} b_{p,n}^2 \right)^d - 2 \left(\sum_{n=0}^{\infty} b_{p,n} b_{q,n} \right)^d + \left(\sum_{n=0}^{\infty} b_{q,n}^2 \right)^d,$$

where coefficients

$$b_{p,n} = \int_{\mathbb{R}} p(x) \cdot \sqrt{\frac{(2\gamma)^n}{n!}} x^n \exp(-\gamma x^2) dx,$$

with $\gamma = \eta^{-2}$ and η is the median of L_2 divergences between samples.

In MMD, only discrepancy between the centers of two classes is considered. When we compare different algorithms using different features, the extents how samples gather around their center are not the same. From the view of pattern recognition, samples with smaller variance are easier to separate.

2.4   Detecting Results by Steganalysis

Many steganalytic algorithms [12,13,14] use Support Vector Machine (SVM) to achieve better accuracy. For SVM, the labels of testing data are decided by the knowledge learned from provided training data. When the detecting result is used as a criterion, it's argued that the selection of testing data affects the reported accuracy significantly [2]. MLEs (SVM [17], neural network [18], etc.) are configured by many parameters, such as the cost function, weights, iterations, etc. All these steganalytic techniques will influence the accuracy. Since detection result criterion relies on many factors, it is not a good choice.

2.5   Existing Problem

Although detection result provides a direct implementation to score the security of steganography, it's affected by too many factors that can be arbitrarily chosen. For this reason, a measure that is independent of steganalytic techniques is more reliable in benchmarking. MMD is easier to estimate than KL divergence. However, it merely reports the discrepancy between two classes.

The within-class variance of samples plays another important role in pattern recognition. Steganalytic features are different in the completeness [19] and aggregation ability. A feature of high aggregation ability has small variance that its sample points are aggregated around its center. In Figs. 1 and 2, the mean of the sample points in two classes are the same. Compared with Fig. 1, the samples in Fig. 2 are gathered around their center more closely and two classes are more separative. If the features from cover and stego signals are more separative, the steganographic system is less secure.

Thus, we suggest that a fair benchmarking criterion satisfy the following conditions.

- It has a solid theoretic base that we can rely on.
- It generates a score to indicate the security or insecurity so that it can be easily compared and sorted in steganographic schemes.
- It is consistent with the best accuracy of current steganalytic schemes when many test images of high diversity are engaged.
- It may be independent to the selection of test images, and eliminate what an operator can arbitrarily control as much as possible.

3   Benchmarking by Kernel Fisher Discriminant Criterion

Since MMD merely concerns the distance between two classes, we propose a benchmarking schemes based on kernel Fisher's discriminant criterion (KFDC) as the maximum ratio of between-class and within-class variances in the form of *Rayleigh coefficient* [20]. In this section, we firstly describe the definition of between-class and within-class variances. Secondly, we expand them to Reproducing Kernel Hilbert Spaces (RKHS) and provide a benchmarking framework via KFDC. A practical implementation is illustrated at the end of this section.

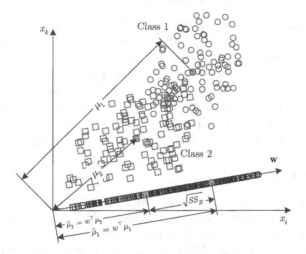

Fig. 1. Between-class scatters in two-dimensional samples. The given samples are placed on two dimensions x_i and x_k. Samples of Class 1 ($\mathcal{X}_1$) are in hollow circles, while those of Class 2 ($\mathcal{X}_2$) are in hollow squares. Their centers are the solid ones. Circles and squares on the projection axis $\mathbf{w}$ are the projections of the ones outside them.

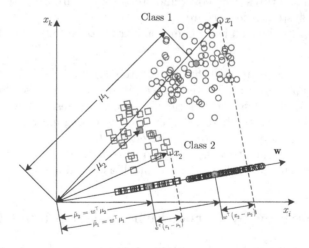

Fig. 2. Within-class scatters in two-dimensional samples. The given samples are placed on two dimensions x_i and x_k. Samples of Class 1 ($\mathcal{X}_1$) are in hollow circles, while those of Class 2 ($\mathcal{X}_2$) are in hollow squares. There are two instances $x_1 \in \mathcal{X}_1, x_2 \in \mathcal{X}_2$. Their centers are the solid ones. Circles and squares on the projection axis $\mathbf{w}$ are the projections of the ones outside them.

3.1   Between-Class and within-Class Variances

Let $\mathcal{X}_1 = \{x_1^{(1)}, x_2^{(1)}, \dots, x_{D_1}^{(1)}\}$ and $\mathcal{X}_2 = \{x_1^{(2)}, x_2^{(2)}, \dots, x_{D_2}^{(2)}\}$ be samples from two different classes, and $\mathcal{X} = \mathcal{X}_1 \bigcup \mathcal{X}_2 = \{x_1, x_2, \dots, x_D\}$. Then the mean vectors of the two classes are

$$\mu_i = \frac{1}{D_i} \sum_{x \in \mathcal{X}_i} x, i = 1, 2.$$

To a vector $\mathbf{w}$, they can be projected as

$$\widetilde{\mu}_i = \mathbf{w}^\top \mu_i = \frac{1}{D_i} \sum_{x \in \mathcal{X}_i} \mathbf{w}^\top x, i = 1, 2.$$

Then, between-class variance SS_B, which is the sum of squares of between-class scatter, is defined as

$$SS_B = (\widetilde{\mu}_1 - \widetilde{\mu}_2)^2 = \mathbf{w}^\top (\mu_1 - \mu_2)(\mu_1 - \mu_2)^\top \mathbf{w} = \mathbf{w}^\top S_B \mathbf{w}. \tag{2}$$

In this equation, we call

$$S_B = (\mu_1 - \mu_2)(\mu_1 - \mu_2)^\top \tag{3}$$

the between-class scatter matrix. Fig. 1 shows the between-class variances in a two-dimensional case. We can find between-class variance plays an important role in indicating the divergence between Class 1 and Class 2. For two classes, the larger SS_B gets, the more separable they are.

Correspondingly, within-class variance SS_W which is the sum of squares of within-class scatter, can be defined as

$$SS_W = \sum_{i=1,2} \sum_{x \in \mathcal{X}_i} [\mathbf{w}^\top (x - \mu_i)]^2$$

$$= \sum_{i=1,2} \mathbf{w}^\top \left[\sum_{x \in \mathcal{X}_i} (x - \mu_i)(x - \mu_i)^\top \right] \mathbf{w} = \mathbf{w}^\top S_W \mathbf{w}. \tag{4}$$

In the equation,

$$S_W = \sum_{i=1,2} \sum_{x \in \mathcal{X}_i} (x - \mu_i)(x - \mu_i)^\top \tag{5}$$

is called the within-class scatter matrix. Fig. 2 shows what the within-class variances are in a two-dimensional case. Within-class variance indicates the cohesiveness of two classes. The smaller SS_W is, the clearer the bound gets, and the better separability they gain.

In the linear case, we can write the Fisher's discriminant [16] in the so-called Rayleigh coefficient form with respect to $\mathbf{w}$,

$$J(\mathbf{w}) = \frac{\mathbf{w}^\top S_B \mathbf{w}}{\mathbf{w}^\top S_W \mathbf{w}}. \tag{6}$$

depending on the between-variances and within-class variances. Fisher Liner Discriminant (FLD) is computed to obtain the maximum $J(\mathbf{w})$ and the best projection $\mathbf{w}$.

3.2   KFDC – FLD in Reproducing Kernel Hilbert Spaces

For real-world data, a linear discriminant is not powerful enough. Therefore, we try to use non-linear model to increase the expressiveness. Kernel idea [20] is originally applied in SVMs and other kernel based algorithms, and RKHS is used yielding a highly flexible algorithm which turns out to be competitive with SVMs [15,21]. Now we introduce kernel based LDA (KDA) [15] to achieve a better result.

Let Φ be a non-linear mapping to $\mathcal{F}$. To find the linear discriminant in $\mathcal{F}$ we need to maximize

$$J(\mathbf{w}) = \frac{\mathbf{w}^\top S_B^\Phi \mathbf{w}}{\mathbf{w}^\top S_W^\Phi \mathbf{w}}. \tag{7}$$

where (3) and (5) are replaced by

$$S_B^\Phi = (\mu_1^\Phi - \mu_2^\Phi)(\mu_1^\Phi - \mu_2^\Phi)^\top, \tag{8}$$

$$S_W^\Phi = \sum_{i=1,2} \sum_{x \in \mathcal{X}_i} (\Phi(x) - \mu_i^\Phi)(\Phi(x) - \mu_i^\Phi)^\top, \tag{9}$$

with $\mu_i^\Phi = \frac{1}{D_i} \sum_{j=1}^{D_i} \Phi(x_j^{(i)})$. If $\mathcal{F}$ is very high-dimensional or even infinitely dimensional, it will be impossible to solve directly. To overcome this limitation, we seek a formulation of the algorithm using only dot-products $\langle \Phi(x) \cdot \Phi(y) \rangle$ of the training patterns instead of mapping the data explicitly.

In kernel FLD, a symmetric and positive finite matrix function called *kernel* $k : \mathcal{X} \times \mathcal{X} \mapsto \mathbb{R}$ is defined. Let $\mathcal{F}$ be a RKHS. To find FLD in RKHS $\mathcal{F}$, we first need a formulation of (7) in terms of only dot-products of input patterns. Then, we replace the dot-product by a certain kernel function. For the theory of reproducing kernels, we know that any solution $\mathbf{w} \in \mathcal{F}$ must lie in the span of all training samples in $\mathcal{F}$. Therefore, we find an expansion for $\mathbf{w}$ of the form

$$\mathbf{w} = \sum_{i=1}^{D} \alpha_i \Phi(x_i). \tag{10}$$

Using the expansion (10) and the definition of μ_i^Φ, we have

$$\mathbf{w}^\top \mu_i^\Phi = \frac{1}{D_i} \sum_{j=1}^{D} \sum_{k=1}^{D_i} \alpha_j k(x_j, x_k^i) = \boldsymbol{\alpha}^\top \mathbf{M}_i. \tag{11}$$

where $(\mathbf{M}_i)_j = \frac{1}{D_i} \sum_{k=1}^{D_i} \alpha_j k(x_j, x_k^{(j)})$ and the dot product is replaced by the kernel function. Then, (2) can be rewritten as

$$SS_B^\Phi = \mathbf{w}^\top S_B^\Phi \mathbf{w} = \boldsymbol{\alpha}^\top \mathbf{M} \boldsymbol{\alpha} \tag{12}$$

where $\mathbf{M} = (\mathbf{M}_1 - \mathbf{M}_2)(\mathbf{M}_1 - \mathbf{M}_2)^\top$. Similarly, we have

$$SS_W^\Phi = \mathbf{w}^\top S_W^\Phi \mathbf{w} = \boldsymbol{\alpha}^\top \mathbf{N} \boldsymbol{\alpha} \tag{13}$$

where $\mathbf{N} = \sum_{j=1,2} \mathbf{K}_j(\mathbf{I} - \mathbf{1}_{D_j})\mathbf{K}_j^\top$, $\mathbf{K}_j$ is a $l \times D_j$ matrix with $(K_j)_{n,m} = k(x_n, x_m^{(j)})$, $\mathbf{I}$ is the identity matrix and $\mathbf{1}_{D_j}$ is the matrix with all entries $1/D_j$.

Combining (12) and (13), we can find FLD in $\mathcal{F}$ called Kernel Fisher Discriminant (KFD) by maximizing

$$J(\boldsymbol{\alpha}) = \frac{\boldsymbol{\alpha}^\top \mathbf{M} \boldsymbol{\alpha}}{\boldsymbol{\alpha}^\top \mathbf{N} \boldsymbol{\alpha}}. \tag{14}$$

In finite sample setting, we now define KFDC as the maximum ratio of variances of between-classes and within-classes in any projection, as the maximum of $J(\boldsymbol{\alpha})$ in the RHKS $\mathcal{F}$.

This problem can be solved by finding the leading eigenvalue of $\mathbf{N}^{-1}\mathbf{M}$, and $\boldsymbol{\alpha}$ is the corresponding eigenvector. Then, we have

$$\text{KFDC}[\mathcal{F}, \mathbf{X}, \mathbf{Y}] = v(\mathbf{N}^{-1}\mathbf{M}), \tag{15}$$

where $v(\mathbf{A})$ is the leading eigenvalue of the matrix $\mathbf{A}$.

But a numerical problem of finding $\mathbf{N}^{-1}$ may occur when the matrix $\mathbf{N}$ is not positive. To solve this problem, a multiple of the identity matrix is simply added to $\mathbf{N}$, i.e. use $\mathbf{N}' = \mathbf{N} + u\mathbf{I}$ with $u \in (0,1]$ instead. This can be also viewed as a regularization on $\|\boldsymbol{\alpha}\|^2$ and decreasing the bias in sample based estimation of eigenvalues [15].

3.3   Practical Implementation

Since the steganographic algorithm itself cannot be directly measured, we take steganography for images as an instance and suggest a practical implementation as follows:

1. A large image database of high diversity is required. Moreover, random messages and random keys are taken in embedding to obtain a stable result.
2. A feature extraction ψ is needed as a low-dimensional modelling because images are in high dimension and they're difficult to estimate. For JPEG steganography we suggest CCMerge [12] feature, while SPAM [13] feature is for spatial steganography.
3. KFDC is calculated on the features from the given cover images and stego images via (15) with $u = 0.1$. Features from cover images are used as $\mathcal{X}_1$ while those from stego images are used as $\mathcal{X}_2$. We take Gaussian Radial Basis Function (RBF) as a specific example, the kernel function is (1) where $\gamma = \eta^{-2}$ with η being the median of L_2 divergences between samples.

We can safely conclude that KFDC values merely depend on the specified steganographic scheme. Compared with the benchmarking by detecting result whose accuracy is highly depends on the selected test images, KFDC is affected by the image database less.

4 Experiments

At the beginning of this section, our experimental setup is described. We observe the relationship between KFDC and SVM test, and explore whether KFDC or MMD is a better fit. Finally, we score 15 popular steganographic algorithms by KFDC and discuss their security.

4.1 Setup of the Experiments

We randomly selected 4000 images from BOSS v0.92 database[1]. Different hidden messages generated by a pseudo-random number generator (PRNG) were embedded in different images. The first 1000 pairs of images (cover images and corresponding stego images) were selected to calculate both MMD in (2) and KFDC in (15). We used the same images for training in SVM, and the other 3000 ones were for testing. CCMerge[12] and SPAM[13] features were utilized as dimension reduction, respectively for JPEG and bitmap files.

There are 15 steganographic schemes engaged in our tests. They are divided into two groups by their embedding domains. Nine of them are in quantized Discrete Cosine Transform (DCT) domain to generate JPEG files. They are:

1. F5 [10], Modified Matrix Encoding (MMEs, including MME and MME3) [6], JSteg[2], JP Hide&Seek (JPHS)[3], Model Based Steganography (MB)[22]. Stego images were generated with the quality factor 90. Images with the same quality factor from bitmaps were created by corresponding JPEG encoders as covers.
2. PQ and its two modifications (PQe and PQt) [7]. Stego images were created with the single-compressed quality factor 85 and the double-compressed one with 70. Double-compressed images with the same quality factors were created as covers.
3. OutGuess[4] with fixed quality factor 75. Images with the same quality factor from bitmaps were created by corresponding JPEG encoders as covers.

The other 6 ones are in spatial domain generating bitmap files (stored in the ".png" format). They are:

1. HUGO [5] (with model correction S2), and StegHide [23].
2. LSBM (Least Significant Bit Matching, or LSB Matching) [24], LSBR (LSB Replacement), DC-DM-QIM (Distortion-Compensated Quantization Index Modulation with Dither Modulation) [25], and SSIS (Spread Spectrum Image Steganalysis) [26] with key-controlled embedding position. In DC-DM-QIM, the Costa parameter was $\alpha = 0.85$ and the step size was 5. In SSIS, a multiplicative noise was generated by hidden messages.

---

[1] ftp://mas22.felk.cvut.cz/PGMs/bossbase_v0.92.tar.gz
[2] http://zooid.org/~paul/crypto/jsteg/
[3] http://linux01.gwdg.de/~alatham/stego.html
[4] http://www.outguess.org/outguess-0.2.tar.gz

The best result of the existed steganalytic methods can be a reliable reference to benchmarking criteria. To approach the best result, LibSVM [17] with Gaussian kernel and C-Supporting Vector Classification was taken as the classifier and a five-fold cross validation on the training set was used to search best parameters in a fixed grid of values. The results from SVM test were reported in the false rate (the probability of error) $P_{FR} = \frac{1}{2}(P_{FP} + P_{FN})$.

4.2   Comparison of MMD, KFDC and Detecting Result

In this experiment, we compare MMD and KFDC values to false rates (FR) in order to observe which is more stable to reflect the detecting results. Considering the most efficient features recently proposed, CCMerge [12] and POMM [14] features were extracted from JPEG images and SPAM [13] was extracted from bitmap images respectively.

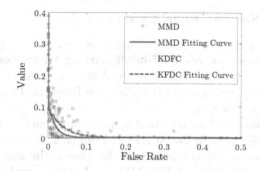

Fig. 3. Comparison of stability of MMD and KFDC to FR of detecting results. CCMerge and POMM were used in testing JPEG steganography and SPAM were used in spatial steganography. Fitting curves are in the two-term exponential formula for their better fits.

Regression method was used to explore the relationship between the criterion value (MMD or KFDC) and FR. We found that a two-term exponential formula $y = a \cdot \exp(b \cdot x) + c \cdot \exp(d \cdot x)$ and a rational formula $y = (a \cdot x + b)/(x^2 + c \cdot x + d)$ were good fits, where x is the criterion value and y is the FR. Sample points and their two-term exponential fitting curves are summarized in Fig. 3. Similar results are shown in KFDC and detecting result, even though they estimate steganographic security in different ways. The smaller KFDC value is, the stronger the steganographic algorithm gets and vice versa.

Tab. 1 lists their best coefficients and corresponding SSE (Sum of Squares due to Error), RMSE (Root Mean Squared Error), R^2 (square of the correlation between the response values and the predicted response values, R-square) and Adjusted R^2 (degree of freedom adjusted R^2) values. In both types, KFDC turns out to be a better fit, because its SSE and RMSE are smaller, in addition, the R^2 and adjusted R^2 values are closer to 1. As a result, KFDC indicates the detectability better than MMD for its better fit.

Table 1. Comparison of best coefficients and goodness of fit for MMD and KFDC. A two-term exponential formula $y = a \cdot \exp(b \cdot x) + c \cdot \exp(d \cdot x)$ and a rational formula $y = (a \cdot x + b)/(x^2 + c \cdot x + d)$ is used respectively.

	MMD	KFDC	MMD	KFDC
Type	Exponential	Exponential	Rational	Rational
a	0.3323	0.3426	3.025×10^{-3}	1.167×10^{-3}
b	-1616	-1458	8.749×10^{-6}	4.786×10^{-6}
c	0.0985	0.1196	4.780×10^{-2}	1.800×10^{-2}
d	-24.75	-56.74	1.965×10^{-5}	1.013×10^{-5}
SSE	0.3121	**0.1300**	0.2725	0.1378
RMSE	0.0481	**0.0310**	0.0449	0.0320
R^2	0.8778	**0.9491**	0.8933	0.9460
Adj. R^2	0.8751	**0.9480**	0.8909	0.9448

4.3   Evaluating Steganography by KFDC

To evaluate specific steganographic algorithms, we utilized the proposed scheme in Sec. 3.3 and plotted the result of benchmarking for steganography in Fig. 4. MMD, KFDC (with their corresponding between-class variances SS_B and within-class variances SS_W) and FR values are listed in Tabs. 2 and 3 using CCMerge and SPAM features.

We obtained a ranking of security of steganographic schemes via KFDC (Figs. 4(c) and 4(d)). HUGO gets the lowest KFDC value, less than 10^{-5}, and it's more secure than any other specified schemes, while JSteg is the weakest one since its KFDC is more than 0.25. PQe, MMEs (MME and MME3) with a low embedding rate (less than 0.20 bpac) are a little more detectable than HUGO, because their KFDC values are in 0.0001–0.005. KFDC values of LSBM, LSBR, StegHide and PQ are in 0.001–0.01 even weaker. F5 with more than 0.10 bpac, JPHS with more than 0.15 bpac, QIM, SSIS, MB and OutGuess are a little better than JSteg and most of their KFDC values exceed 0.02.

Here, we state some detailed analysis on the efficiency of the tested steganographic algorithms via KFDC values (Tabs. 2 and 3). PQe maintains low KFDC values even in high payload for its meticulous selection of embedding in the regions of high energy. By such mechanism, CCMerge feature, especially Markov feature in it, is well preserved because embedding in the regions of low energy may alter small quantized DCT coefficients and arise detectable distortion of the Markov process. The KFDC values of PQs change a little when the embedding rate goes high, because embedding distortion is hidden in the noise of its double-compression. In contrast, the KFDC values of matrix encoding based algorithms, such as F5 and MMEs, raise rapidly as the payload goes high. The main reason is that, for matrix encoding algorithms large embedding block is not enough to support highly efficient matrix encodings and they degenerate into LSB replacement. Overall, F5 and MMEs have low between-class variances for they change less coefficients. The KFDC values of MMEs are smaller as they

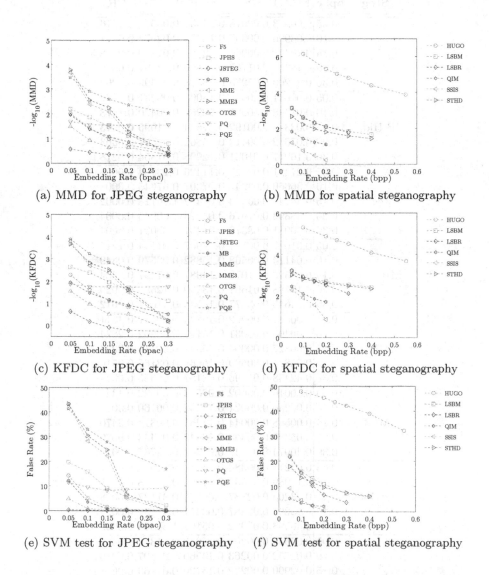

Fig. 4. MMD, proposed KFDC and false rate of SVM test for 9 JPEG and 5 spatial steganographic algorithms and different payloads. MMD and KFDC is shown as $-\log_{10}$ MMD and $-\log_{10}$ KFDC to get a better visual correspondence among figures.

Table 2. Test result of benchmarking for JPEG steganography using CCMerge feature

Steg	bpac	MMD	SS_B	SS_W	KFDC	FR
F5	0.05	0.00973	0.00078	0.14332	0.00546	0.1416
	0.10	0.03906	0.00337	0.12613	0.02674	0.0521
	0.15	0.10409	0.00947	0.12495	0.07580	0.0148
	0.20	0.18354	0.01767	0.11860	0.14897	0.0046
	0.30	0.35200	0.05275	0.08578	0.61499	0.0004
JP Hide	0.05	0.00641	0.00042	0.18002	0.00231	0.1966
	0.10	0.01348	0.00085	0.20269	0.00420	0.1578
	0.15	0.03381	0.00192	0.17544	0.01095	0.0913
	0.20	0.07652	0.00412	0.15862	0.02597	0.0563
	0.30	0.16211	0.01021	0.12998	0.07854	0.0218
JSteg	0.05	0.27491	0.02729	0.11426	0.23884	0.0029
	0.10	0.36660	0.04943	0.07307	0.67645	0.0004
	0.15	0.44741	0.06913	0.05482	1.26118	0.0002
	0.20	0.48893	0.07976	0.04778	1.66945	0.0004
	0.30	0.50011	0.08376	0.04431	1.89021	0.0004
MB	0.05	0.01087	0.00161	0.13907	0.01154	0.1213
	0.10	0.04114	0.00568	0.15882	0.03579	0.0349
	0.15	0.08526	0.01072	0.14687	0.07297	0.0084
	0.20	0.13788	0.01691	0.13430	0.12591	0.0029
	0.30	0.24645	0.03277	0.10545	0.31071	0.0012
MME	0.05	0.00022	0.00002	0.10836	0.00017	0.4311
	0.10	0.00405	0.00031	0.15141	0.00202	0.2834
	0.15	0.00827	0.00064	0.15364	0.00418	0.2224
	0.20	0.06821	0.00509	0.16068	0.03166	0.0516
	0.30	0.42438	0.05596	0.08187	0.68355	0.0011
MME3	0.05	0.00016	0.00002	0.07583	0.00022	0.4323
	0.10	0.00280	0.00021	0.13262	0.00160	0.3041
	0.15	0.00568	0.00044	0.14264	0.00311	0.2470
	0.20	0.05339	0.00398	0.16342	0.02433	0.0679
	0.30	0.40974	0.05248	0.08361	0.62767	0.0014
OutGuess	0.05	0.03271	0.00388	0.13219	0.02935	0.0481
	0.10	0.11989	0.01333	0.11893	0.11208	0.0075
	0.15	0.23205	0.02887	0.09271	0.31137	0.0028
	0.20	0.23205	0.02887	0.09271	0.31137	0.0028
	0.30	0.46598	0.07922	0.05101	1.55304	0.0009
PQ	0.05	0.02050	0.00209	0.15238	0.01372	0.0885
	0.10	0.02752	0.00263	0.14560	0.01807	0.0680
	0.15	0.02900	0.00282	0.15120	0.01863	0.0638
	0.20	0.02986	0.00286	0.15059	0.01897	0.0640
	0.30	0.02861	0.00297	0.16174	0.01833	0.0653
PQe	0.05	0.00014	0.00003	0.29449	0.00010	0.3621
	0.10	0.00050	0.00011	0.23891	0.00044	0.2915
	0.15	0.00107	0.00023	0.20833	0.00112	0.2455
	0.20	0.00179	0.00042	0.20399	0.00204	0.2028
	0.30	0.00918	0.00093	0.15838	0.00584	0.1683

Table 3. Test result of benchmarking for spatial steganography using SPAM feature

Steg	bpp	MMD	SS_B	SS_W	KFDC	FR
HUGO	0.10	0.00000	0.00000	0.13834	0.00000	0.4810
	0.20	0.00000	0.00000	0.09966	0.00001	0.4493
	0.25	0.00001	0.00000	0.09376	0.00002	0.4308
	0.30	0.00001	0.00000	0.09309	0.00003	0.4174
	0.40	0.00004	0.00001	0.08543	0.00007	0.3809
	0.55	0.00012	0.00003	0.13000	0.00020	0.3156
LSBM	0.05	0.00069	0.00009	0.15508	0.00060	0.2191
	0.10	0.00233	0.00038	0.33255	0.00115	0.1614
	0.15	0.00462	0.00070	0.44440	0.00158	0.1344
	0.20	0.00736	0.00094	0.47357	0.00198	0.1108
	0.30	0.01394	0.00127	0.44363	0.00286	0.0710
	0.40	0.02165	0.00158	0.41670	0.00379	0.0589
LSBR	0.05	0.00066	0.00009	0.15254	0.00057	0.2181
	0.10	0.00225	0.00035	0.29971	0.00118	0.1565
	0.15	0.00455	0.00065	0.35190	0.00184	0.1054
	0.20	0.00748	0.00089	0.30869	0.00289	0.0674
	0.30	0.01539	0.00175	0.23903	0.00731	0.0355
DCDMQIM	0.05	0.01490	0.00159	0.38765	0.00411	0.0446
	0.10	0.03643	0.00320	0.33781	0.00947	0.0319
	0.15	0.05900	0.00524	0.33492	0.01566	0.0224
	0.20	0.08221	0.00762	0.34210	0.02229	0.0186
SSIS	0.05	0.06828	0.00319	0.52515	0.00607	0.0823
	0.10	0.18429	0.00753	0.52812	0.01425	0.0408
	0.15	0.33815	0.01533	0.49857	0.03074	0.0200
	0.20	0.57509	0.05369	0.37206	0.14431	0.0045
StegHide	0.05	0.00187	0.00053	0.54306	0.00098	0.1779
	0.10	0.00545	0.00102	0.67387	0.00152	0.1318
	0.15	0.00987	0.00135	0.69481	0.00194	0.1113
	0.20	0.01458	0.00152	0.64509	0.00236	0.0945
	0.30	0.02460	0.00170	0.51059	0.00333	0.0723
	0.40	0.03486	0.00193	0.43691	0.00441	0.0589

achieve minimal distortion to cover. With lower KFDC values, JP Hide, which uses look-up table to scramble the embedding positions, is more undetectable than OutGuess and JSteg. Moreover, JSteg whose SS_B is largest and SS_W is the smallest, is the most detectable that only LSB replacement is used.

In spatial steganography (Fig. 4(d)), HUGO is much better than any other steganographic schemes as it preserves the co-occurrence model where the SPAM feature takes effect. What's more, LSB matching is a little more secure than LSB replacement since its within-class variance gets larger. Graph-theoretic technology based LSB (StegHide) performs worse than key-controlled LSB algorithms. Generally, LSB based algorithms are much better than QIM and SSIS for their less distortion to the image.

Additionally, comparing SS_W in Tabs. 2 and 3, we found that within-class variances of CCMerge are averagely half of those of SPAM. As a merged or fused feature, CCMerge is better to reduce the dimension of images than SPAM in spatial ones.

5   Conclusion

We proposed a novel approach for benchmarking steganographic schemes from the view of pattern recognition. Both between-class and within-class variances are considered to achieve a more consistent result. Compared with KL divergence and Maximum Mean Discrepancy (MMD), kernel Fisher discriminant criterion (KFDC) is more reliable for its low estimation error. In KFDC, we needn't train a classifier or argue whether the given test set is fair or the given configuration is the best. We demonstrate KFDC in 15 popular steganographic algorithms in the quantized DCT and spatial domains and provide some detailed analysis on the benchmarking result.

Besides benchmarking for steganography, KFDC can also be used to benchmark steganalytic features. And it's interesting to benchmark a practical system with different steganographic schemes. We may explore these topics in our future work.

Acknowledgments. This work was supported by the Natural Science Foundation (NSF) of Beijing under Grant 4112063, the NSF of China under Grant 61170281, the Strategic and Pilot Project of Chinese Academy of Sciences (CAS) under Grant XDA06030600, and the Project of Institute of Information Engineering, CAS, under Grant Y1Z0041101.

References

1. Cachin, C.: An Information-Theoretic Model for Steganography. In: Aucsmith, D. (ed.) IH 1998. LNCS, vol. 1525, pp. 306–318. Springer, Heidelberg (1998)
2. Pevný, T., Fridrich, J.: Benchmarking for Steganography. In: Solanki, K., Sullivan, K., Madhow, U. (eds.) IH 2008. LNCS, vol. 5284, pp. 251–267. Springer, Heidelberg (2008)
3. Hopper, N.J., Langford, J., von Ahn, L.: Provably Secure Steganography. In: Yung, M. (ed.) CRYPTO 2002. LNCS, vol. 2442, pp. 77–92. Springer, Heidelberg (2002)
4. Wang, Y., Moulin, P.: Perfectly secure steganography: Capacity, error exponents, and code constructions. IEEE Trans. on Information Theory 54, 2706–2722 (2008)
5. Pevný, T., Filler, T., Bas, P.: Using High-Dimensional Image Models to Perform Highly Undetectable Steganography. In: Böhme, R., Fong, P.W.L., Safavi-Naini, R. (eds.) IH 2010. LNCS, vol. 6387, pp. 161–177. Springer, Heidelberg (2010)
6. Kim, Y., Duric, Z., Richards, D.: Modified Matrix Encoding Technique for Minimal Distortion Steganography. In: Camenisch, J.L., Collberg, C.S., Johnson, N.F., Sallee, P. (eds.) IH 2006. LNCS, vol. 4437, pp. 314–327. Springer, Heidelberg (2007)

7. Fridrich, J., Pevný, T., Kodovský, J.: Statistically undetectable JPEG steganography: Dead ends, challenges, and opportunities. In: Dittmann, J., Fridrich, J. (eds.) Proc. of the 9th ACM Workshop on Multimedia & Security Workshop (MM&Sec 2007), pp. 3–14. ACM Press, New York (2007)
8. Kharrazi, M., Sencar, H.T., Memon, N.D.: Benchmarking steganographic and steganalytic techniques. In: Delp, E.J., Wong, P.W. (eds.) Proc. of SPIE, Electronic Imaging, Security, Steganography, and Watermarking of Multimedia Contents VII, vol. 5681, pp. 252–263 (2005)
9. Kodovský, J., Fridrich, J.: Calibration revisited. In: Dittmann, J., Fridrich, J., Craver, S. (eds.) Proc. of the 11th ACM Workshop on Multimedia & Security Workshop (MM&Sec 2009), pp. 63–74. ACM Press, New York (2009)
10. Westfeld, A.: F5-A Steganographic Algorithm: High Capacity Despite Better Steganalysis. In: Moskowitz, I.S. (ed.) IH 2001. LNCS, vol. 2137, pp. 289–302. Springer, Heidelberg (2001)
11. Kraetzer, C., Dittmann, J., Lang, A.: Transparency benchmarking on audio watermarks and steganography. In: Delp, E.J., Wong, P.W. (eds.) Proc. of SPIE, Electronic Imaging, Security, Steganography, and Watermarking of Multimedia Contents VII, vol. 6072, pp. 610–621 (2005)
12. Pevný, T., Fridrich, J.: Merging Markov and DCT features for multi-class JPEG steganalysis. In: Delp, E.J., Wong, P.W. (eds.) Proc. of SPIE, Electronic Imaging, Security, Steganography, and Watermarking of Multimedia Contents IX, vol. 6505, pp. 3-1–3-14 (2007)
13. Pevný, T., Bas, P., Fridrich, J.: Steganalysis by subtractive pixel adjacency matrix. In: Dittmann, J., Fridrich, J., Craver, S. (eds.) Proc. of the 11th ACM Workshop on Multimedia & Security Workshop (MM&Sec 2009), pp. 63–74. ACM Press, New York (2009)
14. Davidson, J., Jalan, J.: Steganalysis Using Partially Ordered Markov Models. In: Böhme, R., Fong, P.W.L., Safavi-Naini, R. (eds.) IH 2010. LNCS, vol. 6387, pp. 118–132. Springer, Heidelberg (2010)
15. Mika, S., Rätsch, G., Weston, J., Schölkopf, B., Müller, K.: Fisher discriminant analysis with kernels. In: Hu, Y., Larsen, J., Wilson, E., Douglas, S. (eds.) Neural Networks for Signal Processing IX, pp. 41–48. IEEE Press, NJ (1999)
16. Fisher, R.A.: The statistical utilization of multiple measurements. Annals of Eugenics 8, 376–386 (1938)
17. Chang, C., Lin, C.: LIBSVM: a library for support vector machines (2001), software available at http://www.csie.ntu.edu.tw/~cjlin/libsvm
18. Hansen, L., Salamon, P.: Neural network ensembles. IEEE Trans. on Pattern Analysis and Machine Intelligence 12(10), 993–1001 (1990)
19. Kodovský, J., Fridrich, J.: On completeness of feature spaces in blind steganalysis. In: Dittmann, J., et al. (eds.) Proc. of the 10th ACM Workshop on Multimedia & Security Workshop (MM&Sec 2008), pp. 123–132. ACM Press, New York (2008)
20. Müller, K.-R., Mika, S., Rätsch, G., Tsuda, K., Schölkopf, B.: An introduction to kernel-based learning algorithms. IEEE Trans. on Neural Networks 12(2), 181–201 (2001)
21. Steinwart, I.: On the influence of the kernel on the consistency of support vector machines. Journal of Machine Learning Research 2, 67–93 (2001)
22. Sallee, P.: Model-Based Steganography. In: Kalker, T., Cox, I., Ro, Y.M. (eds.) IWDW 2003. LNCS, vol. 2939, pp. 154–167. Springer, Heidelberg (2004)
23. Hetzl, S., Mutzel, P.: A Graph–Theoretic Approach to Steganography. In: Dittmann, J., Katzenbeisser, S., Uhl, A. (eds.) CMS 2005. LNCS, vol. 3677, pp. 119–128. Springer, Heidelberg (2005)

24. Mielikainen, J.: LSB matching revisited. IEEE Signal Processing Letters 13(5), 285–287 (2006)
25. Chen, B., Wornell, G.: Quantization index modulation: a class of provably good methods for digital watermarking and information embedding. IEEE Trans. on Information Theory 47(4), 1423–1443 (2001)
26. Marvel, L., Boncelet, C., Retter, C.: Spread spectrum image steganography. IEEE Trans. on Image Processing 8(8), 1075–1083 (1999)

Improved Tradeoff between Encapsulation and Decapsulation of HK09*

Xianhui Lu[1], Bao Li[1], Qixiang Mei[2], and Yamin Liu[1]

1. State Key Laboratory of Information Security, Graduate University of Chinese Academy of Sciences, Beijing, 100049, China
2. School of Information, Guangdong Ocean University, Zhanjiang, 524088, China
{xhlu,lb,ymliu}@is.ac.cn, nupf@163.com

Abstract. We propose a new variant of HK09 (Proposed by Hofheinz and Kiltz in Eurocrypt2009) which simplifies the decapsulation. Our result is a tradeoff between the efficiency of encapsulation and decapsulation. Compared with original HK09 the efficiency of decapsulation is improved by 38.9% and the efficiency of encapsulation is dropped by 11.4%.

Keywords: public key encryption, chosen ciphertext security, factoring.

1 Introduction

Hofheinz and Kiltz proposed the first practical CCA secure public key encryption scheme based on the factoring assumption [10](HK09). The efficiency of HK09 was later improved by Mei et al. [13]. In [13], the authors instantiated HK09 over the semi-smooth subgroup and also proposed an ElGamal style variant of HK09. The ElGamal style variant of HK09 in [13] can be seen as a tradeoff between the encapsulation and decapsulation. Compared with the original HK09 scheme, the efficiency of encapsulation is dropped by 42.9% and the efficiency of decapsulation is improved by 36.1%. In addition, the key size of the ElGamal style variant is increased by one element.

1.1 Our Contribution

We propose a new variant of HK09 which simplifies the decapsulation without increasing the key size. Our result is also a tradeoff between the efficiency of encapsulation and decapsulation. Compared with original HK09 the efficiency of decapsulation is improved by 38.9% and the efficiency of encapsulation is dropped by 11.4%. Thus our result is better than that of the ElGamal style variant of HK09 in [13].

* Supported by the National Natural Science Foundation of China (No.61070171), the National Basic Research Program of China(973 project) (No.2007CB311201) and the Postdoctoral Science Foundation of China (No.20100480514).

C.-K. Wu, M. Yung, and D. Lin (Eds.): Inscrypt 2011, LNCS 7537, pp. 131–141, 2012.
© Springer-Verlag Berlin Heidelberg 2012

The ciphertext of HK09 is $(R = g^{\mu 2^{l_K + l_H}}, S = |g^{\mu t} X^{\mu}|)$, the encapsulated key is $K = \mathrm{BBS}_r(g^{\mu 2^{l_H}})$, where l_K is the length of K, l_H is the length of the hash value $t = \mathrm{H}(R)$, $\mathrm{BBS}_r()$ is a Blum-Blum-Shub pseudorandom generator [1]. Since the exponent inversion can not be computed directly for hidden order group, the decapsulation algorithm computes $g^{\mu 2^{l_H}}$ by using the gcd (greatest common divisor) skill. To simplify the decapsulation, we derive the encapsulated key from $g^{\mu t 2^{l_H}}$. Thus, we can avoid the computation of exponent inversion and compute $K = \mathrm{BBS}_r((S/R^\rho)^{2^{l_H}})$ directly. Compared with original HK09, the decapsulation is decreased by $3l_K + 4l_H$ multiplications, the encapsulation is increased by $l_K + l_H$ multiplications. Similarly, our new variant can also be instantiated over semi-smooth subgroup [13].

The CCA security of the new variant is easy to understand. The security reduction from CCA security to BBS distinguisher is nearly the same as that of the original HK09. Since the simulator of the original scheme can compute $g^{\mu 2^{l_H}}$, it is easy for the simulator of the new variant to compute $g^{\mu t 2^{l_H}}$. The security reduction from BBS distinguisher to factoring assumption is different from that of the original scheme. In the new variant, the BBS distinguisher needs to distinguish $(N, z, \mathrm{BBS}_r(u^t))$ from (N, z, U). We proof that when $t = \mathrm{H}(z)$ is an odd number, the BBS distinguisher can be reduced to the factoring assumption. It is easy to construct such a hash function. Let H' be a target collision resistant hash function, then $\mathrm{H}(z) = \mathrm{H}'(z) \times 2 + 1$ is a target collision resistant hash function that the output values are odd numbers.

1.2   Related Work

Chosen ciphertext (CCA) security [14,15] is now widely accepted as the standard security notion of public key encryption schemes. During a long period of time, CCA secure schemes were designed based on decisional assumptions, such as Decisional Diffie-Hellman (DDH) assumption [4,6,12], Decisional Composite Residuosity (DCR) assumption [5,6] and Decisional Quadratic Residuosity (DQR) assumption [5,6], whereas the construction of CCA secure schemes based on computational assumptions, such as factoring assumption and Computational Diffie-Hellman (CDH) assumption, remained as an open problem.

The first CCA secure public key encryption scheme based on a computational assumption was proposed by Canetti, Halevi and Katz [2]. The authors obtained a CCA secure scheme from the Computational Bilinear Diffie-Hellman (CBDH) assumption. Later Cash, Kiltz and Shoup proposed a CCA secure scheme under the CDH assumption [3]. The efficiency was later improved in [8,9,16]. In these schemes the encapsulated key is generated by using the hardcore predicate based on the CDH assumption. Thus, one exponentiation can only generate one bit of the key or a few bits of the key (using simultaneous hardcore bits). Hence the computational efficiency of these schemes is not suitable for practice.

2   Definitions

In describing probabilistic processes, $x \stackrel{R}{\leftarrow} X$ denotes x is sampled from the distribution X. If S is a finite set, $s \stackrel{R}{\leftarrow} S$ denotes s is sampled from the uniform distribution on S. If A is a probabilistic algorithm and x an input, then $A(x)$ denotes the output distribution of A on input x. Thus, we write $y \stackrel{R}{\leftarrow} A(x)$ to denote of running algorithm A on input x and assigning the output to the variable y.

2.1   Key Encapsulation Mechanism

A key encapsulation mechanism consists the following algorithms:

- KEM.KeyGen(1^k): A probabilistic polynomial-time key generation algorithm takes as input a security parameter (1^k) and outputs a public key PK and a secret key SK. We write (PK, SK) $\leftarrow$ KEM.KeyGen(1^k)
- KEM.Enc(PK): A probabilistic polynomial-time encapsulation algorithm takes as input the public key PK, and outputs a pair (K, ψ), where $K \in K_D(K_D$ is the key space) is a key and ψ is a ciphertext. We write $(K, \psi) \leftarrow$ KEM.Enc(PK)
- KEM.Dec(SK, ψ): A decapsulation algorithm takes as input a ciphertext ψ and the secret key SK. It returns a key K. We write $K \leftarrow$ KEM.Dec(SK, ψ).

We require that for all (PK,SK) output by KEM.KeyGen(1^k), all $(K, \psi) \in$ [KEM.Enc(PK)], we have KEM.Dec(SK, ψ)=K.

Now we review the adaptive chosen ciphertext security of KEM. Note that we use the definition in [11] which is simpler than the original definition in [6].

Definition 1. *A KEM scheme is secure against adaptive chosen ciphertext attacks if the advantage of any adversary in the following game is negligible in the security parameter k.*

1. The adversary queries a key generation oracle. The key generation oracle computes (PK, SK) $\leftarrow$ KEM.KeyGen(1^k) and responds with PK.
2. The adversary queries an encapsulation oracle. The encapsulation oracle computes:

$$b \stackrel{R}{\leftarrow} \{0, 1\}, (K_0, \psi^*) \leftarrow \text{KEM.Enc(PK)}, K_1 \stackrel{R}{\leftarrow} K_D,$$

   and responds with (K_b, ψ^*).
3. The adversary makes a sequence of calls to the decapsulation oracle. For each query the adversary submits a ciphertext ψ, and the decapsulation oracle responds with KEM.Dec(SK, ψ). The only restriction is that the adversary can not request the decapsulation of ψ^*.
4. Finally, the adversary outputs a guess b'.

The adversary's advantage in the above game is $\text{Adv}_A^{\text{cca}}(k) = |\Pr[b = b'] - 1/2|$. If a KEM is secure against adaptive chosen ciphertext attacks defined in the above game we say it is CCA secure.

2.2 Target Collision Resistant Hash Function

Now we review the definition of target collision resistant (TCR) hash function. We say that a function $H : X \to Y$ is a TCR hash function, if, given a random preimage $x \in X$, it is hard to find $x' \neq x$ with $H(x') = H(x)$. Concretely, the advantage of an adversary $\mathcal{A}$ is defined as:

$$\mathrm{Adv}_{\mathcal{A}}^{\mathrm{tcr}}(k) = \Pr[x \xleftarrow{R} X, x' \leftarrow A(x) : x \neq x' \wedge H(x) = H(x')].$$

We say H is a TCR hash function if $\mathrm{Adv}_{\mathcal{A}}^{\mathrm{tcr}}(k)$ is negligible.

3 New Variant of HK09

Our new variant is described as follows.

- KeyGen: Choose uniformly at random a Blum integer $N = PQ = (2p + 1)(2q + 1)$, where P, Q, p, q are prime numbers. Then compute:

$$g \xleftarrow{R} \mathrm{QR}_N, \rho \xleftarrow{R} [(N-1)/4], X \leftarrow g^{\rho 2^{l_K + l_H}}, r \xleftarrow{R} \{0,1\}^{l_N},$$

$$pk \leftarrow (N, g, X, H, r), sk \leftarrow \rho,$$

where $H : QR_N \to \{0,1\}^{l_H}$ is a TCR hash function that the output values are odd numbers, l_H is the bit length of the output value, l_K is the bit length of encapsulated key K, l_N is the bit length of N.

- Encapsulation: Given pk, the encapsulation algorithm computes:

$$\mu \xleftarrow{R} [(N-1)/4], R \leftarrow g^{\mu 2^{l_K + l_H}}, t \leftarrow H(R), S \leftarrow |g^{\mu t} X^\mu|,$$

$$T \leftarrow g^{\mu t 2^{l_H}}, K \leftarrow \mathrm{BBS}_r(T),$$

where $\mathrm{BBS}_r(x) = B_r(x), \cdots, B_r(x^{l_K - 1})$, $B_r(x)$ denotes the bitwise inner product of r and x.

- Decapsulation: Given a ciphertext (R, S) and sk, the decapsulation algorithm verifies $R \in Z_N^*, S \in Z_N^* \cap [(N-1)/2]$, then computes:

$$t \leftarrow H(R), T \leftarrow (S/R^\rho)^{2^{l_H}},$$

if $T^{2^{l_K + 1}} = R^{2t}$ then compute $K \leftarrow \mathrm{BBS}_r(T)$,

else return the rejection symbol $\perp$.

The correctness of the scheme above can be verified as follows:

$$T = (S/R^\rho)^{2^{l_H}} = \left(\frac{|g^{\mu t} X^\mu|}{g^{\rho \mu 2^{l_K + l_H}}}\right)^{2^{l_H}} = \left(\frac{g^{\mu t} X^\mu}{X^\mu}\right)^{2^{l_H}} = g^{\mu t 2^{l_H}}.$$

$$T^{2^{l_K + 1}} = \left(g^{\mu t 2^{l_H}}\right)^{2^{l_K + 1}} = R^{2t}.$$

Intuitively, we can derive the encapsulated key from g^μ. Since t is an odd number, we have $\gcd(t, 2^{l_K+l_H}) = at + b2^{l_K+l_H} = 1$. Thus we can compute g^μ directly from $S/R^\rho = g^{\mu t}$ and $R = g^{\mu 2^{l_K+l_H}}$ by using the gcd skill as follow:

$$g^\mu = g^{\mu t a} g^{\mu 2^{l_K+l_H} b} = g^{\mu(at+b2^{l_K+l_H})} = g^\mu.$$

Unfortunately, it fails in the security proof. The reason is that, the simulator gets $g^{\mu(t-t^*)}$ instead of $g^{\mu t}$. It is clear that $t - t^*$ is not an odd number and $\gcd(t, 2^{l_K+l_H}) > 1$. So, the simulator can only compute $g^{\mu 2^{l_H}}$. Similarly, we can not derive the encapsulated key from $g^{\mu t}$. As a result, we can only derive the encapsulated key from $g^{\mu t 2^{l_H}}$.

We remark that it is easy to get a TCR hash function that the output values are odd numbers. Let H$'$ be a TCR hash function, then H$(x) = H'(x) \times 2 + 1$ is also a TCR hash function. It is clear that the output values of H are all odd numbers.

3.1 Security Proof

Theorem 1. *If factoring N is hard and H is a TCR hash function that the output values are odd numbers, then the new variant is CCA secure.*

Review the security proof in HK09, the reduction is divided into two steps. In the first step, BBS distinguisher is reduced to factoring assumption. In the second step, CCA security of the scheme is reduced to BBS distinguisher. We remark that the BBS distinguisher in the new variant is different from that of HK09. The experiment for the BBS distinguish problem in our new variant is defined as:

$$\mathrm{Adv}_{\mathcal{A}}^{\mathrm{BBS}} = |\Pr[\mathcal{A}(N, z, \mathrm{BBS}_r(u^t)) = 1] - \Pr[\mathcal{A}(N, z, U) = 1]|,$$

where $t = \mathrm{H}(z), z = u^{2^{l_K}}$, U is a random bit string of length l_K.

It is clear that CCA security of the new variant can also be reduced to the BBS distinguisher above. The only difference is that the simulator need to compute $g^{\mu t 2^{l_H}}$. This is easy since the simulator can compute $g^{\mu 2^{l_H}}$. So we have:

Theorem 2. *If it is hard to distinguish $(N, z, \mathrm{BBS}_r(u^t))$ from (N, z, U), then the new variant is CCA secure.*

Since the proof of theorem 2 above is very similar to HK09, we omit the reduction. Now theorem 1 comes from the following theorem:

Theorem 3. *If factoring N is hard and H is a TCR hash function that the output values are odd numbers, then it is hard to distinguish $(N, z, \mathrm{BBS}_r(u^t))$ from (N, z, U).*

Proof. The reduction can be divided into five steps as follows:

Step 1: BBS distinguish to tag hard-core distinguish

The experiment for tag hard-core distinguish problem is defined as:

1. The challenger sends (N, v, r) to the adversary.
2. The adversary replies with a tag t.
3. The challenger computes:

$$b \xleftarrow{R} \{0,1\}, \alpha_1 \leftarrow B_r(w^t), \alpha_0 \xleftarrow{R} \{0,1\},$$

and responds with α_b. Here $w^2 = v$.
4. Finally, the adversary outputs a guess b'.

The adversary's advantage in the above experiment is:

$$\mathrm{Adv}_{\mathcal{A}}^{\mathrm{THD}} = |\Pr[\mathcal{A}(\alpha_1) = 1] - \Pr[\mathcal{A}(\alpha_0) = 1]|.$$

Since α_0 is randomly selected, we have:

$$\Pr[\alpha_0 = \alpha_1] = \Pr[\alpha_0 = 1 - \alpha_1] = \frac{1}{2}.$$

According to the definition of $\mathrm{Adv}_{\mathcal{A}}^{\mathrm{THD}}$, we have:

$$
\begin{aligned}
\mathrm{Adv}_{\mathcal{A}}^{\mathrm{THD}} &= |\Pr[\mathcal{A}(\alpha_1) = 1] - \Pr[\mathcal{A}(\alpha_0) = 1]| \\
&= |\Pr[\mathcal{A}(\alpha_1) = 1] - (\Pr[\alpha_0 = \alpha_1]\Pr[\mathcal{A}(\alpha_1) = 1] + \\
&\quad \Pr[\alpha_0 = 1 - \alpha_1]\Pr[\mathcal{A}(1 - \alpha_1) = 1])| \\
&= |\Pr[\mathcal{A}(\alpha_1) = 1] - \\
&\quad \tfrac{1}{2}(\Pr[\mathcal{A}(\alpha_1) = 1] + \Pr[\mathcal{A}(1 - \alpha_1) = 1])| \\
&= \tfrac{1}{2}|\Pr[\mathcal{A}(\alpha_1) = 1] - \Pr[\mathcal{A}(1 - \alpha_1) = 1]|.
\end{aligned}
\tag{1}
$$

Lemma 1. *If an adversary A can distinguish $(N, z, BBS_r(u^t))$ from (N, z, U), then there exists an adversary B which can break the tag hard-core distinguish problem.*

$$\mathrm{Adv}_{\mathrm{B}}^{\mathrm{THD}} = \frac{1}{l_K}\mathrm{Adv}_{\mathrm{A}}^{\mathrm{BBS}}.$$

We begin by describing some hybrid experiments associated to B. For $0 \leq k \leq l_K$, experiment $\mathrm{Exp}(k)$ is described as follows:

1. The challenger sends (N, z, V) to the adversary, $V = v_1, \cdots, v_{l_K}$ is constructed as follows:

$$v_i \xleftarrow{R} \{0,1\}, i = 1, \cdots, k,$$

$$v_j \leftarrow B_r(u^{t2^{j-1}}), j = k+1, \cdots, l_K,$$

where $u^{2^{l_K}} = z, t = H(z)$.
2. The adversary outputs a bit b.

Let $\Pr[\mathrm{ExpH}(k) = 1]$ denote the probability that experiment $\mathrm{ExpH}(k)$ returns 1. We have that:

$$
\begin{aligned}
\mathrm{Adv}_{\mathrm{A}}^{\mathrm{BBS}} &= |\Pr[A(N, z, BBS_r(u^t)) = 1] - \Pr[A(N, z, U) = 1]| \\
&= |\Pr[\mathrm{ExpH}(0) = 1] - \Pr[\mathrm{ExpH}(l_K) = 1]|.
\end{aligned}
\tag{2}
$$

Now we show the construction of B. On receiving (N, v, r), B computes:

$$k \xleftarrow{R} [l_K], z \leftarrow v^{2^{l_K-k}}, t \leftarrow H(z).$$

The adversary B then sends t to the challenger of tag hard-core distinguish problem. When receives α_b the adversary B computes:

$$v_i \xleftarrow{R} \{0,1\}, i = 1, \cdots, k-1,$$

$$v_k \leftarrow \alpha_b,$$

$$v_j \leftarrow B_r(v^{t2^{j-k-1}}), j = k+1, \cdots, l_K,$$

$$V \leftarrow v_1, \cdots, v_{l_K}.$$

The adversary B sends (N, z, V) to the adversary A. When A outputs b', B outputs the same b'.

We have that:

$$\begin{aligned}
\text{Adv}_B^{\text{THD}} &= |\Pr[B(\alpha_1) = 1] - \Pr[B(\alpha_0) = 1]| \\
&= \tfrac{1}{l_K}|\textstyle\sum_{i=1}^{l_K}(\Pr[B(\alpha_1) = 1|k = i] - \Pr[B(\alpha_0) = 1|k = i])| \\
&= \tfrac{1}{l_K}|\textstyle\sum_{i=1}^{l_K}(\Pr[\text{ExpH}(i-1) = 1] - \Pr[\text{ExpH}(i) = 1])| \qquad (3) \\
&= \tfrac{1}{l_K}|\Pr[\text{ExpH}(0) = 1] - \Pr[\text{ExpH}(l_K) = 1]| \\
&= \tfrac{1}{l_K}\text{Adv}_A^{\text{BBS}}.
\end{aligned}$$

Step 2: Tag hard-core distinguish to tag hard-core predicate

The experiment for tag hard-core predicate problem is defined as:

$$\text{Adv}_A^{\text{THP}} = |\Pr[A(N, v, r) = (B_r(w^t), t)] - \frac{1}{2}|,$$

where $w^2 = v$, t is an odd number.

Lemma 2. *If an adversary B can break the problem of tag hard-core distinguish, then there exists an adversary C which can break the tag hard-core predicate problem.*

$$\text{Adv}_C^{\text{THP}} = \text{Adv}_B^{\text{THD}}.$$

The construction of C is described as follows:

1. On receiving the challenge (N, v, r), the adversary C sends it to B.
2. On receiving t from B, the adversary C chooses a random bit α and sends it to B.
3. When B outputs b', the adversary C outputs (α, t) if $b' = 1$ and $(1 - \alpha, t)$ if $b' = 0$.

Since α is a random bit, we have $\Pr[B_r(w^t) = \alpha] = \Pr[B_r(w^t) = 1 - \alpha] = \frac{1}{2}$. Consider the advantage of C:

$$
\begin{aligned}
\mathrm{Adv}_C^{\mathrm{THP}} &= |\Pr[C(N, v, r) = (B_r(w^t), t)] - \frac{1}{2}| \\
&= |\Pr[B_r(w^t) = \alpha] \Pr[B(\alpha_1) = 1] + \\
&\quad \Pr[B_r(w^t) = 1 - \alpha] \Pr[B(1 - \alpha_1) = 0] - \frac{1}{2}| \\
&= |\frac{1}{2} \Pr[B(\alpha_1) = 1] + \frac{1}{2} \Pr[B(1 - \alpha_1) = 0] - \frac{1}{2}| \quad\quad (4) \\
&= |\frac{1}{2}(\Pr[B(\alpha_1) = 1] + 1 - \Pr[B(1 - \alpha_1) = 1]) - \frac{1}{2}| \\
&= \frac{1}{2}|\Pr[B(\alpha_1) = 1] - \Pr[B(1 - \alpha_1) = 1]| \\
&= \mathrm{Adv}_B^{\mathrm{THD}}.
\end{aligned}
$$

Step 3: Tag hard-core predicate to tag square root

The experiment for tag square root problem is defined as:

$$
\mathrm{Adv}_{\mathcal{A}}^{\mathrm{TSR}} = \Pr[\mathcal{A}(N, v) = (w^t, t)],
$$

where $w^2 = v$, t is an odd number.

Since $B_r(w^t)$ is the Goldreich-Levin (GL) hard-core predicate [7], according to the reconstruction algorithm of GL hard-core predicate we have:

Lemma 3. *If an adversary C can break the problem of tag hard-core predicate, then there exists an adversary D which can break the tag square root problem.*

$$
\mathrm{Adv}_D^{\mathrm{TSR}} = \mathrm{Adv}_C^{\mathrm{THP}}.
$$

On receiving (N, v), the adversary D randomly selects $r \in \{0, 1\}^{l_N}$ and sends (N, v, r) to adversary C. The adversary C responds with $(B_r(w^t), t)$. According to the reconstruction algorithm of GL hard-core predicate, D can compute (w^t, t) in polynomial time. Note that $t = H(z) = H(v^{2^{l_K - k}})$ is independent of r. Since k is randomly chosen from $[l_K]$, when D submits (N, v, r) repeatedly with different r, the probability that the adversary C returns $(B_r(w^t), t)$ with the same t is $1/l_K$. To get a reply with a certain t, we need to repeatedly run the algorithm of hard-core predicate l_K times on average.

Step 4: Tag square root to square root

The experiment for square root problem is defined as:

$$
\mathrm{Adv}_{\mathcal{A}}^{\mathrm{SR}} = \Pr[\mathcal{A}(N, v) = w],
$$

where $w^2 = v$.

Lemma 4. *If an adversary D can break the problem of tag square root, then there exists an adversary E which can break the square root problem.*

$$
\mathrm{Adv}_E^{\mathrm{SR}} = \mathrm{Adv}_D^{\mathrm{TSR}}.
$$

The construction of E is very simple. On receiving (N, v) from the challenger, E sends it to D directly. On receiving (w^t, t) from D, E computes w as follow:

$$\gcd(t, 2) = at + b2 = 1, w^{at}v^b = w^{at}w^{2b} = w^{at+b2} = w.$$

Step 5: Square root to factoring

The reduction from square root to factoring is a well known result. The experiment for factoring problem is defined as:

$$\text{Adv}_A^{\text{FAC}} = \Pr[\mathcal{A}(N) = (P, Q|N = PQ)].$$

Lemma 5. *If an adversary E can break the problem of square root, then there exists an adversary F which can break the factoring problem.*

$$\text{Adv}_F^{\text{FAC}} = \frac{1}{2}\text{Adv}_E^{\text{SR}}.$$

Since lemma 5 is a well known result, we omit the detail of the proof. According to the five lemmas above, we have:

$$\text{Adv}_F^{\text{FAC}} = \frac{1}{2l_K}\text{Adv}_A^{\text{BBS}}.$$

This completes the proof of theorem 3.   □

3.2   Efficiency

The efficiency of HK09 [10], variants in [13] and our variant is listed in table1.

Table 1. Efficiency comparison

	Encapsulate(mul)	Decapsulate(mul)
HK09	$3272(3l_N + l_K + 1.5l_H)$	$2376(1.5l_N + 4l_K + 6.5l_H)$
S-HK	$1400(3l_{exp} + l_K + 1.5l_H)$	$1440(1.5l_{exp} + 4l_K + 6.5l_H)$
E-HK	$2000(4.5l_{exp} + l_K + 1.5l_H)$	$920(1.5 \times 1.2l_{exp} + 2.5l_H)$
NEW	$3432(3l_N + 2l_K + 2.5l_H)$	$1816(1.5l_N + l_K + 2.5l_H)$
S-NEW	$1560(3l_{exp} + 2l_K + 2.5l_H)$	$880(1.5l_{exp} + l_K + 2.5l_H)$

In table 1, HK09 is the original scheme in [10], S-HK is the variant instantiated over semi-smooth subgroup in [13], E-HK is the ElGamal style variant in [13], NEW is the proposed variant, S-NEW is the proposed variant instantiated over semi-smooth subgroup using the skill in [13]. The parameters are the same as those in [10] and [13], $l_N = 1024, l_K = l_H = 80, l_{exp} = 400$.

Similar to HK09, the encapsulation can first compute $A = g^\mu$ and $B = X^\mu$, which require $3l_N$ multiplications. The computations of $A^{2^{l_H}} = g^{\mu 2^{l_H}}$ and

$S = |A^t B| = |g^{\mu t} X^\mu|$ require $1.5 l_H$ multiplication. The reason is that the computation of $A^{2^{l_H}}$ is a by-product of A^t. Then compute $T = A^{t 2^{l_H}} = g^{\mu t 2^{l_H}}$, which requires l_H multiplications. Finally, compute $R = A^{2^{l_H + l_K}}$ and $K = \mathrm{BBS}_r(T)$, which require $2 l_K$ multiplications. Thus, the encapsulation requires $3 l_N + 2 l_K + 2.5 l_H$ multiplications. In decapsulation, the computation of $T = (S/R^\rho)^{2^{l_H}}$ requires $1.5 l_N + l_H$ multiplications. The computation of $\mathrm{BBS}_r(T)$ is a by-product of $T^{2^{l_K}}$. So the decapsulation only requires $1.5 l_N + l_K + 2.5 l_H$ multiplications.

In [10], the authors claim that the encapsulation requires $3 l_N + 1 l_K + 2.5 l_H$ multiplications. We point out that the computation of $A^{2^{l_H}} = g^{\mu 2^{l_H}}$ and $S = |A^t B| = |g^{\mu t} X^\mu|$ can be further optimized. The computation of $A^{2^{l_H}}$ is a by-product of A^t. Thus, the encapsulation of HK09 requires $3 l_N + 1 l_K + 1.5 l_H$ multiplications.

In [13], the authors claim that the encapsulation requires $4.5 l_{exp} + l_K + 2.5 l_H$ multiplications and the decapsulation requires $1.5 \times 1.2 l_{exp} + l_K + 2.5 l_H$ multiplications. We point out that, g^{2^v} can be precomputed. Thus the computation of $R = g^{\mu 2^v}$ only requires l_{exp} multiplications. As a result, the encapsulation of E-HK requires $4.5 l_{exp} + l_K + 1.5 l_H$ multiplications. For decapsulation, the computation of $K = \mathrm{BBS}_r^+(R^{\rho'})$ is a by-product of $R^{\rho' t}$. So, the decapsulation only requires $1.5 \times 1.2 l_{exp} + 2.5 l_H$ multiplications.

4   Conclusion

We proposed a variant of HK09 in which the decapsulation is simplified. The proposed variant can also be proved to be CCA secure under the factoring assumption. Compared with the original HK09 scheme, the decapsulation operation is decreased by $3 l_K + 4 l_H$ multiplications, while the encapsulation is only increased by $l_K + l_H$ multiplications.

References

1. Blum, L., Blum, M., Shub, M.: A simple unpredictable pseudo-random number generator. SIAM J. Comput. 15(2), 364–383 (1986)
2. Canetti, R., Halevi, S., Katz, J.: Chosen-Ciphertext Security from Identity-Based Encryption. In: Cachin, C., Camenisch, J. (eds.) EUROCRYPT 2004. LNCS, vol. 3027, pp. 207–222. Springer, Heidelberg (2004)
3. Cash, D., Kiltz, E., Shoup, V.: The Twin Diffie-Hellman Problem and Applications. In: Smart, N. (ed.) EUROCRYPT 2008. LNCS, vol. 4965, pp. 127–145. Springer, Heidelberg (2008)
4. Cramer, R., Shoup, V.: A Practical Public Key Cryptosystem Provably Secure against Adaptive Chosen Ciphertext Attack. In: Krawczyk, H. (ed.) CRYPTO 1998. LNCS, vol. 1462, pp. 13–25. Springer, Heidelberg (1998)
5. Cramer, R., Shoup, V.: Universal Hash Proofs and a Paradigm for Adaptive Chosen Ciphertext Secure Public-Key Encryption. In: Knudsen, L.R. (ed.) EUROCRYPT 2002. LNCS, vol. 2332, pp. 45–64. Springer, Heidelberg (2002)

6. Cramer, R., Shoup, V.: Design and analysis of practical public-key encryption schemes secure against adaptive chosen ciphertext attack. SIAM J. Comput. 33, 167–226 (2004), http://dl.acm.org/citation.cfm?id=953065.964243
7. Goldreich, O., Levin, L.A.: A hard-core predicate for all one-way functions. In: Proceedings of the Twenty-First Annual ACM Symposium on Theory of Computing, STOC 1989, pp. 25–32. ACM, New York (1989)
8. Hanaoka, G., Kurosawa, K.: Efficient Chosen Ciphertext Secure Public Key Encryption under the Computational Diffie-Hellman Assumption. In: Pieprzyk, J. (ed.) ASIACRYPT 2008. LNCS, vol. 5350, pp. 308–325. Springer, Heidelberg (2008)
9. Haralambiev, K., Jager, T., Kiltz, E., Shoup, V.: Simple and Efficient Public-Key Encryption from Computational Diffie-Hellman in the Standard Model. In: Nguyen, P.Q., Pointcheval, D. (eds.) PKC 2010. LNCS, vol. 6056, pp. 1–18. Springer, Heidelberg (2010)
10. Hofheinz, D., Kiltz, E.: Practical Chosen Ciphertext Secure Encryption from Factoring. In: Joux, A. (ed.) EUROCRYPT 2009. LNCS, vol. 5479, pp. 313–332. Springer, Heidelberg (2009)
11. Kiltz, E.: Chosen-Ciphertext Secure Key-Encapsulation Based on Gap Hashed Diffie-Hellman. In: Okamoto, T., Wang, X. (eds.) PKC 2007. LNCS, vol. 4450, pp. 282–297. Springer, Heidelberg (2007)
12. Kurosawa, K., Desmedt, Y.: A New Paradigm of Hybrid Encryption Scheme. In: Franklin, M. (ed.) CRYPTO 2004. LNCS, vol. 3152, pp. 426–442. Springer, Heidelberg (2004)
13. Mei, Q., Li, B., Lu, X., Jia, D.: Chosen Ciphertext Secure Encryption under Factoring Assumption Revisited. In: Catalano, D., Fazio, N., Gennaro, R., Nicolosi, A. (eds.) PKC 2011. LNCS, vol. 6571, pp. 210–227. Springer, Heidelberg (2011)
14. Naor, M., Yung, M.: Public-key cryptosystems provably secure against chosen ciphertext attacks. In: Proceedings of the Twenty-Second Annual ACM Symposium on Theory of Computing, STOC 1990, pp. 427–437. ACM, New York (1990)
15. Rackoff, C., Simon, D.R.: Non-interactive Zero-Knowledge Proof of Knowledge and Chosen Ciphertext Attack. In: Feigenbaum, J. (ed.) CRYPTO 1991. LNCS, vol. 576, pp. 433–444. Springer, Heidelberg (1992)
16. Wee, H.: Efficient Chosen-Ciphertext Security via Extractable Hash Proofs. In: Rabin, T. (ed.) CRYPTO 2010. LNCS, vol. 6223, pp. 314–332. Springer, Heidelberg (2010)

Non-interactive Deniable Authentication Protocols

Haibo Tian[1], Xiaofeng Chen[2], and Zhengtao Jiang[3]

[1] School of Information Science and Technology, Sun Yat-Sen University,
Guangzhou, 510275, China
sysutianhb@gmail.com
[2] School of Telecommunications Engineering, Xidian University, Xi'an, 710071, China
xfchen@xidian.edu.cn
[3] School Of Computer, Communication University of China, Beijing, 100024, China
z.t.jiang@163.com

Abstract. This paper gives a security model for non-interactive deniable authentication (NIDA) protocols. This model captures a session-state-reveal attack and a key-compromise-impersonation attack. We analyze some NIDA protocols in the model, and we find that no one is satisfactory. We give a new paradigm to construct an NIDA protocol, which is provably secure in the model.

Keywords: Deniable Authentication, Non-interactive Protocols, security model.

1 Introduction

The deniable authentication (DA) [1] means that a sender not only proves that she/he is the communicating entity with a receiver but also leaves no evidence to the receiver about the participating in a protocol. The deniability feature is desirable in some applications, such as the Off-the-Record Messaging [2], and the Internet Key Exchange protocol [3].

To make a DA protocol more efficient, Shao [4] proposed a concept of non-interactive deniable authentication (NIDA). It claims that a one-pass transcript is enough for the goal of a DA protocol. However, a simple replay attack can be used to falsify the authentication goal of most NIDA protocols. A common countermeasure is to require that each message includes a time stamp by default.

Another problem about NIDA is a gap between its security model and analysis techniques.

- The security model of the NIDA is similar to that of a designated verifier signature (DVS). There is no security model at the beginning [4]. Wang and Song [5] proposed a formal model which is similar to the model of DVS.
- The analysis techniques consider various attacks. The identified attacks include an impersonation attack [4], a session-state-reveal (SSR) attack [6],

C.-K. Wu, M. Yung, and D. Lin (Eds.): Inscrypt 2011, LNCS 7537, pp. 142–159, 2012.
© Springer-Verlag Berlin Heidelberg 2012

a key-compromise-impersonation (KCI) attack [7], and a man-in-the-middle (MITM) attack [8]. An impersonation attack means that an adversary can impersonate an intended receiver to identify the source of a given message. An SSR attack means that an adversary can forge a message if some session-specific values are compromised. A KCI attack means that an adversary who knows a sender's private key can impersonate an honest receiver to identify the source of a message produced by the sender. An MITM attack means that an adversary can establish a session key with either a sender or a receiver.

- The gap is that the security model cannot capture these attacks. The SSR attack and KCI attack are not considered in the model [5]. Sometimes, these attacks are considered by independent proofs [6,7]. The problem is that there is no clear description about an adversary.

This paper focuses on the security model of NIDA protocols. We present a model and analyze some NIDA protocols. Then we give a paradigm to construct satisfactory NIDA protocols.

1.1   Related Works

Lu et al. [9] and Willy et al. [10] proposed protocols similar to a ring signature [11]. The protocol of Lu et al. took a receiver into a signer ring to achieve deniability. The protocol of Willy et al. used chameleon hash functions to separate messages and signatures. Wang et al. [5] proposed a scheme based on the DVS where a simulation procedure was used to achieve deniability. There are many protocols based on a message authentication code (MAC) [6, 8, 12–22]. Generally, there is an MAC key to protect a message. Since the key can be calculated by a receiver or by both a sender and a receiver, the deniability property is achieved.

1.2   Contributions

- **Security Model:** A new model is based on that of DA protocols in [23]. An adversary in the model can deliver messages, corrupt entities and reveal session-state values. There are definitions about authenticator, transcript deniability, and full deniability. There is also a message identification (MI) protocol that is an idea NIDA protocol.
- **Protocol Analysis:** We run some NIDA protocols in the new model. We give a table to summarize their satisfactions to each definitions. There is no satisfactory NIDA protocols. We detail two attacks to show an analysis method in the model.
- **New Paradigm:** A new paradigm emulates an MI protocol in the model. We give a concrete scheme based on the Rabin signature [24]. It is provably secure in the model.

1.3   Organizations

Section 2 is some preliminaries, including some assumptions and a traditional description of NIDA protocols. Section 3 is the new security model, and some analysis about NIDA protocols. Section 4 is the new paradigm to construct NIDA protocols. The concrete scheme is shown in section 5. The comparison is in section 6. The last section concludes the paper.

2   Preliminaries

2.1   Assumptions

- *Computational Diffie-Hellman (CDH) problem:* Given large primes p, q satisfying $q|p-1$, there is a generator $g \in \mathbb{Z}_p^*$ for a group $\mathbb{G}$ with an order q. Given two random elements $g^x, g^y \in_R \mathbb{G}$, the problem is to find $g^z \in \mathbb{G}$ such that $z = xy \bmod q$.
- *Decisional Diffie-Hellman (DDH) problem:* With the same parameters $(p, q, g, \mathbb{G})$, given three random elements g^x, g^y, g^z, the problem is to decide whether $z = xy \bmod q$.

The assumption is that there are no polynomial time algorithms to solve a CDH (DDH) problem with non-negligible probability ϵ in time t when q is big enough.

2.2   NIDA Protocols

An NIDA protocol includes four algorithms $(Setup, Prove, Verify, Sim)$.

- On input of a security parameter $k \in \mathbb{N}$, a *Setup* algorithm generates system parameters and public/private key pairs. The key pair of a sender is usually denoted by (pk_S, sk_S), and a receiver by (pk_R, sk_R);
- A *Prove* algorithm takes as input a message m, the public key pk_R, the secret key sk_S to generate an authenticator *authen*. Then the sender sends $c = m||authen$ to the receiver;
- A *Verify* algorithm takes as input a transcript c, the public key pk_S and the secret key sk_R to produce a decision bit $b \in \{0, 1\}$, where $b = 1$ means that the receiver accepts;
- A *Sim* algorithm takes as input the public key pk_S, the secret key sk_R, and a message m to generate a simulated transcript $\hat{c}$ which is computationally indistinguishable from a real transcript c associated with the given message m.

There are some properties about NIDA protocols. We adopt the descriptions in [5, 8, 25] with some modifications.

1. *Correctness:* If a sender and a receiver follow the description of an NIDA protocol, the receiver is always able to identify the source of the message in a transcript, which means the receiver accepts.

2. *Unforgeability:* An adversary cannot generate a new valid transcript in polynomial time when the adversary can obtain public keys and some qualified transcripts, where messages are determined by the adversary.
3. *Deniability:* An adversary cannot distinguish a simulated transcript from a real one in polynomial time even the adversary can obtain public keys, some real transcripts and simulated transcripts for the adversary's messages.
4. *Resistance to impersonation attack:* An adversary cannot impersonate a qualified receiver to identify the source of a message in a transcript even the adversary can get access to public keys and valid transcripts.
5. *Resistance to SSR:* A disclosed session-specific value does not affect the secure properties of other sessions of an NIDA protocol. Note that a session means one interaction between a sender and a receiver.
6. *Resistance to man-in-the-middle attack:* An adversary cannot establish session keys with either a sender or a receiver even the adversary controls all communication channels between the sender and receiver.
7. *Resistance to KCI attack:* An adversary cannot impersonate a qualified receiver, even if the adversary can get access to the private key of a sender.

3   The Security Model

The current security model [5] does not capture some common attacks to the NIDA protocols. We here give a new model. It is based on an extension framework of Raimondo et al. [23].

Message Driven Non-interactive Protocols. A non-interactive protocol is a process that is initially invoked by a party with some initial state. Once invoked, the protocol waits for an activation that can happen for a message from the network or an external request. Upon activation, the protocol processes the incoming data together with its current internal state generating an outgoing transcript and/or an output. Once the activation is completed, the protocol finishes.

The Authenticated-Links Model (AM). There are n parties $P_1, \ldots, P_n$, each running a copy of a message-driven protocol π. The computation consists of an activation of π within different parties. The adversary $\mathcal{A}$ is a probabilistic polynomial-time (PPT) algorithm with the following abilities:

- *control and schedule activations:* $\mathcal{A}$ can decide who is the next party to activate and which incoming message or external request the activated party is to receive.
- *deliver messages:* $\mathcal{A}$ can change the order of delivery and can choose not to deliver some messages at all. However, $\mathcal{A}$ is restricted to deliver messages faithfully. That is, we assume that each message carries the identities of the sender P_i and of the intended receiver P_j. When a message is sent by a party, it is added to a set M of authentic messages. Whenever $\mathcal{A}$ activates a party P_j on some incoming message m, it must be that m is in the set M and that P_j is the intended receiver of m.

– *corrupt parties:* $\mathcal{A}$ learns the entire current state of the corrupted party P_i and can add to the set M any fake messages on behalf of P_i. A special symbol in the output of P_i is generated to signal the corruption. $\mathcal{A}$ will control all the sequent activations of P_i.

In addition, on the completion of an activation, the outgoing messages, external requests and the output generated by the protocol become known to $\mathcal{A}$. We refer to such an adversary as an AM-adversary.

With all honest parties and the AM-adversary, there is a global output of a running protocol. Let $AUTH_{\pi,\mathcal{A}}(\boldsymbol{x},\boldsymbol{r})$ denote the global output of a running of the protocol π with the n parties and the adversary $\mathcal{A}$ with input $\boldsymbol{x} = x_1,\ldots,x_n$ and random input $\boldsymbol{r} = r_0, r_1, \ldots, r_n$, where r_0 is for $\mathcal{A}$ and x_i and r_i are for a party P_i, $i > 0$. Let $AUTH_{\pi,\mathcal{A}}(\boldsymbol{x})$ denote the random variable describing $AUTH_{\pi,\mathcal{A}}(\boldsymbol{x},\boldsymbol{r})$ when $\boldsymbol{r}$ is uniformly chosen.

Remark 1. Note that the message set M is named authentic messages. The messages are not deleted after a reception. This is due to the nature of non-interactive protocols.

Remark 2. The corrupt ability captures the KCI attack.

The Unauthenticated-Links Model (UM). The computation of unauthenticated-links model is similar to the AM model but the restriction of delivering messages faithfully is removed for the adversary $\mathcal{U}$, referred to as an UM-adversary. Instead, it can deliver arbitrary messages. Besides this, we give the adversary $\mathcal{U}$ an ability to obtain secret information from an honest party's internal state.

– *session-state reveal (SSR):* $\mathcal{U}$ can learn some values in the current state of an uncorrupted party before or after an activation is completed. The *restriction* is that the disclosure of the session-specific values cannot lead to the exposure of the party's long term private key.

Further, there is an initialization function I that models an initial phase out-of-band and authenticated information exchange between the parties.

The random variables $UNAUTH_{\pi,\mathcal{U}}(\boldsymbol{x},\boldsymbol{r})$ and $UNAUTH_{\pi,\mathcal{U}}(\boldsymbol{x})$ are defined analogously to the previous ones $AUTH_{\pi,\mathcal{A}}(\boldsymbol{x},\boldsymbol{r})$ and $AUTH_{\pi,\mathcal{A}}(\boldsymbol{x})$, but with the computation carried out in the unauthenticated-links model.

Remark 3. Note that the restriction of the SSR ability makes the ability different to the corrupt ability. The SSR ability captures the SSR attack.

Emulation of Protocols. When we say that a protocol π' in the unauthenticated-links model emulates a protocol π in the authenticated-links model, we want to capture the idea that the running π' in an unauthenticated network has the same effect as the running π in an authenticated network. Formally speaking:

Definition 1. *Let π' and π be the message-driven protocols for n parties. We say that π' emulates π in unauthenticated networks if for any UM-adversary $\mathcal{U}$ there exists an AM-adversary $\mathcal{A}$ such that for all inputs x,*

$$AUTH_{\pi,\mathcal{A}}(x) \stackrel{c}{=} UNAUTH_{\pi',\mathcal{U}}(x) \tag{1}$$

where $\stackrel{c}{=}$ denotes computationally indistinguishable.

Authenticators. An authenticator is a *compiler* that takes as input protocols designed for authenticated networks, and turns them into *equivalent* protocols for unauthenticated networks.

Definition 2. *A compiler $\mathcal{C}$ is an algorithm that takes as input descriptions of protocols and produces descriptions of protocols. An authenticator is a compiler $\mathcal{C}$ where for any protocol π, the protocol $\mathcal{C}(\pi)$ emulates π in unauthenticated networks.*

In particular, authenticators translate secure protocols in the authenticated-links model into secure protocols in the unauthenticated-links model. The simplest protocol is a message identification (MI) protocol that transports a message from a party to another for identification. It can be described formally as follows:

- On activation within P_i on external request (P_j, m), the party P_i sends the message (P_i, P_j, m) to party P_j and outputs 'P_i sent m to P_j';
- Upon receipt of a message (P_i, P_j, m), P_j outputs 'P_j identified the source of m as P_i'.

A protocol that emulates the above MI protocol in unauthenticated-links model is called an *MI-authenticator*.

Remark 4. The MI-authenticator captures the unforgeability property.

Definition 3. *An MI-authenticator λ is transcript deniable if there exists a simulator S_λ that given a message m sent by a party A to B produces a transcript of a session of λ for m, which is computational indistinguishable from a real one for an adversary who does not corrupt the party B or send this real or simulated transcript to B, and not reveal the session-state of S_λ for this transcript or that of A for the real one.*

Definition 4. *An MI-authenticator λ is full deniable if there exists a simulator $S_\lambda^{pri_B}$ accessing the private key of B that given a message m sent by a party A to B produces a transcript of a session of λ for m, which is computational indistinguishable from a real one for an adversary who does not reveal the session-state of $S_\lambda^{pri_B}$ for this transcript or that of A for the real one.*

Remark 5. The two definitions capture the deniability property of NIDA protocols. The transcript deniability means that an adversary can not distinguish a sender from infinite possible senders. The full deniability means that an adversary can not distinguish a sender from a receiver.

3.1   Protocol Analysis

We give two examples to show an analysis method in the model.

The Protocol of Lee et al. [6] There is a report about the protocol [25]. It reported that the protocol [6] was not KCI secure since an adversary with the private key of a receiver could impersonate a sender. However, this is just the full deniability. It is meaningless to consider this attack if we take the full deniability as a desirable property.

We here give a real attack to show that the scheme is not secure under the SSR attack.

- **The Protocol**
    - **Setup** The system parameter is $(p, q, g, \mathbb{G}, H)$, where $H : \{0,1\}^* \to \mathbb{Z}_q$ and other symbols are the same as those in Section 2.1. For a sender S, $sk_S \in_R \mathbb{Z}_q$ and $pk_S = g^{sk_S} \bmod p$. For a receiver R, (sk_R, pk_R) is computed similarly.
    - **Prove** Select $r \in_R \mathbb{Z}_q$, compute $\Lambda = g^r \bmod p$ and

$$MAC = H((pk_R)^{H(m)sk_S + r\Lambda \bmod q} \bmod p || m),$$

      where "||" denotes bits concatenation. The transcript is $c = (m, \Lambda, MAC)$
    - **Verify** Verify whether $H((pk_S^{H(m)} \Lambda^\Lambda)^{sk_R} \bmod p || m) = MAC$.
- **The Attack**
    - An adversary $\mathcal{A}$ sends a transcript (m, Λ, MAC) to an honest receiver. It reveals a session key $sk = (pk_S^{H(m)} \Lambda^\Lambda)^{sk_R}$ of the receiver.
    - Then $\mathcal{A}$ modifies m arbitrarily to obtain $m' \neq m$ and sends (m', Λ, MAC) to the same receiver. It reveals another session key $sk' = (pk_S^{H(m')} \Lambda^\Lambda)^{sk_R}$.
    - $\mathcal{A}$ computes $g^{sk_S sk_R} = (k/k')^{(H(m)-H(m'))^{-1}}$.
    - $\mathcal{A}$ produces a transcript $(m_\mathcal{A}, \Lambda_\mathcal{A}, MAC_\mathcal{A})$ where $m_\mathcal{A}$ is an arbitrary message, $\Lambda_\mathcal{A} = pk_S^\alpha$ for a random value $\alpha \in_R \mathbb{Z}_q$, and $MAC_\mathcal{A} = H(k_\mathcal{A} || m_\mathcal{A})$ where $k_\mathcal{A} = (g^{sk_S sk_R})^{(H(m_\mathcal{A}) + \alpha \Lambda_\mathcal{A} \bmod q)} \bmod p$.
    - The forged transcript can be accepted according to the protocol description. Thus, the protocol is not an MI-authenticator.

The Protocol of Fan et al. [18] Besides the session key, other session-specific values may also help an adversary. The protocol in [18] is suitable to show the help.

- **The protocol.** We omit the message encryption part of the scheme as it is not related to the unforgeability property.
    - **Setup** A key generation center (KGC) sets groups $(G_1, +)$ and $(G_2, \cdot)$ with order p. The generator of G_1 is P. A paring is $e : G_1 \times G_1 \to G_2$. The KGC randomly selects $s \in_R \mathbb{Z}_p^*$ and sets $P_{pub} = sP$. Three hash functions

are $H_1 : \{0,1\}^* \to G_1$, $H_2 : G_2 \times \mathbb{Z}_p^* \to \mathbb{Z}_p^*$ and $H_3 : G_2 \times \{0,1\}^* \to \mathbb{Z}_p^*$. The KGC computes a user's private key as $D_{ID} = sH_1(ID)$ where ID is the user's identity.

- **Prove** A sender, ID_S, computes $Q_R = H_1(ID_R)$ and $\delta = e(Q_R, Q_R)^r$ for $r \in_R \mathbb{Z}_p^*$. Then the sender computes $\Lambda = H_2(\delta, T)$ where $T \in \mathbb{Z}_p^*$ is a timestamp, and $U = rQ_R - \Lambda D_{ID_S}$, and $MAC = H_3(\delta, m)$. The protocol transcript is $c = (ID_S, \Lambda, U, T, MAC, m)$.
- **Verify** The receiver checks the validity of the timestamp. Then the receiver computes $\delta' = e(U, Q_R)e(Q_S, D_{ID_R})^\Lambda$ and verifies whether $\Lambda = H_2(\delta', T)$ and $MAC = H_3(\delta', m)$.

- **The Attack**
  - $\mathcal{A}$ reveals the value δ of a session and computes

$$e(Q_S, Q_R)^s = (\delta/e(U, Q_R))^{\Lambda^{-1}}.$$

  - $\mathcal{A}$ requests ID_S to send a transcript $(ID_S, \Lambda_S, U_S, T_S, MAC_S, m_S)$.
  - $\mathcal{A}$ computes $\delta_{\mathcal{A}} = e(U_S, Q_R)(e(Q_S, Q_R)^s)^{\Lambda_S}$. A forged transcript is $(ID_S, \Lambda_S, U_S, T_S, MAC', m')$, where m' is an arbitrary message and $MAC' = H_3(\delta_{\mathcal{A}}, m')$.
  - The forged transcript can be accepted according to the protocol. So the protocol is not an MI-authenticator.

Other protocols are analyzed similarly. We give a table in the Section 6 as a summary and comparison.

4   A New Paradigm

4.1   Selectively Unforgeable But Existentially Forgeable Signatures

In the new paradigm, we use a general signature scheme $(KGen, Sign, Ver)$. The scheme is existentially forgeable but not selectively forgeable. The existentially forged signature should be indistinguishable from a real signature. We define its security using the following game. We assume a simulator Sim and a PPT forger $\mathcal{F}$. They play a game as follows:

1. Sim runs $KGen$ to produce a key pair (sk_S, pk_S) for a signer and gives pk_S to $\mathcal{F}$.
2. Sim produces a challenge message m^* and gives it to $\mathcal{F}$;
3. $\mathcal{F}$ produces a signature δ^* for m^*;
4. The forger wins if the pair (m^*, δ^*) is qualified.

We define that a signature scheme is selectively unforgeable but existentially forgeable (SUEF) if a forger cannot win the above game in polynomial time t with a non-negligible probability ϵ, and a PPT adversary cannot distinguish an existentially forged signature from a real one.

4.2 The Construction

We construct a deniable MI-authenticator λ_{DMI} as follows:

- The initialization function I invokes a group generation algorithm to produce the parameters (p, q, g) for a group $\mathbb{G}$, where $p = 2q + 1$, and $g \in_R \mathbb{Z}_p^*$ is a generator with an order q. Let E denote a symmetric encryption algorithm, such that for any key k_e of length l, the function E_{k_e} is a permutation over b-bit strings. Let $H : \{0, 1\}^* \rightarrow \{0, 1\}^l$ be secure hash functions.

  Then I invokes, once for each party, the $KGen$ algorithm to produce key pairs (sk_i, pk_i) for P_i. Each party is assigned a secrete trapdoor key $t_i \in_R \mathbb{Z}_q$ and a public trapdoor key $T_i = g^{t_i}$.

  The public information is the system parameters, all public keys and all public trapdoor keys: $I_0 = (p, q, g, H, E, pk_1, T_1, \ldots, pk_n, T_n)$. The private information for P_i is $I_i = (sk_i, t_i)$.

- When activated, within party P_i and with an external request (m, P_j), the protocol λ_{DMI} invokes a two party protocol $\hat{\lambda}_{DMI}$ that proceeds as follows. P_i sends a transcript: $m, P_i, e = (T_j)^r, \delta = Sign_{sk_i}(E_{H(m, P_i, P_j)}(g^r))'$ to P_j, where $r \in_R \mathbb{Z}_q$. Then P_i produces an output 'P_i sent m to P_j'.

- Upon receipt of 'message: m, P_i, e, δ', party P_j computes $g^r = e^{t_i^{-1}}$ and verifies whether the signature δ is valid for the value $E_{H(m, P_i, P_j)}(g^r)$. If the verification is true, party P_j outputs 'P_j identified the source of m as P_i'.

Pictorially, the protocol is described in Fig.1.

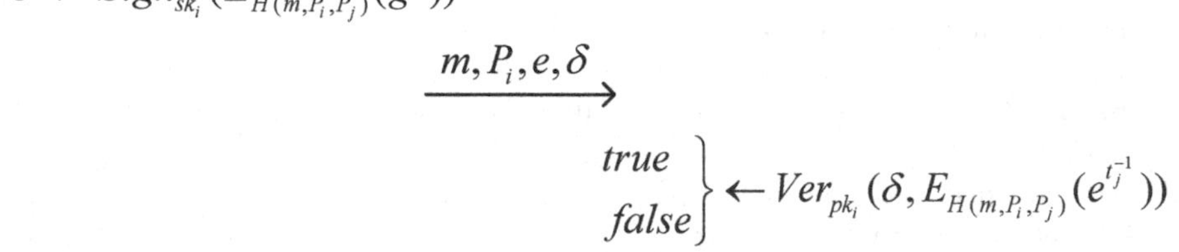

$$P_i \qquad\qquad\qquad\qquad\qquad P_j$$

$$r \in_R \mathbb{Z}_q$$

$$e \leftarrow (T_j)^r$$

$$\delta \leftarrow Sign_{sk_i}(E_{H(m, P_i, P_j)}(g^r))$$

$$\xrightarrow{\quad m, P_i, e, \delta \quad}$$

$$\left.\begin{array}{c} true \\ false \end{array}\right\} \leftarrow Ver_{pk_i}(\delta, E_{H(m, P_i, P_j)}(e^{t_j^{-1}}))$$

Fig. 1. A new paradigm for the non-interactive deniable authentication

4.3   The Proofs

Proposition 1. *If the signature scheme is (t_s, ϵ_s) SUEF secure, the CDH problem is (t_c, ϵ_c) hard, and the symmetric encryption E and decryption E^{-1} are modeled by random oracles, the protocol λ_{DMI} emulates the protocol MI in the unauthenticated-links network.*

Proof. Let $\mathcal{U}$ be an UM-adversary that interacts with λ_{DMI}. We construct an AM-adversary $\mathcal{A}$ such that $AUTH_{MI,\mathcal{A}}() \stackrel{c}{=} UNAUTH_{\lambda_{DMI},\mathcal{U}}()$.

Adversary $\mathcal{A}$ runs $\mathcal{U}$ on a simulated interaction with a set of parties running λ_{DMI}.

- $\mathcal{A}$ chooses and distributes keys for the imitated parties, according to function I.
- When $\mathcal{U}$ activates an imitated party A' for sending a message (m, A', e, δ) to an imitated party B', the adversary $\mathcal{A}$ activates the party A in the authenticated network to send m to B.
- When an imitated party B' produces 'B' identified the source of $\hat{m}$ as A''', the adversary $\mathcal{A}$ activates the party B in the authenticated-links model with the incoming message $\hat{m}$ from A.
- When $\mathcal{U}$ corrupts a party, $\mathcal{A}$ corrupts the same party in the authenticated network and hands the corresponding information from the simulated run to $\mathcal{U}$.
- When $\mathcal{U}$ reveals the session state, $\mathcal{A}$ hands the values from the internal states of imitated parties to $\mathcal{U}$. Finally, $\mathcal{A}$ produces whatever $\mathcal{U}$ produces.

Let $\mathcal{B}$ denotes the event that the imitated party B' produces 'B' identified the source of $\hat{m}$ as A''' where A' and B' are uncorrupted and the message $(\hat{m}, A, B)$ is not currently in the authentic message set M. This implies that A was not activated for sending $\hat{m}$ to B. If the event $\mathcal{B}$ never happens, the simulation of $\mathcal{A}$ is perfect and $AUTH_{MT,\mathcal{A}}() \stackrel{c}{=} UNAUTH_{\lambda_{DMT},\mathcal{U}}()$.

It remains to show that event $\mathcal{B}$ occurs only with negligible probability. Assume the event $\mathcal{B}$ occurs with probability ϵ within time t. We construct a forger $\mathcal{F}$ that breaks the underlying signature scheme or solves a CDH problem. The forger $\mathcal{F}$ interacts with Sim as specified in Section 4.1 to obtain (pk_S, m^*). The forger $\mathcal{F}$ also gets a CDH problem instance (g^x, g^y). The strategy of $\mathcal{F}$ is to run the adversary $\mathcal{U}$.

$\mathcal{F}$ provides $\mathcal{U}$ two random oracles O_E and O_E^{-1} for the computations of E and E^{-1}.

- O_E maintains an E_{list} recording all inputs and outputs. The input to O_E includes a message m, identities of a sender P and a receiver Q, and an element $R \in \mathbb{G}$. If the input is not in the E_{list}, O_E randomly selects a value $c \in \{0,1\}^{|p|}$ as an output, where $|p|$ denotes the bit length of p. The E_{list} is updated by adding the input-output record (m, P, Q, R, c).
- O_E^{-1} maintains an R_{list} which is empty at the beginning. O_E^{-1} takes as input (m, P, Q, c). If there is a match entry in the E_{list} indexed by the input,

O_E returns the value R. Else O_E^{-1} produces an output $R = g^r \in \mathbb{G}$ where $r \in_R \mathbb{Z}_q^*$. O_E^{-1} adds a record (m, P, Q, R, c) in the E_{list} and a record (R, r) in the R_{list}.

Now we specify the game between the forger $\mathcal{F}$ and the adversary $\mathcal{U}$.

- $\mathcal{F}$ runs the function I to set parameters and keys for a set of imitated parties who run the protocol λ_{DMI}. Then the public verification key associated with some party P^*, chosen at random, is replaced by the key pk_S. $\mathcal{F}$ gives all public information to $\mathcal{U}$.
- If during the simulation, P^* is queried to generate a transcript for a message m to a party Q, the forger $\mathcal{F}$ existentially forges a message-signature pair (m_F, δ_F) w.r.t. the key pk_S. Then $\mathcal{F}$ queries the O_E^{-1} oracle with (m, P^*, Q, m_F) to get a reply R. $\mathcal{F}$ computes $e = R^{t_Q}$ and replies to the adversary $\mathcal{U}$ the transcript (m, P^*, e, δ_F).
- Other message delivery queries are responded according to the protocol specification with the oracle access to O_E.
- If $\mathcal{U}$ corrupts a party, the private key of the party is given to $\mathcal{U}$. If $\mathcal{U}$ corrupts P^*, $\mathcal{F}$ fails.
- If $\mathcal{U}$ queries to reveal the session states of one run of a party, $\mathcal{F}$ gives the value r of that run to $\mathcal{U}$. $\mathcal{F}$ will find a value r in the R_{list} as a response if the party is P^*.

If a party Q^* is uncorrupted, and outputs 'Q^* identified the source of m as P^*' but P^* was not activated to send m to Q^*, the forger $\mathcal{F}$ finds the last message received by Q^* such as $(m, P^*, e^* = (T_{Q^*})^{r^*}, \delta^* = Sign_{sk_{P^*}}(E_{H(m,P^*,Q^*)}(g^{r^*})))$. Then $\mathcal{F}$ tries to find a match in the R_{list} indexed by $e^{*t_{Q^*}^{-1}}$.

- If there is no match in the R_{list}, $\mathcal{F}$ rewinds $\mathcal{U}$ to the point where $(m, P^*, Q^*, e^{*t_{Q^*}^{-1}})$ is queried to the oracle O_E. This time the forger $\mathcal{F}$ sets the output of O_E as $c = m^*$. Then the forger $\mathcal{F}$ runs $\mathcal{U}$ again. According to the general forking lemma [26], there is a non-negligible probability for $\mathcal{U}$ to produce another qualified signature for the query $(m, P^*, Q^*, e^{*t_{Q^*}^{-1}})$. The signature is returned to Sim as a response by the forger $\mathcal{F}$.
- If there is a match in the R_{list}, $\mathcal{F}$ resets the public key of P^* as g^x and runs $\mathcal{U}$ again. If a party Q' is uncorrupted, and outputs 'Q' identified the source of m' as P^*' but P^* was not activated to send m' to Q', the forger $\mathcal{F}$ finds out the last message received by Q' such as $(m', P^*, e' = (T_{Q'})^{r^*}, \delta^* = Sign_{sk_{P^*}}(E_{H(m',P^*,Q')}(g^{r^*}))$. Then $\mathcal{F}$ finds the match (R', r') in the R_{list} indexed by $e'^{t_{Q'}^{-1}}$ and the match (m', P^*, Q', R', c') in the E_{list} indexed by (m', P^*, Q', R').

  Then $\mathcal{F}$ rewinds $\mathcal{U}$ to the point when (m', P^*, Q', c') is queried to the oracle O_E^{-1}. This time the forger $\mathcal{F}$ sets the output of O_E^{-1} as g^y. Note that P^* was not activated to send m' to Q'. There is no session state about (m', P^*, Q') in the party P^*. So there is no impact on the session state real quires of $\mathcal{U}$. Then the forger $\mathcal{F}$ runs $\mathcal{U}$ again. According to the general forking lemma, there is a non-negligible probability for $\mathcal{U}$ to produce another qualified signature for the query (m', P^*, Q', c'). $\mathcal{F}$ takes the value e' in the signature as an output about the CDH problem.

Next we analyze the success probability of the forger $\mathcal{F}$ if the forger can finish the game. Suppose the event has a probability ε that $\mathcal{F}$ does not find a match in the R_{list}. In this case, the forger can succeed if the party P^* is just the target for the adversary $\mathcal{U}$ to impersonate, and if $\mathcal{U}$ outputs another qualified transcript for the same $(m^*, P^*, Q^*, e^{*t_{Q^*}^{-1}})$ after the rewinding action. As there are n imitated parties, the probability is $1/n$ that the special P^* is selected as a target. Suppose there are q_e queries to the oracle O_E. Then the probability, according to the general forking lemma, is at least $\epsilon(\epsilon/q_e - 1/q)$ that the adversary $\mathcal{U}$ produces another qualified signature for the same query. So the success probability of the forger $\mathcal{F}$ is $\varepsilon\epsilon/n(\epsilon/q_e - 1/q)$.

The other event has a probability $(1 - \varepsilon)$ that $\mathcal{F}$ finds a match in the R_{list}. Since $\mathcal{F}$ runs $\mathcal{U}$ from the beginning, there is another probability $(1 - \varepsilon)$ that $\mathcal{F}$ finds a match in R_{list} indexed by $e'^{t_{Q'}^{-1}}$. The party P^* is selected as the target by $\mathcal{U}$ with a probability $1/n$. Suppose there are q_r queries to the oracle O_E^{-1}. The successful rewinding probability is still $\epsilon(\epsilon/q_r - 1/q)$. So the success probability in this case is $(1 - \varepsilon)^2\epsilon/n(\epsilon/q_r - 1/q)$.

There is a bad event to make the forger stop the game abnormally. The event is that the P^* is corrupted. Since P^* is selected randomly, the probability to corrupt P^* is $1/n$. The probability of $\mathcal{F}$ to finish the game normally is at least $(1 - 1/n)$.

In summary, the success probability of $\mathcal{F}$ to the SUEF signature is

$$\epsilon_s = \frac{(n-1)\varepsilon\epsilon(q\epsilon - q_e)}{n^2 qq_e} \geq \varepsilon\frac{\epsilon(q\epsilon - q_e)}{2nqq_e}$$

and the success probability to the CDH problem is

$$\epsilon_c = \frac{(n-1)(1-\varepsilon)^2\epsilon(q\epsilon - q_r)}{n^2 qq_r} \geq (1-\varepsilon)^2\frac{\epsilon(q\epsilon - q_r)}{2nqq_r}$$

Finally, we analyze the run time of the forger $\mathcal{F}$. The simulation of O_E^{-1} needs one exponentiation time τ_e for each query. Suppose the existential forgery time of $\mathcal{F}$ is τ_f. When P^* is queried to produce a transcript, there are two times τ_e and one τ_f for each query. Suppose the P^* is queried q_s times. The time is about $t + (q_r + 2q_s)\tau_e + q_s\tau_f$ for $\mathcal{F}$ to wait until the event $\mathcal{B}$ occurs. The rewinding needs about half the above time. So the overall time for $\mathcal{F}$ to break the SUEF signature is about $t_s \approx 1.5(t + (q_r + 2q_s)\tau_e + q_s\tau_f)$. To solve the CDH problem, $\mathcal{F}$ has to run the game again after the event $\mathcal{B}$ occurs. The overall time for $\mathcal{F}$ to solve the CDH problem is about $t_c \approx 2.5(t + (q_r + 2q_s)\tau_e + q_s\tau_f)$. $\quad\square$

Remark 6. It is not new to model a symmetric encryption and decryption as random oracles. This method appeared in [11] when the security of a ring signature was proven.

Remark 7. The general forking lemma is applicable in contexts *other than* standard signature schemes since it only considers the inputs and outputs. We refer our readers to [26] for the detailed reasons.

Proposition 2. *The protocol λ_{DMI} is transcript deniable if the DDH problem is hard.*

Proof. Suppose a simulator S_λ that on input a message m from A to B, produces a transcript as follows:

- Existentially forge a signature δ_F for a random message.
- Randomly select $e_F \in_R \mathbb{G}$.
- Set the simulated transcript as (m, A, e_F, δ_F).

Suppose an adversary $\mathcal{D}$ that claims to distinguish the simulated transcript from a real one without the private key of B and session-state values for the simulated transcript and the real one with a probability ϵ.

Suppose a DDH problem solver S_D which takes as input a DDH problem instance (g, g^x, g^y, g^z). S_D plays with $\mathcal{D}$ using S_λ.

- S_D sets n-imitated parties and runs the function I for them with an exception that the public trapdoor key of a random party B^* is g^y.
- S_D answers queries of $\mathcal{D}$ as follows.
  - When a party is required to send a real message, S_D runs the party according to the protocol specification. When a simulated message is required, S_D runs the S_λ for the party.
  - When a party is required to receive a message, S_D runs according to the protocol specification.
  - When $\mathcal{D}$ corrupts a party, the private key of the party is given to $\mathcal{D}$. If B^* is corrupted, S_D fails.
  - When $\mathcal{D}$ tries to reveal session-state values, S_D gives the values to $\mathcal{D}$.
- S_D produces a challenge message

$$m, A^*, e = g^z, \delta = Sign_{sk_{A^*}}(E_{H(m,A^*,B^*)}(g^x))$$

  using g^x, g^z and the private key of A^*.
- S_D continues to answer queries of $\mathcal{D}$. However, the session-state values about the challenge is not allowed to be revealed. And obviously, the challenge message should not be received by B^*.
- Finally, $\mathcal{D}$ produces a bit $b = 0$ to denote the challenge message is a real transcript, or $b = 1$ otherwise.
- S_D guesses the input tuple is a DDH tuple if $b = 0$ and is not if $b = 1$.

If the input tuple is a DDH tuple, the challenge message is just a qualified transcript. That is, it is a possible real transcript.

Comparatively, if the tuple is not a DDH tuple, the challenge message is not qualified. It is indistinguishable from a simulated one. At first, the signature part is indistinguishable since it is an SUEF signature. Secondly, the value e and e_F are both random values in the group $\mathbb{G}$.

So S_D has the same advantage as $\mathcal{D}$ if the game does not fail. As B^* is selected randomly, the failure probability is $1/n$. So the success probability of S_D is at least $(1 - 1/n)\epsilon \geq \epsilon/2$. $\square$

Proposition 3. *The protocol λ_{DMI} is full deniable.*

Proof. Suppose a simulator $S_\lambda^{pri_B}$ that on input a message m from A to B, produces a transcript as follows:

1. Existentially forge a signature δ_F for a random message m_F.
2. Compute $R = E_{H(m,A,B)}^{-1}(m_F)$. If $R \notin \mathbb{G}$, return to step 1. Else compute $e_F = R^{t_B}$.
3. Set the simulated transcript as (m, A, e_F, δ_F).

The values δ_F and δ are indistinguishable, since we use an SUEF signature.

The randomness of e in a real transcript is determined by the effective random value r. That is, the selecting of r will lead to a valid signature. Suppose the number of effective r is denoted by $\#M_r$.

The randomness of e_F is determined by the random message m_F and the re-computing of a forged message-signature pair. Suppose the number of effective m_F is denoted by $\#M_F$. Then when $\#M_F \approx \#M_r$, the simulated transcripts are indistinguishable from real ones.

Remark 8. The numbers $\#M_F$ and $\#M_r$ are related to concrete protocols. A concrete protocol will prove $\#M_F \approx \#M_r$.

5   The Concrete Protocol

The signature scheme of Rabin [24] is a satisfactory SUEF scheme if the hash function is not used. At first, if an adversary can win the attacking game in section 4.1, the adversary can be used to solve the integer factorization problem. So it is a secure SUEF scheme. Secondly, a forged signature has the same distribution as a real one. We set the big primes in the system parameters as the Blum numbers, and require that the real signature is a quadratic residue, which means that it is the principal square root. A forged signature is also a quadratic residue by design. So it has the indistinguishable property.

The concrete protocol is as follows.

- *Setup:* Assume a sender's public key is (N, p, q, g, H) where $N = p_b q_b$ for two big Blum primes p_b and q_b satisfying $|p_b| = |q_b|$, and (p, q, g, H) is the same as the general construction. The sender's private key is (p_b, q_b). An honest receiver's trapdoor key is $t_R \in \mathbb{Z}_q$. The public trapdoor key is $T_R = g^{t_R}$. We require that $|p| = |N| + 1$.

- *Prove:* To send a message m, the sender randomly selects $r \in \mathbb{Z}_q$ and computes $R_p = g^r$. Then it computes $\kappa = H(m, ID_S, ID_R)$. If $R = E_\kappa(R_p)$ is not bigger than N or $R \mod N$ is not a quadratic residue, another r is selected. Else, the sender calculates $e \leftarrow (T_R)^r$, and $\delta \leftarrow (R)^{1/2} \mod N$, where δ is the principal square root. Then the sender sends (m, ID_S, e, δ) to the receiver.
- *Verify:* The receiver checks the equation $E_{H(m,ID_S,ID_R)}(e^{t_R^{-1}}) = \delta^2 \mod N$. If it holds, the receiver accepts and believes that the message source is ID_S, else rejects.
- *Simulate for full deniability:* With a message m and reviver's trapdoor key t_R, a simulator works as follows. The simulator randomly selects $r_x \in_R \mathbb{Z}_N^*$ and computes $\delta_F = r_x^2 \mod N$, $m_F = \delta_F^2 \mod N$. If $\delta_F^2 \leq N$, another r_x is selected. If $R_p = E_{H(m,ID_S,ID_R)}^{-1}(m_F + \tau N) \notin \mathbb{G}$, another r_x is selected, where $\tau \in \{0, \ldots, \lfloor p/N \rfloor\}$ is random selected if multiple values are satisfactory. Else $e_F = R_p^{t_R}$. The message simulated is (m, ID_S, e_F, δ_F).
- *Simulate for transcript deniability:* It is the same as the above simulation procedure with an exception that the value e_F is now randomly selected from the group $\mathbb{G}$.

We need to prove that $\#M_r \approx \#M_F$ to satisfy the Proposition 3.

According to the simulation method, m_F is a quadratic residue. Considering the re-selecting, the number of effective m_F is $\#M_F = \omega 1/2(p_b - 1)(q_b - 1)/4 \approx \omega N/8$, where $1 < \omega < 2$. That is about half of the number of quadratic residues in the group $\mathbb{Z}_N$. The coefficient ω is for $p > N$ and the real distributions of quadratic residues in $\mathbb{Z}_N$ and of the group $\mathbb{G}$ in $\mathbb{Z}_p$. The number of effective r, $\#M_r$, is about the number of elements in the set

$$\{r | E_\kappa(g^r) \mod N \text{ is a quadratic residue}\}.$$

That number is equivalent to the number of elements in the set

$$\{\delta | \delta \in \mathbb{Z}_N \text{ is a principal square root} \wedge E_\kappa^{-1}(\delta^2 \mod N + \tau N) \in \mathbb{G}\},$$

which is just the total number of δ_F in the simulation algorithm. So $\#M_F \approx \#M_r$.

6   Comparison

We give a table to summarize the analysis results and compare our paradigm with other protocols. In the table, the left column is the literatures. Except the first three rows, all schemes are MAC based. The other three columns are the properties of NIDA protocols. If a protocol is an "MI-Authenticator", it is unforgeable. The meanings of "Transcript Deniability" and "Full Deniability" are defined in the Definitions 3 and 4 in the Section 3. The symbol "Yes" denotes that the protocol in the literature enjoys the property of that column.

Table 1. Analysis Results of NIDA Protocols

	MI-Authenticator	Transcript Deniability	Full Deniability
[9]	Yes	No	Yes
[10]	Yes	No	No
[5]	Yes	No	Yes
[6]	No	Yes	Yes
[8]	No	No	Yes
[12]	No	No	No
[13]	No	No	No
[14]	No	No	No
[15]	No	No	No
[16]	No	Yes	Yes
[17]	No	No	Yes
[18]	No	No	No
[19]	No	No	Yes
[20]	Yes	No	No
[21]	Yes	No	No
[22]	No	No	Yes
Ours	Yes	Yes	Yes

From the table, we observe the following points.

- There are two protocols which enjoy the transcript deniability property.
- There are two MAC based protocols which are MI-authenticators.
- There is no protocol that is an MI-authenticator, and is transcript and full deniable.

The above observations make our scheme unique. It is an MI-authenticator, and enjoys the properties of transcript deniability and full deniability.

7 Conclusion

We describe a formal model for non-interactive deniable authentication protocols, which captures the KCI and SSR attacks. Then we analyze some NIDA protocols in the model, and we show the vulnerabilities of two protocols. Finally, we give a new paradigm to construct a desirable protocol with proofs and a concrete protocol.

Acknowledgment. This work is supported by the National Natural Science Foundation of China (Nos. 60970144, 60803135, 61070168, 61003244, 61103199), Fundamental Research Funds for the Central Universities (Nos. 10lgpy31, 11lgpy71, 11lgzd06, 10lgzd14), Specialized Research Fund for the Doctoral Program of Higher Education for New Teachers (No. 20090171120006), and Beijing Municipal Natural Science Foundation(No. 4112052).

References

1. Dwork, C., Naor, M., Sahai, A.: Concurrent Zero Knowledge. Journal of the ACM 51(6), 851–898 (2004)
2. Borisov, N., Goldberg, I., Brewer, E.: Off-the-record communication, or, why not to use PGP. In: Proceedings of the 2004 ACM Workshop on Privacy in the Electronic Society (WPES 2004), pp. 77–84. ACM, New York (2004)
3. IPSEC Working Group: Design Rationale for IKEv2. INTERNET-DRAFT, draft-ietf-ipsec-ikev2-rationale-00.txt, http://tools.ietf.org/html/draft-ietf-ipsec-ikev2-rationale-00
4. Shao, Z.: Efficient Deniable Authentication Protocol Based On Generalized Elgamal Signature Scheme. Computer Standards & Interfaces 26(5), 449–454 (2004)
5. Wang, B., Song, Z.: A non-interactive deniable authentication scheme based on designated receiver proofs. Information Sciences 179(6), 858–865 (2009)
6. Lee, W., Wu, C., Tsaur, W.: A novel authentication protocol using generalized ElGamal signature scheme. Information Sciences 177(6), 1376–1381 (2007)
7. Chou, J., Chen, Y., Huang, J.: A ID-Based Deniable Authentication Protocol on pairings, http://eprint.iacr.org/2006/335
8. Meng, B.: A secure Non-interactive Deniable Authentication Protocol with Strong Deniability Based on Discrete Logarithm Problem and its Application on Internet Voting Protocol. Information Technology Journal 8(3), 302–309 (2009)
9. Lu, R., Cao, Z., Wang, S., Bao, H.: A New ID-Based Deniable Authentication Protocol. Informatica 18(1), 67–78 (2007)
10. Susilo, W., Mu, Y.: Non-interactive Deniable Ring Authentication. In: Lim, J.-I., Lee, D.-H. (eds.) ICISC 2003. LNCS, vol. 2971, pp. 386–401. Springer, Heidelberg (2004)
11. Rivest, R.L., Shamir, A., Tauman, Y.: How to Leak a Secret. In: Boyd, C. (ed.) ASIACRYPT 2001. LNCS, vol. 2248, pp. 552–565. Springer, Heidelberg (2001)
12. Lu, R., Cao, Z.: Non-interactive deniable authentication protocol based on factoring. Computer Standards & Interfaces 27(4), 401–405 (2005)
13. Lu, R., Cao, Z.: A new deniable authentication protocol from bilinear pairings. Applied Mathematics and Computation 168(2), 954–961 (2005)
14. Qian, H., Cao, Z., Wang, L., Xue, Q.S.: Efficient non-interactive deniable authentication protocols. In: The Fifth International Conference on Computer and Information Technology, CIT 2005, pp. 673–679. IEEE (2005)
15. Shi, Y., Li, J.: Identity-based deniable authentication protocol. Electronics Letters 41(5), 241–242 (2005)
16. Brown, D.: Deniable Authentication with RSA and Multicasting, http://eprint.iacr.org/2005/056
17. Huang, H., Chang, C.: An efficient deniable authentication protocol. In: International Conference on Cyberworlds, pp. 307–310. IEEE (2005)
18. Fan, C., Zhou, S., Li, F.: An Identity-based Restricted Deniable Authentication Protocol. In: 2009 IEEE International Symposium on Parallel and Distributed Processing with Applications, pp. 474–478. IEEE (2009)
19. Wu, T., Zhang, W., Liu, Z., Mu, C.: An efficient deniable authentication protocol. In: International Conference on Management and Service Science, MASS 2009, pp. 1–4 (2009)
20. Xin, X., Chen, D.: A Secure and Efficient Deniable Authentication Protocol. In: WASE International Conference on Information Engineering, ICIE 2009, vol. 2, pp. 172–175 (2009)

21. Xin, X., Chen, D.: ID-based Non-interactive Deniable Authentication Protocol from Pairings. In: International Conference on E-Business and Information System Security, EBISS 2009, pp. 1–4 (2009)
22. Wei, S.: ID-based non-interactive deniable authentication protocol. In: Fifth International Conference on Information Assurance and Security, IAS 2009, pp. 479–482 (2009)
23. Di Raimondo, M., Gennaro, R.: New approaches for deniable authentication. Journal of Cryptology 22(4), 572–615 (2009)
24. Rabin, M.O.: Digitalized signatures and public-key functions as intractable as factorization. MIT Laboratory for Computer Science Technical Report MIT/LCS/TR-212, MIT, MA (1979)
25. Li, G., Xin, X., Li, W.: An Enhanced Deniable Authentication Protocol. In: International Conference on Computational Intelligence and Security, CIS 2008, vol. 1, pp. 336–339. IEEE (2008)
26. Bellare, M., Neven, G.: Multi-Signatures in the Plain Public-Key Model and a General Forking Lemma. In: Proceedings of the 13th Association for Computing Machinery (ACM) Conference on Computer and Communications Security (CCS), pp. 390–399. ACM, Alexandria (2006)

On the Probability Distribution
of the Carry Cells of Stream Ciphers
F-FCSR-H v2 and F-FCSR-H v3[*]

Haixin Song[1,2], Xiubin Fan[1], Chuankun Wu[1], and Dengguo Feng[1]

[1] State Key Laboratory of Information Security, Institute of Software,
Chinese Academy of Sciences, Beijing, 100190, China
[2] Graduate University of Chinese Academy of Sciences, Beijing, 100049, China
{songhaixin,fxb,ckwu,feng}@is.iscas.ac.cn

Abstract. F-FCSR-H v2 is one of the 8 final stream ciphers in the eS-
TREAM portfolio. However, it was broken by M. Hell and T. Johansson
at ASIACRYPT 2008 by exploiting the bias in the carry cells of a Galois
FCSR. In order to resist this attack, at SAC 2009 F. Arnault et $al.$ proposed the new stream cipher F-FCSR-H v3 based upon a ring FCSR. M.
Hell and T. Johansson only presented experimental results but no theoretical results for the success probability of their powerful attack against
F-FCSR-H v2. And so far there are no analytical results of F-FCSR-H
v3. This paper discusses the probability distribution of the carry cells of
F-FCSR-H v2 and F-FCSR-H v3. We build the probability model for the
carry cells of the two stream ciphers and prove that the consecutive output sequence of a single carry cell is a homogeneous Markov chain and
the inverse chain is also a homogeneous Markov chain. We also prove that
the probability of l consecutive outputs of a single carry cell to be zeros
is $(1/2) \cdot (3/4)^{l-1}$, which is a weakness of the carry cells of F-FCSR-H v2
and F-FCSR-H v3, noticing that $(1/2) \cdot (3/4)^{l-1} > 2^{-l}$ for $l > 1$. FCSR is
a finite-state automata, so its distribution is stable. Based on this fact,
we construct a system of equations using the law of total probability,
and present a theoretical probability of breaking F-FCSR-H v2 by solving the equations. Applying this technique to F-FCSR-H v3, we obtain
that the probability of all the 82 carry cells of F-FCSR-H v3 to be zeros
at the same clock is at least $2^{-64.29}$, which is much higher than 2^{-82}.
This is another weakness of the carry cells of F-FCSR-H v3. Our results
provide theoretical support to M.Hell and T.Johansson's cryptanalysis
of F-FCSR-H v2 and establish a theoretical foundation for further cryptanalysis of F-FCSR-H v3.

Keywords: stream cipher, F-FCSR-H v2, F-FCSR-H v3, carry cell,
probability distribution.

---

[*] This work was supported by the Natural Science Foundation of China (Grant No.
60833008 and 60902024).

C.-K. Wu, M. Yung, and D. Lin (Eds.): Inscrypt 2011, LNCS 7537, pp. 160–178, 2012.

1   Introduction

In 1993, Klapper and Goresky initially proposed the idea of using FCSRs to generate sequences for cryptographic applications [7]. F-FCSR-H v2 [1] is a hardware-oriented stream cipher designed by F. Arnault, T.P. Berger, and C. Lauradoux in 2006. It was selected as one of the 4 final hardware-oriented stream cipher candidates in the eSTREAM [3] portfolio. However, M. Hell and T. Johansson broke F-FCSR-H v2 in real time [6] at ASIACRYPT 2008 by exploiting the bias in the carry cells of a Galois FCSR. In order to resist this attack, at SAC 2009 F. Arnault *et al.* proposed the new stream cipher F-FCSR-H v3 [2] based upon a ring FCSR.

An FCSR is similar to LFSRs, but it performs operations with carries. The high non-linearity of the FCSR transition function provides an intrinsic resistance to algebraic attacks. It has several interesting properties: proven long period, non-degenerated states, good statistical properties [5,7,8] and it is simple and efficient, both in hardware and software implementation. However, it also has a weakness: the probability distribution of its carry cells is unbalanced. The reason that F-FCSR-H v2 is broken is just the imbalance of the distribution of the carry cells. In [6], M. Hell and T. Johansson only presented experimental results but no theoretical results for the distribution of the carry cells. And so far there are no analytical results for F-FCSR-H v3.

In this paper, we present the probability distribution of the carry cells of stream ciphers F-FCSR-H v2 and F-FCSR-H v3 and analyze the success probability of breaking F-FCSR-H v2. Although it is claimed in [2] to resist the attack in [6], our analysis shows that the distribution of the carry cells of F-FCSR-H v3 is still unbalanced. Our results provide theoretical support to Hell and Johansson's cryptanalysis and establish a theoretical foundation for further analysis of F-FCSR-H v3.

This paper is organized as follows: Section 2 briefly introduces the F-FCSR-H v2 and F-FCSR-H v3 algorithms. Sections 3 and 4 analyze the probability distribution of the carry cells of F-FCSR-H v2 and F-FCSR-H v3 respectively. Finally, Section 5 concludes this paper.

2   FCSR Architectures

There are three representations of Feedback with Carry Shift Registers(FCSRs): Fibonacci FCSRs [4], Galois FCSRs [4] and ring FCSRs [2]. A Fibonacci FCSR has a single feedback function which depends on multiple inputs. A Galois FCSR has multiple feedbacks which all share one common input. And a ring FCSR can be viewed as a trade-off between the two extreme cases. F-FCSR-H v2 is based on a Galois FCSR and F-FCSR-H v3 is based on a ring FCSR. In the following we briefly introduce the Galois FCSR and the ring FCSR used in F-FCSR-H v2 and F-FCSR-H v3. For more details about F-FCSR-H v2 and F-FCSR-H v3, please refer to [1,2].

2.1 Galois Architecture

A Galois FCSR consists of an r-bit main register $(m_0, \cdots, m_{r-1})$ with some fixed feedback positions $d_0, \cdots, d_{r-1}$. All the feedbacks are controlled by the cell m_0 and $r-1$ binary carry cells $(c_1, \cdots, c_{r-1})$. At time t, the state of a Galois FCSR is updated in the following way:

1. Compute the sums $x_i = m_{i+1} + c_{i+1}d_i + m_0 d_i$ for all i, $0 \le i < r$, here we define $m_r = 0$ and $c_r = 0$.
2. Update the state as follows: $m_i = x_i \bmod 2$ for all i, $0 \le i \le r-1$ and $c_{i+1} = x_i \bmod 2$ for all i, $0 \le i \le r-2$.

For the stream cipher F-FCSR-H v2, the size of the main register is $r = 160$, and the carry register contains 82 active cells. The feedback is determined by
$$d = (AE985DEF26619FC58623DC8AAF46D5903DD4254E).$$

The Galois FCSR architecture of the stream cipher F-FCSR-H v2 is shown in Figure 1.

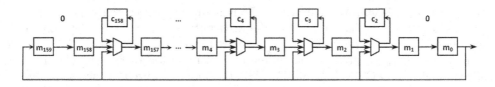

Fig. 1. The Galois FCSR architecture of F-FCSR-H v2

2.2 Ring Architecture

A ring FCSR is composed of a main register of r binary cells $M = (m_0, \cdots, m_{r-1})$, and a carry register of r integer cells $C = (c_0, \cdots, c_{r-1})$. It is updated using the following relations: (1) $M(t+1) = T \cdot M(t) + C(t) \bmod 2$, (2) $C(t+1) = T \cdot M(t) + C(t) \bmod 2$, where T is an $r \times r$ matrix with coefficients 0 or 1 in $\mathbb{Z}$, called transition matrix, $M(t) = (m_0(t), \cdots, m_{r-1}(t))$ is the state of the main register at time t, and $C(t) = (c_0(t), \cdots, c_{r-1}(t))$ is the state of the carry register at time t.

For the stream cipher F-FCSR-H v3, the size of the main shift register M is $r = 160$, and the carry register C contains 82 active cells. The feedback is determined by the transition matrix $T = (t_{i,j})_{0 \le i,j < 160}$, which is defined as follows:

1. For all $0 \le i < 160, t_{i,i+1 \bmod 160} = 1$;
2. For all $(i, j) \in S$, $t_{i,j} = 1$, where $S = \{(1, 121); (2, 133); (4, 44); (5, 82); (9, 38);$
$(11, 40); (12, 54); (14, 105); (15, 42); (16, 63); (18, 80); (19, 136); (20, 2);$
$(21, 35); (23, 28); (25, 137); (28, 131); (31, 102); (36, 41); (39, 138); (40, 31);$
$(42, 126); (44, 127); (45, 77); (46, 110); (47, 86); (48, 93); (49, 45); (51, 17);$
$(54, 8); (56, 7); (57, 150); (59, 25); (62, 51); (63, 129); (65, 130); (67, 122);$
$(73, 148); (75, 18); (77, 46); (79, 26); (80, 117); (81, 1); (84, 72); (86, 60);$

(89, 15); (90, 89); (91, 73); (93, 12); (94, 84); (102, 141); (104, 142); (107, 71);
(108, 152); (112, 92); (113, 83); (115, 23); (116, 32); (118, 50); (119, 43); (121, 34);
(124, 13); (125, 74); (127, 149); (128, 90); (129, 57); (130, 103); (131, 134);
(132, 155); (134, 98); (139, 24); (140, 61); (141, 104); (144, 48); (145, 14);
(148, 112); (150, 59); (153, 39); (156, 22); (157, 107); (158, 30); (159, 78)};
3. Otherwise, $t_{i,j}=0$.

The ring FCSR architecture of the stream cipher F-FCSR-H v3 is shown in
Figure 2.

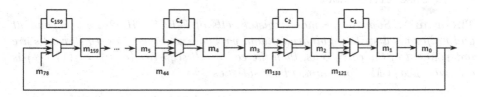

Fig. 2. The ring FCSR architecture of F-FCSR-H v3

3 On the Distribution of the Carry Cells of F-FCSR-H v2

As we know, the stream cipher F-FCSR-H v2 is broken because the carry register
behaves very far from random. Denote the state of the main register of F-FCSR-
H v2 at time t by $M(t) = (m_0(t), \cdots, m_{159}(t))$, and denote the state of the
82 active cells of the carry register at time t by $C(t) = (c_{j_1}(t), \cdots, c_{j_{82}}(t))$,
where $1 \leq j_1 < \cdots < j_{82} \leq 160$. In [6], the event E_{ZERO} is used to break
F-FCSR-H v2, which is given as follows: *Event* E_{ZERO} : $C(t) = C(t + 1) =
\cdots = C(t + 16) = (0, 0, \cdots, 0, 1)$. And the probability of E_{ZERO} is estimated to
be $Prob(E_{ZERO}) \approx 2^{-25.3}$ by experiments. However, no theoretical analysis is
given. In this section, we theoretically discuss the distribution of the carry cells
of F-FCSR-H v2.

Since the filtering function of F-FCSR-H v2 is linear, assume all the active
carry cells to be zeros during a number of consecutive clocks, then the system
would become linear. However, the assumption that a large number of consecutive zero feedback bits would push the weight of C to zero is wrong [6]. So [6]
uses the Event E_{ZERO} as defined above, where all the 82 carry cells except c_2
are zeros for 17 consecutive clocks, to break F-FCSR-H v2.

Although the main register cells may not be statistically independent, for
the convenience of our analysis, here we assume that the main register cells are
independent and uniformly distributed binary random variables defined on the
same probability space, and the main register cells are independent of the carry
cells. Although this assumption is not very correct, the conclusions we get in
this section meet with our experimental results very closely.

Next we will analyze the probability of a single carry cell to be zero for l
consecutive clocks, the probability of n carry cells to be zeros at the same clock,

and the probability of n carry cells to be zeros for l consecutive clocks. Then we will analyze the probability of n carry cells except one to be zeros at the same clock and for l consecutive clocks.

In theory it is possible to analyze the probability of the carry cells to be other values, but it has little relation to breaking the stream ciphers, so we won't discuss it. In this paper we will only discuss the probability of all the carry cells to be zeros and the probability of $n-1$ out of the n carry cells to be zeros.

3.1 The Probability of a Single Carry Cell to Be Zero for l Consecutive Clocks

Theorem 1. *Suppose the main register cells of F-FCSR-H v2 are independent and uniformly distributed binary random variables and the main register cells are independent of the carry cells, then the carry cell sequence $(c_{j_k}(0), c_{j_k}(1), \cdots)$ is a homogeneous Markov chain, which satisfies*

$$Prob(c_{j_k}(t+1) = a \mid c_{j_k}(t) = b) = \begin{cases} 3/4 \ if \ a \oplus b = 0 \\ 1/4 \ if \ a \oplus b = 1 \end{cases},$$

where $a, b \in \{0, 1\}$, $1 \le k \le 82$, $1 \le j_1 < \cdots < j_{82} \le 160$, and the transition probability matrix is $\begin{pmatrix} 3/4 & 1/4 \\ 1/4 & 3/4 \end{pmatrix}$.

Proof. According to the update function of a Galois FCSR, we have

$$c_{j_k}(t+1) = m_0(t)c_{j_k}(t) \ \oplus \ m_{j_k}(t)c_{j_k}(t) \ \oplus \ m_0(t)m_{j_k}(t).$$

This means that the state c_{j_k} at time $t+1$ only depends on the states m_0, m_{j_k} and c_{j_k} at time t. And m_0, m_{j_k} are independent of c_{j_k}, so the sequences $(c_{j_k}(0), c_{j_k}(1), \cdots)$, $1 \le k \le 82$, $1 \le j_1 < \cdots < j_{82} \le 160$ are all Markov chains. If $b = 0$, then $c_{j_k}(t+1) = m_0(t)m_{j_k}(t)$. So,

$$Prob(c_{j_k}(t+1) = a \mid c_{j_k}(t) = 0) = \begin{cases} 3/4 \ if \ a = 0 \\ 1/4 \ if \ a = 1 \end{cases}.$$

If $b = 1$, then $c_{j_k}(t+1) = m_0(t) \oplus m_{j_k}(t) \oplus m_0(t)m_{j_k}(t)$. So,

$$Prob(c_{j_k}(t+1) = a \mid c_{j_k}(t) = 1) = \begin{cases} 3/4 \ if \ a = 1 \\ 1/4 \ if \ a = 0 \end{cases}.$$

Therefore,

$$Prob(c_{j_k}(t+1) = a \mid c_{j_k}(t) = b) = \begin{cases} 3/4 \ if \ a \oplus b = 0 \\ 1/4 \ if \ a \oplus b = 1 \end{cases},$$

so the transition probability matrix is $\begin{pmatrix} 3/4 & 1/4 \\ 1/4 & 3/4 \end{pmatrix}$. And the transition probability doesn't depend on the time, so $(c_{j_k}(0), c_{j_k}(1), \cdots)$ is a homogeneous Markov chain. □

Theorem 2. *Suppose the main register cells of F-FCSR-H v2 are independent and uniformly distributed binary random variables and the main register cells are independent of the carry cells, then the inverse chain of a carry cell sequence $(c_{j_k}(0), c_{j_k}(1), \cdots)$, which is $(\cdots, c_{j_k}(t+1), c_{j_k}(t), \cdots, c_{j_k}(1), c_{j_k}(0))$, is a homogeneous Markov chain, and satisfies*

$$Prob(c_{j_k}(t) = b \mid c_{j_k}(t+1) = a) = \begin{cases} 3/4 \ if \ a \oplus b = 0 \\ 1/4 \ if \ a \oplus b = 1 \end{cases},$$

where $1 \leq k \leq 82$, $1 \leq j_1 < \cdots < j_{82} \leq 160$, and $a, b \in \{0, 1\}$.

Proof. Suppose the current time is $t + 1$. Since the sequence $(c_{j_k}(0), c_{j_k}(1), \cdots)$ is a Markov chain, we can get that $(c_{j_k}(t+2), c_{j_k}(t+3), \cdots)$ are all independent of $c_{j_k}(t)$. So $c_{j_k}(t)$ is also independent of $(c_{j_k}(t+2), c_{j_k}(t+3), \cdots)$. Therefore, the sequence $(\cdots, c_{j_k}(t+1), c_{j_k}(t), \cdots, c_{j_k}(1), c_{j_k}(0))$ is a Markov chain.
According to the update function of a Galois FCSR:

$$c_{j_k}(t+1) = m_0(t)c_{j_k}(t) \ \oplus \ m_{j_k}(t)c_{j_k}(t) \ \oplus \ m_0(t)m_{j_k}(t),$$

we can easily get that:

$$Prob(c_{j_k}(t) = b \mid c_{j_k}(t+1) = a) = \begin{cases} 3/4 \ if \ a \oplus b = 0 \\ 1/4 \ if \ a \oplus b = 1 \end{cases}.$$

The transition probability matrix is $\begin{pmatrix} 3/4 & 1/4 \\ 1/4 & 3/4 \end{pmatrix}$, and it does not depend on the time, so $(\cdots, c_{j_k}(t+1), c_{j_k}(t), \cdots, c_{j_k}(1), c_{j_k}(0))$ is a homogeneous Markov chain. $\qquad \square$

Theorem 3. *Suppose the main register cells of F-FCSR-H v2 are independent and uniformly distributed binary random variables and the main register cells are independent of the carry cells, then the probability of the homogeneous Markov chain $(c_{j_k}(0), c_{j_k}(1), \cdots)$ to be zero for l consecutive clocks is:*

$$Prob(c_{j_k}(t) = 0, c_{j_k}(t+1) = 0, \cdots, c_{j_k}(t+l-1) = 0) = \frac{1}{2} \cdot \left(\frac{3}{4}\right)^{l-1},$$

where $1 \leq k \leq 82$ and $1 \leq j_1 < \cdots < j_{82} \leq 160$.

Proof. If $l = 1$, $Prob(c_{j_k}(t) = 0) = 1/2$, so the theorem holds.

Suppose the theorem holds for $l-1$ consecutive clocks, then

$$Prob(c_{j_k}(t) = 0, c_{j_k}(t+1) = 0, \cdots, c_{j_k}(t+l-1) = 0)$$
$$= Prob(c_{j_k}(t+l-1) = 0 | c_{j_k}(t) = 0, c_{j_k}(t+1) = 0, \cdots, c_{j_k}(t+l-2) = 0) \cdot$$
$$Prob(c_{j_k}(t) = 0, c_{j_k}(t+1) = 0, \cdots, c_{j_k}(t+l-2) = 0)$$
$$= Prob(c_{j_k}(t+l-1) = 0 | c_{j_k}(t+l-2) = 0) \cdot$$
$$Prob(c_{j_k}(t) = 0, c_{j_k}(t+1) = 0, \cdots, c_{j_k}(t+l-2) = 0)$$
$$= \frac{3}{4} \cdot \frac{1}{2} \cdot \left(\frac{3}{4}\right)^{l-2}$$
$$= \frac{1}{2} \cdot \left(\frac{3}{4}\right)^{l-1},$$

which completes our proof. $\square$

As we know, the probability of an independent and uniformly distributed binary random sequence to be zero for l consecutive clocks is 2^{-l}, and $(1/2) \cdot (3/4)^{l-1} > 2^{-l}$ when $l > 1$. This shows that the output sequence of a single carry cell of F-FCSR-H v2 has poor randomness, and it can be distinguished from an independent and uniformly distributed binary random sequence.

3.2   The Probability of n Carry Cells to Be Zeros at the Same Clock

Theorem 4. *Suppose the main register cells of F-FCSR-H v2 are independent and uniformly distributed binary random variables and the main register cells are independent of the carry cells, then the probability of n carry cells to be zeros at the same clock is:*

$$Prob(c_{j_{i_1}}(t) = 0, \cdots, c_{j_{i_n}}(t) = 0) = \frac{1}{n+1},$$

where $1 \le n \le 82$, $1 \le i_1 < \cdots < i_n \le 82$ and $1 \le j_{i_1} < \cdots < j_{i_n} \le 160$.

Proof. If $n = 1$, $Prob(c_{j_{i_1}}(t) = 0) = 1/2$, so the theorem holds.

If $n > 1$, suppose the theorem holds for all $s < n$, where s is the number of carry cells. Let $Prob(c_{j_{i_1}}(t) = 0, \cdots, c_{j_{i_n}}(t) = 0) = x$. Next we will get x by solving equations.

$$x = Prob(c_{j_{i_1}}(t) = 0, \cdots, c_{j_{i_n}}(t) = 0)$$
$$= Prob(c_{j_{i_1}}(t+1) = 0, \cdots, c_{j_{i_n}}(t+1) = 0)$$
$$= Prob\left(\begin{array}{l} m_0(t)c_{j_{i_1}}(t) \oplus m_{j_{i_1}}(t)c_{j_{i_1}}(t) \oplus m_0(t)m_{j_{i_1}}(t) = 0, \\ \cdots \\ m_0(t)c_{j_{i_n}}(t) \oplus m_{j_{i_n}}(t)c_{j_{i_n}}(t) \oplus m_0(t)m_{j_{i_n}}(t) = 0 \end{array}\right)$$
$$= Prob\left(m_{j_{i_1}}(t)c_{j_{i_1}}(t) = 0, \cdots, m_{j_{i_n}}(t)c_{j_{i_n}}(t) = 0, m_0(t) = 0\right) +$$
$$Prob\left(\begin{array}{l} c_{j_{i_1}}(t) \oplus m_{j_{i_1}}(t)c_{j_{i_1}}(t) \oplus m_{j_{i_1}}(t) = 0, \cdots, \\ c_{j_{i_n}}(t) \oplus m_{j_{i_n}}(t)c_{j_{i_n}}(t) \oplus m_{j_{i_n}}(t) = 0, m_0(t) = 1 \end{array}\right)$$
$$= x_1 + x_2$$

Next we compute x_1 and x_2 respectively.

$$x_1 = Prob\big(m_{j_{i_1}}(t)c_{j_{i_1}}(t) = 0, \cdots, m_{j_{i_n}}(t)c_{j_{i_n}}(t) = 0, m_0(t) = 0\big)$$

$$= Prob\left(\begin{array}{l} m_{j_{i_1}}(t)c_{j_{i_1}}(t) = 0, \cdots, m_{j_{i_n}}(t)c_{j_{i_n}}(t) = 0, m_0(t) = 0, \\ m_{j_{i_1}}(t) = 0, \cdots, m_{j_{i_n}}(t) = 0 \end{array}\right) + \cdots +$$

$$Prob\left(\begin{array}{l} m_{j_{i_1}}(t)c_{j_{i_1}}(t) = 0, \cdots, m_{j_{i_n}}(t)c_{j_{i_n}}(t) = 0, m_0(t) = 0, \\ m_{j_{i_1}}(t) = 1, \cdots, m_{j_{i_n}}(t) = 1 \end{array}\right)$$

$$= \frac{1}{2^{n+1}} \cdot \left(\binom{n}{0} + \frac{1}{2}\binom{n}{1} + \frac{1}{3}\binom{n}{2} + \cdots + \frac{1}{n}\binom{n}{n-1} + x \cdot \binom{n}{n}\right)$$

$$= \frac{1}{2^{n+1}} \cdot \left(\frac{2 \cdot (2^n - 1)}{n+1} + x\right)$$

$$= \frac{2^n - 1}{2^n \cdot (n+1)} + \frac{1}{2^{n+1}} \cdot x$$

$$x_2 = Prob\left(\begin{array}{l} c_{j_{i_1}}(t) \oplus m_{j_{i_1}}(t)c_{j_{i_1}}(t) \oplus m_{j_{i_1}}(t) = 0, \cdots, \\ c_{j_{i_n}}(t) \oplus m_{j_{i_n}}(t)c_{j_{i_n}}(t) \oplus m_{j_{i_n}}(t) = 0, m_0(t) = 1 \end{array}\right)$$

$$= Prob\left(\begin{array}{l} c_{j_{i_1}}(t) \oplus m_{j_{i_1}}(t)c_{j_{i_1}}(t) \oplus m_{j_{i_1}}(t) = 0, \cdots, \\ c_{j_{i_n}}(t) \oplus m_{j_{i_n}}(t)c_{j_{i_n}}(t) \oplus m_{j_{i_n}}(t) = 0, m_0(t) = 1, \\ m_{j_{i_1}}(t) = 0, \cdots, m_{j_{i_n}}(t) = 0 \end{array}\right) + \cdots +$$

$$Prob\left(\begin{array}{l} c_{j_{i_1}}(t) \oplus m_{j_{i_1}}(t)c_{j_{i_1}}(t) \oplus m_{j_{i_1}}(t) = 0, \cdots, \\ c_{j_{i_n}}(t) \oplus m_{j_{i_n}}(t)c_{j_{i_n}}(t) \oplus m_{j_{i_n}}(t) = 0, m_0(t) = 1, \\ m_{j_{i_1}}(t) = 1, \cdots, m_{j_{i_n}}(t) = 1 \end{array}\right)$$

$$= \frac{1}{2^{n+1}} \cdot x + 0 + \cdots + 0$$

$$= \frac{1}{2^{n+1}} \cdot x$$

So we get

$$x = x_1 + x_2 = \left(\frac{2^n - 1}{2^n \cdot (n+1)} + \frac{1}{2^{n+1}} \cdot x\right) + \frac{1}{2^{n+1}} \cdot x$$

Then we have $x = \frac{1}{n+1}$. $\square$

As we know, the probability of n independent and uniformly distributed binary random variables to be zeros at the same clock is $\frac{1}{2^n}$. When n is large enough, $\frac{1}{n+1} \gg \frac{1}{2^n}$. Hence Theorem 4 indicates that the distribution of the carry cells of F-FCSR-H v2 is seriously unbalanced.

3.3   The Probability of n Carry Cells to Be Zeros for l Consecutive Clocks

Theorem 5. *Suppose the main register cells of F-FCSR-H v2 are independent and uniformly distributed binary random variables and the main register cells are* *independent of the carry cells. Let $Prob_0(n, l)$ denote the probability of n carry cells $c_{j_{i_1}}, \cdots, c_{j_{i_n}}$ to be zeros for l consecutive clocks, then*

$$Prob_0(n, l) = \frac{1}{n+1} \cdot \left(\frac{2^n + 1}{2^{n+1}}\right)^{l-1},$$

where $1 \leq n \leq 82$, $1 \leq i_1 < \cdots < i_n \leq 82$ and $1 \leq j_{i_1} < \cdots < j_{i_n} \leq 160$.

Proof. From Theorem 4 we know that the probability of n carry cells to be zeros at the same clock is $\frac{1}{n+1}$. Suppose n carry cells are all zeros at clock t. According to the update function of the carry cell c_{j_k}: $c_{j_k}(t+1) = m_0(t)c_{j_k}(t) \oplus m_{j_k}(t)c_{j_k}(t) \oplus m_0(t)m_{j_k}(t)$, next we discuss the values of $\left(m_0(t), m_0(t+1), \cdots, m_0(t+l-2)\right)$.

(1) If $\left(m_0(t), m_0(t+1), \cdots, m_0(t+l-2)\right)$ are all zeros, then the n carry cells will be all zeros for l consecutive clocks.

(2) If $m_0(t+s)$ is 1, where $0 \leq s \leq l-2$, $m_{j_{i_1}}(t+s), m_{j_{i_2}}(t+s), \cdots, m_{j_{i_n}}(t+s)$ must be all zeros to make $c_{j_{i_1}}, c_{j_{i_2}}, \cdots, c_{j_{i_n}}$ be all zeros for l consecutive clocks.

Therefore, the probability of $c_{j_{i_1}}, c_{j_{i_2}}, \cdots, c_{j_{i_n}}$ to be zeros for l consecutive clocks is

$$Prob_0(n, l) = \frac{1}{n+1} \cdot 2^{-(l-1)} \cdot \left(\binom{l-1}{0} + \frac{1}{2^n}\binom{l-1}{1} + \left(\frac{1}{2^n}\right)^2\binom{l-1}{2}\right.$$

$$\left. + \cdots + \left(\frac{1}{2^n}\right)^{l-1}\binom{l-1}{l-1}\right)$$

$$= \frac{1}{n+1} \cdot 2^{-(l-1)} \cdot \left(1 + \frac{1}{2^n}\right)^{l-1}$$

$$= \frac{1}{n+1} \cdot \left(\frac{2^n + 1}{2^{n+1}}\right)^{l-1},$$

which completes our proof. □

When $n = 1$, $Prob_0(1, l) = \frac{1}{2} \cdot \left(\frac{3}{4}\right)^{l-1}$, which is the probability of a signal carry cell to be zero for l consecutive clocks, and this coincides with Theorem 3. So Theorem 3 is a special case of Theorem 5.

The conclusion of Theorem 5 is based on the independence assumption. However, reference [6] points out that the assumption that a large number of consecutive zero feedback bits would push the weight of the carry register to zero is wrong. So in the following we analyze the probability of n carry cells except one to be zeros at the same clock and for l consecutive clocks, which is used in [6] to break F-FCSR-H v2.

3.4 The Probability of n Carry Cells Except One to Be Zeros at the Same Clock

Theorem 6. *Suppose the main register cells of F-FCSR-H v2 are independent and uniformly distributed binary random variables and the main register cells* *are independent of the carry cells, then the probability of n carry cells except one to be zeros at the same clock is $\frac{1}{n \cdot (n+1)}$, where $1 \leq n \leq 82$.*

Proof. Let the n carry cells be $c_{j_{i_1}}, \cdots, c_{j_{i_{n-1}}}, c_{j_{i_n}}$, where $1 \leq n \leq 82, 1 \leq i_1 < \cdots < i_{n-1} < i_n \leq 82$ and $1 \leq j_{i_1} < \cdots < j_{i_{n-1}} < j_{i_n} \leq 160$. Without loss of generality, suppose $c_{j_{i_n}} = 1$ and the other carry cells are all zeros.

Since

$$Prob\left(c_{j_{i_1}}(t) = 0, \cdots, c_{j_{i_{n-1}}}(t) = 0\right)$$

$$= Prob\left(c_{j_{i_1}}(t) = 0, \cdots, c_{j_{i_{n-1}}}(t) = 0, c_{j_{i_n}}(t) = 1\right) +$$

$$Prob\left(c_{j_{i_1}}(t) = 0, \cdots, c_{j_{i_{n-1}}}(t) = 0, c_{j_{i_n}}(t) = 0\right)$$

So from Theorem 4 we have

$$Prob\left(c_{j_{i_1}}(t) = 0, \cdots, c_{j_{i_{n-1}}}(t) = 0, c_{j_{i_n}}(t) = 1\right)$$

$$= Prob\left(c_{j_{i_1}}(t) = 0, \cdots, c_{j_{i_{n-1}}}(t) = 0\right) -$$

$$Prob\left(c_{j_{i_1}}(t) = 0, \cdots, c_{j_{i_{n-1}}}(t) = 0, c_{j_{i_n}}(t) = 0\right)$$

$$= \frac{1}{n} - \frac{1}{n+1}$$

$$= \frac{1}{n \cdot (n+1)},$$

which completes our proof. $\square$

3.5 The Probability of n Carry Cells to Be $(0, \cdots, 0, 1)$ for l Consecutive Clocks

Theorem 7. *Suppose the main register cells of F-FCSR-H v2 are independent and uniformly distributed binary random variables and the main register cells are independent of the carry cells. Let $Prob_1(n, l)$ denote the probability of n carry cells $(c_{j_{i_1}}, \cdots, c_{j_{i_{n-1}}}, c_{j_{i_n}})$ to be $(0, \cdots, 0, 1)$ for l consecutive clocks, then*

$$Prob_1(n, l) = \frac{1}{n \cdot (n+1)} \cdot \left(\left(\frac{1}{2}\right)^{2l-2} + \left(\frac{2^{n-1}+1}{2^n}\right)^{l-1} - \left(\frac{1}{2}\right)^{l-1}\right),$$

where $1 \leq n \leq 82, 1 \leq i_1 < \cdots < i_{n-1} < i_n \leq 82$ and $1 \leq j_{i_1} < \cdots < j_{i_{n-1}} < j_{i_n} \leq 160$.

Proof. From Theorem 6 we know that the probability of n carry cells to be $(0, \cdots, 0, 1)$ at the same clock is $\frac{1}{n \cdot (n+1)}$. Suppose the state of the n carry cells are $(0, \cdots, 0, 1)$ at time t. According to the update function of the carry cell c_{j_k}: $c_{j_k}(t+1) = m_0(t)c_{j_k}(t) \oplus m_{j_k}(t)c_{j_k}(t) \oplus m_0(t)m_{j_k}(t)$, next we discuss the values of $(m_0(t), m_0(t+1), \cdots, m_0(t+l-2))$.

(1) If $(m_0(t), m_0(t+1), \cdots, m_0(t+l-2))$ are all zeros, $m_{j_{i_n}}$ must be 1 to make $c_{j_{i_n}}$ still be 1.

(2) If $m_0(t+s)$ is 1, where $0 \le s \le l-2$, $m_{j_{i_1}}(t+s), \cdots, m_{j_{i_{n-2}}}(t+s), m_{j_{i_{n-1}}}(t+s)$ must be all zeros to make $c_{j_{i_1}}, \cdots, c_{j_{i_{n-1}}}, c_{j_{i_n}}$ be $(0, \cdots, 0, 1)$.

Therefore,

$$
\begin{aligned}
Prob_1(n, l) =& \frac{1}{n \cdot (n+1)} \cdot 2^{-(l-1)} \cdot \left(\left(\frac{1}{2}\right)^{l-1} \binom{l-1}{0} + \frac{1}{2^{n-1}} \binom{l-1}{1} + \right. \\
& \left. \left(\frac{1}{2^{n-1}}\right)^2 \binom{l-1}{2} + \cdots + \left(\frac{1}{2^{n-1}}\right)^{l-1} \binom{l-1}{l-1} \right) \\
=& \frac{1}{n \cdot (n+1)} \cdot 2^{-(l-1)} \cdot \left(\left(\frac{1}{2}\right)^{l-1} + \left(1 + \frac{1}{2^{n-1}}\right)^{l-1} - 1 \right) \\
=& \frac{1}{n \cdot (n+1)} \cdot \left(\left(\frac{1}{2}\right)^{2l-2} + \left(\frac{2^{n-1}+1}{2^n}\right)^{l-1} - \left(\frac{1}{2}\right)^{l-1} \right),
\end{aligned}
$$

which completes our proof.   □

The conclusion of Theorem 7 is a theoretical result based on the independence assumption. When $n = 82$ and $l = 17$, the probability of all the 82 carry cells to be $(0, 0, \cdots, 0, 1)$ for 17 consecutive clocks is $Prob_1(82, 17) = \frac{1}{82 \cdot 83} \cdot \left(\left(\frac{1}{2}\right)^{32} + \left(\frac{2^{81}+1}{2^{82}}\right)^{16} - \left(\frac{1}{2}\right)^{16} \right) \approx 2^{-44.7}$, which is smaller than the experimental probability $Prob(E_{ZERO}) \approx 2^{-25.3}$ in [6]. In the following we will explain why there is such a difference between the theoretical probability and the experimental probability in [6].

Firstly, the independence assumption will bring some bias. We assume that the main register cells are independent and they are independent of the carry cells, but actually they are correlated. Analyzing the Galois FCSR structure of F-FCSR-H v2 carefully(see Figure 1), we can reach the following conclusion. Suppose the values of all the 82 carry cells at time t are $C(t) = (0, 0, \cdots, 0, 1)$. If the event $E_m : (m_l(t), m_{l-1}(t), \cdots, m_2(t), m_1(t), m_0(t)) = (1, 1, \cdots, 1, 0, 0)$ occurs, then m_0 will be 0 during the next $l+1$ clocks, and C will be $(0, 0, \cdots, 0, 1)$ during the next l clocks. Hence the probability of C to be $(0, 0, \cdots, 0, 1)$ for l consecutive clocks is

$$
Prob_1(82, l) \ge Prob\big(C(t) = (0, 0, \cdots, 0, 1)\big) \cdot Prob(E_m) = \frac{1}{82 \cdot 83} \cdot 2^{-(l+1)} \quad (1)
$$

If $l = 17$, then $Prob_1(82, l) \ge \frac{1}{82 \cdot 83} \cdot 2^{-18} \approx 2^{-30.7}$. There is still a bias between it and the experimental result $Prob(E_{ZERO}) \approx 2^{-25.3}$ in [6].

Secondly, let $E_{c_{j_k}}$ denote the event that the carry cell c_{j_k} is 1 and the other 81 carry cells are all zeros, where $1 \le k \le 82$ and $1 \le j_1 < \cdots < j_{82} \le 160$. Using the independence assumption, each event $E_{c_{j_k}}$ occurs with the same probability. However, our experiments show that the event E_{c_2} occurs with higher probability than the other 81 events. Just the event E_{c_2} is used in [6] to attack F-FCSR-H v2. We randomly choose 32 sets of data as the initial states of F-FCSR-H v2, and for each set of data, we run F-FCSR-H v2 for $2^{30} = 1073741824$ clocks. An experimental probability distribution of $E_{c_{j_k}}$ is shown in Table 1.

Table 1. An experimental probability distribution of $E_{c_{j_k}}$

carry cell	frequecnce	$x(Prob = 2^{-x})$	carry cell	frequence	$x(Prob = 2^{-x})$
2	3302174	8.345	148	121393	13.111
3	130	22.972	149	119848	13.129
4	31226	15.070	152	123167	13.090
7	128815	13.025	154	114860	13.190
9	123126	13.090	155	86848	13.594
$\cdots$	$\cdots$	$\cdots$	156	28628	15.195

From the statistical results, we can see that $Prob(E_{c_2}) = 2^{-8.345}$ is the highest, $Prob(E_{c_3}) = 2^{-22.972}$ is small, $Prob(E_{c_{158}}) = 0$, and the probabilities of the other events are very close. The average value of the probabilities of the 82 events is $2^{-12.725}$. Theorem 6 shows that the probability that only one of n carry cells is 1 and the other $n-1$ carry cells are all zeros at the same clock is $\frac{1}{n \cdot (n+1)}$. When $n = 82$, $\frac{1}{n \cdot (n+1)} \approx 2^{-12.733}$, which coincides with the statistical average value $2^{-12.725}$. In formula (1), $Prob\big(C(t) = (0,0,\cdots,0,1)\big) = \frac{1}{82 \cdot 83}$ is the theoretical value computed on the independence assumption. Considering the Galois FCSR structure of F-FCSR-H v2 and the correlations between the main register and the carry cells, put the statistical value $Prob\big(C(t) = (0,0,\cdots,0,1)\big) = Prob(E_{c_2}) = 2^{-8.345}$ and $l = 17$ into formula (1), then we have $Prob_1(82,17) \geq Prob\big(C(t) = (0,0,\cdots,0,1)\big) \cdot Prob(E_m) = 2^{-8.345} \cdot 2^{-18} = 2^{-26.345}$, which is very close to the experimental result $Prob(E_{ZERO}) \approx 2^{-25.3}$ as in [6].

In what follows we discuss the probability distribution of the carry cells of F-FCSR-H v3, which is based on a ring FCSR. Though it is claimed in [2] to resist the attack in [6], our results show that the distribution of the carry cells of F-FCSR-H v3 is still unbalanced.

4   On the Distribution of the Carry Cells of F-FCSR-H v3

F-FCSR-H v3 is based on a ring FCSR (see Figure 2). The main register has 160 cells and the carry register has 82 active cells. Denote the state of the main register at time t by $(m_0(t), \cdots, m_{159}(t))$, and denote the state of the 82 active cells at time t by $(c_{j_1}(t), \cdots, c_{j_{82}}(t))$, where $0 \leq j_1 < \cdots < j_{82} \leq 159$. For the convenience of our analysis, we still assume that the main register cells are independent and uniformly distributed binary random variables defined on the same probability space, and the main register cells are independent of the carry cells. The conclusions we get in this section also meet with our experimental results very closely.

For a single carry cell, the conclusions in Theorem 1, Theorem 2 and Theorem 3 still hold for F-FCSR-H v3. The consecutive output sequence of a single carry cell is a homogeneous Markov chain, and the inverse chain is also a homogeneous Markov chain. The probability of a single carry cell to be zero for l consecutive clocks is $\frac{1}{2} \times \left(\frac{3}{4}\right)^{l-1}$. Therefore, the output sequence of a single carry cell of F-FCSR-H v3 can also be distinguished from an independent and uniformly distributed binary random sequence.

Although the 82 carry cells do not have m_0 as the common input, we found that there are still some correlations between two or more carry cells. First we analyze the correlations between two carry cells. For example, c_2 and c_{132} have a common input m_{133}, so c_2 and c_{132} are correlated at the same clock, and we call this *same-clock-correlation*. The carry cells c_1 and c_{119} do not have a common input at the same clock, however, $c_1(t)$ and $c_{119}(t+1)$ have a common input m_{121}, and we call this *1-clock-delay-correlation*. In the same way, c_{12} and c_{51} have *2-clock-delay-correlation*, c_{21} and c_{31} have *3-clock-delay-correlation*, c_{31} and c_{94} have *7-clock-delay-correlation*, and so on. The *same-clock-correlation* can also be called *0-clock-delay-correlation*. We analyze all the 82 carry cells, and list the correlations between two cells in Table 2.

Table 2. The correlations between two carry cells in F-FCSR-H v3

0-*clock-delay-correlation*: (2,132),(5,81),(11,39),(14,104),(16,62),(18,79),(20,1),(28,130),(36, 40), (42,125),(49, 44),(51, 16),(63, 128),(65,129),(67,121),(77, 45),(79, 25), (80, 116),(86, 59),(89, 14),(93, 11),(102, 140),(104, 141),(112, 91), (116, 31),(118, 49),(119, 42),(124, 12),(125, 73),(127, 148),(128, 89), (129, 56),(130, 102),(139, 23),(144, 47),(156, 21),(159, 77)
1-*clock-delay-correlation*: (1,119),(4, 42),(9, 36),(15, 40),(19,134),(44,125),(45,75),(46,108),(47, 84), (48,91),(56, 5),(57,148),(59, 23),(62, 49),(75,16),(81,159),(108,150),(113,81), (115,21),(131,132),(132,153),(140,59),(141,102),(145, 12),(150, 57),(158, 28), (4,119),(15,36),(21,121),(25,19),(39, 25),(40, 158),(44, 42),(48,112),(54, 56), (57,127),(59, 139),(62,118),(75, 51),(84,107),(91, 84),(94,113),(113,5), (115,156),(131,2),(140,86),(141,130),(145,124),(153,9)
2-*clock-delay-correlation*: (12,51),(23,25),(25,134),(40,28),(54,5),(73,145),(90,86),(94,81),(121,31), (153,36),(157,104),(39,19),(94,5),(121,116),(148,46),(157,14)
3-*clock-delay-correlation*: (21,31),(39,134),(107,67),(134,94),(148,108),(21,116)
4-*clock-delay-correlation*: (84,67),(31,134)
5-*clock-delay-correlation*: (91,67)
7-*clock-delay-correlation*: (31,94)

Now we analyze the correlations of multiple carry cells at the same clock. We found that c_{93} and c_{11} have a common input m_{12}, and c_{11} and c_{39} have a common input m_{40}, so the three carry cells c_{93}, c_{11}, and c_{39} are correlated at the same clock, and we call this 3-cell-correlation. Also we found that c_{28} and c_{130} have a common input m_{131}, c_{130} and c_{102} have a common input m_{103}, and c_{102} and c_{140} have a common input m_{141}, so the four carry cells c_{28}, c_{130}, c_{102}, and c_{140} are correlated at the same clock, and we call this 4-cell-correlation, and so on. We list the correlations of multiple carry cells at the same clock in Table 3.

Table 3. The correlations of multiple carry cells at the same clock in F-FCSR-H v3

3-cell-correlation:
(93,11,39),(51,16,62),(18,79,25),(118,49,44),(65,129,56),(159,77,45),(80,116,31)
4-cell-correlation: (28,130,102,140),(119,42,125,73)
6-cell-correlation: (63,128,89,14,104,141)

For convenience, let $Pr^{(s)}(c_1, \ldots, c_k)$ denote the probability of k carry cells $c_1, \ldots, c_k$ which have s-clock-delay-correlation to be zeros at the same clock, where $s \geq 0, k \geq 1$. If $s = 0$, we write $Pr^{(0)}(c_1, \ldots, c_k)$ as $Pr(c_1, \ldots, c_k)$. For the same-clock-correlation between two carry cells, the conclusion in Theorem 4 still holds for F-FCSR-H v3, i.e. $Pr(c_1, c_2) = \frac{1}{3}$. Next we will analyze the correlations of two or more carry cells, then we will give a preliminary analysis of the probability of all the 82 carry cells to be zeros at the same clock.

4.1   The Correlations between Two Carry Cells

Theorem 8. *Suppose the main register cells of F-FCSR-H v3 are independent and uniformly distributed binary random variables and the main register cells are independent of the carry cells, then the probability of 2 carry cells c_1, c_2 which have s-clock-delay-correlation to be zeros at the same clock is $Pr^{(s)}(c_1, c_2) = Prob\big(c_1(t) = 0, c_2(t) = 0\big) = \frac{3 \cdot 2^s + 1}{3 \cdot 2^{s+2}}$, where $s \geq 0$.*

Proof. For convenience, we write $Pr^{(s)}(c_1, c_2)$ as $Pr^{(s)}$. If $s = 0$, we know that $Pr^{(0)} = Pr(c_1, c_2) = \frac{1}{3}$, so the theorem holds. Next we calculate $Pr^{(s)}, (s \geq 1)$. Suppose the three inputs of the update function of the carry cell c_1 are x_0, x_1 and c_1, then $c_1(t+1) = c_1(t)x_0(t) \oplus c_1(t)x_1(t) \oplus x_0(t)x_1(t)$. Because c_1 and c_2 have s-clock-delay-correlation, we get that $c_1(t)$ and $c_2(t+1)$ have $(s-1)$-clock-delay-correlation, i.e. $Prob\big(c_1(t) = 0, c_2(t+1) = 0\big) = Pr^{(s-1)}$, therefore

$$Pr^{(s)} = Prob\big(c_1(t) = 0, c_2(t) = 0\big)$$
$$= Prob\big(c_1(t+1) = 0, c_2(t+1) = 0\big)$$
$$= Prob\big(c_1(t)x_0(t) \oplus c_1(t)x_1(t) \oplus x_0(t)x_1(t) = 0, c_2(t+1) = 0\big)$$
$$= Prob\big(c_1(t)x_0(t) \oplus c_1(t)x_1(t) \oplus x_0(t)x_1(t) = 0, c_2(t+1) = 0,$$
$$x_0(t) = 0, x_1(t) = 0\big)+$$
$$Prob\big(c_1(t)x_0(t) \oplus c_1(t)x_1(t) \oplus x_0(t)x_1(t) = 0, c_2(t+1) = 0,$$
$$x_0(t) = 0, x_1(t) = 1\big)+$$
$$Prob\big(c_1(t)x_0(t) \oplus c_1(t)x_1(t) \oplus x_0(t)x_1(t) = 0, c_2(t+1) = 0,$$
$$x_0(t) = 1, x_1(t) = 0\big)+$$
$$Prob\big(c_1(t)x_0(t) \oplus c_1(t)x_1(t) \oplus x_0(t)x_1(t) = 0, c_2(t+1) = 0,$$
$$x_0(t) = 1, x_1(t) = 1\big)$$
$$= Prob\big(0 = 0, c_2(t+1) = 0, x_0(t) = 0, x_1(t) = 0\big)+$$
$$Prob\big(c_1(t) = 0, c_2(t+1) = 0, x_0(t) = 0, x_1(t) = 1\big)+$$
$$Prob\big(c_1(t) = 0, c_2(t+1) = 0, x_0(t) = 1, x_1(t) = 0\big)+$$
$$Prob\big(1 = 0, c_2(t+1) = 0, x_0(t) = 1, x_1(t) = 1\big)$$
$$= \frac{1}{8} + \frac{1}{4} \cdot Pr^{(s-1)} + \frac{1}{4} \cdot Pr^{(s-1)} + 0 = \frac{1}{2} \cdot Pr^{(s-1)} + \frac{1}{8}$$

From formula $Pr^{(s)} = \frac{1}{2} \cdot Pr^{(s-1)} + \frac{1}{8}$ and $Pr^{(0)} = \frac{1}{3}$ we have that

$$Pr^{(s)} = \frac{3 \cdot 2^s + 1}{3 \cdot 2^{s+2}},$$

which completes our proof.   □

4.2   The Correlations of Multiple Carry Cells at the Same Clock

As defined before, $Pr(c_1, \ldots, c_k)$ denotes the probability of k carry cells $c_1, \ldots, c_k$ which have k-cell-correlation to be all zeros at the same clock. If $k = 1$, $Pr(c_1) = Prob(c_1(t) = 0) = \frac{1}{2}$. If $k = 2$, we know that $Pr(c_1, c_2) = \frac{1}{3}$. Next we calculate $Pr(c_1, \ldots, c_k)$, $3 \leq k \leq 6$ (see Table 3).

Theorem 9. *Suppose the main register cells of F-FCSR-H v3 are independent and uniformly distributed binary random variables and the main register cells are independent of the carry cells, then $Pr(c_1, \ldots, c_3) = \frac{5}{24}, Pr(c_1, \ldots, c_4) = \frac{2}{15}, Pr(c_1, \ldots, c_5) = \frac{61}{720}$, and $Pr(c_1, \ldots, c_6) = \frac{17}{315}$.*

Proof. For convenience, we write $Pr(c_1, \ldots, c_k)$ as $Prob_k$, $k \geq 1$. First we calculate $Prob_3$. Suppose the update function of c_1 is $c_1(t+1) = c_1(t)x_0(t) \oplus c_1(t)x_1(t) \oplus x_0(t)x_1(t)$, the update function of c_2 is $c_2(t+1) = c_2(t)x_1(t) \oplus$

$c_2(t)x_2(t) \oplus x_1(t)x_2(t)$, and the update function of c_3 is $c_3(t+1) = c_3(t)x_2(t) \oplus c_3(t)x_3(t) \oplus x_2(t)x_3(t)$. c_1 and c_2 have a common input x_1, and c_2 and c_3 have a common input x_2. c_1 and c_3 are independent. Then we can get:

$$Prob\big(c_1(t) = 0\big) = Prob\big(c_2(t) = 0\big) = Prob\big(c_3(t) = 0\big) = Prob_1 = \frac{1}{2},$$

$$Prob\big(c_1(t) = 0, c_2(t) = 0\big) = Prob\big(c_2(t) = 0, c_3(t) = 0\big) = Prob_2 = \frac{1}{3},$$

$$Prob\big(c_1(t) = 0, c_3(t) = 0\big) = Prob_1 \cdot Prob_1 = \frac{1}{4}.$$

Therefore,

$$
\begin{aligned}
&Prob_3 \\
&= Prob(c_1(t) = 0, c_2(t) = 0, c_3(t) = 0) \\
&= Prob(c_1(t+1) = 0, c_2(t+1) = 0, c_3(t+1) = 0) \\
&= prob \begin{pmatrix} c_1(t)x_0(t) \oplus c_1(t)x_1(t) \oplus x_0(t)x_1(t) = 0, \\ c_2(t)x_1(t) \oplus c_2(t)x_2(t) \oplus x_1(t)x_2(t) = 0, \\ c_3(t)x_2(t) \oplus c_3(t)x_3(t) \oplus x_2(t)x_3(t) = 0 \end{pmatrix} \\
&= prob \begin{pmatrix} c_1(t)x_0(t) \oplus c_1(t)x_1(t) \oplus x_0(t)x_1(t) = 0, \\ c_2(t)x_1(t) \oplus c_2(t)x_2(t) \oplus x_1(t)x_2(t) = 0, \\ c_3(t)x_2(t) \oplus c_3(t)x_3(t) \oplus x_2(t)x_3(t) = 0, \\ x_0(t) = 0, x_1(t) = 0, x_2(t) = 0, x_3(t) = 0 \end{pmatrix} + \cdots + \\
&\quad prob \begin{pmatrix} c_1(t)x_0(t) \oplus c_1(t)x_1(t) \oplus x_0(t)x_1(t) = 0, \\ c_2(t)x_1(t) \oplus c_2(t)x_2(t) \oplus x_1(t)x_2(t) = 0, \\ c_3(t)x_2(t) \oplus c_3(t)x_3(t) \oplus x_2(t)x_3(t) = 0, \\ x_0(t) = 1, x_1(t) = 1, x_2(t) = 1, x_3(t) = 1 \end{pmatrix} \\
&= Prob(0 = 0, 0 = 0, 0 = 0, x_0(t) = 0, x_1(t) = 0, x_2(t) = 0, x_3(t) = 0) + \cdots + \\
&\quad Prob(1 = 0, 1 = 0, 1 = 0, x_0(t) = 1, x_1(t) = 1, x_2(t) = 1, x_3(t) = 1) \\
&= \frac{1}{2^4} \begin{pmatrix} 1 + Prob_1 + Prob_2 + 0 + Prob_2 + Prob_3 + 0 + 0 + \\ Prob_1 + Prob_1 \cdot Prob_1 + Prob_3 + 0 + 0 + 0 + 0 + 0 \end{pmatrix} \\
&= \frac{1}{2^4}\left(\frac{35}{12} + 2Prob_3\right)
\end{aligned}
$$

Solve the equation, and we get $Prob_3 = \frac{5}{24}$.
Similarly, we can calculate: $Prob_4 = \frac{2}{15}$, $Prob_5 = \frac{61}{720}$, and $Prob_6 = \frac{17}{315}$.   □

4.3   The Probability of All the 82 Carry Cells to Be Zeros at the Same Clock

In this section, we make a preliminary analysis of the probability of all the 82 carry cells of F-FCSR-H v3 to be zeros at the same clock. According to the ring FCSR architecture of F-FCSR-H v3, Table 2 and Table 3, the correlations of the 82 carry cells are shown in Figure 3. They are divided into 2 groups. Group 1 contains 76 carry cells, and Group 2 contains 6 carry cells. We take Group 2 as an example to illustrate. (c_{148}, c_{127}) have 0-*clock-delay-correlation*, (c_{46}, c_{108}), (c_{108}, c_{150}), (c_{150}, c_{57}), (c_{57}, c_{148}), and (c_{57}, c_{127}) all have 1-*clock-delay-correlation*, (c_{148}, c_{46}) have 2-*clock-delay-correlation*, and (c_{148}, c_{108}) have 3-*clock-delay-correlation*.

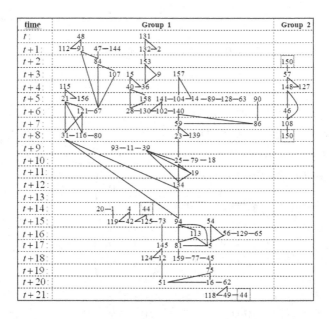

Fig. 3. The correlations of the 82 carry cells of F-FCSR-H v3

In Figure 3, we can see that the carry cells $(c_{48}, c_{112}, c_{91})$, (c_{131}, c_{132}, c_2), $(c_{115}, c_{21}, c_{156})$ and $(c_{57}, c_{148}, c_{127})$ have a similar structure. Let's take $(c_{48}, c_{112}, c_{91})$ as an example to illustrate. (c_{48}, c_{112}) and (c_{48}, c_{91}) have 1-*clock-delay-correlation*, and (c_{112}, c_{91}) have 0-*clock-delay-correlation*. We call $(c_{48}, c_{112}, c_{91})$ having 1-*clock-triangle-correlation*. Using the law of total probability, we can get the probability of (c_1, c_2, c_3) which have 1-*clock-triangle-correlation* to be zeros at the same clock on the independence assumption, which is:

$$Prob(c_1(t) = 0, c_2(t) = 0, c_3(t) = 0) = \frac{5}{24}.$$

We can also see in Figure 3 that $(c_{56}, c_{129}, c_{65})$ have 0-*clock-delay-correlation*, and (c_{54}, c_{56}) have 1-*clock-delay-correlation*. While $(c_{28}, c_{130}, c_{102}, c_{140})$ have 0-*clock-delay-correlation*, and (c_{158}, c_{28}) have 1-*clock-delay-correlation*. They also have a similar structure. On the independence assumption, we can prove that

$$Prob(c_{54}(t) = 0, c_{56}(t) = 0, c_{129}(t) = 0, c_{65}(t) = 0) = \frac{57}{480},$$

$$Prob\big(c_{158}(t) = 0, c_{28}(t) = 0, c_{130}(t) = 0, c_{102}(t) = 0, c_{140}(t) = 0\big) = \frac{109}{1440}.$$

To analyze the probability of the 82 carry cells to be zeros at the same clock, according to Figure 3, we divide the 82 carry cells into nine categories(see Table 4). Now we make a preliminary analysis. Suppose the carry cells of different categories are independent, and the carry cells of different groups in the same category are also independent. Let E_0 denote the event of all the 82 carry cells of F-FCSR-H v3 to be zeros at the same clock. Then from the above analysis, we have

$$Prob\big(E_0\big) \geq \big(Prob_2\big)^4 \cdot \big(Prob_3\big)^6 \cdot \big(Prob_6\big) \cdot \big(Pr^{(1)}\big)^4 \cdot \big(Pr^{(2)}\big).$$

$$\left(\frac{1}{2}\right)^4 \cdot \left(\frac{5}{24}\right)^9 \cdot \frac{109}{1440} \cdot \frac{57}{480}$$

$$= \left(\frac{1}{3}\right)^4 \cdot \left(\frac{5}{24}\right)^6 \cdot \left(\frac{17}{315}\right) \cdot \left(\frac{7}{24}\right)^4 \cdot \left(\frac{13}{48}\right).$$

$$\left(\frac{1}{2}\right)^4 \cdot \left(\frac{5}{24}\right)^9 \cdot \frac{109}{1440} \cdot \frac{57}{480}$$

$$\approx 2^{-64.29}$$

But for independent and uniformly distributed binary random sequences, the probability of 82 cells to be all zeros at the same clock is 2^{-82}. Our results show that the distribution of F-FCSR-H v3's carry cells is still unbalanced.

Table 4. Classification of the correlations of F-FCSR-H v3's 82 carry cells

Classification		Carry cells
1st class: 4 groups	same-clock-correlation	(144,47),(67,121), (20, 1),(125,73)
2nd class: 6 groups	3-cell-correlation	(80,116,31),(93,11,39), (18,79,25),(159,77,45), (51,16,62),(118,49,44)
3rd class: 1 group	6-cell-correlation	(63,128,89,14,104,141)
4th class: 4 groups	1-clock-delay-correlation	(84,107),(153,9), (19,134),(46,108)
5th class: 1 group	2-clock-delay-correlation	(90,86)
6th class: 4 groups	independent carry cells	157,150, 94,75
7th class: 9 groups	1-clock-triangle-correlation	(48,112,91),(131,132,2), (15,40,36),(115,21,156), (59,23,139),(4,119,42), (113,81,5),(145,124,12), (57,148,127)
8th class: 1 group		(158,28,130,102,140)
9th class: 1 group		(54,56,129,65)

5   Conclusion

In [6], M. Hell and T. Johansson breaks F-FCSR-H v2 in real time using the biased property of the carry cells. In order to resist this powerful attack, F. Arnault *et al.* proposed the new stream cipher F-FCSR-H v3 in [2]. Reference [6] only gives the experimental results of the success probability, but no theoretical results about the distribution of F-FCSR-H v2's carry cells. In this paper, we analyze the carry cells' probability distribution of F-FCSR-H v2 and F-FCSR-H v3, and build a probability model for the two stream ciphers. Under the probability model, we prove that the consecutive output sequence of a single carry cell is a homogeneous Markov chain, and the inverse chain is also a homogeneous Markov chain. The probability of a single carry cell to be zero for l consecutive clocks is $\frac{1}{2} \cdot \left(\frac{3}{4}\right)^{l-1}$, and when $l > 1$, $\frac{1}{2} \cdot \left(\frac{3}{4}\right)^{l-1} > 2^{-l}$, which is a weakness of F-FCSR-H v2 and F-FCSR-H v3's carry cells. We give theoretical results of the carry cells' probability distribution that are needed for breaking F-FCSR-H v2 in [6], and explain why there exists a bias between theoretical results and experimental results. For F-FCSR-H v3, we also analyze the correlations of the carry cells, and prove that the probability of all 82 carry cells to be zeros at the same clock is at least $2^{-64.29}$, which is much higher than 2^{-82}. This is another weakness of F-FCSR-H v3's carry cells. Our results provide theoretical support to M.Hell and T.Johansson's cryptanalysis of F-FCSR-H v2 and establish a theoretical foundation for further cryptanalysis of F-FCSR-H v3.

References

1. Arnault, F., Berger, T., Lauradoux, C.: Update on F-FCSR stream cipher. eS-TREAM, ECRYPT Stream Cipher Project, Report 2006/025 (2006), http://www.ecrypt.eu.org/stream
2. Arnault, F., Berger, T., Lauradoux, C., Minier, M., Pousse, B.: A New Approach for FCSRs. In: Jacobson Jr., M.J., Rijmen, V., Safavi-Naini, R. (eds.) SAC 2009. LNCS, vol. 5867, pp. 433–448. Springer, Heidelberg (2009)
3. eSTREAM: Ecrypt stream cipher project, http://www.ecrypt.eu.org/stream/
4. Goresky, M., Klapper, A.: Fibonacci and Galois representations of feedback-with-carry shift registers. IEEE Transactions on Information Theory 48(11), 2826–2836 (2002)
5. Goresky, M., Klapper, A.: Periodicity and distribution properties of combined FCSR sequences. In: Gong, G., Helleseth, T., Song, H.-Y., Yang, K. (eds.) SETA 2006. LNCS, vol. 4086, pp. 334–341. Springer, Heidelberg (2006)
6. Hell, M., Johansson, T.: Breaking the F-FCSR-H Stream Cipher in Real Time. In: Pieprzyk, J. (ed.) ASIACRYPT 2008. LNCS, vol. 5350, pp. 557–569. Springer, Heidelberg (2008)
7. Klapper, A., Goresky, M.: 2-Adic Shift Registers. In: Anderson, R. (ed.) FSE 1993. LNCS, vol. 809, pp. 174–178. Springer, Heidelberg (1994)
8. Klapper, A., Goresky, M.: Feedback Shift Registers, 2-Adic Span, and Combiners with Memory. J. Cryptol. 10(2), 111–147 (1997)

Efficient Self-certified Signatures with Batch Verification*

Nan Li, Yi Mu, and Willy Susilo**

Centre for Computer and Information Security Research
School of Computer Science and Software Engineering
University of Wollongong
Wollongong, NSW 2522, Australia
{nl864,ymu,wsusilo}@uow.edu.au

Abstract. To eliminate the need of public-key certificates from Public Key Infrastructure (PKI) and the problem of key escrow in identity-based cryptography, the concept of *self-certified* public key was put forth by Girault. In this paper, we propose an efficient and novel self-certified signature scheme, which requires only one modular multiplication in signing with pre-computation. One of features of our scheme lies in its batch verification in both single-signer and multi-signer settings. Pairing computations in the batch verification are independent from the number of signatures. Our scheme is proven secure in the random oracle model.

Keywords: Digital Signature, Self-certified Signature, Batch Verification.

1 Introduction

Digital signature is an important primitive in modern cryptography. A valid digital signature can be seen as a receipt of a message from the particular sender and can be applied to many security services such as authentication and non-repudiation. Signature verification relies on public key or signature verification key; therefore, proving the relationship between a public key and its owner is essential for security of signatures. In practice, it relies on the Public Key Infrastructure (PKI). That is, Certificate authority (CA) as a part of PKI issues public key certificates to its users. Nevertheless, PKI might not be desirable. Often, a signature has to be distributed along with its public-key certificate. Prior to the signature verification, a signature receiver needs to check the validity of the corresponding certificate and store the certificate for later communications. Certificate distribution, verification and storage add additional cost to communication, computation and storage.

The notion of identity-based signature (IBS) was introduced by Shamir in 1984 [17]. Problems of certificate verification and management are solved by using the

---

* This work is partially supported by the Australian Research Council Discovery Project DP110101951.
** This work is supported by ARC Future Fellowship FT0991397.

C.-K. Wu, M. Yung, and D. Lin (Eds.): Inscrypt 2011, LNCS 7537, pp. 179–194, 2012.
© Springer-Verlag Berlin Heidelberg 2012

signer's identity as his public key. This idea has been applied to various signature schemes, including several multi-user signatures (e.g., [23,9]). An identity-based signature scheme secure in the standard model was proposed by Paterson and Schuldt [14]. In identity-based signatures, a user's private key is generated by a trusted authority (TA), as a private key generator (PKG). As a drawback of identity-based systems, PKG can sign a message on behalf of any user. It is referred to as the so-called *key escrow* problem. The problem may be avoided by sharing master secret key among several authorized parties [21], but a potential collusion of the authorities could still be a problem. Some other efforts are also presented in [22,5].

To fill the gap between the PKI based and identity-based signatures, Girault [10] introduced the notion of *Self-certified Public Keys*, where certificate verification and management are not required and the key escrow problem can be eliminated. The idea is that the certificate is replaced by a *witness* and the public key is embeded in it. Anyone who holds a witness along with an attributive identity can recover a correct public key for signature verification. The amount of communication, computation and storage are also reduced. Unlike identity-based schemes, the trusted third party (TTP) cannot extract user's private key. The scheme captures a strong security (level-3) defined by Girault [10]. Notice that IBS only reaches level-1 security.

Saeednia [16] found a problem in the Girault's scheme, namely, a malicious TTP can compromise user private key by using a specific composite modular of RSA. Roughly speaking, the TTP chooses two "small" prime numbers to compute the RSA modulus n and it is helpful to solve the discrete logarithm problem. For a more complete account, we refer the readers to [16]. Zhou, Cao and Lu [25] prevented this attack by utilizing different user chosen modular, whereas the size of signature is increased and the public key recovery must be separated from the signature verification. Self-certified public key generation protocol based on discrete logarithm was also proposed in [15].

1.1   Our Contribution

In this paper, we proposed an efficient and novel self-certified signature (SCS) scheme, which achieves the level-3 security as defined by Girault [10]. The scheme is based on the discrete logarithm rather than RSA. Hence, the private key exposure problem has been resolved. In Our scheme, there is no need to separate a certificate and a public key. Instead, we embed user's public key in a witness, which can be seen as a *lightweight* certificate. The public key can be implicitly verified in the signature verification, while anyone who has the user identity and the witness can explicitly extract the public key. We present both cases in our scheme.

The efficiency of a signature scheme is normally evaluated by two aspects: signing efficiency and verification efficiency. In the signing phase, our self-certified signature scheme only requires one exponent and two multiplication computations with no pairing calculation. We also show that our SCS scheme can be made more efficient by utilizing the idea of pre-computation so that only one multiplication computation is needed. In the verification phase, our scheme requires two pairing computations. However, it is reduced to one pairing computation when the signer's public key has been recovered explicitly. Additionally, we show that our scheme is especially suitable for verifying large number of signatures by batch verification. The result shows that our scheme achieves a constant number of pairing computations in multi-signer setting. We prove that our scheme is secure in the random oracle model.

1.2   Related Work and Comparison

The notion of *certificateless public key cryptography* (CL-PKC) was introduced by Al-Riyami and Paterson [1] in 2003. The idea is similar to self-certified public keys, since the signer is implicitly certified in signature verification and no certificate involved the scheme. Similar to TTP in SCS scheme, an authority called *Key Generation Centre* (KGC) that generates partial private keys for users. An efficient certificateless signature scheme was proposed by Choi, Park, Hwang and Lee [4] (or CPHL for short). An efficient pairing-free security mediated certificateless signature scheme was proposed by Yap, Chow, Heng and Goi [20]. While the signing algorithm is an interactive protocol between a signer and an online semi-trusted server. The signature generation needs the help of a third party. Gentry [8] introduced *Certificate-Based Cryptography* (CBC) as another paradigm to remove certificate and solve private key escrow problem. Indeed, the CL-PKC and CBC schemes can easily transfer from the one to the other [19]. Liu, Baek, Susilo and Zhou [12] (or LBSZ for short) proposed a certificate-based signature scheme without pairing computations in random oracle.

The main difference between self-certified signatures and certificateless or certificate-based signatures is the key recoverable property. In self-certified signatures, the user's public key is computable by anyone who has his witness along with a set of public parameters. Once the user's public key has been recovered, the TTP's public key is no longer required. It implies that the cost of key certification and calculation is only needed at the initial stage of a communication as conventional signature schemes. If we treat the witness as a "public key", then it can be used along with the TTP's public key to verify a signature. In both certificateless signatures and certificate-based signatures, on the other hand, the signature verification always needs the KGC's public key and the user's public key is uncomputable except the KGC.

We compare some efficient schemes that solved the same problems as SCS schemes in Table 1.

1.3   Organization

The rest of this paper is organized as follows. The definition of our scheme and complexity assumptions are given in Section 2. A formal security model of our scheme is defined in Section 3. Our proposed scheme along with a formal

Table 1. P: one pairing computation; E: one exponentiation computation; M: one multiplication computation; Size: number of elements; SCS-1: our basic scheme; SCS-2: public key is already recovered by a verifier

	Signing	Verification	Signature Size	Public Key Size
CPHL	2E	1P+2E+1M	2	1
LBSZ	1E+2M	3E+4M	3	3
Our SCS-1	1E+2M	2P+3E+1M	2	1
Our SCS-2	1E+2M	1P+2E	2	1

security proof of our scheme is given in Section 4. Further discussions on pre-computation and batch verification are presented in Section 5 and 6, respectively. Finally, Section 7 concludes the paper.

2   Definitions

In this section, we present the definition of self-certified signatures and the underlying mathematical definitions.

2.1   Self-certified Signature

Digital signature schemes are basically consisted of three algorithms: key generation (**KeyGen**), signing algorithm (**Sign**) and verification algorithm (**Verify**). Besides the basic algorithms, a self-certified signature scheme has two additional algorithms: the system setup algorithm (**Setup**) for generating system parameters and the witness registration algorithm (**WitReg**) for registering a user. The five algorithms in SCS are defined as follows:

- **Setup**(k_1): is a PPT algorithm run by a Trusted Third Party (TTP) that takes as input a security parameter k_1, outputs the public system parameters *param* and a master secret key *msk*.
- **KeyGen**(k_2): is a PPT algorithm run by a user that takes as input a security parameter k_2, outputs a pair of public and private keys (pk, sk).
- **WitReg**(ID, pk, v): is a PPT algorithm run by the TTP that takes as input a user's identity ID, public key pk and the proof of the knowledge of private key v, outputs a witness W if the proof v is valid, otherwise rejects.
- **Sign**(m, sk): is a PPT algorithm that takes as input a message m, private key sk, outputs a signatures $\sigma = (u, t)$.
- **Verify**(m, σ, ID, W): is a deterministic algorithm that takes as input a message m, a signature σ, user's identity ID and the witness W, outputs *true* if it is valid, otherwise outputs *false*.

2.2   Bilinear Maps

Let $\mathbb{G}_1$, $\mathbb{G}_2$ and $\mathbb{G}_T$ be three multiplicative cyclic groups of same prime order p. ψ is an isomorphism from $\mathbb{G}_2$ to $\mathbb{G}_1$. Let g_1 be a generator of $\mathbb{G}_1$ and

$\psi(g_2) = g_1$. The map $e : \mathbb{G}_1 \times \mathbb{G}_2 \to \mathbb{G}_T$ is a bilinear mapping (pairing) and $(g_1, g_2, p, e, \mathbb{G}_1, \mathbb{G}_2, \mathbb{G}_T)$ is a bilinear group. Simply, we let $\mathbb{G} = \mathbb{G}_1 = \mathbb{G}_2$ in this paper. Some properties of bilinear pairings are as follows:

- **Bilinearity**: for all $u \in \mathbb{G}_1$, $v \in \mathbb{G}_2$ and $a, b \in \mathbb{Z}_p^*$, we have the equation $e(u^a, v^b) = e(u, v)^{ab}$.
- **Non-Degeneracy**: for all $g_1 \in \mathbb{G}_1$, $g_2 \in \mathbb{G}_2$, if g_1, g_2 are generators respectively, we have $e(g_1, g_2) \neq 1$ is a generator of $\mathbb{G}_T$.
- **Efficiency**: There is an efficient algorithm to calculate $e(u, v)$ for all $u \in \mathbb{G}_1$, $v \in \mathbb{G}_2$.

2.3 Complexity Assumptions

Definition 1 (Discrete Logarithm assumption). *The discrete logarithm problem (DLP) is (t, ϵ)-hard if given a tuple $< g, g^a >$ that g is a generator of a group $\mathbb{G}$ and $a \in_R \mathbb{Z}_p^*$, there is no probabilistic polynomial time (PPT) algorithm $\mathcal{A}$ to compute a in t-time with advantage at least ϵ.*

Definition 2 (Computational Diffie-Hellman assumption). *The computational Diffie-Hellman problem (CDHP) is (t, ϵ)-hard if given a tuple $< g, g^a, g^b >$ that g is a generator of a group $\mathbb{G}$ and $a, b \in_R \mathbb{Z}_p^*$, there is no PPT algorithm $\mathcal{A}$ to compute g^{ab} in t-time with advantage at least ϵ.*

Definition 3 ($k+1$ exponent assumption). *The $(k+1)$-exponent problem is (t, ϵ)-hard, if given $k+1$ values $< g, g^a, g^{a^2}, \ldots, g^{a^k} >$ that g is a generator of a group $\mathbb{G}$ and $a \in_R \mathbb{Z}_p^*$, there is no PPT algorithm $\mathcal{A}$ to compute $g^{a^{k+1}}$ in t-time with advantage at least ϵ.*

The $(k+1)$-exponent problem $((k+1)$-EP) is firstly introduced by Zhang, Safavi-Naini and Susilo [24]. $(k+1)$-EP is proved that it is polynomial time equal to the k-wCDHP presented by Mitsunari, Sakai and Kasahara [13]. Note that both $(k+1)$-exponent problem and k-wCDHP are no harder than the CDHP.

3   Security Models

Goldwasser, Micali and Rivest [11] introduced the strongest security notion of digital signature schemes: existential unforgeability against adaptive chosen-message attacks (EUF-CMA). A self-certified signature scheme needs to satisfy EUF-CMA as normal signature schemes. However, there are some differences according to the using of self-certified public keys. Girault [10] defined the security of self-certified public keys as three levels: 1) the TTP knows a user's private key; 2) the attacker cannot know a user's private key, but it can forge a false witness without being detected by users; 3) anyone cannot know a user's private key and cannot forge a witness without being detected. Hence, the identity-based signature schemes are only reach the level 1. A self-certified signature scheme should satisfy the level 3. Following this notion, we define a security model of self-certified signature schemes. There are two cases in our security model and the SCS scheme is EUF-CMA iff it is secure in both cases.

- *Type I adversary* ($\mathcal{A}_I$): plays as a malicious user who does not get a valid witness from the TTP. The adversary tries to forge a witness that cannot be detected in the verification phase.
- *Type II adversary* ($\mathcal{A}_{II}$): is considered as a corrupted TTP who tries to reveal the user's private key.

The security of self-certified signatures is defined by two games.

Game 1: This is a game defined as *Type I attack*. The challenger runs **Setup** and gives public parameters to $\mathcal{A}_I$. $\mathcal{A}_I$ has an ability to access user private keys, but the master secret key is unknown. The adversary makes **Corruption**, **WitReg**, **Sign** queries and outputs a forgery.

- **Setup:** The challenger $\mathcal{C}$ runs the algorithm **Setup** to generate public parameters *param* and returns to $\mathcal{A}_I$.
- **Queries:** $\mathcal{A}_I$ has the ability to adaptively submit three types of query defined as follows.
  - **Corruption Query:** On an $\mathcal{A}_I$'s query ID, $\mathcal{C}$ returns the corresponding private key. $\mathcal{A}_I$ can make this query at most q_1 times.
  - **WitReg Query:** On an $\mathcal{A}_I$'s query (ID, pk, v), $\mathcal{C}$ runs the algorithm **WitReg** and returns a valid witness W. $\mathcal{A}_I$ can make this query at most q_2 times.
  - **Sign Query:** On an $\mathcal{A}_I$'s query (m, ID), $\mathcal{C}$ runs the algorithm **Sign** and returns a signature σ of message m. $\mathcal{A}_I$ can make this query at most q_3 times.
- **Forgery:** $\mathcal{A}_I$ outputs a signature $\sigma^* = (u^*, t^*)$ of a message m^* that the pair (m^*, ID^*) is not queried in **Sign Query** and W^* is not an output of **WitReg Query**. $\mathcal{A}_I$ wins the game if the **Verify**$(m^*, \sigma^*, ID^*, W^*)$ =*true*. The advantage of $\mathcal{A}_I$ is defined as

$$Adv_{\mathcal{A}_I} = \Pr[\mathcal{A}_I \ wins].$$

Definition 4. *A self-certified signature scheme is $(t, q_1, q_2, q_3, \epsilon)$-secure against an adaptively chosen message Type I attack, if there is no $\mathcal{A}_I$ who wins Game 1 in polynomial time t with advantage at least ϵ after q_1, q_2, q_3 queries.*

Game 2: This is a game defined as *Type $\mathcal{A}_{II}$ attack*. The challenger runs **Setup** and gives public parameters to $\mathcal{A}_{II}$. Due to $\mathcal{A}_{II}$ is considered as a dishonest TTP, a master secret key is also returned, but $\mathcal{A}_{II}$ has no ability to access user private key. Then the adversary makes **Public-Key**, **Sign** queries and outputs a forgery.

- **Setup:** The challenger runs the algorithm **Setup**, outputs public parameters *param* and a master secret key *msk*. $\mathcal{C}$ gives *param* and *msk* to the adversary.
- **Public-Key Query:** On $\mathcal{A}_{II}$'s query ID, the challenger $\mathcal{C}$ runs the algorithm **KeyGen** and returns a public key. $\mathcal{A}_{II}$ can make this query at most q_1 times.

- **Sign Query**: On $\mathcal{A}_{II}$'s query (m, ID), $\mathcal{C}$ runs the algorithm **Sign** and returns a signature σ of a message m. $\mathcal{A}_{II}$ can make this query at most q_2 times.
- **Forgery**: $\mathcal{A}_{II}$ outputs a signature $\sigma^* = (u^*, t^*)$ of a message m^* that the pair (m^*, ID^*) is not queried in **Sign Query**. $\mathcal{A}_{II}$ wins the game if the **Verify**$(m^*, \sigma^*, ID^*, W^*)$=*true*. The advantage of $\mathcal{A}_{II}$ is defined as

$$Adv_{\mathcal{A}_{II}} = \Pr[\mathcal{A}_{II} \ wins].$$

Definition 5. *A self-certified signature scheme is a* (t, q_1, q_2, ϵ)-*secure against an adaptively chosen message Type II attack, if there is no* $\mathcal{A}_{II}$ *who wins Game 2 in polynomial time t with advantage at least* ϵ *after* q_1, q_2 *queries.*

4   The Proposed Scheme

In PKI based schemes, a certificate can be seen as a part of a signature when the two parties initiate a communication. The verification of a certificate is required prior to the signature verification. For stable partners who communicate frequently, the cost of certificate transmission and verification are negligible. However, in most cases, the participants barely know each other personally, and hence, the verification process becomes essential. We present a novel and efficient self-certified signature scheme that the cost of computations, transmission and storage are all reduced.

4.1   Construction

Setup: Select a pairing $e : \mathbb{G} \times \mathbb{G} \to \mathbb{G}_T$, where the order of group $\mathbb{G}$ and $\mathbb{G}_T$ are the same prime p. Let g be a generator of $\mathbb{G}$. The TTP then chooses two collision-resistant cryptographic hash functions that $h_1 : \{0, 1\}^* \to \mathbb{G}$, $h_2 : \{0, 1\}^* \to \mathbb{Z}_p^*$. Randomly select a number $\alpha \in_R \mathbb{Z}_p^*$, set $msk = \alpha$ and the master public key $mpk = g^\alpha$. The public parameters are $(\mathbb{G}, \mathbb{G}_T, g, p, e, h_1, h_2, mpk)$.
KeyGen: Randomly chooses $x \in_R \mathbb{Z}_p^*$ and computes $e(g, g)^x$. Sets the public and private keys as $(pk, sk) = (e(g, g)^x, x)$.
WitReg: A user interact with a TTP in this algorithm as follows.

- The user computes a proof of knowledge of private key $v = g^{\alpha x}$, where x is the user private key, and sends (ID, pk, v) to TTP.
- TTP verifies the equation $e(v, g) \overset{?}{=} pk^\alpha$, if it holds, then generates a witness

$$W = (v^{\frac{1}{\alpha}} h_1(ID))^{\frac{1}{\alpha}}.$$

- The user accepts the witness if the following equations holds:

$$\begin{aligned}
&e(W, mpk)e(h_1(ID)^{-1}, g) \\
&= e(v^{\frac{1}{\alpha}} h_1(ID), g)e(h_1(ID)^{-1}, g) \\
&= pk.
\end{aligned} \tag{1}$$

Sign: To sign a message $m \in \{0,1\}^*$, the signer randomly selects $r \in_R \mathbb{Z}_p^*$ and computes

$$\sigma = (g^r, \frac{1 - rh_2(m||g^r)}{x})$$
$$= (u, t).$$

Verify: On input a signature $\sigma = (u, t)$ on a message m under a witness W of the identity ID, the verifier checks whether

$$e(W^t, mpk)e(u^{h_2(m||u)}h_1(ID)^{-t}, g) \stackrel{?}{=} e(g, g) \tag{2}$$

or

$$e(g, g)^{xt}e(u^{h_2(m||u)}, g) \stackrel{?}{=} e(g, g). \tag{3}$$

Outputs *true* if the equation holds, otherwise outputs *false*. The equation (3) is to utilize once the user public key was recovered as in (1).

Correctness: Our self-certified signature scheme is correct as shown in follows:

$$e(W^t, mpk)e(u^{h_2(m||u)}h_1(ID)^{-t}, g)$$
$$= e((v^{\frac{1}{a}}h_1(ID))^t, g)e(u^{h_2(m||u)}h_1(ID)^{-t}, g)$$
$$= e(g^{xt}g^{rh_2(m||u)}, g)$$
$$= e(g, g).$$

4.2   Security Analysis

A self-certified signature is unforgeable if it is against two types of attacks defined in Section 3. We show that our signature scheme is secure under the strongest security notion for signature schemes (EUF-CMA).

Theorem 1. *Our SCS scheme is $(t, q_{h_1}, q_2, q_3, \epsilon)$-secure against an existential forgery under Type I chosen message attack, q_{h_1} is the number of queries on h_1 hash function, assuming that the $(k+1)$-exponent problem is (t', ϵ')-hard, where,*

$$\epsilon' \geq \frac{1}{q_2} \cdot (1 - \frac{1}{q_2 + 1})^{q_2+1} \cdot \epsilon, \qquad t' = t + O(q_{h_1} + q_2 + q_3).$$

Proof. Suppose a *Type I adversary* $\mathcal{A}_I$ who can $(t, q_1, q_2, q_3, \epsilon)$-break our SCS scheme. We can construct an algorithm $\mathcal{B}$ run by the challenger to use $\mathcal{A}_I$ to solve the $(k+1)$-exponent problem. The algorithm $\mathcal{B}$ is given the $(k+1)$-EP instance $(g, g^a, g^{a^2}, g^{a^3})$, where $k = 3$, and the goal is to output g^{a^4}. $\mathcal{B}$ interacts with $\mathcal{A}_I$ in game 1 as follows.

Setup: $\mathcal{B}$ sets g^a as the generator of a group $\mathbb{G}$ and the master public key $mpk = g$. Let the master secret key $msk = a^{-1}$, which is unknown to $\mathcal{B}$. $\mathcal{B}$ maintains four lists $L_{h1} = \{< ID, b, coin \in \{0, 1\} >\}$, $L_{h2} = \{< M, c >\}$, $L_c = \{< ID, sk >\}$ and $L_w = \{< ID, pk, v, W >\}$, which are initially empty.

h_1 **Query:** $\mathcal{A}_I$ issues an h_1 query on input ID_i at most q_{h_1} times, where $1 \leq i \leq q_{h_1}$. $\mathcal{B}$ outputs $h_1(ID_i)$ if ID_i is in the list L_{h1}. Otherwise, $\mathcal{B}$ tosses a coin with the probability $\Pr[coin = 1] = \xi$ ($\Pr[coin = 0] = 1 - \xi$), selects $b_i \in_R \mathbb{Z}_p^*$ and answers the query as follows.

$$\begin{cases} coin_i = 0 : \ h_1(ID_i) = g^{ab_i}, \\[2mm] coin_i = 1 : \ h_1(ID_i) = g^{a^3 b_i}, \end{cases}$$

$\mathcal{B}$ outputs $h_1(ID_i)$ and adds $< ID_i, b_i, coin_i >$ in the list L_{h1}

h_2 **Query:** $\mathcal{A}_I$ issues an h_2 query on input string M_i at most q_{h_2} times, where $1 \leq i \leq q_{h_2}$. $\mathcal{B}$ outputs $h_2(M_i)$ if M_i is in the list L_{h2}. Otherwise, $\mathcal{B}$ randomly selects $c_i \in_R \mathbb{Z}_p^*$ and sets $h_2(M_i) = c_i$. Then, $\mathcal{B}$ outputs $h_2(M_i)$ and adds $< M_i, c_i >$ into the list L_{h2}.

Corruption Query: $\mathcal{A}_I$ issues a corruption query on input identity ID_i, where $1 \leq i \leq q_1$. $\mathcal{B}$ outputs sk_i if ID_i is in the list L_c. Otherwise, $\mathcal{B}$ outputs a random choice $sk_i \in_R \mathbb{Z}_p^*$ and adds $< ID_i, sk_i >$ in the list L_c.

WitReg Query: $\mathcal{A}_I$ issues a witness query on input (ID_i, pk_i, v_i), where $1 \leq i \leq q_2$. $\mathcal{B}$ outputs a witness W_i if ID_i is in the list L_w. Otherwise, $\mathcal{B}$ retrieves the private key sk_i and b_i in L_c and L_{h1}, respectively. If $coin_i = 0$, $\mathcal{B}$ sets and outputs witness W_i as

$$W_i = g^{a^2(sk_i + b_i)}.$$

$\mathcal{B}$ adds $< ID_i, pk_i, v_i, W_i >$ into the list L_w. If $coin_i = 1$, $\mathcal{B}$ outputs FAIL and aborts the simulation.

Sign Query: $\mathcal{A}_I$ issues a signing query on input (m_i, ID_i), where $1 \leq i \leq q_3$. $\mathcal{B}$ retrieves the private key sk_i from the list L_c. If it exists, runs the algorithm **Sign** and outputs a signature σ on message m_i. Otherwise, $\mathcal{B}$ runs **Corruption Query** first, then generates a signature as before.

Forgery: Eventually, $\mathcal{A}_I$ outputs a forgery $\sigma^* = (u^*, t^*)$ on message m^* under the witness W^* of identity ID^*. $\mathcal{A}_I$ wins the game if **Verify**$(m^*, \sigma^*, ID^*, W^*)$ outputs *true*, the pair (m^*, ID^*) does not be an input of **Sign Query** and W^* is not an output of **WitReg Query**. We assume that sk^* and b^* are in L_c and L_{h1}, respectively. $\mathcal{B}$ computes a solution of $(k+1)$-exponent problem ($k = 3$) as follows

$$g^{a^4} = (W^* g^{-a^2 sk^*})^{\frac{1}{b^*}}.$$

Probability: The simulator $\mathcal{B}$ outputs FAIL only if $coin_i = 1$ when the adversary queries a witness. Hence, the challenger can solve the $(k + 1)$-exponent problem in condition of the simulation is success and the forgery witness is related to the index i. The probability is $\epsilon' \geq \frac{1}{q_2} \cdot (1 - \frac{1}{q_2+1})^{q_2+1} \cdot \epsilon$ and the reduction process is as [3]. The time of an exponentiation in each query is denoted as $O(1)$, so the simulation time is $t' = t + O(q_{h_1} + q_2 + q_3)$. $\qquad\square$

Theorem 2. *Our SCS scheme is (t, q_1, q_2, ϵ)-secure against an existential forgery under Type II chosen message attack, assuming that the DL problem is (t', ϵ')-hard, where*

$$\epsilon' = \epsilon, \qquad t' \geq t + O(q_{h_1} + q_1 + 2q_2).$$

Proof. Suppose a *Type II adversary* $\mathcal{A}_{II}$ who can (t, q_1, q_2, ϵ)-break our SCS scheme. We can construct an algorithm $\mathcal{B}$ run by the challenger to use $\mathcal{A}_{II}$ to solve the DL problem. The algorithm $\mathcal{B}$ is given the DL instance (g, g^a), and the goal is to output a. $\mathcal{B}$ interacts with $\mathcal{A}_{II}$ in game 2 as follows.

Setup: $\mathcal{B}$ sets g as the generator of a group $\mathbb{G}$ and the master public key $mpk = g^\alpha$. Let the master secrete key $msk = \alpha$ and give it to $\mathcal{A}_{II}$. $\mathcal{B}$ maintains three list $L_{h1} = \{< ID, b >\}$, $L_{h2} = \{< M, c >\}$ and $L_{pk} = \{< ID, pk, s >\}$, which are initially empty.

h_1 **Query:** $\mathcal{A}_{II}$ issues an h_1 query on input ID_i at most q_{h_1} times, where $1 \leq i \leq q_{h_1}$. $\mathcal{B}$ outputs $h_1(ID_i)$ if ID_i is in the list L_{h1}. Otherwise, $\mathcal{B}$ randomly chooses $b_i \in \mathbb{Z}_p^*$ and sets $h_1(ID_i) = g^{b_i}$. Then, $\mathcal{B}$ outputs $h_1(ID_i)$ and adds $< ID_i, b_i >$ in the list L_{h1}.

h_2 **Query:** $\mathcal{A}_{II}$ issues an h_2 query on input string M_i at most q_{h_2} times, where $1 \leq i \leq q_{h_2}$. $\mathcal{B}$ answers the query as h_2 **Query** in game 1 and adds $< M_i, c_i >$ in the list L_{h2}.

Public-key Query: $\mathcal{A}_{II}$ issues a public-key query on input ID_i, where $1 \leq i \leq q_1$. $\mathcal{B}$ outputs pk_i if ID_i is in the list L_{pk}. Otherwise, $\mathcal{B}$ randomly chooses $s_i \in_R \mathbb{Z}_p^*$ and computes public key

$$pk_i = e(g^a, g)^{s_i}.$$

$\mathcal{B}$ then outputs pk_i and adds $< ID_i, pk_i, s_i >$ into the list L_{pk}.

Sign Query: $\mathcal{A}_{II}$ issues a signing query on input (m_i, ID_i), where $1 \leq i \leq q_2$. $\mathcal{B}$ answers queries as follows:

- If ID_i is not in L_{pk}, $\mathcal{B}$ runs **Public-Key Query**.
- Otherwise, $\mathcal{B}$ randomly selects $c_i, r_i \in_R \mathbb{Z}_p^*$ and computes

$$u_i = g^{\frac{1}{c_i}} (g^a)^{-s_i r_i}, \quad t_i = c_i r_i.$$

Let $M_i = m_i \| u_i$ and $h_2(M_i) = c_i$, $\mathcal{B}$ adds $< M_i, c_i >$ into the list L_{h_2} and outputs the signature $\sigma_i = (u_i, t_i)$.

Forgery: Eventually, $\mathcal{A}_{II}$ outputs a forgery $\sigma^* = (u^*, t^*)$ on message m^* under a witness W^* of the identity ID^*. $\mathcal{A}_{II}$ wins the game if **Verify**$(m^*, \sigma^*, ID^*, W^*)$ outputs *true* and the pair (m^*, ID^*) is never queried to the **Sign Query**. Then, $\mathcal{B}$ can run the same random tape and a different h_2 to output another valid signature $\sigma^{*\prime} = (u^{*\prime}, t^{*\prime})$. The outputs of two h_2 hash functions are respectively c^* and $c^{*\prime}$, where $c^* \neq c^{*\prime}$. We assume that s^* is in the list L_{pk}. $\mathcal{B}$ can compute

$$\begin{cases} 1 - r^*c^* = as^*t^*, \\ 1 - r^*c^{*\prime} = as^*t^{*\prime}, \end{cases} \qquad a = \frac{c^{*\prime} - c^*}{s^*(t^*c^{*\prime} - t^{*\prime}c^*)} ,$$

as a solution of DL problem.

Probability: The simulator $\mathcal{B}$ does not outputs FAIL in any queries. The challenger can solve the DL problem in condition of the successful simulation. Hence, the probability is $\epsilon' = \epsilon$. The time consuming of an exponentiation is considered as $O(1)$. Therefore, the simulation time is $t' = t + O(q_{h_1} + q_1 + 2q_2)$. $\square$

5   Self-certified Signatures with Precomputations

Even, Goldreich and Micali introduced the notion of online/offline signatures [6] to improve the signature generation efficiency. Their main idea is to split the signature generation into two stages, namely offline stage and online stage. Most heavy computations are carried out in the offline stage prior to the availability of the message. Once the message is received, the algorithm can output a signature quickly by conducting the online stage. They proposed a method which converts any signature schemes into an online/offline signature scheme. However, it is impractical. Subsequently, Shamir and Tauman presented an efficient "*hash-sign-switch*" paradigm [18]. The size of signatures are largely reduced while the efficiency is maintained.

Our scheme provides pre-computations in the signing stage as some other schemes mentioned in [18]. It is easy to partition our scheme into two parts: offline stage and online stage. In the offline stage, the signer picks a random choice r', where $r' \in_R \mathbb{Z}_p^*$. Then he/she computes $u' = g^{r'}$ and $t' = \frac{r'}{x}$. The pair (u', t') should be securely stored. In the online stage, the signer retrieves a pair (u', t'), and computes $u = u', t = x^{-1} - t'h_2(m||u')$ as a signature on the message m. Hence, in the online signature operations, it only requires a modular multiplication and a subtraction, provided that the signer stores the inverse of his private key x^{-1}. In addition, the length of our self-certified signature scheme is as short as [18].

6   Batch Verification

The notion of batch verification was introduced by Fiat in 1989 [7]. Generally, the motivation of batch verification is to improve the verification efficiency when verifying large number of signatures. According to the three paradigms of batch verification scheme proposed in [2], we apply the *Small Exponent Test* in this paper. The length l of the exponent is a security parameter that depends on the security requirement in practice. Batch verification for single-signer and multi-signer settings are both provided in this section.

6.1   Single-Signer Batch Verification

In the single-signer setting, there is no need to implicitly verify signer public keys in all signatures, since all public keys are the same. Therefore, we assume that the signer's public key has been recovered and the equation (3) is used in the verification. Nevertheless, the equation (2) can be used in a similar way if the public key is not computed.

Let $(\mathbb{G}, \mathbb{G}_T, g, p, e, h_1, h_2, mpk)$ be public parameters and $k = |\mathbb{G}| = |\mathbb{G}_T|$. Given a set of signatures $S = \{\sigma_1, \sigma_2, \ldots, \sigma_n\}$, where $\sigma_i = (u_i, t_i)$, on messages $M = \{m_1, m_2, \ldots, m_n\}$ from the same singer in which $pk = e(g, g)^x$. The verifier checks S as follows.

- If $u_i \notin \mathbb{G}$, where $i = 1, 2, \ldots, n$, rejects all signatures and outputs *false*.
- Otherwise, randomly selects l-bits elements $(\lambda_1, \lambda_2, \ldots, \lambda_n) \in \mathbb{Z}_p^n$, where $l < k$, and computes:

$$T = \lambda_1 t_1 + \lambda_2 t_2 + \ldots + \lambda_n t_n = \sum_{i=1}^{n} \lambda_i t_i \ ,$$

$$U = u_1^{\lambda_1 h_2(m_1 || u_1)} \cdot u_2^{\lambda_2 h_2(m_2 || u_2)} \ldots u_i^{\lambda_i h_2(m_i || u_i)} = \prod_{i=1}^{n} u_i^{\lambda_i h_2(m_i || u_i)} \ ,$$

$$C = \lambda_1 + \lambda_2 + \ldots + \lambda_i = \sum_{i=1}^{n} \lambda_i.$$

Accepts all signatures and outputs *true* if the equation holds

$$e(g, g)^{xT} e(U, g) = e(g, g)^C.$$

Correctness

$$e(g, g)^{xT} e(U, g)$$
$$= e(g, g)^{x \sum_{i=1}^{n} \lambda_i t_i} e(g, g)^{\sum_{i=1}^{n} r_i \lambda_i h_2(m_i || u_i)}$$
$$= e(\prod_{i=1}^{n} g^{\lambda_i - r_i \lambda_i h_2(m_i || u_i)}, g) e(\prod_{i=1}^{n} g^{r_i \lambda_i h_2(m_i || u_i)}, g)$$
$$= e(g, g)^C.$$

Let A be a modular addition in $\mathbb{Z}_p^*$ and Pa is a pairing calculation. Mul_s is a modular multiplication in group s. An l-bits exponentiation in group s is denoted as $Ex_s(l)$ and a test of a group member is Gt. Computational cost of has functions in both types of verification are ignored since they are the same. The cost of native verification and batch verification on n signatures in single-signer setting are respectively,

$$n Ex_{\mathbb{G}}(k) + n Ex_{\mathbb{G}_T}(k) + n Pa + n Mul_{\mathbb{G}_T}$$

and

$$n Gt + 2n Mul_{\mathbb{Z}_p^*} + 2(n-1)A + n Ex_{\mathbb{G}}(k) + 1 Ex_{\mathbb{G}_T}(k)$$
$$+ 1 Pa + 1 Ex_{\mathbb{G}_T}(l) + (n-1) Mul_{\mathbb{G}} + 1 Mul_{\mathbb{G}_T}.$$

Theorem 3. *The batch verification of our self-certified signature scheme in single-signer setting is secure, if there is no adversary with probability at least 2^{-l}, where l is the length of a small exponent.*

Proof. Suppose that an adversary outputs a forgery (M^*, S^*) accepted by batch verification under identity ID. We show that the probability of a valid forgery depends on the length l of a small exponent.

Without losing generality, we assume that the public key $pk = e(g, g)^x$ has been recovered from (1). A signature $\sigma_i^* = (u_i^*, t_i^*)$ can be considered as

$$\sigma_i^* = (g^{r_i}, \frac{1 - r_i h_2(m_i^* \| g^{r_i}) + k_i}{x}),$$

where $r_i, k_i \in_R \mathbb{Z}_p^*$. If $k_i = 0$, the signature is valid. Otherwise, it is invalid. Then, we can compute that

$$T^* = \lambda_1 t_1^* + \lambda_2 t_2^* + \ldots + \lambda_n t_n^* = \sum_{i=1}^n \lambda_i t_i^*, \quad U^* = U, \quad C^* = C.$$

If the following equation holds

$$e(g, g)^{xT^*} e(U^*, g)$$
$$= e(g^x, g)^{\sum_{i=1}^n \lambda_i t_i^*} e(g, g)^{\sum_{i=1}^n r_i \lambda_i h_2(m_i^* \| u_i)}$$
$$= e(\prod_{i=1}^n g^{\lambda_i - r_i \lambda_i h_2(m_i^* \| u_i) + \lambda_i k_i}, g) e(\prod_{i=1}^n g^{r_i \lambda_i h_2(m_i^* \| u_i)}, g)$$
$$= e(g, g)^{C^*},$$

then $\sum_{i=1}^n \lambda_i k_i \equiv 0 \pmod{p}$. Assuming that at least one signature σ_j^* is invalid. It implies the adversary can find a k_j such that

$$\lambda_j \equiv -k_j^{-1} \sum_{i=1, i \neq j}^n \lambda_i k_i \pmod{p}, \quad k_j \neq 0.$$

However, small exponents λ_i, where $i = 1, 2, \ldots, n$, are l-bits random choices selected by the verifier. Hence, the probability of an adversary break the batch verification is equal to the probability of the equation hold, where

$$\Pr\left[\lambda_j \equiv -k_j^{-1} \sum_{i=1, i \neq j}^n \lambda_i k_i \pmod{p} \,\middle|\, \sum_{i=1}^n \lambda_i k_i \equiv 0 \pmod{p}\right] \leq 2^{-l}.$$

$\square$

6.2   Multi-signer Batch Verification

Generally speaking, the batch verification in a single-signer setting is a special case of that in a multi-signer setting. The amount of pairing computations normally depend on the number of signers in the multi-signer batch verification. However, we show that our scheme only needs constant pairing computations.

Suppose that public keys have not been recovered in this case. Let $(\mathbb{G}, \mathbb{G}_T, g, p,$ $e, h_1, h_2, mpk)$ be public parameters and $k = |\mathbb{G}| = |\mathbb{G}_T|$. Given a set of signatures $S = \{\sigma_1, \sigma_2, \ldots, \sigma_n\}$, where $\sigma_i = (u_i, t_i)$, on messages $M = \{m_1, m_2, \ldots, m_n\}$ with witnesses $WT = \{W_1, W_2, \ldots, W_n\}$ under identity $I = \{ID_1, ID_2 \ldots, ID_n\}$, respectively. The verifier checks S as follows.

- If $u_i \notin \mathbb{G}$, where $i = 1, 2, \ldots, n$, rejects all signatures and outputs *false*.
- Otherwise, randomly selects l-bits elements $(\lambda_1, \lambda_2, \ldots, \lambda_n) \in \mathbb{Z}_p^n$, where $l < k$, and computes:

$$T = W_1^{\lambda_1 t_1} \cdot W_2^{\lambda_2 t_2} \ldots W_n^{\lambda_n t_n} = \prod_{i=1}^{n} W_i^{\lambda_i t_i},$$

$$U = (u_1^{h_2(m_1\|u_1)} h_1(ID_1)^{-t_1})^{\lambda_1} \cdot (u_2^{h_2(m_2\|u_2)} h_1(ID_2)^{-t_2})^{\lambda_2}$$
$$\ldots (u_i^{h_2(m_i\|u_i)} h_1(ID_i)^{-t_i})^{\lambda_i}$$
$$= \prod_{i=1}^{n} (u_i^{h_2(m_i\|u_i)} h_1(ID_i)^{-t_i})^{\lambda_i},$$

$$C = \lambda_1 + \lambda_2 + \ldots + \lambda_i = \sum_{i=1}^{n} \lambda_i.$$

Accepts all signatures and outputs *true* if the equation holds

$$e(T, mpk)e(U, g) = e(g, g)^C.$$

Correctness

$$e(T, mpk)e(U, g)$$
$$= e(g^{x_i} h(ID_i), g)^{\sum_{i=1}^{n} \lambda_i t_i} e(\prod_{i=1}^{n} (u_i^{h_2(m_i\|u_i)} h_1(ID_i)^{-t_i})^{\lambda_i}, g)$$
$$= e(g, g)^{\sum_{i=1}^{n} x_i \lambda_i t_i} e(g, g)^{\sum_{i=1}^{n} r_i \lambda_i h_2(m_i\|u_i)}$$
$$= e(\prod_{i=1}^{n} g^{\lambda_i - r_i \lambda_i h_2(m_i\|u_i)}, g) e(\prod_{i=1}^{n} g^{r_i \lambda_i h_2(m_i\|u_i)}, g)$$
$$= e(g, g)^C.$$

The cost of the original verification and the batch verification on n signatures in a multi-signer setting are respectively,

$$3nEx_{\mathbb{G}}(k) + nMul_{\mathbb{G}} + 2nPa + nMul_{\mathbb{G}_T}$$

and

$$nGt + nMul_{\mathbb{Z}_p^*} + 3nEx_{\mathbb{G}}(k) + (3n - 2)Mul_{\mathbb{G}} + nEx_{\mathbb{G}}(l)$$
$$+ (n - 1)A + 2Pa + 1Mul_{\mathbb{G}_T} + 1Ex_{\mathbb{G}_T}(l).$$

Theorem 4. *The batch verification of our self-certified signature scheme in multi-signer setting is secure, if there is no adversary with probability at least 2^{-l}, where l is the length of a small exponent.*

Proof. The proof is similar to the proof of Theorem 3 and we omit it.

7 Conclusion

In this paper, we proposed an efficient and novel self-certified signature scheme. With pre-computation, our scheme requires only one modular multiplication for signature generation. Our scheme allows the batch verification in both single-singer and multi-signer settings. We showed that in the multi-signer setting, the verification of n signatures requires only two pairing computations regardless of the size of n. Our self-certified signature scheme was proven secure in the random oracle model.

References

1. Al-Riyami, S.S., Paterson, K.G.: Certificateless Public Key Cryptography. In: Laih, C.-S. (ed.) ASIACRYPT 2003. LNCS, vol. 2894, pp. 452–473. Springer, Heidelberg (2003)
2. Bellare, M., Garay, J.A., Rabin, T.: Fast Batch Verification for Modular Exponentiation and Digital Signatures. In: Nyberg, K. (ed.) EUROCRYPT 1998. LNCS, vol. 1403, pp. 236–250. Springer, Heidelberg (1998)
3. Boneh, D., Lynn, B., Shacham, H.: Short signatures from the weil pairing. J. Cryptology 17(4), 297–319 (2004)
4. Choi, K.Y., Park, J.-H., Hwang, J.Y., Lee, D.-H.: Efficient Certificateless Signature Schemes. In: Katz, J., Yung, M. (eds.) ACNS 2007. LNCS, vol. 4521, pp. 443–458. Springer, Heidelberg (2007)
5. Chow, S.S.M.: Removing Escrow from Identity-Based Encryption. In: Jarecki, S., Tsudik, G. (eds.) PKC 2009. LNCS, vol. 5443, pp. 256–276. Springer, Heidelberg (2009)
6. Even, S., Goldreich, O., Micali, S.: On-Line/Off-Line Digital Signatures. In: Brassard, G. (ed.) CRYPTO 1989. LNCS, vol. 435, pp. 263–275. Springer, Heidelberg (1990)
7. Fiat, A.: Batch RSA. In: Brassard, G. (ed.) CRYPTO 1989. LNCS, vol. 435, pp. 175–185. Springer, Heidelberg (1990)
8. Gentry, C.: Certificate-Based Encryption and the Certificate Revocation Problem. In: Biham, E. (ed.) EUROCRYPT 2003. LNCS, vol. 2656, pp. 272–293. Springer, Heidelberg (2003)
9. Gentry, C., Ramzan, Z.: Identity-Based Aggregate Signatures. In: Yung, M., Dodis, Y., Kiayias, A., Malkin, T. (eds.) PKC 2006. LNCS, vol. 3958, pp. 257–273. Springer, Heidelberg (2006)
10. Girault, M.: Self-certified Public Keys. In: Davies, D.W. (ed.) EUROCRYPT 1991. LNCS, vol. 547, pp. 490–497. Springer, Heidelberg (1991)
11. Goldwasser, S., Micali, S., Rivest, R.L.: A digital signature scheme secure against adaptive chosen-message attacks. SIAM Journal on Computing 17(2), 281–308 (1988)

12. Liu, J.K., Baek, J., Susilo, W., Zhou, J.: Certificate-Based Signature Schemes without Pairings or Random Oracles. In: Wu, T.-C., Lei, C.-L., Rijmen, V., Lee, D.-T. (eds.) ISC 2008. LNCS, vol. 5222, pp. 285–297. Springer, Heidelberg (2008)
13. Mitsunari, S., Sakai, R., Kasahara, M.: A new traitor tracing. IEICE Tran. E85-A(2), 481–484 (2002)
14. Paterson, K.G., Schuldt, J.C.N.: Efficient Identity-Based Signatures Secure in the Standard Model. In: Batten, L.M., Safavi-Naini, R. (eds.) ACISP 2006. LNCS, vol. 4058, pp. 207–222. Springer, Heidelberg (2006)
15. Petersen, H., Horster, P.: Self-certified keys - concepts and applications. In: Proceeding of Communications and Multimedia Security 1997, pp. 102–116. Chapman & Hall (1997)
16. Saeednia, S.: A note on girault's self-certified model. Inf. Process. Lett. 86(6), 323–327 (2003)
17. Shamir, A.: Identity-Based Cryptosystems and Signature Schemes. In: Blakely, G.R., Chaum, D. (eds.) CRYPTO 1984. LNCS, vol. 196, pp. 47–53. Springer, Heidelberg (1985)
18. Shamir, A., Tauman, Y.: Improved Online/Offline Signature Schemes. In: Kilian, J. (ed.) CRYPTO 2001. LNCS, vol. 2139, pp. 355–367. Springer, Heidelberg (2001)
19. Wu, W., Mu, Y., Susilo, W., Huang, X.: Certificate-based signatures revisited. J. UCS 15(8), 1659–1684 (2009)
20. Yap, W.-S., Chow, S.S.M., Heng, S.-H., Goi, B.-M.: Security Mediated Certificateless Signatures. In: Katz, J., Yung, M. (eds.) ACNS 2007. LNCS, vol. 4521, pp. 459–477. Springer, Heidelberg (2007)
21. Yoon, H., Cheon, J.H., Kim, Y.: Batch Verifications with ID-Based Signatures. In: Park, C., Chee, S. (eds.) ICISC 2004. LNCS, vol. 3506, pp. 233–248. Springer, Heidelberg (2005)
22. Yuen, T.H., Susilo, W., Mu, Y.: How to Construct Identity-Based Signatures without the Key Escrow Problem. In: Martinelli, F., Preneel, B. (eds.) EuroPKI 2009. LNCS, vol. 6391, pp. 286–301. Springer, Heidelberg (2010)
23. Zhang, F., Kim, K.: ID-Based Blind Signature and Ring Signature from Pairings. In: Zheng, Y. (ed.) ASIACRYPT 2002. LNCS, vol. 2501, pp. 533–547. Springer, Heidelberg (2002)
24. Zhang, F., Safavi-Naini, R., Susilo, W.: An Efficient Signature Scheme from Bilinear Pairings and Its Applications. In: Bao, F., Deng, R., Zhou, J. (eds.) PKC 2004. LNCS, vol. 2947, pp. 277–290. Springer, Heidelberg (2004)
25. Zhou, Y., Cao, Z., Lu, R.: An efficient digital signature using self-certified public keys. In: Proceedings of the 3rd International Conference on Information Security, vol. 85, pp. 44–47. ACM (2004)

A Generic Construction from Selective-IBE to Public-Key Encryption with Non-interactive Opening*

Jiang Zhang, Xiang Xie, Rui Zhang, and Zhenfeng Zhang

State Key Laboratory of Information Security,
Institute of Software, Chinese Academy of Sciences, Beijing, 100190, China
{zhangjiang,xiexiang,r-zhang,zfzhang}@is.iscas.ac.cn

Abstract. Public-key encryption schemes with non-interactive opening (PKENO) allow a receiver who received a ciphertext c to non-interactively convince third parties that the decryption of c is what he has claimed, without compromising the scheme's security. In this work, we present a generic construction from identity-based encryption scheme, which is secure against selective-ID and chosen plaintext attack (IND-sID-CPA), to PKENO with chameleon hash instead of the one-time signature technology. Our construction gives new view of IBE-to-PKENO technique, and some previously known PKENO schemes can be viewed as concrete instantiations of our generic construction. At last, we also give a new instantiation, which is (slightly) more efficient than the best known scheme [13].

1 Introduction

Public-key encryption (PKE) allows a receiver Bob to generate a pair of public key and private key (pk_B, sk_B), then he makes pk_B public and keeps sk_B secret. Anyone can use the public key pk_B to encrypt message m, but only Bob who knows the secret key sk_B can decrypt the ciphertext under pk_B. Identity Based Encryption (IBE) was introduced by Shamir [14]. The motivation of this concept was to simplify key management and avoid the use of digital certificates. The public key can be any information non-ambiguously identifying its owner (e.g., e-mail address) while the associated private keys can only be computed by a trusted Key Generation Center (KGC) with the help of a master secret.

Consider the following situation in multiparty computations, player Alice sends a secret message to player Bob, then Bob checks what he receives to proceed. Otherwise, Bob can't move forward and needs to do some "exception handling". A solution to this problem is to have Bob broadcast a complaint, and Alice must broadcast what she has sent to Bob, then all players can check the information. This solution is reasonable, but it has an important drawback that

* The work is supported by the National Natural Science Foundation of China under Grant No. 60873261, 61170278, and the National Basic Research Program (973) of China under Grant No. 2007CB311202.

C.-K. Wu, M. Yung, and D. Lin (Eds.): Inscrypt 2011, LNCS 7537, pp. 195–209, 2012.

interaction is required. In particular, Alice must be present to help resolve the conflict. In some cases, this is unpractical.

In 2007, Damgård and Thorbek [8] introduced the notion of Public-key encryption schemes with non-interactive opening (PKENO), which is a special kind of PKE and can efficiently solve the above problem. By using PKENO, the secret key's owner (i.e., Bob) can convincingly prove to a verifier (e.g., Victor) that the result of decrypting ciphertext c is actually m, without interaction and compromising the confidentiality of non-opened ciphertexts. In particular, Damgård and Thorbek [8] used PKENO as a building block in their scheme to prove that a given party did not follow the protocol, namely, has sent fake ciphertext.

Technically, there is a straightforward solution to implement PKENO. We can use a PKE combining a non-interactive zero knowledge (NIZK) to implement PKENO, since the receiver can prove a message m is the result of decrypting c by using NIZK. Unfortunately, with the known techniques, the above solution is very inefficient and essentially useless in practice. Though, we can construct efficient NIZKs in the random oracle model, but it is well-known that a security proof in the random oracle model does not guarantee its security in the real world, thus, should be avoided whenever possible.

Damgård and Thorbek [8] suggested that PKENO can be implemented from identity-based encryption. And in [7], Damgård, Hofheinz, Kiltz and Thorbek present a generic construction using IBEs scheme and one-time signatures. Their method is basically adopted from CHK technique [6], which transforms any chosen plaintext secure (CPA) IBE into a chosen ciphertext secure (CCA) PKE scheme. Their construction is direct, but the strongly unforgeable one-time signature makes the construction inefficient. They also gave a concrete construction based on Boyen, Mei and Waters' CCA PKE [5]. But unfortunately, their concrete scheme was shown to be insecure by Galindo [9]. Galindo thus presented a fixed scheme based on the adaptive-IBE version in [5]. Galindo's new scheme is secure under decision bilinear Diffie-Hellman (DBDH) assumption in standard model with a price of long public keys and secret keys.

Recently, Galindo et al. [10] gave a new generic construction from any robust non-interactive threshold encryption (TPKE) to PKENO, together with two concrete PKENO schemes. The first one is efficient, but its security is only guaranteed in the random oracle model. The second one uses one-time signature, thus it is not efficient in the sense of ciphertext overhead. Lai, Deng, Liu and Kou [13] proposed an efficient PKENO scheme, and they stated that their scheme took advantage of the techniques in [6] and [5]. Namely, they use two types of "identities", one is chosen randomly for each ciphertext as in [6] (i.e., the verification key), the other is uniquely determined by the first two elements of a ciphertext as in [5]. It seems that Lai et al.'s strategy highly relies on particular mathematical structure of the underlying IBE.

Our Contribution. In this paper, we demonstrate that one can achieve better efficiency by taking advantage of underlying IBEs. In particular, we use IBEs with special structure called separability [15]. In a separable IBE, the encryption algorithm can be separated into two parts. One part is uniquely determined by the master public key mpk, the message m and the random coin r, in brief $u \leftarrow f_1(mpk, m, r)$, and the other part is uniquely determined by the master public key mpk, identity id and the random coin r, in brief $v \leftarrow f_2(mpk, id, r)$. For our purpose, we emphasize that the two deterministic functions f_1, f_2 use the same randomness (i.e, r) and (u, id) uniquely determines v.

In our generic construction, we use a similar technique as [15,1]. The idea is that we use IBE's master public key mpk as PKENO's public key pk, and use IBE's master secret key msk as PKENO's secret key sk. To encrypt message m, we first compute $u \leftarrow f_1(pk, m, r_1)$, then we hash u by using a chameleon hash H and a random coin r_2, in brief, $id \leftarrow H(u, r_2)$. Next, we compute $v \leftarrow f_2(pk, id, r_1)$. The triple (u, v, r_2) is the ciphertext of m. To decrypt ciphertext $c = (u, v, r_2)$, we just need to extract the secret sk_{id} corresponding to $id = H(u, r_2)$, and use the IBE's decryption algorithm to decrypt c. The receiver just outputs a secret key sk_{id} corresponding to $id = H(u, r_2)$ as a proof for $(c = (u, v, r_2), m)$. Note that anyone can verify whether the decryption of c is m by decrypting c using sk_{id}.

The correctness of our generic PKENO construction is guaranteed by the correctness of underlying IBEs. The security of the PKENO can be reduced to the chosen plaintext security of selective-IBE or the collision resistance of chameleon hash. Our generic scheme benefits from the chameleon hash function in two aspects. First it makes our generic construction achieved chosen-ciphertext and prove attacks (CCPA) security and proof soundness only by using a weaker primitive, say selective-IBE. Second, since the trapdoor of the chameleon hash function is only used in the security proof, and never used in the real world, in practice, we can further improve the efficiency by using practical hash functions, say SHA-1. Compared to the generic transform in [7], which needs strong unforgeable one-time signature, we greatly improve the efficiency.

Moreover, our generic construction gives a seemingly more succinct explanation of Lai et al.'s PKENO scheme [13], and we will review this later. In addition, we also give a new construction based on the well known Boneh-Boyen IBE [2]. The resulting scheme achieves slightly better efficiency and lower computation costs than Lai et al.'s. Finally, we summarize our methodology and compare it with previous ones, and conclude that our methodology is very efficient.

2 Preliminaries

2.1 Notation

If x is a string, $|x|$ denotes its length, and if S is a set, $|S|$ denotes its size. Denote $x\|y$ as the bit concatenation of two strings $x, y \in \{0, 1\}^*$. We use 1^k to denote the string of k ones for some positive integer k. We use the notation $\leftarrow$ to denote randomly choosing an element from some set (distribution) or indicate the output of some algorithm. For example, $s \leftarrow S$ means that we randomly choose an element s from the set (distribution) S, and $z \leftarrow \mathcal{A}(x, y, \dots)$ means that the output of algorithm $\mathcal{A}$ with inputs $x, y, \dots,$ is z. We say a function $f(n)$

is negligible if for every $c > 0$, there exists a N such that $f(n) < 1/n^c$ for all $n > N$. Usually, we denote an unspecific negligible function by $negl(n)$. We say a probability is overwhelming if it is $1 - negl(n)$.

2.2   Bilinear Groups and Assumptions

Let positive integer k be the security parameter. $\mathbb{G}_1$ and $\mathbb{G}_2$ are two cyclic groups of the same prime order q $(2^k < q < 2^{k+1})$. A bilinear pairing is a map $\hat{e} : \mathbb{G}_1 \times \mathbb{G}_1 \to \mathbb{G}_2$ which satisfies the following properties:

- Bilinear: $\hat{e}(u^a, v^b) = \hat{e}(u, v)^{ab}$ for all $u, v \in \mathbb{G}_1$ and $a, b \in Z_q^*$.
- Non-degenerate: there exists $u, v \in \mathbb{G}_1$ such that $\hat{e}(u, v) \neq 1$.
- Computable: there is an efficient algorithm to compute $\hat{e}(u, v)$ for all $u, v \in \mathbb{G}_1$.

Throughout the paper, we use $\mathbb{G}_1^*$ to denote $\mathbb{G}_1 \backslash \{0\}$, i.e. the set of all group elements except the neutral element, and use $\mathcal{PG} = \{\mathbb{G}_1, \mathbb{G}_2, q, \hat{e}\}$ as shorthand for the description of bilinear groups.

The DBDH Assumption. Let $\mathcal{PG} = \{\mathbb{G}_1, \mathbb{G}_2, q, \hat{e}\}$ be the description of bilinear groups and g be a generator of $\mathbb{G}_1$. The decisional bilinear Diffie-Hellman assumption (DBDH) states that the two distributions $(g^x, g^y, g^z, \hat{e}(g, g)^{xyz})$ and $(g^x, g^y, g^z, \hat{e}(g, g)^r)$, where x, y, z, r are randomly and independently chosen from $\mathbb{Z}_q$, are indistinguishable for any polynomial time adversary. Formally, for any polynomial time adversary $\mathcal{A}$, its advantage

$$\mathrm{Adv}_{\mathcal{PG}, \mathcal{A}}^{\mathrm{dbdh}}(k) = |\Pr[\mathcal{A}(g^x, g^y, g^z, \hat{e}(g, g)^{xyz}) = 1] - \Pr[\mathcal{A}(g^x, g^y, g^z, \hat{e}(g, g)^r) = 1]|$$

is negligible in security parameter k, where the probability is over the random choice of x, y, z, r in $\mathbb{Z}_q$ and the random bits of $\mathcal{A}$.

The q-DBDHI Assumption. Let $\mathcal{PG} = \{\mathbb{G}_1, \mathbb{G}_2, q, \hat{e}\}$ be the description of bilinear groups and g be a generator of $\mathbb{G}_1$. The q-decision bilinear Diffie-Hellman inversion assumption (q-DBDHI) states that the two distributions $(g, g^x, \ldots, g^{x^q}, \hat{e}(g, g)^{1/x})$ and $(g, g^x, \ldots, g^{x^q}, \hat{e}(g, g)^r)$, where x, r are randomly and independently chosen from $\mathbb{Z}_q$, are indistinguishable for any polynomial time adversary. Formally, for any polynomial time adversary $\mathcal{A}$, its advantage

$$\mathrm{Adv}_{\mathcal{PG}, \mathcal{A}}^{q\text{-dbdhi}}(k) = |\Pr[\mathcal{A}\,(g, g^x, \ldots, g^{x^q}, \hat{e}(g, g)^{1/x}) = 1] \\ - \Pr[\mathcal{A}(g, g^x, \ldots, g^{x^q}, \hat{e}(g, g)^r) = 1]|$$

is negligible in security parameter k, where the probability is over the random choice of x, r in $\mathbb{Z}_q$ and the random bits of $\mathcal{A}$.

2.3   Chameleon Hash Function

A chameleon hash function is a trapdoor collision resistant hash function, which is associated with a key pair (hk, td). Anyone who knows the public key hk can efficiently compute the hash value for each input. However, there exists no efficient algorithm for anyone without the secret key td to find collisions for every given input.

Formally, a chameleon hash function consists of three algorithms $\mathcal{CMH} =$ (CMkg, CMhash, CMswch). The randomized key generation algorithm CMkg takes a security parameter k as input, outputs a hash key hk and a trapdoor td, denoted as $(hk, td) \leftarrow \text{CMkg}(1^k)$. The randomized hashing algorithm takes as input a public key hk, an auxiliary random coin w drawn from space $\mathcal{R}$ and a value $x \in \{0, 1\}^*$, outputs a binary string y of fixed length l, denoted as $y \leftarrow \text{CMhash}(hk, x, w)$. The switch algorithm CMswch takes as input the trapdoor td, a pair (x, w) and a message $x^* \neq x$, outputs w^*, such that $\text{CMhash}(hk, x, w) = \text{CMhash}(hk, x^*, w^*)$, denoted as $w^* \leftarrow \text{CMswch}(td, x, w, x^*)$. Finally, for all $x, x^* \in \{0, 1\}^*$ and $w \in \mathcal{R}$, we require $w^* \leftarrow \text{CMswch}(td, x, w, x^*)$ is uniformly distributed in $\mathcal{R}$ and we call this property the uniformness of a chameleon hash function. We next give the security requirements for a chameleon hash, namely collision resistance (CR).

Collision Resistance. We say a chameleon hash function is $(\epsilon_{\mathcal{H}}, T_{\mathcal{H}})$-collision resistant (CR) if any adversary $\mathcal{A}$ without access to the trapdoor td, the success probability of finding collisions is at most ϵ_H within time $T_{\mathcal{H}}$ in the following experiment.

$$\text{Succ}^{cr}_{\mathcal{CMH}, \mathcal{A}}(k) = \Pr[(hk, td) \leftarrow \text{CMkg}(1^k); x \leftarrow \mathcal{A}(hk); w \leftarrow \mathcal{R};$$
$$y \leftarrow \text{CMhash}(hk, x, w); (x', w') \leftarrow \mathcal{A}(hk, x, w)$$
$$: (x'; w') \neq (x; w) \wedge y = \text{CMhash}(hk, x', w')].$$

We say a chameleon hash function is collision resistant, if for any polynomially bounded $T_{\mathcal{H}}$, $\epsilon_{\mathcal{H}}$ is negligible.

Implementation of chameleon hash. In 1998, Krawczyk and Rabin [12] proposed several efficient chameleon hash constructions based on Factoring and Discrete Log (DL). And the most well known construction is the one based on the chameleon commitment scheme [4]. Intuitively, for prime number $p = kq + 1$ (q is also a prime number) and $g \in \mathbb{Z}_p^*$ is an element of order q, choose $x \in \mathbb{Z}_q^*$ and compute $y = g^x \bmod p$. Set the hash key $hk = (p, q, g, y)$ and trapdoor $td = x$. Given message $m \in \mathbb{Z}_q^*$, choose a random number $r \in \mathbb{Z}_q^*$ and compute the hash value $\text{CMhash}(hk, m, r) = g^m y^r \bmod p$. For more details, please refer to [12].

2.4   Identity Based Encryption

An IBE scheme consists of four algorithms $\mathcal{IBE} =$ (IBEkg, IBEext, IBEenc, IBEdec). The randomized key generation algorithm IBEkg, taking a security parameter k as input, outputs a public parameter mpk and a master secret key msk, denoted as $(pk, msk) \leftarrow$ IBEkg(1^k). The extract algorithm, possibly randomized, takes inputs of mpk, msk and an identity id, outputs a secret key sk_{id} for id, denoted as $sk_{id} \leftarrow$ IBEext(mpk, msk, id), in brief $sk_{id} \leftarrow$ IBEext(msk, id). The randomized encryption algorithm IBEenc takes pk, an identity id and a plaintext m taken from the message space as inputs, with internal coin flipping r, outputs a ciphertext c, which is denoted as $c \leftarrow$ IBEenc(mpk, id, m, r), in brief $c \leftarrow$ IBEenc(mpk, id, m). The deterministic algorithm IBEdec takes a secret key sk_{id}, an identity id and a ciphertext c as inputs, outputs a plaintext m, or a special symbol $\perp$, which is denoted $m \leftarrow$ IBEdec(sk_{id}, id, c). We require for all $(mpk, msk) \leftarrow$ IBEkg(1^k), $sk_{id} \leftarrow$ IBEext(msk, id) and $\forall$ message m, we have IBEdec$(sk_{id}, id,$ IBEenc$(mpk, id, m)) = m$.

Separability. An $\mathcal{IBE}$ is said to be sparable if the encryption algorithm can be arranged in two parts, such that one part is uniquely determined by mpk, m and the random coin r, in brief $u \leftarrow f_1(mpk, m, r)$, and the other part is uniquely determined by the mpk, id and r, in brief $v \leftarrow f_2(mpk, id, r)$. Moreover, we require that (u, id) uniquely determines v, and this property, which was called Unique Split Property by Abe et al. [1] , is very important in our security proof. The ciphertext is $c = \langle u, v \rangle$. We insist that r is essentially used in both parts, since some trivial functions, e.g., an identity function may not follow our discussion herein.

IND-sID-CPA *Security.* We consider the security of indistinguishability against selective-ID and chosen plaintext attack (IND-sID-CPA). We say an identity based encryption with security parameter k is (ϵ, q, T)-IND-sID-CPA-secure if the advantage of any adversary $\mathcal{A}$ is at most ϵ, with access q times to an extraction oracle $\mathcal{EO}$ within time T in the following experiment.

$$
\begin{aligned}
\mathrm{Adv}_{\mathcal{IBE}, \mathcal{A}}^{\text{ind-sid-cpa}}(k) = |\Pr[& (id^*, s_0) \leftarrow \mathcal{A}(1^k); (mpk, msk) \leftarrow \text{IBEkg}(1^k); \\
& (m_0, m_1, s_1) \leftarrow \mathcal{A}^{\mathcal{EO}(\cdot)}(mpk; s_0); b \leftarrow \{0, 1\}; \\
& c^* \leftarrow \text{IBEenc}(mpk, id^*, m_b); b' \leftarrow \mathcal{A}^{\mathcal{EO}(\cdot)}(c^*, s_1) \\
& : b' = b] - 1/2|
\end{aligned}
$$

where $\mathcal{EO}(\cdot)$ returns the corresponding secret key on a query on identity id, whereas $\mathcal{A}$ is forbidden to query id^* at $\mathcal{EO}$. For non-triviality, we also require that $|m_0| = |m_1|$. We say an $\mathcal{IBE}$ is IND-sID-CPA-Secure, if for polynomially bounded q and T, ϵ is negligible.

As in [7], we require that there exists an efficient algorithm IBEver that can publicly and efficiently verify whether a given user secret key sk_{id} was properly generated for identity id. Namely, the algorithm IBEver takes a master public key mpk, an identity id and a secret key sk_{id} as input, outputs *accept* or *reject*. We require that for all honestly generated key pair $(mpk, msk) \leftarrow$ IBEkg(1^k) satisfies the following: For all identities $id \in \{0, 1\}^*$ and strings $s \in \{0, 1\}^*$, we have IBEver$(id, s) = accept$ iff $s = sk_{id}$, where $sk_{id} \leftarrow$ IBEext(mpk, msk, id). This property seems a little bit strong, but almost all known IBE systems, to the best of our knowledge, can efficiently do such a verification by utilizing the underlying mathematical structure, such as [3,2,11]. For convenience, we implicitly assume that IBEver exists for all IBEs, and anyone with public information can run the algorithm efficiently.

3 Public Key Encryption with Non-interactive Opening

Now, we review a definition of PKENO [7]. A PKENO scheme $\mathcal{PKENO}$ consists of five algorithms: (Gen, Enc, Dec, Prove, Ver). Gen is a randomized algorithm which takes a security parameter k as input, outputs a key pair (pk, sk). The probabilistic algorithm Enc takes as input a public key pk and a message m, returns a ciphertext c of m. Dec is a deterministic algorithm that takes as input a ciphertext c and a secret sk, outputs a message m or a special symbol $\perp$. The probabilistic algorithm Prove takes a ciphertext c and a secret key sk as input, outputs a proof π of the results of decrypting c with sk. Ver is a deterministic algorithm that takes as input a public key pk, a ciphertext c, a plaintext m and a proof π. It outputs a bit $b \in \{0,1\}$, meaning the proof is correct or not.

For correctness, we require that for any key pair $(pk, sk) \leftarrow \text{Gen}(1^k)$, the following two conditions hold with overwhelming probability.

1. For any messages m, we have $\text{Dec}(sk, \text{Enc}(pk, m)) = m$.
2. For any ciphertexts c, $\text{Ver}(pk, c, \text{Dec}(sk, c), \text{Prove}(sk, c)) = 1$.

We give the security definitions of PKENO, which we adapted from [10]. Consider the following game between a challenger and an adversary $\mathcal{A}$.

Setup: Given the security parameter k, the challenger generates $(pk, sk) \leftarrow \text{Gen}(1^k)$ and gives the public key pk to $\mathcal{A}$.

Phase 1: The adversary $\mathcal{A}$ may adaptively make a number of decryption or proof queries on ciphertext c, the challenger responds with $\text{Dec}(sk, c)$ or $\text{Prove}(sk, c)$.

Challenge: At some point, $\mathcal{A}$ outputs two equal-length messages m_0, m_1. The challenger chooses a random bit $b \in \{0,1\}$ and returns $c^* \leftarrow \text{Enc}(pk, m_b)$.

Phase 2: The adversary $\mathcal{A}$ makes more decryption or proof queries as in phase 1, but with a constraint that decryption or proof queries on c^* are not allowed.

Guess: Eventually, The adversary $\mathcal{A}$ outputs a guess $b' \in \{0,1\}$.

The adversary wins the game if $b = b'$. The advantage of $\mathcal{A}$ in the above game is defined as $\text{Adv}^{\text{ind-ccpa}}_{\mathcal{PKENO}, \mathcal{A}}(k) = |Pr[b = b'] - 1/2|$.

Definition 1 (IND-CCPA). *We say a PKENO scheme $\mathcal{PKENO}$ is secure under chosen-ciphertext and prove attacks (IND-CCPA), if for any polynomial time probabilistic $\mathcal{A}$, its advantage in the above game is negligible.*

For the application of PKENO, the above security is not enough. We also need that any adversarial prover can't prove a false claim. That's what we called proof soundness [7].

Definition 2 (Proof Soundness). *We say a PKENO scheme is proof sound, if for any polynomial time probabilistic algorithm $\mathcal{B}$, its advantage defined below is negligible.*

$$\mathrm{Adv}_{PKENO,\mathcal{B}}^{\mathrm{proof\text{-}snd}}(\mathrm{k}) = \Pr[(pk, sk) \leftarrow \mathsf{Gen}(1^k), m \leftarrow \mathcal{B}(pk, sk),$$
$$c = \mathsf{Enc}(pk, m), (m', \pi') \leftarrow \mathcal{B}(pk, sk, c)$$
$$: \mathsf{Ver}(pk, c, m', \pi') = 1 \wedge m \neq m'].$$

In [10], Galindo et al. gave two strong soundness definitions, which they called strong proof soundness and strongly committing. In the strong proof soundness setting, the adversary outputs the public key pk, and he might produce it incorrectly and might not know the secret key. And in the strongly committing setting, the adversary not only outputs the public key pk but also the ciphertext c, and both might be produced inappropriately.

Here, we review the two definitions of soundness in Definition 3 and 4.

Definition 3 (Strong Proof Soundness [10]). *A PKENO scheme is strongly proof sound if for any PPT adversary $\mathcal{B}$, his advantage defined below is negligible*

$$\mathrm{Adv}_{PKENO,\mathcal{B}}^{\mathrm{sproof\text{-}snd}}(\mathrm{k}) = \Pr[(pk, m) \leftarrow \mathcal{B}(1^k), c \leftarrow \mathsf{Enc}(pk, m), (m', \pi') \leftarrow \mathcal{B}(c) :$$
$$\mathsf{Ver}(pk, c, m', \pi') = 1 \wedge m \neq m']$$

Definition 4 (Strongly Committing [10]). *A PKENO scheme is strongly committing if for any PPT adversary $\mathcal{B}$, his advantage defined below is negligible*

$$\mathrm{Adv}_{PKENO,\mathcal{B}}^{\mathrm{sproof\text{-}com}}(\mathrm{k}) = \Pr[(pk, c, m, \pi, m', \pi') \leftarrow \mathcal{B}(1^k) :$$
$$\mathsf{Ver}(pk, c, m, \pi) = 1 = \mathsf{Ver}(pk, c, m', \pi') \wedge m \neq m']$$

Galindo et al. [10] showed that Definition 3 and 4 are much stronger than Definition 2. In this paper, our generic construction achieves proof soundness. However, our practical scheme achieves strong proof soundness and strongly committing.

4   A Generic Construction from Selective-IBE to PKENO

In this section, we present our generic construction from a separable selective IBE to PKENO and its formal security proof. We review the PKENO scheme in [13] and give an explanation using our framework.

Let $\mathcal{IBE} =$ (IBEkg, IBEext, IBEenc, IBEdec) be an IBE scheme and $\mathcal{CMH} =$ (CMkg, CMhash, CMswch) be a chameleon hash function which is collision resistant. We give our PKENO scheme $\mathcal{PKENO} = $(Gen, Enc, Dec, Prove, Ver) as follows.

$\mathsf{Gen}(1^k)$: The key generation algorithm runs $(mpk, msk) \leftarrow \mathsf{IBEkg}(1^k)$ and $(hk, td) \leftarrow \mathsf{CMkg}(1^k)$. Then it sets $pk = (mpk, hk)$ and $sk = msk$ (td is only needed in security proof) and returns (pk, sk).

Enc(pk, m): Given $pk = (mpk, hk)$ and a message m, the encryption algorithm randomly chooses $r_1 \leftarrow \mathcal{R}_1$, $r_2 \leftarrow \mathcal{R}_2{}^1$ for IBEenc and CMhash, and then it computes $u \leftarrow f_1(mpk, m, r_1)$, $id \leftarrow$ CMhash(hk, u, r_2) and $v \leftarrow f_2(mpk, id, r_1)$. Finally, it returns the ciphertext $C = (u, v, r_2)$.

Dec(sk, C): The decryption algorithm parses $C = (u, v, r_2)$, and then it computes $id \leftarrow$ CMhash(hk, u, r_2) and $sk_{id} \leftarrow$ IBEext(sk, id). Next, it uses the $\mathcal{IBE}$ decryption algorithm to decrypt the message $m \leftarrow$ IBEdec$(sk_{id}, id, u||v)$. Finally, it returns m.

Prove(sk, C): The prove algorithm parses $C = (u, v, r_2)$, and then it computes $id \leftarrow$ CMhash(hk, u, r_2) and $sk_{id} \leftarrow$ IBEext(sk, id) and returns $\pi = sk_{id}$.

Ver(C, m, π): The verification algorithm parses $C = (u, v, r_2)$. Next, it computes $id \leftarrow$ CMhash(hk, u, r_2) and checks if π is a valid secret key for id. If not, it returns 0. Otherwise it decrypts C by running $\hat{m} \leftarrow$ IBEdec$(\pi, id, u||v)$, where $\hat{m} \in \mathcal{M}_k \cup \{\perp\}$. If $\hat{m} \neq m$, it returns 0, else returns 1.

It is easy to check that the above scheme satisfies correctness.

4.1 Security

In this subsection, we show our generic PKENO scheme is CCPA secure and proof sound, if the underlying separable IBE is selectively secure and the chameleon hash is collision resistant. Formally,

Theorem 1. *Assume $\mathcal{IBE}$ is* IND-sID-CPA *secure and $\mathcal{CMH}$ is collision resistant. Then $\mathcal{PKENO}$ constructed above is* IND-CCPA *secure and Proof Sound.*

First note that the Ver algorithm will call the IBEver algorithm to check whether the secret key π is correctly generated. If the IBEver outputs "reject", we will always reject the proof. And if it outputs "accept", the secret key π can be used to decrypt all properly generated ciphertexts that are encrypted under id with overwhelmingly probability. The adversary cannot output another message that is not equal to the message which it submits to the challenger for encryption. Thus, the proof soundness of our construction is obvious.

Therefore, in the following proof, we only consider an adversary $\mathcal{A}$ that breaks the IND-CCPA security of our scheme.

Proof. We show how to build an algorithm $\mathcal{B}$ breaks either the $\mathcal{IBE}$ or the chameleon hash by interacting with $\mathcal{A}$. Note that a ciphertext in our construction consists of three parts u, v, r_2, where r_2 is the randomness used to compute $id = H(u, r_2)$. Let q denote the total number of decryption queries and proof queries made by $\mathcal{A}$. Let $C^{(i)} = (u^{(i)}, v^{(i)}, r_2^{(i)})$ be the i-th query (decryption or proof) and $id^{(i)} =$ CMhash$(hk, u^{(i)}, r_2^{(i)})$. Let $C^* = (u^*, v^*, r_2^*)$ be the challenge ciphertext and $id^* =$ CMhash(hk, u^*, r_2^*).

We distinguish the following two types of adversaries:

---

[1] $\mathcal{R}_1$ and $\mathcal{R}_2$ are corresponding spaces of random coins for IBEenc and CMhash.

Type 1: For all all valid query $C^{(i)} = (u^{(i)}, v^{(i)}, r_2^{(i)})$, $1 \leq i \leq q$, there is $id^{(i)} \neq id^*$.

Type 2: There is at least one valid query $C^{(i)} = (u^{(i)}, v^{(i)}, r_2^{(i)})$ such that $id^{(i)} = id^*$ and $(u^{(i)}, r_2^{(i)}) \neq (u^*, r_2^*)$ for some $1 \leq i \leq q$.

Note that, the probability that an adversary makes a query $C^{(i)}$ that is equal to C^* in phase 1 is negligible. And it can't query the challenge ciphertext C^* in the phase 2 by our security model (if he does query one, it's invalid and the challenger just simply reject it). So without loss of generality, we assume that $C^{(i)} \neq C^*$ always holds for all the queries.

Since each pair (u, r_2) determines an unique "identity" $id = H(u, r_2)$, and (u, id) uniquely determines v by the assumption of underlying separable IBE, (u, r_2) uniquely determines v in our context. Thus for all the valid queries, we always have $(u^{(i)}, r_2^{(i)}) \neq (u^*, r_2^*)$. Hence, if an adversary only queries valid ciphertext (u, v, r_2) that $id = H(u, r_2) \neq id^*$, then it must be a Type 1 adversary. Otherwise, he must make at least one valid query (u, v, r_2) that $id = H(u, r_2) = id^*$, it's a Type 2 adversary.

As the discussions we give above, two types of adversaries include all the adversaries that attack our construction. Now, for the type 1 adversary, we construct an algorithm that breaks the *IND-sID-CPA* security of $\mathcal{IBE}$, and for the type 2 adversary, we construct an algorithm that breaks the collision resistance of chameleon hash.

Type 1 Adversary: Define $\mathcal{B}$ as follows.

Setup: $\mathcal{B}$ runs $(hk, td) \leftarrow$ CMhash(1^k). Then he randomly chooses u' from the domain f_1, and r_2' from $\mathcal{R}_2$, and computes $id^* =$ CMhash(hk, u', r_2'), where r_2' is an auxiliary random coin for chameleon hash. $\mathcal{B}$ then submits id^* to its own challenger as the identity to be challenged. After receiving public parameters mpk from its challenger, $\mathcal{B}$ sets $pk = (mpk, hk)$ and sends pk as the public key to $\mathcal{A}$.

Phase 1: After giving pk to $\mathcal{A}$, $\mathcal{B}$ answers $\mathcal{A}$'s decryption queries and proof queries as follows:
Decryption: For decryption query $C^{(i)} = (u^{(i)}, v^{(i)}, r_2^{(i)})$, $\mathcal{B}$ first computes $id^{(i)} =$ CMhash$(hk, u^{(i)}, r_2^{(i)})$, if $id^{(i)} = id^*$, $\mathcal{B}$ outputs a random bit and halts. Otherwise, he sends $id^{(i)}$ to its own extraction oracle and obtain $sk_{id^{(i)}}$. Then $\mathcal{B}$ computes $m^{(i)} =$ IBEdec$(sk_{id^{(i)}}, id^{(i)}, u^{(i)}||v^{(i)})$, and sends $m^{(i)}$ to $\mathcal{A}$.
Proof: For proof query $C^{(i)} = (u^{(i)}, v^{(i)}, r_2^{(i)})$, $\mathcal{B}$ computes $id^{(i)} =$ CMhash $(hk, u^{(i)}, r_2^{(i)})$, if $id^{(i)} = id^*$, $\mathcal{B}$ outputs a random bit and halts. Otherwise, he sends $id^{(i)}$ to its own extraction oracle and forwards to $\mathcal{A}$ whatever its extraction oracle replies.

Challenge: When $\mathcal{B}$ receives from $\mathcal{A}$ a pair of plaintexts (m_0, m_1) that $\mathcal{A}$ wants to be challenged on, $\mathcal{B}$ forwards (m_0, m_1) to its own challenge oracle. After receiving its challenge ciphertext (u^*, v^*) (under identity id^*), $\mathcal{B}$ computes $r_2^* \leftarrow \text{CMswch}(td, u', r_2', u^*)$. $\mathcal{B}$ then sends $C^* = (u^*, v^*, r_2^*)$ to $\mathcal{A}$ as the challenge ciphertext. Due to the uniformness of the chameleon hash, the distribution of the challenge is exactly as the real attack.

Phase 2: In this phase, $\mathcal{B}$ answers $\mathcal{A}$'s queries as in phase 1:

Guess: When $\mathcal{A}$ outputs a guess b', $\mathcal{B}$ outputs the same bit as its answer.

From the description of $\mathcal{B}$, it is easy to verify that the key generation is simulated perfectly. And because of the uniformness property, r_2^* is uniformly distributed, the challenge oracle is also perfectly simulated. Besides, in this case, $\mathcal{A}$ is a type 1 adversary, we always have $id^{(i)} \neq id^*$ for all valid query, thus the probability that $\mathcal{B}$ halts is zero. In conclusion, $\mathcal{B}$ simulates a perfect environment for $\mathcal{A}$ as in the real attack, and if $\mathcal{A}$ succeeds in attacking our construction with non-negligible probability, $\mathcal{B}$ will succeed in attacking the underlying PKENO with the same probability.

Type 2 adversary: We only give the sketch. For setup, $\mathcal{B}$ receives hk from its challenger. $\mathcal{B}$ generates $(mpk, msk) \leftarrow \text{IBEkg}(1^k)$ and sets the public key as (mpk, hk). $\mathcal{B}$ keeps msk as the secret key. Since $\mathcal{B}$ has msk, all decryption queries and proof queries can be answered perfectly. For challenge, upon receiving (m_0, m_1) from $\mathcal{A}$, $\mathcal{B}$ first picks $b \leftarrow \{0, 1\}$ and sets $u^* = f_1(params, m_b, r_1)$, where r_1 is chosen uniformly from the randomness space of IBEenc. $\mathcal{B}$ then outputs u^* to its hash challenger. After receiving r_2^* from the challenger, $\mathcal{B}$ sets $id^* \leftarrow \text{CMhash}(hk, u^*, r_2^*)$ and $v^* = f_2(params, id^*, r_1)$, and sends (u^*, v^*, r_2^*) to $\mathcal{A}$ as the challenge ciphertext. One can verify this is a valid challenge. Finally, when decryption query or proof query $(u^{(i)}, v^{(i)}, r_2^{(i)})$ is queried for some i, where $\text{CMhash}(hk, u^{(i)}, r_2^{(i)}) = id^*$ and $(u^{(i)}, r_2^{(i)}) \neq (u^*, r_2^*)$, $\mathcal{B}$ outputs $(u^{(i)}, r_2^{(i)})$ as a collision for its challenger. We conclude that $\mathcal{B}$ breaks collision resistance with the same probability as $\mathcal{A}$'s advantage in guessing b.

Summarizing the two cases, we obtain the claimed results.

4.2 A New Explanation of Lai et al.'s PKENO Scheme

In CT-RSA 2010, Lai, Deng, Liu and Kou gave an efficient PKE/PKENO scheme [13] from identity-based techniques. Our generic construction gives a new explanation of their PKENO scheme. For completeness, we review their scheme in Table 1.

Lai et al. stated that they used two types of "identities", one is uniquely determined by the first two elements of a ciphertext (i.e., t), the other is chosen randomly for each ciphertext (i.e., r). By using two "identities", their scheme obtained a good computation and communication efficiency. In fact, from the view of our generic construction, this two "identities" are two inputs of chameleon hash $H(t, r) = u^t v^r$, where $t \in \mathbb{Z}_q$ is its input, and $r \in \mathbb{Z}_q$ is its random coin.

First of all, their scheme based on the first Boneh and Boyen's selective-(H)IBE [2], and which is selective-ID secure and has separable property. In fact, if we set $f_1(pk, m, s) = (m \cdot Z^s, g^s)$ and $f_2(pk, id, s) = (h(id) \cdot d)^s$, where h is some collision resistant (encoding) hash function (w.l.o.g, we can set $h(id) = g^{id}$). Obviously, these two functions "used" in their scheme satisfy our conditions. Secondly, note that if we replace the hash function h in f_2 by $H(t, r) = u^t v^r$, we obtain Lai et al.'s encryption function. Now we only need to prove that $H(t, r) = u^t v^r$ is a chameleon hash. Actually, H's collision resistant property is guaranteed by DL assumption. And if someone knows x, y where $u = g^x$ and $v = g^y$, he can easily find a collision. More precisely, for any hash triple $(t, r, H(t, r))$ and any message $t' \neq t$, the one who knows x, y can compute $r' = y^{-1}x(t - t') + r$ and have $H(t, r) = H(t', r')$.

Table 1. Lai et al.'s PKENO scheme [13]. (Let $\mathcal{PG} = \{\mathbb{G}_1, \mathbb{G}_2, q, \hat{e}\}$ be a bilinear group and g be a generator of $\mathbb{G}_1$. Let $\mathcal{H} : \{0, 1\}^* \to \mathbb{Z}_q$ be a collision resistant cryptographic hash family.)

$\mathbf{Gen}(1^k)$	$\alpha, x, y, z \leftarrow \mathbb{Z}_q; g_2 \leftarrow \mathbb{G}_1; H \leftarrow \mathcal{H}; g_1 = g^\alpha, u = g^x, v = g^y, d = g^z;$ $Z = \hat{e}(g_1, g_2); pk = (u, v, d, Z, H), sk = (g_2^\alpha, x, y, z);$ Return (pk, sk).
$\mathbf{Enc}(pk, m)$	$s, r \leftarrow \mathbb{Z}_q; C_0 = m \cdot Z^s, C_1 = g^s; t = H(C_0, C_1); C_2 = (u^t v^r d)^s;$ Return $C = (C_0, C_1, C_2, r)$.
$\mathbf{Dec}(sk, C)$	Parse C as $(C_0, C_1, C_2, r); t = H(C_0, C_1);$ If $(C_1)^{tx+ry+z} \neq C_2$ then return $\perp$. Else return $C_0 / \hat{e}(C_1, g_2^\alpha)$.
$\mathbf{Prove}(sk, C)$	Parse C as $(C_0, C_1, C_2, r); t = H(C_0, C_1);$ If $(C_1)^{tx+ry+z} \neq C_2$ then return $\pi = \perp$. Else $\gamma \leftarrow \mathbb{Z}_q; d_C^1 = g_2^\alpha (u^t v^r d)^\gamma, d_C^2 = g^\gamma;$ Return $\pi = (d_C^1, d_C^2)$.
$\mathbf{Ver}(pk, C, m, \pi)$	Parse $C = (C_0, C_1, C_2, r), \pi = (d_C^1, d_C^2); t = H(C_0, C_1);$ If $\hat{e}(C_1, u^t v^r d) = \hat{e}(g, C_2), \hat{e}(g, d_C^1) = Z \cdot \hat{e}(u^t v^r d, d_C^2)$ and $m = C_0 \cdot \hat{e}(C_2, d_C^2) / \hat{e}(C_1, d_C^1)$ then return 1. Else return 0.

5   A New PKENO Scheme

In this section, we present a new instantiation of our transform by employing the second Boneh-Boyen selective-IBE [2].

Let $\mathcal{PG} = \{\mathbb{G}_1, \mathbb{G}_2, q, \hat{e}\}$ be a bilinear group as described in section 2, and g be a generator of $\mathbb{G}_1$. Here we instantiate the chameleon hash by using Krawczyk and Rabin's chameleon hash combined with a collision resistant hash function $H : \{0, 1\}^* \to \mathbb{Z}_q^*$. We also assume that the plaintext space is $\mathbb{G}_2$. By using Boneh and Boyen's scheme, we obtain our PKENO scheme $\mathcal{PKENO}$=(Gen, Enc, Dec, Prove, Ver) as follows.

Gen(1^k): Randomly choose $x, y, z \in \mathbb{Z}_q^*$ and compute $X = g^x, Y = g^y, Z = \hat{e}(g, g)$, and $h = g^z$. Select a collision resistant hash function H. Set the public key $pk = (g, X, Y, Z, h, H)$ and secret key $sk = (x, y)$ (z is only needed in our security proof).

Enc(pk, m): Parse $pk = (g, X, Y, Z, h, H)$. Randomly choose $r, s \leftarrow \mathbb{Z}_q^*$. Compute $c_1 = m \cdot Z^s$, $c_2 = Y^s$, $id = H(2\|g^{H(1\|c_1\|c_2)}h^r)$ and $c_3 = (g^{id}X)^s$. Return $C = (c_1, c_2, c_3, r)$.

Dec(sk, C): First parse $sk = (x, y)$ and $C = (c_1, c_2, c_3, r)$. Then compute $id = H(2\|g^{H(1\|c_1\|c_2)}h^r)$, and check whether $c_2^{(id+x)/y} = c_3$. If no, this is an invalid ciphertext and return $\perp$. Otherwise, compute $m = c_1/\hat{e}(c_2, g^{1/y})$ and return m.

Prove(sk, C): Parse $sk = (x, y)$ and $C = (c_1, c_2, c_3, r)$. Then compute $id = H(2\|g^{H(1\|c_1\|c_2)}h^r)$ and check whether $c_2^{(id+x)/y} = c_3$. If no, this is an invalid ciphertext and return $\pi = \perp$. Otherwise, randomly choose $t \in \mathbb{Z}_q$ such that $id + x + ty \neq 0 \mod q$, and compute $K = g^{1/(id+x+ty)}$. Finally return $\pi = (t, K)$.

Ver(C, m, π): Parse $C = (c_1, c_2, c_3, r)$ and $\pi = (t, K)$. Then compute $id = H(2\|g^{H(1\|c_1\|c_2)}h^r)$ and check if $\hat{e}(K, g^{id}XY^t) = Z$ and $\hat{e}(c_2, g^{id}X) = \hat{e}(c_3, Y)$. If not, return 0. Otherwise, compute $m' = c_1/e(c_3c_2^t, K)$. If $m \neq m'$, return 0. Else return 1.

The correctness of our scheme can be easily verified. Since the underlying IBE [2] we used here is IND-sID-CPA secure, and the collision resistance of chameleon hash $h(m, r) = H(2\|g^{H(1\|m)}h^r))$ can be reduced to DL assumption or the collision resistance of H, we can obtain the CCPA security and proof soundness of our new scheme simply by Theorem 1.

Moreover, though our generic construction only satisfies proof soundness, our concrete construction above can achieve strong proof soundness and strongly committing. It is because we can check whether a secret key or ciphertext is created properly by pairings.

5.1 Comparisons

In Table 2, we give a comparison of known PKENO schemes in the literature. This first column indicates what methodology the corresponding scheme has employed, as we show that there are three methodologies, and compared to the other two methodologies, our generic construction from selective IBE to PKENO is more efficient.

Here, we don't list the second scheme proposed in [7], since Galindo showed that it is insecure [9]. Galindo also gave a fixed scheme, which employed the KEM/DEM mechanism. But as shown in Table 2, it needs long public keys linear to the security parameters n. Though, compared to other schemes in the list, it can accept arbitrary length of plaintexts. Galindo et al. [10] proposed two PKENO schemes based on threshold public key (TPK). The first one enjoys a security reduction to DDH assumption in the random oracle model. The second employed one-time signatures, which needs more computation and communication cost. Recently, Lai, Deng, Liu and Kou [13] proposed an efficient PKENO scheme, which can be viewed as an instantiation of our generic construction.

Table 2. Comparisons of schemes (σ denotes the one time signature and Signkey denotes the one time signature verify key. h denotes the hash function used in each scheme. R denotes the random space in our scheme used by chameleon hash function.)

Methodology	Schemes	Public Key	Secret Key	Ciphertext overhead	Assumption	Standard Model?
Adaptive IBE $\longrightarrow$ PKENO	[9]	$(n+2)\mathbb{G}_1$ $+ \mathbb{G}_2 + h$	$(n+2)\mathbb{Z}_q$	$2\mathbb{G}_1+$ DEM	DBDH	$\checkmark$
TPKE $\longrightarrow$ PKENO	[10]	$3\mathbb{G} + 2h$	$\mathbb{Z}_q$	$3\mathbb{G} + 2\mathbb{Z}_q$	DDH	$\times$
		$5\mathbb{G}_1$	$4\mathbb{Z}_q$	$5\mathbb{G}_1 + \sigma$ $+$ Signkey	D-linear	$\checkmark$
Selective IBE $\overset{Ours}{\longrightarrow}$ PKENO	[13]	$4\mathbb{G}_1 + \mathbb{G}_2 + h$	$\mathbb{G}_1 + 3\mathbb{Z}_q^*$	$2\mathbb{G}_1 + \mathbb{G}_2$ $+\mathbb{Z}_q$	DBDH	$\checkmark$
	Ours	$4\mathbb{G}_1 + \mathbb{G}_2 + h$	$2\mathbb{Z}_q$	$2\mathbb{G}_1 + \mathbb{G}_2$ $+\mathbb{Z}_q$	q-DBDHI	$\checkmark$

6   Conclusion

In this paper, a generic construction from selective-IBE to public key encryption with non-interactive opening is proposed. The proposed construction benefits from chameleon hash functions, since it makes our transform achieved its security from a weaker cryptographic primitive (i.e., selective-IBE), compared to adaptive-IBE. There is a gap [9] between adaptive secure and selective secure, thus the generic construction does have its practical meaning in this view. In addition, our generic construction gives a new explanation of an efficient PKENO scheme [13], and it specifies the relationship among some known primitives.

Acknowledgments. We thank Cheng Chen, Yu Chen, Wenhao Wang, and the anonymous reviewers for their helpful comments and suggestions.

References

1. Abe, M., Cui, Y., Imai, H., Kiltz, E.: Efficient hybrid encryption from ID-based encryption. Designs, Codes and Cryptography 54(3), 205–240 (2010)
2. Boneh, D., Boyen, X.: Efficient Selective-ID Secure Identity-Based Encryption Without Random Oracles. In: Cachin, C., Camenisch, J. (eds.) EUROCRYPT 2004. LNCS, vol. 3027, pp. 223–238. Springer, Heidelberg (2004)
3. Boneh, D., Franklin, M.: Identity-Based Encryption from the Weil Pairing. In: Kilian, J. (ed.) CRYPTO 2001. LNCS, vol. 2139, pp. 213–229. Springer, Heidelberg (2001)
4. Boyar, J.F., Kurtz, S.A., Krentel, M.W.: A discrete logarithm implementation of perfect zero-knowledge blobs. Journal of Cryptology 2, 63–76 (1990)
5. Boyen, X., Mei, Q., Waters, B.: Direct chosen ciphertext security from identity-based techniques. In: Proceedings of the 12th ACM Conference on Computer and Communications Security, CCS 2005, pp. 320–329. ACM, New York (2005)

6. Canetti, R., Halevi, S., Katz, J.: Chosen-Ciphertext Security from Identity-Based Encryption. In: Cachin, C., Camenisch, J. (eds.) EUROCRYPT 2004. LNCS, vol. 3027, pp. 207–222. Springer, Heidelberg (2004)
7. Damgård, I., Hofheinz, D., Kiltz, E., Thorbek, R.: Public-Key Encryption with Non-interactive Opening. In: Malkin, T. (ed.) CT-RSA 2008. LNCS, vol. 4964, pp. 239–255. Springer, Heidelberg (2008)
8. Damgård, I., Thorbek, R.: Non-interactive Proofs for Integer Multiplication. In: Naor, M. (ed.) EUROCRYPT 2007. LNCS, vol. 4515, pp. 412–429. Springer, Heidelberg (2007)
9. Galindo, D.: Breaking and Repairing Damgård et al. Public Key Encryption Scheme with Non-interactive Opening. In: Fischlin, M. (ed.) CT-RSA 2009. LNCS, vol. 5473, pp. 389–398. Springer, Heidelberg (2009)
10. Galindo, D., Libert, B., Fischlin, M., Fuchsbauer, G., Lehmann, A., Manulis, M., Schröder, D.: Public-Key Encryption with Non-Interactive Opening: New Constructions and Stronger Definitions. In: Bernstein, D.J., Lange, T. (eds.) AFRICACRYPT 2010. LNCS, vol. 6055, pp. 333–350. Springer, Heidelberg (2010)
11. Gentry, C., Silverberg, A.: Hierarchical ID-Based Cryptography. In: Zheng, Y. (ed.) ASIACRYPT 2002. LNCS, vol. 2501, pp. 548–566. Springer, Heidelberg (2002)
12. Krawczyk, H., Rabin, T.: Chameleon hashing and signatures. Preprint, Theory of Cryptography Library (1998)
13. Lai, J., Deng, R.H., Liu, S., Kou, W.: Efficient CCA-Secure PKE from Identity-Based Techniques. In: Pieprzyk, J. (ed.) CT-RSA 2010. LNCS, vol. 5985, pp. 132–147. Springer, Heidelberg (2010)
14. Shamir, A.: Identity-Based Cryptosystems and Signature Schemes. In: Blakely, G.R., Chaum, D. (eds.) CRYPTO 1984. LNCS, vol. 196, pp. 47–53. Springer, Heidelberg (1985)
15. Zhang, R.: Tweaking TBE/IBE to PKE Transforms with Chameleon Hash Functions. In: Katz, J., Yung, M. (eds.) ACNS 2007. LNCS, vol. 4521, pp. 323–339. Springer, Heidelberg (2007)

Fast Tate Pairing Computation on Twisted Jacobi Intersections Curves[*]

Xusheng Zhang[1,2], Shan Chen[1,2], and Dongdai Lin[1]

[1] SKLOIS, Institute of Software, Chinese Academy of Sciences, Beijing, China
[2] Graduate University of Chinese Academy of Sciences, Beijing, China
xszhang.is@gmail.com

Abstract. Recently there are lots of studies on the Tate pairing computation with different coordinate systems, such as twisted Edwards curves and Hessian curves coordinate systems. However, Jacobi intersections curves coordinate system, as another useful one, is overlooked in pairing-based cryptosystems.

This paper proposes the explicit formulae for the doubling and addition steps in Miller's algorithm to compute the Tate pairing on twisted Jacobi intersections curves, as a larger class containing Jacobi intersections curves. Although these curves are not plane elliptic curves, our formulae are still very efficient and competitive with others. When the embedding degree is even, our doubling formulae are the fastest except for the formulae on Hessian/Selmer curves, and the parallel execution of our formulae are even more competitive with the Selmer curves case in the parallel manner. Besides, we give the detailed analysis of the fast variants of our formulae with other embedding degrees, such as the embedding degree 1, and the embedding degree dividing 4 and 6. At last, we analyze the relation between the Tate pairings on two isogenous elliptic curves, and show that the Tate pairing on twisted Jacobi intersections curves can be substituted for the Tate pairing on twisted Edwards curves completely.

Keywords: Twisted Jacobi intersections curves, Tate pairing, Miller's function.

1 Introduction

Pairings on elliptic curves have been used to construct new elliptic curve cryptosystems which were not only based on discrete logarithm groups, such as identity-based encryption scheme, one round protocol for tripartite Diffie-Hellman key exchange, short signature and so on.

Miller's algorithm [20] is the first effective algorithm to calculate the Weil and Tate pairings in the double-and-add manner. Due to various cryptographic applications, lots of effort have gone into efficient computation of pairings

---

[*] This work was supported by the National 973 Program of China under Grant 2011CB302400, the National Natural Science Foundation of China under Grant 60970152, the Grand Project of Institute of Software under Grant YOCX285056.

C.-K. Wu, M. Yung, and D. Lin (Eds.): Inscrypt 2011, LNCS 7537, pp. 210–226, 2012.

by improving Miller's algorithm. To our knowledge, different forms of elliptic curves over finite fields with different coordinate systems have been studied to improve the efficiency of the scalar multiplication, in which Edwards form is the fastest at present. Analogously, different forms have been considered to improve the efficiency of the pairing computation by optimizing the formulae of Miller's algorithm. First, Chatterjee *et al.* [4] gave fast Tate pairing computation in projective coordinates of Weierstrass curves. Later, several further optimizations were proposed on other equivalent or special forms of elliptic curves, such as (twisted) Edwards curves [8][15][1], Weierstrass curves of the form $y^2 = x^3 + c^2$ [6], Jacobi quartic curves [21], Huff curves [16], Hessian curves [12] and Selmer curves [23] as the generalized Hessian curves [9] with j-invariant being 0. Almost all improvements are presented in the context of the Tate pairing on elliptic curves with even embedding degrees, since the nature of the Tate pairing allows for a relatively simple exposition and improves efficiency through the denominator elimination and twist techniques.

The state of the art Miller's formulae, as the faster substitutions for the formulae on Weierstrass curves, are proposed on twisted Edwards curves [1] and Hessian/Selmer curves [12][23]. It is well known that every Weierstrass curve with a point of order 3 over a finite field (char>3) is birationally equivalent to a Hessian curve, and every Weierstrass curve with a point of order 4 over a finite field (char>2) is birationally equivalent to an Edwards curve. In [2], Bernstein *et al.* showed that every elliptic curve with three points of order 2 is 2-isogenous to a twisted Edwards curve, especially it is birationally equivalent to a twisted Edwards curve over $\mathbb{F}_p$ with $p \equiv 1 \pmod 4$. But the only overlooked form with some similar properties is the Jacobi intersections curve (see [5][18][13][14] for the fast addition and doubling formulae for this form). Lately, Feng *et al.* [10] presented twisted Jacobi intersections curves, as a larger class containing Jacobi intersections curves, which are birationally equivalent to elliptic curves with three points of order 2, and they gave many fast addition and doubling formulae in projective coordinates on twisted Jacobi intersections curves.

In this paper, we propose explicit Miller's formulae for the Tate pairing on twisted Jacobi intersections curves, which are very efficient and competitive with others although twisted Jacobi intersections curves are not plane curves. Specially, when the embedding degree is even, our Miller's doubling formulae are fastest except for the formulae on Hessian/Selmer curves. Moreover, we present the parallel execution of our formulae which can also be competitive with the formulae on Selmer curves case in the parallel manner. Besides, elliptic curves with embedding degree 1 are applied in pairing-based cryptosysytems over composite-order bilinear groups [11], so we modify our formulae in this case so that they are faster than the formulae on Weierstrass forms given in [17]. According to [7], the pairing computation can benefit a lot from the high-degree twists. For example, there are sextic twists of Weierstrass curves, cubic twists of Selmer curves, quartic twists of twised Jacobi quartic curves, but only quadratic twists can be defined on twisted Edwards and twisted Jacobi intersections curves. To make up for the lack of the high-degree twists, we use the mixed coordinates and the birational map to accelerate the computation of our Miller's formulae when the embedding degree divides 4 and 6. At last, we analyze the relation between the Tate pairings on two isogenous elliptic curves, and show that the faster Tate pairing on twisted Jacobi intersections curves can be substituted for that on twisted Edwards curves completely.

The organization is as follows: Section 2 recalls some basics of Tate pairing and twisted Jacobi intersections curves. Section 3 presents our formulae of Miller's functions on twisted Jacobi intersections curves. In Section 4, we analyze the fast calculation of our Miller's formulae in the case of even embedding degree. In Section 5, a further analysis of our formulae is given in the cases of other embedding degrees. At last, we analyze the relation between the Tate pairings on twisted Jacobi intersections and twisted Edwards curves in Section 6.

2   Preliminaries

2.1   Tate Pairing and Miller's Algorithm

Let E be an elliptic curve over the finite field $\mathbb{F}_q$, where q is a power of an odd prime, and let $\mathcal{O}$ denote the neutral element of $E(\mathbb{F}_q)$. Let $n \mid \#E(\mathbb{F}_q)$ be coprime to q, if $k \geq 1$ is the smallest integer such that $n \mid q^k - 1$, then k is called the embedding degree with respect to n.

Let $\mathrm{Div}(E)$ be the divisor group of E. Given $D = \sum_{P \in E} n_p(P) \in \mathrm{Div}(E)$ and a nonzero rational function f such that $\mathrm{div}(f)$ and D have disjoint supports, the evaluation of f at D is defined by $f(D) = \prod_{P \in E} f(P)^{n_p}$. For $P, Q \in E[n]$, there exist $D_P, D_Q \in \mathrm{Div}_0(E)$ such that $D_P \sim (P) - (\mathcal{O})$ and $D_Q \sim (Q) - (\mathcal{O})$ have disjoint supports, and rational functions f_P and f_Q such that $\mathrm{div}(f_P) = nD_P$ and $\mathrm{div}(f_Q) = nD_Q$. Let $\mu_n \subset \mathbb{F}_{q^k}^*$ denote the group of n-th roots of unity. The reduced Tate pairing is given by [22]

$$\tau_n : E(\mathbb{F}_{q^k})[n] \times E(\mathbb{F}_{q^k})/nE(\mathbb{F}_{q^k}) \to \mu_n, \quad (P, Q) \mapsto f_P(D_Q)^{(q^k-1)/n}.$$

For cryptographic applications, we usually assume $k > 1$, and take $G_1 = E[n] \cap \mathrm{Ker}(\pi_q - 1)$ and $G_2 = E[n] \cap \mathrm{Ker}(\pi_q - [q])$ as the eigenspaces of the Frobenius endomorphism π_q with $E[n] = G_1 \times G_2$. Let $f_{n,P} \in \mathbb{F}_q(E)$ satisfy $\mathrm{div}(f_{n,P}) = n(P) - n(\mathcal{O})$, the reduced Tate pairing can be simplified as

$$\tau_n : G_1 \times G_2 \to \mu_n, \quad (P, Q) \mapsto f_{n,P}(Q)^{(q^k-1)/n}.$$

Miller [20] suggested computing $f_{n,P}$ from the rational function $f_{i,P}$ satisfying $\mathrm{div}(f_{i,P}) = i(P) - ([i]P) - (i-1)(\mathcal{O})$ recursively. For the Weierstrass curves, one can compute $f_{i_1+i_2,P} = f_{i_1,P} \cdot f_{i_2,P} \cdot l_{[i_1]P,[i_2]P}/v_{[i_1+i_2]P}$, where $l_{[i_1]P,[i_2]P}$ is the line passing through the points $[i_1]P, [i_2]P$ and $v_{[i_1+i_2]P}$ is the vertical line passing through the point $[i_1 + i_2]P$.

Algorithm: Miller's algorithm for Weierstrass curve

Input: $s = \sum_{j=0}^{L} s_j 2^j \in \mathbb{N}$ with $s_j \in \{0, 1\}$, $s_L = 1$; $P, Q \in E[r]$ with $P \neq Q$

Output: $f_{s,P}(Q)$

1: $T \leftarrow P$; $f \leftarrow 1$
2: **for** j from $L - 1$ downto 0 **do**
3:      $f \leftarrow f^2 \cdot l_{T,T}(Q)/v_{2T}(Q)$; $T \leftarrow 2T$ (Doubling step)
4:      **if** $s_j = 1$ **then**
5:          $f \leftarrow f \cdot l_{T,P}(Q)/v_{T+P}(Q)$; $T \leftarrow T + P$ (Addition step)
6: **return** $f^{(q^k-1)/n}$.

2.2 Twisted Jacobi Intersections Curves

Let K be a field whose characteristic is not 2. The projective *twisted Jacobi intersections curve* over K proposed by Feng *et al.* [10] is defined by

$$E_{a,b} : \begin{cases} aU^2 + V^2 = Z^2 \\ bU^2 + W^2 = Z^2, \end{cases} \tag{1}$$

where $a, b \in K$ with $ab(a - b) \neq 0$. A Jacobi intersections curve given in [5] is a twisted Jacobi intersections curve with $a = 1$.

The neutral element is $\mathcal{O} = (0, 1, 1, 1)$, and the negative of (U, V, W, Z) is $(-U, V, W, Z)$. A point (U, V, W, Z) on $E_{a,b}$ can also be represented in affine coordinates as $(u, v, w) = (U/Z, V/Z, W/Z)$. There are always four infinite points on the intersection of $E_{a,b}$ and the plane $Z = 0$ in $\mathbb{P}^3(\overline{K})$, namely $\infty_1 = (1, \alpha, \beta, 0)$, $\infty_2 = (1, -\alpha, \beta, 0)$, $\infty_3 = (1, \alpha, -\beta, 0)$, $\infty_4 = (1, -\alpha, -\beta, 0)$, where $\pm\alpha$ and $\pm\beta$ are the roots of $x^2 + a = 0$ and $y^2 + b = 0$ in $\overline{K}$ respectively. Besides, there are always three non-neutral K-rational points of order 2, namely $\mathcal{O}_2 = (0, -1, 1, 1)$, $\mathcal{O}_3 = (0, 1, -1, 1)$, and $\mathcal{O}_4 = (0, -1, -1, 1)$. From the group law in Theorem 2, $[2]\infty_1 = [2]\infty_2 = [2]\infty_3 = [2]\infty_4 = \mathcal{O}_4$, and $\infty_1 + \infty_2 = \infty_3 + \infty_4 = \mathcal{O}_2$.

The twisted Jacobi intersections curve $E_{a,b}$ is called a quadratic twist of the Jacobi intersection curve $E_{1,b/a} : U^2 + V^2 = Z^2, (b/a)U^2 + W^2 = Z^2$, i.e. $E_{a,b}$ is isomorphic to $E_{1,b/a}$ over $K(\sqrt{a})$ under the isogeny $(U, V, W, Z) \rightarrow (\sqrt{a} \cdot U, V, W, Z)$, if and only if a is a quadratic non-residue in K^*.

Theorem 1. *([10], Theorem 1) Let K be a field with $char(K) \neq 2$. Then every elliptic curve over K having three K-rational points of order 2 is isomorphic to a twisted Jacobi intersections curve over K. Especially, let $E : y^2 = x(x - a)(x - b)$ and $E_{a,b} : au^2 + v^2 = 1, bu^2 + w^2 = 1$ (in affine form), there exist isomorphisms $\psi : E \rightarrow E_{a,b}, (x, y) \mapsto (-\frac{2y}{x^2 - ab}, \frac{x^2 - 2ax + ab}{x^2 - ab}, \frac{x^2 - 2bx + ab}{x^2 - ab})$ and $\varphi : E_{a,b} \rightarrow E, (u, v, w) \mapsto (-\frac{a(w+1)}{v-1}, \frac{au}{v-1}(x - b))$.*

Theorem 2. *([10], Theorem 8) Let $P = (U_1, V_1, W_1, Z_1)$, $Q = (U_2, V_2, W_2, Z_2)$ be two points on the twisted Jacobi intersections curve $E_{a,b}$ defined over K with $ab(a - b) \neq 0$, let $R = (U_3, V_3, W_3, Z_3)$ and $S = (U_3', V_3', W_3', Z_3')$, where*

$$\begin{cases} U_3 = U_1 Z_1 V_2 W_2 + V_1 W_1 U_2 Z_2, & V_3 = V_1 Z_1 V_2 Z_2 - a U_1 W_1 U_2 W_2, \\ W_3 = W_1 Z_1 W_2 Z_2 - b U_1 V_1 U_2 V_2, & Z_3 = Z_1^2 V_2^2 + a U_2^2 W_1^2, \end{cases} \tag{2}$$

and

$$\begin{cases} U_3' = U_1^2 Z_2^2 - Z_1^2 U_2^2, & V_3' = U_1 V_1 W_2 Z_2 - W_1 Z_1 U_2 V_2, \\ W_3' = U_1 W_1 V_2 Z_2 - V_1 Z_1 U_2 W_2, & Z_3' = U_1 Z_1 V_2 W_2 - V_1 W_1 U_2 Z_2. \end{cases} \quad (3)$$

Then $P + Q = R$ if $R \neq 0$, and $P + Q = S$ if $S \neq 0$.

Theorem 3. *([10]) Let $P = (U_1, V_1, W_1, Z_1)$ be a point on the twisted Jacobi intersections curve $E_{a,b}$ defined over K with $ab(a - b) \neq 0$, and $S = [2]P = (U_3, V_3, W_3, Z_3)$, then*

$$\begin{cases} U_3 = 2U_1 V_1 W_1 Z_1, & V_3 = V_1^2 Z_1^2 - Z_1^2 W_1^2 + V_1^2 W_1^2, \\ W_3 = Z_1^2 W_1^2 - V_1^2 Z_1^2 + V_1^2 W_1^2, & Z_3 = Z_1^2 W_1^2 + V_1^2 Z_1^2 - V_1^2 W_1^2. \end{cases} \quad (4)$$

There are also other fast doubling formulae dependent of a and b given in [10]. However, for constructing more efficient Miller's formulae for the Tate pairing, only the addition and doubling formulae independent of a and b are considered.

3 Miller's Formulae on Twisted Jacobi Intersections Curves

3.1 The Geometric Group Law

The chord-tangent law [22] is the famous geometric group law on Weierstrass, Hessian and Huff curves. Recently, more complicated geometric group laws on Edwards curves and Jacobi quartic curves are given by Arène *et al.* [1] and Wang *et al.* [21], respectively. Luckily, there is a much simpler geometric group law (as the spatial chord-tangent law) on twisted Jacobi intersections curves [19].

We review it as follows: Let $E_{a,b}$ be defined by (1) in §2.2. For arbitrary $P_1, P_2 \in E_{a,b}(K)$, there is a plane through $\mathcal{O}$, P_1 and P_2. Then the plane intersects $E_{a,b}$ at the fourth point R according to the Bézout theorem, and R is the negation of $P_1 + P_2$, i.e. $R = -P_1 - P_2$. The negation of a point $-R$ is given as the residual intersection of the plane through R containing the tangent line to $E_{a,b}$ at $\mathcal{O}$. Let P_3 denote the point $P_1 + P_2$, then $P_3 = -R$.

3.2 Miller's Formulae

Given $P_1, P_2 \in E_{a,b}(K)$ and $P_3 = P_1 + P_2$, we can characterize the Miller's function $f_{P_1, P_2} \in \overline{K}(E_{a,b})$ with $\text{div}(f_{P_1, P_2}) = (P_1) + (P_2) - (P_3) - (\mathcal{O})$ as the rational function $h_{P_1, P_2}/h_{P_3}$ satisfying

$$\begin{cases} \text{div}(h_{P_1, P_2}) = (P_1) + (P_2) + (P_3) + (\mathcal{O}) - (\infty_1) - (\infty_2) - (\infty_3) - (\infty_4), \\ \text{div}(h_{P_3}) = (P_3) + (-P_3) + 2(\mathcal{O}) - (\infty_1) - (\infty_2) - (\infty_3) - (\infty_4). \end{cases}$$

Lemma 1. *Assume K is a finite field $\mathbb{F}_q$, where q is a power of an odd prime. Let $D = (\infty_1) + (\infty_2) + (\infty_3) + (\infty_4) \in \text{Div}(E_{a,b})$. If $E_{a,b}$ is defined over K, then D is defined over K, i.e. $D^{(q)} = D$. Specially, the above functions h_{P_1, P_2} and h_{P_3} can be constructed in $K(E_{a,b})$.*

Proof. Let α, β be defined as in §2.2. Then $K(\alpha, \beta)$ is a finite normal extension with $[K(\alpha, \beta) : K] \leq 2$, and q-th Frobenius map π_q generates $\mathrm{Gal}_{K(\alpha,\beta)/K}$ with $\pi_q(\alpha) = \alpha^q = a^{(q-1)/2}\alpha$ and $\pi_q(\beta) = \beta^q = b^{(q-1)/2}\beta$. Note that $a^{(q-1)/2} = b^{(q-1)/2} = 1$ if and only if a, b are quadratic residues. Thus D is defined over K, i.e. $D^{(q)} = D$. So both $\mathrm{div}(h_{P_1,P_2})$ and $\mathrm{div}(h_{P_3})$ are defined over K with $\mathrm{div}(h_{P_1,P_2}^{(q)}) = \mathrm{div}(h_{P_1,P_2})^{(q)} = \mathrm{div}(h_{P_1,P_2})$ and $\mathrm{div}(h_{P_3}^{(q)}) = \mathrm{div}(h_{P_3})^{(q)} = \mathrm{div}(h_{P_3})$. So there exist $c_1, c_2 \in \overline{K}$ s.t. $c_1 = h_{P_1,P_2}^{(q)}/h_{P_1,P_2}$ and $c_2 = h_{P_3}^{(q)}/h_{P_3}$. There also exist $d_1, d_2 \in \overline{K}$ s.t. $d_1^q/d_1 = c_1$ and $d_2^q/d_2 = c_2$. Let $H_{P_1,P_2} = h_{P_1,P_2}/d_1$ and $H_{P_3} = h_{P_3}/d_2$, then $H_{P_1,P_2}^{(q)} = H_{P_1,P_2}$ and $H_{P_3}^{(q)} = H_{P_3}$, i.e. $H_{P_1,P_2}, H_{P_3} \in K(E_{a,b})$. $\square$

According to the geometric group law, we can give the explicit formulae of h_{P_1,P_2} and h_{P_3} in the following theorems.

Theorem 4. *Let $P_1 = (U_1, V_1, W_1, Z_1)$ and $P_2 = (U_2, V_2, W_2, Z_2)$ be two non-neutral points with $P_1 \neq P_2$. Then $h_{P_1,P_2} = A_a U + B_a V + C_a W + D_a Z$, where*

$$
\begin{aligned}
A_a &= V_1 W_2 - V_2 W_1 + V_2 Z_1 - V_1 Z_2 + W_1 Z_2 - W_2 Z_1, \\
B_a &= U_2 W_1 - U_1 W_2 + U_1 Z_2 - U_2 Z_1, \\
C_a &= U_1 V_2 - U_2 V_1 + U_2 Z_1 - U_1 Z_2, \\
D_a &= -B_a - C_a = U_1 W_2 - U_2 W_1 + U_2 V_1 - U_1 V_2.
\end{aligned}
\tag{5}
$$

Assume $P_3 = (U_3, V_3, W_3, Z_3)$ is not a 2-torsion point, then $h_{P_3} = BV + CW + DZ$, where

$$
\begin{aligned}
B &= Z_3 - W_3, \\
C &= V_3 - Z_3, \\
D &= -B - C = W_3 - V_3.
\end{aligned}
\tag{6}
$$

Proof. Let $h_{P_1,P_2} = A_a U + B_a V + C_a W + D_a Z = 0$ be the plane through $\mathcal{O}, P_1, P_2$. Then we can compute these coefficients A_a, B_a, C_a, D_a by solving the equation

$$
\begin{pmatrix} 0 & 1 & 1 & 1 \\ U_1 & V_1 & W_1 & Z_1 \\ U_2 & V_2 & W_2 & Z_2 \end{pmatrix} \begin{pmatrix} A_a \\ B_a \\ C_a \\ D_a \end{pmatrix} = \begin{pmatrix} 0 \\ 0 \\ 0 \end{pmatrix}.
\tag{7}
$$

Thus, we get these coefficients (not unique) as

$$
A_a = \begin{vmatrix} 1 & 1 & 1 \\ Z_1 & V_1 & W_1 \\ Z_2 & V_2 & W_2 \end{vmatrix}, B_a = \begin{vmatrix} 0 & 1 & 1 \\ U_1 & Z_1 & W_1 \\ U_2 & Z_2 & W_2 \end{vmatrix}, C_a = \begin{vmatrix} 0 & 1 & 1 \\ U_1 & V_1 & Z_1 \\ U_2 & V_2 & Z_2 \end{vmatrix}, D_a = -B_a - C_a.
$$

Similarly, let $h_{P_3} = AU + BV + CW + DZ = 0$ be the plane through P_3 containing the tangent line to $E_{a,b}$ at $\mathcal{O}$. According to the geometric group law, it is equivalent to the plane through $\mathcal{O}, P_3, -P_3$. Since $-P_3 = (-U_3, V_3, W_3, Z_3)$, then we can solve A, B, C, D by substituting $P_3, -P_3$ for P_1, P_2 in the equations (7). Then we have

$$A = \begin{vmatrix} 1 & 1 & 1 \\ Z_3 & V_3 & W_3 \\ Z_3 & V_3 & W_3 \end{vmatrix} = 0, B = \begin{vmatrix} 0 & 1 & 1 \\ U_3 & Z_3 & W_3 \\ -U_3 & Z_3 & W_3 \end{vmatrix}, C = \begin{vmatrix} 0 & 1 & 1 \\ U_3 & V_3 & Z_3 \\ -U_3 & V_3 & Z_3 \end{vmatrix}, D = -B - C.$$

Note that B, C and D have the common factor $2U_3$. Since $\mathrm{char}(K)$ is not 2, and P_3 is not a 2-torsion point, then $U_3 \neq 0$. Thus $2U_3$ can be eliminated. □

Theorem 5. Let $P_0 = (U_0, V_0, W_0, Z_0)$ is a non-neutral point with $Z_0 \neq 0$. Then $h_{P_0, P_0} = A_d U + B_d V + C_d W + D_d Z$, where

$$\begin{aligned} A_d &= aU_0 W_0^2 - bU_0 V_0^2 + bU_0 V_0 Z_0 - aU_0 W_0 Z_0, \\ B_d &= bU_0^2 V_0 + V_0 W_0^2 - V_0 W_0 Z_0, \\ C_d &= V_0 W_0 Z_0 - aU_0^2 W_0 - V_0^2 W_0, \\ D_d &= -B_d - C_d = aU_0^2 W_0 - bU_0^2 V_0 + V_0^2 W_0 - V_0 W_0^2. \end{aligned} \tag{8}$$

Proof. Let $h_{P_0, P_0} = A_d U + B_d V + C_d W + D_d Z = 0$ be the plane through $\mathcal{O}$ containing the tangent line to $E_{a,b}$ at P_0. In the affine space $\mathbb{A}^3$, denote $P = (u_0, v_0, w_0) = (U_0/Z_0, V_0/Z_0, W_0/Z_0)$ and the affine curve

$$E_{a,b} : \begin{cases} F(u, v, w) = au^2 + v^2 - 1 = 0 \\ G(u, v, w) = bu^2 + w^2 - 1 = 0. \end{cases} \tag{9}$$

The tangent line at P_0 is given by $\frac{u - u_0}{\tau_u^0} = \frac{v - v_0}{\tau_v^0} = \frac{w - w_0}{\tau_w^0}$, where

$$\begin{aligned} \tau_u^0 &= \frac{\partial F^0}{\partial v} \frac{\partial G^0}{\partial w} - \frac{\partial F^0}{\partial w} \frac{\partial G^0}{\partial v} = 4v_0 w_0, \\ \tau_v^0 &= \frac{\partial F^0}{\partial w} \frac{\partial G^0}{\partial u} - \frac{\partial F^0}{\partial u} \frac{\partial G^0}{\partial w} = -4au_0 w_0, \\ \tau_w^0 &= \frac{\partial F^0}{\partial u} \frac{\partial G^0}{\partial v} - \frac{\partial F^0}{\partial v} \frac{\partial G^0}{\partial u} = -4bv_0 u_0. \end{aligned}$$

Fixing a new point $(\tau_u^0 + u_0, \tau_v^0 + v_0, \tau_w^0 + w_0)$ on the tangent line, we can construct the equation

$$\begin{pmatrix} 0 & 1 & 1 & 1 \\ u_0 & v_0 & w_0 & 1 \\ \tau_u^0 + u_0 & \tau_v^0 + v_0 & \tau_w^0 + w_0 & 1 \end{pmatrix} \begin{pmatrix} A_d \\ B_d \\ C_d \\ D_d \end{pmatrix} = \begin{pmatrix} 0 \\ 0 \\ 0 \end{pmatrix}.$$

The above equation can be simplified and transformed in the projective coordinates as

$$\begin{pmatrix} 0 & 1 & 1 & 1 \\ U_0 & V_0 & W_0 & Z_0 \\ V_0 W_0 & -aU_0 W_0 & -bV_0 U_0 & 0 \end{pmatrix} \begin{pmatrix} A_d \\ B_d \\ C_d \\ D_d \end{pmatrix} = \begin{pmatrix} 0 \\ 0 \\ 0 \end{pmatrix}.$$

Then we can obtain

$$A_a = \begin{vmatrix} 1 & 1 & 1 \\ Z_0 & V_0 & W_0 \\ 0 & -aU_0W_0 & -bV_0U_0 \end{vmatrix}, \quad B_a = \begin{vmatrix} 0 & 1 & 1 \\ U_0 & Z_0 & W_0 \\ V_0W_0 & 0 & -bV_0U_0 \end{vmatrix},$$

$$C_a = \begin{vmatrix} 0 & 1 & 1 \\ U_0 & V_0 & Z_0 \\ V_0W_0 & -aU_0W_0 & 0 \end{vmatrix}, \quad D_a = -B_d - C_d.$$

$\square$

4   Operation Counts with Even Embedding Degree

In this section, we give a detailed analysis of the Tate pairing computation on twisted Jacobi intersections curves in the case of the even embedding degree.

Let K be a finite field $\mathbb{F}_q$ with $\text{char}(\mathbb{F}_q) > 2$, and let $\mathbf{M}, \mathbf{S}$ and $\mathbf{m}, \mathbf{s}$ denote multiplication and squaring in $\mathbb{F}_{q^k}$ and $\mathbb{F}_q$, respectively. Besides, $\mathbf{m}_a$ and $\mathbf{m}_b$ denote multiplication in $\mathbb{F}_q$ by constants a and b.

Let $\mathbb{F}_{q^k}$ have the basis $\{1, \alpha\}$ over $\mathbb{F}_{q^{k/2}}$ with $\alpha^2 = \delta \in \mathbb{F}_{q^{k/2}}$. The right argument $Q \in G_2$ of the Tate pairing $\tau_n(P, Q)$ can be chosen using the quadratic twist technique as shown in [7]. Since $E_{a\delta, b\delta}$ is the quadratic twist of $E_{a,b}$, $Q' = (U_Q, V_Q, W_Q, Z_Q) \in G_1' = E_{a\delta, b\delta}(\mathbb{F}_{q^{k/2}})[n]$ can be chosen with $U_Q, V_Q, W_Q, Z_Q \in \mathbb{F}_{q^{k/2}}$. Then the point $Q = (U_Q\alpha, V_Q, W_Q, Z_Q) \in E_{a,b}(\mathbb{F}_{q^k})$ is twisted from Q'. On the other side, the left argument can be chosen as $P = (U_P, V_P, W_P, Z_P) \in G_1$, where $U_P, V_P, W_P, Z_P \in \mathbb{F}_q$.

Given $P_1, P_2, P_0 \in \langle P \rangle$. According to the denominator elimination technique, since Q is not a 2-torsion point, then $U_Q \neq 0$. Thus one only needs to compute

$$f_{P_1,P_2}(Q) = \frac{A_a U_Q \alpha + B_a(V_Q - Z_Q) + C_a(W_Q - Z_Q)}{B(V_Q - Z_Q) + C(W_Q - Z_Q)}$$

$$= \frac{A_a \frac{U_Q}{W_Q - Z_Q}\alpha + B_a \frac{V_Q - Z_Q}{W_Q - Z_Q} + C_a}{B\frac{V_Q - Z_Q}{W_Q - Z_Q} + C} \in (A_a\xi\alpha + B_a\zeta + C_a)\mathbb{F}_{q^{k/2}},$$

$$f_{P_0,P_0}(Q) = \frac{A_d U_Q \alpha + B_d(V_Q - Z_Q) + C_d(W_Q - Z_Q)}{B(V_Q - Z_Q) + C(W_Q - Z_Q)}$$

$$= \frac{A_d \frac{U_Q}{W_Q - Z_Q}\alpha + B_d \frac{V_Q - Z_Q}{W_Q - Z_Q} + C_d}{B\frac{V_Q - Z_Q}{W_Q - Z_Q} + C} \in (A_d\xi\alpha + B_d\zeta + C_d)\mathbb{F}_{q^{k/2}},$$

where $\xi = \frac{U_Q}{W_Q - Z_Q}$ and $\zeta = \frac{V_Q - Z_Q}{W_Q - Z_Q}$.

Since A_a, B_a, C_a and A_d, B_d, C_d are defined over $\mathbb{F}_q$, and $\xi, \zeta \in \mathbb{F}_{q^{k/2}}$ can be precomputed, the each of $B_a\xi, C_a\zeta, B_d\xi$, and $C_d\zeta$ can be computed in $\frac{k}{2}\mathbf{m}$. So, given A_a, B_a, C_a and A_d, B_d, C_d, both the evaluations of Miller's function f_{P_1,P_2} and f_{P_0,P_0} at Q can be computed in $k\mathbf{m}$. Hence, the calculations in one Miller's addition and doubling step are $1\mathbf{M} + k\mathbf{m}$ and $1\mathbf{M} + 1\mathbf{S} + k\mathbf{m}$, respectively.

4.1   Addition Step

Given $P_1 = (U_1, V_1, W_1, Z_1)$ and $P_2 = (U_2, V_2, W_2, Z_2)$ with $P_1 \neq P_2$, and $P_3 = P_1 + P_2 = (U_3, V_3, W_3, Z_3)$, Formulae (5) and Formulae (3) can be used to compute (A_a, B_a, C_a) and (U_3, V_3, W_3, Z_3) respectively. In order to minimize the total operations, however, we use the variants of Formulae (3) and Formulae (5) instead in the addition step. First, we rewrite Formulae (3) as

$$\begin{cases} U_3 = (U_1 Z_2 + Z_1 U_2)(U_1 Z_2 - Z_1 U_2), & V_3 = U_1 V_1 W_2 Z_2 - W_1 Z_1 U_2 V_2, \\ W_3 = U_1 W_1 V_2 Z_2 - V_1 Z_1 U_2 W_2, & Z_3 = U_1 Z_1 V_2 W_2 - V_1 W_1 U_2 Z_2. \end{cases}$$

The direct computation of the above formulae takes redundant operations. Instead, we use the following explicit formulae to compute $(2U_3, 2V_3, 2W_3, 2Z_3)$, which is equal to (U_3, V_3, W_3, Z_3) and cannot change the final value of the Tate pairing.

$$\begin{cases} V_3 - W_3 = (V_1 W_2 - V_2 W_1)(U_1 Z_2 + Z_1 U_2) = (①-②)(⑫+⑦), \\ Z_3 + W_3 = (U_1 V_2 - U_2 V_1)(Z_1 W_2 + W_1 Z_2) = (⑧-⑨)(④+⑩), \\ V_3 - Z_3 = (U_2 W_1 + U_1 W_2)(V_1 Z_2 - Z_1 V_2) = (⑤+⑥)(⑪-③), \\ 2U_3 = 2(U_1 Z_2 + Z_1 U_2)(U_1 Z_2 - Z_1 U_2) = 2(⑫+⑦)(⑫-⑦). \end{cases}$$

In one addition step, one needs 12m to compute ① ∼ ⑫, and 3m to compute $2V_3, 2W_3, 2Z_3$ by the linear combination of $V_3 - W_3$, $Z_3 + W_3$, and $V_3 - Z_3$. The computation of $2U_3$ needs 1m. From Formulae (5), A_a, B_a, C_a can be computed only with the additions of ① ∼ ⑫. Thus the cost of A_a, B_a, C_a and $(2U_3, 2V_3, 2W_3, 2Z_3)$ is 16m. The explicit formulae are given as follows.

$$① = V_1 W_2, ② = V_2 W_1, ③ = Z_1 V_2, ④ = Z_1 W_2, ⑤ = U_2 W_1, ⑥ = U_1 W_2, \quad \text{6m}$$
$$⑦ = Z_1 U_2, ⑧ = U_1 V_2, ⑨ = U_2 V_1, ⑩ = W_1 Z_2, ⑪ = V_1 Z_2, ⑫ = U_1 Z_2, \quad \text{6m}$$
$$E = (①-②)(U_1+⑦), F = (⑧-⑨)(④+W_1), G = (⑤+⑥)(V_1-③), \quad \text{3m}$$
$$A_a = ①-②+③-④+W_1-V_1, B_a = ⑤-⑥-⑦+U_1,$$
$$C_a = ⑧-⑨+⑦-U_1, 2V_3 = E+F+G, 2W_3 = F-E+G,$$
$$2Z_3 = F+E-G, 2U_3 = 2(⑫+⑦)(⑫-⑦). \quad \text{1m}$$

Usually, $P_2 = P = (U_2, V_2, W_2, Z_2)$ is fixed in the calculation of the Tate pairing, so we can suppose $Z_2 = 1$. Then the cost for computing (A_a, B_a, C_a) and $(2U_3, 2V_3, 2W_3, 2Z_3)$ can be reduced to 13m. Hence, the total cost for one Miller's mixed addition step is $1M + km + 13m$. Finally, we list the costs for one Miller's addition step in different forms of elliptic curves ignoring the common cost $1M + km$ in Table 1.

4.2   Doubling Step

Given $P_0 = (U_0, V_0, W_0, Z_0)$ and $P_3 = [2]P_0 = (U_3, V_3, W_3, Z_3)$, Formulae (8) and Formulae (4) can be used to compute (A_d, B_d, C_d) and (U_3, V_3, W_3, Z_3). However, we use a variant of Formulae (8) to minimize the total operations in the Miller's doubling step. First, using the equation of twisted Jacobi intersections curves

$aU_0^2 + V_0^2 = Z_0^2, bU_0^2 + W_0^2 = Z_0^2$, we have $aW_0^2 - bV_0^2 = (a-b)Z_0^2$. Then Formulae (8) can be transformed as follows:

$$A_d = U_0(aW_0^2 - aW_0Z_0 + bV_0Z_0 - bV_0^2) = U_0((a-b)Z_0^2 + bV_0Z_0 - aW_0Z_0)$$
$$= (U_0Z_0)(a(Z_0 - W_0) + b(V_0 - Z_0)),$$
$$B_d = V_0(bU_0^2 + W_0^2 - W_0Z_0) = V_0(Z_0^2 - W_0Z_0) = (V_0Z_0)(Z_0 - W_0),$$
$$C_d = W_0(V_0Z_0 - aU_0^2 - V_0^2) = V_0(V_0Z_0 - Z_0^2) = (W_0Z_0)(V_0 - Z_0).$$

Note that the common factor Z_0 of (A_d, B_d, C_d) for the intermediate point P_0 must belong to $\mathbb{F}_q$. Thus Z_0 can be eliminated under the final exponentiation of the Tate paring. So one only needs to calculate

$$A_d' = U_0(a(Z_0 - W_0) + b(V_0 - Z_0)), \quad B_d' = V_0Z_0 - V_0W_0, \quad C_d' = V_0W_0 - W_0Z_0.$$

In one doubling step, first, B_d' and C_d' can be computed in $3\mathbf{m}$, and A_d' can be computed in $1\mathbf{m} + 1\mathbf{m}_a + 1\mathbf{m}_b$. Then, the calculation of Formulae (4) requires additional $2\mathbf{m}$ and $3\mathbf{s}$ to compute (U_3, V_3, W_3, Z_3). Thus the cost of A_d', B_d', C_d' and (U_3, V_3, W_3, Z_3) is $6\mathbf{m} + 3\mathbf{s} + 1\mathbf{m}_a + 1\mathbf{m}_b$. The explicit formulae are given as follows.

$①' = V_0Z_0, ②' = W_0Z_0, ③' = V_0W_0, E = ①'^2, F = ②'^2, G = ③'^2,$	$3\mathbf{m} + 3\mathbf{s}$
$A_d' = U_0(a(Z_0 - W_0) + b(V_0 - Z_0)),$	$1\mathbf{m} + 1\mathbf{m}_a + 1\mathbf{m}_b$
$B_d' = ①' - ③', C_d' = ③' - ②', U_3 = 2Z_0U_0③',$	$2\mathbf{m}$
$V_3 = E - F + G, W_3 = F - E + G, Z_3 = F + E - G.$	

The total cost for one Miller's doubling step is $1\mathbf{M} + 1\mathbf{S} + k\mathbf{m} + 6\mathbf{m} + 3\mathbf{s} + 1\mathbf{m}_a + 1\mathbf{m}_b$. We list the calculations for one Miller's doubling step in different forms of elliptic curves ignoring the common cost $1\mathbf{M} + 1\mathbf{S} + k\mathbf{m}$ in Table 1.

Table 1. Costs of Miller's formulae for Tate pairing with different coordinate systems. (Denote projective coordinates by $\mathcal{P}$, and Jacobian coordinates by $\mathcal{J}$.)

Forms of EC	Mixed Addition (mADD)	Doubling (DBL)
Weierstrass ($\mathcal{J}$), [15] or [1]	$9\mathbf{m} + 3\mathbf{s}$ or $6\mathbf{m} + 6\mathbf{s}$	$1\mathbf{m} + 11\mathbf{s} + 1$
Weierstrass ($\mathcal{P}$), $a_4 = -3$ [1]	$6\mathbf{m} + 6\mathbf{s}$	$6\mathbf{m} + 5\mathbf{s}$
Weierstrass ($\mathcal{P}$), $a_4 = 0$ [1]	$6\mathbf{m} + 6\mathbf{s}$	$3\mathbf{m} + 8\mathbf{s}$
Edwards ($\mathcal{P}$), [15]	$14\mathbf{m} + 4\mathbf{s} + 1\mathbf{m}_d$	$8\mathbf{m} + 4\mathbf{s} + 1\mathbf{m}_d$
twisted Edwards ($\mathcal{P}$), [1]	$12\mathbf{m} + 1\mathbf{m}_a$	$6\mathbf{m} + 5\mathbf{s} + 2\mathbf{m}_a$
Huff ($\mathcal{P}$), [16]	$13\mathbf{m}$	$11\mathbf{m} + 6\mathbf{s}$
Hessian ($\mathcal{P}$), [12]	$10\mathbf{m}$	$3\mathbf{m} + 6\mathbf{s} + 3\mathbf{m}_d$
Selmer ($\mathcal{P}$), [23]	$10\mathbf{m}$	$5\mathbf{m} + 3\mathbf{s}$
twisted Jacobi quartic ($\mathcal{P}$), [21]	$16\mathbf{m} + 1\mathbf{s} + 3\mathbf{m}_a + 1\mathbf{m}_d$	$4\mathbf{m} + 8\mathbf{s} + 1\mathbf{m}_a$
twisted Jacobi intersections ($\mathcal{P}$)	$13\mathbf{m}$	$6\mathbf{m} + 3\mathbf{s} + 1\mathbf{m}_a + 1\mathbf{m}_b$

Note that the calculation for DBL is much more importance, since the group order usually has light Hamming weight. Thus, if the total costs for DBL and mADD in two different forms are the same, we recommend the form with the less cost for DBL. In addition, the constants a and b could be chosen as smaller integers, we therefore can omit $\mathbf{m}_a$ and $\mathbf{m}_b$ in Table 1. So our formulae are efficient and competitive.

4.3   Parallel Execution

Be similar to the parallel computation of the Tate pairing on Selmer curves, our formulae can also be performed in a parallel way. Assume that three multiprecision multiplications can be performed in parallel, the costs of DBL and DBL+mADD can be reduced to $1\mathbf{M} + 1\mathbf{S} + \frac{k}{2}\mathbf{m} + 3\mathbf{m} + 1\mathbf{s}$ and $1\mathbf{M} + 1\mathbf{S} + k\mathbf{m} + 10\mathbf{m} + 1\mathbf{s}$ respectively, which are competitive with the costs on Selmer curves in parallel, namely $1\mathbf{M} + 1\mathbf{S} + \frac{k}{2}\mathbf{m} + 2\mathbf{m} + 1\mathbf{s}$ for DBL, and $1\mathbf{M} + \frac{k}{2}\mathbf{m} + 4\mathbf{m}$ for mADD, and therefore $2\mathbf{M} + 1\mathbf{S} + k\mathbf{m} + 6\mathbf{m} + 1\mathbf{s}$ for DBL+mADD. The details are given in Appendix B.

5   Operation Counts with Other Embedding Degree

In the pairing computations, elliptic curves with twists of high degree can bring many advantages. Unfortunately, there are only quadratic twists of twisted Jacobi intersections curves. Instead, however, we can use the mixed coordintes constituting of the left argument chosen on the Weierstrass form and the right argument chosen on the corresponding twisted Jacobi intersections form. In this section, we analyze the computations of the Tate pairing on twisted Jacobi intersections curves with different embedding degrees.

5.1   Embedding Degree 1

Let $z \in \mathbb{F}_q(E)$ be a fixed local uniformizer at $\mathcal{O}$. For $f \in \mathbb{F}_{q^k}(E)$, f is called monic or normalized, if $(fz^{-v})(\mathcal{O}) = 1$, where v is the order of f at $\mathcal{O}$. In the computation of the Tate pairing, the Miller's functions have to be monic when the embedding degree is 1.

Proposition 1. *Let* h_{P_1,P_2}, h_{P_3} *and* h_{P_0,P_0} *be defined in Theorem 4 and Theorem 5, respectively. Since U is a local uniformizer at $\mathcal{O}$, then the orders of $\frac{h_{P_1,P_2}}{U}$, $\frac{h_{P_3}}{U^2}$, $\frac{h_{P_0,P_0}}{U}$ at $\mathcal{O}$ are all zeros. Furthermore,* $\frac{h_{P_1,P_2}}{U}(\mathcal{O}) = A_a$, $\frac{h_{P_3}}{U^2}(\mathcal{O}) = \frac{-aB-bC}{2}$, $\frac{h_{P_0,P_0}}{U}(\mathcal{O}) = A_d$.

Proof. Since $\mathrm{ord}_{\mathcal{O}}(U) = 1$, and $\mathrm{ord}_{\mathcal{O}}(h_{P_1,P_2}) = 1$, and $\mathrm{ord}_{\mathcal{O}}(h_{P_3}) = 2$, and $\mathrm{ord}_{\mathcal{O}}(h_{P_0,P_0}) = 1$. Then $\mathrm{ord}_{\mathcal{O}}(\frac{h_{P_1,P_2}}{U}) = \mathrm{ord}_{\mathcal{O}}(\frac{h_{P_3}}{U^2}) = \mathrm{ord}_{\mathcal{O}}(\frac{h_{P_0,P_0}}{U}) = 0$. Since $V - Z = \frac{-aU^2}{V+Z}$ and $W - Z = \frac{-bU^2}{W+Z}$, then $\mathrm{ord}_{\mathcal{O}}(V - Z) = \mathrm{ord}_{\mathcal{O}}(W - Z) = 2$. Thus we have that $\frac{h_{P_1,P_2}}{U}(\mathcal{O}) = \frac{A_a U + B_a(V-Z) + C_a(W-Z)}{U}(\mathcal{O}) = A_a$, $\frac{h_{P_0,P_0}}{U}(\mathcal{O}) = \frac{A_d U + B_d(V-Z) + C_d(W-Z)}{U}(\mathcal{O}) = A_d$, $\frac{h_{P_3}}{U^2}(\mathcal{O}) = \frac{(V+Z)(W+Z)(B(V-Z)+C(W-Z))}{(V+Z)(W+Z)U^2}(\mathcal{O})$
$= \frac{-aB(W+Z)-bC(V+Z)}{(V+Z)(W+Z)}(\mathcal{O}) = \frac{-aB-bC}{2}$. $\square$

Hence, the new Miller's functions $\bar{h}_{P_0,P_0} = \frac{1}{A_d}h_{P_0,P_0}$, $\bar{h}_{P_1,P_2} = \frac{1}{A_a}h_{P_1,P_2}$, $\bar{h}_{P_3} = \frac{-2}{aB+bC}h_{P_3}$ are monic. Given $P_0, P_1, P_2, P_3 \in E(\mathbb{F}_q)[r]$ with $P_1 = [2]P_0$ and $P_3 = P_1 + P_2$ with $P_1 \neq P_2$, then the explicit Miller's formulae are given by

$$f_{P_0,P_0} = \frac{\bar{h}_{P_0,P_0}}{\bar{h}_{P_1}} = \frac{(aB+bC)(A_d\frac{U}{W-Z} + B_d\frac{V-Z}{W-Z} + C_d)}{-2A_d(B\frac{V-Z}{W-Z} + C)}$$

$$= \frac{(aB+bC)(A_d'\frac{U}{W-Z} + B_d'\frac{V-Z}{W-Z} + C_d')}{-2A_d'(B\frac{V-Z}{W-Z} + C)} = \frac{(aB+bC)(A_d'\xi + B_d'\zeta + C_d')}{-2A_d'(B\zeta + C)},$$

and

$$f_{P_1,P_2} = \frac{\bar{h}_{P_1,P_2}}{\bar{h}_{P_3}} = \frac{(aB+bC)(A_a\frac{U}{W-Z} + B_a\frac{V-Z}{W-Z} + C_a)}{-2A_a(B\frac{V-Z}{W-Z} + C)}$$

$$= \frac{(aB+bC)(A_a\xi + B_a\zeta + C_a)}{-2A_a(B\zeta + C)},$$

where $\xi = \frac{U}{W-Z}$ and $\zeta = \frac{V-Z}{W-Z}$.

Since the embedding degree is 1, all multiplications and squarings take place in $\mathbb{F}_q$, i.e. $\mathbf{M} = \mathbf{m}$ and $\mathbf{S} = \mathbf{s}$. When A_d, B_d, C_d and A_a, B_a, C_a and B, C are given, and ξ, ζ are precomputed, the Miller's doubling and addition steps cost $7\mathbf{M} + 2\mathbf{S} + 1\mathbf{M}_a + 1\mathbf{M}_b$ and $7\mathbf{M} + 1\mathbf{M}_a + 1\mathbf{M}_b$, respectively.

Besides, as analyzed in §4.1 and §4.2, we need $13\mathbf{M}$ to compute A_a, B_a, C_a and $P_3 = (2U_3, 2V_3, 2W_3, 2Z_3)$ in one mixed addition step, and $6\mathbf{M}+3\mathbf{S}+1\mathbf{M}_a+1\mathbf{M}_b$ to compute A_d', B_d', C_d' and $P_1 = (U_1, V_1, W_1, Z_1)$ in one doubling step. Note that B, C, D can be computed without any multiplications and squarings. Hence, the total costs for one Miller's doubling and addition step are $13\mathbf{M}+5\mathbf{S}+2\mathbf{M}_a+2\mathbf{M}_b$ and $20\mathbf{M} + 1\mathbf{M}_a + 1\mathbf{M}_b$.

Example 1. The currently known elliptic curves over $\mathbb{F}_p$ with embedding degree 1 are very rare. Koblitz and Menezes [17] first gave two families of such elliptic curves over $\mathbb{F}_p$, where $p = A^2 + 1$ is prime, which are defined by

$$E_1 : y^2 = x^3 - x , \text{ if } A \equiv 0 \pmod 4,$$
$$E_2 : y^2 = x^3 - 4x , \text{ if } A \equiv 2 \pmod 4.$$

Koblitz and Menezes showed that $E_i(\mathbb{F}_p) \cong \mathbb{Z}/A\mathbb{Z} \times \mathbb{Z}/A\mathbb{Z}$ for $i = 1, 2$. Note that $E_1 \cong E_{1,-1}$ and $E_2 \cong E_{2,-2}$, where $E_{1,-1}$ and $E_{2,-2}$ are two twisted Jacobi intersections curves defined by (1). Since $a = -b$ is very small, the total costs for one Miller's doubling and addition step are $13\mathbf{M} + 5\mathbf{S}$ and $20\mathbf{M}$, which are less than the costs in Weierstrass form given in [17].

5.2 Embedding Degree Divided by 4

For choosing the right argument Q from a Weierstrass curve with a quartic twist, the twisted Jacobi intersections curve need be chosen as

$$E_{a,-a} : aU^2 + V^2 = Z^2, \quad -aU^2 + W^2 = Z^2,$$

which is isomorphic to the Weierstrass curve $E : y^2 = x^3 - a^2 x$ under ψ given in Theorem 1. Let $D \in \mathbb{F}_q$ be a quadratic non-residue, then $E^t : y^2 = x^3 - \frac{a^2}{D}x$ is the quartic twist of E with $\phi_4(x, y) = (D^{1/2}x, D^{3/4}y) \in \mathrm{Hom}(E^t, E)$. Choosing $Q' = (x_Q, y_Q) \in E^t(\mathbb{F}_q^{k/4})[n]$, one has

$$Q = \psi \circ \phi_4(Q')$$
$$= \left(\frac{-2D^{3/4}y_Q}{Dx_Q^2 + a^2}, \frac{Dx_Q^2 - 2aD^{1/2}x_Q - a^2}{Dx_Q^2 + a^2}, \frac{Dx_Q^2 + 2aD^{1/2}x_Q - a^2}{Dx_Q^2 + a^2} \right)$$
$$= (-2D^{3/4}y_Q, Dx_Q^2 - 2aD^{1/2}x_Q - a^2, Dx_Q^2 + 2aD^{1/2}x_Q - a^2, Dx_Q^2 + a^2)$$
$$\in E_{a,-a}(\mathbb{F}_q^k)[n].$$

Then the Miller's addition and doubling functions only need to be computed as

$$f_{P_1,P_2}(Q) \in \left(A_a \frac{y_Q}{a^2} D^{3/4} + (B_a - C_a)\frac{x_Q}{a}D^{1/2} + (B_a + C_a) \right)\mathbb{F}_{q^{k/4}}$$
$$f_{P_0,P_0}(Q) \in \left(A_d \frac{y_Q}{a^2} D^{3/4} + (B_d - C_d)\frac{x_Q}{a}D^{1/2} + (B_d + C_d) \right)\mathbb{F}_{q^{k/4}}$$

Since A_a, B_a, C_a and A_d, B_d, C_d are all defined over $\mathbb{F}_q$, and $y_Q/a^2, x_Q/a \in \mathbb{F}_{q^{k/4}}$ can be precomputed, then the calculations of $f_{P_1,P_2}(Q)$ and $f_{P_0,P_0}(Q)$ need $1\mathbf{M} + \frac{k}{2}\mathbf{m} + 13\mathbf{m}$ and $1\mathbf{M} + 1\mathbf{S} + \frac{k}{2}\mathbf{m} + 6\mathbf{m} + 3\mathbf{s} + 1\mathbf{m}_a$.

5.3   Embedding Degree Divided by 6

For choosing the right argument Q from a Weierstrass curve with a sextic twist, the twisted Jacobi intersections curve needs to be defined by

$$E_{a,b} : aU^2 + V^2 = Z^2, \quad bU^2 + W^2 = Z^2,$$

with $a = e_2 - e_1$, $b = e_3 - e_1$ for some $e_1, e_2, e_3 \in \mathbb{F}_q$, which is isomorphic to the Weierstrass curve $E : y^2 = (x - e_1)(x - e_2)(x - e_3) = x^3 + B$ under $\psi' = \psi \circ \phi$, where ψ is given in Theorem 1 and $\phi : E \to E' : y^2 = x(x + e_1 - e_2)(x + e_1 - e_3), (x, y) \mapsto (x - e_1, y)$. Let $D \in \mathbb{F}_q$ be a quadratic and cubic non-residue, then $E^t : y^2 = x^3 + \frac{B}{D}x$ is the sextic twist of E with $\phi_6(x, y) = (D^{1/3}x, D^{1/2}y) \in \mathrm{Hom}(E^t, E)$. Choosing $Q' = (x_Q, y_Q) \in E^t(\mathbb{F}_q^{k/6})[n]$, one has

$$Q = \psi' \circ \phi_6(Q') = \psi(D^{1/3}x_Q - e_1, D^{1/2}y_Q) = (U_Q, V_Q, W_Q, Z_Q) \in E_{a,b}(\mathbb{F}_q^k)[n]$$

where $U_Q = -2D^{\frac{1}{2}}y_Q$, $V_Q = D^{\frac{2}{3}}x_Q^2 - 2e_2 D^{\frac{1}{3}}x_Q + e_2 e_3 + e_1 e_2 - e_1 e_3$, $W_Q = D^{\frac{2}{3}}x_Q^2 - 2e_3 D^{\frac{1}{3}}x_Q + e_2 e_3 + e_1 e_3 - e_1 e_2$, $Z_Q = D^{\frac{2}{3}}x_Q^2 - 2e_1 D^{\frac{1}{3}}x_Q - e_2 e_3 + e_1 e_2 + e_1 e_3$. Then the Miller's addition and doubling functions only need to be computed as

$$f_{P_1,P_2}(Q) \in \left(A_a \frac{y_Q}{e_2 b}D^{\frac{1}{2}} + (B_a + C_a)\frac{ax_Q}{e_2 b}D^{\frac{1}{3}} - B_a \frac{e_3 a}{e_2 b} - C_a \right)\mathbb{F}_{q^{k/6}},$$
$$f_{P_0,P_0}(Q) \in \left(A_d \frac{y_Q}{e_2 b}D^{\frac{1}{2}} - (B_d + C_d)\frac{ax_Q}{e_2 b}D^{\frac{1}{3}} - B_d \frac{e_3 a}{e_2 b} - C_d \right)\mathbb{F}_{q^{k/6}}.$$

Note that $A_a, B_a, C_a, A_d, B_d, C_d \in \mathbb{F}_q$, and since $\frac{y_Q}{e_2 b}, \frac{a x_Q}{e_2 b} \in \mathbb{F}_{q^{k/6}}, \frac{e_3 a}{e_2 b} \in \mathbb{F}_q$ can be precomputed, then the calculations of $f_{P_1,P_2}(Q)$ and $f_{P_0,P_0}(Q)$ require $1\mathbf{M} + \frac{k}{3}\mathbf{m} + 13\mathbf{m} + 2\mathbf{m}_c$ and $1\mathbf{M} + 1\mathbf{S} + \frac{k}{3}\mathbf{m} + 6\mathbf{m} + 3\mathbf{s} + 3\mathbf{m}_c$, where $\mathbf{m}_c$ denotes multiplication by a constant in $\mathbb{F}_q$.

6 Relation between the Tate Pairings on Twisted Jacobi Intersections Curves and Twisted Edwards Curves

First, there exists a close relation between twisted Jacobi intersections curves and twisted Edwards curves. Bernstein *et al.* [2] showed that an elliptic curve with three points of order 2 might not be birationally equivalent to a twisted Edwards curve. However, they gave the following statement.

Theorem 6. *([2], Theorem 5.1) Fix a field K with $\mathrm{char}(K) \neq 2$. Every elliptic curve over K having three K-rational points of order 2 is 2-isogenous over K to a twisted Edwards curve.*

Indeed, we can construct the 2-isogeny and the dual 2-isogeny directly (in Appendix A), and conclude that every twisted Edwards curve is also 2-isogenous over K to an elliptic curve over K having three K-rational points of order 2. From Theorem 1 and Theorem 6, we can obtain the following corollary.

Corollary 1. *For a field K with $\mathrm{char}(K) \neq 2$, every twisted Jacobi intersections curve is 2-isogenous over K to a twisted Edwards curve, and vice versa.*

Proof. The specific 2-isogeny and dual 2-isogeny are given in Appendix A. □

Let ϕ be the 2-isogeny from the twisted Jacobi intersections curve $E_{a,b}$ to the twisted Edwards curve $E_{E,A,B}$, and let $\hat{\phi}$ be the dual 2-isogenous. We will show the relation between the Tate pairings on $E_{a,b}$ and $E_{E,A,B}$.

Theorem 7. *([3], Theorem IX.9) Let $\phi : E \to E'$ be an isogeny, where E and E' are elliptic curves over $\mathbb{F}_q$. Let $n \mid \gcd(\#E(\mathbb{F}_q), \#E'(\mathbb{F}_q))$ and suppose the embedding degree corresponding to q and n is k. Then, up to nth powers,*

$$\tau_n(\phi(P), \phi(Q)) = \tau_n(P, Q)^{\deg \phi}.$$

According to the above theorem, twisted Jacobi intersections curves can be completely substituted for twisted Edwards curves in the Tate pairing computation. Concretely, given the twisted Edwards curve $E_{E,A,B}$, compute the twisted Jacobi intersections curve $E_{a,b}$ with the isogeny $\phi : E_{E,A,B} \to E_{a,b}$ in Appendix A. Given $P, Q \in E_{E,A,B}[n]$, compute $\phi(P), \phi(Q) \in E_{a,b}[n]$, and therefore compute the Tate pairing on twisted Jacobi intersections curves $\tau_{n,J}(\phi(P), \phi(Q))^{1/2}$ instead of the Tate pairing on twisted Edwards curves $\tau_{n,E}(P, Q)$.

In practical pairing-based cryptosystems, the extraction of the square root for computing $\tau_{n,J}(\phi(P), \phi(Q))^{1/2}$ can be omitted, since $\tau_{n,J}(\phi(P), \phi(Q))$ also defines a bilinear pairing. Thus $\tau_{n,J}(\phi(P), \phi(Q))$ can be completely substituted for $\tau_{n,E}(P, Q)$ in practice.

Usually, the group order has light Hamming weight, our formulae for twisted Jacobi intersections curves with less cost for the doubling step, may be better than the formulae for twisted Edwards curves.

7 Conclusion

In this paper, explicit formulae for the Miller's addition and doubling steps on twisted Jacobi intersections curves have been presented to compute the Tate pairing. We show that our Miller's formulae are very efficient not only in the case of even embedding degree but also in the case of embedding degree 1. Moreover, we propose fast Miller's formulae in the case of embedding degrees dividing 4 and 6 by using the high-degree twists of Weierstrass curves. In addition, we give an analysis of the relation between the Tate pairings on two isogenous elliptic curves and substitute the Tate pairing on twisted Jacobi intersections curves for that on twisted Edwards curves completely. At last, we hope that pairings on twisted Jacobi intersections curves would draw more attentions and become a good choice in practice.

References

1. Arène, C., Lange, T., Naehrig, M., Ritzenthaler, C.: Faster computation of the Tate pairing. Journal of Number Theory 131, 842–857 (2011)
2. Bernstein, D.J., Birkner, P., Joye, M., Lange, T., Peters, C.: Twisted Edwards Curves. In: Vaudenay, S. (ed.) AFRICACRYPT 2008. LNCS, vol. 5023, pp. 389–405. Springer, Heidelberg (2008)
3. Blake, I.F., Seroussi, G., Smart, N.P.: Advance in Elliptic Curve Cryptogtaphy. LMS Lecture Note Series, vol. 317. Cambridge University Press (2005)
4. Chatterjee, S., Sarkar, P., Barua, R.: Efficient Computation of Tate Pairing in Projective Coordinate over General Characteristic Fields. In: Park, C., Chee, S. (eds.) ICISC 2004. LNCS, vol. 3506, pp. 168–181. Springer, Heidelberg (2005)
5. Chudnovsky, D.V., Chudnovsky, G.V.: Sequences of Numbers Generated by Addition in Formal Groups and New Primality and Factorization Tests. Advances in Applied Mathematics 7(4), 385–434 (1986)
6. Costello, C., Hisil, H., Boyd, C., Gonzalez Nieto, J., Wong, K.K.-H.: Faster Pairings on Special Weierstrass Curves. In: Shacham, H., Waters, B. (eds.) Pairing 2009. LNCS, vol. 5671, pp. 89–101. Springer, Heidelberg (2009)
7. Costello, C., Lange, T., Naehrig, M.: Faster Pairing Computations on Curves with High-Degree Twists. In: Nguyen, P.Q., Pointcheval, D. (eds.) PKC 2010. LNCS, vol. 6056, pp. 224–242. Springer, Heidelberg (2010)
8. Das, M.P.L., Sarkar, P.: Pairing Computation on Twisted Edwards Form Elliptic Curves. In: Galbraith, S.D., Paterson, K.G. (eds.) Pairing 2008. LNCS, vol. 5209, pp. 192–210. Springer, Heidelberg (2008)
9. Farashahi, R.R., Joye, M.: Efficient Arithmetic on Hessian Curves. In: Nguyen, P.Q., Pointcheval, D. (eds.) PKC 2010. LNCS, vol. 6056, pp. 243–260. Springer, Heidelberg (2010)

10. Feng, R., Nie, M., Wu, H.: Twisted Jacobi Intersections Curves. In: Kratochvil, J., Li, A., Fiala, J., Kolman, P. (eds.) TAMC 2010. LNCS, vol. 6108, pp. 199–210. Springer, Heidelberg (2010)
11. Freeman, D., Scott, M., Teske, E.: A Taxonomy of Pairing-Friendly Elliptic Curves. Journal of Cryptology 23(2), 224–280 (2010)
12. Gu, H., Gu, D., Xie, W.L.: Efficient Pairing Computation on Elliptic Curves in Hessian Form. In: Rhee, K.-H., Nyang, D. (eds.) ICISC 2010. LNCS, vol. 6829, pp. 169–176. Springer, Heidelberg (2011)
13. Hisil, H., Carter, G., Dawson, E.: New Formulae for Efficient Elliptic Curve Arithmetic. In: Srinathan, K., Pandu Rangan, C., Yung, M. (eds.) INDOCRYPT 2007. LNCS, vol. 4859, pp. 138–151. Springer, Heidelberg (2007)
14. Hisil, H., Wong, K.K.H., Carter, G., Dawson, E.: Faster Group Operations on Elliptic Curves. In: Brankovic, L., Susilo, W. (eds.) AISC 2009 (CRPIT), vol. 98, pp. 7–20. Australian Computer Society, Inc. (2009)
15. Ionica, S., Joux, A.: Another Approach to Pairing Computation in Edwards Coordinates. In: Chowdhury, D.R., Rijmen, V., Das, A. (eds.) INDOCRYPT 2008. LNCS, vol. 5365, pp. 400–413. Springer, Heidelberg (2008)
16. Joye, M., Tibouchi, M., Vergnaud, D.: Huff's Model for Elliptic Curves. In: Hanrot, G., Morain, F., Thomé, E. (eds.) ANTS-IX 2010. LNCS, vol. 6197, pp. 234–250. Springer, Heidelberg (2010)
17. Koblitz, N., Menezes, A.: Pairing-Based Cryptography at High Security Levels. In: Smart, N.P. (ed.) Cryptography and Coding 2005. LNCS, vol. 3796, pp. 13–36. Springer, Heidelberg (2005)
18. Liardet, P., Smart, N.P.: Preventing SPA/DPA in ECC Systems Using the Jacobi Form. In: Koç, Ç.K., Naccache, D., Paar, C. (eds.) CHES 2001. LNCS, vol. 2162, pp. 391–401. Springer, Heidelberg (2001)
19. Merriman, J.R., Siksek, S., Smart, N.P.: Explicit 4-Descents on an Elliptic Curve. Acta Arith. 77(4), 385–404 (1996)
20. Miller, V.S.: The Weil Pairing, and Its Efficient Calculation. Journal of Cryptology 17(4), 235–261 (2004)
21. Wang, H., Wang, K., Zhang, L., Li, B.: Pairing Computation on Elliptic Curves of Jacobi Quartic Form. Technical report, Cryptology ePrint Archive Report 2010/475 (2010), http://eprint.iacr.org/2010/475
22. Washington, L.C.: ELLIPTIC CURVES: Number Theory and Cryptography, vol. 50. Chapman & Hall (2008)
23. Zhang, L., Wang, K., Wang, H., Ye, D.: Another Elliptic Curve Model for Faster Pairing Computation. In: Bao, F., Weng, J. (eds.) ISPEC 2011. LNCS, vol. 6672, pp. 432–446. Springer, Heidelberg (2011)

A   2-Isogeny between Twisted Jacobi Intersections Curves and Twisted Edwards Curves

For every twisted Edwards curve $E_{E,a,d} : ax^2 + y^2 = 1 + dx^2y^2$, there exits a twisted Jacobi intersections curve $E_{a,d} : au^2 + v^2 = 1, du^2 + w^2 = 1$ with the 2-isogeny

$$\phi : E_{E,a,d} \to E_{a,d},$$
$$(x,y) \mapsto \left(\frac{2(a-d)x^3y}{(adx^4-1)(y^2-1)}, \frac{1-2ax^2+adx^4}{1-adx^4}, \frac{1-2dx^2+adx^4}{1-adx^4} \right).$$

Conversely, for every twisted Jacobi intersections curve $E_{a,b} : au^2 + v^2 = 1, bu^2 + w^2 = 1$, there exits a twisted Edwards curve $E_{E,a,b} : ax^2 + y^2 = 1 + bx^2 y^2$ with the 2-isogeny

$$\psi : E_{a,b} \to E_{E,a,b}, \quad (u,v,w) \mapsto \left(u, \frac{v}{w} \right).$$

It can be verified that $\psi = \widehat{\phi}$ easily.

B   Parallel Execution

For the further reduction of the cost, we give the explicit expression of the product of doubling function and addition function in the addition step.

Given $P_0 = (U_0, V_0, W_0, Z_0)$, $P_1 = [2]P_0 = (U_1, V_1, W_1, Z_1)$, $P_2 = P = (U_2, V_2, W_2, Z_2)$ (is fixed), and $Q = (U_Q\alpha, V_Q, W_Q, Z_Q)$, where $U_Q, V_Q, W_Q, Z_Q \in \mathbb{F}_{q^{k/2}}$. In stead of the product of $f_{P_0,P_0}(Q)$ and $f_{P_1,P_2}(Q)$ in the addition step, one only need to compute $(A_d\xi\alpha + B_d\zeta + C_d)(A_a\xi\alpha + B_a\zeta + C_a) = ((A_dB_a + A_aB_d)\xi\zeta + (A_dC_a + A_aC_d)\xi)\alpha + A_dA_a\xi^2\delta + (B_dC_a + C_dB_a)\zeta + B_dB_a\zeta^2 + C_dC_a$.

Note that $\xi, \zeta, \xi^2\delta, \zeta^2, \xi\zeta \in \mathbb{F}_{q^{k/2}}$ can be precomputed. Given the values of A_d, B_d, C_d and A_a, B_a, C_a, the above product can be computed in $\frac{5}{2}km + 9\mathbf{m}$ instead of $1\mathbf{M} + 2km$. Then the cost of one doubling plus one addition step is $1\mathbf{M} + 1\mathbf{S} + \frac{5}{2}km + 9\mathbf{m}$, which is less than $2\mathbf{M} + 1\mathbf{S} + 2km$ when $k \geq 4$.

Assume that three multiprecision multiplications can be performed in parallel, then the parallel execution is given as follows:

Processor 1	Processor 2	Processor 3
Doubling step:		
$a_1 = V_0 Z_0$;	$a_2 = W_0 Z_0$;	$a_3 = V_0 W_0$;
$a_4 = a_1^2$;	$a_5 = a_2^2$;	$a_6 = a_3^2$;
$V_3 = a_4 - a_5 + a_6$;	$W_3 = a_5 - a_4 + a_6$;	$Z_3 = a_4 + a_5 - a_6$;
$B_d = a_1 - a_3$;	$a_7 = Z_0 - W_0$;	$a_8 = V_0 - Z_0$;
$a_9 = a_7 a$;	$a_{10} = a_8 b$;	$a_{11} = U_0 Z_0$;
$C_d = a_3 - a_2$;	$a_{12} = a_9 + a_{10}$;	$a_{13} = 2a_{11}$;
$A_d = U_0 a_{10}$;	$U_3 = a_{13} a_3$;	$- - -$
If addition step is needed:		
$b_1 = V_1 V_2$;	$b_2 = W_1 V_2$;	$b_3 = Z_1 V_2$;
$b_4 = Z_1 W_2$;	$b_5 = W_1 U_2$;	$b_6 = U_1 W_2$;
$b_7 = Z_1 U_2$;	$b_8 = U_1 V_2$;	$b_9 = V_1 U_2$;
$b_{10} = W_1 Z_2$ ($Z_2 = 1$);	$b_{11} = V_1 Z_2$ ($Z_2 = 1$);	$b_{12} = U_1 Z_2$ ($Z_2 = 1$);
$b_{13} = (b_1 - b_2)(b_7 + b_{12})$;	$b_{14} = (b_5 + b_6)(b_{11} - b_3)$;	$b_{15} = (b_8 - b_9)(b_4 + b_{10})$;
$A_a = b_1 - b_2 + b_3 - b_{11} - b_4 + b_{10}$;	$B_a = b_5 - b_6 - b_7 + b_{12}$;	$C_a = b_8 - b_9 + b_7 - b_{12}$;
$2V_3 = b_{13} + b_{14} + b_{15}$;	$2W_3 = b_{13} - b_{14} + b_{15}$;	$2Z_3 = b_{13} + b_{14} - b_{15}$;
$c_1 = A_d B_a$;	$c_2 = A_d C_a$;	$c_3 = B_d C_a$;
$c_4 = A_a B_d$;	$c_5 = A_a C_d$;	$c_6 = B_a C_d$;
$c_7 = A_d A_a$;	$c_8 = B_d B_a$;	$c_9 = C_d C_a$;
$d_1 = (c_1 + c_4)\xi\zeta$;	$d_2 = (c_2 + c_5)\xi$;	$d_3 = (c_3 + c_6)\zeta$;
$d_4 = c_7 \xi^2 \delta$;	$d_5 = c_8 \zeta^2$;	$2U_3 = 2(b_{12} + b_7)(b_{12} - b_7)$;
Else:		
$d_1 = A_d \xi$;	$d_2 = B_d \zeta$;	$- - -$

With parallel execution, the cost of one doubling step plus one mixed addition step (DBL+mADD) is $1\mathbf{M} + 1\mathbf{S} + km + 10\mathbf{m} + 1\mathbf{s}$, and the cost of one doubling step is $1\mathbf{M} + 1\mathbf{S} + \frac{k}{2}m + 3\mathbf{m} + 1\mathbf{s}$. In fact, the real cost is less, since $1\mathbf{M} + 1\mathbf{S}$ can also be computed in parallel.

Weak-Key Class of MISTY1 for Related-Key Differential Attack

Yi-bin Dai and Shao-zhen Chen

Zhengzhou Information Science and Technology Institute , Zhengzhou 450002, China
dybin321@163.com, chenshaozhen@vip.sina.com

Abstract. MISTY1 is a Feistel block cipher with presence in many cryptographic standards and applications. In this paper, according to analyzing the key schedule algorithm, a weak-key class encompassing $2^{102.57}$ weak keys of MISTY1 is found. Then we present 7-round related-key differential characteristics of MISTY1 under the weak-key class, which lead to the attacks on the 8-round MISTY1 without the first FL lay. The attack requires 2^{61} chosen ciphertexts, and the time complexities is $2^{84.6}$. To the best of our knowledge, the attack reported in this paper is the most powerful attack against MISTY1 with two related keys.

Keywords: MISTY1, weak-key, related-key, differential attack.

1 Introduction

The block cipher MISTY1 was proposed by M.Matsui [10], which was designed based on the principle of provable security against differential and linear cryptanalysis. MISTY1 is a 64-bit block cipher that has a key size of 128 bits. MISTY1 is used in many cryptographic standards and applications. For example, MISTY1 was selected to be in the final NESSIE portfolio of block ciphers, as well as an ISO standard.

Several cryptanalyses of MISTY1 have been reported. Slicing attack [7], collision search attack [6], integral attack [5], impossible differential attack [3,9], higher order differential attack [1,13,12,14,15] and the related-key amplified boomerang attack [8] can attack on reduced-round MISTY1. All of these attack can not attack on 8-round MISTY1. And the effective attack of these methods are higher order differential attack and related-key amplified boomerang attack, which lead to the attacks on 7-round MISTY1.

This paper concentrates on the key schedule algorithm since it is considered to be simple. According to our analysis of the key schedule, a weak-key class which has 2^{105} pairs related keys is found. Then combining the related-key attack [4,11] with the differential attack [2], we present a 7-round related-key differential characteristic of MISTY1, which lead to the attack on the 8-round MISTY1(without the first FL lay). Compared with the probability of 2^{-55} that the related keys exist in [8], the probability existing in this paper is 2^{-23}. Besides the attack requires two keys and can attack on the 8-round MISTY1(without the first FL lay).

C.-K. Wu, M. Yung, and D. Lin (Eds.): Inscrypt 2011, LNCS 7537, pp. 227–236, 2012.
© Springer-Verlag Berlin Heidelberg 2012

We summarize our results along with previously known results on MISTY1 in Table 1.

This paper is organized as follows: In Section 2, we give a brief description of the structure of MISTY1. We describe the some Propositions of MISTY1 and introduce the related weak-key class in Section 3. In Section 4, we present the attack on 8-round MISTY1. Section 5 concludes the paper.

Table 1. Summary of the Attacks on MISTY1

Attack	Rounds	FL lays	Data	Time
Slice attack[7]	4	3	$2^{22.25}$CP	2^{45}
Collision attack[6]	4	3	2^{20}CP	2^{89}
Integral attack[5]	4	3	25CP	2^{27}
Integral attack[5]	5	3	2^{34}CP	2^{48}
Impossible differential attack[3]	5[†]	4	$2^{41.36}$CP	$2^{46.35}$
Higher order differential attack(weak key)[13]	6	4	$2^{18.9}$CP	$2^{80.6}$
Higher order differential attack[14]	6	4	$2^{53.7}$CP	$2^{64.4}$
Higher order differential attack[15]	6	4	$2^{53.7}$CP	$2^{53.7}$
Impossible differential attack[3]	6	4	2^{51}CP	$2^{123.4}$
Related-key amplified boomerang attack[8]$(2^{-55})^*$	7	3	2^{54}CP	$2^{55.3}$
Higher order differential attack[15]	7	4	$2^{54.1}$KP	$2^{120.7}$
Related-key differential attack$(2^{-23})^*$	7	4	2^{39}CC	$2^{39.5}$
Related-key differential attack(Sec[4])$(2^{-25.43})^*$	8	4	2^{61}CC	$2^{84.6}$

CP-Chosen plaintext; CC-Chosen ciphertext; KP-Known plaintext; 5[†]-the attack retrieve 41.36 bits of information about the key; $(2^{-55})^*$ and $(2^{-25.43})^*$-the probability of the keys that exists in the attack.

2   The MISTY1 Cipher

In this section, we briefly describe the encryption and key schedule algorithm of MISTY1.

2.1   The Encryption Algorithm of MISTY1

MISTY1 [10] is a 64-bit block cipher with 128-bit keys. It has a recursive Feistel structure. The cipher has eight Feistel rounds. MISTY1 is composed of two functions: the non-linear function FO which is in itself close to a 3-round 32-bit Feistel construction and the function FL that mixes a 32-bit subkey with the data in a linear way.

The FO function also has a recursive structure: its round function called FI, is a three round Feistel construction. The FI function uses two non-linear S-boxes S7 and S9 (where S7 is a 7-bit to 7-bit permutation and S9 is a 9-bit to 9-bit permutation) . There is 112-bit subkey enters FO in each round 48 subkey bits are used in the FI functions and 64 subkey bits is used in the key mixing states.

The FL function is a simple linear transformation which accepts a 32-bit input and two 16-bit subkey words. One subkey word affects the data using the OR operation, while another subkey affects the data using the AND operation. We outline the structure of MISTY1 and its parts in Figure 1.

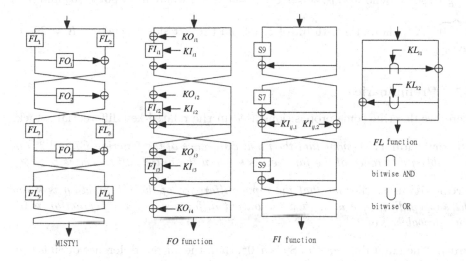

Fig. 1. Outline of MISTY1

2.2 The Key Schedule Algorithm of MISTY1

The key schedule of MISTY1 takes the 128-bit key, and treats it as eight 16-bit words:

$$K = K_1 || K_2 || K_3 || K_4 || K_5 || K_6 || K_7 || K_8$$

From this set of subkeys, another eight 16-bit words are generated according to the non-linear FI function:

$$K_i' = FI_{K_{i+1}}(K_i), 1 \leq i \leq 8$$

Table 2. The Key Schedule Algorithm of MISTY1

KO_{i1}	KO_{i2}	KO_{i3}	KO_{i4}	KI_{i1}	KI_{i2}	KI_{i3}	KL_{i1}	KL_{i2}
K_i	K_{i+2}	K_{i+7}	K_{i+4}	K'_{i+5}	K'_{i+1}	K'_{i+3}	$K_{\frac{i+1}{2}}(odd\ i)$	$K'_{\frac{i+1}{2}+6}(odd\ i)$
							$K'_{\frac{i}{2}+2}(even\ i)$	$K_{\frac{i}{2}+4}(even\ i)$

In each round, there are seven 16-bit words used in the FO function as the round subkey, and each of the FL functions accepts two subkey words. We give the exact schedule of MISTY1 in Table 2.

3   Preliminaries and Weak-Key Class of MISTY1

In this section, we will refer to some propositions of MISTY1. Then we find a weak-key class of MISTY1 for the 8-round related-key differential attack. Firstly, we give some denotations: $k = a^7 0^9$, $\beta = a^7 0^2 a^7$, where $a^7 = 0010000_2$ and $0^t = \overbrace{0 \cdots 0}^{t}$; $(K)_j$ shows the j-th bit of K (from the left side) , such as $K = 2000_x$, $(K)_3 = 1$.

3.1   Preliminaries

Here, we describe some propositions used in the related-key differential attack.

Observation 1. *Assume that the input difference of the function FI is 0^{16}, and the subkey difference of the function is k, then the output difference is β.*

Proposition 1. *Assume that the input difference of the FI function is k and the subkey difference is β, then the output difference of the FI function is 0^{16} with probability of 2^{-8}.*

Proof. The input difference of S9 is $a^7 0^2$, then the output difference of S9 is $0^2 a^7$ with probability of 2^{-8} which can kill the subkey difference, so that the output difference of the FI function is 0^{16} with probability of 2^{-8}.

Proposition 2. *Assume that the input bit difference of AND(or OR) operation is 1, and the key bit difference is 0, then the output bit difference is 1(or 0) with probability of 2^{-1}.*

Proposition 3. *Assume that the input difference of the FI function is k and the subkey difference is 0, then the output difference of the FI function is k with probability of 2^{-16} (The proposition can be verified experimentally).*

All of the propositions and observation described above are effectively used in the construction of the weak-key class and the related-key differential characteristic.

3.2   Weak-Key Class of MISTY1

We define the two 128-bit master keys K_a and K_b of MISTY1 that satisfy the following assumptions:

$$K_a = K_1 || K_2 || K_3 || K_4 || K_5 || K_6 || K_7 || K_8$$

$$K_b = K_1 || K_2 || K_3 || K_4 || K_5 || K_6^* || K_7 || K_8,$$

where $K_6 \oplus K_6^* = k$.

According to the function FI, another two keys are generated:

$$K'_a = K'_1||K'_2||K'_3||K'_4||K'_5||K'_6||K'_7||K'_8$$

$$K'_b = K'_1||K'_2||K'_3||K'_4||K'^*_5||K'^*_6||K'_7||K'_8,$$

where $K'_i = FI_{K_{i+1}}(K_i)$, $1 \leq i \leq 8$, especially $K'^*_5 = FI_{K^*_6}(K_5)$, $K'^*_6 = FI_{K_7}(K'^*_6)$. Besides $K'_6 \oplus K'^*_6 = k$, $K'_5 \oplus K'^*_5 = \beta$. Obversely, the two keys K_a and K_b satisfy the following conditions:

$$\Delta K_{ab} = (0,0,0,0,0,k,0,0), \Delta K'_{ab} = (0,0,0,0,\beta,k,0,0)$$

Then assume that we give the following 7-bit keys:

$$(K_7)_3 = 1, (K_7)_{12} = 0, (K_8)_3 = 1, (K'_4)_3 = 1, (K'_4)_{12} = 1, (K_6)_{12} = 0,$$
$$(K'_7)_3 = 0,$$

i.e. we know the following 7-bit key:
$(KL_{62})_3 = 1$, $(KL_{62})_{12} = 0$, $(KL_{82})_3 = 1$, $(KL_{41})_3 = 1$, $(KL_{41})_{12} = 1$, $(KL_{42})_{12} = 0$, $(KL_{10\ 1})_3 = 0$.
Besides, in order to construct the related-key differential characteristics, the following conditions should be ensure:

$$Pr[FI_{(\bullet,K_{2'})}(k \longrightarrow k)] > 0$$

$$Pr[FI_{(\bullet,K_{7'})}(\beta \longrightarrow k)] > 0$$

[1] Consequently, the number of the keys (K_6, K_7, K_8) and (K_2, K_3) which satisfy the conditions are $2^{29.57}$, that is to say, the probability is $2^{-2.43}$.

The set of all the key pairs satisfied the conditions above is called a weak-key class. The probability of the weak-key class is 2^{-23} ($= 2^{-16} \cdot 2^{-7}$) , since

$$Pr[K'_6 \oplus K'^*_6 = k|K_6 \oplus K^*_6 = k] = 2^{-16}$$

$$Pr[K'_5 \oplus K'^*_5 = \beta|K_6 \oplus K^*_6 = k] = 1,$$

according to the Proposition.3, and $Pr[(K_7)_3 = 1, (K_7)_{12} = 0, (K_8)_3 = 1, (K'_4)_3 = 1, (K'_4)_{12} = 1, (K_6)_{12} = 0, (K'_7)_3 = 0] = 2^{-7}$, which can be verified experimentally. Hence, the number of the weak keys of the weak-key class is about $2^{102.57}$($= 2^{128} \cdot 2^{-23} \cdot 2^{-2.43}$).

4   Related-Key Differential Attack on 8-Round MISTY1 without the First *FL* Lay

In this section, we present a 7-round related-key differential characteristic of MISTY1 under the weak-key class. Then we attack on the 8-round MISTY1 without the first FL lay. The attack requires 2^{61} chosen ciphertexts and the time complexity is $2^{84.6}$.

---

[1] Thanks Jiqiang Lu presents the conditions.

Table 3. The Subkeys Difference of MISTY1

Round	ΔKO_{i1}	ΔKO_{i2}	ΔKO_{i3}	ΔKO_{i4}	ΔKI_{i1}	ΔKI_{i2}	ΔKI_{i3}	ΔKL_{i1}	ΔKL_{i2}
1	0	0	0	0	k	0	0	0	0
2	0	0	0	k	0	0	β	0	0
3	0	0	0	0	0	0	k	0	0
4	0	k	0	0	0	β	0	0	k
5	0	0	0	0	0	k	0	0	0
6	k	0	0	0	0	0	0	β	0
7	0	0	k	0	0	0	0	0	0
8	0	0	0	0	β	0	0	k	0
9	–	–	–	–	–	–	–	0	0
10	–	–	–	–	–	–	–	0	0

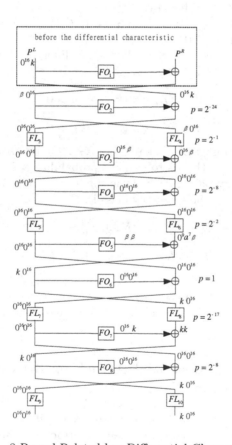

Fig. 2. 8-Round Related-key Differential Characteristics

4.1   The 7-Round Related-Key Differential Characteristic

Let the key pair (K_a, K_b) satisfies the following conditions:

$$\Delta K_{ab} = (0,0,0,0,0,k,0,0), \Delta K'_{ab} = (0,0,0,0,\beta,k,0,0)$$

and $(KL_{62})_3 = 1$, $(KL_{62})_{12} = 0$, $(KL_{82})_3 = 1$, $(KL_{41})_3 = 1$, $(KL_{41})_{12} = 1$, $(KL_{42})_{12} = 0$, $(KL_{10\ 1})_3 = 0$, $Pr[FI_{(\bullet, K_{2'})}(k \longrightarrow k)] > 0$, $Pr[FI_{(\bullet, K_{7'})}(\beta \longrightarrow k)] > 0$ i.e. the pair (K_a, K_b) is in the weak-key class. Then we can construct a 7-round related-key differential characteristic of MISTY1: $(\beta 0^{16}, 0^{16}k) \longrightarrow (0^{16}0^{16}, k0^{16})$ (See Figure 2) with probability of 2^{-58}, and the Table 3 gives the subkey difference of MISTY1.

Figure 2 and Table 4 illustrate the family and the probabilities of about 7-round differential characteristics in detail. The Proposition 1, 2, 3 are effectively used in the differential characteristics. Moreover, the given seven bits $(KL_{62})_3 = 1$, $(KL_{62})_{12} = 0$, $(KL_{82})_3 = 1$, $(KL_{41})_3 = 1$, $(KL_{41})_{12} = 1$, $(KL_{42})_{12} = 0$, $(KL_{10\ 1})_3 = 0$ ensure the following equations right: $FL_4(\beta 0^{16}) = 0^{16}\beta$, $FL_6(0^{16}0^{16}) = 0^9 a^7 \beta$, $FL_8(k0^{16}) = kk$, $FL_{10}(k0^{16}) = k0^{16}$. These elements correspond to some 7-round differential characteristics with probability of 2^{-58}, which is better than the random permutation, so that, the characteristic can lead to an attack on the full MISTY1 without the first FL lay.

Table 4. The 7-Round Related-Key Differential Characteristic

Round(i)	Difference	Probability
1	$(\beta 0^{16}, 0^{16}k)$	-
2	$(0^{16}0^{16}, \beta 0^{16})$	2^{-23}(Prop.1 and experiment)
3	$(0^{16}0^{16}, 0^{16}0^{16})$	2^{-1}(Prop.2)
4	$(0^{16}0^{16}, 0^{16}0^{16})$	2^{-8}(Prop.1)
5	$(k0^{16}, 0^{16}0^{16})$	2^{-2}(Prop.2, 2 bits)
6	$(0^{16}0^{16}, k0^{16})$	1
7	$(k0^{16}, 0^{16}0^{16})$	2^{-16}(Prop.1 and experiment)
8	$(0^{16}0^{16}, k0^{16})$	2^{-8}(Prop.1)
$output^\dagger$	$(0^{16}0^{16}, k0^{16})$	1

$\dagger$: the output difference of the last FL lay.

4.2   Attack on 8-Round MISTY1 without the First FL Lay

According to the 7-round related-key differential characteristics of MISTY1, we attack the 7-round MISTY1.

The attack algorithm is as follows:

1. Choose m ciphertext pairs (C_a, C_b) that satisfy $C_a \oplus C_b = (0^{16}0^{16}, k0^{16})$. Ask for the decryption of all the ciphertexts under the keys K_a and K_b respectively and denote the plaintexts corresponding to (P_a, P_b);

2. For each plaintext pair (P_a, P_b), check $P_a^L \oplus P_b^L = 0^{16}k$. If this is not the case, discard the pair. After this test, about $m \cdot 2^{-32}$ pairs are expected remain;

3. For every guess KO_{11}, KO_{12}, KO_{13}, KI_{11}, $KI_{12,2}$ and $KI_{13,2}$, partially encrypt the FO_1, we can get the output difference of the FO_1. Then if the output difference does not match the corresponding bits of $P_a^R \oplus P_b^R \oplus 0^{32}$, discard the pairs. Do as follow :

   (a) Guess KO_{11} and KO_{12}, we get the left 7-bit output difference of the FI_{11} and FI_{12} respectively, then we can compute the 7-bit output difference of the FO_1. Compared with the corresponding bits of $(P_a^R \oplus P_b^R)^2$. Discard all pairs if they do not pass the test. After the test, about $m \cdot 2^{-32} \cdot 2^{-7} = m \cdot 2^{-39}$ pairs are expected to remain.

   (b) Guess $KI_{11,2}$ and $KI_{12,2}$, we get the right 9-bit output difference of the FI_{11} and FI_{12} respectively, then we can compute the 9-bit output difference of the FO_1. Compared with the corresponding bits of $(P_a^R \oplus P_b^R)$. Discard all pairs if they do not pass the test. After the test, about $m \cdot 2^{-39} \cdot 2^{-9} = m \cdot 2^{-48}$ pairs are expected to remain.

   (c) Guess $KI_{11,1}$ and KO_{13}(only guess 15 bits, since $(KO_{13})_3 = (K_8)_3 = 1$), we get two output values of the FI_{13}. Then we can compute the 7-bit output difference of the FI_{13}, according to (a), we get the 7-bit output difference of the FO_1. Compared with the corresponding bits of $P_a^R \oplus P_b^R$. Discard all pairs if they do not pass the test. After the test, about $m \cdot 2^{-48} \cdot 2^{-7} = m \cdot 2^{-55}$ pairs are expected to remain.

   (d) Guess $KI_{13,2}$, we compute the right 9-bit output difference of the FI_{13}. According to (b), we can get the 9-bit output difference of the FO_1. Compared with the corresponding bits of $P_a^R \oplus P_b^R$. Discard all pairs if they do not pass the test; After the test, about $m \cdot 2^{-55} \cdot 2^{-9} = m \cdot 2^{-64}$ pairs are expected to remain. If $m = 2^{60}$, thus the expectation of the remaining plaintext pairs for the wrong key guess is about $2^{60} \cdot 2^{-64} = 2^{-4}$; the expectation of the remaining plaintext pairs for the right key guess is about $2^{60} \cdot 2^{-58} = 2^2$;

   (e) Output the subkey guess KO_{11}, KO_{12}, KO_{13}, KI_{11}, $KI_{12,2}$ and $KI_{13,2}$ as the correct subkey, if the number of the remaining pairs is bigger than 2. Otherwise, go to Step (3).

The attack requires about $2 \cdot 2^{60} = 2^{61}$ chosen ciphertexts.

We analyze the time complexity of the attack. There remains $2^{60} \cdot 2^{-32} = 2^{28}$ pairs after the step (2). In Step (a), the remaining pairs are treated with 2^{32} subkey candidates for KO_{11} and KO_{12}, so the time complexity is about $2 \cdot 2^{28} \cdot 2^{32} \cdot 1/8 = 2^{58}$ and about $2^{28} \cdot 2^{-7} = 2^{21}$ pairs remain; In Step (b), the remaining pairs are treated with 2^{18} subkey candidates for $KI_{11,2}$ and $KI_{12,2}$, so the time complexity is about $2 \cdot 2^{32} \cdot 2^{21} \cdot 2^{18} \cdot 1/8 = 2^{69}$ and about $2^{21} \cdot 2^{-9} = 2^{12}$ pairs remain; In Step (c), the remaining pairs are treated with 2^{22} subkey candidates for $KI_{11,1}$ and KO_{13}, so the time complexity is about $2 \cdot 2^{50} \cdot 2^{12} \cdot 2^{22} \cdot 1/8 = 2^{82}$ and about $2^{12} \cdot 2^{-7} = 2^5$ pairs remain; In Step (d), the remaining pairs are

---

2 We replace $P_a^R \oplus P_b^R$ with $(P_a^R \oplus P_b^R \oplus 0^{32})$ for short.

treated with 2^9 subkey candidates for $KI_{13,2}$, so the time complexity is about $2 \cdot 2^{72} \cdot 2^5 \cdot 2^9 \cdot 1/8 = 2^{84}$ and about $2^5 \cdot 2^{-9} = 2^{-4}$ pairs remain.

Hence, the attack requires 2^{63} chosen ciphertexts and the complexity is $2^{58} + 2^{69} + 2^{82} + 2^{84} + 2 \cdot 2^{60} \approx 2^{84.6}$. Besides, by the *Possion* distribution, the success rate of the attack is 0.76.

Remark 1. The related-key differential characteristic can be used to attack on the 7-round MISTY1. The attack requires 2^{38} chosen ciphertexts, the time complexity is $2^{38.5}$ encryption.

5   Summary

In this paper, we analyze the key schedule algorithm of MISTY1 and describe a weak-key class. Then we present a 7-round related-key differential distinguisher of MISTY1 under the weak-key class. According to the distinguisher, we attack the 8-round MISTY1 which requires 2^{61} chosen ciphertexts and the time complexity is about $2^{84.6}$. Since our target, reduce round MISTY1, has FL function, this algorithm is more realistic and powerful than existing methods. We require the least number of chosen ciphertexts and the time complexity is smallest. Moreover, the attack requires two related keys and can attack on 8-round MISTY1 without the first FL lay.

Acknowledgement. This paper is supported by the National Natural Science Foundation of China (NO. 60673081), the opening Foundation of Key Laboratory of Information Security of China and the postgraduate subject of the strategics.

References

1. Babbage, S., Frisch, L.: On MISTY1 Higher Order Differential Cryptanalysis. In: Won, D. (ed.) ICISC 2000. LNCS, vol. 2015, pp. 22–36. Springer, Heidelberg (2001)
2. Biham, E.: New types of Cryptanalytic Attack Using Related Keys. J. Cryptology 7(4), 229–246 (1994)
3. Dunkelman, O., Keller, N.: An Improved Impossible Differential Attack on MISTY1. In: Pieprzyk, J. (ed.) ASIACRYPT 2008. LNCS, vol. 5350, pp. 441–454. Springer, Heidelberg (2008)
4. Knudsen, L.R.: Cryptanalysis of LOKI91. In: Zheng, Y., Seberry, J. (eds.) AUSCRYPT 1992. LNCS, vol. 718, pp. 196–208. Springer, Heidelberg (1993)
5. Knudsen, L.R., Wagner, D.: Integral Cryptanalysis. In: Daemen, J., Rijmen, V. (eds.) FSE 2002. LNCS, vol. 2365, pp. 112–127. Springer, Heidelberg (2002)
6. Kühn, U.: Cryptanalysis of Reduced-Round MISTY. In: Pfitzmann, B. (ed.) EUROCRYPT 2001. LNCS, vol. 2045, pp. 325–339. Springer, Heidelberg (2001)
7. Kühn, U.: Improved Cryptanalysis of MISTY1. In: Daemen, J., Rijmen, V. (eds.) FSE 2002. LNCS, vol. 2365, pp. 61–75. Springer, Heidelberg (2002)
8. Lee, E., Kim, J., Hong, D., Lee, C., Sung, J., Lim, J.: Weak-key Classes of 7-Round MISTY1 and 2 for Related-Key Amplified Boomerang Attack. IEICE Transactions 91-A(2), 642–649 (2008)

9. Lu, J., Kim, J., Keller, N., Dunkelman, O.: Improving the Efficiency of Impossible Differential Cryptanalysis of Reduced Camellia and MISTY1. In: Malkin, T. (ed.) CT-RSA 2008. LNCS, vol. 4964, pp. 370–386. Springer, Heidelberg (2008)
10. Matsui, M.: New Block Encryption Algorithm MISTY. In: Biham, E. (ed.) FSE 1997. LNCS, vol. 1267, pp. 54–68. Springer, Heidelberg (1997)
11. Kelsey, J., Kohno, T., Schneier, B.: Amplified Boomerang Attacks Against Reduced-Round MARS and Serpent. In: Schneier, B. (ed.) FSE 2000. LNCS, vol. 1978, pp. 75–93. Springer, Heidelberg (2001)
12. Sugita, M.: Higher Order Differential Attack of Block Cipher MISTY1, 2. In: ISEC 1998, IEICE (1998)
13. Tanaka, H., Hatano, Y., Sugio, N., Kaneko, T.: Security Analysis of MISTY1. In: Kim, S., Yung, M., Lee, H.-W. (eds.) WISA 2007. LNCS, vol. 4867, pp. 215–226. Springer, Heidelberg (2008)
14. Tsunoo, Y., Saito, T., Nakashima, H., Shigeri, M.: Higher Order Differential Attack on 6-Round MISTY1. IEICE Transactions 92-A(2) (2009)
15. Tsunoo, Y., Saito, T., Shigeri, M., Kawabata, T.: Higher Order Differential Attacks on Reduced-Round MISTY1. In: Lee, P.J., Cheon, J.H. (eds.) ICISC 2008. LNCS, vol. 5461, pp. 415–431. Springer, Heidelberg (2009)

Cryptanalysis of Reduced-Round KLEIN Block Cipher

Xiaoli Yu[1,2], Wenling Wu[1], Yanjun Li[1], and Lei Zhang[1]

[1] State Key Laboratory of Information Security,
Institute of Software, Chinese Academy of Sciences, Beijing 100190, P.R. China
[2] Graduate University of Chinese Academy of Sciences, Beijing 100049, P.R. China
{yuxiaoli,wwl}@is.iscas.ac.cn

Abstract. KLEIN is a lightweight block cipher proposed in RFIDSec 2011 which combines 4-bit S-box with Rijndael's byte-oriented MixColumn. In this paper, we first investigate the security of KLEIN against truncated differential analysis. We construct a 6-round truncated differential distinguisher based on a careful observation about the characteristic of KLEIN round function. With the help of this new distinguisher, we give a truncated differential analysis of 8-round KLEIN-64 with the data complexity of 2^{32} and time complexity of $2^{46.8}$ encryptions. Furthermore, we study the security of KLEIN against integral analysis and present an integral analysis of 7-round KLEIN-64 and 8-round KLEIN-80 using a 5-round distinguisher, which is constructed by utilizing higher-order integral and higher-order differential properties.

Keywords: lightweight block cipher, KLEIN, integral analysis, differential cryptanalysis, complexity.

1 Introduction

With the development of electronic and communication applications, RFID technology has been used in many aspects of life, such as access control, parking management, identification, goods tracking *etc.* This kind of new cryptography environments is ubiquitous but constrained. Traditional block ciphers such as AES are not suitable for this kind of extremely constrained environments. Hence, in recent years, a number of lightweight block ciphers have been proposed, e.g. PRESENT[2], HIGHT[8], mCrypton[18], DESL[16], CGEN[20], MIBS[9], KATAN & KTANTAN[3], TWIS[19], SEA[21], LBlock[22], KLEIN[7] etc. All of these ciphers are designed and targeted specifically for extremely constrained environments.

KLEIN[7] is a family of block ciphers, with a fixed 64-bit block size and variable key length-64, 80 or 96-bits. Until now, there are no cryptanalytic results on KLEIN as far as we know. Previous cryptanalysis of KLEIN, presented by designers, concerned differential and linear attacks on 4 rounds, integral attack on up to 5 rounds. Key schedule attack, algebraic attack and side-channel attack were also considered by the designers, but the truncated differentials analysis

C.-K. Wu, M. Yung, and D. Lin (Eds.): Inscrypt 2011, LNCS 7537, pp. 237–250, 2012.
© Springer-Verlag Berlin Heidelberg 2012

was not taken into account. And the result of the integral analysis proposed by the designers can be improved using the high order integral and the high order differential properties.

A differential that predicts only parts of an n bit value is called a truncated differential, which has more advantages than differential analysis in some certain case[1]. In fact, truncated differentials have led to some successful attacks on ciphers with a pronounced word-oriented structure[11–13].

Integral attack is extended from square attack, which is first introduced to attack the block cipher Square[4]. And the designers of AES[5] used this technology to study the security of AES. Ferguson et al.[6] improved this attack to 8 rounds version of Rijndael-128 with the partial sum technique and the herd technique. Knudsen and Wagner first proposed the definition of integral and analyzed it as a dual to differential attacks particularly applicable to block ciphers with bijective components[14]. Later, Muhammad et al. presented bit-pattern based integral attack [23]. Integral attack applied to many kinds of block ciphers, such as Rijndeal, ARIA [17], Serpent [23]. Higher-order differential attack and Square like attack are different from integral attack, however, their distinguisher length can be extended by using the integral property.

In this paper, a 6-round truncated differential distinguisher is constructed. Based on this distinguisher, we present a truncated differential analysis of 8-round KLEIN-64. Furthermore, we present an integral analysis of 7-round KLEIN-64 and 8-round KLEIN-80 by using a 5-round distinguisher, which is constructed by utilizing higher-order integral and higher-order differential properties.

This paper is organized as follows: Section 2 provides a brief description of KLEIN and the notations used throughout this paper. Section 3 presents a 6-round truncated differential distinguisher and describes truncated differential cryptanalysis of KLEIN. Section 4 presents a 5-round integral distinguisher and describes integral cryptanalysis of KLEIN. Finally, Section 5 concludes this paper.

2   A Brief Description of KLEIN

KLEIN is a family of block ciphers, with a fixed 64-bit block size and variable key length-64, 80 or 96-bits. According to the different key length, we denote the ciphers by KLEIN-64/80/96 respectively. The number of rounds is 12/16/20 corresponding to KLEIN-64/80/96. The structure of KLEIN is a typical Substitution-Permutation Network(SPN). The round function of KLEIN includes four basic operations: AddRoundKey, SubNibbles, RotateNibbles and MixNibbles. All internal operations except MixNibbles are nibble-wise, that is, on 4-bit words. The last round has an additional AddRoundKey operation after MixNibbles. Note that in the last round, MixNibbles is not omitted, unlike MixColumns in Rijndael.

AddRoundKey(AK): The 64-bit round key is XORed to the state. The round keys are derived from the master key by means of key scheduling. For the details of key scheduling algorithm, the interested readers can refer to [7].

SubNibbles(SN): A non-linear nibble substitution operation is applied to each nibble of the state independently. Each nibble is input to the same 16 S-boxes. The KLEIN S-box S is a 4×4 involutive permutation.

RotateNibbles(RN): The 16 nibbles in the state are rotated left two bytes in every round. The RotateNibbles step is illustrated in Figure 1.

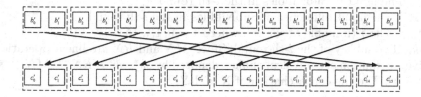

Fig. 1. RotateNibbles of KLEIN Round Function

MixNibbles(MN): MixNibbles is a bricklayer permutation of the state. The i-th round input nibbles are divided into 2 tuples, which will be proceeded the same as MixColumns in Rijndael[5]. MixNibbles operation is byte-wise, that is, on 8-bit words. The detail of MixNibbles is illustrated in Figure 2.

$$
\begin{bmatrix} s_0^{i+1} \| s_1^{i+1} \\ s_2^{i+1} \| s_3^{i+1} \\ s_4^{i+1} \| s_5^{i+1} \\ s_6^{i+1} \| s_7^{i+1} \end{bmatrix}
=
\begin{bmatrix} 2 & 3 & 1 & 1 \\ 1 & 2 & 3 & 1 \\ 1 & 1 & 2 & 3 \\ 3 & 1 & 1 & 2 \end{bmatrix}
\times
\begin{bmatrix} c_0^i \| c_1^i \\ c_2^i \| c_3^i \\ c_4^i \| c_5^i \\ c_6^i \| c_7^i \end{bmatrix}
,
\quad
\begin{bmatrix} s_8^{i+1} \| s_9^{i+1} \\ s_{10}^{i+1} \| s_{11}^{i+1} \\ s_{12}^{i+1} \| s_{13}^{i+1} \\ s_{14}^{i+1} \| s_{15}^{i+1} \end{bmatrix}
=
\begin{bmatrix} 2 & 3 & 1 & 1 \\ 1 & 2 & 3 & 1 \\ 1 & 1 & 2 & 3 \\ 3 & 1 & 1 & 2 \end{bmatrix}
\times
\begin{bmatrix} c_8^i \| c_9^i \\ c_{10}^i \| c_{11}^i \\ c_{12}^i \| c_{13}^i \\ c_{14}^i \| c_{15}^i \end{bmatrix}
$$

Fig. 2. MixNibbles of KLEIN Round Function

The matrix MC used in MixNibbles and its inverse matrix MC^{-1} are as follows,

$$
MC = \begin{pmatrix} 2 & 3 & 1 & 1 \\ 1 & 2 & 3 & 1 \\ 1 & 1 & 2 & 3 \\ 3 & 1 & 1 & 2 \end{pmatrix}, MC^{-1} = \begin{pmatrix} 0e & 0b & 0d & 09 \\ 09 & 0e & 0b & 0d \\ 0d & 09 & 0e & 0b \\ 0b & 0d & 09 & 0e \end{pmatrix}.
$$

In the following, we introduce some notations used throughout this paper. The state of the encryption is denoted by Table 1, and the encryption round is denoted by $i = 1, ..., N_R$, where $N_R = 12/16/20$.

Table 1. The state of the Encryption

0	1	8	9
2	3	10	11
4	5	12	13
6	7	14	15

$-X_i$: The input of the i-th round.

$-\Delta X_i$: The input difference of the i-th round.

$-Y_i$: The input of SubNibbles in the i-th round .

$-\Delta Y_i$: The input difference of SubNibbles in the i-th round .

$-X_{i,j}$: The j-th nibble of the X_i, where $j = 0, 1, ...15$.

$-sk_i$: The subkey of the i-th round. Since MN and RN are linear operations, we give a definition of equivalent subkey denoted by sk_i^*, $sk_i^* = RN^{-1}(MN^{-1}(sk_i))$.

$-X \parallel Y$: The the concatenation of X and Y.

3   Truncated Differential Cryptanalysis of KLEIN

As described in Section 2, all internal operations in KLEIN are nibble-wise except for MixNibbles which is byte-wise. In this section, we use this characteristic to construct a 6-round truncated differential distinguisher, based on which we present a truncated differential analysis of 8-round KLEIN-64.

3.1   6-Round Truncated Differential Distinguisher

In this subsection, we construct a 6-round truncated differential distinguisher with the probability of 2^{-29}. Firstly, we give some observations of MixNibbles which will be used in the construction of the distinguisher.

MixNibbles proceeds the same as MixColumns in Rijndael, which includes multiplication in $GF(2^8)$. The finite field used in Rijndael is $GF(2^8)$ using $m(x) = x^8 + x^4 + x^3 + x + 1$.

Property 1. Consider a polynomial in $GF(2^8)$, which has the form $f(x) = b_7x^7 + b_6x^6 + b_5x^5 + b_4x^4 + b_3x^3 + b_2x^2 + b_1x + b_0$. If we multiply it by x,we get:

$$x \times f(x) = \begin{cases} (b_6b_5b_4b_3b_2b_1b_00) & \text{if } b_7 = 0 \\ (b_6b_5b_4b_3b_2b_1b_00) \oplus (00011011) & \text{if } b_7 = 1 \end{cases}$$

Lemma 1. *If two 4-bit tuples satisfy the form* $(0, z)$, *where z is a 4-bit string and the highest bit of z is 0, then $(0, z)$ multiply by x is equal to $(0, z')$, where z' is a 4-bit string, that is the highest 4 bits of the result will stay 0.*

Proof. Let $f(x) = b_7x^7 + b_6x^6 + b_5x^5 + b_4x^4 + b_3x^3 + b_2x^2 + b_1x + b_0$, where $b_7b_6b_5b_4 = 0000$. According to Property 1, we have $x \times f(x) = (000b_3b_2b_1b_00)$.

Because the highest bit of z is 0, that is $b_3 = 0$, $x \times f(x) = (0000b_2b_1b_00)$. Then the highest 4 bits of the result will stay 0. □

Based on Lemma 1, we obtain three observations as follows,

Observation 1. Equ.(1) holds with the probability of 2^{-1}.

$$
\begin{pmatrix} 2\,3\,1\,1 \\ 1\,2\,3\,1 \\ 1\,1\,2\,3 \\ 3\,1\,1\,2 \end{pmatrix} \times \begin{pmatrix} 0z \\ 00 \\ 00 \\ 00 \end{pmatrix} = \begin{pmatrix} 0z'_1 \\ 0z'_2 \\ 0z'_3 \\ 0z'_4 \end{pmatrix}
\tag{1}
$$

where $z, z'_1, z'_2, z'_3, z'_4$ are 4-bit strings.
    Proof. Based on Lemma 1, Equ.(1) holds if and only if the highest bit of z is 0. So Equ.(1) holds with the probability of 2^{-1}. □

Observation 2. Equ.(2) holds with the probability of 2^{-2}.

$$
\begin{pmatrix} 2\,3\,1\,1 \\ 1\,2\,3\,1 \\ 1\,1\,2\,3 \\ 3\,1\,1\,2 \end{pmatrix} \times \begin{pmatrix} 00 \\ 00 \\ 0z_1 \\ 0z_2 \end{pmatrix} = \begin{pmatrix} 0z'_1 \\ 0z'_2 \\ 0z'_3 \\ 0z'_4 \end{pmatrix}
\tag{2}
$$

where $z_1, z_2, z'_1, z'_2, z'_3, z'_4$ are 4-bit strings.
    Proof. According to the matrix product rule,

$$
\begin{pmatrix} 2\,3\,1\,1 \\ 1\,2\,3\,1 \\ 1\,1\,2\,3 \\ 3\,1\,1\,2 \end{pmatrix} \times \begin{pmatrix} 00 \\ 00 \\ 0z_1 \\ 0z_2 \end{pmatrix} = \begin{pmatrix} (0z_1) \oplus (0z_2) \\ 3(0z_1) \oplus (0z_2) \\ 2(0z_1) \oplus 3(0z_2) \\ (0z_1) \oplus 2(0z_2) \end{pmatrix}.
\tag{3}
$$

Based on Lemma 1, Equ.(2) holds if and only if the highest bit of z_1 and z_2 are both 0. So Equ.(2) holds with the probability of 2^{-2}. □

Observation 3. Equ.(4) holds with the probability of 2^{-3}.

$$
\begin{pmatrix} 2\,3\,1\,1 \\ 1\,2\,3\,1 \\ 1\,1\,2\,3 \\ 3\,1\,1\,2 \end{pmatrix} \times \begin{pmatrix} 0z_1 \\ 0z_2 \\ 0z_3 \\ 0z_4 \end{pmatrix} = \begin{pmatrix} 0z'_1 \\ 0z'_2 \\ 0z'_3 \\ 0z'_4 \end{pmatrix}
\tag{4}
$$

where $z_1, z_2, z_3, z_4, z'_1, z'_2, z'_3, z'_4$ are 4-bit strings.

Proof. According to the matrix product rule,

$$\begin{pmatrix} 2\,3\,1\,1 \\ 1\,2\,3\,1 \\ 1\,1\,2\,3 \\ 3\,1\,1\,2 \end{pmatrix} \times \begin{pmatrix} 0z_1 \\ 0z_2 \\ 0z_3 \\ 0z_4 \end{pmatrix} = \begin{pmatrix} 2(0z_1) \oplus 3(0z_2) \oplus (0z_3) \oplus (0z_4) \\ (0z_1) \oplus 2(0z_2) \oplus 3(0z_3) \oplus (0z_4) \\ (0z_1) \oplus (0z_2) \oplus 2(0z_3) \oplus 3(0z_4) \\ 3(0z_1) \oplus (0z_2) \oplus (0z_3) \oplus 2(0z_4) \end{pmatrix}. \tag{5}$$

According to Lemma 1, if the highest bit of z_1, z_2, z_3 and z_4 are all 0, Equ.(4) holds. Furthermore, if the highest bit of z_1, z_2, z_3 and z_4 are all 1, Equ.(4) also holds. So Equ.(4) holds with the probability of $2^{-4} + 2^{-4} = 2^{-3}$.   □

Based on the observations of MixNibbles discussed above, a 6-round truncated differential distinguisher with the probability of 2^{-29} is constructed.(Figure 3.)

Proposition 1. *If the input difference of 6-round KLEIN are all zero except for the 13-th nibble, after 6-round encryption, the first and the third column will stay 0 with the probability of 2^{-29}.*

Because MixNibbles operation is byte-wise, while other operations are all nibble-wise, observation 1–3 ensure that the difference in one column will stay in the same column after MixNibbles. Using this characteristic, we construct a 6-round distinguisher with high probability.

3.2   Truncated Differential Analysis of 8-Round KLEIN-64

In this subsection, the 6-round distinguisher discussed above is used in 2–7 round when we present the truncated differential analysis of 8-round KLEIN-64. Since AddRoundKey, RotateNibbles and MixNibbles are linear operations, the order of the AddRoundKey, RotateNibbles and MixNibbles operations can be changed[24].

By choosing plaintexts, we add one round before the 6-round distinguisher. Furthermore, we set the nonzero input difference in the 13-th nibble of the 6-round distinguisher as 0001. According to the matrix product rule,

$$MC^{-1} \times \begin{pmatrix} 00 \\ 00 \\ 01 \\ 00 \end{pmatrix} = \begin{pmatrix} 0d \\ 0b \\ 0e \\ 09 \end{pmatrix}. \tag{6}$$

The additional round before the 6-round distinguisher is illustrated in Figure 4.

One can refer to Figure 3 and 4 for the following analysis. The postwhitening subkey of 8-round KLEIN is denoted by sk_9.

The Analysis Procedure

Step 1. Choose a set of 2^{16} plaintexts which have certain fixed values in all but four nibbles $X_{1,1}, X_{1,3}, X_{1,13}, X_{1,15}$. We call this a structure, and one structure can form $(2^{16} \times (2^{16} - 1))/2 \approx 2^{31}$ plaintext pairs. Generate m structures, thus $2^{16}m$ plaintexts, and $2^{31}m$ plaintext pairs.

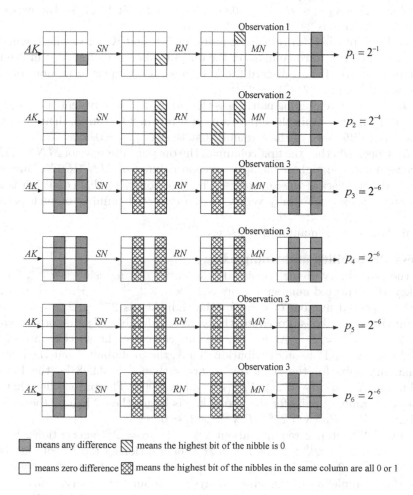

Fig. 3. 6-round Truncated Differential Distinguisher of KLEIN

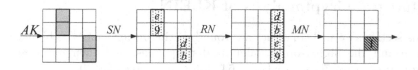

Fig. 4. The First Round of 8-round KLEIN

Step 2. Guess the values of the subkey nibbles $sk_{1,1}, sk_{1,3}, sk_{1,13}, sk_{1,15}$ to make sure $\Delta S(X_{1,1} \oplus sk_{1,1}) = 0xe$, $\Delta S(X_{1,3} \oplus sk_{1,3}) = 0x9$, $\Delta S(X_{1,13} \oplus sk_{1,13}) = 0xd$ and $\Delta S(X_{1,15} \oplus sk_{1,15}) = 0xb$. This is a 16-bit filter, so the expected number of pairs is $2^{31} \times m \times 2^{-16} = 2^{15}m$.

Step 3. Encrypt all $2^{15}m$ remaining pairs for 7-round KLEIN. Check whether the first and the third columns of the output difference of MN^{-1} in the last round are zero. If not, discard the key guess. The expected number of such pairs is $2^{15} \times m \times (2^{-16})^2 = 2^{-17}m$.

Step 4. For every remaining pair, guess the value of the equivalent subkey $sk_{9,j}^*$, $j = 0, 1, ..., 7$ to obtain the input value of S-box in 8-th round, then we obtain the input difference of the 8-round, that is $\Delta X_{8,j}$, $j = 0, 1, ..., 7$.

Step 5. Check whether the first column of the output difference of $MN^{-1}(\Delta X_8)$ are zero and the highest bit of the second column of $MN^{-1}(\Delta X_8)$ are all 0 or 1. If not, discard the key guess. The probability of this condition is 2^{-7} as one can experimentally verify. So the expected number of such pairs is $2^{-17} \times m \times 2^{-7} = 2^{-24}m$.

Step 6. Guess the remaining 16 bits key.

Success Probability and Complexity

Since the probability of the truncated differential distinguisher is 2^{-29}, for the right key, the expected number of pairs is $2^{15} \times m \times 2^{-29} = 2^{-14}m$. Let $m = 2^{16}$, then the expected number of pairs for the right key is $2^{-14} \times 2^{16} = 2^2$. Thus, according to the analysis procedure, the expected number of pairs for the wrong key is $2^{-24} \times 2^{16} = 2^{-8}$. As in [10], we can calculate the success rate of the attack by using the Poisson distribution. Thus, the probability that the number of remaining pairs for the right key is larger than 2 is 0.908 by the Poisson distribution, $X \sim Poi(\lambda = 2^2)$, $Pr_X[X > 2] \approx 0.908$. The probability that the number of remaining pairs for the wrong key is larger than 2 is 0 by the Poisson distribution, $Y \sim Poi(\lambda = 2^{-8})$, $Pr_Y[Y > 2] \approx 0$.

For $m = 2^{16}$, Step 2 requires about $2^{16} \times 2^{16}/8 = 2^{29}$ encryptions. Step 3 requires about $2^{15} \times 2^{16} \times 2^{16} \times 7/8 = 2^{46.8}$ encryptions. Step 4 requires about $2^{-17} \times 2^{16} \times 2^{16} \times 2^{32}/8 = 2^{44}$ encryptions. Step 6 requires about 2^{16} encryptions. So the time complexity of the whole analysis is about $2^{46.8}$ encryptions.

In summary, the data complexity of the analysis of 8-round KLEIN is $2^{16} \times m = 2^{32}$ chosen plaintexts and the time complexity is $2^{46.8}$ encryptions.

4 Integral Cryptanalysis of KLEIN

In this section, we will construct a 5-round distinguisher using the higher-order integral and the higher-order differential properties, and then we present an integral analysis of 7-round KLEIN-64 and 8-round KLEIN-80.

4.1 5-Round Distinguisher

Firstly, according to the higher-order differential cryptanalysis introduced by [11, 15], a 3.5-round distinguisher is constructed as follows.

Proposition 2. *If we select 2^{32} input values of RotateNibbles, after 3.5-round KLEIN encryption[2], the sum of the outputs in each nibble is 0.*

Proof. Since the algebra degree of KLEIN S-box is 3, the algebra degree of 3-round KLEIN encryption is at most $3^3 = 27$. As we know, the linear operations will not affect the algebra degree and another RotateNibbles and MixNibbles operations are added before 3-round KLEIN encryption. Thus the algebra degree of 3.5-round KLEIN encryption is at most 27. Since we select 2^{32} input values, the sum of the outputs in each nibble is 0.   □

Secondly, we construct a 1.5-round integral distinguisher using higher-order integral properties as follows. We will denote two concatenation of Sbox operation by T in the following, that is $T = S \parallel S$.

Proposition 3. *If the input state is active[3] in the i-th nibbles, where $i = 0, 1, 2, 3, 12, 13, 14, 15$, after 1.5-round KLEIN encryption[4], the output is active in the j-th nibbles, where $j = 8, 9, 10, 11, 12, 13, 14, 15$.*

Proof. Assume the input state is M, so the active nibbles are M_i, where $i = 0, 1, 2, 3, 12, 13, 14, 15$, let $x'_0 = M_0 \parallel M_1$, $x'_1 = M_2 \parallel M_3$, $x'_2 = M_{12} \parallel M_{13}$, $x'_3 = M_{14} \parallel M_{15}$, then x'_0, x'_1, x'_2, x'_3 are all active bytes. Each of them takes 2^8 values independently. Since S-box is a permutation, we denote $x_i = T(x'_i \oplus c_i)$, where $i = 0, 1, 2, 3$, c_i's are some constant values. Thus $x_i, (i = 0, 1, 2, 3)$ are active, that is, each of them takes 2^8 values independently.

We denote the nonzero output bytes of MixNibbles operations by y'_0, y'_1, y'_2, y'_3, then $y'_0 = 2x_2 \oplus 3x_3 \oplus x_0 \oplus x_1$, $y'_1 = x_2 \oplus 2x_3 \oplus 3x_0 \oplus x_1$, $y'_2 = x_2 \oplus x_3 \oplus 2x_0 \oplus 3x_1$, $y'_3 = 3x_2 \oplus x_3 \oplus x_0 \oplus 2x_1$. Since $x_i(i = 0, 1, 2, 3)$ takes 2^8 values independently, for each value of x_0, the x_1, x_2, x_3 can take any fixed value, so y'_0 takes 2^8 different values. Similarly $y'_i, (i = 1, 2, 3)$ takes 2^8 different values.

Since $y'_0 \oplus y'_1 = 3x_2 \oplus x_3 \oplus 2x_0$, where x_0, x_2, x_3 are independent active bytes, y'_0 and y'_1 are independent active bytes. Thus, y'_0, y'_1, y'_2 and y'_3 are independent active bytes. They together take 2^{32} values.

After one AddRoundKey operation and one SubNibbles operation, denote the nonzero output bytes by $y_j, (j = 0, 1, 2, 3)$, where $y_j = T(y'_j \oplus c'_j), (j = 0, 1, 2, 3)$ they also take 2^{32} values because S-box is a permutation.   □

According to higher-order integral and higher-order differential properties discussed above, a 5-round integral distinguisher is constructed.(Figure 5.)

Proposition 4. *If the input state is active in the i-th nibbles, where $i = 0, 1, 2, 3, 12, 13, 14, 15$, after 5-round KLEIN encryption, the sum of the outputs in each nibble is 0.*

---

[2] 3.5-round means one RotateNibbles operation and one MixNibbles operation plus 3-round KLEIN encryptions.

[3] Active means it takes all different values.

[4] 1.5-round means 1-round KLEIN encryption plus one AddRoundKey operation and one SubNibbles operation.

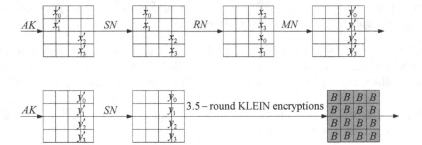

Fig. 5. The 5-round integral distinguisher

Based on this 5-round integral distinguisher, if we select 2^{32} plaintexts $P^i, i = 1, 2, ..., 2^{32}$, which are active in $X_{1,0}$, $X_{1,1}$, $X_{1,2}$, $X_{1,3}$, $X_{1,12}$, $X_{1,13}$, $X_{1,14}$ and $X_{1,15}$ nibbles, we obtain

$$\bigoplus_{i=1}^{2^{32}} X_{6,j}^i = 0, j = 0, 1, ...15. \tag{7}$$

4.2   Integral Analysis of 7-Round KLEIN-64

In this subsection, we present an integral analysis of 7-round KLEIN-64, by adding two rounds at the end of 5-round distinguisher. Since the property of balance[5] is not affected by Round Key Addition Layer, we obtain

$$\bigoplus_{i=1}^{2^{32}} Y_{6,j}^i = 0, j = 0, 1, ...15. \tag{8}$$

To reduce the time complexity, we will use the partial sum technique[6]. Denote the postwhitening subkey of 7-round KLEIN by sk_8 and the result of $RN^{-1}(MN^{-1}(C))$ by Z_7. For convenience, we rewrite some notations as follows,

$$\theta_1 = S^{-1}(Z_{7,0} \oplus sk_{8,0}^*) \parallel S^{-1}(Z_{7,1} \oplus sk_{8,1}^*) \tag{9}$$

$$\theta_2 = S^{-1}(Z_{7,2} \oplus sk_{8,2}^*) \parallel S^{-1}(Z_{7,3} \oplus sk_{8,3}^*) \tag{10}$$

$$\theta_3 = S^{-1}(Z_{7,4} \oplus sk_{8,4}^*) \parallel S^{-1}(Z_{7,5} \oplus sk_{8,5}^*) \tag{11}$$

$$\theta_4 = S^{-1}(Z_{7,6} \oplus sk_{8,6}^*) \parallel S^{-1}(Z_{7,7} \oplus sk_{8,7}^*). \tag{12}$$

Then

$$Y_{6,4} \parallel Y_{6,5} = T^{-1}(R^{-1}(0e \cdot \theta_1 \oplus 0b \cdot \theta_2 \oplus 0d \cdot \theta_3 \oplus 09 \cdot \theta_4) \oplus sk_{7,4}^* \parallel sk_{7,5}^*). \tag{13}$$

---

[5] Balance means the sum of all values is zero.

The Analysis Procedure

Step 1. Select 2^{32} plaintexts $P^i, i = 1, 2, ..., 2^{32}$, which are active in $X_{1,0}$, $X_{1,1}$, $X_{1,2}$, $X_{1,3}$, $X_{1,12}$, $X_{1,13}$, $X_{1,14}$ and $X_{1,15}$ nibbles. We call this a structure, and one structure has 2^{32} plaintexts. Generate 5 structures, thus $5 \times 2^{32} \approx 2^{34.3}$ plaintexts. For each structure, encrypt all 2^{32} plaintexts for 7 round KLEIN. Denote all the ciphertexts by $C_7^i, i = 1, 2, ..., 2^{32}$.

Step 2. For each structure, we will calculate $\bigoplus_{i=1}^{2^{32}} Y_{6,4}^i \parallel Y_{6,5}^i = \bigoplus_{(\theta_1, \theta_2, \theta_3, \theta_4)} Y_{6,4} \parallel Y_{6,5}$ in the following steps. We start with a list of 2^{32} ciphertexts.

1. We guess the values of $sk_{8,0}^*, sk_{8,1}^*, sk_{8,2}^*, sk_{8,3}^*$ and compute how often each triple $(m_1, \theta_3, \theta_4)$ occurs in the list, where $m_1 = 0e \cdot \theta_1 \oplus 0b \cdot \theta_2$. That is, for each i, we compute the three-byte value $(m_1, \theta_3, \theta_4)$ as a function of the i-th ciphertext and the guessed key material, and we count how many times each three-byte value appears during this computation. As there are only 2^{24} possible values for three bytes, we do not have to list all $(m_1, \theta_3, \theta_4)$ values, rather, we count how often each triple occurs.

2. We guess the values of $sk_{8,4}^*, sk_{8,5}^*$, and compute how often each tuple (m_2, θ_4) occurs, where $m_2 = m_1 \oplus 0d \cdot \theta_3$. There are only 2^{16} possible values for two bytes.

3. We guess the values of $sk_{8,6}^*, sk_{8,7}^*$, and compute how often each value (m_3) occurs, where $m_3 = m_2 \oplus 09 \cdot \theta_4$. There are only 2^8 possible values for one byte.

4. We guess the values of $sk_{7,4}^*, sk_{7,5}^*$, and compute the desired sum $\bigoplus_{i=1}^{2^{32}} Y_{6,4}^i \parallel Y_{6,5}^i$, where $Y_{6,4} \parallel Y_{6,5} = S^{-1}(R^{-1}(m_3 \oplus sk_{7,4}^* \parallel sk_{7,5}^*))$.

Step 3. Check whether $\bigoplus_{i=1}^{2^{32}} Y_{6,4}^i \parallel Y_{6,5}^i$ is equal to 0. If not, discard the key guess. The wrong key can pass this condition with the probability of 2^{-8}, we use 5 structures to make sure only right key can remain.

Step 4. Guess the remaining 24 bits key.

Complexity

The data complexity of the analysis is $2^{34.3}$ chosen plaintexts. For each structure,

Step 2.1 requires about $2^{32} \times 2^{16} = 2^{48}$ S-box operations.

Step 2.2 requires about $2^{24} \times 2^{16} \times 2^8 = 2^{48}$ S-box operations.

Step 2.3 requires about $2^{16} \times 2^{16} \times 2^8 \times 2^8 = 2^{48}$ S-box operations.

Step 2.4 requires about $2^8 \times 2^{16} \times 2^8 \times 2^8 \times 2^8 = 2^{48}$ S-box operations.

So Step 2 requires about $4 \times 2^{48} = 2^{50}$ S-box operations. There are 16 S-box operations in one round encryption, so Step 2 requires about $2^{50}/(16 \times 7) = 2^{43.2}$ encryptions.

Step 4 requires about 2^{24} encryptions.

So the total time complexity of the analysis is $5 \times 2^{43.2} \approx 2^{45.5}$ encryptions.

In summary, the data complexity of the analysis of 7-round KLEIN-64 is $2^{34.3}$ chosen plaintexts and the time complexity is $2^{45.5}$ encryptions.

4.3 Integral Analysis of 8-Round KLEIN-80

The procedure of the integral analysis of 8-round KLEIN-80 is similar to the integral analysis of 7-round KLEIN-64. We can guess 2^{32} subkeys in the 8-th round to partly decrypt. The data complexity of the analysis of 8-round KLEIN-80 is $2^{34.3}$ chosen plaintexts and the time complexity is $2^{77.5}$ encryptions.

5   Conclusion

In this paper, we described the truncated differential and integral cryptanalysis against reduced-round variants of the KLEIN block cipher[7]. According to the properties of KLEIN round function, a 6-round truncated differential distinguisher was constructed. Based on this distinguisher, we gave a truncated differential analysis of 8-round KLEIN-64. Furthermore, we proposed an integral analysis of 7-round KLEIN-64 and 8-round KLEIN-80 by using a 5-round distinguisher, which was constructed by utilizing higher-order integral and higher-order differential properties.

Table 2 summarized the complexities of all analysis results of reduced-round KLEIN described in this paper.

Table 2. Attacks Complexities on reduced-round KLEIN block cipher

KLEIN-b	Rounds	Data	Time	Attacks	Source	Success Prob.
KLEIN-64	7	$2^{34.3}$CP	$2^{45.5}$	Integral	Sec.4.2	–
	8	2^{32}CP	$2^{46.8}$	TD	Sec.3.2	90.8%
KLEIN-80	8	$2^{34.3}$CP	$2^{77.5}$	Integral	Sec.4.3	–

† CP: Chosen Plaintext; TD: Truncated Differential Cryptanalysis.
† Time complexity is measured in encryption units.

Acknowledgments. We would like to thank anonymous referees for their helpful comments and suggestions. The research presented in this paper is supported by the National Natural Science Foundation of China (No.60873259) and The Knowledge Innovation Project of The Chinese Academy of Sciences.

References

[1] Biryukov, A., De Canniere, C., Lano, J., Ors, S.B., Preneel, B.: Security and performance analysis of ARIA. Final report, KU Leuven ESAT/SCD-COSIC, 3 (2004)

[2] Bogdanov, A., Knudsen, L.R., Leander, G., Paar, C., Poschmann, A., Robshaw, M.J.B., Seurin, Y., Vikkelsoe, C.: PRESENT: An Ultra-Lightweight Block Cipher. In: Paillier, P., Verbauwhede, I. (eds.) CHES 2007. LNCS, vol. 4727, pp. 450–466. Springer, Heidelberg (2007)

[3] De Cannière, C., Dunkelman, O., Knežević, M.: KATAN and KTANTAN — A Family of Small and Efficient Hardware-Oriented Block Ciphers. In: Clavier, C., Gaj, K. (eds.) CHES 2009. LNCS, vol. 5747, pp. 272–288. Springer, Heidelberg (2009)

[4]   Daemen, J., Knudsen, L.R., Rijmen, V.: The Block Cipher SQUARE. In: Biham,
      E. (ed.) FSE 1997. LNCS, vol. 1267, pp. 149–165. Springer, Heidelberg (1997)
[5]   Daemen, J., Rijmen, V.: The Design of Rijndael: AES - The Advanced Encryption
      Standard. Springer (2002)
[6]   Ferguson, N., Kelsey, J., Lucks, S., Schneier, B., Stay, M., Wagner, D., Whiting,
      D.: Improved Cryptanalysis of Rijndael. In: Schneier, B. (ed.) FSE 2000. LNCS,
      vol. 1978, pp. 213–230. Springer, Heidelberg (2001)
[7]   Gong, Z., Nikova, S., Law, Y.W.: KLEIN: A New Family of Lightweight Block
      Ciphers. In: Juels, A., Paar, C. (eds.) RFIDSec 2011. LNCS, vol. 7055, pp. 1–18.
      Springer, Heidelberg (2012)
[8]   Hong, D., Sung, J., Hong, S., Lim, J., Lee, S., Koo, B.-S., Lee, C., Chang, D., Lee,
      J., Jeong, K., Kim, H., Kim, J., Chee, S.: HIGHT: A New Block Cipher Suitable
      for Low-Resource Device. In: Goubin, L., Matsui, M. (eds.) CHES 2006. LNCS,
      vol. 4249, pp. 46–59. Springer, Heidelberg (2006)
[9]   Izadi, M., Sadeghiyan, B., Sadeghian, S.S., Khanooki, H.A.: MIBS: A New
      Lightweight Block Cipher. In: Garay, J.A., Miyaji, A., Otsuka, A. (eds.) CANS
      2009. LNCS, vol. 5888, pp. 334–348. Springer, Heidelberg (2009)
[10] Kim, J., Hong, S., Preneel, B.: Related-Key Rectangle Attacks on Reduced
      AES-192 and AES-256. In: Biryukov, A. (ed.) FSE 2007. LNCS, vol. 4593, pp.
      225–241. Springer, Heidelberg (2007)
[11] Knudsen, L.R.: Truncated and Higher Order Differentials. In: Preneel, B. (ed.)
      FSE 1994. LNCS, vol. 1008, pp. 196–211. Springer, Heidelberg (1995)
[12] Knudsen, L.R., Berson, T.A.: Truncated Differentials of SAFER. In: Gollmann,
      D. (ed.) FSE 1996. LNCS, vol. 1039, pp. 15–26. Springer, Heidelberg (1996)
[13] Knudsen, L.R., Robshaw, M.J.B., Wagner, D.: Truncated Differentials and
      Skipjack. In: Wiener, M. (ed.) CRYPTO 1999. LNCS, vol. 1666, pp. 165–180.
      Springer, Heidelberg (1999)
[14] Knudsen, L.R., Wagner, D.: Integral Cryptanalysis. In: Daemen, J., Rijmen, V.
      (eds.) FSE 2002. LNCS, vol. 2365, pp. 112–127. Springer, Heidelberg (2002)
[15] Lai, X.: Higher order derivatives and differential cryptanalysis. In:
      Communications and Cryptography: Two Sides of One Tapestry, p. 227
      (1994)
[16] Leander, G., Paar, C., Poschmann, A., Schramm, K.: New Lightweight DES
      Variants. In: Biryukov, A. (ed.) FSE 2007. LNCS, vol. 4593, pp. 196–210. Springer,
      Heidelberg (2007)
[17] Li, Y., Wu, W., Zhang, L.: Integral Attacks on Reduced-Round ARIA Block
      Cipher. In: Kwak, J., Deng, R.H., Won, Y., Wang, G. (eds.) ISPEC 2010. LNCS,
      vol. 6047, pp. 19–29. Springer, Heidelberg (2010)
[18] Lim, C.H., Korkishko, T.: mCrypton - A Lightweight Block Cipher for Security of
      Low-Cost RFID Tags and Sensors. In: Song, J., Kwon, T., Yung, M. (eds.) WISA
      2005. LNCS, vol. 3786, pp. 243–258. Springer, Heidelberg (2006)
[19] Ojha, S.K., Kumar, N., Jain, K., Sangeeta: TWIS – A Lightweight Block Cipher.
      In: Prakash, A., Sen Gupta, I. (eds.) ICISS 2009. LNCS, vol. 5905, pp. 280–291.
      Springer, Heidelberg (2009)
[20] Robshaw, M.J.B.: Searching for Compact Algorithms: CGEN. In: Nguyen, P.Q.
      (ed.) VIETCRYPT 2006. LNCS, vol. 4341, pp. 37–49. Springer, Heidelberg (2006)
[21] Standaert, F.-X., Piret, G., Gershenfeld, N., Quisquater, J.-J.: SEA: A Scalable
      Encryption Algorithm for Small Embedded Applications. In: Domingo-Ferrer, J.,
      Posegga, J., Schreckling, D. (eds.) CARDIS 2006. LNCS, vol. 3928, pp. 222–236.
      Springer, Heidelberg (2006)

[22] Wu, W., Zhang, L.: LBlock: A Lightweight Block Cipher. In: Lopez, J., Tsudik, G. (eds.) ACNS 2011. LNCS, vol. 6715, pp. 327–344. Springer, Heidelberg (2011)

[23] Z'aba, M.R., Raddum, H., Henricksen, M., Dawson, E.: Bit-Pattern Based Integral Attack. In: Nyberg, K. (ed.) FSE 2008. LNCS, vol. 5086, pp. 363–381. Springer, Heidelberg (2008)

[24] Zhang, W., Wu, W., Feng, D.: New Results on Impossible Differential Cryptanalysis of Reduced AES. In: Nam, K.-H., Rhee, G. (eds.) ICISC 2007. LNCS, vol. 4817, pp. 239–250. Springer, Heidelberg (2007)

An Efficient RSA Implementation
without Precomputation

Wuqiong Pan[1], Jiwu Jing[1], Luning Xia[1], Zongbin Liu[1], and Meng Yu[2]

[1] State Key Laboratory Of Information Security,
Graduate University of Chinese Academy of Sciences, Beijing, China
{wqpan,jing,halk,zbliu}@lois.cn
[2] Computer Science, Virginia Commonwealth University,
Richmond, Virginia, America
myu@vcu.edu

Abstract. Modular multiplication is widely used in cryptographic algorithms. In order to improve the efficiency, most of the recent implementations adopt precomputation. Precomputation improves the speed and in the meanwhile makes the algorithms more complex. The complex algorithms are not suitable for hardware implementation. We propose a new algorithm without precomputation, which is more efficient even compared with the ones with precomputation. Our algorithm is based on interleaving modular algorithm. The modulus in our algorithm is enlarged, and this modification greatly reduces the number of subtractions. By a small change of the multiplier, our algorithm does not need the last subtraction. We also propose a pipeline scheme which can achieve high frequency. Compared with existing work (including the precomputation ones), our implementation improves the *throughput/area* by 47%.

Keywords: RSA, hardware implementation, Field Programmable Gate Arrays, modular multiplication.

1 Introduction

Modular multiplication is widely used in cryptographic algorithms, especially in ECC and RSA. In the past, these algorithms are mainly used in severs and PCs. Nowadays, they are used more widely. For example, many POS, pay cards and mobile phones have security functions. These devices usually do not have abundant power supply and computing resources as severs and PCs do. The implementation of the security functions should be more efficient, both faster and smaller.

Most of the modular multiplication algorithms adopt precomputation to speed up. Especially in recent days, the adopted precomputation is more complex than before. Precomputation is the initial computation of an algorithm, the results of which are then used to speed up later parts of that algorithm. Although precomputation can speed up the algorithm, it also makes the algorithm more complex. The results of the initial computation need more communication and storage.

C.-K. Wu, M. Yung, and D. Lin (Eds.): Inscrypt 2011, LNCS 7537, pp. 251–268, 2012.

For example, the modular multiplication has three inputs, while Montgomery multiplication has four inputs.

Another problem is how to process the initial computation. The initial computation is only required for precomputation algorithms, not in the original algorithm. The initial computation is different from the later computation. It requires extra hardware resources. The published work [1–3] rarely mention how to process the initial computation and its consuming resources. The usual way is to use a CPU. But sometimes the systems do not have a CPU or the CPU is not powerful enough. For example, most smart cards still adopt 8-bit CPUs. We can also implement a special module for precomputation, but the special module will need a lot of hardware resources. Therefore the efficiency of the whole algorithm will be compromised.

According to above discussion, an algorithm with precomputation is complex and needs extra hardware resources. We propose an efficient modular multiplication algorithm which does not need precomputation. Our implementation is small and fast. Disregard the portion of initial computation, algorithms with precomputation are still less efficient than ours. Our algorithm is based on interleaving modular multiplication [4, 5]. One of our improvements is enlarging the modulus, which significantly reduces the number of subtractions. By a small change of the multiplier, our algorithm does not need the last subtraction. We also propose a pipeline scheme, which can achieve high frequency. Compared with existing RSA implementations, ours improves the *throughput/area* by 47%.

2   Related Work

The main computation of RSA is modular exponentiation: $C = M^D \pmod{N}$. The main computation of modular exponentiation is modular multiplication: $C = A \cdot B \pmod{N}$. Many algorithms have been proposed to improve the modular multiplication. Interleaving modular multiplication [4, 5] is an early one. Many techniques have been used to improve it. For examples, carry save adders [6] can avoid long carry delay, and sign estimation algorithm [7] is used to replace the comparison. An important improvement is proposed by Koç in [8]. He proposed a more accurate sign estimation technique which greatly reduces the mount of computation. But its logic is complex and not suitable for hardware implementation.

Montgomery algorithm [9] is proposed just after interleaving modular multiplication. Now, most of the modular multiplication algorithms [2, 10, 11] are based on Montgomery algorithm. A recent improved algorithm is called Multiple-Word Radix-2 Montgomery Multiplication [2, 10]. These algorithms process every word separately, which consumes very small area. Another excellent work is Shieh's [1], which is highly efficient.

Some work [12, 13] adopt high-radix Montgomery algorithms. They are much faster than the 2-radix algorithm. However, they need many special resources, for example, DSP, Multiplier and RAM. These resources may be insufficient in some cases. The high-radix algorithms also need a lot of other resource, which make them less applicable than 2-radix algorithms.

Recently some researchers adopt look-up table to improve the algorithms. Bunimov first proposed it [14, 15]. Many recent proposals are based on it [16, 17]. These algorithms need more complex precomputation than Montgomery Multiplication. The precomputation of Montgomery Multiplication only depends on modulus, while that of the new ones depends on both modulus and multiplier. The multiplier is variable. Every time the multiplier changes, the look-up table should be recomputed.

The algorithms without precomputation are rare. Knezevic improved Barrett algorithm and Montgomery algorithm to discard precomputation [18, 19]. But this improvement is only applicable to a specific set of modulus.

Our algorithm has no restriction on the modulus, and does not need extra hardware resources to process precomputation. It is easier to apply. Our algorithm is based on interleaving modular algorithm [4] which also adopts carry save adder [6] and sign estimation algorithm [7]. Our algorithm reduces calculation much. The amount of our calculation is almost the same as that of Montgomery's, while our algorithm is simpler and more suitable for hardware implementation.

3   Modular Multiplication

We introduce our algorithm in this section. In Section 3.1 and Section 3.2, we introduce the previous algorithms. In Section 3.3 - 3.5, we introduce our improvement. In Section 3.6, we give the amount of the calculation of our algorithm.

3.1   Interleaving Modular Multiplication

Interleaving modular multiplication is a simple algorithm.

$$
\begin{aligned}
C = A \cdot B &= A \cdot \sum_{i=0}^{k-1} B_i 2^i = \sum_{i=0}^{k-1} (A \cdot B_i) 2^i \\
&= 2(\ldots 2(2(0 + A \cdot B_{k-1}) + A \cdot B_{k-2}) + \ldots) + A \cdot B_0
\end{aligned}
\tag{1}
$$

In equation (1), B_i is the ith bit of B. Multiplication, addition and shifting execute alternately. We can do modular operation after each addition. The algorithm is as follows.
Before Step 4, we have

$$
C < N
\tag{2}
$$

After Step 4, we have

$$
C = 2C + A \cdot B_i < 3N
\tag{3}
$$

On Step 5, we subtract N twice at most. The process is as follows.

Algorithm 1. Interleaving modular multiplication

Input: A, B, N : k-bit **Integer**, where $A < N, B < N$
Output: $C = A \cdot B \pmod{N}$
1 **begin**
2   initialization: $C = 0$
3   **for** $i = k - 1$ **to** 0 **do**
4         $C = 2C + A \cdot B_i$
5         $C = C \pmod{N}$
6   **end**
7 **end**

---

if $C >= n$ **then**
  | $C = C - n$
end
if $C >= n$ **then**
  | $C = C - n$
end

3.2   Using Carry Save Adders and Estimation Technique

The interleaving algorithm is not an efficient scheme for big numbers. The subtraction and addition have long carry delay, and they can not execute in one cycle. The redundant number system can resolve this problem. We adopt Carry Save Adders (CSA), the most used redundant number system, in our algorithm.

The interleaving algorithm needs to compare C with N. The comparison causes long delay. We use an estimation function to replace the comparison, which gives the right result when C is not close to N.

First, we introduce an estimation function of number X: $T(X, t)$. $T(X, t)$ replaces the least significant t bits of X with t zeros. This means

$$T(X, t) = X_{m-1} X_{m-2} \ldots X_t \underbrace{0 \ldots 0}_{t} \tag{4}$$

In other words,

$$T(X, t) = X - (X \pmod{2^t}) \tag{5}$$

$T(X, t)$ is the estimated value of X. The relation between $T(X)$ and X can be expressed as

$$T(X, t) \leq X < T(X, t) + 2^t \tag{6}$$

$$X - 2^t < T(X) \leq X \tag{7}$$

Then, we define an estimate function of the comparison.

$$E(C, S, N, t) = \begin{cases} 1 \text{ if } T(C, t) + T(S, t) > T(N, t) \\ 0 \text{ others} \end{cases} \tag{8}$$

$E(C, S, N, t)$ is an estimated value of the comparison between $C + S$ and N.

Theorem 1. *If $E(C, S, N, t) == 1$, then $C+S > N$; Else, then $C+S < N+2^{t+1}$*

Proof. If $E(C, S, N, t) == 1$ we have

$$T(C, t) + T(S, t) > T(N, t) \tag{9}$$

Because the least significant t bits of $T(C), T(S), T(N)$ are all zeros, we have

$$T(C, t) + T(S, t) \geq T(N, t) + 2^t \tag{10}$$

Because $T(N, t) + 2^t > N$, we have

$$T(C, t) + T(S, t) > N \tag{11}$$

Then we have

$$C + S > N \tag{12}$$

If $E(C, S, N, t) == 0$, we have

$$T(C, t) + T(S, t) \leq T(N, t) \tag{13}$$

Because $T(X, t) \leq X < T(X, t) + 2^t$, we have

$$C + S < T(C, t) + 2^t + T(S, t) + 2^t \leq T(N, t) + 2^{t+1} \leq N + 2^{t+1} \tag{14}$$

We use CSA and the estimate function to improve the interleaving modular multiplication.

Algorithm 2. CSA and estimation technique algorithm

Input: A, B, N : k-bit **Integer**, where $A < N, B < N$
Output: C, S : (k+1)-bit **Integer**, where $(C, S) = A \cdot B \pmod{N}$,
            and $(C, S) < N + 2^{k-3}$

1 **begin**
2 $\quad$ initialization: $(C, S) = (0, 0)$
3 $\quad$ **for** $i = k - 1$ **to** 0 **do**
4 $\quad\quad$ $(C, S) = 2C + 2S + A \cdot B_i$
5 $\quad\quad$ **While** $E(C, S, N, k - 4) == 1$ **then** $(C, S) = C + S - N$
6 $\quad$ **end**
7 **end**

Step 4 adopts CSA. Step 5 adopts CSA and the estimate function. When $C + S$ is greater than N, we subtract N from $C + S$.

From Theorem 1, $E(C, S, N, k - 4) == 1$ means that $C + S > N$, so the subtraction does not cause overflow.

For the first time of Step 4, C and S are zeros. For other situations, C and S are the results of Step 5. So we have $E(C, S, N, k - 4) == 0$ before Step 4. It means

$$T(C, t) + T(S, t) \leq T(N, t) \tag{15}$$

N is k-bit integer, and C , S are $(k + 1)$-bit integers. Then the kth bits(most significant bit) of C and S are both zero, and the $(k - 1)^{th}$ bits of C and S cannot be ones simultaneously. So the kth bits of $2C$ and $2S$ cannot be ones simultaneously. $A \cdot B_i$ only has k bits, so the kth bit of $A \cdot B_i$ is zero. On Step 4, we use CSA to compute $2C + 2S + A \cdot B_i$, and the carry-out bit of the kth bit is zero. So the addition does not cause overflow.

Since neither the subtraction or the addition causes overflow, the whole algorithm will not have overflow.

We estimate the calculation of this algorithm. After Step 5, we have

$$E(C, S, N, k - 4) = 0 \tag{16}$$

From Theorem 1, we know

$$C + S < N + 2^{k-3} \tag{17}$$

After Step 4, we have

$$2C + 2S + A \cdot B_{k-1-i} < 2(C+S) + 2^k < 2N + 2^{k-2} + 2^k < 2N + N + 2N = 5N \tag{18}$$

So Step 5 needs $4k$ subtractions totally. And Step 4 needs k additions totally. One substraction or one addition needs one CSA. The whole calculation is $5k$ CSA. This algorithm needs $5k$ cycles if one cycle is needed for one CSA.

3.3   Enlarging Modulus

In previous algorithm, most of the calculation are subtractions. We enlarge the modulus, which significantly reduces the number of subtractions.

The modulus is enlarged by 2^e times. e is a variable parameter. Usually, we select $e = \lfloor \log_2 k \rfloor$.

Algorithm 3. Enlarging modulus algorithm

Input: A, B, N : k-bit **Integer**, where $A < N, B < N$
Output: C, S : (k+1+e)-bit **Integer**, where $(C, S) = A \cdot B \quad (\text{mod } N)$,
$\qquad (C, S) < N + 2^{k-3}$, $e = max(\lfloor \log_2 k \rfloor, 6)$

1 **begin**
2 $\quad$ initialization: $(C, S) = (0, 0), N' = N \cdot 2^e, B' = B \cdot 2^e$
3 $\quad$ **for** $i = k + e - 1$ **to** 0 **do**
4 $\quad\quad$ $(C, S) = 2C + 2S + A \cdot B'_i$
5 $\quad\quad$ **While** $E(C, S, N', k + e - 4) == 1$ **then** $(C, S) = C + S - N'$
6 $\quad$ **end**
7 $\quad$ $(C, S) = (C/2^e, S/2^e)$
8 **end**

Compared with the previous algorithm, N and B are enlarged by 2^e times at the beginning, while the (C, S) is divided by 2^e at the end. e cannot be too small, and it is bigger than 6.

Theorem 2. *In the enlarging modulus algorithm, after Step 6, both C and S are divisible by 2^e.*

Proof. When $i = e$, C and S are divisible by 2^0.

Assume when $i = e - u$(u is an integer, $0 \le u \le e - 1$), both C and S are divisible by 2^u.

When $i = e - u - 1$, B'_i is zero, and $A \cdot B'_i$ is zero. After Step 4, both C and S are divisible by 2^{u+1}. The least significant e bits of N' are zero, so after Step 5, both C and S are still divisible by 2^{u+1}.

From the induction, we know after $i = 0$, both C and S are divisible by 2^e.

Steps from 3 to 6 are similar to those in the previous algorithm. After step 6, we have

$$(C, S) \equiv A \cdot B' \quad (\text{mod } N') \tag{19}$$

$$(C, S) \equiv A \cdot B \cdot 2^e \quad (\text{mod } N \cdot 2^e) \tag{20}$$

$$(C/2^e, S/2^e) \equiv A \cdot B \quad (\text{mod } N) \tag{21}$$

After Step 7, we have

$$(C, S) \equiv A \cdot B \quad (\text{mod } N) \tag{22}$$

Compared with the previous algorithm, this algorithm increases little hardware resource. Enlarging by 2^e and dividing by 2^e are shift operations, which do not need extra hardware resources.

Before we estimate the calculation of this algorithm, we show a theorem.

Theorem 3. *In the enlarging modulus algorithm, at most two subtractions execute on Step 5 when $i = m$(m is an integer,$0 \le m < k + e$); When $i = m$, if two subtractions execute on Step 5, then when $i = m - 1$ no subtraction will execute on Step 5.*

Proof. We firstly prove the first part of the theorem. After Step 5, we have

$$E(C, S, N', k + e - 4) = 0 \tag{23}$$

Form Theorem 1, we know

$$C + S < N' + 2^{k+e-3} \tag{24}$$

After Step 4, we have

$$(C, S) = 2C + 2S + A \cdot B_i < 2(N' + 2^{k+e-3}) + 2^k = 2N' + 2^{k+e-2} + 2^k \tag{25}$$

Because N' has $k + e$ bits,

$$(C, S) < 3N' \tag{26}$$

So, at most two subtractions execute on Step 5.

Now, we prove the second half. Assume two subtractions execute on Step 5 when $i = m$.

Before Step 5, from the proof of the first half, we know

$$(C, S) = 2C + 2S + A \cdot B_i < 2(N' + 2^{k+e-3}) + 2^k = 2N' + 2^{k+e-2} + 2^k \quad (27)$$

On Step 5, two subtractions execute. We have

$$(C, S) < 2^{k+e-2} + 2^k \quad (28)$$

After Step 5, the algorithm goes back to Step 4, and $i = m - 1$. On Step 4, we have

$$(C, S) = 2C + 2S + A \cdot B_i < 2(2^{k+e-2} + 2^k) + 2^k = 2^{k+e-1} + 2^{k+1} + 2^k \quad (29)$$

The most significant bits of (C, S) are less than those of $2^{k+e-1} + 2^{k+1} + 2^k$.

$$T(C, k + e - 4) + T(S, k + e - 4) \le T(2^{k+e-1} + 2^{k+1} + 2^k, k + e - 4) \quad (30)$$

Because $e \ge 6$, we have

$$T(C, k + e - 4) + T(S, k + e - 4) \le 2^{k+e-1} \quad (31)$$

$$T(C, k + e - 4) + T(S, k + e - 4) \le N' \quad (32)$$

$$E(C, S, N', k + e - 4) = 0 \quad (33)$$

So, no subtraction executes on Step 5 when $i = m - 1$.

Theorem 4. *The number of subtractions on Step 5 for $i = k + e - 1$ to $i = 0$ is no more than $k + e + 1$.*

Proof. Step 5 may have no subtraction, one subtraction or two subtractions, by which the steps are divided into three parts. $n0$, $n1$ and $n2$ are the number of respective parts. Step 5 executes $k + e$ times. So

$$n0 + n1 + n2 = k + e \quad (34)$$

And the number of the total subtractions on Step 5 is

$$0 \cdot n0 + 1 \cdot n1 + 2 \cdot n2 = n1 + 2 \cdot n2 \quad (35)$$

From Theorem 3, we have

$$n2 \le n0 + 1 \quad (36)$$

Thus,

$$n1 + 2 \cdot n2 \le n1 + n2 + (n0 + 1) = k + e + 1 \quad (37)$$

So, the number of the total subtractions on Step 5 is no more than $k + e + 1$.

e is much less than k. The number of the subtractions on Step 5 is about k, which is $1/4$ of that of the previous algorithm.

Step 4 needs $k+e$ additions. One substraction or one addition needs one CSA. The whole calculation is $(k+e+1)+(k+e)=2(k+e)+1$ CSA at most. This algorithm needs $2(k+e)+1$ cycles if one cycle is needed for one CSA.

3.4 Pipeline

In function $E(C, S, N', k+e-4)$, the most significant 5 bits of (C, S) are compared with the corresponding bits of N, while others are not. The CSA number is not suitable for comparison. We should add C and S before the comparison. We use one number to replace the most significant 5 bits of (C, S), called $head$. The other $k+e-4$ bits are still expressed by two numbers (C, S). We use expression $(head, C, S)$ to replace the original (C, S). $(head, C, S) = head \cdot 2^{k+e-4} + C + S$. The assignment is shown in Fig.1. In the figure, $head$ is in red color.

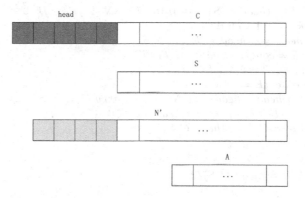

Fig. 1. The alignment of C, S, N' and A

In the new expression, $E(C, S, N', k+e-4)$ is $E(head, 0, N', k+e-4)$. It is the comparison between $head$ and $T(N', k+e-4)$.

We use a new register $nextE$ to storage the comparison result. The new algorithm adopts two-stage pipeline. The first stage is the computation of $nextE$. The second stage is the computation of $(head, C, S)$. The algorithm is shown in Algorithm 4.

Step 5 and Step 6 execute in parallel. Step 9 and Step 10 execute in parallel. On Step 4, $newhead$ has the same value as $head$ after Step 6. On Step 5 $nextE$ is the value of $(newhead > T_4(N'))$. It is also the estimation of $((head, C, S) > N')$ after Step 6. On Step 8, $newhead$ has the same value as $head$ after Step 10. On Step 9 $nextE$ is the value of $(newhead > T_4(N'))$. It is also the estimation of $((head, C, S) > N')$ after Step 10. $nextE$ is similar to $E(C, S, N', k+e-4)$ in the previous algorithm. The only difference is computing sequence. In the previous algorithm, we compute (C, S) first, then compute $E(C, S, N', k+e-4)$. In this algorithm, we compute the two parts in parallel.

The critical path of the previous algorithm contains $E(C, S, N', k+e-4)$ and one CSA. In this algorithm, the two parts execute in parallel, and the critical path is much shorter. The $E(C, S, N', k+e-4)$ of the previous algorithm needs to add the most five significant bits of C and S, while the new algorithm only needs to add one or two bits of C and S. The implementation of the pipeline algorithm can achieve high frequency. The proof of the algorithm is the same as the previous one, and the calculation is also the same. It needs $2(k+e)+1$ CSA at most. It needs $2(k+e)+1$ cycles if one cycle is needed for one CSA.

Algorithm 4. Pipeline algorithm

Input: A, B, N : k-bit **Integer**, where $A < N, B < N$
Output: $head$:5-bit **Integer**, C,S : (k+e-4)-bit **Integer**, where
$\quad\quad\quad (head, C, S) = A \cdot B \pmod{N}, (head, C, S) < N + 2^{k-3}$,
$\quad\quad\quad e = max(\lfloor \log_2 k \rfloor, 6)$

1 **begin**
2 $\quad$ initialization: $(head, C, S) = (0, 0, 0), N' = N \cdot 2^e, B' = B \cdot 2^e$
3 $\quad$ **for** $i = k + e - 1$ **to** 0 **do**
4 $\quad\quad$ $newhead = 2 \cdot head + C_{k+e-5} + S_{k+e-5} + carry(C_{k+e-6}, S_{k+e-6}, 0)$
5 $\quad\quad$ $nextE = compare(newhead, T_4(N'))$
6 $\quad\quad$ $(head, C, S) = 2(head, C, S) + A \cdot B'_i$
7 $\quad\quad$ **while** $nextE == 1$ **do**
8 $\quad\quad\quad$ $newhead = head - T_4(N') - 1 + carry(C_{k+e-5}, S_{k+e-5}, \sim N'_{k+e-5})$
9 $\quad\quad\quad$ $nextE = compare(newhead, T_4(N'))$
10 $\quad\quad\quad$ $(head, C, S) = (head, C, S) - N'$
11 $\quad\quad$ **end**
12 $\quad$ **end**
13 $\quad$ $(head, C, S) = (head, C, S)/2^e$
14 **end**
15 Note:
16 Function $carry(X, Y, Z) = X\&Y|Y\&Z|Z\&X$
17 $T_4(N') = T(N', k + e - 4)/2^{k+e-4}$
18 Function $compare(newhead, T_4(N')$ is the comparison result of $newhead$ and $T_4(N')$

3.5   Implementation of Modular Multiplication

The output of a modular multiplication may be an input of another modular multiplication. As the input requirement, it must be a single number and less than N. The output of Algorithm 4 is $(head, C, S)$, which is not qualified. The typical steps to solve this are as follow.

$S = (head, C, S)$
if $S >= N$ **then**
$\quad$ $S = S - N$

From theorem 1, we know $S < N + 2^{k-3}$ after the addition. So we need to subtract N once at most.

We have an improved scheme. We do not do the subtraction, but release the restriction on the input. After the addition, the output is one single number, but it may be more than N. We adjust the input of Algorithm 4, and we allow that the input are $k + 1$ bits. The new one is shown in Algorithm 5. It has one more i loop because of the enlarging of A and B. We use signal $isfinal$ to indicate whether we need the final result. If we need the final result, we do the last subtraction, and the result is less than N.

Algorithm 5. Modular multiplication algorithm

Input: A, B: k+1-bit **Integer**; N : k-bit **Integer**;
Input: $isfinal$: 1-bit **Integer**
Output: S : (k+e+1)-bit **Integer**, where $S = A \cdot B \pmod{N}$, If ($isfinal$)
$\quad\quad\quad S < N$,else $S < N + 2^{k-3}$, $e = max(\lfloor \log_2 k \rfloor, 6)$

1 **begin**
2 $\quad$ initialization: $(head, C, S) = (0, 0, 0), N' = N \cdot 2^e, B' = B \cdot 2^e$
3 $\quad$ **for** $i = k + e$ **to** 0 **do**
4 $\quad\quad$ $newhead = 2head + C_{k+e-5} + S_{k+e-5} + carry(C_{k+e-6}, C_{k+e-6}, 0)$
5 $\quad\quad$ $nextE = compare(newhead, T_4(N'))$
6 $\quad\quad$ $(head, C, S) = 2(head, C, S) + A \cdot B'_i$
7 $\quad\quad$ **while** $nextE == 1$ **do**
8 $\quad\quad\quad$ $newhead = head - T_s(N') - 1 + carry(C_{k+e-5}, C_{k+e-5}, \sim N'_{k+e-5})$
9 $\quad\quad\quad$ $nextE = compare(newhead, T_4(N'))$
10 $\quad\quad\quad$ $(head, C, S) = (head, C, S) - N'$
11 $\quad\quad$ **end**
12 $\quad$ **end**
13 $\quad$ $S = (head, C, S)/2^e$
14 $\quad$ **if** $isfinal$ & $S \geq N$ **then**
15 $\quad\quad$ $S = S - N$
16 $\quad$ **end**
17 **end**
18 Note:
19 Function $carry(X, Y, Z) = X\&Y|Y\&Z|Z\&X$
20 $T_4(N') = T(N', k + e - 4)/2^{k+e-4}$
21 Function $compare(newhead, T_4(N')$ is the comparison result of $newhead$ and $T_4(N')$

The last addition, comparison and subtraction rarely execute, so the speed of this part is not critical. We just use one 32-bit addition to realize them. The operands are divided into $k/32$ groups, and one group has 32 bits. These groups are added sequentially, from the low-order group to the high-order group. It needs $k/32$ cycles. The comparison and subtraction can transform to addition. So they can use the same hardware resources.

The architecture of modular multiplication is shown in Fig.2. It has three main parts: the addition (Step 6), the subtraction (Step 10), and the last addition (Steps from 13 to 16). The first two parts are two CSA, and consume most of the whole area. The last addition is a 32-bit addition.

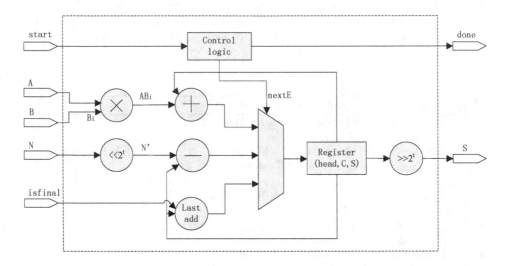

Fig. 2. The architecture of modular multiplication

Because i loops increase one, both the addition and the subtraction increase one. The calculation is about $2(k + e + 1) + 1$ CSA. If $isfinal == 0$, it needs $2(k + e + 1) + 1 + k/32$ cycles at most;else, it needs $2(k + e + 1) + 1 + 3k/32$ cycles at most.

3.6 The Average Number of Cycles of Modular Multiplication

The number of cycles of the previous algorithm is $2(k+e+1)+1+k/32$, which is about $2k$. The additions consume about k cycles, and the subtractions consume about k cycles. From Theorem 4, the subtractions consume no more than $k+e+1$ cycles (it is $k + e + 2$ in Algorithm 5). Next, we estimate the average number of subtractions.

From the proof of Theorem 3, after Step 4 of Algorithm 3,

$$C + S < 2N' + 2^{k+e-2} + 2^k$$

$2^{k+e-2} + 2^k$ is much less than N'. If $C + S$ is evenly distributed, it has about 50% chance to exceed N'. So Step 5 has 50% chance to have one subtraction. The average subtractions are $(k + e)/2$ (it is $(k + e + 1)/2$ in Algorithm 5). The average number of cycles of Algorithm 5 is $3(k + e + 1)/2 + k/32$.

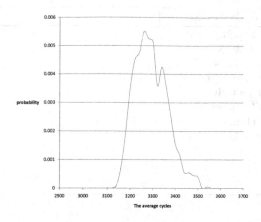

Fig. 3. The average number of cycles for 2048-bit multiplication

Table 1. The statics of the average number of cycles

k	512	1024	2048	4096
cycles	832	1650	3282	6551
cycles	1.63k	1.61k	1.60k	1.60k

This is only a rough estimation. We have also done experiments to evaluate it. We selected $k = 2048$. We produced three random integers: A, B and N, where A and B are $(k+1)$ bits, and N is k bits. Then, we replaced the most significant and the least significant of N by 1. A,B and N are input to Algorithm 5. We produced one thousand groups of A,B,N for test. The numbers of cycles are shown in Fig.3.

The average number of cycles is 3282, about $1.60k$. It is very closed to our previous estimated value $3(k+e+1)/2 + k/32 = 3154$. The range of the numbers is very small, which has 99% chance in $(1.5k, 1.7k)$. We also do the experiments for $k = 512$ and $k = 1024$. The result is shown in the Table 1. Generally, the average number of cycles is about $1.6k$.

4   RSA

In work [5], the author reviewed the most popular modular exponentiation algorithms: Left-to-Right (LR) and Right-to-Left (RL). The difference is the direction in which the bits of e are scanned. The LR binary method is more widely used (shown in Algorithm 6).

The RL binary method used twice as much area as LR's, but only increases 50% speed. So we adopt LR binary method. LR binary method uses one modular multiplication, which executes $1.5h$ times. h equals to k in our algorithm.

Algorithm 6. LR Binary Method

    Input: M, N: k bits **Integer**
    Input: e : h bits **Integer**
    Output: $C = M^e \pmod{N}$
1 initialization:$C = 1$ **begin**
2   **for** $i = h - 1$ **to** 0 **do**
3         $C = C \cdot C \pmod{N}$
4   **if** $e_i = 1$ **then**
5            $C = C \cdot M \pmod{N}$
6   **end**
7   **end**
8 **end**

The input $is final$ is 1 for only once, in the last multiplication of RSA. The last comparison and subtraction (Steps from 13 to 16) just execute once in the whole RSA.

5   Result and Comparison

5.1   Analysis

The calculation of the original interleaving modular algorithm (Algorithm 2) has $5k$ CSA at most, while that of our improved algorithm has $2k$ CSA at most. The calculation of Montgomery algorithm has also $2k$ CSA. Although Montgomery algorithm adopts precomputation, it does not have advantage in calculation over our algorithm. The comparison between Montgomery algorithm and our algorithm are shown in Table 2.

Montgomery multiplication needs one more input than our algorithm. Montgomery RSA needs twice domain transitions. The transitions do not increase the calculation much, but they make the algorithm more complex, which also needs more hardware resources. If a system contains Montgomery RSA, it must process the initial computation, and needs extra communication and storage for the result of the initial computation. These disadvantages make Montgomery algorithm less efficient. One advantage of Montgomery algorithm is that it does not have comparison, but this is not important for 2-radix algorithm. We can use the estimate function to replace the comparison.

5.2   Comparison

We select Xilinx XC2V6000 as our hardware platform, which is the most used platform by other researchers. Our RSA implementation is very small, only half of other implementations. Our implementation improves the $Throughput/Area$ by 47%. Other implementations do not include the consuming resource of the initial computation, even if they adopt precomputation.

Table 2. Comparison between Montgomery algorithm and our algorithm

	Montgomery	Proposal
Modular multiplication	four inputs	three inputs
	none	need comparison
RSA	need domain transition	none
whole system	need initial computation	none
	extra communication and storage	none

Montgomery algorithm is currently the most efficient modular multiplication algorithm. Huang [2] proposes an improved one based on multiple words. Shieh [1] proposes an improved one based on CSA. The efficiency is shown in Table 3.

Amanor implements the look-up table algorithm [17] proposed by [14, 15]. These algorithms need initial computation for each multiplication, which need a lot of resources. The actual efficiency is not as good as that shown in the table.

AbdelFattah implements an improved interleaving modular algorithm [20], which does not need the precomputation. His implementation only has half throughput as ours, and needs double slices. Its *Throughput/Area* is 1/4 of ours.

Table 3. Comparison for modular multiplication implementation

Key size	Work	Freq (MHz)	Latency cycles	Area (slices)	Throughput (Mbps)	Throughput/Area $(Mbps/slice))$
1024	McIvor [3]	123.6	1025	8294	123.5	0.015
1024	Huang [2]	100	1088	4178	94.1	0.023
1024	Shieh [1]	219.06	1028	8000	218.2	0.027
1024	Amanor [17]	69.4	1025	4608	69.5	0.015
1024	AbdelFattah [20]	181.0	4078	7546	45.4	0.006
1024	Proposed	181.6	1650	4534	112.7	0.025
2048	McIvor [3]	110.6	2049	12490	110.5	0.009
2048	Huang [2]	100	2176	8337	94.1	0.011
2048	Proposed	181.6	3282	8950	113.3	0.012
4096	McIvor [3]	92.81	4049	25474	92.7	0.004
4096	Huang [2]	100	4176	16648	98.1	0.0059
4096	Proposed	181.6	6551	17765	113.5	0.0064

Our modular multiplication has the highest efficiency among existing works expect Shieh's, which is a little higher than ours. Actually, Shieh's algorithm is less efficient than ours. This can be known from RSA implementation, shown in Table 4. His RSA adopts LR binary method, which is the same as ours. His implementation consumes twice as much area as ours, and the speed is similar to

Table 4. Comparison for RSA implementation

Key size	Work	Freq (MHz)	Latency cycles	Area (slices)	Throughput (Kbps)	Throughput/Area $(bps/slice))$
1024	Mclvor [21]	95.9	1025*1024	23208	93.5	4.0
1024	Shieh [1]	152.49	1028*1536	12537	98.9	7.9
1024	Proposed	176.6	1650*1536	6174	71.4	11.6

ours. Our *throughput/area* is 47% more than Shieh's. Our RSA is implemented according to LR Binary Method. It does not need precomputation, while Shieh's needs precomputation which is not implemented in his work.

The reason of the comparison result has been shown in Table 2. Shieh's algorithm needs twice domain transition, which makes the algorithm more complex. Its implementation needs more area, and the frequency decreases significantly. From modular multiplication to RSA, Shieh's implementation increases 57% area, while ours increases only 36% area, and Shieh's implementation decreases 30% frequency, while ours is almost unchanged. These comparisons are shown in Table 5.

Table 5. From modular multiplication implementation to RSA implementation

Key size	Work	Freq decreases	Area increases
1024	Shieh[1]	30%	57%
1024	Proposed	2.8%	36%

Our algorithm is highly efficient. Compared with the algorithms without precomputation, *throughput/area* of our RSA implementation improves three times. Compared with the algorithms with precomputation, *throughput/area* of our RSA implementation improves 47%. Our algorithm does not need precomputation, and does not need extra hardware resource, which is easier to apply.

6   Conclusion

In this paper, we present an efficient RSA algorithm. Our algorithm is based on interleaving modular multiplication, and significantly reduces the calculation. Our algorithm has a great improvement compared with other algorithms without precomputation. Even compared to algorithms with precomputation, our algorithm is still more efficient. The algorithms without precomputation have many advantages. They do not need initial computation, extra communication and storage. They usually are simple and suitable for hardware implementation. If precomputation can not bring more advantages, we can try algorithms without precomputation.

References

1. Shieh, M., Chen, J., Wu, H., Lin, W.: A new modular exponentiation architecture for efficient design of RSA cryptosystem. IEEE Transactions on Very Large Scale Integration (VLSI) Systems 16(9), 1151–1161 (2008)
2. Huang, M., Gaj, K., Kwon, S., El-Ghazawi, T.: An Optimized Hardware Architecture for the Montgomery Multiplication Algorithm. In: Cramer, R. (ed.) PKC 2008. LNCS, vol. 4939, pp. 214–228. Springer, Heidelberg (2008)
3. McIvor, C., et al.: FPGA Montgomery Multiplier Architectures -A Comparison. IEEE Computer Society (2004)
4. Blakely, G.: A computer algorithm for calculating the product AB modulo M. IEEE Transactions on Computers 100(5), 497–500 (1983)
5. Koç, Ç.: Rsa hardware implementation. Tech. rep. RSA Laboratories (1996)
6. Koç, Ç., Hung, C.: Carry-save adders for computing the product AB modulo N. Electronics Letters 26(13), 899–900 (1990)
7. Koç, Ç., Hung, C.: Bit-level systolic arrays for modular multiplication. The Journal of VLSI Signal Processing 3(3), 215–223 (1991)
8. Koç, Ç., Hung, C.: A Fast algorithm for modular reduction. IEE Proceedings-Computers and Digital Techniques 145(4), 265–271 (1998)
9. Montgomery, P.: Modular multiplication without trial division. Mathematics of Computation 44(170), 519–521 (1985)
10. Tenca, A.F., Koç, Ç.K.: A Scalable Architecture for Montgomery Multiplication. In: Koç, Ç.K., Paar, C. (eds.) CHES 1999. LNCS, vol. 1717, pp. 94–108. Springer, Heidelberg (1999)
11. Harris, D., Krishnamurthy, R., Anders, M., Mathew, S., Hsu, S.: An improved unified scalable radix-2 montgomery multiplier. IEEE Computer Society (2005)
12. Mesquita, D., Perin, G., Herrmann, F., Martins, J.: An efficient implementation of montgomery powering ladder in reconfigurable hardware. In: Proceedings of the 23rd Symposium on Integrated Circuits and System Design, pp. 121–126. ACM (2010)
13. Perin, G., Mesquita, D., Herrmann, F., Martins, J.: Montgomery modular multiplication on reconfigurable hardware: fully systolic array vs parallel implementation. In: 2010 VI Southern Programmable Logic Conference (SPL), pp. 61–66. IEEE (2010)
14. Bunimov, V., Schimmler, M., Tolg, B.: A complexity-effective version of montgomery's algorithm. In: Workshop on Complexity Effective Designs, ISCA, vol. 2. Citeseer (2002)
15. Bunimov, V., Schimmler, M.: Area and time efficient modular multiplication of large integers. In: Proceedings of the IEEE International Conference on Application-Specific Systems, Architectures, and Processors, pp. 400–409. IEEE (2003)
16. Schimmler, M., Bunimov, V.: Fast modular multiplication by operand changing. IEEE Computer Society (2004)
17. Narh Amanor, D., Paar, C., Pelzl, J., Bunimov, V., Schimmler, M.: Efficient hardware architectures for modular multiplication on FPGAs. In: Field Programmable Logic and Applications, pp. 539–542. IEEE (2005)
18. Knezevic, M., Batina, L., Verbauwhede, I.: Modular reduction without precomputational phase. In: IEEE International Symposium on Circuits and Systems, ISCAS 2009, pp. 1389–1392. IEEE (2009)

19. Knežević, M., Sakiyama, K., Fan, J., Verbauwhede, I.: Modular Reduction in $GF(2^n)$ without Pre-computational Phase. In: von zur Gathen, J., Imaña, J.L., Koç, Ç.K. (eds.) WAIFI 2008. LNCS, vol. 5130, pp. 77–87. Springer, Heidelberg (2008)
20. AbdelFattah, A.M., Bahaa El-Din, A.M., Fahmy, H.M.A.: An Efficient Architecture for Interleaved Modular Multiplication. World Academy of Science, Engineering and Technology (2009)
21. McIvor, C., McLoone, M., McCanny, J.: Modified Montgomery modular multiplication and RSA exponentiation techniques. In: IEE Proceedings - Computers and Digital Techniques, vol. 151, pp. 402–408. IET (2004)

The Stream Cipher Core of the 3GPP Encryption Standard 128-EEA3: Timing Attacks and Countermeasures

Gautham Sekar

Temasek Laboratories, National University of Singapore
5A, Engineering Drive 1, Singapore 117411, Singapore
tslgs@nus.edu.sg

Abstract. The core of the 3rd Generation Partnership Project (3GPP) encryption standard 128-EEA3 is a stream cipher called ZUC. It was designed by the Chinese Academy of Sciences and proposed for inclusion in the cellular wireless standards called "Long Term Evolution" or "4G". The LFSR-based cipher uses a 128-bit key. In this paper, we first show timing attacks on ZUC that can recover, with about 71.43% success rate, *(i)* one bit of the secret key immediately, and *(ii)* information involving 6 other key bits. The time, memory and data requirements of the attacks are negligible. While we see potential improvements to the attacks, we also suggest countermeasures.

Keywords: Stream cipher, cache timing attack, key recovery.

1 Introduction

ZUC [8] is a stream cipher designed by the Data Assurance and Communication Security Research Center (DACAS) of the Chinese Academy of Sciences. The cipher forms the core of the 3GPP mobile standards 128-EEA3 (for encryption) and 128-EIA3 (for message integrity) [7]. It is presently being proposed by the European Telecommunications Standards Institute (ETSI) for inclusion in the Long Term Evolution (LTE) or the 4th generation of cellular wireless standards (4G).[1] ZUC is LFSR-based and uses a 128-bit key and a 128-bit initialization vector (*IV*). Some key points in the evolution of ZUC are listed in the following timeline.

Timeline:

- 18th *June 2010:* The Security Algorithms Group of Experts (SAGE) of the ETSI published a document providing the specifications of the first version of ZUC. The document was indexed "Version 1.0".

---

[1] Strictly speaking, LTE is not 4G as it does not fully comply with the International Mobile Telecommunications Advanced (IMT-Advanced) requirements for 4G. Put differently, LTE is beyond 3G but pre-4G.

C.-K. Wu, M. Yung, and D. Lin (Eds.): Inscrypt 2011, LNCS 7537, pp. 269–288, 2012.

- 26th–30th *July 2010:* Improvements and minor corrections were made successively to the C implementation of the ZUC algorithm of Version 1.0. These resulted in versions 1.2 and 1.3 of the ETSI/SAGE document. The preface to Version 1.3 was corrected and the resulting document released as Version 1.4.
- 02nd–03rd *December 2010 (First International Workshop on ZUC Algorithm):* A few observations on the algorithm of Version 1.4 were reported (see [6]) but none of these posed any immediate threat to its security.
- 05th–09th *December 2010 (ASIACRYPT):* The algorithm of Version 1.4 was cryptanalysed by Wu *et al.* [20] and the results were presented at the rump session of ASIACRYPT 2010.

  The attack reduces the effective key size of ZUC to about 66 bits by exploiting the fact that a difference set between a pair of *IV*s may result in identical keystreams.
- 08th *December 2010:* Gilbert *et al.* reported an existential forgery attack on the 128-EIA3 MAC algorithm.

  The attack allows, given any message and its MAC value under an unknown integrity key and an initialization vector, to predict the MAC value of a related message under the same key and the same initialization vector with a success probability of 1/2.

  Gilbert *et al.* also gave a modified version of the 128-EIA3 algorithm (*cf.* [9, Algorithm 2]).

  In the original 128-EIA3 construction, some 32-bit keystream words are used in computing the universal hash function, and then the next whole word of keystream is used as a mask. But in [9, Algorithm 2], the first keystream word is used as the mask. The latter algorithm better fits the standard Carter-Wegman construction [5].
- 04th *January 2011:* In response to Wu *et al.*'s key recovery attack, the initialization of ZUC was modified. Version 1.5 contains the new algorithm [8]. This algorithm is the one we analyse in this paper; we have been and shall henceforth be simply calling it "ZUC" (i.e., without any accompanying version numbers).
- 05th–06th *June 2011 (The 2nd International Workshop on ZUC Algorithm and Related Topics):* Gilbert *et al.* presented an updated version (*cf.* [9]) of their paper. In this they argue that [9, Algorithm 2] might have slightly greater resistance against nonce reuse.
- 07th *June 2011 – present:* Changing the ZUC integrity algorithm of 128-EIA3 to [9, Algorithm 2] was being considered by the ETSI/SAGE in June 2011. Although [9, Algorithm 2] offers some advantages, they appear to be marginal. To the best of our knowledge, it is not yet decided by the ETSI/SAGE as to which keystream word will be used as the mask word.

  In this paper, we present two timing attacks on ZUC, each of can (in the best case) recover with (nearly) 0.7143 success probability, *(i)* one bit of the key immediately, and *(ii)* information involving 6 other bits of the key. Before describing how this paper is organised, we shall discuss timing attacks briefly.

Timing attack: This is a side-channel attack in which the attacker exploits timing measurements of (parts of) the cryptographic algorithm's implementation. For example, in the case of unprotected AES implementations based on lookup tables, the dependence of the lookup time on the table index can be exploited to speed up key recovery [4]. A *cache timing attack* is a type of timing attack which is based on the idea that the adversary can observe the cache accesses of a legitimate party. The cache is an intermediate memory between the CPU and the RAM and is used to store frequently used data fetched from the RAM. The problem with the cache memory is that, unlike the RAM, it is shared among users sharing a CPU.[2] Hence, if Bob and Eve are sharing a CPU and Eve is aware that Bob is about to encrypt, Eve may initiate her cache timing attack as follows. She first fills the cache memory with values of her choice and waits for Bob to run the encryption algorithm. She then measures the time taken to load the earlier cache elements into the CPU; loading is quick if the element is still in cache (such an event is called a *cache hit*; its complement is a *cache miss*) and not overwritten by one of Bob's values. This technique is known as Prime+Probe [15]. Cache timing attacks have been successfully mounted on several ciphers, notably the AES [4,15,22,11].

In [15], two types of cache timing attacks are introduced – *synchronous* and *asynchronous*. In a synchronous attack, the adversary can make cache measurements only after certain operations of the cipher (e.g., a full update of a stream cipher's internal state) have been performed. In this attack scenario, the plaintext or the ciphertext is assumed to be available to the adversary. An asynchronous cache adversary, on the other hand, is able to make cache measurements in parallel to the execution of the routine. She is able to obtain a list of all cache accesses made *in chronological order* [22]. Here, there are different viewpoints on the resources available to the adversary. According to Osvik *et al.*, the adversary has only the distribution of the plaintext/ciphertext and not sample values [15]. Zenner differs in [22] where he argues that the adversary can (partially) control input/output data and observe cache behaviour. Asynchronous attacks are particularly effective on processors with simultaneous multithreading. One of the timing attacks in this paper is an asynchronous cache timing attack, and the other is a straightforward timing attack that does not involve the cache.

Organisation: Section 2 provides the specifications of ZUC along with some notation and convention. The preliminary observations that lead us to timing attacks are listed in Sect. 3 and the attacks are detailed in Sect. 4. We follow this with an analysis of some design/implementation modifications that resist the attacks, in Sect. 5. In Sect. 6, we see possible improvements to the timing attacks and find that the proposed design modifications resist these improved attacks too. In addition, we see several highlights of our attacks such as the

---

[2] Actually, in most modern CPUs the cache is simply the static RAM (SRAM) and the dynamic RAM (DRAM) is the other, predominant type of computer memory that we simply call "the RAM".

novelty of an employed technique. The paper concludes with a suggestion for future work, in the same section.

2   Specifications of ZUC

In this paper, we use several of the notation and convention followed in [8] in addition to that provided in Table 1.

Table 1. Notation and convention

Notation	Meaning
LSB	Least significant bit
MSB	Most significant bit
$\odot$	Multiplication modulo $(2^{31} - 1)$
$t_{i(j)}$	The jth bit ($j = 0$ denoting the LSB) of t_i
$[\beta_1\beta_2 \ldots \beta_n]$	$\beta_1 \| \beta_2 \| \ldots \| \beta_n$
Y_H	$[Y_{(30)}Y_{(29)} \ldots Y_{(15)}]$, when $\|Y\| = 31$ bits $[Y_{(31)}Y_{(29)} \ldots Y_{(16)}]$, when $\|Y\| = 32$ bits
Y_L	$[Y_{(15)}Y_{(14)} \ldots Y_{(0)}]$

As previously mentioned, the inputs to the ZUC cipher are a 128-bit key and a 128-bit *IV*. The algorithm has three parts or "layers" – a linear feedback shift register (LFSR) layer, a bit-reorganisation ("BR") layer and a nonlinear function F. The execution of the algorithm proceeds in two stages – an initialization stage and a "working" stage. Each iteration of the algorithm in the working stage generates 32 bits of keystream output. We shall now detail the layers and stages to the level that is required for the understanding of the results to follow. For the complete specifications, the interested reader is referred to [8, Sect. 3].

The LFSR layer: ZUC uses one LFSR that contains sixteen 32-bit cells containing 31-bit values $s_0, s_1, \ldots, s_{15}$. However, none of the 31-bit elements can assume the value 0; the remaining $2^{31} - 1$ values are allowed. The steps of the LFSR layer in the initialization mode comprise Algorithm 1.

Algorithm 1. The LFSR layer in the initialization mode

1: $v := 2^{15} \odot s_{15} + 2^{17} \odot s_{13} + 2^{21} \odot s_{10} + 2^{20} \odot s_4 + 2^8 \odot s_0 + s_0 \bmod (2^{31} - 1)$;
2: $s_{16} := (v + u) \bmod (2^{31} - 1)$; /* u is derived from the output of F */
3: **if** $s_{16} = 0$ **then**
4:     $s_{16} \leftarrow 2^{31} - 1$;
5: $(s_1, s_2, \ldots, s_{15}, s_{16}) \rightarrow (s_0, s_1, \ldots, s_{14}, s_{15})$;

The steps of the LFSR layer in the working mode comprise Algorithm 2.

Algorithm 2. The LFSR layer in the working mode

1: $s_{16} = 2^{15} \odot s_{15} + 2^{17} \odot s_{13} + 2^{21} \odot s_{10} + 2^{20} \odot s_4 + 2^8 \odot s_0 + s_0 \bmod (2^{31} - 1)$;
2: **if** $s_{16} = 0$ **then**
3:    $s_{16} \leftarrow 2^{31} - 1$;
4: $(s_1, s_2, \ldots, s_{15}, s_{16}) \rightarrow (s_0, s_1, \ldots, s_{14}, s_{15})$;

The BR layer: In this layer, 128 bits are extracted from the cells of the LFSR and four 32-bit words are formed. Three of these words (X_0, X_1, X_2) are used by the nonlinear function F, and the fourth word (X_3) is used in producing the keystream.

The nonlinear function F: This function involves two 32-bit values in memory cells (R_1, R_2), one 32×32 S-box (S), two linear transforms (L_1, L_2) and the aforementioned three 32-bit words produced by the BR layer. The output of the function F is a 32-bit word W. The 32-bit keystream word Z, that is produced in every iteration of the working mode of the ZUC algorithm, is simply $W \oplus X_3$. The F function is defined as follows:

$F(X_0, X_1, X_2)\{$
  1: $W = (X_0 \oplus R_1) + R_2 \bmod 2^{32}$;
  2: $W_1 := R_1 \oplus X_1$;
  3: $W_2 := R_2 \oplus X_2$;
  4: $R_1 = S(L_1(W_{1L} || W_{2H}))$;
  5: $R_2 = S(L_2(W_{2L} || W_{1H}))$;$\}$

Key loading: The key loading procedure expands the 128-bit secret key and the 128-bit IV to form the initial state of the LFSR. In [8], this key is denoted as k ($= k_0 || k_1 || \ldots || k_{15}$, where each k_i is a byte) and the IV as iv ($= iv_0 || iv_1 || \ldots || iv_{15}$, where each iv_i is a byte). In addition to k and iv, a 240-bit constant D ($= d_0 || d_1 || \ldots || d_{15}$) is used in the key loading procedure. We shall now provide the binary representations of the d_i's first (in Table 2), followed by the key loading procedure.

Given this, the key loading is a set of very simple and straightforward steps given by:

$$s_i = k_i || d_i || iv_i, \text{ for } i \in \{0, 1, \ldots, 15\}. \tag{1}$$

The execution of ZUC: As mentioned earlier, the execution of the ZUC algorithm proceeds in two stages. We shall now describe these stages.

The initialization stage: This stage is given by Algorithm 3.
The working stage: This stage, in turn, has two sub-stages that are given by Algorithms 4 and 5.

Table 2. The constants d_i, $i \in \{0, 1, \ldots, 15\}$, used in the key loading procedure

d_0	100010011010111	d_8	100110101111000
d_1	010011010111100	d_9	010111100010011
d_2	110001001101011	d_{10}	110101111000100
d_3	001001101011110	d_{11}	001101011110001
d_4	101011110001001	d_{12}	101111000100110
d_5	011010111100010	d_{13}	011110001001101
d_6	111000100110101	d_{14}	111100010011010
d_7	000100110101111	d_{15}	100011110101100

Algorithm 3. The initialization stage of ZUC execution

1: $ctr = 0$;
2: **repeat**
3:    Execute the BR layer;
4:    Compute the nonlinear function F taking as inputs the outputs X_0, X_1 and X_2 of the BR layer;
5:    Run Algorithm 1;
6:    $ctr \leftarrow ctr + 1$;
7: **until** ctr = 32

Algorithm 4. First sub-stage of the working stage of ZUC execution

1: Execute the BR layer;
2: Compute the nonlinear function F taking as inputs the outputs X_0, X_1 and X_2 of the BR layer;
3: Discard the output W of F;
4: Run Algorithm 2;

Algorithm 5. Keystream generating sub-stage of the working stage of ZUC execution

1: **repeat**
2:    Execute the BR layer;
3:    Compute the nonlinear function F taking as inputs the outputs X_0, X_1 and X_2 of the BR layer;
4:    Compute the keystream as $Z = W \oplus X_3$;
5:    Run Algorithm 2;
6: **until** one 32-bit keystream word more than the required number of words is generated

3 Motivational Observations

We start with the following two trivial observations.

Observation 1. *The ZUC key is initially loaded directly into the 16 LFSR cells.*

Observation 2. *Multiplication and addition in the initialization mode and working mode of the LFSR layer are modulo $(2^{31} - 1)$. Other additions and multiplications are modulo 2^{32}.*

Addition modulo $(2^{31} - 1)$ of two 31-bit integers x and y is performed in [8] as follows. First, they are stored in 32-bit cells and $z = x + y \bmod 2^{32}$ is computed. If the *end carry*, meaning the carry-in at the MSB position of a 32-bit word/register/memory cell, is b, the MSB of the 32-bit z is first discarded and then this 31-bit word is incremented by b. This is implemented in C in [8] as:

```
u32 Add(u32 x, u32 y) {
  u32 z = x + y;
  if (z & 0x80000000)
   z = (z & 0x7FFFFFFF) + 1;
  return z;
}
```

It is to be noted that the increment step in *Add()* cannot regenerate end carry[3] because $x, y \in \{1, 2, \ldots, 2^{31} - 1\}$ implies that $u32\,z$ has at least one zero in its 31 LSBs.

An end carry of 1 brings in one extra 32-bit *AND* operation and one 32-bit addition in the software implementation (in hardware implementation, we have 32 bitwise *AND* operations and one 32-bit ripple carry addition). Let T_{carry} denote the total time taken by the processor to perform these additional operations and T denote the time taken to run the *Add()* subroutine without the step where z is incremented. We now have the following simple observation that forms the base of our timing analysis.

Observation 3. *If the attacker observes that the time taken to run the Add() subroutine is $T + T_{carry}$, then she necessarily concludes that the end carry is 1, and can use this to retrieve some information on the summands x and y in general and their MSBs in particular.*

In Sect. 4, we shall show how we exploit Observations 1–3 to mount (partial) key recovery attacks on ZUC.

---

[3] Throughout this paper, a 'generated' or 'produced' end carry is always 1 unless otherwise stated.

4 The Timing Attacks

In this section, we shall examine the first invocation of the LFSR layer in the initialization mode. Recall that the first step of Algorithm 1 is:

$$v := 2^{15} \odot s_{15} + 2^{17} \odot s_{13} + 2^{21} \odot s_{10} + 2^{20} \odot s_4 + 2^8 \odot s_0 + s_0 \bmod (2^{31} - 1). \quad (2)$$

Given a 32-bit cell containing a 31-bit integer δ, the product $2^n \odot \delta$ is implemented in C in [8] as $((\delta \ll n) | (\delta \gg (31 - n))) \,\&\, 0x7FFFFFFF$. Given this and the manner in which the key bits are loaded into the cells initially (see [8, Sect. 3]), we see that the 31-bit summands on the RHS of (2) in the first round of the initialization mode are:

$$z_1 := [k_{0(7)} k_{0(6)} \dots k_{0(0)} d_{0(14)} d_{0(13)} \dots d_{0(0)} iv_{0(7)} iv_{0(6)} \dots iv_{0(0)}],$$
$$z_2 := [d_{0(14)} \dots d_{0(0)} iv_{0(7)} \dots iv_{0(0)} k_{0(7)} \dots k_{0(0)}],$$
$$z_3 := [d_{4(2)} d_{4(1)} d_{4(0)} iv_{4(7)} \dots iv_{4(0)} k_{4(7)} \dots k_{4(0)} d_{4(14)} \dots d_{4(3)}],$$
$$z_4 := [d_{10(1)} d_{10(0)} iv_{10(7)} \dots iv_{10(0)} k_{10(7)} \dots k_{10(0)} d_{10(14)} \dots d_{10(2)}],$$
$$z_5 := [d_{13(5)} \dots d_{13(0)} iv_{13(7)} \dots iv_{13(0)} k_{13(7)} \dots k_{13(0)} d_{13(14)} \dots d_{13(6)}],$$
$$z_6 := [d_{15(7)} \dots d_{15(0)} iv_{15(7)} \dots iv_{15(0)} k_{15(7)} \dots k_{15(0)} d_{15(14)} \dots d_{15(8)}].$$

In the C implementation of ZUC in [8], the z_i's are added modulo $(2^{31} - 1)$ as $((((z_1 + z_2) + z_3) + z_4) + z_5) + z_6$,[4] using the $Add()$ subroutine. Recall that the $d_i(j)$'s are known (see Table 2). There is no vector $[z_{1(30)} z_{2(30)} \dots z_{6(30)}]$ such that an end carry is not produced. This is because $d_{0(14)} = 1$ and $d_{15(7)} = 1$. Let c_1 denote the carry bit produced by the addition of $z_{1(29)}$, $z_{2(29)}$ and the carry coming in from bit position 28 (bit position 0 denotes the LSB), in the first step of the $Add()$ subroutine. The sum bit in this addition is added with $z_{3(29)}$ and the corresponding carry coming in from bit position 28.[5] Let c_2 denote the carry bit produced therefrom. Similarly c_3, c_4 and c_5 are defined. The only binary vectors $\Gamma := [c_1 c_2 \dots c_5 z_{1(30)}]$ that are capable of producing end carry exactly once are:

$$\Gamma_1 := [0\,0\,0\,0\,0\,0],$$
$$[\Gamma_2 \Gamma_3 \Gamma_4 \Gamma_5 \Gamma_6 \Gamma_7]^T := \mathbf{I}_6,$$

where $\mathbf{I}_6$ is the identity matrix of size 6.

---

[4] Evidently there are other orders in performing the modular additions; e.g., $((((z_1 + z_3) + z_2) + z_4) + z_5) + z_6$. However, a similar analysis as that in this paper can be performed for each of these orders.

[5] Strictly speaking, the sum bit may be flipped before it is added with $z_{3(29)}$ and the carry-in from bit position 28. This is because of the increment-by-1 step in $Add()$. However, the sum bit is flipped only (i) when there is an end carry and (ii) if all the 29 LSBs in the sum are 1's. The probability for such an event is intuitively negligible, even considering that many bits of the z_i's are constants. We therefore ignore such bit flips.

Clarification: Among the MSBs of the 31-bit z_i's, all but the MSB of z_1 are known to us. Let us, for example, suppose that this unknown bit is 1. Then, we are bound to have a carry-out (in other words, carry-in at the bit position 31 or 'end carry'). Since the z_i's are added progressively modulo $(2^{31} - 1)$, we can have end carry produced many times (λ, say, in total). If the MSBs of the z_i's are all variables, λ is bounded from above by 5, the number of additions modulo 2^{32}. (For the case at hand, though, this upper bound is conjectured to be 3 by means of a simulation.)

Now, what must be the carry-in's at the bit position 30, for each of these additions, such that we have only one carry-out? It is rather straightforward to see that the answer is [00000] for the 5 additions. If one of these bits is 1 instead of 0, then we would certainly have one more carry-out. Thus, when the MSB of z_1 is 1, the only *favourable* carry vector is [00000]. This is what Γ_7 means. We similarly have $\Gamma_1, \Gamma_2, \ldots, \Gamma_6$ as the favourable binary vectors for the case when the MSB of z_1 is 0.   □

Reverting back to the Γ_i's, one can see that in 5 out of 7 cases, $z_{1(30)} = 0$ and $c_1 = 0$. In each of $z_1, z_2, \ldots, z_6$, we have the unknown key bits, (un)known IV bits and known d-bits. If all the 31 z-bits are unknown variables, one could assume that they are uniformly distributed at random[6] and evaluate the likelihood of the occurrence of each of $\Gamma_1, \Gamma_2, \ldots, \Gamma_7$.[7] Because at least 15 bits of each of $z_1, z_2, \ldots, z_6$ are constants, the assumption of uniform distribution cannot be right away made anymore. If the IV is a known constant, one can assume that the 40 key bits $k_0||k_4||k_{10}||k_{13}||k_{15}$ are uniformly distributed at random and compute $Pr(\Gamma_i)$, for $i \in \{1, 2, \ldots, 7\}$, by running a simulation. Otherwise, the 40 IV bits $iv_0||iv_4||iv_{10}||iv_{13}||iv_{15}$ may also be assumed to be uniformly distributed at random, and the probabilities $Pr(\Gamma_i)$ estimated theoretically. However, the latter approach appears to be highly involved, so we instead performed Experiment 1.

Experiment 1. *The key/IV bytes k_0 and iv_0 are exhaustively varied, setting every other key/IV byte to 0x00, and the cases where end carry is produced exactly once, when the $z_1, z_2, \ldots, z_6$ are added modulo $(2^{31} - 1)$, are examined.*

We found 6995 such cases (out of a total of $256 \times 256 = 65536$ cases). In 3444 of the cases, the vector was Γ_6; in 3030 cases, Γ_5; and in the remaining 521 cases, the vector was Γ_3. (A few of these cases are listed in Appendix A.) Firstly, this affirms that there are binary vectors that occur in practice. Next, if these are the only such vectors that occur in practice, then we have recovered $z_{1(30)}$, or the MSB of k_0, with probability 1 when the time taken to execute (2) is at

---

[6] The probability distribution here is *a priori*.

[7] Here, one may choose to ignore negligible biases in the carry probabilities. For example, when two 32-bit words are added modulo 2^{32}, the carry-in at the MSB position is likely to be 0 with a very small bias probability of 2^{-32}. Bias probabilities of the carries generated in modular sums have been examined in several works [19,14,17,16].

its minimum. This minimum time period would naturally be $T_{const} + T_{carry}$, with T_{const} being the *constant time* component (i.e., the sum total of the execution times of the steps, of the $Add()$'s invoked for (2), that are independent of the respective x's and y's). With this, let us proceed to the second step of the initialization mode, viz.,

$$s_{16} = v + u \bmod (2^{31} - 1), \tag{3}$$

where $u = W \gg 1$ (see Sect. 2). We shall now argue that there are significantly many cases where (3) does not involve an end carry generation.

We performed Experiment 1 again, this time counting the frequency at which the MSB of v took the value 0. The total number of such cases was 32840, translating to a probability of 0.5011. Therefore, v_{30} appears to be uniformly distributed at random. The first value that u takes after it is initialised is $W = (X_0 \oplus R_{1(ini)}) + R_{2(ini)} \bmod 2^{32}$, where $R_{1(ini)}$ and $R_{2(ini)}$ are the initial values of R_1 and R_2, respectively. From [8, Sect. 3.6.1], we infer that $R_{1(ini)} = 0$ and $R_{2(ini)} = 0$. Hence, $W = X_0$ and

$$\begin{aligned}
u = W \gg 1 &= X_0 \gg 1 \\
&= s_{15H} \| s_{14L} \gg 1 \\
&= [s_{15(30)} s_{15(29)} \cdots s_{15(15)}] \| [s_{14(15)} s_{14(14)} \cdots s_{14(1)}] \\
&= k_{15(7)} \| \{0,1\}^{30};
\end{aligned} \tag{4}$$

and this is value of u that goes into step 2 of the first invocation of Algorithm 1. Since $k_{15(7)}$ is an unknown key bit, u_{30} can be reasonably assumed to be uniformly distributed at random. Given this, even if the carry-in at the bit position 30 were to be heavily biased towards 1, with 0.25 probability we would still have the carry-out to be 0. In summary, the minimum execution time of Algorithm 1 can reasonably be expected to be $T'_{const} + T_{carry}$, T'_{const} being the constant time component, for anywhere between 25% and 50% of the key-*IV* pairs. We shall now show two ways to measure the execution time of Algorithm 1 and, using it, recover key-dependent information.

1. Through Cache Measurements: In [22], Zenner makes a mention of a side-channel oracle ACT_KEYSETUP() that provides an asynchronous cache adversary a list of all cache accesses made by KEYSETUP(), the key setup algorithm of HC-256, in chronological order. Similarly, we introduce an oracle ACT_Algorithm-3() that provides the adversary with a chronologically ordered list of all cache accesses made by Algorithm 3. Zenner does not mention in [22] whether or not such an ordered list normally contains the time instants of the cache accesses as well. We assume that the instants are contained in the list. This is a rather strong assumption because in the absence of the oracle, the adversary has to have considerable control over the CPU of the legitimate party, in order to obtain the cache access times.

Given this assumption, the adversary scans through the list and calculates the time difference between the third and the fourth accesses of the S-box S.

The first access to S is when it is initialised. Before Algorithm 1 is invoked for the first time, the nonlinear function F is computed (see Algorithm 3). During this computation, S is accessed twice (see the definition of F in Sect. 2). The next (i.e., the fourth) access of S happens after a few constant-time operations (e.g., executing the BR layer, computing W) that follow the first invocation of Algorithm 1. Let the time taken to perform these operations be denoted by T''_{const}. Then, the aforesaid time difference between the third and the fourth cache accesses of S provides the adversary with $T'_{const} + \lambda T_{carry} + T''_{const}$, $\lambda \in \{1, 2, 3\}$. The adversary can easily measure T_{carry}, T'_{const} and T''_{const} by simulating with an arbitrarily chosen key-IV pair (in practice, quite a few pairs will be required for precision). Thereby, the adversary obtains the value of λ. When $\lambda = 1$, the adversary is able to recover the MSB of k_0 immediately with probability 1.

Now, since Experiment 1 cannot be performed over all key-IV pairs, we reasonably assume that $\Gamma_1, \Gamma_2, \ldots, \Gamma_7$ are equally likely to occur in practice. Under this assumption, $Pr(k_{0(7)} = 0)$ falls to $6/7 = 0.8571$. This probability is further reduced to $5/7 = 0.7143$ if we are to additionally have $c_1 = 0$.

The timing analysis above assumes that S is in cache. This is a very realistic assumption for the following reason. In [8, Appendix A], the S-box S is implemented using two 8×8 lookup tables, viz., $S0$ and $S1$. Encryption performed many times on a single CPU would ideally result in the elements of these tables to be frequently accessed. And, every element of $S0$ and $S1$ could be expected to be accessed frequently if each encryption, in turn, invokes Algorithm 5 multiple times (i.e., long keystream is generated). This would ideally place the lookup tables in the cache.

2. Using Statistical Methods That Do Not Involve Any Cache Measurement:

The execution time of Algorithm 1 can also be estimated without performing cache measurements. Let us recall that Algorithm 1 is run 32 times during the initialization process (see Algorithm 3). Following this, Algorithm 2 is run once (along with constant time steps of Algorithm 4 and Algorithm 5) before the first 32-bit keystream word is output (see Algorithms 4 and 5). Now, the first step of Algorithm 2 is identical to the first step of Algorithm 1. The subsequent steps of Algorithm 2 are constant time operations.[8] Thereby, the total execution time till the first keystream word is generated is

$$T'''_{const} + T_{carry} \cdot \left(\sum_{j=0}^{31} \lambda_j\right) + T^{(w)}_{const} + \lambda_1^{(w)} \cdot T_{carry}, \tag{5}$$

where

---

[8] Throughout this paper, we ignore steps 3 and 4 of Algorithm 1 (and, naturally, steps 2 and 3 of Algorithm 2) because the event $s_{16} = 0$ occurs randomly with probability 2^{-31} which is negligible when compared to the probability that end carry is generated exactly once. Besides, the step 4 of Algorithm 1 is just an assignment operation and consumes only a small fraction of the time it takes to perform one 32-bit AND and one 32-bit addition. Therefore, we can safely assume that steps 3 and 4 of Algorithm 1 have negligible influence on the timing analysis.

1. T'''_{const} is the sum total of $32 \cdot T'_{const}$ and the constant-time steps of Algorithm 3;

2. λ_j, $j \in \{0, 1, \ldots, 31\}$, is the number of times end carry is generated in the $(j+1)$th iteration of Algorithm 1;

3. $T^{(w)}_{const}$ is the sum total of the execution times of the constant time steps of Algorithm 2, plus the time to compute steps 1–3 of Algorithm 4 and steps 2–4 of Algorithm 5;

4. $\lambda_1^{(w)}$ is the λ of the first run of Algorithm 2;

5. $\lambda_j, \lambda_1^{(w)} \in \{0, 1, \ldots, 5\}$, $\forall j \in \{0, 1, \ldots, 31\}$.

Let us now try to estimate the mean of the λ's assuming the z-terms are uniformly distributed from iteration 17 of Algorithm 1 onwards. This assumption is very reasonable at iteration 17, when every LFSR element has been updated once, and the subsequent iterations. We performed Experiment 2 to determine the mean.

Experiment 2. *The new $[z_{1(30)} z_{2(30)} \cdots z_{6(30)}]$ is exhaustively varied, and so is $[c_1 c_2 \ldots c_5]$. The λ for each $[z_{1(30)} z_{2(30)} \cdots z_{6(30)} c_1 c_2 \ldots c_5]$ is counted.*

We obtained the frequencies 12, 220, 792, 792, 220, and 12 for $\lambda = 0, 1, 2, 3, 4, 5$, and 6 respectively.

From these frequencies we obtain that the mean λ,

$$\bar{\lambda} = \frac{0 \cdot 12 + 1 \cdot 220 + 2 \cdot 792 + 3 \cdot 792 + 4 \cdot 220 + 5 \cdot 12}{2^{11}} = 2.5. \tag{6}$$

For the iterations 17–32 of Algorithm 1 and iteration 1 of Algorithm 2, the expected cumulative λ is $17 \cdot \bar{\lambda} = 42.5$. The cumulative λ (expected) can be computed for iterations 2–16, but in these computations one needs to make certain assumptions. This is because, in any iteration before the 17th, at least one of the z-vectors is composed of bits loaded directly from the key, IV and the d-constants. Assuming that the incoming carries at the bit position 30 are uniformly distributed can make the λ calculations erroneous. One may instead resort to simulations, but even then would have to perform extrapolations. For example, if the IV is unknown, then in iteration 2, to determine

- $Pr(c_1 = 0)$, the simulation takes $O(2^{15})$ time (15 unknown key and IV bits);
- $Pr(c_2 = 0)$, the simulation takes $O(2^{15} \cdot 2^{16}) = O(2^{31})$ time (16 unknown key and IV bits and 2^{15} possible outputs of the previous simulation);
- $Pr(c_3 = 0)$ or $Pr(c_4 = 0)$, the simulation takes $O(2^{31} \cdot 2^{16}) = O(2^{47})$ time (similar reasoning as the above);
- $Pr(c_5 = 0)$, the simulation takes $O((2^{31} - 1) \cdot 2^{31}) = O(2^{62})$ time (because s_{15} has been changed at the end of iteration 1 and the new s_{15} can assume any value in the set $\{1, 2, \ldots, 2^{31} - 1\}$).

From these probabilities, it is rather easy to compute the average λ by building a truth table of the λ-values and the corresponding vectors $[z_{1(30)} \ z_{2(30)} \ \cdots \ z_{6(30)} \ c_1 \ c_2 \ \ldots \ c_5]$. Such a table would consist of 2^7 rows because $z_{2(30)}, z_{3(30)}$,

$z_{4(30)}$ and $z_{5(30)}$ are known constants. Looking at the $O(2^{62})$ time complexity, however, one can at the best perform a partial simulation and extrapolate the result. This means that there is always an error in computing the expected λ for each of the iterations 2–16. Hence, we can instead assume that the expected λ is $\bar{\lambda}$ for each of these iterations. This is also error-prone, but we can construct an appropriate credible interval to mitigate the error. This is done as follows. First, upon performing Experiment 2 with more z- (and hence c-) bits and observing the resultant frequencies (i.e., similar to those corresponding to (6)), we will observe that λ is near-normally distributed. Given this, we first choose a confidence level[9] (say, α) and construct a credible interval around $\bar{\lambda}$. To reduce the error in assuming that the λ's of iterations 2–16 are also near-normally distributed, we widen the credible interval corresponding to α while maintaining that the confidence level is α.

Let λ_{min} and λ_{max} denote the lower and upper limits of the resulting credible interval around $\bar{\lambda}$. Now, let us suppose that the attacker clocks the encryption up to the generation of the first keystream word. If this duration falls within the interval (see (5)):

$$[T'''_{const} + 31 \cdot T_{carry} \cdot (\bar{\lambda} - \lambda_{min}) + T^{(w)}_{const} + T_{carry} \cdot (\bar{\lambda} - \lambda_{min}) + T_{carry},$$

$$T'''_{const} + 31 \cdot T_{carry} \cdot (\bar{\lambda} - \lambda_{min}) + T^{(w)}_{const} + T_{carry} \cdot (\bar{\lambda} - \lambda_{min}) + 2 \cdot T_{carry})$$

$$= [T'''_{const} + T^{(w)}_{const} + 81 \cdot T_{carry} - 32 \cdot \lambda_{min} \cdot T_{carry},$$

$$T'''_{const} + T^{(w)}_{const} + 82 \cdot T_{carry} - 32 \cdot \lambda_{min} \cdot T_{carry}), \tag{7}$$

then the attacker concludes that the λ for iteration 1 of Algorithm 1 is 1 (just like T'_{const} and T_{carry}, the attacker can measure $T^{(w)}_{const}$). When this is the case, the attacker concludes that $k_{0(7)} = 0$ and $c_1 = 0$ with probability 5/7.   □

Given that $k_{0(7)}$ and c_1 are recovered, using $[d_{0(14)}d_{0(13)} \cdots d_{0(7)}] = [10001001]$, we arrive at Theorem 1.

Theorem 1. *When $c_1 = 0$ and $k_{0(7)} = 0$, we have:*

$$(k_{0(1)} \cdot k_{0(2)} \cdot \bar{k}_{0(3)} + k_{0(3)}) \cdot k_{0(4)} \cdot k_{0(5)} \cdot k_{0(6)} = 0, \tag{8}$$

with the '+' symbol denoting standard integer addition.

Proof. We begin by examining the addition of $[k_{0(7)}k_{0(6)} \cdots k_{0(0)}]$ and $[d_{0(14)}d_{0(13)} \cdots d_{0(7)}]$ while performing the first step of $Add(u32\ z_1, u32\ z_2)$. We know that the incoming carry at the MSB position (of the 31-bit z_1 or z_2) is c_1. Let $c_{1[-1]}, c_{1[-2]}, \ldots, c_{1[-7]}$ denote the incoming carries at the bit positions of $k_{0(6)}, k_{0(5)}, \ldots, k_{0(0)}$, respectively. For the sake of simplicity and clarity, we denote c_1 by $c_{1[0]}$. Now, we know that

$$c_{1[i+1]} = k_{0(i+7)} \cdot d_{0(i+14)} + c_{1[i]} \cdot (k_{0(i+7)} \oplus d_{0(i+14)}), i = -1, -2, \ldots, -7, \tag{9}$$

where the '+' denotes standard integer addition. Solving the recurrence equation (9), we arrive at (8).   □

---

[9] The term 'confidence level' is accepted in Bayesian inference also.

4.1 Complexities and Success Probabilities

The cache attack requires a few cache timing measurements for precision. If the S-boxes $S0$ and $S1$ are not in the cache, then Eve performs a few encryptions, using key-IV pairs of her choice, until the instant when Bob starts encrypting. We recall from Sect. 2 that the S-boxes are accessed twice in every iteration of Algorithm 5. From [8, Appendix A], we infer that 4 elements of $S0$ and $S1$ are used in every iteration of Algorithm 5. In the initialization mode, we have 32 similar iterations where F is computed and, hence, $S0$ and $S1$ accessed. Let η denote the number of iterations of Algorithm 5. Then, the total number of iterations per key-IV pair is $32 + 1 + \eta = 33 + \eta$ (includes one iteration of Algorithm 4). This translates to a total of $2 \cdot (33 + \eta)$ ($= \eta'$, say) draws of elements from each of $S0$ and $S1$. Assuming that the draws are uniform and independent, the probability that every 8-bit S-box element appears at least θ times in the list of draws is given by:

$$\frac{1}{256^{\eta'}} \cdot \left(\sum_{\substack{\omega_0, \omega_1, \ldots, \omega_{255} \in \mathbb{N}, \\ \omega_0 + \omega_1 + \ldots + \omega_{255} = \eta', \\ \omega_0 \geq \theta, \omega_1 \geq \theta, \ldots, \omega_{255} \geq \theta}} \binom{\eta'}{\omega_0, \omega_1, \ldots, \omega_{255}} \right), \qquad (10)$$

where θ is the number of quickly successive RAM-fetches after which the concerned memory element is placed in the cache. The problem now is to find the smallest η such that the probability given by (10) is reasonably close to 1. We are not aware of any simple method to solve this problem. However, when $\eta' = 256 \cdot \theta$, one *expects* that every element appears θ times in the list of *uniform and independent* draws. Given this, $\eta = 128 \cdot \theta - 33$. Therefore, the attack requires $128 \cdot \theta - 33$ keystream words to be generated with one key-IV pair. The time cost is $(128 \cdot \theta - 33) \cdot T_{KGA} + T_{ini}$, where T_{KGA} is the execution time of one iteration of the keystream generating algorithm (i.e., Algorithm 5) and T_{ini} is the initialization time. Alternatively, the attack can be performed with many key-IV pairs with each generating fewer keystream words. The time complexity in this case will obviously be higher than $(128 \cdot \theta - 33) \cdot T_{KGA} + T_{ini}$. But since the attacker does not require the keystream words for the attack (so it is an asynchronous attack even in the stricter viewpoint of Osvik et al. [15]), the data complexity is irrelevant here. Hence, we choose one key-IV pair and mount the attack in order to minimise its time complexity.

As an example, when $\theta = 100$, the pre-computation phase of the single-(key, IV) attack is expected to require $2^{13.64} \cdot T_{KGA} + T_{ini}$ time. In practice, θ is such that the time complexity is not significantly larger than that for $\theta = 100$, we believe. Besides, if the S-boxes are already in the cache, key recovery is almost immediate.

For the statistical timing attack, when the IV is unknown, the attack requires one 32-bit keystream word and the time needed to generate it. The success probability is less than $5/7$ because of the errors caused by the approximations involved in the attack. While it seems extremely tedious to accurately compute the error, its magnitude can intuitively be made negligible by choosing a wide credible interval as stated earlier.

4.2   Implications of the Attacks to 128-EEA3

The 3GPP encryption algorithm 128-EEA3 is also a stream cipher that is built around ZUC [7]. It uses a 128-bit "confidentiality key" (denoted in [7] as CK) and encrypts data in blocks of size ranging from 1 bit to 20 kbits. Aside from the ZUC algorithm, the 128-EEA3 contains the following main steps.

Key Initialization: The confidentiality key CK initialises the ZUC key in a straightforward manner as follows [7].
Let $CK = CK_0||CK_1||\ldots||CK_{15}$, where each CK_i is a byte. Then,

$$k_i = CK_i, \text{ for } i \in \{0, 1, \ldots, 15\}. \tag{11}$$

IV **Initialization:** The IV of ZUC is initialised using three parameters of ZUC, viz., $COUNT$, $BEARER$ and $DIRECTION$. The parameter $COUNT$ ($= COUNT_0||COUNT_1||\ldots||COUNT_4$, where each $COUNT_i$ is a byte) is a counter, $BEARER$ is a 5-bit "bearer identity" token and $DIRECTION$ is a single bit that indicates the direction of message transmission [7]. Given these, the IV of ZUC is initialised as:

$$iv_i = COUNT_i, \text{ for } i \in \{0, 1, 2, 3\},$$
$$iv_4 = BEARER||DIRECTION||00_2,$$
$$iv_5 = iv_6 = iv_7 = 00000000_2,$$
$$iv_j = iv_{j-8}, \text{ for } j \in \{8, 9, \ldots, 15\}.$$

From (11), it trivially follows that the timing attacks on ZUC are also attacks on the 128-EEA3, with the corresponding bits of the confidentiality key CK being (partially) recovered. In other words, if bit $k_{i(j)}$ of the ZUC key is recovered then the bit $CK_{i(j)}$ of the 128-EEA3's confidentiality key is recovered as well.

5   Countermeasures

In the previous sections, we described timing weaknesses that are mainly attributable to the design/implementation flaws listed in Observations 1 and 2. Consequently, we see the following countermeasures for the attacks that stem from these weaknesses:

1. A constant-time implementation of the modulo $(2^{31} - 1)$ addition in software and hardware.
2. A more involved key loading procedure.

Of course, a conservative approach would be to complicate the key loading procedure as well as implement the modulo $(2^{31} - 1)$ addition as a constant-time operation.

For the key loading procedure, we suggest the following alternatives:

1. *Applying a secure hash function to the s_i's of (1):* A preimage and timing attack resistant hash function would solve our problem, ideally, if applied to the s_i's of (1). The size of the string $[s_{15}s_{14} \ldots s_0]$ is 496 bits. For the countermeasure, this string is fed (after padding) into the compression function of a secure hash function, such as SHA-512 [13], on which there is no known preimage or timing attack despite years of scrutiny.[10] The 512-bit output is truncated to 496 bits, replacing $[s_{15}s_{14} \ldots s_0]$.

2. *Employing 16 carefully chosen, secret $N \times 31$ ($N \geq 31$) S-boxes:* The inputs to the S-boxes (call them B_i, $i \in \{0, 1, \ldots, 15\}$) are the s_i's of (1). When the S-boxes are all secret, $N = 31$ can suffice even though at least 15 input bits are known constants. This is because *(i)* S-boxes are secret, and *(ii)* S-boxes with outputs larger than inputs can still accomplish Shannon's *confusion* [18] (note that Shannon's *diffusion*, as interpreted by Massey in [12], does not apply to stream ciphers) [1].

   Recall that the timing attacks of Sect. 4 can recover only one bit of $B_0(s_0)$ and some information on 6 other bits. While these may be improved in the future (directions for this are provided in Sect. 6) to possibly recover more key bits, recovering an entire 31-bit block seems far-fetched. Actually, with the use of secret S-boxes it is no longer possible, in the first place, to perform the exact same analysis as in Sect. 4. This is because we will have unknown bits in place of the $d_{i(j)}$'s that constitute the MSBs of $z_1, z_2, \ldots, z_6$ (see Sect. 4). Therefore, even upon making precise timing measurements, the attacker will very likely have to guess the bits in place of the $d_{i(j)}$'s before trying to determine the bits in the LFSR. The attacker can, given precise timing measurements, find the number of 0's in $[z_{1(30)}z_{2(30)} \cdots z_{6(30)}]$, but is unlikely to be able to ascertain which bits are 0's. For example, the six z-bits being uniformly distributed (given that the S-boxes are secret) and the carries into the bit position 30 being distributed close to uniformly (see footnote 4), there is about $2^{-7.42}$ probability that there is no end carry.[11] Given that there is no end carry, the attacker deduces that there are fewer than two 1's in $[z_{1(30)}z_{2(30)} \cdots z_{6(30)}]$. Consequently, the attacker is able to recover at least 4 of the 6 z-bits but she cannot immediately ascertain if a particular bit guess is correct.

   Despite the seeming infeasibility, even if an entire 31-bit block $B_i(s_i)$ is recovered somehow, the input key bits cannot be recovered because B_i is secret.

   Caveat: As mentioned earlier, an S-box implemented as a lookup table is stored in the cache if its elements are used frequently. One should therefore

---

[10] There are, however, preimage attacks on step-reduced SHA-512 (see e.g. [2,10]). The best of these, due to Aoki *et al.* [2], works on 46 steps (out of the total 80), has a time complexity of $2^{511.5}$ and requires a memory of about 2^6 words.

[11] This probability is simply the ratio of the frequency corresponding to $\lambda = 0$ to the total of the frequencies corresponding to (6). The probability was 0 in the timing attacks of Sect. 4 because $d_{0(14)} = 1$ and $d_{15(7)} = 1$.

ensure that the B_i, $i \in \{0, 1, \ldots, 15\}$, are placed directly in the processor registers so that memory accesses are avoided. We borrow this idea from [15] where the authors also state that some architectures like the x86-64 and PowerPC AltiVec have register files sufficiently large to store large lookup tables.

Secret S-boxes have previously been used in ciphers (see e.g. GOST [21]). However, *security through obscurity* is in direct violation of the Shannon's maxim [18]. Using a hash function like SHA-512 may be practical provided that the ZUC key is not changed very often.

For the constant-time implementation in software, our suggestion is to change the *Add*() subroutine to the following (we call it "*AddC*()", with the 'C' denoting 'constant-time'):

```
u32 AddC(u32 x, u32 y) {
 u32 z = x + y;
 z = (z & 0x7FFFFFFF) + ((z & 0x80000000) >> 31);
 return z;
}
```

Osvik *et al.* provide some generic countermeasures against cache timing attacks in [15, Sect. 5]. We have already stated one of them, i.e., avoiding memory accesses by placing lookup tables in CPU registers wherever the architecture permits to do so. Some of the other suggestions of [15, Sect. 5] that are relevant to our cache timing analysis are:

1. disabling cache sharing,
2. disabling the cache mechanism per se,
3. adding noise to the cache access pattern (only mitigates the cache timing attack),
4. adding noise to the timing information (again, only mitigates the attack), and
5. providing secure execution of cryptographic primitives as operating system services.

Nomenclature: To facilitate future reference, we label some of the above, secure modifications of ZUC in Appendix B.

6 Conclusions

In this paper, we have presented timing attacks on the stream cipher ZUC that recover, under certain practical circumstances, one key bit along with some key-dependent information with about 0.7 success probability and negligible time, memory and data. To the best of our knowledge, these are the first attacks on the ZUC cipher of Version 1.5. The following are other highlights of this paper.

– This is one of the very few and early papers analysing the cache timing resistance of stream ciphers. As noted in [11], block ciphers (mainly the AES) have been the prominent targets of cache timing attacks. Besides, cache

timing analyses of stream ciphers are recent additions to the cryptanalysis literature, with the first paper (viz., [22]) being published as late as 2008 [11].
- The statistical timing attack is novel, to the best of our knowledge.
- The timing attacks of this paper warn that algorithms must be designed or implemented to resist single-round/iteration timing weaknesses. This single round can even belong to the key/IV setup of the cipher.

The weaknesses we have found that lead us to the attacks may be certificational. Nonetheless, we see a possibility for improving the attacks to recover a few other key bits by, for example, examining the cases where end carry is generated twice.

We have also proposed modifications to ZUC that resist not only the initiatory timing attacks but, evidently, also their potential improvements suggested above. Analysis of these new schemes comes across to us as an interesting problem for future research.

Acknowledgements. The author would like to thank Steve Babbage, Hongjun Wu, Erik Zenner and the anonymous referees of Inscrypt 2011 for their useful comments and suggestions.

References

1. Adams, C.M.: Constructing Symmetric Ciphers Using the CAST Design Procedure. Designs, Codes and Cryptography 12, 283–316 (1997)
2. Aoki, K., Guo, J., Matusiewicz, K., Sasaki, Y., Wang, L.: Preimages for Step-Reduced SHA-2. In: Matsui, M. (ed.) ASIACRYPT 2009. LNCS, vol. 5912, pp. 578–597. Springer, Heidelberg (2009)
3. Bellare, M., Kohno, T.: Hash Function Balance and Its Impact on Birthday Attacks. In: Cachin, C., Camenisch, J. (eds.) EUROCRYPT 2004. LNCS, vol. 3027, pp. 401–418. Springer, Heidelberg (2004)
4. Bernstein, D.J.: Cache-timing attacks on AES, Preprint (April 14, 2005), http://cr.yp.to/antiforgery/cachetiming-20050414.pdf
5. Carter, J.L., Wegman, M.N.: Universal Classes of Hash Functions. Journal of Computer and System Sciences 18(2), 143–154 (1979)
6. Data Assurance and Communication Security Research Center: "Workshop Presentations". First International Workshop on ZUC Algorithm, December 02-03 (2010), http://www.dacas.cn/zuc10/
7. Data Assurance and Communication Security Research Center: Specification of the 3GPP Confidentiality and Integrity Algorithms 128-EEA3 & 128-EIA3. Document 1: 128-EEA3 and 128-EIA3 Specification. ETSI/SAGE Specification, Version 1.5 (Latest) (January 04, 2011), http://www.gsmworld.com/documents/EEA3_EIA3_specification_v1_5.pdf
8. Data Assurance and Communication Security Research Center: Specification of the 3GPP Confidentiality and Integrity Algorithms 128-EEA3 & 128-EIA3. Document 2: ZUC Specification. ETSI/SAGE Specification, Version 1.5 (Latest) (January 04, 2011), http://gsmworld.com/documents/EEA3_EIA3_ZUC_v1_5.pdf

9. Fuhr, T., Gilbert, H., Reinhard, J.-R., Videau, M.: A Forgery Attack on the Candidate LTE Integrity Algorithm 128-EIA3. Cryptology ePrint Archive, Report 2010/618 (December 08, 2010), http://eprint.iacr.org/2010/618.pdf
10. Isobe, T., Shibutani, K.: Preimage Attacks on Reduced Tiger and SHA-2. In: Dunkelman, O. (ed.) FSE 2009. LNCS, vol. 5665, pp. 139–155. Springer, Heidelberg (2009)
11. Leander, G., Zenner, E., Hawkes, P.: Cache Timing Analysis of LFSR-Based Stream Ciphers. In: Parker, M.G. (ed.) Cryptography and Coding 2009. LNCS, vol. 5921, pp. 433–445. Springer, Heidelberg (2009)
12. Massey, J.L.: An Introduction to Contemporary Cryptology. Proceedings of the IEEE 76(5), 533–549 (1988)
13. National Institute of Standards and Technology: US Department of Commerce, "Secure Hash Standard (SHS)". Federal Information Processing Standards Publication, FIPS PUB 180-3 (October 2008),
    http://csrc.nist.gov/publications/fips/fips180-3/fips180-3_final.pdf
14. Nyberg, K., Wallén, J.: Improved Linear Distinguishers for SNOW 2.0. In: Robshaw, M.J.B. (ed.) FSE 2006. LNCS, vol. 4047, pp. 144–162. Springer, Heidelberg (2006)
15. Osvik, D.A., Shamir, A., Tromer, E.: Cache Attacks and Countermeasures: The Case of AES (Extended Version) (revised November 20, 2005), http://www.osvik.no/pub/cache.pdf; Original version: Pointcheval, D. (ed.) CT-RSA 2006. LNCS, vol. 3860, pp. 1–20. Springer, Heidelberg (2006)
16. Sarkar, P.: On Approximating Addition by Exclusive OR. Cryptology ePrint Archive, Report 2009/047 (February 03, 2009),
    http://eprint.iacr.org/2009/047.pdf
17. Sekar, G., Paul, S., Preneel, B.: New Weaknesses in the Keystream Generation Algorithms of the Stream Ciphers TPy and Py. In: Garay, J.A., Lenstra, A.K., Mambo, M., Peralta, R. (eds.) ISC 2007. LNCS, vol. 4779, pp. 249–262. Springer, Heidelberg (2007)
18. Shannon, C.E.: Communication Theory of Secrecy Systems. Bell Systems Technical Journal 28(4), 656–715 (1949)
19. Staffelbach, O., Meier, W.: Cryptographic Significance of the Carry for Ciphers Based on Integer Addition. In: Menezes, A., Vanstone, S.A. (eds.) CRYPTO 1990. LNCS, vol. 537, pp. 602–614. Springer, Heidelberg (1991)
20. Wu, H., Nguyen, P.H., Wang, H., Ling, S.: Cryptanalysis of the Stream Cipher ZUC in the 3GPP Confidentiality & Integrity Algorithms 128-EEA3 & 128-EIA3. Presentation at the Rump Session of ASIACRYPT 2010 (December 07, 2010),
    http://www.spms.ntu.edu.sg/Asiacrypt2010/
    Rump%20Session-%207%20Dec%202010/wu_rump_zuc.pdf
21. Gosudarstvennyi Standard: Cryptographic Protection for Data Processing Systems. Government Committee of the USSR for Standards, GOST 28147-89 (1989)
22. Zenner, E.: A Cache Timing Analysis of HC-256. In: Avanzi, R.M., Keliher, L., Sica, F. (eds.) SAC 2008. LNCS, vol. 5381, pp. 199–213. Springer, Heidelberg (2009)

A   Practical Occurrences of Γ_3, Γ_5 and Γ_6

Table 3 provides some example key-IV values that produce the favourable Γ-vectors (i.e., the vectors that generate end carry exactly once).

Table 3. Some practical occurrences of the vectors Γ_3, Γ_5 and Γ_6 (all entries except those in the last column are in hexadecimal); in each of these examples, $k_i, iv_i = 0 \, \forall \, i \neq 0$

k_0	iv_0	z_1	z_2	z_3	z_4	z_5	z_6	$[c_1 c_2 \ldots c_5 z_{1(30)}]$
0	0	44D700	44D70000	10000AF1	1AF1	1A0000F1	56000047	$[000010]$ (Γ_6)
5	5	2C4D705	44D70505	10000AF1	1AF1	1A0000F1	56000047	$[000010]$ (Γ_6)
2F	2B	17C4D72B	44D72B2F	10000AF1	1AF1	1A0000F1	56000047	$[000100]$ (Γ_5)
31	2E	18C4D72E	44D72E31	10000AF1	1AF1	1A0000F1	56000047	$[000100]$ (Γ_6)
6E	5C	3744D75C	44D75C6E	10000AF1	1AF1	1A0000F1	56000047	$[010000]$ (Γ_3)
75	E	3AC4D70E	44D70E75	10000AF1	1AF1	1A0000F1	56000047	$[010000]$ (Γ_3)

B   ZUC Modifications

We list our proposed algorithm/implementation modifications in Table 4.

Table 4. ZUC modifications: To each label we suffix a '+' if one or more of the generic countermeasures suggested by Osvik *et al.* in [15] are applied

Label	Reference
ZUC-1.5C	Constant-time software implementation of modulo $(2^{31} - 1)$ addition
ZUC-1.5H	Involved key loading: hash function
ZUC-1.5S	Involved key loading: S-boxes
ZUC-1.5CH	Constant-time implementation of modulo $(2^{31} - 1)$ addition along with involved key loading using a hash function
ZUC-1.5CS	Constant-time implementation of modulo $(2^{31} - 1)$ addition along with involved key loading using S-boxes

Batching Multiple Protocols to Improve Efficiency of Multi-Party Computation

Naoto Kiribuchi[1], Ryo Kato[1], Takashi Nishide[2], and Hiroshi Yoshiura[1]

[1] The University of Electro-Communications, 1-5-1 Chofugaoka, Chofu-shi, Tokyo,
182-8585, Japan
[2] Kyushu University, 744 Motooka Nishi-ku, Fukuoka, 819-0395, Japan

Abstract. It is becoming more and more important to make use of personal or classified information while keeping it confidential. A promising tool for meeting this challenge is secure multi-party computation (MPC). It enables multiple parties, each given a snippet of a secret s, to compute a function $f(s)$ by communicating with each other without revealing s. However, one of the biggest problems with MPC is that it requires a vast amount of communication. Much research has gone into making each protocol (equality testing, interval testing, etc.) more efficient. In this work, we make a set of multiple protocols more efficient by transforming these protocols to be batched and propose four protocols: "Batch Logical OR," "Batch Logical AND," "Batch Logical OR-AND," and "Batch Logical AND-OR." Existing logical OR and logical AND protocols consisting of t equality testing invocations have a communication complexity of $O(\ell t)$, where ℓ is the bit length of the secret. Our batched versions of these protocols reduce it to $O(\ell+t)$. For t interval testing invocations, they reduce both communication complexity and round complexity. Thus they can make the queries on a secret shared database more efficient. For example, the use of the proposed protocols reduces the communication complexity for a query consisting of equality testing and interval testing by approximately 70% compared to the use of the corresponding existing protocols. The concept of the proposed protocols is versatile and can be applied to logical formulas consisting of protocols other than equality testing and interval testing, thereby making them more efficient as well.

Keywords: Multi-party Computation, Secret Sharing, Secret Shared Database.

1 Introduction

Although gathering personal information (e.g., age, address, and buying history) and using it directly or via data mining enable the provision of higher quality services, leakage of such information has become a serious problem. Likewise, sensor logs can provide valuable information, but data leakage can be a problem. Moreover, in cloud computing, the confidentiality of remotely located personal or classified information must be guaranteed. It has thus become more important to balance data availability against information confidentiality.

C.-K. Wu, M. Yung, and D. Lin (Eds.): Inscrypt 2011, LNCS 7537, pp. 289–308, 2012.
© Springer-Verlag Berlin Heidelberg 2012

A promising tool for meeting this challenge is secure multi-party computation(MPC). Here we focus on MPC based on Shamir's (k, n) threshold secret sharing [9] in which a "share," or snippet, of secret information is distributed to n parties, and the parties can reconstruct the secret by gathering k shares.

MPC based on Shamir's scheme enables multiple parties to obtain a function value for secrets without revealing them. Various existing protocols (e.g., addition, multiplication, equality testing, and comparison) [1, 4–7, 10] enable the construction of such a function for using personal or classified information and thus can be used to balance data availability against information confidentiality.

However, one of the biggest problems with MPC is that it requires a vast amount of communication. The multiplication protocol, which obtains the product of secrets $a, b \in \mathbb{Z}_p$, requires $n(n-1)$ times communication since n parties communicate with each other. The complexity of MPC for protocols other than multiplication, such as comparison and equality testing, is evaluated in terms of communication complexity and round complexity. The communication complexity indicates the number of times the multiplication protocol is used. The round complexity indicates the number of invocations of the parallelized multiplication protocol.

Much research has gone into reducing the communication and round complexity of each protocol. For example, the communication complexity of equality testing for secrets $a, b \in \mathbb{Z}_p$ is 81ℓ multiplication invocations, and the round complexity is 8 parallelized multiplication invocations (8 rounds), where ℓ is the bit length of prime number p [7]. However, in the case of a 32-bit secret, the equality testing requires $2,592$ multiplication invocations, and the total amount of communicated data reaches 202.5 Kbytes for five participants. Hence, to execute larger computation in practical applications, MPC will need to be made more efficient.

Our Contribution. In this work, we make such logical formulas as formula (1) more efficient.

$$F_1 \vee F_2 \vee \cdots \vee F_t \tag{1}$$

These logical formulas consist of multiple protocols (F_i) that are connected by logical operators ($\vee$ and $\wedge$). The symbol F_i denotes a Boolean protocol (e.g., equality testing, comparison, interval testing) that outputs truth value. The logical formulas taken up are used in many applications such as querying for a secret shared database, searching a file for a character string, and determining whether the given information is included in a list or not. It is therefore important to make such a logical formula more efficient.

Existing Boolean protocols (F_i) output shares of 1 as true or shares of 0 as false. The proposed batched protocols use F_i', which outputs shares of 0 as true or shares of non-zero value as false. We refer to the *alternative protocol of F_i* as F_i'. The basic concept in this approach is to represent truth values by shares of 0 and shares of a non-zero value using alternative protocols F_i' that are more efficient than F_i, and to make a logical formula consisting of multiple protocols

Table 1. Complexities of logical formulas using existing or proposed protocols

Logical formula	Communication		Round	
	Existing	Proposed	Existing	Proposed
$\bigvee_{i=1}^{t} F_i$ $\bigwedge_{i=1}^{t} F_i$	$\sum_{i=1}^{t} c_i$ $+t-1$	$\sum_{i=1}^{t} c'_i$ $+t+c_{\mathbf{EQ}}-1$	$\max(r_1,\ldots,r_t)$ $+\lceil \log_2 t \rceil$	$\max(r'_1,\ldots,r'_t)$ $+r_{\mathbf{EQ}}+\lceil \log_2 t \rceil$
$\bigvee_{i=1}^{u}\bigwedge_{j=1}^{v} F_{i,j}$ $\bigwedge_{i=1}^{u}\bigvee_{j=1}^{v} F_{i,j}$	$\sum_{i,j=1}^{u,v} c_{i,j}$ $+uv-1$	$\sum_{i,j=1}^{u,v} c'_{i,j}$ $+uv+c_{\mathbf{EQ}}-1$	$\max(r_{1,1},\ldots,r_{u,v})$ $+\lceil \log_2 uv \rceil$	$\max(r'_{1,1},\ldots,r'_{u,v})$ $+r_{\mathbf{EQ}}+\lceil \log_2 uv \rceil$

Table 2. Complexities of the logical formula consisting of equality testing or interval testing in Table 1

F_i	Communication		Round	
	Existing	Proposed	Existing	Proposed
$x_i = y_i$	$81\ell t + t - 1$	$81\ell + t - 1$	$8 + \lceil \log_2 t \rceil$	$8 + \lceil \log_2 t \rceil$
$d_i < x_i < e_i$	$110\ell t + 2t - 1$	$\sum_{i=1}^{t}(e_i - d_i)$ $-t + 81\ell - 1$	$13 + \lceil \log_2 t \rceil$	$8 + \lceil \log_2 t \rceil$ $+ \max(\lceil \log_2(e_i - d_i - 1)\rceil)$

more efficient by batching the truth values and converting them into shares of 1 and shares of 0.

Suppose the complexities for Boolean protocol F_i are c_i multiplications and r_i rounds, and the complexities for its alternative protocol F'_i are c'_i multiplications and r'_i rounds. Moreover, the complexities for equality testing are $c_{\mathbf{EQ}}$ multiplications and $r_{\mathbf{EQ}}$ rounds. Table 1 shows that the complexities of the logical formulas depend on F_i and F'_i. If $t = u \times v$, the effects of using the proposed protocols are equal since both the complexities of the existing and proposed protocols are represented by the same formula. As shown in Table 2, if all the F_i protocols in a logical formula are equality testing ($x_i = y_i$), although proposed protocols do not reduce round complexity, they reduce the upper bound of the communication complexity from $O(\ell t)$ to $O(\ell + t)$, where ℓ is the bit length of prime number p used in $x_i, y_i \in \mathbb{Z}_p$. For example, for equality testing with $\ell = 32$ bits and $t = 3$, the proposed protocols reduce the communication complexity by approximately 67%. If all the F_i protocols in the formula are interval testing ($d_i < x_i < e_i$), proposed protocols reduce both communication and round complexity for some d_i and e_i. For interval testings with $\ell = 32$ bits and $t = 3$, proposed protocols reduce the communication complexity and round complexity by approximately 75% and 3 rounds.

The proposed protocols are applied to a secret shared database in Section 5. A search example shows that a proposed protocol reduces the communication complexity and round complexity by approximately 70% and 1 round for a query consisting of equality testing and interval testing. An information presence example shows that a proposed protocol reduces the communication complexity to approximately $\frac{1}{81\ell}$ for a query designed to determine whether the given information is in a list or not.

The organization of this paper is as follows. In Section 2, we explain MPC based on Shamir's (k, n) threshold secret sharing scheme. In Section 3, we introduce our batched protocols and discuss their complexity, correctness, and security. In Section 4, we describe how the logical protocols are modified, enabling them to be batched, and discuss the complexity, correctness, and security of the batched protocols. In Section 5, we describe two example applications of these protocols and their complexities. We conclude in Section 6 with a summary of the key points.

2   Related Work

2.1   Notation

- p: an ℓ-bit prime number
- $[a]_p$: a set of shares of secret $a \in \mathbb{Z}_p$
- $[a]_p + [b]_p$: shares of addition $[a + b \pmod{p}]_p$, where secrets $a, b \in \mathbb{Z}_p$
- $[a]_p \times [b]_p$: shares of multiplication $[a \times b \pmod{p}]_p$, where secrets $a, b \in \mathbb{Z}_p$
- $[a = b]_p$: shares of result of equality testing $a = b$, where secrets $a, b \in \mathbb{Z}_p$

2.2   Shamir's (k, n) Threshold Secret Sharing

Given a secret $s \in \mathbb{Z}_p$, Shamir's (k, n) threshold secret sharing scheme generates a polynomial,

$$f(x) = s + r_1 x + r_2 x^2 + \cdots + r_{k-1} x^{k-1} \pmod{p}, \qquad (2)$$

where $r_i \in \mathbb{Z}_p$ is a random number $(1 \leq i \leq k - 1)$. Each of n parties P_d is given a share, $f(d)$ $(1 \leq d \leq n)$. To reconstruct the secret, the parties must gather k shares.

2.3   Multi-Party Computation Based on Secret Sharing Scheme

Because MPC requires a vast amount of communication, complexity for MPC is evaluated in terms of communication. Basic protocols for MPC are addition and multiplication.

Addition Protocol. Given secrets $a, b \in \mathbb{Z}_p$, the addition protocol obtains $[c]_p = [a + b \pmod{p}]_p$ without revealing a, b. To compute $[c]_p$, each party simply adds $[a]_p$ and $[b]_p$ on $\mathbb{Z}_p$ independently. The complexity of the addition protocol is negligible since communication is unnecessary.

Multiplication Protocol. Given secrets $a, b \in \mathbb{Z}_p$, the multiplication protocol obtains $[c]_p = [a \times b \pmod{p}]_p$ without revealing a, b. The details are reported elsewhere [1, 5]. The communication complexity of the multiplication protocol is evaluated on the basis of the number of times the parties communicate with each other. As mentioned above, one invocation of the multiplication protocol requires $n(n-1)$ communications since n parties communicate with each other. However, if secret $a \in \mathbb{Z}_p$ and public value $e \in \mathbb{Z}_p$ are given, the computation of $[c]_p = [a \times e]_p$ requires no communication. Moreover, the complexity of computing any second-order polynomial, such as $[c]_p = [a^2 + b^2]_p$, is one multiplication operation [8].

Communication and Round Complexity. The complexities of MPC are evaluated in term of the communication complexity and round complexity. The communication complexity is represented as the number of multiplication protocol invocations. The round complexity represents the parallelized number of multiplication protocols. For example, the complexities of $[a]_p \times [b]_p \times [c]_p \times [d]_p$ are 3 (invocations of) multiplications and 3 rounds if we obtain $[a]_p \times [b]_p$, $[a]_p \times [b]_p \times [c]_p$, and $[a]_p \times [b]_p \times [c]_p \times [d]_p$ in sequence. On the other hand, if we obtain $[a]_p \times [b]_p$ and $[c]_p \times [d]_p$ in parallel, the complexities are 3 multiplications and 2 rounds. We evaluate the round complexity of a protocol by performing the multiplication protocol in parallel as much as possible.

Equality Testing Protocol. Given secrets $a, b \in \mathbb{Z}_p$, this protocol outputs $[1]_p$ if $a = b$ and $[0]_p$ if $a \neq b$ without revealing a, b.

Cramer and Damgård proposed an equality testing protocol using Fermat's little theorem [3]. It was implemented by Burkhart et al. [2]. The complexities of this protocol are $O(\ell)$ multiplications and $O(\ell)$ rounds, and round complexity depends on ℓ. Damgård et al. proposed an equality testing protocol that requires $98\ell + 94\ell \log_2 \ell$ multiplications and 39 rounds and that uses a bit-decomposition protocol [4]. The round complexity of this protocol is independent of ℓ. Nishide and Ohta proposed an equality testing protocol that requires 81ℓ multiplications and 8 rounds [7]. However, in the case of a 32-bit secret, it requires $2,592$ multiplications, and the total amount of communicated data is 202.5 Kbytes for five participants. Hence, as mentioned above, MPC will need to be more efficient for larger computation with practical efficiency.

Although much research has gone into reducing the complexity of each protocol, there have been no proposals for making operations that require multiple protocols more efficient.

3   Proposed Protocols

3.1   Key Ideas

Existing Boolean protocols (F_i) output $[1]_p$ as true or $[0]_p$ as false. The proposed protocols use secure MPC protocols (F_i') that output $[0]_p$ as true or a set of shares of a non-zero value as false. We call protocol F_i' the alternative protocol of protocol F_i. The key ideas are to represent truth values by $[0]_p$ and a set of

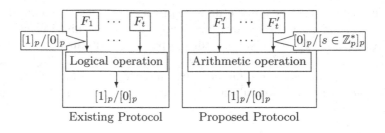

Fig. 1. Key ideas of proposed protocols

shares of non-zero value by using the alternative protocols (F_i') that are more efficient than F_i, and to make a logical formula consisting of multiple protocols (F_i) more efficient by batching the truth values and converting them into $[1]_p$ and $[0]_p$ using arithmetic operations (Fig. 1).

In this section, we describe four protocols that make a logical formula consisting of Boolean protocols (F_i's) more efficient by using alternative protocols (F_i'''s).

3.2   Batch Logical OR Protocol

The Batch Logical OR protocol obtains the result of the following logical formula consisting of F_i's by using alternative protocols F_i'''s for $1 \le i \le t$.

$$F_1 \vee F_2 \vee \cdots \vee F_t \tag{3}$$

It outputs $[1]_p$ if the formula is true and $[0]_p$ if the formula is false. Protocol 1 shows the steps in this protocol. Let F_i' be as follows.

$$F_i' = \begin{cases} [0]_p & \text{if } F_i = \textbf{true} \\ \left[v \in \mathbb{Z}_p^*\right]_p & \text{if } F_i = \textbf{false} \end{cases} \tag{4}$$

Protocol 2 shows the sub protocol used in the proposed ones. Given an operation $\circ$ and shares $[x_1]_p, \ldots, [x_t]_p$, it obtains shares of $(x_1 \circ x_2) \circ \cdots \circ (x_{t-1} \circ x_t)$ in parallel with $t - 1$ multiplications and $\lceil \log_2 t \rceil$ rounds.

Correctness of Batch Logical OR Protocol. If logical formula (3) is true, there exists j such that F_j is true. Thus, there exists F_j' such that $F_j' = [0]_p$. Hence, the output of the Batch Logical OR protocol is as follows.

Protocol 1. Batch Logical OR

1: $[temp]_p \leftarrow \textbf{DoParallel}(\times, F_1', \ldots, F_t')$ // **DoParallel** is defined in **Protocol 2**
2: **return** $[0 = temp]_p$

Protocol 2. DoParallel($\circ, [x_1]_p, \ldots, [x_t]_p$)

1: **if** $1 < t$ **then**
2:     **foreach** $i \in \{1, \ldots, \lfloor \frac{t}{2} \rfloor\}$ **do in parallel**
3:         $[y_i]_p \leftarrow [x_{2i-1}]_p \circ [x_{2i}]_p$
4:     **end foreach**
5:     **if** t is even **then**
6:         $[z]_p \leftarrow$ **DoParallel**($\circ, [y_1]_p, \ldots, [y_{\lfloor \frac{t}{2} \rfloor}]_p$)
7:     **else**
8:         $[z]_p \leftarrow$ **DoParallel**($\circ, [y_1]_p, \ldots, [y_{\lfloor \frac{t}{2} \rfloor}]_p, [x_t]_p$)
9:     **end if**
10: **else**
11:     $[z]_p \leftarrow [x_1]_p$
12: **end if**
13: **return** $[z]_p$ // $z = (x_1 \circ x_2) \circ \cdots \circ (x_{t-1} \circ x_t)$

1: $[temp]_p \leftarrow$ **DoParallel**($\times, F'_1, \ldots, F'_t$) // $[temp]_p = [0]_p$
2: **return** $[0 = temp]_p$ // $[0 = temp]_p =$ **true**$= [1]_p$

Therefore, the Batch Logical OR protocol outputs "true" if logical formula (3) is true.

If logical formula (3) is false, all F_i's output "false". Thus, all F'_i's output a non-zero value. Although **DoParallel**($\times, F'_1, \ldots, F'_t$) is computed over $\mathbb{Z}_p$, the product is a non-zero value since p is a prime number. Hence, the output of the Batch Logical OR protocol is as follows.

1: $[temp]_p \leftarrow$ **DoParallel**($\times, F'_1, \ldots, F'_t$) // $[temp]_p = [v \in \mathbb{Z}_p^*]_p$
2: **return** $[0 = temp]_p$ // $[0 = temp]_p =$ **false**$= [0]_p$

Therefore, the Batch Logical OR protocol outputs "false" if logical formula (3) is false.

Since the output of Batch Logical OR is equal to that of formula (3), the Batch Logical OR protocol is correct.

Complexity of Batch Logical OR Protocol. Let the complexities of a protocol F_i be c_i multiplications and r_i rounds, and let the complexities of its alternative protocol F'_i be c'_i multiplications and r'_i rounds. Moreover, let the complexities of equality testing be $c_{\mathbf{EQ}}$ multiplications and $r_{\mathbf{EQ}}$ rounds.

For the existing protocols, the complexities of logical formula (3) are as follows. First, the parties obtain t F_i's in parallel. The complexities of this step are $\sum_{i=1}^{t} c_i$ multiplications and $\max(r_1, \ldots, r_t)$ rounds, where $\max(x_1, \ldots, x_t)$ is the maximum of $x_1, \ldots, x_t$. Then, the parties obtain logical OR in parallel. For sets of shares $[a]_p, [b]_p$ of truth values $a, b \in \{0, 1\}$, the logical OR $[a \vee b]_p$ is computed using $[a \vee b]_p = [a]_p + [b]_p - [a \times b]_p$. Thus, the complexities of a set of logical OR $[a \vee b]_p$ are 1 multiplication and 1 round. For logical formula (3), the complexities of $t - 1$ sets of logical OR are $t - 1$ multiplications and

Table 3. Complexities of logical formula (3)

Protocol	Communication	Round
Existing	$(\sum_{i=1}^{t} c_i) + t - 1$	$\max(r_1, \ldots, r_t) + \lceil \log_2 t \rceil$
Batch Logical OR	$(\sum_{i=1}^{t} c_i') + t + c_{\mathbf{EQ}} - 1$	$\max(r_1', \ldots, r_t') + r_{\mathbf{EQ}} + \lceil \log_2 t \rceil$

$\lceil \log_2 t \rceil$ rounds. Therefore, the total complexities of logical formula (3) with the existing protocols are $(\sum_{i=1}^{t} c_i) + t - 1$ multiplications and $\max(r_1, \ldots, r_t) + \lceil \log_2 t \rceil$ rounds.

On the other hand, the complexities of logical formula (3) using the Batch Logical OR protocol are as follows. First, the parties obtain t F_i'''s in parallel. The complexities of this step are $\sum_{i=1}^{t} c_i'$ multiplications and $\max(r_1', \ldots, r_t')$ rounds. Then, the parties obtain $[temp]_p$ by multiplying the F_i'''s in parallel, as shown in Figure 2. The complexities of this step are $t - 1$ multiplications and $\lceil \log_2 t \rceil$ rounds. Finally, the parties obtain the result $[0 = temp]_p$. The complexities of this step are $c_{\mathbf{EQ}}$ multiplications and $r_{\mathbf{EQ}}$ rounds. Therefore, the total complexities are $(\sum_{i=1}^{t} c_i') + t + c_{\mathbf{EQ}} - 1$ multiplications and $\max(r_1', \ldots, r_t') + r_{\mathbf{EQ}} + \lceil \log_2 t \rceil$ rounds. Table 3 shows the complexities of logical formula (3).

The conditions for the Batch Logical OR protocol to be more efficient than the existing protocols are as follows. The condition for communication complexity is

$$\left(\sum_{i=1}^{t} c_i' \right) + t + c_{\mathbf{EQ}} - 1 < \left(\sum_{i=1}^{t} c_i \right) + t - 1 \tag{5}$$

$$\left(\sum_{i=1}^{t} c_i' \right) + c_{\mathbf{EQ}} < \sum_{i=1}^{t} c_i. \tag{6}$$

This inequality means that the sum of the communication complexity of alternative protocols F_i'''s and equality testing is less than that of the original protocols F_i's. The condition for round complexity is

$$\max(r_1', \ldots, r_t') + r_{\mathbf{EQ}} + \lceil \log_2 t \rceil < \max(r_1, \ldots, r_t) + \lceil \log_2 t \rceil \tag{7}$$

$$\max(r_1', \ldots, r_t') + r_{\mathbf{EQ}} < \max(r_1, \ldots, r_t). \tag{8}$$

This inequality means that the sum of the round complexity of equality testing and the maximum of the round complexity of alternative protocols F_i'''s is less than the maximum of the original protocols F_i's.

3.3 Batch Logical AND Protocol

The Batch Logical AND protocol obtains the result of the following logical formula consisting of F_i's by using alternative protocols F_i'''s for $1 \le i \le t$.

$$F_1 \wedge F_2 \wedge \cdots \wedge F_t \tag{9}$$

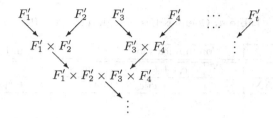

Fig. 2. Parallelized operation of Batch Logical OR (Step 1)

Protocol 3. Batch Logical AND

Require: $p \equiv 3 \pmod 4$
1: $[temp]_p \leftarrow$ **DoParallel**$(\star, F_1', \ldots, F_t')$ $//$ $[a]_p \star [b]_p := [a]_p^2 + [b]_p^2$
2: **return** $[0 = temp]_p$

It outputs $[1]_p$ if the formula is true and $[0]_p$ if the formula is false. We construct this protocol assuming prime number $p \equiv 3 \pmod 4$ and then modify it to remove the requirement for prime number p. Protocol 3 shows steps in this protocol.

Correctness of Batch Logical AND Protocol. If logical formula (9) is true, all F_i''s output $[0]_p$. Thus, $[temp]_p$ in Protocol 3 is always $[0]_p$, and the output is $[1]_p$. Therefore, the Batch Logical AND protocol outputs "true" if logical formula (9) is true.

If logical formula (9) is false, there exists j such that $F_j' \neq [0]_p$. We rewrite the operation $\star$ in Protocol 3 as follows for simplicity.

$$\gamma \leftarrow \alpha^2 + \beta^2 \pmod p \tag{10}$$

Let $0 \leq \alpha < p$ and $0 < \beta = F_j' < p$. We show that γ is a non-zero value.

For $\alpha = 0$, $\gamma \neq 0$ since $\gamma = \beta^2 \pmod p$, $\beta \neq 0$.

For $\alpha \neq 0$, if $\gamma = 0$, the following equation is true.

$$-\alpha^2 = \beta^2 \pmod p \tag{11}$$

The Legendre symbol on the left-hand side of equation (11) is as follows since $p \equiv 3 \pmod 4$.

$$\left(\frac{-\alpha^2}{p}\right) = \left(\frac{-1}{p}\right) = (-1)^{\frac{p-1}{2}} = -1 \tag{12}$$

The Legendre symbol on the right-hand side of the equation is as follows.

$$\left(\frac{\beta^2}{p}\right) = 1 \tag{13}$$

We now have a contradiction between the left-hand side and the right-hand side. Hence, $\gamma \neq 0$.

Table 4. Complexities of logical formula (9)

Protocol	Communication	Round
Existing	$(\sum_{i=1}^{t} c_i) + t - 1$	$\max(r_1, \ldots, r_t) + \lceil \log_2 t \rceil$
Batch Logical AND	$(\sum_{i=1}^{t} c_i') + t + c_{\mathbf{EQ}} - 1$	$\max(r_1', \ldots, r_t') + r_{\mathbf{EQ}} + \lceil \log_2 t \rceil$

Thus, $\gamma \neq 0$ for $0 \leq \alpha < p$ and $0 < \beta = F_j' < p$. This means $temp$ is a non-zero value if there exists j such that $F_j' \neq [0]_p$. Therefore, the Batch Logical AND protocol outputs "false" if logical formula (9) is false.

Since the output of the Batch Logical AND is equal to that of formula (9), the Batch Logical AND protocol is correct.

Complexity of Batch Logical AND Protocol. For the existing protocols, the complexities of logical formula (9) are as follows. First, the parties obtain t F_i's in parallel. The complexities of this step are $\sum_{i=1}^{t} c_i$ multiplications and $\max(r_1, \ldots, r_t)$ rounds. Then, the parties obtain logical AND in parallel. For sets of shares of $[a]_p, [b]_p$, where truth values $a, b \in \{0, 1\}$, the logical AND $[a \wedge b]_p$ is computed using $[a \wedge b]_p = [a \times b]_p$. Thus, the complexities of a set of logical AND $[a \wedge b]_p$ are 1 multiplication and 1 round. For logical formula (9), the complexities of $t - 1$ sets of logical AND are $t - 1$ multiplications and $\lceil \log_2 t \rceil$ rounds. Therefore, the total complexities of logical formula (9) with the existing protocols are $(\sum_{i=1}^{t} c_i) + t - 1$ multiplications and $\max(r_1, \ldots, r_t) + \lceil \log_2 t \rceil$ rounds.

On the other hand, the complexities of logical formula (9) for the Batch Logical AND protocol are as follows. First, the parties obtain t F_i'''s in parallel. The complexities of this step are $\sum_{i=1}^{t} c'$ multiplications and $\max(r_1', \ldots, r_t')$ rounds. Then, the parties obtain $[temp]_p$ at Step 1 in Protocol 3 in parallel. Since $[a]_p^2 + [b]_p^2$ is second-order, the complexity of this formula is 1 multiplication, as mentioned in Section 2. Thus, the complexities of this step are $t - 1$ multiplications and $\lceil \log_2 t \rceil$ rounds. Finally, the parties obtain the result $[0 = temp]_p$. The complexities of this step are $c_{\mathbf{EQ}}$ multiplications and $r_{\mathbf{EQ}}$ rounds. Therefore, the total complexities of formula (9) with the Batch Logical AND protocol are $(\sum_{i=1}^{t} c_i') + t + c_{\mathbf{EQ}} - 1$ multiplications and $\max(r_1', \ldots, r_t') + r_{\mathbf{EQ}} + \lceil \log_2 t \rceil$ rounds. Table 4 shows the complexities of logical formula (9).

As shown in Tables 3 and 4, the complexities of the Batch Logical AND are equal to those of the Batch Logical OR, and the complexities of the corresponding existing protocols are also equal. Hence, the conditions for the Batch Logical AND protocol to be more efficient than the existing protocols are the same as those for the Batch Logical OR protocol. Therefore, the condition for communication complexity is formula (6), and the condition for round complexity is formula (8).

Protocol 4. Batch Logical OR-AND

Require: $p \equiv 3 \pmod 4$
1: **foreach** $i \in \{1, \ldots, u\}$ **do in parallel**
2:     $[row_i]_p \leftarrow$ **DoParallel**$(\star, F'_{i,1}, \ldots, F'_{i,v})$ // $[a]_p \star [b]_p := [a]_p^2 + [b]_p^2$
3: **end foreach**
4: $[temp]_p \leftarrow$ **DoParallel**$(\times, [row_1]_p, \ldots, [row_u]_p)$
5: **return** $[0 = temp]_p$

Requirement Removal. Protocol 3 requires $p \equiv 3 \pmod 4$. We can modify Step 1 of Protocol 3 as follows for $p \equiv 1 \pmod 4$.

$$[temp]_p \leftarrow \textbf{DoParallel}(\diamond, F'_1, \ldots, F'_t), \tag{14}$$

where $[a]_p \diamond [b]_p := [a]_p^2 + y[b]_p^2$ and y is a public value defined such that $\left(\dfrac{y}{p} \right) = -1$. We can see that the correctness of this protocol is the same as above. Furthermore, its complexity is the same as above.

3.4   Batch Logical OR-AND Protocol

The Batch Logical OR-AND protocol obtains the result of the following logical formula consisting of $F_{i,j}$'s by using alternative protocols $F'_{i,j}$'s for $1 \le i \le u, 1 \le j \le v$.

$$
\begin{aligned}
\{F_{1,1} \wedge F_{1,2} \wedge \cdots \quad &\wedge F_{1,v}\} \vee \\
\{F_{2,1} \wedge F_{2,2} \wedge \cdots \quad &\wedge F_{2,v}\} \vee \\
\cdots \quad &\vee \\
\{F_{u,1} \wedge F_{u,2} \wedge \cdots \quad &\wedge F_{u,v}\}
\end{aligned}
\tag{15}
$$

It outputs $[1]_p$ if the formula is true and $[0]_p$ if the formula is false. Protocol 4 shows the steps in this protocol for prime number $p \equiv 3 \pmod 4$. We can modify these steps for $p \equiv 1 \pmod 4$ by applying the same technique as in Section 3.3.

Correctness of Batch Logical OR-AND Protocol. The Batch Logical OR-AND protocol is a combination of the Batch Logical OR and Batch Logical AND protocols. $[row_i]_p$ is $[0]_p$ if the following logical formula is true and is a set of shares of a non-zero value if it is false.

$$F_{i,1} \wedge F_{i,2} \wedge \cdots \wedge F_{i,v} \tag{16}$$

This step is part of the Batch Logical AND protocol, and its correctness is shown in Section 3.3. The remaining steps, which determine whether $[0]_p$ is present in u sets of shares, are the same as those in the Batch Logical OR protocol. Since the correctness of the Batch Logical OR protocol is shown in Section 3.2, the Batch Logical OR-AND protocol is correct.

Complexity of Batch Logical OR-AND Protocol. For the existing protocols, the complexities of logical formula (15) are as follows. First, the parties obtain $u \times v$ $F_{i,j}$'s in parallel. The complexities of this step are $\sum_{i=1}^{u} \sum_{j=1}^{v} c_{i,j}$ multiplications and $\max(r_{1,1}, r_{1,2}, \ldots, r_{u,v})$ rounds. Then, the parties obtain $(v-1)u$ sets of logical AND in parallel. The complexities of this step are $(v-1)u$ multiplications and $\lceil \log_2 uv \rceil$ rounds. Finally, the parties obtain $u-1$ sets of logical OR in parallel. The complexities of this step are $u-1$ multiplications and $\lceil \log_2 u \rceil$ rounds. Therefore, the total complexities are $(\sum_{i=1}^{u} \sum_{j=1}^{v} c_{i,j}) + uv - 1$ multiplications and $\max(r_{1,1}, r_{1,2}, \ldots, r_{u,v}) + \lceil \log_2 uv \rceil$ rounds.

On the other hand, the complexities of logical formula (15) using the Batch Logical OR-AND protocol are as follows. Since the step that obtains $[row_i]_p$ for each i is the same as that in the Batch Logical AND protocol, the complexities of this step are $\sum_{i=1}^{u} \sum_{j=1}^{v} c'_{i,j} + (v-1)u$ multiplications and $\max(r'_{1,1}, \ldots, r'_{u,v}) + \lceil \log_2 v \rceil$ rounds. Then, the parties obtain logical OR in parallel. Since this step is the same as that in the Batch Logical OR protocol for u sets of F_i's, the complexities of this step are $u-1$ multiplications and $\lceil \log_2 u \rceil$ rounds. Finally, the parties obtain the result $[0 = temp]_p$. The complexities of this step are $c_{\mathbf{EQ}}$ multiplications and $r_{\mathbf{EQ}}$ rounds. Therefore, the total complexities are $(\sum_{i=1}^{u} \sum_{j=1}^{v} c'_{i,j}) + uv + c_{\mathbf{EQ}} - 1$ multiplications and $\max(r'_{1,1}, r'_{1,2}, \ldots, r'_{u,v}) + r_{\mathbf{EQ}} + \lceil \log_2 uv \rceil$ rounds.

The conditions for the Batch Logical OR-AND protocol to be more efficient than the existing protocols are as follows. The condition for communication complexity is

$$\left(\sum_{i=1}^{u} \sum_{j=1}^{v} c'_{i,j} \right) + c_{\mathbf{EQ}} < \sum_{i=1}^{u} \sum_{j=1}^{v} c_{i,j}. \tag{17}$$

The condition for round complexity is

$$\max(r'_{1,1}, r'_{1,2}, \ldots, r'_{u,v}) + r_{\mathbf{EQ}} < \max(r_{1,1}, r_{1,2}, \ldots, r_{u,v}). \tag{18}$$

3.5   Batch Logical AND-OR Protocol

The Batch Logical AND-OR protocol obtains the result of the following logical formula consisting of $F_{i,j}$'s by using alternative protocol $F'_{i,j}$'s for $1 \leq i \leq u, 1 \leq j \leq v$.

$$
\begin{aligned}
\{F_{1,1} \vee F_{1,2} \vee \cdots && \vee F_{1,v}\} \wedge \\
\{F_{2,1} \vee F_{2,2} \vee \cdots && \vee F_{2,v}\} \wedge \\
\cdots && \wedge \\
\{F_{u,1} \vee F_{u,2} \vee \cdots && \vee F_{u,v}\}
\end{aligned}
\tag{19}
$$

It outputs $[1]_p$ if the formula is true and $[0]_p$ if the formula is false. Protocol 5 shows the steps in this protocol for prime number $p \equiv 3 \pmod 4$. We can modify these steps for $p \equiv 1 \pmod 4$ by applying the same technique as in Section 3.3.

Protocol 5. Batch Logical AND-OR

Require: $p \equiv 3 \pmod 4$
1: **foreach** $i \in \{1, \ldots, u\}$ **do in parallel**
2:    $[row_i]_p \leftarrow \textbf{DoParallel}(\times, F'_{i,1}, \ldots, F'_{i,v})$
3: **end foreach**
4: $[temp]_p \leftarrow \textbf{DoParallel}(\star, [row_1]_p, \ldots, [row_u]_p)$ // $[a]_p \star [b]_p := [a]_p^2 + [b]_p^2$
5: **return** $[0 = temp]_p$

Correctness of Batch Logical AND-OR Protocol. The Batch Logical AND-OR protocol is a combination of the Batch Logical OR and Batch Logical AND protocols. $[row_i]_p$ is $[0]_p$ if the following logical formula is true and is a set of shares of a non-zero value if it is false.

$$F_{i,1} \vee F_{i,2} \vee \cdots \vee F_{i,v} \tag{20}$$

This step is part of the Batch Logical OR protocol, and its correctness is shown in Section 3.2. The remaining steps, which determine whether a set of shares of a non-zero value is present in u sets of shares, are the same as those in the to Batch Logical AND protocol. Since the correctness of Batch Logical AND is shown in Section 3.3, the Batch Logical AND-OR protocol is correct.

Complexity of Batch Logical AND-OR Protocol. For the existing protocols, the complexities of logical formula (19) are as follows. First, the parties obtain $u \times v$ $F_{i,j}$'s in parallel. The complexities of this step are $\sum_{i=1}^{u} \sum_{j=1}^{v} c_{i,j}$ multiplications and $\max(r_{1,1}, r_{1,2}, \ldots, r_{u,v})$ rounds. Then, the parties obtain $(v-1)u$ sets of logical OR in parallel. The complexities of this step are $(v-1)u$ multiplications and $\lceil \log_2 v \rceil$ rounds. Finally, the parties obtain $u-1$ sets of logical AND in parallel. The complexities of this step are $u-1$ multiplications and $\lceil \log_2 u \rceil$ rounds. Therefore, the total complexities are $(\sum_{i=1}^{u} \sum_{j=1}^{v} c_{i,j}) + uv - 1$ multiplications and $\max(r_{1,1}, r_{1,2}, \ldots, r_{u,v}) + \lceil \log_2 uv \rceil$ rounds.

On the other hand, the complexities of logical formula (19) using the Batch Logical AND-OR protocol are as follows. Since the step that obtains $[row_i]_p$ for each i is the same as that in the Batch Logical OR protocol, the complexities of this step are $\sum_{i=1}^{u} \sum_{j=1}^{v} c'_{i,j} + (v-1)u$ multiplications and $\max(r'_{1,1}, \ldots, r'_{u,v}) + \lceil \log_2 v \rceil$ rounds. Then, the parties obtain logical AND in parallel. Since this step is the same as that in the Batch Logical AND protocol for u sets of F''_i's, the complexities of this step are $u-1$ multiplications and $\lceil \log_2 u \rceil$ rounds. Finally, the parties obtain the result $[0 = temp]_p$. The complexities of this step are $c_{\textbf{EQ}}$ multiplications and $r_{\textbf{EQ}}$ rounds. Therefore, the total complexities are $(\sum_{i=1}^{u} \sum_{j=1}^{t} c'_{i,j}) + uv + c_{\textbf{EQ}} - 1$ multiplications and $\max(r'_{1,1}, r'_{1,2}, \ldots, r'_{u,v}) + r_{\textbf{EQ}} + \lceil \log_2 uv \rceil$ rounds.

Since the complexities of the Batch Logical AND-OR are equal to those of the Batch Logical OR-AND and the complexities of the corresponding existing protocols are also equal, the conditions for the Batch Logical AND-OR protocol to be more efficient than the existing protocols are the same as those for the Batch Logical OR-AND protocol. Thus, the condition for communication complexity is

$$\left(\sum_{i=1}^{u}\sum_{j=1}^{v} c'_{i,j}\right) + c_{\mathbf{EQ}} < \sum_{i=1}^{u}\sum_{j=1}^{v} c_{i,j}, \tag{21}$$

and the condition for round complexity is

$$\max(r'_{1,1}, r'_{1,2}, \ldots, r'_{u,v}) + r_{\mathbf{EQ}} < \max(r_{1,1}, r_{1,2}, \ldots, r_{u,v}). \tag{22}$$

3.6   Summary of Proposed Protocol Complexities

As shown in Sections 3.2 and 3.3, the Batch Logical OR protocol and the Batch Logical AND protocol both require $(\sum_{i=1}^{t} c'_i) + t + c_{\mathbf{EQ}} - 1$ multiplications and $\max(r'_1, \ldots, r'_t) + r_{\mathbf{EQ}} + \lceil \log_2 t \rceil$ rounds.

Furthermore, as shown in Sections 3.4 and 3.5, the Batch Logical AND-OR and the Batch Logical OR-AND protocols both require $(\sum_{i=1}^{u}\sum_{j=1}^{v} c'_{i,j}) + uv + c_{\mathbf{EQ}} - 1$ multiplications and $\max(r'_{1,1}, \ldots, r'_{u,v}) + r_{\mathbf{EQ}} + \lceil \log_2 uv \rceil$ rounds.

By setting $t = u \times v, c'_{(i-1)v+j} = c'_{i,j}, r'_{(i-1)v+j} = r'_{i,j}$, we can represent the communication complexity of the four proposed protocols in one equation and the round complexity in another. The communication complexity for the proposed protocols is

$$(\sum_{i=1}^{t} c'_i) + t + c_{\mathbf{EQ}} - 1, \tag{23}$$

and the round complexity is

$$\max(r'_1, \ldots, r'_t) + r_{\mathbf{EQ}} + \lceil \log_2 t \rceil. \tag{24}$$

Similarity, by setting $c_{(i-1)v+j} = c_{i,j}, r_{(i-1)v+j} = r_{i,j}$, we can do likewise for the corresponding existing protocols. The communication complexity for the existing protocols is

$$(\sum_{i=1}^{t} c_i) + t - 1, \tag{25}$$

and the round complexity is

$$\max(r_1, \ldots, r_t) + \lceil \log_2 t \rceil. \tag{26}$$

Furthermore, the conditions for the four proposed protocols to be more efficient than the corresponding existing protocols are as follows. The condition for communication complexity is

$$(\sum_{i=1}^{t} c'_i) + c_{\mathbf{EQ}} < \sum_{i=1}^{t} c_i, \tag{27}$$

and that for the round complexity is

$$\max(r'_1, \ldots, r'_t) + r_{\mathbf{EQ}} < \max(r_1, \ldots, r_t). \tag{28}$$

3.7   Security

The proposed protocols consist of addition, multiplication, equality testing, and an alternative protocol. As mentioned in Section 3.1, the alternative protocol is an MPC protocol, so the proposed protocols are based on (k, n) threshold secret sharing. Therefore, the security of the proposed protocols is reduced to that of (k, n) threshold secret sharing. That is, for secret s, no information about s is leaked without k shares of s.

4   Alternative Protocols and Their Complexities

As mentioned in Section 3.1, one of the key ideas of the proposed protocols is to make a logical formula consisting of multiple Boolean protocols F_i's more efficient by using alternative protocols F_i''s instead of F_i's where alternative protocol F_i' of F_i is an MPC function.

$$F_i' = \begin{cases} [0]_p & \text{if } F_i = \textbf{true} \\ [v \in \mathbb{Z}_p^*]_p & \text{if } F_i = \textbf{false} \end{cases} \tag{29}$$

In this section, we construct an alternative protocol for equality testing and evaluate its complexities. Similarly, we construct an alternative protocol for interval testing and evaluate its complexities.

4.1   Equality Testing

Given shares of secrets $[a]_p, [b]_p$, the equality testing protocol obtains $[a = b]_p$ without revealing them, where $a, b \in \mathbb{Z}_p$. The equality testing of Nishide and Ohta requires $c_{\textbf{EQ}} = 81\ell$ multiplications and $r_{\textbf{EQ}} = 8$ rounds [7].

The alternative protocol of equality testing F is

$$F' = [a - b]_p. \tag{30}$$

The complexities of F' are 0 multiplications and 0 rounds. Now we show that F' is an alternative protocol of F. If F is true, $F' = [0]_p$ since $a = b$. If F is false, $F' = [v \in \mathbb{Z}_p^*]_p$ since $a \neq b$. Note that the operation "$-$" is done over $GF(p)$. Thus, F' is an alternative protocol of F.

If all F_i's are equality testing for the Batch Logical OR protocol, the logical formula is

$$(a_1 = b_1) \vee (a_2 = b_2) \vee \cdots \vee (a_t = b_t). \tag{31}$$

The complexities of this formula for the existing protocols are $81\ell t + t - 1$ multiplications and $8 + \lceil \log_2 t \rceil$ rounds since $c_i = c_{\textbf{EQ}}$ and $r_i = r_{\textbf{EQ}}$ in Table 3. On the other hand, its complexities for the Batch Logical OR protocol are $81\ell + t - 1$ multiplications and $8 + \lceil \log_2 t \rceil$ rounds since $c_i' = 0$ and $r_i' = 0$ in Table 3. Thus, the Batch Logical OR protocol reduces the upper bound of the communication complexity from $O(\ell t)$ to $O(\ell + t)$ though it does not reduce round complexity. As shown in Section 3.6, the complexities of the Batch Logical OR protocol are equal to those of the other proposed protocols. Thus, the other proposed protocols similarly reduce communication complexity.

4.2   Interval Testing

Given shares of a secret $[a]_p$ and public values d, e, the interval testing protocol obtains $[d < a < e]_p$ without revealing a, where $a, d, e \in \mathbb{Z}_p, d < e$. The interval testing protocol of Nishide and Ohta requires $110\ell + 1$ multiplications and 13 rounds [7].

The alternative protocol of interval testing[1] F is

$$F' = (a - (d + 1)) \times (a - (d + 2)) \times \cdots \times (a - (e - 2)) \times (a - (e - 1)). \quad (32)$$

The complexities are $e - d - 2$ multiplications and $\lceil \log_2(e - d - 1) \rceil$ rounds. Now we show that F' is an alternative protocol of F. If F is true, $F' = [0]_p$ since a is an integer from $d + 1$ to $e - 1$. If F is false, $F' = [v \in \mathbb{Z}_p^*]_p$ since all factors have a non-zero value. Thus, F' is an alternative protocol of F.

If all F_i's are interval testing for the Batch Logical OR protocol, the logical formula is

$$(d_1 < a_1 < e_1) \vee (d_2 < a_2 < e_2) \vee \cdots \vee (d_t < a_t < e_t). \quad (33)$$

The complexities of this formula for the existing protocols are as follows since $c_i = 110\ell + 1$ and $r_i = 13$ in Table 3. The communication complexity is

$$\left(\sum_{i=1}^{t} c_i \right) + t - 1 = 110\ell t + 2t - 1, \quad (34)$$

and the round complexity is

$$\max(r_1, \ldots, r_t) + \lceil \log_2 t \rceil = 13 + \lceil \log_2 t \rceil. \quad (35)$$

On the other hand, the complexities of this formula for the Batch Logical OR protocol are as follows. Since $c_i' = e_i - d_i - 2$ and $r_i' = \lceil \log_2(e_i - d_i - 1) \rceil$ in Table 3, the communication complexity is

$$\left(\sum_{i=1}^{t} c_i' \right) + c_{\mathbf{EQ}} + t - 1 = \sum_{i=1}^{t}(e_i - d_i) - t + 81\ell - 1, \quad (36)$$

and the round complexity is

$$\max(r_1, \ldots, r_t) + r_{\mathbf{EQ}} + \lceil \log_2 t \rceil = \\ \max(\lceil \log_2(e_1 - d_1 - 1) \rceil, \ldots, \lceil \log_2(e_t - d_t - 1) \rceil) + 8 + \lceil \log_2 t \rceil. (37)$$

Now we show the conditions for the Batch Logical OR protocol to be more efficient than the existing protocols. Let $c_{\mathbf{EQ}} = 81\ell, c_i = 110\ell + 1, r_{\mathbf{EQ}} = 8$ and

---

[1]   Though we deal with interval testing here, it can be generalized to set membership testing easily where the set includes non-consecutive values.

$r_i = 13$ for the protocols of Nishide and Ohta [7]. The condition for communication complexity is

$$\left(\sum_{i=1}^{t} c_i'\right) + c_{\mathbf{EQ}} < \sum_{i=1}^{t} c_i \tag{38}$$

$$\sum_{i=1}^{t}(e_i - d_i - 2) + 81\ell < (110\ell + 1)t \tag{39}$$

$$\frac{\sum_{i=1}^{t}(e_i - d_i)}{t} < \left(110 - \frac{81}{t}\right)\ell + 3, \tag{40}$$

and that for round complexity is

$$\max(r_1', \ldots, r_t') + r_{\mathbf{EQ}} < \max(r_1, \ldots, r_t) \tag{41}$$
$$\max(r_1', \ldots, r_t') < 5 \tag{42}$$
$$\lceil \log_2(e_i - d_i - 1) \rceil < 5 \tag{43}$$
$$e_i - d_i < 17, \tag{44}$$

where $\max(r_1', \ldots, r_t') = r_i' = \lceil \log_2(e_i - d_i - 1) \rceil$. These results are equal to the those of the other proposed protocols as they were for equality testing above.

5   Application of Proposed Protocols

We apply the proposed protocols to two example applications using a secret shared database and evaluate their complexities for the example queries. For the database, we suppose that

- each value is distributed by (k, n) threshold secret sharing as a secret and that
- n database servers store each share as parties

The secret shared database leaks no information about the values even if an adversary breaks into $k - 1$ database servers.

5.1   Example 1: Patient Database Searches

In the first example, the proposed protocols are used to search a patient database (Table 5) for a male with heart disease aged between 10 and 19. The values for patient ID, age, gender, and disease in the ith row of the table are id_i, a_i, g_i, and d_i, respectively. The values representing male and heart disease are m and h, respectively.

If the existing protocols are used straightforwardly, the steps are as follows.

1. The parties perform the following steps in parallel for each row i.
2. The parties obtain $[A_i]_p \leftarrow [10 \leq a_i \leq 19]_p$, $[G_i]_p \leftarrow [g_i = m]_p$, and $[D_i]_p \leftarrow [d_i = h]_p$ using the equality testing and interval testing protocols in parallel.

Table 5. Patient database

Patient ID	Age	Gender	Disease
001	43	female	pneumonia
002	16	male	heart disease
003	59	male	stomach cancer
⋮	⋮	⋮	⋮

Table 6. Results of patient information search

Patient ID	Age	Gender	Disease
0	0	0	0
002	16	male	heart disease
0	0	0	0
⋮	⋮	⋮	⋮

3. The parties obtain $[T_i]_p \leftarrow [A_i \wedge G_i \wedge D_i]_p = [A_i]_p \times [G_i]_p \times [D_i]_p$.
4. To record values of 0 if the record does not satisfy the condition, the parties perform the following operations in parallel.
$[id_i]_p \leftarrow [id_i]_p \times [T_i]_p$, $[a_i]_p \leftarrow [a_i]_p \times [T_i]_p$, $[g_i]_p \leftarrow [g_i]_p \times [T_i]_p$, $[d_i]_p \leftarrow [d_i]_p \times [T_i]_p$

The results of this search are shown in Table 6.

On the other hand, since the query can be represented as $(10 \le a_i \le 19) \wedge (g_i = m) \wedge (d_i = h)$, the Batch Logical AND protocol can be used as follows.

1. The parties perform the following steps in parallel for each row i.
2. The parties obtain the results of the following alternative protocols in parallel.
$[A'_i]_p \leftarrow [a_i - 10]_p \times [a_i - 11]_p \times \cdots \times [a_i - 19]_p$
$[G'_i]_p \leftarrow [g_i - m]_p$
$[D'_i]_p \leftarrow [d_i - h]_p$
3. The parties obtain the result of $[A'_i]_p \wedge [G'_i]_p \wedge [D'_i]_p$ in the form of $[0]_p$ or shares of a non-zero value
$[T'_i]_p \leftarrow ([A'_i]_p^2 + [G'_i]_p^2)^2 + [D'_i]_p^2$
4. The parties convert $[T'_i]_p$ into the form of $[0]_p$ or $[1]_p$.
$[T_i]_p \leftarrow [T'_i = 0]_p$
5. To record values of 0 if the record does not satisfy the condition, the parties perform the following operations in parallel.
$[id_i]_p \leftarrow [id_i]_p \times [T_i]_p$, $[a_i]_p \leftarrow [a_i]_p \times [T_i]_p$, $[g_i]_p \leftarrow [g_i]_p \times [T_i]_p$, $[d_i]_p \leftarrow [d_i]_p \times [T_i]_p$

Complexity. We evaluate the complexities for this query using existing and the proposed protocols assuming that the equality testing protocol requires 81ℓ multiplications and 8 rounds and that the interval testing protocol requires $110\ell + 1$ multiplications and 13 rounds. These protocols were proposed by Nishide and Ohta [7].

With the existing protocols, Step 2 requires $110\ell + 1 + 81\ell \times 2 = 272\ell + 1$ multiplications and 13 rounds, Step 3 requires 2 multiplications and 2 rounds, and Step 4 requires 4 multiplications and 1 round. Thus the total complexities are $(272\ell + 7)x$ multiplications and 16 rounds, where x is the number of rows.

On the other hand, with the Batch Logical AND protocol, Step 2 requires $19 - 10 = 9$ multiplications and $\lceil \log_2(19 - 10 + 1) \rceil = 4$ rounds, Step 3 requires 2 multiplications and 2 rounds, Step 4 requires 81ℓ multiplications and 8 rounds, and Step 5 requires 4 multiplications and 1 round. Thus, the total complexities are $(81\ell + 15)x$ multiplications and 15 rounds. Therefore, for this example, the Batch Logical AND protocol reduces the communication complexity by approximately 70% and the round complexity by 1 round.

5.2   Example 2: Information Presence Search

In the second example application, the proposed protocols are used to determine whether information is present in a list. An immigration officer might want to search a terrorist watch list to see whether a person entering the country is on the list. The values for the person's name, nationality, gender, and age are $a, b, c,$ and d, corresponding to $x_i, y_i, z_i,$ and w_i in the ith row. The number of rows is v. The query is represented as a logical formula:

$$\{(a = x_1) \wedge (b = y_1) \wedge (c = z_1) \wedge (d = w_1)\} \vee$$
$$\{(a = x_2) \wedge (b = y_2) \wedge (c = z_2) \wedge (d = w_2)\} \vee$$
$$\vdots$$
$$\{(a = x_v) \wedge (b = y_v) \wedge (c = z_v) \wedge (d = w_v)\}. \qquad (45)$$

The complexities with the existing protocols are $(\sum_{i=1}^{u} \sum_{j=1}^{v} c_{i,j}) + uv - 1$ multiplications and $\max(r_{1,1}, \ldots, r_{u,v}) + \lceil \log_2 uv \rceil$ rounds as shown in Section 3.4. Since $c_{i,j} = 81\ell, u = 4,$ and $r_{i,j} = 8$, the complexities are $324\ell v + 4v - 1$ multiplications and $10 + \lceil \log_2 v \rceil$ rounds. On the other hand, we can apply the Batch Logical OR-AND protocol to this logical formula straightforwardly. If we do, the complexities are $(\sum_{i=1}^{u} \sum_{j=1}^{v} c'_{i,j}) + uv + c_{\mathbf{EQ}} - 1$ multiplications and $\max(r'_{1,1}, \ldots, r'_{u,v}) + r_{\mathbf{EQ}} + \lceil \log_2 uv \rceil$ rounds. Since $c'_{i,j} = 0, u = 4, c_{\mathbf{EQ}} = 81\ell, r'_{i,j} = 0,$ and $r_{\mathbf{EQ}} = 8$, the complexities are $81\ell + 4v - 1$ multiplications and $10 + \lceil \log_2 v \rceil$ rounds. Since v is dominant in practical use, the Batch Logical OR-AND protocol reduces the communication complexity for this query to $\frac{1}{81\ell}$. As shown by these two examples, the proposed protocols are practically applicable to database queries and reduce the complexities drastically.

6   Conclusion

The biggest problem with multi-party computation is that it requires a vast amount of communication. Much research has gone into reducing the communication and round complexity of each protocol (equality testing, interval testing, etc.). In this work, we proposed following four efficient protocols.

- $\bigvee_{i=1}^{t} F_i$: Batch Logical OR protocol
- $\bigwedge_{i=1}^{t} F_i$: Batch Logical AND protocol
- $\bigvee_{i=1}^{u} \bigwedge_{j=1}^{v} F_{i,j}$: Batch Logical AND-OR protocol
- $\bigwedge_{i=1}^{u} \bigvee_{j=1}^{v} F_{i,j}$: Batch Logical OR-AND protocol

If all F_i's ($F_{i,j}$'s) in the logical formulas are equality testing protocols and $uv = t$, the proposed protocols reduce the upper bound of the communication complexity from $O(\ell t)$ to $O(\ell + t)$, where ℓ is the bit length of a prime number p and secrets are over $\mathbb{Z}_p$. If all F_i's ($F_{i,j}$'s) are interval testing ($d_i < x_i < e_i$), the proposed protocols reduce both communication and round complexity depending on d_i and e_i.

We applied the proposed protocols to a secret shared database and presented two examples. The first showed that a proposed protocol reduces the communication complexity by approximately 70% and the round complexity by 1 round for a query consisting of equality testing and interval testing. The second showed that a proposed protocol reduces the communication complexity to approximately $\frac{1}{81\ell}$ for a query that determines whether the given information is included in a list. The concept of the proposed protocols is versatile and can be applied to protocols other than equality testing and interval testing, thereby making them more efficient as well.

References

1. Ben-Or, M., Goldwasser, S., Wigderson, A.: Completeness theorems for non-cryptographic fault-tolerant distributed computation. In: Proc. of the 20th Annual ACM Symposium on Theory of Computing, pp. 1–10 (1988)
2. Burkhart, M., Strasser, M., Many, D., Dimitropoulos, X.: SEPIA: Privacy-Preserving Aggregation of Multi-Domain Network Events and Statistics. In: 19th USENIX Security Symposium (2010)
3. Cramer, R., Damgård, I.: Secure Distributed Linear Algebra in a Constant Number of Rounds. In: Kilian, J. (ed.) CRYPTO 2001. LNCS, vol. 2139, pp. 119–136. Springer, Heidelberg (2001)
4. Damgård, I., Fitzi, M., Kiltz, E., Nielsen, J.B., Toft, T.: Unconditionally Secure Constant-Rounds Multi-party Computation for Equality, Comparison, Bits and Exponentiation. In: Halevi, S., Rabin, T. (eds.) TCC 2006. LNCS, vol. 3876, pp. 285–304. Springer, Heidelberg (2006)
5. Gennaro, R., Rabin, M.O., Rabin, T.: Simplified VSS and fast-track multiparty computations with applications to threshold cryptography. In: Proc. of the 17th Annual ACM Symposium on Principles of Distributed Computing, pp. 101–111 (1998)
6. Ning, C., Xu, Q.: Multiparty Computation for Modulo Reduction without Bit-Decomposition and a Generalization to Bit-Decomposition. In: Abe, M. (ed.) ASIACRYPT 2010. LNCS, vol. 6477, pp. 483–500. Springer, Heidelberg (2010)
7. Nishide, T., Ohta, K.: Multiparty Computation for Interval, Equality, and Comparison Without Bit-Decomposition Protocol. In: Okamoto, T., Wang, X. (eds.) PKC 2007. LNCS, vol. 4450, pp. 343–360. Springer, Heidelberg (2007)
8. SecureSCM, "Security Analysis," Technical Report D9.2, SecureSCM (2009)
9. Shamir, A.: How to Share a Secret. Commun. ACM 22(11), 612–613 (1979)
10. Toft, T.: Constant-Rounds, Almost-Linear Bit-Decomposition of Secret Shared Values. In: Fischlin, M. (ed.) CT-RSA 2009. LNCS, vol. 5473, pp. 357–371. Springer, Heidelberg (2009)

Towards Attack Resilient Social Network Based Threshold Signing

Jian Zhou*, Ji Xiang, and Neng Gao

The State Key Laboratory of Information Security,
Graduate University of Chinese Academy of Sciences, China
{jzhou,jixiang,gaoneng}@is.ac.cn

Abstract. The idea exploiting social networks for threshold signing was proposed to help average users better protect their private keys. In order to investigate the attack-resilience of the whole system, we propose a weight based attack strategy, which is more powerful than those previously proposed. We also investigate some important factors affecting the attack-resilience of the system, and based on the results, we propose a new design for delegate selection which can efficiently improve the attack-resilience of the whole system.

Keywords: social networks, threshold cryptography, attack-resilience.

1 Introduction

A threshold secret sharing scheme enables a dealer to distribute a secret among a set of users, by giving each user a piece of information called a share such that only a sufficient number of users will be able to reconstruct the secret, while a smaller number of users gain no information on the secret. Because of this significant security feature, threshold cryptography techniques play an important role in protecting cryptographic keys [1] [2] [3]. In general, a user can employ multiple servers to run a threshold cryptosystem. However, in order to make such techniques more widely available in the real world, allowing average users better protect their private keys, there have been some work [4] [5] [6] proposing employing threshold cryptography in social networks.

Our work is mainly based on [4] that proposed exploiting social networks for threshold signing whereby users take advantage of their trusted ones to help secure their private keys. The attack-resilience of the resulting system has been studied in [4] under various attack strategies, due to the compromise of some computers and thus the compromise of the cryptographic key shares stored on them. However, while identifying the optimal attack strategy is known to be NP-hard [7], there is a problem how to heuristically identify a relatively powerful

---

* This work was supported by National Natural Science Foundation of China (Grant No. 70890084/G021102 and 61003274), Knowledge Innovation Program of Chinese Academy of Sciences (Grant No. YYYJ-1013), and National Science & Technology Pillar Program of China (Grant No. 2008BAH32B00 and 2008BAH32B04).

C.-K. Wu, M. Yung, and D. Lin (Eds.): Inscrypt 2011, LNCS 7537, pp. 309–323, 2012.

attack. Although [4] proposed an attack strategy called *RemainderDegreeBased Attack* which always picks the highest degree node in remainder graphs to compromise, it is not powerful enough in most cases. Besides, [4] carried out all its experiments only with simulated data and didn't give any advice of how to improve the attack-resilience of the resulting system based on a given network.

Following the work of [4], we further investigate the attack-resilience of exploiting social networks for threshold signing. Our work and contributions include:

- We propose an attack strategy called *WeightBased Attack*. It is more powerful than those already known. Moreover the adversary doesn't need to know the topology of the whole network beforehand. The adversary can launch the attack just with the local knowledge of those compromised nodes.
- We study the factors affecting the attack-resilience of the whole system, including network topology and network average degree.
- For a given network, we propose a new design for delegate selection in order to improve the attack-resilience. Experiments show that our design exhibits better attack-resilience than the one defined in [4].
- We carry out our experiments not only with simulated data but also with real data of social networks. In fact, we do experiments with three types of data. One follows Watts-Strogatz small world model [8]; another follows power law model [9]; and the third is a facebook data set [10].

The remainder of the paper is organized as follows: in section 2 we introduce the background knowledge and system model. In section 3 we propose our attack strategy. In section 4 we investigate some important factors affecting the attack-resilience of the whole system. In Section 5, we propose a new design to improve the attack-resilience for given social networks. In Section 6, we introduce some related works. At last, in section 7 we make a conclusion and discuss some open problems.

2   Background and System Model

In this section, we introduce the system model and some important notions of [4] on which our work is mainly based.

Social networks can be modeled as an undirected graph $G = (V, E)$, where each node or vertex $u \in V$ represents a user, and an edge $(u, v) \in E$ means that there is a strong mutual trust between u and v. When exploiting social networks for threshold signing, each $u \in V$ picks some nodes he trusts in the network to hold his private key shares. We let $Delegates(u)$ denote the set of nodes whom u picks to hold his private key shares , and $Principals(u)$ the set of nodes who pick u to hold their shares. In both $Delegates(u)$ and $Principals(u)$, u itself is not included. In [4], the author assume a user only trusts his direct friends and picks all his direct friends as delegates. In such a design, $Delegates(u)$ and $Principals(u)$ are symmetric, such that if $v \in Delegates(u)$, then it is true $u \in Principals(v)$.

We define $\alpha = \frac{k}{n}$ for a (k,n)-threshold scheme, and suppose it is a system-wide parameter. If we directly apply secret sharing schemes to social networks, there may be an undesirable situation that compromising T nodes results in compromising $S \geq T$ private keys. For example, consider the simple case of $|V| = 3$ and $\alpha = 0.5$, where each node shares his private key to all the three nodes using a $(2,3)$ secret sharing. In this case, compromising any two nodes immediately causes the compromise of all three private keys. So the resulting security is worse than the one where each user holds his own private key. To avoid this drawback, it is proposed in [4] each user distributes his secret shares using a two-tier secret sharing method. A user $u \in V$ first uses a $(2,2)$ threshold secret sharing method to split his private key sk_u into two shares sk_{u1} and sk_{u2}. Then, a $(\lceil \alpha \cdot deg(u) \rceil, deg(u))$ threshold secret sharing method is used to split sk_{u2} into $deg(u)$ shares $(sk_{u2,1}, \ldots, sk_{u2,deg(u)})$, where $deg(u)$ denotes the degree of node u. As a result, u holds sk_{u1} and erases sk_u as well as sk_{u2}, and each neighbor of u holds a share of sk_{uu2}. Using the above two-tier secret sharing method, in order to comprise the private key of u, an adversary has to comprise u and a sufficient number of u's friends.

In the adversary model, an adversary who wants to steal private keys of users can compromise user computers, and thus the secret shares stored on the computers. We assume the adversary has the ability to compromise any other users in the social network and we don't consider the price of compromising a single user. All the compromised nodes are under control of the adversary. It is also assumed that the adversary knows the topology of the social networks and compromising of a node by an adversary doesn't jeopardize its availability. This assumption is realistic since unavailability of infected machines can signal to the owner to scan and clean his computer from malicious software.

There are three states for each node: not yet compromised; compromised but the private key is not compromised; compromised and also the private key. We respectively use S_h, S_{nc} and S_{kc} to denote the three sets of nodes. Note the intersection of any two sets is empty. We let S_c denote those compromised nodes despite the states of their private keys, so we have $S_c = S_{nc} \bigcup S_{kc}$.

Intuitively, if the adversary can only compromise a few private keys when he compromise lots of nodes, we say the security of the system is high, and vice versa. Precisely, the security of the resulting system is measured by the definition of attack-resilience:

$$AR(G, D, A) = \frac{\frac{1}{|V|} \sum_{0 < T \leq |V|} (S(G, D^*, A, T) - S(G, D, A, T))}{(|V| - 1)/2}$$

$$= \frac{2}{|V||V - 1|} \sum_{0 < T \leq |V|} (T - S(G, D, A, T))$$

In the above equation, $G = (V, E)$ is a given social network. D denotes the set of possible designs on how the users hold private keys shares of each other, and A denotes the set of possible attacks. $S(G, D, A, T)$: $\mathbb{G} \times \mathbb{D} \times \mathbb{A} \times \mathbb{N} \to \mathbb{N}$ is the function that returns the number of compromised private keys when $0 \leq T \leq |V|$ nodes are compromised according to $A \in \mathbb{A}$. D^* is the benchmark design where

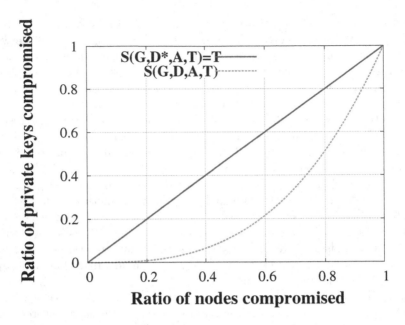

Fig. 1. Attack-resilience

each user holds his own private key. It is obvious that $S(G, D^*, A, T) = T$ for any $A \in \mathbb{A}$. The definition of attack-resilience can be explained by the average distance between the line $S(G, D^*, A, T) = T$ and the curve $S(G, D, A, T)$ as shown in figure 1.

We focus our study on the attack-resilience of the whole system, and the availability is not within the scope of our work, which means we don't consider the situation when computers are not responsive. In fact, we can make the same assumption as [5] : a user sending a request to an off-line delegate simply waits till the latter is available.

3   Our Weight Based Attack

3.1   Motivation

To accommodate the worst-case scenario, it makes sense to identify the most powerful attack strategy, which turns out to be NP-hard. We thus need to heuristically present an often powerful attack strategy. However, although some attack strategies have been presented, they are far from the optimal attack strategy. In other words, they are not powerful enough. The most powerful attack defined in [4] is called *RemainderDegreeBased Attack*. The adversary heuristically picks the highest degree node in remainder graphs to compromise. Remainder graphs are referred to the subgraphs after removing the nodes whose private keys have been compromised and relevant edges. The intuition behind this attack is that compromising the highest degree nodes in remainder graphs means the compromise of many private key shares, and thus may cause the compromise of many private keys that have yet to be compromised. However, compromising more shares doesn't actually mean the compromise of more private keys. In fact, given α is a system-wide parameter, it is more difficult to compromise the private key of the node with a higher degree, which is at odds with the intuition. For example, in a specified network topology, the adversary following *RemainderDegreeBased Attack* may compromise some nodes all holding many shares, but most of their friends are not compromised, so the adversary has actually compromised few private keys.

A powerful attack strategy implies that the adversary tries to compromise as many private keys as possible by compromising as few nodes as possible. Because of the two-tier secret sharing method, compromising n nodes results in at most n private keys compromised. This ideal situation happens if and only if for each $u \in S_c$, it has at least $\alpha \cdot deg(u)$ friends in S_c. So intuitively the adversary should compromise those nodes preferentially: those who have a large fraction of friends in S_c, and those who are friends of $u \in S_{nc}$ whose large fraction of friends are in S_c. For example, in the case of figure 2, supposing $\alpha = 1$, all friends of N7 belong to S_c, and N10 is a friend of N6 whose most friends belong to S_c, so N7 and N10 should be compromised preferentially. In fact, compromising N7 leads to the compromise of N7's private key immediately, and compromising N10 leads to the compromise of N6's private key immediately. Based on this idea, we propose our attack strategy. Experiment results show it is more powerful than those previously proposed.

3.2 Attack Algorithm

In our attack strategy, the adversary heuristically decides the node next to be compromised based on S_c. S_h can be viewed as a candidate list from which the adversary picks node to compromise. For each $u \in S_h$, we assign u a value $weight(u)$ measuring if we compromise u, its effect on the current system, which is composed of two parts: one measuring how much its own private key is compromised, the other measuring how much the private keys of these nodes in S_{nc} are compromised. We let $W(u, v)$ denote the function which returns the effect on the safety of v's private key if u is compromised. Denote by $nd(u)$ the number of delegates of u, $ncd(u)$ the number of compromised delegates of u. Define $k(u) = \alpha * nd(u)$, where $k(u)$ represents the threshold number of shares needed to compromise u's private key, then the curves of $W(u, v)$ are shown in Figure 3 when v respectively is u itself and $v \in Principals(u) \cap S_{nc}$; otherwise, $W(u, v) = 0$, which means compromising u has no effect on the safety of v's private key. Here we ignore the effect if $v \in S_h$ because compromising v is the precondition of compromising the private key of v. So if $u \neq v$ we only consider the nodes in S_{nc}. From the curves we can see that we put more attention to the nodes whose private keys are approximately compromised. In other words, our attack is a local optimal or greedy algorithm that gives priority to the nodes who currently contribute most to compromising private keys.

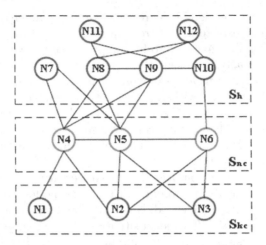

Fig. 2. A simple example of social network being compromised

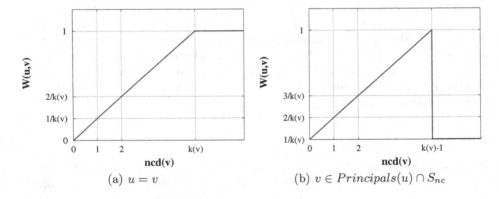

(a) $u = v$ (b) $v \in Principals(u) \cap S_{nc}$

Fig. 3. Effect on v if compromising u

We have: $weight(u) = W(u, u) + \sum_{v \in Principals(u) \cap S_{nc}} W(u, v)$ and $weight(u)$ can be treated as the priority of u to be compromised.

Our attack strategy is processed as the following steps:

1. Pick the node with the maximum value of weight in S_h(the candidate list) to compromise. If there are multiple ones eligible, a random one is chosen.
2. Remove the node from S_h, and update the weights of those nodes in S_h
3. Repeat the above two steps until the number of compromised nodes reaches the previous assigned value.

Algorithm 1 gives the process of our attack strategy in detail and algorithm 2 elaborately describes the update process. Note Algorithm 1 is also applicable to the directed situation where u is v's friend but v is not u's friend so $u \in Delegates(v)$ but $v \notin Delegates(u)$. In fact, any edge in undirected graphs can be represented by two directed edges.

Algorithm 1. WeightBasedAttack

Input: $G = (V, E), 0 < \alpha \leq 1, T$(the number of allowed compromised nodes,$T \leq |V|$)

1 **begin**
2      $S_h = V, S_{nc} = \varnothing, S_{kc} = \varnothing, cnt = 0$
3   **foreach** $u \in S_h$ **do** /*Initialize weights for each node*/
4          $weight(u) = 0$
5   **end**
6   **while** $cnt \leq T$ **do**
7          $u = Random\{v \in S_h | weight(v) == max_{x \in S_h}\{weight(x)\}\}$
8          $S_h = S_h - u$
9          $UpdateWeight(G, u, \alpha, S_h, S_{nc}, S_{kc})$
10         $cnt = cnt + 1$
11   **end**
12 **end**

Algorithm 2. UpdateWeight

Input: $G = (V, E), n \in V$(the node just compromised), $0 < \alpha \leq 1, S_h, S_{nc}, S_{kc}$

1 **begin**
2      $k = \alpha * nd(n)$
3   **if** $ncd(n) \geq k$ **then**
4          $S_{kc} = S_{kc} \cup \{n\}$
5   **else**
6          $S_{nc} = S_{nc} \cup \{n\}$
7   **foreach** $u \in Delegates(n) \cap S_h$ **do**
8              $weight(u) = weight(u) + \frac{ncd(n)+1}{k}$
9   **end**
10   **foreach** $u \in Principals(n)$ **do**
11         $k = \alpha * nd(u)$
12         $ncd(u) = ncd(u) + 1$
13   **if** $u \in S_h$ **and** $ncd(u) \leq k$ **then**
14             $weight(u) = weight(u) + \frac{1}{k}$
15   **else if** $u \in S_{nc}$ **then**
16             $w = 0$
17   **if** $ncd(u) < k$ **then**
18                 $w = \frac{1}{k}$
19   **else**
20                 $w = -1$
21                 $S_{nc} = S_{nc} - u$
22                 $S_{kc} = S_{kc} \cup \{u\}$
23   **foreach** $v \in Delegates(u) \cap S_h$ **do**
24                 $weight(v) = weight(v) + w$
25   **end**
26   **end**
27 **end**

3.3   Experiments and Analysis

In order to identify our attack strategy, we carry out our experiments with three types of data set. One follows Watts-Strogatz small world model, with average degree 10 and rewiring probability 0.8 (thus this network has short average path length and a small clustering coefficient). Another follows power law model, with average degree approximately 10 and power law exponent -2.5. Both graphs are generated with $|V| = 1000$. The third is a facebook data set with $63,731$ nodes and $817,090$ edges.

We compare our attack strategy which is called *WeightBased Attack* with two other strategies:

- **Random Attack**: The adversary always randomly picks a non-compromised node in S_h to compromise.
- **RemainderDegreeBased Attack**: The adversary heuristically picks the highest degree node in remainder graphs to compromise.

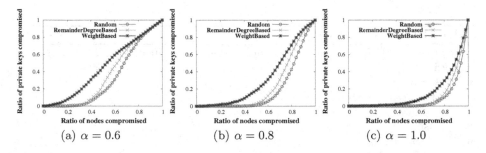

Fig. 4. Ratio of compromised keys vs. Ratio of compromised nodes: Small World

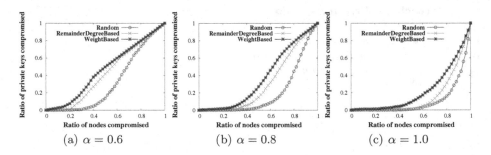

Fig. 5. Ratio of compromised keys vs. Ratio of compromised nodes: Power Law

Figure 4 plots the simulated ratio of compromised keys vs. the ratio of compromised nodes in the small world graph case. It is shown that our attack is always more powerful than *RemainderDegreeBased Attack*, which in turn is always more powerful than *Random Attack*. Specially, when α is low ($\alpha = 0.6$ in our experiments), the curve of our attack is close a straight line, indicating

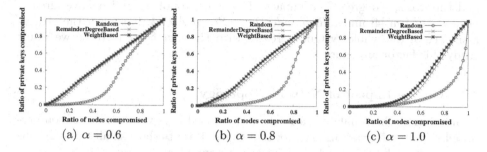

(a) $\alpha = 0.6$ (b) $\alpha = 0.8$ (c) $\alpha = 1.0$

Fig. 6. Ratio of compromised keys vs. Ratio of compromised nodes: Facebook

the effect of our attack is almost ideal. Besides, our attack starts to compromise private keys after compromising a much smaller number of nodes than the other attacks, which is particularly significant when there is an upper limit on the number of nodes that can be compromised. Taking $\alpha = 0.6$ for example, *Random Attack* and *RemainderDegreeBased Attack* starts to compromise private keys after compromising about 30 percents of nodes, while our attack starts to compromise private keys almost at the beginning. That is because our attack can be regarded as a local optimal or greedy strategy which is eager to compromise private keys as early as possible. Figure 5 plots the simulated ratio of compromised keys vs. the ratio of compromised nodes in the power law graph case, where the results are almost the same as in Figure 4. Figure 6 plots the simulated ratio of compromised keys vs. the ratio of compromised nodes in facebook case. However, although our attack is still powerful than *RemainderDegreeBased Attack*, the difference between them is not obvious. This may be because the facebook data set we use exhibits the power law characteristic whose absolute value of power law exponent is rather small. In such a graph, after compromising a small number of nodes with high degree, it is likely that when compromising a node its private key is also compromised since a large fraction of its friends belong to S_c, which is the ideal situation. So, when using facebook data set, *RemainderDegreeBased Attack* performs well and the effect is close to our attack.

In conclusion, our attack strategy are more powerful than others under various social network topologies and various values of α. Besides, compared with *RemainderDegreeBased Attack*, ours just make use of the local knowledge of the already compromised nodes. The adversary doesn't need to know the topology of the whole network beforehand. In the rest of the paper, we will only consider our attack so as to accommodate the worst-case scenario.

4   Important Factors Affecting the Attack-Resilience of System

In this section we investigate the factors affecting the attack-resilience of the whole system under our *WeightBased Attack*, including the network topology and the average degree. The impact of network topology and α have already been studied in [4] under *RemainderDegreeBased Attack*. It is clear the attack-resilience of the whole system increases with the increasing of α, so we won't study this factor any more.

4.1   On the Impact of Network Topology

Figure 7 plots the simulated ratio of compromised keys vs. the ratio of compromised nodes under various network topologies. Results show small world graphs always exhibit better attack-resilience than power law graphs.

Here we try to give some explanations of the results from the perspective of graph theory. When $\alpha = 1$, identifying the optimal attack strategy can be translated to the NP-hard problem known as vertex expansion [4]. Meanwhile, expander graphs for which any small subset of nodes has a relatively large neighborhood have high value of vertex expansion according to its definition. Thus, we suppose an expander graph is more likely to have good attack-resilience. On the other hand, expander graphs are well local connected. For small world graphs, any node arrives another node in a few steps while for power law graphs, lots of nodes have only few friends. So small world graphs are much more well local connected than power law graphs, which cause small world graphs exhibit better attack-resilience than power law graphs.

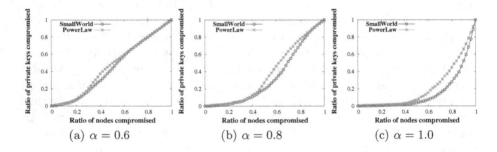

(a) $\alpha = 0.6$ (b) $\alpha = 0.8$ (c) $\alpha = 1.0$

Fig. 7. The Impact of Network Topology

4.2   On the Impact of Average Degree

Figure 8 plots the simulated attack-resilience vs. the average degree respectively for small world graph topology and power law graph topology. Results show that the attack-resilience increases with the increase of average degree at a dropping rate.

Here we also give some explanations of the results from the perspective of graph theory: for a well local connected graph, increasing its average degree contribute less to its local connectivity, and vice versa. So when average degree is low, the attack-resilience increases quickly. On the contrary, when average degree is high, the increase is not obvious.

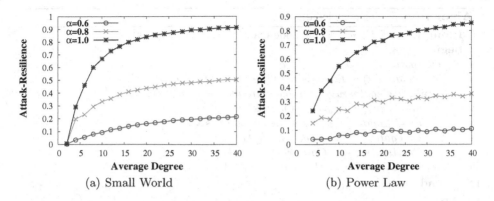

Fig. 8. The Impact of Average Degree

5 Delegate Selection Model and Design

For a given social network, how can we improve the attack-resilience of the whole system? In this section, we give a possible design which will increase the attack-resilience efficiently.

From the results of section 4, we know network topology and average degree have significant impacts on the attack-resilience, so we consider improving the attack-resilience by constructing an overlay over the original topology. If we make sure the overlay has a higher average degree and a better topology, the attack-resilience of the whole system under the new design will increase.

5.1 Delegate Selection Algorithm

The key point of our new design is to construct such an overlay. In the design of [4], the author assumes a user only trusts his direct friends and he picks all the friends as his delegates. Here we extend the limitation such that a user not only trusts his friends but also the friends of his friends based on the acknowledge that people are more likely to trust a friend of a friend than a random stranger [11] [12]. Now a user's trust list includes his friends and friends of friends whom can be regarded as the candidates where the user selects his delegates. And we are able to construct an overlay by the selection of delegates. We observe that the overlay can be modeled as a directed graph.

Now the problems are:

- Is it necessary to select all candidates as one's delegates?
- If not, how to select delegates to make system have better attack-resilience?

It is known from the experiment results that the increase of the attack-resilience is not obvious when average degree is high. At the same time, for a user, the communication consumption increases proportionally to the number of his delegates. Here we suppose a user can directly communicate with his delegates, so

---

Algorithm 3. SelectDelegates

Input: $G = (V, E), u \in V$(the node ready to select delegates)
1 **begin**
2    $Delegates(u) = \varnothing$
3    $Candidates(u) = Friends(u) \bigcup FriendsOfFriends(u)$
4   **while** $|Delegates(u)| \leq 20$ *and* $Candidates(u) \neq \varnothing$ **do**
5       $m = min_{x \in Candidates(u)}\{sharesNum(x)\}$
6       $v = Random\{x \in Candidates(u)|sharesNum(x) == m\}$
7       $Delegates(u) = Delegates(u) \bigcup \{v\}$
8       $Candidates(u) = Candidates(u) - \{v\}$
9       $sharesNum(v) = sharesNum(v) + 1$
10   **end**
11 **end**

---

the communication consumption is unrelated with the number of hops in social networks. Thus, it is necessary for us to set a value indicating the maximum number of delegates a user can select. Here we let the value be 20 as an experiment parameter. Of course other appropriate values are available according to the experiment result of figure 8. On the other hand, in order to make the overlay well local connected, we try to make each node hold approximately the same number of shares.

Based on the above considerations, for each node, we process our delegate selection algorithm as follows, which is described detailedly in algorithm 3:

– In each round, a node select the candidate which currently keeps the minimum number of shares until its delegate number reaches 20 or the candidate list is empty.
– When there are more than one nodes possessing the minimum number of shares, randomly select one.

5.2   Experiments and Analysis

We compare our design with the design in [4] in which a user selects all the friends as his delegates. Figure 9 plots the simulated ratio of compromised keys vs. the

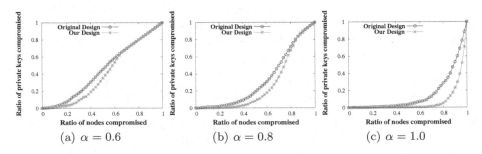

(a) $\alpha = 0.6$ (b) $\alpha = 0.8$ (c) $\alpha = 1.0$

Fig. 9. Ratio of compromised keys vs. Ratio of compromised nodes: Small World

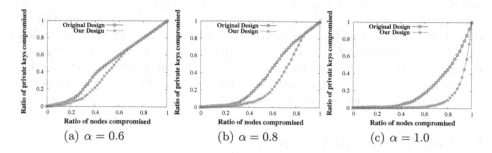

Fig. 10. Ratio of compromised keys vs. Ratio of compromised nodes: Power Law

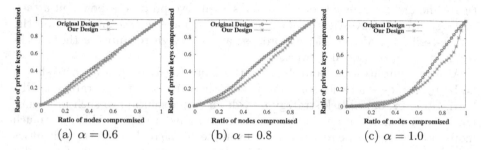

Fig. 11. Ratio of compromised keys vs. Ratio of compromised nodes: Facebook

ratio of compromised nodes in the small world graph case. Figure 10 plots the simulated ratio of compromised keys vs. the ratio of compromised nodes in the power law graph case. And Figure 11 plots the simulated ratio of compromised keys vs. the ratio of compromised nodes in facebook case. It is observed that our design performs better under various network topologies and various values of α.

6 Related Work

Employing threshold cryptography to improve the security of system has been discussed in various scenarios. For example, [1], [2], [3] respectively proposed utilizing threshold cryptography to improve Kerberos, protect private keys of networked cryptographic devices, and revoke certificates quickly and safely. The main idea of [1], [2] and [3] is simply to split a private key into two pieces such that one piece is kept on the user's computer and the other on some remote server. In addition, [13] discussed applications and usability of threshold cryptography in P2P and mobile ad hoc networks, and [14] presented a distributed certification system for decentralized varying-size P2P networks, in which signing a certificate needs the collaboration of a fixed ratio of the nodes.

Besides [4], there are also some other works employing threshold cryptography in social networks. [5] proposed employing threshold-based secret sharing schemes in distributed online social networks for the purpose of key recovery, which is different from ours. On the other hand, [5] discussed the security of the whole system only under some simple attack strategies, including *Random Attack* and *DegreeBased Attack*. [6] introduced a social secret sharing scheme in which shares are allocated based on a play's reputation and the way he interacts with other participants. However, the scheme in [6] is designed from the perspective of a single user. The security of the whole system is not studied.

7 Conclusion and Discussion

When exploiting social networks for threshold cryptography, in order to investigate the attack-resilience of the whole system, we propose a powerful attack strategy. We also investigate some factors which have significant effects on the attack-resilience. Meanwhile, we propose a new design to improve the attack-resilience for given social networks.

Although our attack is powerful than those previously proposed, there should be better attack strategies since identifying the optimal attack strategy is NP-hard. However, our attack strategy provides a closer solution to such problems. On the other hand, in our model some assumptions are ideal, which are much more complicated in the real world. For example, in the real world, the difficulties of compromising various nodes are different. So, when each node is assigned a value indicating the difficulty to be compromised, how to compromise as many private keys as possible with as low price as possible is an interesting problem and may be our future work.

References

1. Ganesan, R.: Yaksha: augmenting kerberos with public key cryptography. In: Proceedings of the 1995 Symposium on Network and Distributed System Security (SNDSS 1995), p. 132. IEEE Computer Society, Washington, DC (1995)
2. Philip, M., Michael, K.R.: Networked cryptographic devices resilient to capture. Technical report (2001)
3. Boneh, D., Ding, X., Tsudik, G., Wong, C.M.: A method for fast revocation of public key certificates and security capabilities. In: Proceedings of the 10th Conference on USENIX Security Symposium, SSYM 2001, vol. 10, p. 22. USENIX Association, Berkeley (2001)
4. Xu, S., Li, X., Parker, P.: Exploiting social networks for threshold signing: attack-resilience vs. availability. In: Proceedings of the 2008 ACM Symposium on Information, Computer and Communications Security, ASIACCS 2008, pp. 325–336. ACM, New York (2008)
5. Vu, L.H., Aberer, K., Buchegger, S., Datta, A.: Enabling secure secret sharing in distributed online social networks. In: Proceedings of the 2009 Annual Computer Security Applications Conference, ACSAC 2009, pp. 419–428. IEEE Computer Society, Washington, DC (2009)
6. Nojoumian, M., Stinson, D., Grainger, M.: Unconditionally secure social secret sharing scheme. IET Information Security 4, 202–211 (2010)

7. Alon, N.: Spectral Techniques in Graph Algorithms. In: Lucchesi, C.L., Moura, A.V. (eds.) LATIN 1998. LNCS, vol. 1380, pp. 206–215. Springer, Heidelberg (1998)
8. Watts, D.J., Strogatz, S.H.: Collective dynamics of 'small-world' networks. Nature 393, 440–442 (1998)
9. Bu, T., Towsley, D.F.: On distinguishing between internet power law topology generators. In: INFOCOM (2002)
10. Viswanath, B., Mislove, A., Cha, M., Gummadi, K.P.: On the evolution of user interaction in facebook. In: Proceedings of the 2nd ACM Workshop on Online Social Networks, WOSN 2009, pp. 37–42. ACM, New York (2009)
11. Golbeck, J.A.: Computing and applying trust in web-based social networks. PhD thesis, College Park, MD, USA (2005) AAI3178583
12. Massa, P., Avesani, P.: Trust metrics on controversial users: balancing between tyranny of the majority and echo chambers. International Journal on Semantic Web and Information Systems (2007)
13. Saxena, N., Tsudik, G., Yi, J.H.: Threshold cryptography in P2P and manets: The case of access control. Comput. Netw. 51, 3632–3649 (2007)
14. Lesueur, F., Mé, L., Viet Triem Tong, V.: A Distributed Certification System for Structured P2P Networks. In: Hausheer, D., Schönwälder, J. (eds.) AIMS 2008. LNCS, vol. 5127, pp. 40–52. Springer, Heidelberg (2008)

A Ciphertext Policy Attribute-Based Encryption Scheme without Pairings*

Jiang Zhang and Zhenfeng Zhang

State Key Laboratory of Information Security,
Institute of Software, Chinese Academy of Sciences, Beijing, 100190, China
{zhangjiang,zfzhang}@is.iscas.ac.cn

Abstract. Sahai and Waters [34] proposed Attribute-Based Encryption
(ABE) as a new paradigm of encryption algorithms that allow the sender
to set a policy to describe who can read the secret data. In recent years,
lots of attribute-based schemes appeared in literatures, but almost all the
schemes, to the best of our knowledge, are constructed from pairings. In
this work, we present a ciphertext policy attribute-based encryption (CP-
ABE) scheme, which supports and-gates without pairings. Our scheme
is defined on q-ary lattices, and has a very strong security proof based
on worst-case hardness. More precisely, under the learning with errors
(LWE) assumption, our CP-ABE scheme is secure against chosen plaintext attack in the selective access structure model. Though our scheme
only encrypts one bit at a time, we point out that it can support multi-
bit encryption by using a well-known technique. Besides, our result can
be easily extended to ideal lattices for a better efficiency.

1 Introduction

Sahai and Waters [34] introduced the notion of attribute-based encryption as
an extension of identity-based encryption (IBE), where users' secret keys are
produced by a trust authority according to a set of attributes. In an ABE system,
a user's secret keys, and ciphertexts are labeled with sets of descriptive attributes
and a particular key can decrypt a particular ciphertext only if there is a match
between the attributes of the ciphertext and the user's key.

Goyal, Pandey, Sahai and Waters [14] further extended the idea of ABE and
introduced two variants: key policy attribute-based encryption (KP-ABE) and
ciphertext policy attribute-based encryption (CP-ABE). In a KP-ABE system,
the ciphertext is associated with a set of descriptive attributes, while the private
key of a party is associated with an access policy which is defined over a set of
attributes and specifies which type of ciphertexts the key can decrypt. A CP-
ABE system can be seen as a complementary form to KP-ABE system, where the
private keys are associated with a set of attributes, while a policy defined over a

---

* The work is supported by the National Natural Science Foundation of China under
Grant No. 60873261, 61170278, and the National Basic Research Program (973) of
China under Grant No. 2007CB311202.

C.-K. Wu, M. Yung, and D. Lin (Eds.): Inscrypt 2011, LNCS 7537, pp. 324–340, 2012.

set of attributes is attached to the ciphertext. A ciphertext can be decrypted by a party if the attributes associated with its private keys satisfy the ciphertext's policy.

Cheung and Newport [9] proposed the first CP-ABE system that supports and-gates, and proved its security under decision bilinear Diffie-Hellman (DBDH) assumption. Since then, there are many attribute-based encryptions that support various access structures. Such as and-gates schemes in [9,27,10], tree-based schemes in [13,19,16], and directly linear secret sharing scheme (LSSS) based constructions in [17,18,36].

All the schemes mentioned above are constructed from pairings, and there are no implications that an (efficient) ABE scheme can be constructed based on other cryptographic assumptions than pairings. Moreover, those pairing related assumptions are known to be vulnerable as we step into a post-quantum era. In contrast, lattice is an ideal choice to construct secure cryptographic schemes according to the following two facts:

- There is no known algorithm that can efficiently solve lattice hard problems even for quantum computers;
- Lattice based cryptographic constructions enjoy several potential advantages: asymptotic efficiency, conceptual simplicity and security proofs based on worst-case hardness.

Unfortunately, there are few attribute-based cryptographic constructions from lattices, though lattice cryptography has gained fruitful results in recent years.

The seminal work of Ajtai [5] brought lattice cryptography into our sight. He gave the first collision-resistant hash function on random lattices in 1996. Later in 2002, Micciancio [25] constructed a hash function on ideal lattices and proved its one-wayness. In 2006, Lyubashevsky and Micciancio [21], Peikert and Rosen [29] independently proved that the hash function in [25] is collision-resistant with some restriction on the domain. As for public encryption setting, in 2005, Regev [31] introduced the learning with error (LWE) problem, and proved that its average-case hardness could be reduced by a quantum algorithm to some standard lattice problems in the worst-case. He also proposed an elegant encryption scheme based on LWE. Later, plenty of constructions based on LWE were proposed (e.g.,[30,32]). In 2009, Peikert [28] gave a classic reduction for LWE problem under an extension hard problem on lattices. In 2008, Gentry, Peikert and Vaikuntanathan [11] gave a famous algorithm that could efficiently sample elements from the distribution (i.e., $D_{\Lambda,s,c}$, see section 3.1). They also gave a digital signature scheme on lattices which was proved to be secure in the random oracle model. Some other signature schemes on lattices have appeared in literatures (e.g., [22,20,12]). Based on the sample algorithm in [11] and the LWE assumption in [31], many IBE and Hierarchical IBE schemes have been proposed (e.g.,[1,2,8]).

More recently, two schemes [3,4] were posted on eprint.iacr.org. Agrawal et al. [3] constructed a fuzzy identity based encryption from lattices. Their construction employed the technique in [1] together with Shamir secret-sharing scheme. If we consider each identity "bit" in their scheme as an attribute, then we obtain a KP-ABE that supports threshold gate policy. They also pointed out that it was difficult to generalize their construction to support more expressive policies. In addition, Agrawal, Freeman and Vaikuntanathan constructed a functional encryption for inner product predicates based on the LWE assumption. They utilized the technique in [1], and also presented a new technique that could transform the ciphertext lattice into a lattice that matches the key lattice (while two lattices are already matched once they are generated in [1]). Their scheme can also be viewed as a ABE scheme that supports inner product policy.

Our contribution. In this paper, we investigate ciphertext policy attribute-based encryption (CP-ABE), which supports and-gates on positive and negative attributes. In this setting, each attribute is associated with two types of attributes, namely positive attribute and negative attribute. And if a user has attribute i, we say he has positive attribute i. Otherwise, we say he has negative attribute i. Actually, positive attribute i and negative attribute i are two different attributes, and denoted by i^+ and i^- respectively. Each user in this system has one and only one of the two attributes, since a user either has attribute i or doesn't. For instance, for a real attribute system which has four attributes $\{att_1, att_2, att_3, att_4\}$, we extend these four attributes into $\{att_1^+, att_1^-, att_2^+, att_2^-, att_3^+, att_3^-, att_4^+, att_4^-\}$ in our system. If a user has attributes $\{att_1, att_3\}$ in the real world, we implicitly define his attributes set as $\{att_1^+, att_2^-, att_3^+, att_4^-\}$. Moreover, all access structures are organized by and-gates in this setting. E.g., a user can decrypt a ciphertext if he has all the positive attributes and doesn't have any negative attributes, which are specified in the ciphertext's policy. For instance, a ciphertext encrypted under access structure $W = (att_1^+$ and att_2^- and $att_3^+)$ can only be decrypted by those who have attributes att_1, att_3 and doesn't have attributes att_2, and we don't care about whether he has att_4.

We propose a ciphertext policy attribute-based encryption that supports and-gates on positive and negative attributes. The basic idea of our construction is that, in the positive and negative setting, each user in this system has an "identity" (i.e., the set of his positive and negative attributes), which is unique in the sense of attribute sets, thus we can use this "identity" to do some things as we do in IBE systems. Specifically, we associate each (positive or negative) attribute with a matrix, actually a matrix uniquely defines a lattice by a well-known definition in lattice cryptography [5]. Thus a user's "identity" uniquely defines a set of lattices. When we generate secret keys for a user with attribute set S, we use his lattices set determined by S to share a public vector, which is used for encryption, by utilizing a trapdoor (i.e., short basis) of these lattices, and the secret key for each attribute in S is a short vector in a lattice (strictly, a coset defined by the lattice) determined by the attribute. As two users with different attribute sets have different "identities", they share the same public vector in two different methods (i.e., in two different lattice sets). The security of this method is guaranteed by Inhomogeneous Small Integer Solution (ISIS) problem [26], which was shown to be as hard as some lattice hard problems. For details see section 4.

To the best of our knowledge, our construction is the first CP-ABE scheme without pairings. Though our construction seems to be not much efficient, it gives light to the possibility of constructing attribute schemes under other hard problem assumptions (e.g., lattice problems), instead of the pairing-related assumptions. Our scheme has a very strong security proof based on worst-case hardness. More precisely, under the learning with errors (LWE) assumption, our CP-ABE scheme is secure against chosen plaintext attack in the selective access structure model.

Our basic construction only encrypts one bit at a time, but as we show later, one can obtain a multi-bit encryption with a small ciphertext expansion (respect to the one bit setting) by using a well-known technique [1]. We also point out that our result can be easily extended to ideal lattices for a better efficiency.

2 Preliminaries

2.1 Notation

The set of real numbers (integers) is denoted by $\mathbb{R}$ ($\mathbb{Z}$, resp.). The function log denotes the natural logarithm. Vectors are in column form and denoted by bold lower-case letters (e.g., $\mathbf{x}$). We view a matrix simply as the set of its column vectors and denoted by bold capital letters (e.g., $\mathbf{X}$).

Denote l_2 and l_∞ norm by $\|\cdot\|$ and $\|\cdot\|_\infty$ respectively. Define the norm of a matrix $\mathbf{X}$ as the norm of its longest column (i.e., $\|\mathbf{X}\| = \max_i \|\mathbf{x}_i\|$). If the columns of $\mathbf{X} = \{\mathbf{x}_1, \ldots, \mathbf{x}_k\}$ are linearly independent, let $\widetilde{\mathbf{X}} = \{\widetilde{\mathbf{x}}_1, \ldots, \widetilde{\mathbf{x}}_k\}$ denote the Gram-Schmidt orthogonalization of vectors $\mathbf{x}_1, \ldots, \mathbf{x}_k$ taken in that order. For $\mathbf{X} \in \mathbb{R}^{n \times m}$ and $\mathbf{Y} \in \mathbb{R}^{n \times m'}$, $[\mathbf{X}\|\mathbf{Y}] \in \mathbb{R}^{n \times (m+m')}$ denotes the concatenation of the columns of $\mathbf{X}$ followed by the columns of $\mathbf{Y}$. And for $\mathbf{X} \in \mathbb{R}^{n \times m}$ and $\mathbf{Y} \in \mathbb{R}^{n' \times m}$, $[\mathbf{X}; \mathbf{Y}] \in \mathbb{R}^{(n+n') \times m}$ is the concatenation of the rows of $\mathbf{X}$ followed by the rows of $\mathbf{Y}$. If S is an attribute set and W is an access structure, $S \vdash W$ means that S satisfies W.

The natural security parameter throughout the paper is n, and all other quantities are implicitly functions of n. Let $poly(n)$ denote an unspecified function $f(n) = O(n^c)$ for some constant c. We use standard notation O, ω to classify the growth of functions. If $f(n) = O(g(n) \cdot \log^c n)$, we denote $f(n) = \tilde{O}(g(n))$. We say a function $f(n)$ is negligible if for every $c > 0$, there exists a N such that $f(n) < 1/n^c$ for all $n > N$. We use $negl(n)$ to denote a negligible function of n, and we say a probability is overwhelming if it is $1 - negl(n)$.

2.2 Ciphertext Policy Attribute-Based Encryption

A ciphertext policy attribute-based encryption (CP-ABE) scheme $\mathcal{ABE} = \{\text{Setup}, \text{KeyGen}, \text{Enc}, \text{Dec}\}$ consists of four algorithms:

- Setup($\lambda, \mathcal{R}$). Given a security parameter λ and an attribute set $\mathcal{R}$, the algorithm returns a public key pk and a master key msk. The public key is used for encryption. The master key, held by the central authority, is used to generate users' secret keys.

- KeyGen(msk, S). The algorithm takes as input the master key msk and an attribute set $S \subseteq \mathcal{R}$, returns a secret key sk_S.
- Enc(pk, W, M) Given the public key pk, an access structure W, and a message M, Enc returns the ciphertext C.
- Dec(sk_S, C) The algorithm takes a secret key sk_S and a ciphertext C as input, it first checks whether the attribute set of sk_S satisfies the access structure W in C. If not, the algorithm returns $\perp$. Otherwise, it decrypts C and returns the result.

For correctness, we require that, for any message $M \in \{0,1\}^*$, access structure W, attribute $S \subseteq \mathcal{R}$ that $S \vdash W$, Dec(ENC(pk, W, M), sk_S) $= M$ holds with overwhelming probability.

Here, we review the security model for CP-ABE in [9,15], in which the attacker specifies the challenge access structure before the setup phase. The formal description of this model is given below:

Init. The adversary chooses the challenge access structure W^* and gives it to the challenger.

Setup. The challenger runs the Setup algorithm, gives pk to the adversary and keeps the master key msk secret.

Key Generation Query: The adversary can adaptively make a number of key generation queries on attribute sets S except that he is not allowed to query an attribute set S that satisfies W^*.

Challenge. At some time, the adversary outputs two messages M_0, M_1, and $|M_0| = |M_1|$. The challenger randomly chooses one bit $b \in \{0,1\}$, computes $C^* = $ Enc(pk, W^*, M_b), and returns C^* to the adversary.

Guess. The adversary makes more key generation queries on any attribute set S with a restriction that S doesn't satisfy W^*. Finally, the adversary will output a bit b'.

The advantage of an adversary $\mathcal{A}$ in the above IND-sCPA game is defined as

$$\mathrm{Adv}_{ABE,\mathcal{A}}^{\text{ind-scpa}}(\lambda) = |\Pr[b = b'] - \frac{1}{2}|$$

Definition 1. *A CP-ABE scheme $\mathcal{ABE}$ is said to be secure against selective chosen plaintext attack (sCPA) if the advantage $Adv_{ABE,\mathcal{A}}^{\text{ind-scpa}}(\lambda)$ is a negligible function in λ for all polynomial time adversary $\mathcal{A}$.*

3 Lattices

Let $\mathbb{R}^n$ be the n-dimensional Euclidean space. A lattice in $\mathbb{R}^n$ is the set

$$\mathcal{L}(\mathbf{b}_i, \ldots, \mathbf{b}_m) = \left\{ \sum_{i=1}^m x_i \mathbf{b}_i : x_i \in \mathbb{Z} \right\}$$

of all integral combinations of m linearly independent vectors $\mathbf{b}_1, \ldots, \mathbf{b}_m \in \mathbb{R}^n$. The integers m and n are called the rank and dimension of the lattice, respectively. The sequence of vectors $\mathbf{b}_1, \ldots, \mathbf{b}_m$ is called a lattice basis and it is conveniently represented as a matrix

$$\mathbf{B} = [\mathbf{b}_1, \ldots, \mathbf{b}_m] \in \mathbb{R}^{n \times m}.$$

The dual lattice of $\mathbf{\Lambda}$, denoted $\mathbf{\Lambda}^*$, is defined to be

$$\mathbf{\Lambda}^* = \left\{ \mathbf{x} \in \mathbb{R}^n : \forall \, \mathbf{v} \in \mathbf{\Lambda}, \ \langle \mathbf{x}, \mathbf{v} \rangle \in \mathbb{Z} \right\}$$

Let $\mathcal{B}_m(\mathbf{0}, r) = \{ \mathbf{x} \in \mathbb{R}^m : \|\mathbf{x}\| < r \}$ be the m-dimensional open ball of radius r centered in $\mathbf{0}$. For any m-dimensional lattice $\mathbf{\Lambda}$, the ith minimum $\lambda_i(\mathbf{\Lambda})$ is the shortest radius r such that $\mathcal{B}_m(\mathbf{0}, r)$ contains i linearly independent lattice vectors. Formally,

$$\lambda_i(\mathbf{\Lambda}) = \inf\{ r : dim(span(\mathbf{\Lambda} \cap \mathcal{B}_m(\mathbf{0}, r))) \geq i \}.$$

For any rank n lattice $\mathbf{\Lambda}$, $\lambda_1(\mathbf{\Lambda}), \ldots, \lambda_n(\mathbf{\Lambda})$ are constants, and $\lambda_1(\mathbf{\Lambda})$ is the length of the shortest vector in $\mathbf{\Lambda}$.

There are some well-known standard hard problems related to λ_i on lattices, and SIVP is one of those problems.

Definition 2 (Shortest Independent Vector Problem, SIVP). *Given a basis $\mathbf{B}$ of an n-dimensional lattice $\mathbf{\Lambda} = \mathcal{L}(\mathbf{B})$, the goal of a $SIVP_\gamma$ problem is to find a set of n linearly independent lattice vectors $\mathbf{S} = \{ \mathbf{s}_1, \ldots, \mathbf{s}_n \} \subset \mathbf{\Lambda}$, such that $\|\mathbf{S}\| \leq \gamma(n) \cdot \lambda_n(\mathbf{\Lambda})$, where $\gamma = \gamma(n)$ is the approximation factor as a function of the dimension.*

Let $\mathbf{A} \in \mathbb{Z}_q^{n \times m}$ for some positive integers n, m, q, we consider two kinds of full-rank m-dimensional integer lattices defined by $\mathbf{A}$:

$$\mathbf{\Lambda}_q^{\perp}(\mathbf{A}) = \left\{ \mathbf{e} \in \mathbb{Z}^m \ s.t. \ \mathbf{A}\mathbf{e} = 0 \ (\bmod \ q) \right\}$$

$$\mathbf{\Lambda}_q(\mathbf{A}) = \left\{ \mathbf{y} \in \mathbb{Z}^m \ s.t. \ \exists \mathbf{s} \in \mathbb{Z}^n, \ \mathbf{A}^{\mathbf{T}}\mathbf{s} = \mathbf{y} \ (\bmod \ q) \right\}$$

The two lattices defined above are dual when properly scaled, as $\mathbf{\Lambda}_q^{\perp}(\mathbf{A}) = q\mathbf{\Lambda}_q(\mathbf{A})^*$ and $\mathbf{\Lambda}_q(\mathbf{A}) = q\mathbf{\Lambda}_q^{\perp}(\mathbf{A})^*$.

For any fixed $\mathbf{u}$, define the coset of $\mathbf{\Lambda}_q^{\perp}(\mathbf{A})$ as

$$\mathbf{\Lambda}_q^{\mathbf{u}}(\mathbf{A}) = \left\{ \mathbf{e} \in \mathbb{Z}^m \ s.t. \ \mathbf{A}\mathbf{e} = \mathbf{u} \ (\bmod \ q) \right\}.$$

The following hard-on-average problem was first proposed by Ajtai [5], and then was formalized by Micciancio and Regev in [26].

Definition 3 (Small Integer Solution Problem). *The Small Integer Solution (SIS) problem in l_2 norm is: Given an integer q, a random matrix $\mathbf{A} \in \mathbb{Z}_q^{n \times m}$, and a real β, find a non-zero integer vector $e \in \mathbb{Z}^m$ such that $\mathbf{A}e = \mathbf{0}$ (mod q) and $\|e\| \leq \beta$. Equivalently, the SIS problem asks to find a vector $e \in \Lambda_q^\perp(\mathbf{A}) \backslash \{\mathbf{0}\}$ with $\|e\| \leq \beta$.*

Micciancio and Regev also defined a variant problem, called ISIS problem, which is to find a short solution to a random inhomogeneous system.

Definition 4 (Inhomogeneous Small Integer Solution Problem). *The Inhomogeneous Small Integer Solution (ISIS) problem in l_2 norm is: Given an integer q, a random matrix $\mathbf{A} \in \mathbb{Z}_q^{n \times m}$, a syndrome $\mathbf{u} \in \mathbb{Z}_q^n$, and a real β, find a non-zero integer vector $e \in \mathbb{Z}^m$ such that $\mathbf{A}e = \mathbf{u}$ (mod q) and $\|e\| \leq \beta$. The average-case problem $ISIS_{q,m,\beta}$ is defined similarly, where $\mathbf{A}$ and $\mathbf{u}$ are uniformly random and independent.*

The SIS and ISIS problems were shown to be as hard as certain worst-case lattice problems in [11].

Proposition 1 ([11]). *For any poly-bounded $m, \beta = poly(n)$ and any prime $q \geq \beta \omega(\sqrt{n \log n})$, the average-case problems $SIS_{q,m,\beta}$ and $ISIS_{q,m,\beta}$ are as hard as approximating the SIVP problem in the worst case to within certain $\gamma = \beta \cdot \widetilde{O}(\sqrt{n})$ factors.*

3.1 Discrete Gaussians

For any $s > 0$, define the Gaussian function on $\Lambda \subset \mathbb{Z}^n$ centered at $\mathbf{c}$ with parameter s:

$$\forall \mathbf{x} \in \Lambda, \ \rho_{s,\mathbf{c}}(\mathbf{x}) = \exp\left(-\pi \frac{\|\mathbf{x} - \mathbf{c}\|^2}{s^2}\right).$$

Let $\rho_{s,\mathbf{c}}(\Lambda) = \sum_{\mathbf{x} \in \Lambda} \rho_{s,\mathbf{c}}(\mathbf{x})$. Define the discrete Gaussian distribution over Λ with center $\mathbf{c}$, and parameter s as:

$$\forall \mathbf{y} \in \Lambda, D_{\Lambda,s,c}(\mathbf{y}) = \frac{\rho_{s,\mathbf{c}}(\mathbf{y})}{\rho_{s,\mathbf{c}}(\Lambda)}.$$

The subscripts s and $\mathbf{c}$ are taken to be 1 and $\mathbf{0}$ (respectively) when omitted.

Micciancio and Regev [26] proposed a lattice quantity called smoothing parameter:

Definition 5 ([26]). *For any n-dimensional lattice Λ and positive real $\epsilon > 0$, the smoothing parameter η_ϵ is the smallest real $s > 0$ such that $\rho_{1/s}(\Lambda^* \backslash \{\mathbf{0}\}) \leq \epsilon$.*

3.2 Learning with Errors

The learning with errors problem on lattices was proposed by Regev [31]. The hardness of the problem can be reduced by a quantum algorithm to some standard lattices problems (i.e., SIVP) in the worst case. For any $\alpha \in \mathbb{R}^+$, Ψ_α is defined to be the distribution on $\mathbb{T}$ of a normal variable with mean 0 and standard $\alpha/\sqrt{2\pi}$, reduced modulo 1.

$$\forall r \in [0,1), \ \Psi_\alpha(r) := \sum_{k=-\infty}^{\infty} \frac{1}{\alpha} \cdot \exp(-\pi(\frac{r-k}{\alpha})^2).$$

For any probability distribution $\phi : \mathbb{T} \to \mathbb{R}^+$ and some integer $q \geq 1$, the discrete distribution $\bar{\phi}$ over $\mathbb{Z}_q$ is the random variable $\lfloor q \cdot X_\phi \rceil \bmod q$, where X_ϕ has distribution ϕ. By the standard tail inequality: a normal variable with variance σ^2 is within distance $t \cdot \sigma$ of its mean, except with probability at most $\frac{1}{t}\exp(-t^2/2)$. We have that, for any $m = poly(n)$ independent variables $\mathbf{e} = (e_1, \ldots, e_m)$ from $\bar{\Psi}_\alpha$ over $\mathbb{Z}_q$, $\|\mathbf{e}\| \leq \alpha q\sqrt{m}\omega(\sqrt{\log m})$ with overwhelming probability, since each $\|e_i\| \leq \alpha q \omega(\sqrt{\log m})$ holds with probability negligible to 1.

For $q \geq 2$ and some probability distribution χ over $\mathbb{Z}_q$, an integer $n \in \mathbb{Z}^+$ and a vector $\mathbf{s} \in \mathbb{Z}_q^n$, define $A_{\mathbf{s},\chi} \subseteq \mathbb{Z}_q^n \times \mathbb{Z}_q$ as the distribution of variable $(\mathbf{a}, \mathbf{a}^T\mathbf{s}+x)$, where $\mathbf{a}$ and x are informally chosen from $\mathbb{Z}_q^n$ and χ respectively, and all operations are performed in $\mathbb{Z}_q$. For any m independent samples $(\mathbf{a}_1, y_1), \ldots, (\mathbf{a}_m, y_m)$ from $A_{\mathbf{s},\chi}$, we simply denote it by $(\mathbf{A}, \mathbf{y}) \in \mathbb{Z}_q^{n \times m} \times \mathbb{Z}_q^m$, where $\mathbf{A} = (\mathbf{a}_1, \ldots, \mathbf{a}_m)$ and $\mathbf{y} = (y_1, \ldots, y_m)^T$.

Learning with Errors (LWE). For an integer $q = q(n)$ and a distribution χ on $\mathbb{Z}_q$, we say that an algorithm solves $\text{LWE}_{q,\chi}$ if, for any $\mathbf{s} \in \mathbb{Z}_q^n$, given samples from $A_{\mathbf{s},\chi}$ it outputs $\mathbf{s}$ with probability exponentially close to 1.

The decisional variant of the LWE problem is to distinguish samples chosen according to $A_{\mathbf{s},\chi}$ for a uniformly random $\mathbf{s} \in \mathbb{Z}_q^n$ from samples chosen according to the uniform distribution over $\mathbb{Z}_q^n \times \mathbb{Z}_q$. Regev [31] showed that for $q = poly(n)$ prime, LWE and its decisional version are polynomially equivalent. He proved that for certain modulus q and Gaussian error distribution χ, $\text{LWE}_{q,\chi}$ is as hard as solving SIVP problems using a quantum algorithm.

Proposition 2 ([31]). *Let $\alpha = \alpha(n) \in (0,1)$ and let $q = q(n)$ be a prime such that $\alpha \cdot q > 2\sqrt{n}$. If there exists an efficient (possibly quantum) algorithm that solves $\text{LWE}_{q,\bar{\Psi}_\alpha}$, then there exists an efficient quantum algorithm for approximating SIVP in the l_2 norm, in the worst case, to within $\tilde{O}(n/\alpha)$ factors.*

3.3 Some Facts

Here, we list several facts about lattices in literatures.

Lemma 1 ([26]). *For any n-dimensional lattice Λ, vector $\mathbf{c} \in \mathbb{R}^n$, and reals $0 < \epsilon < 1, s \geq \eta_\epsilon(\Lambda)$, we have*

$$\Pr_{\mathbf{x} \sim D_{\Lambda,s,\mathbf{c}}} [\|\mathbf{x} - \mathbf{c}\| > s\sqrt{n}] \leq \frac{1-\epsilon}{1+\epsilon} \cdot 2^{-n}.$$

For a lattice Λ, define the Gram-Schmidt minimum as $\tilde{bl}(\Lambda) = \min_{\mathbf{B}} \|\tilde{\mathbf{B}}\|$, where the minimum is taken over all (ordered) bases $\mathbf{B}$ of Λ.

Lemma 2 ([11]). *For any n-dimensional lattice Λ and real $\epsilon > 0$, we have $\eta_\epsilon(\Lambda) \leq \tilde{bl}(\Lambda) \cdot \sqrt{(\log(2n(1 + 1/\epsilon))/\pi}$. Then for any $\omega(\sqrt{\log n})$ function, there is a negligible $\epsilon(n)$ for which $\eta_\epsilon(\Lambda) \leq \tilde{bl}(\Lambda) \cdot \omega(\sqrt{\log n})$.*

Proposition 3 ([11]). *There is a probabilistic polynomial-time algorithm that, given a basis $\mathbf{B}$ of an n-dimensional lattice $\Lambda = \mathcal{L}(\mathbf{B})$, a parameter $s \geq \|\widetilde{\mathbf{B}}\| \cdot \omega(\sqrt{\log n})$, and a center $\mathbf{c} \in \mathbb{R}^n$, outputs a sample from a distribution that is statistically close to $D_{\Lambda,s,\mathbf{c}}$.*

We refer to the algorithm of Proposition 3 as SampleGaussian$(\mathbf{B}, s, \mathbf{c})$, which takes a basis $\mathbf{B}$ for a lattice $\Lambda \subset \mathbb{R}^m$, a positive real $s \geq \|\widetilde{\mathbf{B}}\| \cdot \omega(\sqrt{\log m})$, and a vector $\mathbf{c} \in \mathbb{R}^m$ as input, outputs a random vector $\mathbf{x} \in \Lambda$ drawn from a distribution statistically close to $D_{\Lambda,s,\mathbf{c}}$.

Proposition 4 ([11]). *Let n and q be a positive integers with q prime, and let $m \geq 2n \log q$. Then for all but a $2q^{-n}$ fraction of all $\mathbf{A} \in \mathbb{Z}_q^{n \times m}$ and for any $s \geq \omega(\sqrt{\log m})$, the distribution of the syndrome $\mathbf{u} = \mathbf{Ae} \bmod q$ is statistically close to uniform over $\mathbb{Z}_q^n$, where $\mathbf{e} \backsim D_{\mathbb{Z}^m,s}$.*

Gentry, Peikert and Vaikuntanathan [11] showed that, for any $\mathbf{u} \in \mathbb{Z}_q^n$, $\mathbf{t} \in \mathbb{Z}^m$ such that $\mathbf{At} = \mathbf{u} \bmod q$, the conditional distribution of $\mathbf{e} \backsim D_{\mathbb{Z}^m,s}$ given $\mathbf{Ae} = \mathbf{u} \bmod q$ is exactly $\mathbf{t} + D_{\Lambda_q^\perp(\mathbf{A}),s,-\mathbf{t}}$. Furthermore, there is an algorithm SamplePre$(\mathbf{A}, \mathbf{T_A}, s, \mathbf{u})$, that takes input a short basis $\mathbf{T_A}$ for $\Lambda_q^\perp(\mathbf{A})$, a real $s \geq \|\widetilde{\mathbf{T_A}}\| \cdot \omega(\sqrt{\log m})$, and a vector $\mathbf{u} \in \mathbb{Z}^n$, outputs a vector $\mathbf{e} \backsim D_{\mathbb{Z}^m,s}$ condition on $\mathbf{Ae} = \mathbf{u}$.

Proposition 5 ([6]). *For any $\delta_0 > 0$, there is a probabilistic polynomial-time algorithm that, on input a security parameter n, an odd prime $q=poly(n)$, and integer $m \geq (5 + 3\delta_0)n \log q$, outputs a statistically $(mq^{-\delta_0 n/2})$-close to uniform matrix $\mathbf{A} \in \mathbb{Z}_q^{n \times m}$ and a basis $\mathbf{T_A} \subset \Lambda_q^\perp(\mathbf{A})$ such that with overwhelming probability $\|\mathbf{T_A}\| \leq O(n \log q)$ and $\|\widetilde{\mathbf{T_A}}\| \leq O(\sqrt{n \log q})$.*

For concreteness, we use TrapGen(n, m, q) to denote the algorithm in Proposition 5. Note that if we let $\delta_0 = \frac{1}{3}$, we can choose $m \geq \lceil 6n \log q \rceil$.

Lemma 3 ([1]). *Let $\mathbf{e}$ be some vector in $\mathbb{Z}^m$ and let $\mathbf{y} \leftarrow \bar{\Psi}_\alpha^m$. Then the quantity $|\mathbf{e}^T\mathbf{y}|$ treated as an integer in $[0, q-1]$ satisfies*

$$|\mathbf{e}^T\mathbf{y}| \leq \|\mathbf{e}\| q\alpha\omega(\sqrt{\log m}) + \|\mathbf{e}\|\sqrt{m}/2$$

with all but negligible probability in m. In particularly, if $x \leftarrow \bar{\Psi}_\alpha$ is treated as an integer in $[0, q-1]$ then $|x| \leq q\alpha\omega(\sqrt{\log m}) + 1/2$ with all but negligible probability in m.

For convenience, we give the following lemma, which is implied by Theorem 3.4 in [7].

Lemma 4. *There exists an algorithm that takes* $\mathbf{A}_1 \in \mathbb{Z}_q^{n \times m}, \ldots, \mathbf{A}_k \in \mathbb{Z}_q^{n \times m}$, *a basis* $\mathbf{S}_i$ *of* $\Lambda_q^{\perp}(\mathbf{A}_i)$, *and a vector* $\mathbf{u} \in \mathbb{Z}_q^n$, *a real* $s \geq \|\tilde{\mathbf{S}}_i\| \cdot \omega(\sqrt{\log km})$ *as input, outputs a vector* $\mathbf{e} \sim D_{\Lambda_q^{\mathbf{u}}(\mathbf{A}),s}$ *with overwhelming probability, where* $\mathbf{A} = [\mathbf{A}_1 \| \ldots \| \mathbf{A}_k]$, *and each* $\mathbf{A}_i$ *is randomly chosen from* $\mathbb{Z}_q^{n \times m}$.

The algorithm first randomly chooses $\mathbf{e}_j$ from $D_{\mathbb{Z}^{m_j},s}$ for all $j \neq i$, then it computes $\mathbf{u}' = \mathbf{u} - \sum_{j \neq i} \mathbf{A}_j \mathbf{e}_j$. Finally, it computes $\mathbf{e}_i \leftarrow \mathtt{SamplePre}(\mathbf{A}_i, \mathbf{S}_i, s, \mathbf{u}')$ and outputs $\mathbf{e} = [\mathbf{e}_1; \ldots; \mathbf{e}_k]$.

For simplicity of notation, we denote the new algorithm by $\mathtt{SamplePre}$ as before.

4   A CP-ABE Scheme on Lattices

In this section, we present our CP-ABE scheme in which the access structures are and-gates on positive and negative attributes. Basically, each negative attribute is considered as a new attribute [9]. Namely, if a user has attribute set $S \subseteq \mathcal{R}$ in the real system, we consider all of his attributes in S as positive attributes, and the other attributes in $\mathcal{R} \setminus S$ are implicitly considered as his negative ones. Hence, each user in our system actually has $|\mathcal{R}|$ attributes. Without loss of generality, we denote $\mathcal{R} = \{1, \ldots, |\mathcal{R}|\}$.

Our construction is defined below, which is parameterized by modulus q, dimension m, Gaussian parameter s, and α that determines the error distribution χ. Usually, all these parameters are functions of security parameter n, and all of these will be instantiated later. All the additions here are performed in $\mathbb{Z}_q$.

$\mathtt{Setup}(n, m, q, \mathcal{R})$: Given positive integers n, m, q, and an attribute set $\mathcal{R}$, first compute $(\mathbf{B}_0, \mathbf{T}_{\mathbf{B}_0}) \leftarrow \mathtt{TrapGen}(n, m, q)$. Then for each $i \in \mathcal{R}$, randomly choose $\mathbf{B}_{i+} \leftarrow \mathbb{Z}_q^{n \times m}$, $\mathbf{B}_{i-} \leftarrow \mathbb{Z}_q^{n \times m}$. Next, randomly choose a vector $\mathbf{u} \leftarrow \mathbb{Z}_q^n$, and set public key $pk = (\mathbf{B}_0, \{\mathbf{B}_{i+}, \mathbf{B}_{i-}\}_{i \in \mathcal{R}}, \mathbf{u})$, and master secret key $msk = (pk, \mathbf{T}_{\mathbf{B}_0})$. Finally, return (pk, msk).

$\mathtt{KGen}(msk, S)$: Given the master secret key msk and a user's attribute set $S \subseteq \mathcal{R}$, for each $i \in \mathcal{R}$, if $i \in S$, define $\tilde{\mathbf{B}}_i = \mathbf{B}_{i+}$, else define $\tilde{\mathbf{B}}_i = \mathbf{B}_{i-}$. Then for each $i \in \mathcal{R}$, randomly choose $\mathbf{e}_i \leftarrow D_{\mathbb{Z}^m,s}$, and compute $\mathbf{y} = \mathbf{u} - \sum_{i \in R} \tilde{\mathbf{B}}_i \mathbf{e}_i$. Finally, compute $\mathbf{e}_0 \leftarrow \mathtt{SamplePre}(\mathbf{B}_0, \mathbf{T}_{\mathbf{B}_0}, s, \mathbf{y})$, and return secret key $\mathbf{sk}_S = [\mathbf{e}_0; \ldots; \mathbf{e}_{|\mathcal{R}|}]$.

Observe that, if let $\mathbf{D} = [\mathbf{B}_0 \| \tilde{\mathbf{B}}_1 \| \ldots \| \tilde{\mathbf{B}}_{|\mathcal{R}|}]$, we have $\mathbf{D} \cdot \mathbf{sk}_S = \mathbf{u}$.

$\mathtt{Enc}(pk, W, M)$: Given the public key $pk = (\{\mathbf{B}_{i+}, \mathbf{B}_{i-}\}_{i \in \mathcal{R}}, \mathbf{u})$, an access structure W, and a message bit $M \in \{0, 1\}$, denote $S^+(S^-)$ as the set of positive (negative) attributes in W, and $S' = S^+ \cup S^-$. Then for each $i \in S'$, if $i \in S^+$, define $\tilde{\mathbf{B}}_i = \mathbf{B}_{i+}$, else, define $\tilde{\mathbf{B}}_i = \mathbf{B}_{i-}$. Next, randomly choose $\mathbf{s} \leftarrow \mathbb{Z}_q^n$ and compute:
- $z = \mathbf{u}^T \mathbf{s} + x_z + M \lfloor \frac{q}{2} \rfloor$, where $x_z \leftarrow \chi$,
- $\mathbf{c}_0 = \mathbf{B}_0^T \mathbf{s} + \mathbf{x}_0$, where $\mathbf{x}_0 \leftarrow \chi^m$,
- $\mathbf{c}_i = \tilde{\mathbf{B}}_i^T \mathbf{s} + \mathbf{x}_i$ for each $i \in S'$, where $\mathbf{x}_i \leftarrow \chi^m$,
- $\mathbf{c}_{i+} = \mathbf{B}_{i+}^T \mathbf{s} + \mathbf{x}_{i+}$ and $\mathbf{c}_{i-} = \mathbf{B}_{i-}^T \mathbf{s} + \mathbf{x}_{i-}$ for each $i \in \mathcal{R} \setminus S'$, where $\mathbf{x}_{i+}, \mathbf{x}_{i-} \leftarrow \chi^m$.

Finally, return ciphertext $C = (W, z, \mathbf{c}_0, \{\mathbf{c}_i\}_{i \in S'}, \{\mathbf{c}_{i+}, \mathbf{c}_{i-}\}_{i \in \mathcal{R} \setminus S'})$.

Dec($C, \mathbf{sk}$): Given the ciphertext C and the secret key $\mathbf{sk} = [\mathbf{e}_0; \ldots; \mathbf{e}_{|\mathcal{R}|}]$, let S be the attribute set associated to $\mathbf{sk}$, if S doesn't satisfy W, then return $\bot$. Otherwise $S \vdash W$. Define $S^+(S^-)$ as the set of positive (negative) attributes in W, and $S' = S^+ \cup S^-$. Obliviously, $S^+ \subset S$ and $S^- \cap S = \emptyset$. Parse C into $(W, z, \mathbf{c}_0, \{\mathbf{c}_i\}_{i \in S'}, \{\mathbf{c}_{i+}, \mathbf{c}_{i-}\}_{i \in \mathcal{R} \setminus S'})$. Then let $\mathbf{y}_i = \mathbf{c}_i$ for each $i \in S' \cup \{0\}$, and for each $i \in \mathcal{R} \setminus S'$, if $i \in S$, let $\mathbf{y}_i = \mathbf{c}_{i+}$, else let $\mathbf{y}_i = \mathbf{c}_{i-}$. Define $\mathbf{y} = [\mathbf{y}_0; \mathbf{y}_1; \ldots; \mathbf{y}_{|\mathcal{R}|}]$, and compute $a = \mathbf{sk}^T \mathbf{y} = \mathbf{u}^T \mathbf{s} + x'$, $b = z - a = x_z - x' + M\lfloor \frac{q}{2} \rfloor$. Finally, If $|b - \lfloor \frac{q}{2} \rfloor| \leq \lfloor \frac{q}{4} \rfloor$ in $\mathbb{Z}$, return 1, otherwise return 0.

4.1   Parameters and Correctness

Let $\mathbf{D}$ be the matrix determined by the attribute set in $\mathbf{sk}$, thus $\mathbf{D} \cdot \mathbf{sk} = \mathbf{u}$. By the method we choose vector $\mathbf{y}$, we have $\mathbf{y} = \mathbf{D}^T \mathbf{s} + \mathbf{x}_y$, where $\mathbf{s} \in \mathbb{Z}_q^n, \mathbf{x}_y \in \chi^{m(|\mathcal{R}|+1)}$ are chosen in the encryption. Thus, $a = \mathbf{sk}^T \mathbf{y} = \mathbf{sk}^T (\mathbf{D}^T \mathbf{s} + \mathbf{x}_y) = \mathbf{u}^T \mathbf{s} + \mathbf{sk}^T \mathbf{x}_y = \mathbf{u}^T \mathbf{s} + x'$. And if $|x_z - x'| \leq q/5$ holds (with overwhelming probability), it is easy to check that our decryption algorithm always outputs plaintext M correctly.

Now we set the parameters to achieve our goal.

- For algorithm TrapGen, we need $m \geq \lceil 6n \log q \rceil$ (i.e., by Proposition 5).
- For the security proof and SamplePre, we need $s \geq \|\tilde{\mathbf{T}}_{\mathbf{B}_0}\| \cdot \omega(\sqrt{\log(m(|\mathcal{R}| + 1))})$ (i.e., by Lemma 4).
- For the hardness of LWE, we need $\alpha q > 2\sqrt{n}$ (i.e., by Proposition 2).
- For the decryption algorithm works correctly, we need $|x_z - x'| \leq q/5$.

Note that $\|\tilde{\mathbf{T}}_{\mathbf{B}_0}\| \leq O(\sqrt{n \log q})$ by Proposition 5, $\|\mathbf{sk}\| \leq s\sqrt{m(|\mathcal{R}| + 1)}$ by Lemma 1, $|x_z| \leq q\alpha\omega(\sqrt{\log m}) + 1/2$ and $|x'| \leq \|\mathbf{sk}\| q\alpha\omega(\sqrt{\log(m(|\mathcal{R}| + 1))}) + \|\mathbf{sk}\|\sqrt{m(|\mathcal{R}| + 1)}/2$ by Lemma 3. We obtain $|x_z - x'| \leq sq\alpha\sqrt{m(|\mathcal{R}| + 1)} \cdot \omega(\sqrt{\log(m(|\mathcal{R}| + 1))}) + sm(|\mathcal{R}| + 1)$.

To satisfy all the conditions above, we assume δ is real such that $n^\delta > \lceil \log q \rceil$, and set m, s, q, α as below:

$$m = 6n^{1+\delta}$$
$$s = \sqrt{m}\omega(\sqrt{\log(m(|\mathcal{R}| + 1))})$$
$$q = sm(|\mathcal{R}| + 1) \cdot w(\sqrt{\log(m(|\mathcal{R}| + 1))})$$
$$\alpha = (s\sqrt{m(|\mathcal{R}| + 1)} \cdot \omega(\sqrt{\log(m(|\mathcal{R}| + 1))}))^{-1}$$

4.2   Security

Theorem 1. *Let m, s, q, α as above, and let $\chi = \bar{\Psi}_\alpha$. Then if $LWE_{q,\chi}$ is hard, our CP-ABE scheme is secure against selective chosen ciphertext attack (sCPA).*

In particularly, if there exists an adversary $\mathcal{A}$ that breaks the sCPA security of our scheme with advantage ϵ, then there exists an algorithm $\mathcal{B}$ solves $LWE_{q,\chi}$ with probability ϵ.

Proof. Suppose there exists a polynomial time adversary $\mathcal{A}$ that breaks the sCPA security of our CP-ABE scheme with advantage ϵ and makes at most q key generation queries. We construct an algorithm $\mathcal{B}$ that solves the LWE problem with probability negligible to ϵ.

Note that algorithm $\mathcal{B}$ has an oracle $\mathcal{O}(\cdot)$, and he wants to decide whether the samples output by $\mathcal{O}(\cdot)$ is from $A_{\mathbf{s},\chi}$ or uniform. $\mathcal{B}$ runs adversary $\mathcal{A}$ and simulates $\mathcal{A}$'s view in the sCPA security experiment as follows:

Init. Adversary $\mathcal{A}$ chooses a challenge access structure W^* and gives it to $\mathcal{B}$. Let $S^+(S^-)$ be the set of positive (negative) attributes in W^*, and let $S' = S^+ \cup S^-$.

Setup. After receiving W^*, $\mathcal{B}$ compute:
- $\mathcal{B}$ obtains $(\mathbf{B}_0, \mathbf{v}_0) \in \mathbb{Z}_q^{n \times m} \times \mathbb{Z}_q^m$ and $(\mathbf{u}, v_u) \in \mathbb{Z}_q^n \times \mathbb{Z}_q$ from $\mathcal{O}(\cdot)$.
- For each $i \in \mathcal{R} \backslash S'$, $\mathcal{B}$ obtains $(\mathbf{B}_{i+}, \mathbf{v}_{i+}), (\mathbf{B}_{i-}, \mathbf{v}_{i-}) \in \mathbb{Z}_q^{n \times m} \times \mathbb{Z}_q^m$ from $\mathcal{O}(\cdot)$.
- For each $i \in S^+$, $\mathcal{B}$ obtains $(\mathbf{B}_{i+}, \mathbf{v}_{i+}) \in \mathbb{Z}_q^{n \times m} \times \mathbb{Z}_q^m$ from $\mathcal{O}(\cdot)$, then compute $(\mathbf{B}_{i-}, \mathbf{T}_{\mathbf{B}_{i-}}) \leftarrow \mathtt{TrapGen}(n, m, q)$.
- For each $i \in S^-$, $\mathcal{B}$ obtains $(\mathbf{B}_{i-}, \mathbf{v}_{i-}) \in \mathbb{Z}_q^{n \times m} \times \mathbb{Z}_q^m$ from $\mathcal{O}(\cdot)$, then compute $(\mathbf{B}_{i+}, \mathbf{T}_{\mathbf{B}_{i+}}) \leftarrow \mathtt{TrapGen}(n, m, q)$.

Finally, $\mathcal{B}$ sets $pk = (\mathbf{B}_0, \{\mathbf{B}_{i+}, \mathbf{B}_{i-}\}_{i \in R}, \mathbf{u})$, and keeps $(\{\mathbf{T}_{\mathbf{B}_{i-}}, \mathbf{v}_{i+}\}_{i \in S^+},$ $\{\mathbf{T}_{\mathbf{B}_{i+}}, \mathbf{v}_{i-}\}_{i \in S^-}, \{\mathbf{v}_{i+}, \mathbf{v}_{i-}\}_{i \in \mathcal{R} \backslash S'})$ secret.

Key Generation Queries. After receiving a query with attribute set $S \subseteq \mathcal{R}$. If $S \vdash W^*$, $\mathcal{B}$ simply outputs $\bot$. Otherwise, for each $i \in \mathcal{R}$, if $i \in S$, $\mathcal{B}$ lets $\tilde{\mathbf{B}}_i = \mathbf{B}_{i+}$, else lets $\tilde{\mathbf{B}}_i = \mathbf{B}_{i-}$. Since S doesn't satisfy W^*, namely $S^+ \cap S \neq S^+$ or $S^- \cap S \neq \emptyset$,
there must exists a $j \in \mathcal{R}$, such that $\tilde{\mathbf{B}}_j$ is generated by $\mathtt{TrapGen}$. Hence, $\mathcal{B}$ knows its trapdoor $\mathbf{T}_{\tilde{\mathbf{B}}_j}$. Let $\mathbf{D} = [\mathbf{B}_0 \| \tilde{\mathbf{B}}_1 \| \ldots \| \tilde{\mathbf{B}}_n \|]$, $\mathcal{B}$ computes $\mathbf{e}_S \leftarrow \mathtt{SamplePre}(\mathbf{D}, \mathbf{T}_{\tilde{\mathbf{B}}_j}, s, \mathbf{u})$, and returns $sk_S = \mathbf{e}_S$ to $\mathcal{A}$.

Challenge. When $\mathcal{A}$ submits $M_0, M_1 \in \{0, 1\}$, $\mathcal{B}$ randomly chooses $b \in \{0, 1\}$, and computes $z = v_u + M_b \lfloor \frac{q}{2} \rfloor$ and $\mathbf{c}_0 = \mathbf{v}_0$. For each $i \in S^+$, let $\mathbf{c}_i = \mathbf{v}_{i+}$. For each $i \in S^-$, let $\mathbf{c}_i = \mathbf{v}_{i-}$. For each $i \in \mathcal{R} \backslash S'$, let $\mathbf{c}_{i+} = \mathbf{v}_{i+}$ and $\mathbf{c}_{i-} = \mathbf{v}_{i-}$. Finally, $\mathcal{B}$ returns $C^* = (W, z, \mathbf{c}_0, \{\mathbf{c}_i\}_{i \in S'}, \{\mathbf{c}_{i+}, \mathbf{c}_{i-}\}_{i \in \mathcal{R} \backslash S'})$.

$\mathcal{A}$ can make more key generation queries on attribute set S that doesn't satisfy W^*. Eventually, $\mathcal{A}$ outputs a bit b' as a guess for b. if $b' = b$, $\mathcal{B}$ outputs 1, else outputs 0.

Note that $\mathcal{B}$ answers the key generation queries almost the same as the challenger does in the real game by Lemma 4. On one hand, if $\mathcal{O}(\cdot)$ is a LWE oracle for some $\mathbf{s}^*$, C^* is a valid ciphertext, thus the distribution of $\mathcal{A}$'s view is statistically close to that in the real game. On the other hand, if $\mathcal{O}(\cdot)$ is chosen from uniform, then the ciphertext z is uniform on $\mathbb{Z}_q$, thus the probability that $\mathcal{A}$ guesses the right b is exactly $1/2$. So if $\mathcal{A}$ can break our system, $\mathcal{B}$ can break the LWE assumption, which yields our claim.

5   Multi-bit Encryption

Note that, our basic construction only encrypts one bit at a time, but as many other encryption schemes based on LWE (e.g., [11,1]), it is secure to reuse the same random coin $\mathbf{s}$ to encrypt multiple message bits.

Basically, in the ciphertext there is only one element $z \in \mathbb{Z}_q$ that contains the message information (i.e., $z = \mathbf{u}^T\mathbf{s} + x_z + M\lfloor\frac{q}{2}\rfloor$). In order to encrypt N bits message, a matrix $\mathbf{U} = (\mathbf{u}_1, \ldots, \mathbf{u}_N) \in \mathbb{Z}_q^{n \times N}$ is chosen instead of a vector $\mathbf{u} \in \mathbb{Z}_q^n$ in the public key. And for the jth bit of message $(M_1, \ldots, M_N) \in \{0,1\}^N$, compute $z_j = \mathbf{u}_j^T\mathbf{s} + x_{zj} + M_j\lfloor\frac{q}{2}\rfloor$. For a user whose attributes satisfy a ciphertext's policy can decrypt the ciphertext, the key generation has to generate secret keys $sk_1, \ldots, sk_N$ for him, where each sk_j are independently produced as in our basic construction by using $\mathbf{u}_j$ instead of $\mathbf{u}$. For completeness, we present our multi-bit encryption in Table 1.

We claim that the multi-bit encryption is also secure under the LWE assumption. As in the security proof of our basic scheme, $(\mathbf{u}, v_u)$ are drawn from the oracle $\mathcal{O}(\cdot)$. Here, we can simply get a matrix $(\mathbf{U}, \mathbf{v}_U) \in \mathbb{Z}_q^{n \times N} \times \mathbb{Z}_q^N$ by independently drawing from the same oracle N times, and set $z_j = v_j + M_j\lfloor\frac{q}{2}\rfloor$ in the challenge ciphertext. Thus, we can simulate the security experiment perfectly as in the one bit setting.

Note that, the total ciphertext with this technique is 1 element of $\mathbb{Z}_q$ for each bit of messages, plus at least $m|\mathcal{R}|$ elements of $\mathbb{Z}_q$ regardless of the message length. Thus the ciphertext size is at least $N + m|\mathcal{R}|$ (at most $N + 2m|\mathcal{R}|$) elements of $\mathbb{Z}_q$.

6   On Ideal Lattices

In 2002, Micciancio constructed a hash function [25] based on a kind of special structure lattices which called cyclic lattices or ideal lattices. Since then, many works on ideal lattices have appeared (e.g., [23,33,24]). Usually, the schemes based on ideal lattices have asymptotical computation efficiency and require small storage. Using the known results showed below with some more subtle considerations, our result can be extended to the ideal lattices with a shorter key and ciphertext size.

Stehlé, Steinfeld, Tanaka and Xagawa [35] constructed an efficient public key encryption algorithm on ideal lattices. In their work, they gave an algorithm TrapGen, which can be considered as similar version of the one in Proposition 5 in the ideal lattice setting. Namely, the algorithm outputs a random vector $\mathbf{g} \in (\mathbb{Z}_q[x]/f)^m$, and a short basis for the lattice $rot_f(\mathbf{g})^\perp$, where f is a degree n polynomial $f \in \mathbb{Z}[x]$ and $rot_f(\mathbf{g})^\perp = \{\mathbf{b} \in (\mathbb{Z}[x]/f)^m | \langle \mathbf{b}, \mathbf{g} \rangle = 0 \mod q\}$. Recently, Lyubashevsky, Peikert and Regev [24] introduced Ring-LWE and gave a similar quantum reduction as for the classic LWE problem. They also showed that computational Ring-LWE can be reduced to decisional Ring-LWE.

Combining the above two facts and the results in Proposition 3, we can obtain a secure CP-ABE scheme on ideal lattices. For more details, please refer to [35,24].

Table 1. Multi-bit Encryption

$\texttt{Setup}(n, m, q, \mathcal{R})$	$(\mathbf{B}_0, \mathbf{T}_{\mathbf{B}_0}) \leftarrow \texttt{TrapGen}(n, m, q)$; Choose $\mathbf{U} = (\mathbf{u}_1, \ldots, \mathbf{u}_N) \leftarrow \mathbb{Z}_q^{n \times N}$; For each $i \in \mathcal{R}$, choose $\mathbf{B}_{i+} \leftarrow \mathbb{Z}_q^{n \times m}$ and $\mathbf{B}_{i-} \leftarrow \mathbb{Z}_q^{n \times m}$; $pk = (\{\mathbf{B}_{i+}, \mathbf{B}_{i-}\}_{i \in \mathcal{R}}, \mathbf{U})$, $msk = (pk, \mathbf{T}_{\mathbf{B}_0})$; Return (pk, msk).
$\texttt{KGen}(msk, S)$	For each $i \in \mathcal{R}$, if $i \in S$, $\tilde{\mathbf{B}}_i = \mathbf{B}_i^+$, else $\tilde{\mathbf{B}}_i = \mathbf{B}_i^-$; For each $j \in \{1, \ldots, N\}$ and $i \in \mathcal{R}$, choose $\mathbf{e}_{j,i} \leftarrow D_{\mathbb{Z}^m, s}$; Compute $\mathbf{y}_j = \mathbf{u}_j - \sum_{i \in \mathcal{R}} \tilde{\mathbf{B}}_i \mathbf{e}_{j,i}$, $\mathbf{e}_{j,0} \leftarrow \texttt{SamplePre}(\mathbf{B}_0, \mathbf{T}_{\mathbf{B}_0}, s, \mathbf{y}_j)$; Set $\mathbf{sk}_j = [\mathbf{e}_{j,0}; \ldots; \mathbf{e}_{j,\|\mathcal{R}\|}]$; Return $\mathbf{sk}_S = (\mathbf{sk}_0, \ldots, \mathbf{sk}_N)$.
$\texttt{Enc}(pk, W, M)$	// Denote $S^+(S^-)$ be the set of positive (negative) attributes in W. // Denote $S' = S^+ \cup S^-$ and $\bar{S}' = \mathcal{R} \backslash S'$. // $M = \{M_1, \ldots, M_N\} \in \{0, 1\}^N$. Choose $\mathbf{s} \leftarrow \mathbb{Z}_q^n$; For each $j \in \{1, \ldots, N\}$, compute $z_j = \mathbf{u}_j^T \mathbf{s} + x_{zj} + M_j \lfloor \frac{q}{2} \rfloor$, where $x_{zj} \leftarrow \chi$; For each $i \in S^+$, compute $\mathbf{c}_i = \mathbf{B}_{i+}{}^T \mathbf{s} + \mathbf{x}_{i+}$, where $\mathbf{x}_{i+} \leftarrow \chi^m$; For each $i \in S^-$, compute $\mathbf{c}_i = \mathbf{B}_{i-}{}^T \mathbf{s} + \mathbf{x}_{i-}$, where $\mathbf{x}_{i-} \leftarrow \chi^m$; For each $i \in \bar{S}'$, compute $\mathbf{c}_{i+} = \mathbf{B}_{i+}^T \mathbf{s} + \mathbf{x}_{i+}$ and $\mathbf{c}_{i-} = \mathbf{B}_{i-}^T \mathbf{s} + \mathbf{x}_{i-}$, where $\mathbf{x}_{i+}, \mathbf{x}_{i-} \leftarrow \chi^m$; Finally, compute $\mathbf{c}_0 = \mathbf{B}_0^T \mathbf{s} + \mathbf{x}_0$, where $\mathbf{x}_0 \leftarrow \chi^m$; Return $C = (W, \{z_j\}_{j \in \{1, \ldots, N\}}, \mathbf{c}_0, \{\mathbf{c}_i\}_{i \in S'}, \{\mathbf{c}_{i+}, \mathbf{c}_{i-}\}_{i \in \bar{S}'})$.
$\texttt{Dec}(C, sk)$	// Denote S be the attribute set associated to sk. // Denote W be the access structure in C. // Denote $S^+(S^-)$ as the set of positive (negative) attributes in W. // Denote $S' = S^+ \cup S^-$ and $\bar{S}' = \mathcal{R} \backslash S'$. If S doesn't satisfy W, return $\perp$. Parse C into $(W, \{z_j\}_{j \in \{1, \ldots, N\}}, \mathbf{c}_0, \{\mathbf{c}_i\}_{i \in S'}, \{\mathbf{c}_{i+}, \mathbf{c}_{i-}\}_{i \in \bar{S}'})$; Parse $\mathbf{sk}$ into $(\mathbf{sk}_0; \ldots; \mathbf{sk}_N)$; For each $i \in S'$, let $\mathbf{y}_i = \mathbf{c}_i$; For each $i \in \bar{S}'$, if $i \in S$, let $\mathbf{y}_i = \mathbf{c}_{i+}$, else $\mathbf{y}_i = \mathbf{c}_{i-}$; Let $\mathbf{y} = [\mathbf{c}_0; \mathbf{y}_1; \ldots; \mathbf{y}_{\|\mathcal{R}\|}]$; For each $j \in \{1, \ldots, N\}$, compute $a_j = \mathbf{sk}_j^T \mathbf{y}$, $b_j = z_j - a_j$; If $|b_j - \lfloor \frac{q}{2} \rfloor| \leq \lfloor \frac{q}{4} \rfloor$ in $\mathbb{Z}$, let $M_j = 1$, else $M_j = 0$; Return $M = \{M_0, \ldots, M_N\}$.

7 Conclusion

In this paper, a selective secure ciphertext policy attribute-based encryption (CP-ABE) without pairings is proposed. To the best of our knowledge, it is the first CP-ABE scheme from lattices. The security of the proposed scheme is proved in standard model under the LWE assumption. Our constructions only support and-gate access policy, and it remains an open problem to obtain a CP-ABE scheme that can support more general access structure from lattices.

Acknowledgments. We thank Yanfei Guo, Wenhao Wang, Xiang Xie, Rui Zhang, and the anonymous reviewers for their helpful comments and suggestions.

References

1. Agrawal, S., Boneh, D., Boyen, X.: Efficient Lattice (H)IBE in the Standard Model. In: Gilbert, H. (ed.) EUROCRYPT 2010. LNCS, vol. 6110, pp. 553–572. Springer, Heidelberg (2010)
2. Agrawal, S., Boneh, D., Boyen, X.: Lattice Basis Delegation in Fixed Dimension and Shorter-Ciphertext Hierarchical IBE. In: Rabin, T. (ed.) CRYPTO 2010. LNCS, vol. 6223, pp. 98–115. Springer, Heidelberg (2010)
3. Agrawal, S., Boyen, X., Vaikuntanathan, V., Voulgaris, P., Wee, H.: Fuzzy identity based encryption from lattices. Cryptology ePrint Archive, Report 2011/414 (2011), http://eprint.iacr.org/
4. Agrawal, S., Freeman, D.M., Vaikuntanathan, V.: Functional encryption for inner product predicates from learning with errors. Cryptology ePrint Archive, Report 2011/410 (2011), http://eprint.iacr.org/
5. Ajtai, M.: Generating hard instances of lattice problems (extended abstract). In: Proceedings of the Twenty-Eighth Annual ACM Symposium on Theory of Computing, STOC 1996, pp. 99–108. ACM, New York (1996)
6. Alwen, J., Peikert, C.: Generating shorter bases for hard random lattices. In: STACS, pp. 75–86 (2009)
7. Cash, D., Hofheinz, D., Kiltz, E.: How to delegate a lattice basis. Cryptology ePrint Archive, Report 2009/351 (2009), http://eprint.iacr.org/
8. Cash, D., Hofheinz, D., Kiltz, E., Peikert, C.: Bonsai Trees, or How to Delegate a Lattice Basis. In: Gilbert, H. (ed.) EUROCRYPT 2010. LNCS, vol. 6110, pp. 523–552. Springer, Heidelberg (2010)
9. Cheung, L., Newport, C.: Provably secure ciphertext policy ABE. In: Proceedings of the 14th ACM Conference on Computer and Communications Security, CCS 2007, pp. 456–465. ACM, New York (2007)
10. Emura, K., Miyaji, A., Nomura, A., Omote, K., Soshi, M.: A Ciphertext-Policy Attribute-Based Encryption Scheme with Constant Ciphertext Length. In: Bao, F., Li, H., Wang, G. (eds.) ISPEC 2009. LNCS, vol. 5451, pp. 13–23. Springer, Heidelberg (2009)
11. Gentry, C., Peikert, C., Vaikuntanathan, V.: Trapdoors for hard lattices and new cryptographic constructions. In: Proceedings of the 40th Annual ACM Symposium on Theory of Computing, STOC 2008, pp. 197–206. ACM, New York (2008)
12. Dov Gordon, S., Katz, J., Vaikuntanathan, V.: A Group Signature Scheme from Lattice Assumptions. In: Abe, M. (ed.) ASIACRYPT 2010. LNCS, vol. 6477, pp. 395–412. Springer, Heidelberg (2010)
13. Goyal, V., Jain, A., Pandey, O., Sahai, A.: Bounded Ciphertext Policy Attribute Based Encryption. In: Aceto, L., Damgård, I., Goldberg, L.A., Halldórsson, M.M., Ingólfsdóttir, A., Walukiewicz, I. (eds.) ICALP 2008, Part II. LNCS, vol. 5126, pp. 579–591. Springer, Heidelberg (2008)
14. Goyal, V., Pandey, O., Sahai, A., Waters, B.: Attribute-based encryption for fine-grained access control of encrypted data. In: Proceedings of the 13th ACM Conference on Computer and Communications Security, CCS 2006, pp. 89–98. ACM, New York (2006)
15. Herranz, J., Laguillaumie, F., Ràfols, C.: Constant Size Ciphertexts in Threshold Attribute-Based Encryption. In: Nguyen, P.Q., Pointcheval, D. (eds.) PKC 2010. LNCS, vol. 6056, pp. 19–34. Springer, Heidelberg (2010)
16. Ibraimi, L., Tang, Q., Hartel, P., Jonker, W.: Efficient and Provable Secure Ciphertext-Policy Attribute-Based Encryption Schemes. In: Bao, F., Li, H., Wang, G. (eds.) ISPEC 2009. LNCS, vol. 5451, pp. 1–12. Springer, Heidelberg (2009)

17. Lewko, A., Okamoto, T., Sahai, A., Takashima, K., Waters, B.: Fully Secure Functional Encryption: Attribute-Based Encryption and (Hierarchical) Inner Product Encryption. In: Gilbert, H. (ed.) EUROCRYPT 2010. LNCS, vol. 6110, pp. 62–91. Springer, Heidelberg (2010)

18. Lewko, A., Waters, B.: Decentralizing Attribute-Based Encryption. In: Paterson, K.G. (ed.) EUROCRYPT 2011. LNCS, vol. 6632, pp. 568–588. Springer, Heidelberg (2011)

19. Liang, X., Cao, Z., Lin, H., Xing, D.: Provably secure and efficient bounded ciphertext policy attribute based encryption. In: Proceedings of the 4th International Symposium on Information, Computer, and Communications Security, ASIACCS 2009, pp. 343–352. ACM, New York (2009)

20. Lyubashevsky, V.: Fiat-Shamir with Aborts: Applications to Lattice and Factoring-Based Signatures. In: Matsui, M. (ed.) ASIACRYPT 2009. LNCS, vol. 5912, pp. 598–616. Springer, Heidelberg (2009)

21. Lyubashevsky, V., Micciancio, D.: Generalized Compact Knapsacks Are Collision Resistant. In: Bugliesi, M., Preneel, B., Sassone, V., Wegener, I. (eds.) ICALP 2006, Part II. LNCS, vol. 4052, pp. 144–155. Springer, Heidelberg (2006)

22. Lyubashevsky, V., Micciancio, D.: Asymptotically Efficient Lattice-Based Digital Signatures. In: Canetti, R. (ed.) TCC 2008. LNCS, vol. 4948, pp. 37–54. Springer, Heidelberg (2008)

23. Lyubashevsky, V., Micciancio, D., Peikert, C., Rosen, A.: SWIFFT: A Modest Proposal for FFT Hashing. In: Nyberg, K. (ed.) FSE 2008. LNCS, vol. 5086, pp. 54–72. Springer, Heidelberg (2008)

24. Lyubashevsky, V., Peikert, C., Regev, O.: On Ideal Lattices and Learning with Errors over Rings. In: Gilbert, H. (ed.) EUROCRYPT 2010. LNCS, vol. 6110, pp. 1–23. Springer, Heidelberg (2010)

25. Micciancio, D.: Generalized compact knapsacks, cyclic lattices, and efficient one-way functions from worst-case complexity assumptions. In: Proceedings of the 43rd Annual IEEE Symposium on Foundations of Computer Science, pp. 356–365 (2002)

26. Micciancio, D., Regev, O.: Worst-case to average-case reductions based on gaussian measures. SIAM J. Comput. 37, 267–302 (2007)

27. Nishide, T., Yoneyama, K., Ohta, K.: Attribute-Based Encryption with Partially Hidden Encryptor-Specified Access Structures. In: Bellovin, S.M., Gennaro, R., Keromytis, A., Yung, M. (eds.) ACNS 2008. LNCS, vol. 5037, pp. 111–129. Springer, Heidelberg (2008)

28. Peikert, C.: Public-key cryptosystems from the worst-case shortest vector problem: extended abstract. In: Proceedings of the 41st Annual ACM Symposium on Theory of Computing, STOC 2009, pp. 333–342. ACM, New York (2009)

29. Peikert, C., Rosen, A.: Efficient Collision-Resistant Hashing from Worst-Case Assumptions on Cyclic Lattices. In: Halevi, S., Rabin, T. (eds.) TCC 2006. LNCS, vol. 3876, pp. 145–166. Springer, Heidelberg (2006)

30. Peikert, C., Waters, B.: Lossy trapdoor functions and their applications. In: Proceedings of the 40th Annual ACM Symposium on Theory of Computing, STOC 2008, pp. 187–196. ACM, New York (2008)

31. Regev, O.: On lattices, learning with errors, random linear codes, and cryptography. In: Proceedings of the Thirty-Seventh Annual ACM Symposium on Theory of Computing, STOC 2005, pp. 84–93. ACM, New York (2005)

32. Rosen, A., Segev, G.: Chosen-Ciphertext Security via Correlated Products. In: Reingold, O. (ed.) TCC 2009. LNCS, vol. 5444, pp. 419–436. Springer, Heidelberg (2009)

33. Rückert, M.: Lattice-Based Blind Signatures. In: Abe, M. (ed.) ASIACRYPT 2010. LNCS, vol. 6477, pp. 413–430. Springer, Heidelberg (2010)
34. Sahai, A., Waters, B.: Fuzzy Identity-Based Encryption. In: Cramer, R. (ed.) EUROCRYPT 2005. LNCS, vol. 3494, pp. 457–473. Springer, Heidelberg (2005)
35. Stehlé, D., Steinfeld, R., Tanaka, K., Xagawa, K.: Efficient Public Key Encryption Based on Ideal Lattices. In: Matsui, M. (ed.) ASIACRYPT 2009. LNCS, vol. 5912, pp. 617–635. Springer, Heidelberg (2009)
36. Waters, B.: Ciphertext-Policy Attribute-Based Encryption: An Expressive, Efficient, and Provably Secure Realization. In: Catalano, D., Fazio, N., Gennaro, R., Nicolosi, A. (eds.) PKC 2011. LNCS, vol. 6571, pp. 53–70. Springer, Heidelberg (2011)

Cryptanalysis of Randomized Arithmetic Codes Based on Markov Model

Liang Zhao[1], Takashi Nishide[1], Avishek Adhikari[3], Kyung-Hyune Rhee[2], and Kouichi Sakurai[1]

[1] Graduate School of Information Science and Electrical Engineering
Kyushu University, Fukuoka, Japan 819-0395
zhaoliang@itslab.csce.kyushu-u.ac.jp,
nishide@inf.kyushu-u.ac.jp,
sakurai@csce.kyushu-u.ac.jp
[2] Department of IT Convergence Applications Engineering
Pukyong National University, Busan, Republic of Korea 608-737
yisecure@gmail.com
[3] Department of Pure Mathematics
University of Calcutta, Kolkata, India 700019
avishek.adh@gmail.com

Abstract. An improvement of arithmetic coding based on Markov model (ACMM) has been proposed in the paper (Duan L.L., Liao X. F., Xiang T., Communications in Nonlinear Science and Numerical Simulation, 2011, 16(6):2554-2562). Though, a methodology to construct the ACMM is proposed in the above mentioned paper, it really lacks the formal definition of the ACMM. In the current paper, we not only investigate the security analysis of the ACMM, but also put forward formal definitions of the ACMM as well as its different security notions. Based on those definitions, a chosen-plaintext attack is proposed to reveal the used pseudorandom bit sequence for the encryption under the condition that the same pseudorandom bit sequence is used to encrypt the different messages. We also show that the ACMM does not have indistinguishable encryptions under the ciphertext-only attack (i.e., does not have indistinguishable encryptions in the presence of an eavesdropper) even if the different pseudorandom bit sequences are used to encrypt the different messages. Moreover, when the ACMM is combined with the randomized arithmetic code (RAC) (Grangetto M., Magli E., Olmo G., IEEE Trans. Multimedia, 2006 8(5):905-917), we also explore the insecurity of this combined encryption scheme. The analysis demonstrates that the ACMM+RAC is also insecure. Finally, the simulated experimental results show the correctness of all the proposed attacks.

Keywords: Randomized arithmetic code, Markov model, Chosen-plaintext attack, Ciphertext-only attack, Indistinguishable.

1 Introduction

1.1 Research Background

With the development of the information processing technology, affording the compression and security is of significance as the increased use of the multimedia

C.-K. Wu, M. Yung, and D. Lin (Eds.): Inscrypt 2011, LNCS 7537, pp. 341–362, 2012.
© Springer-Verlag Berlin Heidelberg 2012

files in many applications such as the digital cameras and internet [1]. Specially, the compression removes the redundancy of the data by analyzing the statistics of the input. The size of the output is shortened compared with the size of the input. The typical compression algorithms are the Huffman Coding and Arithmetic Coding (AC) [3–5]. The security makes the adversary difficult to obtain the plaintext information without the permission. Generally speaking, it is provided by cryptography. However, as a good cryptographic scheme provides the output to have a pseudorandom distribution for the symbol probability, the compression, in general, needs to be applied for dealing with the multimedia data prior to the cryptography. This method can be called first-compression-then-encryption approach.

In recent years, there exists another trend that the encryption and compression are performed in one single step for acting on the multimedia data [1–7]. Compared with the traditional first-compression-then-encryption approach, the major merit of joint compression-encryption hybrid method is that the goal of compression and encryption can be achieved simultaneously. This can simplify the design of the system for reducing the time and computation. Moreover, it makes the system flexible for the advanced multimedia processing [8].

1.2   Previous Works

The compression based encryption is seen as one of the choices for the multimedia encryption. In general, the algorithm which incorporates the security into the compression can improve the efficiency for the practical applications. Two compression algorithms namely the Huffman Coding and the Arithmetic Coding (AC) are always considered to be modified for encryption. However, according to the viewpoint of Witten et al. [9], the AC has the better compression ratio than the Huffman coding. Therefore, the AC is widely used in the recent multimedia compression standards (e.g., JPEG2000, H.264/AVC), which brings the AC based encryption into focus on a large scale.

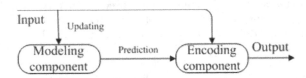

Fig. 1. Tow components of compression: modeling and encoding component

Moreover, according to [9], the compression is separated into the modeling component and the encoding component (see Fig. 1), where the modeling component is used to provide, in any given context, a probability distribution for the forthcoming symbol. Hence, there are two main kinds of methods for incorporating the security into the AC, namely, the model based encryption and coder based encryption [2]. In Table 1, some detailed works about the modified AC along with the corresponding attacks are listed.

Table 1. Some existing works on modified AC and the corresponding attacks

Previous works	Corresponding attack
Adaptive model based AC encryption [9]	CPA [10]; ABFA [2]
Combination of model and coder based encryption [13]	BHA [14]
Randomized AC (RAC) [1]	COA [11]
AC with key-based interval splitting [5]	ACCA [8]; ACPA/COA [12]
Markov model based AC encryption [15]	Our work

CPA: Chosen-plaintext attack; ABFA: Adaptive brute-force attack; BHA: Bergen/Hogan analysis [10] based attack; COA: Ciphertext-only attack; ACCA/ACPA: Adaptive chosen-plaintext/ciphertext attack.

1.3   Our Contributions

In 2011, Duan et al. [15] proposed a randomized AC based on the first-order Markov model (ACMM). This algorithm can be seen as a model based randomized AC. The randomness is achieved by choosing the probability of the binary symbol from the Markov model. Specially, the used Markov model is expressed as the tree structure which has two orders, namely, order-0 model and order-1 model. The order-0 model is the single symbol (i.e., 0 or 1) model without context which has two values corresponding to $\Pr[s_i=0]$ and $\Pr[s_i=1]$, while the order-1 model for the binary symbol has four values of conditional probabilities of the form $\Pr[s_i=0|s_{i-1}=0]$, $\Pr[s_i=1|s_{i-1}=0]$, $\Pr[s_i=0|s_{i-1}=1]$ and $\Pr[s_i=1|s_{i-1}=1]$ (see Fig. 2(a)). In the current work, we formally define the ACMM scheme and its different security notions at first. Based on these security notions, we address some security issues about the ACMM as follows:

- Firstly, we suppose that the same pseudorandom bit sequence is generated for encrypting different plaintext messages, and the lower bound of the encoding interval is considered as the ciphertext message. With this setup, we establish that the ACMM is insecure under the chosen-plaintext attack (CPA) by revealing the used pseudorandom bit sequence.
- Secondly, if different pseudorandom bit sequences are used to encrypt different plaintext messages, we show that the ACMM does not have indistinguishable encryptions under the ciphertext-only attack (COA). i.e., the ACMM does not have indistinguishable encryptions in the presence of an eavesdropper (see [11] about this concept).
- Thirdly, even if the two steps of the arithmetic coding (i.e., the modeling and encoding component) are encrypted simultaneously by the ACMM and RAC respectively, then also it can be shown that the combined scheme ACMM+RAC is still insecure under the COA.

Moreover, the simulation experiments are implemented for the above analyses. The experiments results (see Tables 4 and 5) confirm our analyses which show that both the ACMM and ACMM+RAC are insecure.

2   Arithmetic Coding Based on Markov Model Proposed by Duan/Liao/Xiang and Corresponding Drawbacks

2.1   Scheme Description

The ACMM [15] is a modified AC which makes use of the first-order Markov model to predict the encoding probability for each symbol s_i of the binary plaintext message $S=s_1s_2...s_N$ of length N. It introduces the pseudorandom bit sequence $q=q_1q_2...q_N$, generated by a pseudorandom bit generator (PRBG), for the encryption ($r=q$ which denotes the pseudorandom bit sequence in [15].). This encryption is the permutation of the probability which is produced by the Markov model and used to encode the binary plaintext message S. Specially, the process for encrypting each symbol s_i is shown in Fig. 2(b).

Moreover, the ACMM does not do the encryption on the encoding process. Then, the standard arithmetic coder (i.e., SAC) [13] can be used to encode the binary plaintext message S. This implies that it is different from the RAC [1] which does the encryption on the encoding process with the pseudorandom bit sequence q. Specially, according to [15], the initial model of the Markov model can be as Fig. 2(a), in which all the symbol counts (SC) are equal to 1. See [15], for detailed description.

2.2   Drawbacks of ACMM

The encryption mechanism of the ACMM is the 'randomized' Markov model controlled by the pseudorandom bit sequence q. According to the value of each pseudorandom bit q_i, the probability that arises from the Markov model can be decided to encode the i-th symbol s_i. However, two potential drawbacks exist in the ACMM, and have a significant effect on the security of the ciphertext C.

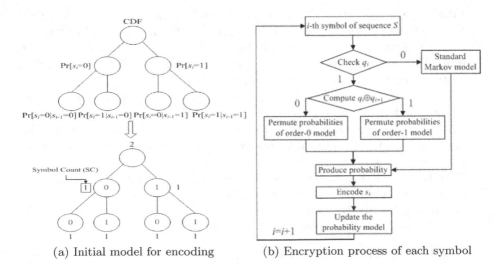

(a) Initial model for encoding   (b) Encryption process of each symbol

Fig. 2. Initial model and encryption process of ACMM

- The initial model in Fig. 2(a) is used to encode the 1-st symbol s_1 of the plaintext message S. However, probabilities from the order-0 model (i.e., $\Pr[s_1=0]$ and $\Pr[s_1=1]$) correspond to the same SC (e.g., 1). This implies that no matter what pseudorandom bit q_1 is, the probability for encoding the 1-st symbol s_1 is $1/2$, and the interval $[0, 1)$ is divided into $[0, 0.5)$ and $[0.5, 1)$ for 0 and 1, respectively.
- Let $I(S)$ represent the interval of the plaintext message S. According to the value of the pseudorandom bit q_i (or $q_i \oplus q_{i+1}$), probabilities of the order-0 model or the order-1 model are permutated. However, the positions of the symbols 0 and 1 in the interval $I(S)$ are not scrambled. This implies that for an interval $[x, y)$, $I(0):=[x, z)$ and $I(1):=[z, y)$ for any pseudorandom bit q_i, where x, y and z are real numbers between 0 and 1 or integers between 0 and a sufficiently large integer (e.g., 65535), and z is decided by the current pseudorandom bit q_i.

3   Insecurity of ACMM

In this section, two attacks are presented for the ACMM [15]. Note that the pseudorandom bit sequences play an important role in the security of the ACMM. Depending on the use of the pseudorandom bit sequences, we propose two attacks: one is the CPA, in which the same pseudorandom bit sequence is used to encrypt different plaintext messages (defined as **Case 1**), and the other one is the COA, in which different pseudorandom bit sequences are used to encrypt different plaintext messages (defined as **Case 2**). Before stating the attacks, we first present some general assumptions for the convenience of the following analysis:

- The initial interval of encoding is the most commonly used interval, i.e., the interval $[0, 1)$.
- The expression of the ciphertext C is seen as a real number (e.g., $C=0.628$). Specially, for a pair of plaintext messages (S_0 and S_1) of same length N, the expression precision of the ciphertexts ($C(S_0)$ and $C(S_1)$) is the same.

The formal definition of ACMM and the related security notions are presented in the next subsection following [11, 16].

3.1   Formal Definitions of ACMM and Related Security Notions

Formal Definition of ACMM under Case 1. The ACMM can be viewed as a symmetric-key encryption algorithm which is a triple of probabilistic polynomial-time algorithm $\prod=(\mathsf{Enc}, \mathsf{Dec}, \mathsf{Gen})$[16]. In this definition, Enc is the encryption function, Dec is the decryption function and Gen is the probabilistic key-generation function. Specially, under **Case 1**, every plaintext message S is encrypted by a fixed pseudorandom bit sequence q obtained through the pseudorandom function F.

Definition 1. *Let n be the security parameter and $N=\ell(n)$ be a polynomial in n. Then $\prod=$(Enc, Dec, Gen) can be defined as follows:*

- Gen (*This step is executed once*): *On input 1^n, choose $k\leftarrow\{0,1\}^n$ uniformly and randomly. Then, output k as the key.*
- Enc: *On input $k\in\{0,1\}^n$ and a plaintext message $S\in\{0,1\}^N$, output the set of probabilities $\bigcup_{i=1}^N \mathrm{Pr}^a[s_i] :=$ACMM$(F(k), S)$. Let $F(k) = q$. Then, generate the ciphertext $C:=$SAC$(\bigcup_{i=1}^N \mathrm{Pr}^a[s_i], S)$, where F is a pseudorandom function which outputs a pseudorandom bit sequence of length N. ACMM(q, S) implies performing the ACMM algorithm on the plaintext message S using the pseudorandom bit sequence q, and SAC(p, S) implies the standard arithmetic coding is used for the plaintext S with the probability set $\mathrm{Pr}^a[S] :=\{\mathrm{Pr}^a[s_i]|i\in\{1, 2,\ldots, N\}\}$. $\mathrm{Pr}^a[s_i]$ is the permuted probability (see notations in Subsection 3.2).*
- Dec: *On input k, and the ciphertext C, the plaintext message S is decrypted by producing $F(k)$ and decoded using standard AC.*

In the subsequent sections we are going to use the notions of **negligible** function and pseudorandom function as defined in [16].

Definition of Security under Case 1. Let n be a security parameter and $N=\ell(n)$ be a polynomial in n. We define the experiment $\mathsf{Privk}_{\mathcal{A},\prod}^{\mathrm{cpa}}(n)$ for the ACMM as follow:

Experiment $\mathsf{Privk}_{\mathcal{A},\prod}^{\mathrm{cpa}}(n)$:

- *A key k is produced by using* Gen(1^n).
- *The adversary $\mathcal{A}$ is given input 1^n and access to the encryption oracle, and output a pair of messages S_0 and S_1 of the same length N, where S_0 and $S_1\in\{0,1\}^N$. Note that the adversary $\mathcal{A}$ can choose any pair of (S_0, S_1).*
- *The fixed $F(k) = q\in\{0,1\}^N$ is used and a random bit $b\leftarrow\{0,1\}$ is chosen. The ciphertext $C:=$SAC$(\bigcup_{i=1}^N \mathrm{Pr}^a[s_i^b], S_b)$, $\bigcup_{i=1}^N \mathrm{Pr}^a[s_i^b] :=$ACMM$(q, S_b)$ is generated by the challenger and given to the adversary $\mathcal{A}$. This C is called the* **challenge** ciphertext.
- *The adversary $\mathcal{A}$ is given access to the encryption oracle and request for the encryption of a polynomial number of chosen plaintexts.*
- *The adversary $\mathcal{A}$ outputs a bit b'. If $b'=b$, the output of this experiment is 1, otherwise, the output is 0. In case $\mathsf{Privk}_{\mathcal{A},\prod}^{\mathrm{cpa}}(n)=1$, we say that $\mathcal{A}$ succeeded.*

Based on this experiment, the definition of the indistinguishability of ACMM encryption under the CPA is presented below.

Definition 2. *The fixed-length symmetric-key encryption algorithm $\prod=$(Enc, Dec, Gen) is CPA-secure if for any probabilistic polynomial-time adversary $\mathcal{A}$, there exists a negligible function* negl$(\cdot)$ *which satisfies $|\mathrm{Pr}[\mathsf{Privk}_{\mathcal{A},\prod}^{\mathrm{cpa}}(n)= 1]-1/2|$ $\leq$negl(n), where the probability is taken over the random coins used by the adversary $\mathcal{A}$, as well as the random coins used in the experiment.*

The above security definition (Definition 2) actually implies that the adversary $\mathcal{A}$ can not tell which message was used to achieve the ciphertext C except making a random guess even if $\mathcal{A}$ is given access to the encryption oracle. However, in the Subsection 3.2, we shall show that for ACMM, when the adversary $\mathcal{A}$ can have access to the encryption oracle, the used pseudorandom bit sequence can be revealed according to the ciphertexts from some suitable plaintexts. Therefore, for this condition, the adversary $\mathcal{A}$ always succeeds in the above game with probability 1. The details of this attack is presented in Subsection 3.2.

Definition of ACMM and Its Security Notions under Case 2. For the ACMM, the difference between **Case 1** and **Case 2** is the used pseudorandom bit sequences for the encryption. Under **Case 2**, for each encryption of a message S, a new pseudorandom bit sequence is used. Therefore, the formal definition of the ACMM under **Case 2**, i.e., $\prod'=(\text{Enc}', \text{Dec}', \text{Gen}')$, is almost similar to that of the ACMM under **Case 1**, i.e., $\prod$. The only difference is listed below:

- Gen': *On input 1^n, and for each encryption of a binary plaintext message S, choose $k \leftarrow \{0, 1\}^n$ uniformly and randomly. Then, output k as the key corresponding S.*

For **Case 2**, the definition of the COA indistinguishability experiment $\text{Privk}_{\mathcal{A},\prod'}^{\text{coa}}(n)$ is also similar to the experiment $\text{Privk}_{\mathcal{A},\prod}^{\text{cpa}}(n)$. However, in the COA, the adversary $\mathcal{A}$ is not allowed to access the encryption oracle, and for each encryption of a message S, a new pseudorandom bit sequence is used. Moreover, the definition of the security under the COA is the same as in Definition 2. This is based on the fact that $\text{Privk}_{\mathcal{A},\prod'}^{\text{coa}}(n)$ is a special case of $\text{Privk}_{\mathcal{A},\prod}^{\text{cpa}}(n)$ [16]. In Subsection 3.3, the details of the COA are presented based on the above definitions, which show that ACMM does not have indistinguishable encryptions under the COA.

3.2   Insecurity of ACMM under CPA

In this subsection, we show that the ACMM is not CPA-secure by revealing the used pseudorandom bit sequence q that is used to encrypt different plaintexts. Before presenting the details of this attack, we state the following assumption:

- If the current interval $I(S)$ of the plaintext message S is $[C(S), C(S)+E(S))$, where $E(S)$ is the product of probabilities of the whole symbols in S (i.e., $E(S)=\prod_{i=1}^{N}\text{Pr}^a[s_i]$), the endpoint $C(S)$ is stored as the ciphertext C.

Notations and Properties. We first present some notations and results that are important for our proposed attack.

- $n^i(0)$, $n^i(1)$: the current SC of order-0 model after updating the i-th symbol in the Markov model.
- $n_0{}^i(0)$, $n_0{}^i(1)$, $n_1{}^i(0)$, $n_1{}^i(1)$: the current SC of order-1 model after updating the i-th symbol in the Markov model.

- $\Pr[s_i=0]$, $\Pr[s_i=1]$: the order-0 probabilities of the Markov model for encoding the i-th symbol s_i.
- $\Pr[s_i=0|s_{i-1}=0]$, $\Pr[s_i=1|s_{i-1}=0]$, $\Pr[s_i=0|s_{i-1}=1]$, $\Pr[s_i=1|s_{i-1}=1]$: the order-1 probabilities of the Markov model for encoding the i-th symbol s_i.
- $\Pr^a[s_i=0]$, $\Pr^a[s_i=1]$: the permuted probabilities for encoding the symbol s_i. They belong to the set $\{\Pr[s_i=0]$, $\Pr[s_i=1]$, $\Pr[s_i=0|s_{i-1}=0]$, $\Pr[s_i=1|s_{i-1}=0]$, $\Pr[s_i=0|s_{i-1}=1]$, $\Pr[s_i=1|s_{i-1}=1]\}$.

Definition 3. *For the initial encoding interval as* $[0,1)$, *when the i-th symbol s_i needs to be encoded, the probability in the Markov model can be expressed as:*

$$
\begin{cases} \Pr[s_i = 0] = \frac{n^{i-1}(0)}{n^{i-1}(0)+n^{i-1}(1)} \\ \Pr[s_i = 1] = \frac{n^{i-1}(1)}{n^{i-1}(0)+n^{i-1}(1)} \end{cases},
\begin{cases} \Pr[s_i = 0|s_{i-1} = 0] = \frac{n_0^{i-1}(0)}{n_0^{i-1}(0)+n_0^{i-1}(1)} \\ \Pr[s_i = 1|s_{i-1} = 0] = \frac{n_0^{i-1}(1)}{n_0^{i-1}(0)+n_0^{i-1}(1)} \end{cases},
$$
$$
\begin{cases} \Pr[s_i = 0|s_{i-1} = 1] = \frac{n_1^{i-1}(0)}{n_1^{i-1}(0)+n_1^{i-1}(1)} \\ \Pr[s_i = 1|s_{i-1} = 1] = \frac{n_1^{i-1}(1)}{n_1^{i-1}(0)+n_1^{i-1}(1)}, \end{cases}
\tag{1}
$$

where $\Pr[s_i= 0]+\Pr[s_i= 1]=1$, $\Pr[s_i= 0|s_{i-1}= 0]+\Pr[s_i= 1|s_{i-1}= 0]=1$ *and* $\Pr[s_i= 0|s_{i-1}= 1]+\Pr[s_i= 1|s_{i-1}= 1]=1$.

Lemma 1. *Let us consider the binary plaintext message* $S=s_1s_2...s_{N-1}s_N=00...$ $.01$ *of length N, where $N\geq2$. Then, during the encryption of $s_N=1$, $\Pr[s_N=d_1]\neq$* $\Pr[s_N=d_2|s_{N-1}= 0]$, *where d_1, $d_2\in\{0,1\}$.*

Proof. See appendix A for the proof.

Lemma 2. *Let the two binary plaintext messages* $S_1=s_1s_2...s_m$ *and* $S_2=s'_1s'_2..$ $.s'_ms'_{m+1}$ *be encrypted by using the same pseudorandom bit sequence q, where* $s_i=s'_i$, $i\in\{1,..., m\}$. *Then, $C(S_1)\leq C(S_2)$. The equality is achieved when* $s'_{m+1}= 0$.

Proof. This result follows from the fact that $I(S_2)\subseteq I(S_1)$. Specially, if $s'_{m+1}=0$, according to the above assumption on the representation of the cipher text corresponding to the plaintext interval, we have, $C(S_1)=C(S_2)$.

Based on *Lemma* 2 and the definition in [17], the **ACMM** can be presented as a formula.

Theorem 1. *Let us consider two plaintext messages* $S_1=s_1...s_m$ *and* $S_2=S_1s_{m+1}$, *where $m\geq1$. Then, the encoder of the ACMM can be described through Eq. (2):*

$$
C(S_2) = C(S_1) + s_{m+1} \times \Pr^a[s_{m+1} = 0] \times E(S_1),
\tag{2}
$$

where $E(S_1)$ is given by Eq. (3):

$$
E(S_1) = \prod_{i=1}^{m} (\Pr^a[s_i = 1])^{s_i} \times (\Pr^a[s_i = 0])^{1-s_i}.
\tag{3}
$$

In particular, when $m= 1$, $\Pr[s_0= 0] =\Pr[s_0= 1] = 0.5$. $C(S_1)=s_0\times0.5$.

Proof. According to *Lemma 2*, $C(S_1) \leq C(S_2)$, and if $s_{m+1}=0$, $C(S_1)=C(S_2)$. Hence, we have $C(S_1 1)-C(S_1 0)=E(S_1 0)$. This implies that $C(S_2)=C(S_1)+s_{m+1} \times E(S_1 0)$. Specially, as $E(S_1 0)$ is the product of the whole probabilities corresponding to the symbols of $S_1 0$, $E(S_1 0)=E(S_1) \times \Pr^a[s_{m+1}=0]=\Pr^a[s_1=t_1] \times \Pr^a[s_2=t_2]... \times \Pr^a[s_N=t_m] \times \Pr^a[s_{m+1}=0]$, where $t_1, t_2,...,t_m \in \{0, 1\}$. This implies that the above equations can be achieved. When $m=1$, as $\Pr[s_0= 0] =\Pr[s_0= 1] = 0.5$, $C(S_1)=s_0 \times 0.5$.

Method of Attack. The security of ACMM depends on the encryption of the Markov model by the pseudorandom bit sequence q. Therefore, the proposed attack should try to reveal the probability for encoding each symbol at first, and then, unveil the corresponding pseudorandom bit q_i.

$\Pr^a[s_i=0]$ Recovery: Let the chosen plaintext messages, each of length N, be $S_1=100...0$, $S_2=010...0$, ..., $S_N=000...1$. According to the Theorem 1, the corresponding cipher text is given by $C(S_i)=0+s_i \times \Pr^a[s_i=0] \times E(S_j)=s_i \times \Pr^a[s_i=0] \times \prod_{k=0}^{i-1} \Pr^a[s_k=0]$. Therefore, after $S_1, S_2,..., S_N$ are encoded by the ACMM, the corresponding ciphertexts $C(S_1), C(S_2),..., C(S_N)$ are expressed as follows:

$$C(S_1) = 0.5, \ C(S_2) = 0.5 \times \Pr^a[s_2 = 0], \ C(S_3) = 0.5 \times \Pr^a[s_2 = 0]$$
$$\times \Pr^a[s_3 = 0], ..., \ C(S_N) = 0.5 \times \Pr^a[s_2 = 0] \cdots \times \Pr^a[s_N = 0]$$

Based on the relationship among $C(S_1), C(S_2),..., C(S_N)$, we can compute $\Pr^a[s_2=0]$, $\Pr^a[s_3=0]$,..., $\Pr^a[s_N=0]$ by using Eq. (4).

$$\Pr^a[s_i = 0] = \frac{C(S_i)}{C(S_{i-1})}, \quad i \in \{2, 3, ..., N\}. \tag{4}$$

Pseudorandom Bit Recovery: According to the *Lemma 1*, it can be found that $\forall i \in \{1, 2,...,N\}$, the revealed $\Pr^a[s_i=0]$ belongs to either the set $\{\Pr[s_i=0], \Pr[s_i=1]\}$ or the set $\{\Pr[s_i=0|s_{i-1}=0], \Pr[s_i=1|s_{i-1}=0]\}$. To estimate the order of $\Pr^a[s_i=0]$ which is used to recover the pseudorandom bit q_i, a Detector $f_{det}(\cdot, \cdot, \cdot)$ is defined as follow:

Definition 4. *For an adversary $\mathcal{A}$ who obtains the set of probabilities $\{\Pr^a[s_i= 0]|i \in \{1, 2,...,N\}\}$, a Detector is a function $f_{det}(\cdot, \cdot, \cdot)$ which is used to reveal the pseudorandom bit sequence q. This function can be presented as $(q, \{CM_i|i \in \{1, 2, ...,N\}) = f_{det}(S_{azp}, IM, \{\Pr^a[s_i= 0]|i \in \{1, 2,...N\}\})$, where IM is the initial model as in Fig. 2(a), $S_{azp}= 00...0$ is the all zero plaintext, and CM_i is the updated Markov model for encoding the i-th symbol.*

According to the definition of the Detector, if the adversary $\mathcal{A}$ obtains the set of probabilities $\{\Pr^a[s_i=0]|i \in \{1, 2,...,N\}\}$, he/she can reveal the pseudorandom bit sequence q through this Detector. In fact, the Detector can be seen as the constructor of the updated Markov model for each symbol s_i. When the pseudorandom bit q_i is revealed, the corresponding Markov model can also be updated.

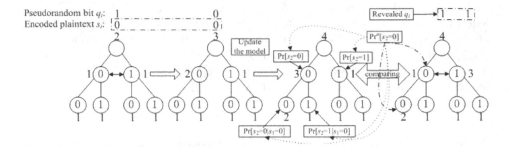

Fig. 3. Example of pseudorandom bit recovery (S=0010...0), suppose that q_1 and q_2 are revealed

Fig. 3 is an example on the work principle of the Detector. Suppose that the first two symbols are 00. The Markov model is updated and output after the 2-nd symbol 0 is encoded. Then, the revealed $\Pr^a[s_2=0]$ is compared with the probabilities $\Pr[s_2=0]$, $\Pr[s_2=1]$, $\Pr[s_2=0|s_1=0]$, and $\Pr[s_2=1|s_1=0]$ in this model to decide the used pseudorandom bit q_2 (see Fig. 3). The construction of every model CM_i reveals each pseudorandom bit q_i. Table 2 lists the revealed pseudorandom bit q_i and possible q_{i+1} according to the $\Pr^a[s_i=0]$ and the probabilities $\Pr[s_i=0]$, $\Pr[s_i=1]$, $\Pr[s_i=0|s_{i-1}=0]$, and $\Pr[s_i=1|s_{i-1}=0]$ in the Markov model.

Table 2. Four states of pseudorandom bit recovery

	$\Pr^a[s_i=0]$	q_i	q_{i+1}
$\Pr[s_i=0]$	$\Pr^a[s_i=0]=\Pr[s_i=0]$	0	0/1
$\Pr[s_i=1]$	$\Pr^a[s_i=0]=\Pr[s_i=1]$	1	1
$\Pr[s_i=0|s_{i-1}=0]$	$\Pr^a[s_i=0]=\Pr[s_i=0|s_{i-1}=0]$	0	0/1
$\Pr[s_i=1|s_{i-1}=0]$	$\Pr^a[s_i=0]=\Pr[s_i=1|s_{i-1}=0]$	1	0

Specially, in the Markov model, if $\Pr[s_i=0]=\Pr[s_i=1]$ after the $(i-1)$-th symbol 0 is encoded (suppose that $\Pr^a[s_i=0]=\Pr[s_i=0]$), the pseudorandom bit q_i can be 0 or 1. However, if $q_i=0$ and there has existed sequence '00' in front of the $(i-1)$-th symbol 0, the coder should use the order-1 probability to encode the $(i-1)$-th symbol 0. Hence, according to this rule, we can ensure that $q_i=1$ when $\Pr^a[s_i=0]=\Pr[s_i=0]$. Moreover, if $\Pr[s_i=0|s_{i-1}=0]=\Pr[s_i=1|s_{i-1}=0]$ after the $(i-1)$-th symbol 0 is encoded (suppose that $\Pr^a[s_i=0]=\Pr[s_i=0|s_{i-1}=0]$), the pseudorandom bit q_i can also be 0 or 1. Under this situation, we can check that whether there is an 'escape symbol' which is used in the standard Markov model for telling the decoder to use order-1 probability to decode. If there exists such an 'escape symbol', the encoder use the standard Markov model (i.e., $q_i=0$), otherwise, $q_i=1$. Algorithm 1 is used to describe the revealing process for the whole pseudorandom bit sequence q.

Algorithm 1. Recovery of the Pseudorandom Bit Sequence q

1: **Input:** $S_{azp}=s_1s_2...s_N=00...0$, IM, $\{0.5, \Pr^a[s_2=0], \Pr^a[s_3=0],..., \Pr^a[s_N=0]\}$
2: **Output:** q, $\{CM_1, CM_2,..., CM_N\}$
3: $z \leftarrow S_{azp}$;
4: $ES \leftarrow ACMM(S_{azp})$; /* Returning escape symbol of q */
5: **for** $g = 1$ to N **do**
6:    **if** $g=1$ **then**
7:       $(q_g, CM_g) \leftarrow f_{det}(z(g), IM, 0.5)$;
8:    **else**
9:       $(q_g, CM_g) \leftarrow f_{det}(z(g), CM_{g-1}, \Pr^a[s_g=0])$; /* $q_g \in \{0, 1, 2\}$. $q_g=2$ implies that q_g can be 0 or 1. */
10:   **end if**
11:   **if** $q_g=2$ **then**
12:      **if** $\Pr^a[s_g=0]=\Pr[s_g=0]=\Pr[s_g=1]$ and $g \geq 2$ **then**
13:         **if** $g < N$ **then**
14:            $(q_g, q_{g+1})=(1, 1)$;
15:         **else if** $g=N$ **then**
16:            $(q_g, q_0)=(1, 1)$;
17:         **end if**
18:      **else if** $\Pr^a[s_g=0]=\Pr[s_g=0|s_{g-1}=0]=\Pr[s_g=1|s_{g-1}=0]$ **then**
19:         escape symbol $\leftarrow ES(s_g)$;
20:         **if** $g < N$ **then**
21:            f_{check}(escape symbol)$=1?(q_g=0):((q_g, q_{g+1})=(1, 0))$; /* Checking escape symbol for recovering q_g */
22:         **else if** $g=N$ **then**
23:            f_{check}(escape symbol)$=1?(q_g=0):((q_g, q_0)=(1, 0))$; /* Checking escape symbol for recovering q_g */
24:         **end if**
25:      **end if**
26:   **end if**
27: **end for**
28: **return** q, $\{CM_1, CM_2,..., CM_N\}$;

Attack Complexity. Based on the method of the proposed CPA as the above description, we state the following propositions on the data complexity and time complexity.

Proposition 1. *For a binary sequence $S=s_1s_2...s_N$ of length N, if the length of the corresponding pseudorandom bit sequence q is also N, the data complexity of the CPA is $N+1$ chosen plaintext messages.*

Proof. This proof is immediate from the description of the attack processes in Subsection 3.2.

Proposition 2. *If the encryption for one binary symbol s_i is considered as one computation, the time complexity of this proposed attack is $\mathcal{O}(N^2)$.*

Proof. Two steps of the proposed attack should be considered. Specially, the computation load of the $\Pr^a[s_i=0]$ recovery is N^2 (more accurately, the computation load is $N \times (N\text{-}1)$). For the pseudorandom bit recovery, the computation load is N. If there is an extra encryption for obtaining the escape symbol, the corresponding computation load is $2 \times N$. Therefore, the total time complexity is $\mathcal{O}(N^2+N)$ (or $\mathcal{O}(N^2+2 \times N)$) which can be simplified to $\mathcal{O}(N^2)$.

3.3 Insecurity of ACMM under COA

In Subsection 3.2, the CPA is proposed for revealing the fixed pseudorandom bit sequence q used in ACMM. In this section, the security of the ACMM is explored if the different pseudorandom bit sequences are used to encrypt the different binary plaintext messages. The analysis proves that the ACMM does not have indistinguishable encryptions under the COA.

For the following analyses, two plaintext messages of the same length N are defined as $0x_1$ and $1x_2$, where x_1 and $x_2 \in \{0, 1\}^{N-1}$. Moreover, based on the initial model as Fig. 2(a), the interval $[0, 1)$ is divided into the subinterval as $J_1 = [0, 0.5)$ and $J_2 = [0.5, 1)$.

Lemma 3. *Let $S_0 = 0x_1$ and $S_1 = 1x_2$. Choose a key $k \leftarrow \{0,1\}^n$ uniformly at random and select a random bit $b \leftarrow \{0, 1\}$. Let $q = F(k)$ be the pseudorandom bit sequence of length N. Generate the ciphertext $C := \mathsf{SAC}(\bigcup_{i=1}^{N} \mathrm{Pr}^a[s_i^b], S_b)$, $\bigcup_{i=1}^{N} \mathrm{Pr}^a[s_i^b] := \mathsf{ACMM}(q, S_b)$. Then, if $C \in J_1$, $\mathrm{Pr}[S_b = S_0 | C \in J_1] = 1$, and if $C \in J_2$, $\mathrm{Pr}[S_b = S_1 | C \in J_2] = 1$. Therefore, $\mathrm{Pr}[\mathsf{Privk}_{\mathcal{A},\prod'}^{coa}(n) = 1 | C \in J_1] = 1$ and $\mathrm{Pr}[\mathsf{Privk}_{\mathcal{A},\prod'}^{coa}(n) = 1 | C \in J_2] = 1$.*

Proof. See appendix B for the proof.

According to *Lemma* 3, the following theorem can be achieved.

Theorem 2. *The $\prod'$ does not have indistinguishable encryptions under the COA.*

Proof. A distinguisher $\mathcal{D}$ is constructed for the adversary $\mathcal{A}$ who uses it in the experiment $\mathsf{Privk}_{\mathcal{A},\prod'}^{coa}(n)$. The challenge ciphertext is denoted as $C := \mathsf{SAC}(\bigcup_{i=1}^{N} \mathrm{Pr}^a[s_i^b], S_b)$, $\bigcup_{i=1}^{N} \mathrm{Pr}^a[s_i^b] := \mathsf{ACMM}(q, S_b)$. Define the intervals as $CI_0 = [0, 1/2)$ and $CI_1 = [1/2, 1)$, respectively. The distinguisher $\mathcal{D}$ can be described as:

Distinguisher $\mathcal{D}$:

- If the value of the challenge ciphertext C is in CI_0, S_0 is used to generate C. The adversary $\mathcal{A}$ outputs $b' = 0$.
- If the value of the challenge ciphertext C is in CI_1, S_1 is used to generate C. The adversary $\mathcal{A}$ outputs $b' = 1$.

It can be denoted that if $|\mathrm{Pr}[\mathsf{Privk}_{\mathcal{A},\prod'}^{coa}(n) = 1] - 1/2| \nleq \mathsf{negl}(n)$, the ACMM does not have indistinguishable encryptions under the COA. In the following, this result can be shown.

$$\mathrm{Pr}[\mathsf{Privk}_{\mathcal{A},\prod'}^{coa}(n) = 1] = \mathrm{Pr}[\mathsf{Privk}_{\mathcal{A},\prod'}^{coa}(n) = 1 | C \in J_1] \times \mathrm{Pr}[C \in J_1]$$
$$+ \mathrm{Pr}[\mathsf{Privk}_{\mathcal{A},\prod'}^{coa}(n) = 1 | C \in J_2] \times \mathrm{Pr}[C \in J_2]$$

From *Lemma* 3, i.e., $\Pr[\mathrm{Privk}_{\mathcal{A},\prod'}^{\mathrm{coa}}(n)=1|C \in J_1]=1$ and $\Pr[\mathrm{Privk}_{\mathcal{A},\prod'}^{\mathrm{coa}}(n)=1|C \in J_2]$ $=1$. The above equation is simplified to

$$\Pr[\mathrm{Privk}_{\mathcal{A},\prod'}^{\mathrm{coa}}(n) = 1] = \Pr[C \in J_1] + \Pr[C \in J_2].$$

As $\Pr[C \in J_1]+\Pr[C \in J_2]=1$, we can obtain that $\Pr[\mathrm{Privk}_{\mathcal{A},\prod'}^{\mathrm{coa}}(n)=1]=1=1/2+$ $1/2>1/2$, which demonstrates that the ACMM does not have indistinguishable encryptions under the COA.

3.4   Remark

For the ACMM, if the initial model is not as the Fig. 2(a) (e.g., in the initial model, $n^0(0)=3$, $n^0(1)=2$, $n_0{}^0(0)=2$, $n_0{}^0(1)=1$, $n_1{}^0(0)=2$, $n_1{}^0(1)=1$), the ACMM is also insecure under the proposed attack. This is due to the fact that the proposed attack is not based on the initial model as Fig. 2(a). If the initial model is known to the adversary $\mathcal{A}$, the pseudorandom bits sequence q can be revealed completely.

4   Security Analysis of **ACMM+RAC** under COA

Note that ACMM is a particular type of AC where the encryption is done in the modeling component whereas RAC is again a particular type of AC in which the encryption is done in the encoding component, both by using the pseudorandom bit sequence. The Section 3 demonstrates that ACMM is insecure while Katti et al. [11] demonstrate that RAC is also insecure. Hence, intuitively, it seems that combination of these two encryptions, i.e., encryption at both modeling as well as at encoding component synchronously by using different pseudorandom bit sequences may enhance the security of the combined scheme. We refer this combined scheme as ACMM+RAC. Let us demonstrate the combined scheme through an example. Let the plaintext message be 11 and the corresponding pseudorandom bit sequences be $q = 11$ (for ACMM) and $q' = 10$ (for RAC), the final interval for 11 is given by $I(11) = [1/3, 1/2)$ (see Fig. 4).

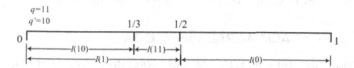

Fig. 4. Encryption example according to q=11 and q'=10

Though, intuitively, it seems that ACMM+RAC gives security, the following analysis can shows that the ACMM+RAC does not also have indistinguishable encryptions under the COA. Let us first provide the formal definition of the ACMM+RAC.

4.1   Formal Definition on ACMM+RAC

We are now going to define formally the ACMM+RAC scheme denoted by $\widetilde{\prod}=(\widetilde{\mathsf{Enc}}, \widetilde{\mathsf{Dec}}, \widetilde{\mathsf{Gen}})$.

Definition 5. *Let n be the security parameter and $N=\ell(n)$ be a polynomial in n. Then $\widetilde{\prod}= (\widetilde{\mathsf{Enc}}, \widetilde{\mathsf{Dec}}, \widetilde{\mathsf{Gen}})$ can be defined as follows:*

- *$\widetilde{\mathsf{Gen}}$: On input 1^n and for each encryption of a binary plaintext message S of length N, choose $k \leftarrow \{0, 1\}^n$, $k' \leftarrow \{0, 1\}^n$ uniformly and randomly. Then, output k, k' as the keys.*
- *$\widetilde{\mathsf{Enc}}$: On input k, k' and the message S, compute $q = F(k)$, $q' = F(k')$ and output the set of probabilities $\bigcup_{i=1}^{N}\Pr^a[s_i] :=$ACMM$(q, S)$. Then, generate the ciphertext $C:=$RAC$(q', \bigcup_{i=1}^{N}\Pr^a[s_i], S)$, where the notations ACMM is already defined in Definition 1, and RAC(q', p, S) implies the randomized arithmetic coding which is used to encrypt the plaintext message S with the pseudorandom bit sequence q' and probabilities set $\Pr^a[S] :=\{\Pr^a_i[s_i]|i\in\{1, 2,\ldots, N\}\}$.*
- *$\widetilde{\mathsf{Dec}}$: On input k, k' and ciphertext C, the plaintext message S is decrypted by producing $F(k)$ and $F(k')$ and decoded through standard AC.*

To analyze the security of $\widetilde{\prod}$, the experiment $\mathsf{Privk}^{coa}_{\mathcal{A},\widetilde{\prod}'}(n)$ can also be used. However, some modifications are required which are listed below:

- *For each encryption of a binary plaintext message S of length N, two keys k and k' are generated by running the $\widetilde{\mathsf{Gen}}(1^n)$. Using these two keys for S, two pseudorandom bit sequences q and q' are generated. The ciphertext $C:=$RAC$(q', \bigcup_{i=1}^{N}\Pr^a[s_i], S)$, $\bigcup_{i=1}^{N}\Pr^a[s_i] :=$ACMM$(q, S)$ is generated by the challenger and given to the adversary $\mathcal{A}$. This C is called the* challenge cipher-text.

Then, this experiment $\mathsf{Privk}^{coa}_{\mathcal{A},\widetilde{\prod}'}(n)$ is redefined as $\mathsf{Privk}^{coa}_{\mathcal{A},\widetilde{\prod}}(n)$ for the following analysis. The security definition in Subsection 3.1 can be used for the analysis of the ACMM+RAC. Moreover, for the convenience of the analysis, the assumptions in Section 3 are still fit for the ACMM+RAC, and we also suppose that any real number in the final interval $I(S)$ can be seen as the ciphertext C.

4.2   Insecurity of ACMM+RAC under COA

In this section, we state that the ACMM+RAC does not satisfy the security requirements as mentioned above. For the following analysis, two plaintext messages $10x_3$ and $11x_4$ of the same length N are considered, where x_3, $x_4\in\{0, 1\}^{N-2}$. The interval $[0, 1)$ is divided into the subintervals as $[0, 1/6)\bigcup[1/6, 1/4)\bigcup[1/4, 1/3)\bigcup[1/3, 1/2)\bigcup[1/2, 2/3)\bigcup[2/3, 3/4)\bigcup[3/4, 5/6)\bigcup[5/6, 1)$ according to the observation of Table 3 which is the interval distribution of the encryption of $s_1s_2=10$ and $s'_1s'_2=11$. Specially, $s_1s_2=10$ and $s'_1s'_2=11$ belong to the messages $10y_1$ and $11y_2$ of length N $(N\geq3)$, respectively.

Table 3. Interval partition of $s_1s_2=10$ and $s'_1s'_2=11$ with different q and q'

q'	q	$I(10)$	$I(11)$	q'	q	$I(11)$	$I(10)$
10	000	[0, 1/6)	[1/6, 1/2)	11	000	[0, 1/3)	[1/3, 1/2)
	001	[0, 1/6)	[1/6, 1/2)		001	[0, 1/3)	[1/3, 1/2)
	010	[0, 1/4)	[1/4, 1/2)		010	[0, 1/4)	[1/4, 1/2)
	011	[0, 1/3)	[1/3, 1/2)		011	[0, 1/6)	[1/6, 1/2)
	100	[0, 1/6)	[1/6, 1/2)		100	[0, 1/3)	[1/3, 1/2)
	101	[0, 1/6)	[1/6, 1/2)		101	[0, 1/3)	[1/3, 1/2)
	110	[0, 1/4)	[1/4, 1/2)		110	[0, 1/4)	[1/4, 1/2)
	111	[0, 1/3)	[1/3, 1/2)		111	[0, 1/6)	[1/6, 1/2)
00	000	[1/2, 2/3)	[2/3, 1)	01	000	[1/2, 5/6)	[5/6, 1)
	001	[1/2, 2/3)	[2/3, 1)		001	[1/2, 5/6)	[5/6, 1)
	010	[1/2, 3/4)	[3/4, 1)		010	[1/2, 3/4)	[3/4, 1)
	011	[1/2, 5/6)	[5/6, 1)		011	[1/2, 2/3)	[2/3, 1)
	100	[1/2, 2/3)	[2/3, 1)		100	[1/2, 5/6)	[5/6, 1)
	101	[1/2, 2/3)	[2/3, 1)		101	[1/2, 5/6)	[5/6, 1)
	110	[1/2, 3/4)	[3/4, 1)		110	[1/2, 3/4)	[3/4, 1)
	111	[1/2, 5/6)	[5/6, 1)		111	[1/2, 2/3)	[2/3, 1)

Lemma 4. *Let $S_0= 10x_3$ and $S_1= 11x_4$. Produce two random keys k, k'. Let $q = F(k)$ and $q' = F(k')$. Select a random bit $b \leftarrow \{0, 1\}$. Then, generate the ciphertext $C:=\mathsf{RAC}(q', \bigcup_{i=1}^{N}\mathrm{Pr}^a[s_i^b], S_b)$, $\bigcup_{i=1}^{N}\mathrm{Pr}^a[s_i^b]:=\mathsf{ACMM}(q, S_b)$. If C is in the interval J_3, where $J_3 \in \{[0,1/6), [1/3, 1/2), [1/2, 2/3), [5/6, 1)\}$, $\mathrm{Pr}[\mathrm{Privk}_{\mathcal{A}, \widetilde{\prod}}^{coa}(n)= 1|C \in J_3]= 19/35$, $b'= 0$ is chosen as the output of the adversary $\mathcal{A}$. If C is in J_4, where $J_4 \in \{[1/6, 1/4), [1/4, 1/3), [2/3, 3/4), [3/4, 5/6)\}$, $\mathrm{Pr}[\mathrm{Privk}_{\mathcal{A}, \widetilde{\prod}}^{coa}(n)= 1|C \in J_4]= 8/13$, $b'= 1$ is chosen as the output of the adversary $\mathcal{A}$.*

Proof. See appendix C for the proof.

According to *Lemma 4*, the following theorem can be achieved.

Theorem 3. *The $\widetilde{\prod}$ does not have indistinguishable encryptions under the COA.*

Proof. A distinguisher $\mathcal{D}'$ is constructed for the adversary $\mathcal{A}$ which is used in the experiment $\mathrm{Privk}_{\mathcal{A}, \widetilde{\prod}}^{coa}(n)$. Generate the challenge ciphertext $C:=\mathsf{RAC}(q', \bigcup_{i=1}^{N}\mathrm{Pr}^a[s_i^b], S_b)$, $\bigcup_{i=1}^{N}\mathrm{Pr}^a[s_i^b]:=\mathsf{ACMM}(q, S_b)$. Define the intervals $CI_2=[0, 1/6)\bigcup[1/3, 1/2)\bigcup[1/2, 2/3)\bigcup[5/6, 1)$ and $CI_3=[1/6, 1/3)\bigcup[2/3, 5/6)$. The distinguisher $\mathcal{D}'$ is described as follow:

Distinguisher $\mathcal{D}'$:

- If the value of the challenge ciphertext C is in CI_2, S_0 is used to generate C. The adversary $\mathcal{A}$ outputs $b'=0$.
- If the value of the challenge ciphertext C is in CI_3, S_1 is used to generate C. The adversary $\mathcal{A}$ outputs $b'=1$.

Then, for the $\text{Privk}^{\text{coa}}_{\mathcal{A},\widetilde{\prod}}(n)$, $\Pr[\text{Privk}^{\text{coa}}_{\mathcal{A},\widetilde{\prod}}(n)=1]$ can be expressed as

$$\Pr[\text{Privk}^{\text{coa}}_{\mathcal{A},\widetilde{\prod}}(n) = 1] = \sum\nolimits_{i=1}^{8} \Pr[\text{Privk}^{\text{coa}}_{\mathcal{A},\widetilde{\prod}}(n) = 1 | C \in [x_i, \, y_i)] \times \Pr[C \in [x_i, \, y_i)]$$

where $[x_1, \, y_1)=[0, 1/6)$, $[x_2, \, y_2)=[1/6, 1/4)$, $[x_3, \, y_3)=[1/4, 1/3)$, $[x_4, \, y_4)=[1/3, 1/2)$, $[x_5, \, y_5)=[1/2, 2/3)$, $[x_6, \, y_6)=[2/3, 3/4)$, $[x_7, \, y_7)=[3/4, 5/6)$, $[x_8, \, y_8)=[5/6, 1)$. Then, according to *Lemma 4*,

$$\begin{aligned}
\Pr[\text{Privk}^{\text{coa}}_{\mathcal{A},\widetilde{\prod}}(n) = 1] = {}^{19}\!/\!_{35} &\times (\Pr[C \in [0, \, {}^{1}\!/\!_6)] + \Pr[C \in [{}^{1}\!/\!_3, \, {}^{1}\!/\!_2)] \\
&+ \Pr[C \in [{}^{1}\!/\!_2, \, {}^{2}\!/\!_3)] + \Pr[C \in [{}^{5}\!/\!_6, \, 1)]) + {}^{8}\!/\!_{13} \times (\Pr[C \in [{}^{1}\!/\!_6, \, {}^{1}\!/\!_4)] \\
&+ \Pr[C \in [{}^{1}\!/\!_4, \, {}^{1}\!/\!_3)] + \Pr[C \in [{}^{2}\!/\!_3, \, {}^{3}\!/\!_4)] + \Pr[C \in [{}^{3}\!/\!_4, \, {}^{5}\!/\!_6)])
\end{aligned}$$

According to Eq. (6) (see Appendix C), the computation of $\Pr[C \in J_3]$ and $\Pr[C \in J_4]$ can come from the condition $S_b=S_0$ and $S_b=S_1$, respectively. Then, based on Table 3, we can obtain that $\Pr[C \in [0, 1/6)]=\Pr[C \in [1/3, 1/2)]=\Pr[C \in [1/2, 2/3)]=\Pr[C \in [5/6, 1)]=35/192$, $\Pr[C \in [1/6, 1/4)]=\Pr[C \in [1/4, 1/3)]=\Pr[C \in [2/3, 3/4)]=\Pr[C \in [3/4, 5/6)]=13/192$. Then,

$$\Pr[\text{Privk}^{\text{coa}}_{\mathcal{A},\widetilde{\prod}}(n) = 1] = {}^{19}\!/\!_{35} \times {}^{140}\!/\!_{192} + {}^{8}\!/\!_{13} \times {}^{52}\!/\!_{192} = {}^{108}\!/\!_{192}$$

As $108/192=1/2+12/192>1/2$, it demonstrates that the $\widetilde{\prod}$ does not have indistinguishable encryptions under the COA.

5   Experimental Results for Proposed Attacks

This section presents the corresponding experimental results about our analyses on both the ACMM and ACMM+RAC.

5.1   Simulation Results of CPA on ACMM

To show the success of the CPA on ACMM, the following two simulations are presented. Firstly, according to the attack process, the used pseudorandom bit

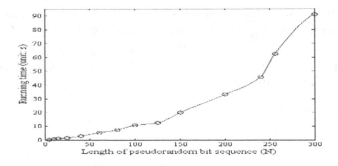

Fig. 5. Running time of proposed CPA

sequences of different length N are revealed and listed in Table 4. Specially, $Value(q)$ and $Value(q^{rv})$ are the decimal number of the original and revealed pseudorandom bit sequences, respectively. i.e., $Value(q)=q_1 \times 2^0 + q_2 \times 2^1 + q_3 \times 2^2 \ldots + q_N \times 2^{N-1}$. From this table, it can be found that the revealed pseudorandom bit sequences are nearly the same as the original pseudorandom bit sequences. In some results, $Value(q)$ and $Value(q^{rv})$ are 1 apart. (e.g., when $N=18$, $Value(q)=22531$, $Value(q^{rv})=22530$). This is based on the fact that the first pseudorandom bit q_1 is not revealed. For the first pseudorandom bit q_1, the unique method to reveal it is related to the formula $k_N = q_N \oplus q_1$ when $q_N = 1$. If $q_N = 0$, q_1 can not be revealed according to the proposal.

Table 4. Comparison between $Value(q)$ and $Value(q^{rv})$

N	$Value(q)$	$Value(q^{rv})$	N	$Value(q)$	$Value(q^{rv})$
5	30	30	24	11073787	11073787
18	22531	22530	31	1381678966	1381678966
22	1624471	1624470	34	2576196589	2576196588
39	496095156996	496095156996	40	744640262774	744640262774
44	5852185964842	5852185964842	46	36910857133194	36910857133194
51	31408458593527	31408458593526	53	3334307707163655	3334307707163654

Secondly, we test the running time of the proposed CPA for the different values of the lengths N. Fig. 5 is the variation trend of the running time for the different values of the lengths N. The test length of the pseudorandom bit sequence q is in the set $\{5, 10, 15, 25, 40, 60, 80, 100, 125, 150, 200, 240, 256, 300\}$. For each length N, 10 times experiments are performed for obtaining the average value. Note that all the experiments were done by Matlab2009 running on Core 2 Duo CPU 1.40GHz with 2.00GB RAM.

5.2 Simulation Results of COA on ACMM and ACMM+RAC

For the COA, we implement the experiments by computing the probability that the adversary $\mathcal{A}$ answers correctly. This probability corresponds to a real number in $[0, 1]$. Specially, in this experiment, the adversary $\mathcal{A}$ chooses two kinds of plaintext message pairs for analyzing the ACMM and ACMM+RAC, respectively, i.e., $(S_0, S_1)=(0x_1, 1x_2)$ and $(S_0, S_1)=(10x_3, 11x_4)$. $x_1, x_2 \in \{0, 1\}^{N-1}$ and $x_3, x_4 \in \{0, 1\}^{N-2}$. For each plaintext message pair, the lengths are the same. In each experiment, the new pseudorandom bit sequence (q or (q and q')) is used to encrypt the plaintext message S_b. The length of S_0 and S_1 is from 20 to N' ($N' \in \{2019, 4019, 6019, 8019, 9019, 10019\}$). This implies that the adversary $\mathcal{A}$ did 2000 experiments $\mathrm{Privk}^{\mathrm{coa}}_{\mathcal{A}, \prod'}(n)$ (or $\mathrm{Privk}^{\mathrm{coa}}_{\mathcal{A}, \widetilde{\prod}}(n)$), 4000 experiments $\mathrm{Privk}^{\mathrm{coa}}_{\mathcal{A}, \prod'}(n)$ (or $\mathrm{Privk}^{\mathrm{coa}}_{\mathcal{A}, \widetilde{\prod}}(n)$),..., 10000 experiments $\mathrm{Privk}^{\mathrm{coa}}_{\mathcal{A}, \prod'}(n)$ (or $\mathrm{Privk}^{\mathrm{coa}}_{\mathcal{A}, \widetilde{\prod}}(n)$), respectively. Table 5 lists the corresponding results about this simulation.

Table 5. Simulation results on the $\Pr[\text{Privk}_{\mathcal{A},\prod'}^{\text{coa}}(n){=}1]$ and $\Pr[\text{Privk}_{\mathcal{A},\widetilde{\prod}}^{\text{coa}}(n){=}1]$

Experiment times	ACMM:$(S_0, S_1){=}(0x_1, 1x_2)$			ACMM+RAC:$(S_0, S_1){=}(10x_2, 11x_3)$		
	$N(b'{=}b)$	$N(b'{\neq}b)$	$\Pr[\cdot]$	$N(b'{=}b)$	$N(b'{\neq}b)$	$\Pr[\cdot]$
2000	2000	0	1	1115	885	0.5575
4000	4000	0	1	2235	1765	0.5587
6000	6000	0	1	3323	2677	0.5538
8000	8000	0	1	4428	3572	0.5535
9000	9000	0	1	4987	4013	0.5541
10000	10000	0	1	5526	4474	0.5526

In Table 5, $\Pr[\cdot]$ is $\Pr[\text{Privk}_{\mathcal{A},\prod'}^{\text{coa}}(n){=}1]$ (or $\Pr[\text{Privk}_{\mathcal{A},\widetilde{\prod}}^{\text{coa}}(n){=}1]$). $N(b'{=}b)$ denotes the number of times that the adversary $\mathcal{A}$ answers correctly within a fixed experiment. $N(b'{\neq}b)$ denotes the number of times the adversary fails to answer correctly within the same experiment. From the values of this table, it can be found that for the ACMM, if $(S_0, S_1){=}(0x_1, 1x_2)$, the values of the $\Pr[\text{Privk}_{\mathcal{A},\prod'}^{\text{coa}}(n){=}1]$ match the deduction value of Theorem 2 in Subsection 3.3. Moreover, for the ACMM+RAC, when $(S_0, S_1){=}(10x_2, 11x_3)$, the values of the $\Pr[\text{Privk}_{\mathcal{A},\widetilde{\prod}}^{\text{coa}}(n){=}1]$ are near to the deduction value of Theorem 3 (i.e, 108/192).

6   Conclusions

An improved AC called ACMM was presented in [15]. In the current paper, we put forward the formal definition of ACMM. Along with the definition, we discussed various security notions related to ACMM. Based on these security notions, a chosen-plaintext attack was proposed to reveal the used pseudorandom bit sequence for the encryption under the condition that the same pseudorandom bit sequence is used to encrypt the different messages. We also showed that the ACMM does not have indistinguishable encryptions under the COA even if the different pseudorandom bit sequences are used to encrypt the different messages. To improve the security of AC, the authors Grangetto et al. [1] proposed another variant of AC, known as randomized arithmetic coding (RAC). Unfortunately, the authors Katti et al. [11] demonstrated that RAC is also insecure. Hence, intuitively, it seems that combination of these two encryptions, i.e., encryption at both modeling as well as at encoding component synchronously by using different pseudorandom bit sequences may enhance the security of the combined scheme referred as ACMM+RAC. However, we proved that ACMM+RAC does not have indistinguishable encryptions under the COA. Moreover, the authors Katti et al. [11] provided a scheme using AES in the counter mode. Nevertheless, according to the opinion from the authors Katti et al. [11], this use can increase the overhead. Therefore, as a future work, we will investigate the possibilities of proposing a secure randomized arithmetic coding scheme.

Acknowledgments. This research including the visit of Dr. Avishek Adhikari to Kyushu University and the visit of Mr. Liang Zhao to Indian Statistical

Institute is supported by Strategic Japanese-Indian Cooperative Programme on Multidisciplinary Research Field, which combines Information and Communications Technology with Other Fields Supported by Japan Science and Technology Agency and Department of Science and Technology of the Government of India. The first author of this research Liang Zhao is supported by the governmental scholarship from China Scholarship Council. The fourth author Professor Kyung-Hyune Rhee is supported by Basic Science Research Program through the National Research Foundation of Korea (NRF) funded by the Ministry of Education, Science and Technology (2011-0012849).

References

1. Grangetto, M., Magli, E., Olmo, G.: Multimedia selective encryption by means of randomized arithmetic coding. IEEE Trans. Multimedia 8(5), 905–917 (2006)
2. Lim, J., Boyd, C., Dawson, E.: Cryptanalysis of Adaptive Arithmetic Coding Encryption Schemes. In: Varadharajan, V., Pieprzyk, J., Mu, Y. (eds.) ACISP 1997. LNCS, vol. 1270, pp. 216–227. Springer, Heidelberg (1997)
3. Wu, C., Kuo, C.: Design of integrated multimedia compression and encryption systems. IEEE Trans. Multimedia 7(5), 828–839 (2005)
4. Jakimoski, G., Subbalakshmi, K.P.: Cryptanalysis of some multimedia encryption shcemes. IEEE Trans. Multimedia 10(3), 330–338 (2008)
5. Kim, H., Wen, J., Villasenor, J.D.: Secure arithmetic coding. IEEE Trans. Signal Process. 55(5), 2263–2272 (2007)
6. Wen, J., Kim, H., Villasenor, J.D.: Binary arithmetic coding with key-based interval splitting. IEEE Signal Process. Let. 13(2), 69–72 (2006)
7. Bergen, H.A., Hogan, J.M.: Data security in a fixed-model arithmetic coding compression algorithm. Comput. Secur. 11(5), 445–461 (1992)
8. Zhou, J., Au, O.C., Wong, P.H.: Adaptive chosen-ciphertext attack on secure arithmetic coding. IEEE Trans. Signal Process. 57(5), 1825–1838 (2009)
9. Witten, I.H., Cleary, J.G.: On the privacy afforded by adaptive text compression. Comput. Secur. 7(4), 397–408 (1988)
10. Bergen, H.A., Hogan, J.M.: A chosen plaintext attack on an adaptive arithmetic coding compression algorithm. Comput. Secur. 12(2), 157–167 (1993)
11. Katti, R.S., Srinivasan, S.K., Vosoughi, A.: On the security of randomized arithmetic codes against ciphertext-only attack. IEEE Trans. Inf. Forensics Security 6(1), 19–27 (2011)
12. Sun, H.M., Wang, K.H., Ting, W.C.: On the security of the secure arithmetic code. IEEE Trans Inf. Forensics Security 4(4), 781–789 (2009)
13. Liu, X., Farrell, P.G., Boyd, C.A.: Resisting the Bergen-Hogan Attack on Adaptive Arithmetic Coding. In: Darnell, M. (ed.) Cryptography and Coding 1997. LNCS, vol. 1355, pp. 199–208. Springer, Heidelberg (1997)
14. Uehara, T., Naini, R.S.: Attack on Liu/Farrell/Boyd arithmetic coding encryption scheme. In: Preneel, B. (ed.) CMS 1999. IFIP, vol. 152, pp. 273–290. Kluwer Academic, Norwell (1999)
15. Duan, L.L., Liao, X.F., Xiang, T.: A secure arithmetic coding based on Markov model. Commun. Nonlinear Sci. Numer. Simulat. 16(6), 2554–2562 (2011)
16. Katz, J., Lindell, Y.: Introduction of modern cryptography. Chapman & Hall/CRC, London (2008)

17. Zhao, F.G., Jiang, E.X., Ni, X.F.: On the specific expression of bit-level arithmetic coding. Numerical Mathematics, A Journal of Chinese Universities 7(2), 211–220 (1998)

Appendix

Appendix A: Proof of Lemma 1

Proof. For the sake of the simplicity, we only prove the case for $d_1=0$ and $d_2=0$. The other cases follow the similar proof and obtain the same deduction. To prove this *Lemma*, it is sufficient to show that $\Pr[s_N=0]-\Pr[s_N=0|s_{N-1}=0]\neq0$. According to Eq. (1), $\Pr[s_N=0]-\Pr[s_N=0|s_{N-1}=0]$ can be changed to

$$\frac{n_0^{N-1}(0)}{n_0^{N-1}(0) + n_0^{N-1}(1)} - \frac{n^{N-1}(0)}{n^{N-1}(0) + n^{N-1}(1)}. \tag{5}$$

When the N–1 many 0s have been encoded (i.e., the Markov model has been updated for encoding the N-th symbol), $n^{N-1}(0)$, $n^{N-1}(1)$, $n_0^{N-1}(0)$ and $n_0^{N-1}(1)$ should satisfy:

$$\begin{cases} n_0^{N-1}(1) + n_0^{N-1}(0) + 1 = n^{N-1}(0) + n^{N-1}(1) = N+1 \\ n_0^{N-1}(1) \geq 1,\, n_0^{N-1}(0) \geq 1,\, n^{N-1}(0) \geq 1,\, n^{N-1}(1) \geq 1 \end{cases}$$

Therefore, Eq. (5) is equivalent to the following transformation:

$$\frac{n_0^{N-1}(0) \times (N+1) - n^{N-1}(0) \times N}{(n_0^{N-1}(0) + n_0^{N-1}(1)) \times (n_0^{N-1}(0) + n_0^{N-1}(1) + 1)}$$

where $n_0^{N-1}(1)+n_0^{N-1}(0))\times(n_0^{N-1}(1)+n_0^{N-1}(0)+1)\neq0$. To estimate the value of $n_0^{N-1}(0)\times(N+1)-n^{N-1}(0)\times N$, the apagoge is used. Suppose that $n_0^{N-1}(0)\times(N+1)-n^{N-1}(0)\times N=0$, then, $n_0^{N-1}(0)/n^{N-1}(0)=N/(N+1)$. However, as $\gcd(N, N+1)=1$, $n_0^{N-1}(0)<N$ and $n^{N-1}(0)<(N+1)$, $n_0^{N-1}(0)/n^{N-1}(0)\neq N/(N+1)$. Hence, $n_0^{N-1}(0)\times(N+1)-n^{N-1}(0)\times N\neq0$, i.e., $\Pr[s_N=0]\neq\Pr[s_N=0|s_{N-1}=0]$.

Appendix B: Proof of Lemma 3

Proof. Suppose that the plaintext message is S_0, the ciphertext is $C_0:=\mathrm{SAC}(\bigcup_{i=1}^{N} \Pr^a[s_i^0], S_0)$, $\bigcup_{i=1}^{N}\Pr^a[s_i^0]:=\mathrm{ACMM}(q, S_0)$. If only the encryption of the first symbol s_1 is considered, according to the encryption steps of the ACMM, $\Pr^a[s_0=0]=\Pr^a[s_0=1]=0.5$ for encrypting the s_1. Moreover, as the encoding component is the standard AC, for the $s_1=0$, the corresponding interval must be $[0, 0.5)$. Then, based on the fact that $I(0x_1)\subseteq I(0)$, C_0 must be in J_1. Similarly, if the plaintext message is S_1, it can show that the corresponding ciphertext C_1 must be in J_2.

Therefore, if the ciphertext C is in J_1, the C must correspond to the plaintext message S_0, otherwise, it must be the encryption of S_1. This implies that for such plaintext messages S_0 and S_1, the adversary $\mathcal{A}$ will succeed in the proposed experiment.

Appendix C: Proof of Lemma 4

Proof. For the experiment $\mathsf{Privk}^{coa}_{\mathcal{A},\widetilde{\Pi}}(n)$, the success of the adversary $\mathcal{A}$ is dependent on the value of b, i.e., $\Pr[\mathsf{Privk}^{coa}_{\mathcal{A},\widetilde{\Pi}}(n)=1]$ is decided by the condition $S_{b'}=S_b$. For the intervals J_3 and J_4, both the encryptions of S_0 and S_1 can be within them. Then, for these intervals, the probabilities under the condition $S_b=S_0$ and $S_b=S_1$ should be compared. e.g., for the interval J_3, if the probability $\Pr[C\in J_3|S_b=S_0]=\Pr[C\in J_3|S_b=S_1]$, $\Pr[\mathsf{Privk}^{coa}_{\mathcal{A},\widetilde{\Pi}}(n)=1|C\in J_3]=1/2$. Otherwise, the adversary $\mathcal{A}$ should output the $S_{b'}$ which has the bigger probability for producing the ciphertext within the interval J_3. This implies that if $\Pr[C\in J_3|S_b=S_0]>\Pr[C\in J_3|S_b=S_1]$, the adversary $\mathcal{A}$ outputs $b'=0$. To obtain the probabilities of $C\in J_3$ and $C\in J_4$ under the condition $S_b=S_0$ and $S_b=S_1$, the adversary $\mathcal{A}$ draws the interval distribution table of first two binary symbols 10 and 11 (see Table 3) for the analysis, where q is $F(k)$ and q' is $F(k')$. This analysis is based on the fact that as $I(10x_3)\subseteq I(10)$ and $I(11x_4)\subseteq I(11)$, $C(S_0)\in I(10)$ and $C(S_1)\in I(11)$. Then, these probabilities can be produced by computing the following formula:

$$\Pr[C\in[x,y)|S_b=S_w]$$
$$=\sum_{d'=1}^{e'}\frac{1}{4}\times\sum_{d=1}^{e}\frac{|[x,y)|}{|I_d(s_0s_1)|}\times\frac{\#\{I_d^{F(k_1)}(s_0s)=I_d^{F(k_2)}(s_0s_1):F(k_1)\neq F(k_2)\}}{8}, \qquad (6)$$

where $|\cdot|$ denotes the length of the interval, $I(s_0s_1)$ corresponds to the plaintext $S_b=S_w$, $w\in\{0,1\}$, $e'\in\{1,2\}$, $e\in\{1,2,3\}$, $\#\{I^{F(k_1)}(s_0s_1)=I^{F(k_2)}(s_0s_1):F(k_1)\neq F(k_2)\}$ is the number of the same interval (e.g., for $F(k_1)=000$ and $F(k_2)=001$, the intervals of $I(10)$ or $I(11)$ are the same. Then, $\#\{10\}=\#\{11\}=2$). Specially, $[x,y)\in\{J_3,J_4\}$.

To achieve the $\Pr[\mathsf{Privk}^{coa}_{\mathcal{A},\widetilde{\Pi}}(n)=1]$, each sub-interval should be considered separately. In this proof, two examples are given in details. For $J_3=[0,1/6)$, if $s_0s_1=10$, when $F(k)\in\{000,001,010,011,100,101,110,111\}$ and $F(k')=10$, $J_3\subseteq I(10)$. According to Eq. (6), $\Pr[C\in[0,1/6)|S_b=S_0]=1/4\times(1/2+2/3\times1/4+1/2\times1/4)=19/96$. Moreover, if $s_0s_1=11$, when $F(k)\in\{000,001,010,011,100,101,110,111\}$ and $F(k')=11$, $J_3\subseteq I(11)$. Then, for S_1, $\Pr[C\in[0,1/6)|S_b=S_1]=1/4\times(1/4+1/2\times1/2+2/3\times1/4)=1/6$.

As $\Pr[C\in[0,1/6)|S_b=S_0]>\Pr[C\in[0,1/6)|S_b=S_1]$, $b'=0$ is chosen as the output of the adversary $\mathcal{A}$. The $\Pr[\mathsf{Privk}^{coa}_{\mathcal{A},\widetilde{\Pi}}(n)=1|C\in[0,1/6)]$ should be computed as follow,

$$\Pr[\mathsf{Privk}^{coa}_{\mathcal{A},\widetilde{\Pi}}(n)=1|C\in[0,1/6)]=\frac{\Pr[C\in[0,1/6)|S_b=S_0]\times\Pr[S_b=S_0]}{\Pr[C\in[0,1/6)]}=\frac{19}{35}$$

where $\Pr[C\in[0,1/6)]=\Pr[C\in[0,1/6)|S_b=S_0]\times\Pr[S_b=S_0]+\Pr[C\in[0,1/6)|S_b=S_1]\times\Pr[S_b=S_1]$. For $J_4=[1/6,1/4)$, if $s_0s_1=10$, when $F(k)\in\{010,011,110,111\}$, $F(k')=10$, and when $F(k)\in\{011,111\}$, $F(k')=11$, it is within $I(10)$. Then, $\Pr[C\in[1/6,1/4)|S_b=S_0]=1/4\times(1/3\times1/4+1/4\times1/4)+1/4\times(1/4\times1/4)=5/96$. If

$s_0 s_1 = 11$, when $F(k) \in \{000, 001, 100, 101\}$, $F(k') = 10$, and when $F(k) \in \{000, 001, 010, 100, 101, 110\}$, $F(k') = 11$, $J_4 \in I(11)$. Then, $\Pr[C \in [1/6, 1/4)|S_b = S_1] = 1/4 \times (1/2 \times 1/4 + 1/3 \times 1/4) + 1/4 \times (1/2 \times 1/4) = 1/12$.

As $\Pr[C \in [0, 1/6)|S_b = S_1] > \Pr[C \in [0, 1/6)|S_b = S_0]$, $b' = 1$ is chosen as the output of the adversary $\mathcal{A}$. The $\Pr[\mathsf{Privk}_{\mathcal{A},\widetilde{\Pi}}^{coa}(n) = 1|C \in [1/6, 1/4)]$ should be computed as follow,

$$\Pr[\mathsf{Privk}_{\mathcal{A},\widetilde{\Pi}}^{coa}(n) = 1|C \in [\frac{1}{6}, \frac{1}{4})] = \frac{\Pr[C \in [1/6, 1/4)|S_b = S_1] \times \Pr[S_b = S_1]}{\Pr[C \in [1/6, 1/4)]} = \frac{8}{13}$$

where $\Pr[C \in [1/6, 1/4)] = \Pr[C \in [1/6, 1/4)|S_b = S_0] \times \Pr[S_b = S_0] + \Pr[C \in [1/6, 1/4)|S_b = S_1] \times \Pr[S_b = S_1]$. The same method can be used to analyze the other sub-intervals, i.e., $\{[1/3, 1/2), [1/2, 2/3), [5/6, 1), [1/4, 1/3), [2/3, 3/4), [3/4, 5/6)\}$. Then, the conclusion is achieved

$$\begin{cases} \Pr[\mathsf{Privk}_{\mathcal{A},\widetilde{\Pi}}^{coa}(n) = 1|C \in J_3] = 19/35, \ b' = 0 \\ \Pr[\mathsf{Privk}_{\mathcal{A},\widetilde{\Pi}}^{coa}(n) = 1|C \in J_4] = 8/13, \ b' = 1 \end{cases}.$$

Concurrent Non-Malleable Witness Indistinguishable Argument from Any One-Way Function*

Guifang Huang and Lei Hu

State Key Laboratory of Information Security,
Graduate University of Chinese Academy of Sciences, Beijing, 100049, P.R. China
{gfhuang,hu}@is.ac.cn

Abstract. *Non-malleable witness indistinguishability* (NMWI) is a security notion against man-in-the-middle attacks which requires that the witness encoded in the right interaction is computationally independent of that used by honest prover in the left. In STOC 2009, Lin et al. defined *strongly non-malleable witness indistinguishability* (SNMWI) which is similar in spirit to NMWI, and proposed a SNMWI scheme based on one-way function. In this paper, we firstly show that the two notions NMWI and SNMWI are incomparable: there exists a SNMWI argument which is not NMWI, and vice versa. Furthermore, it is pointed out that the SNMWI construction given in STOC 2009 is not NMWI. Then, we present a variant of LPV08 scheme [17] and show that this variant is a concurrent NMWI argument. Compared with the concurrent NMWI argument of [22] which was shown to be non-malleable by using non-black-box techniques and whose difficulty assumption was claw-free permutation, our new scheme is based on the existence of one-way functions and its proof of security relies on black-box techniques.

Keywords: concurrent non-malleable witness indistinguishability, strong non-malleable witness indistinguishability, commitment, special-sound WI proofs:

1 Introduction

Witness indistinguishability (WI), a relaxed notion of zero knowledge proofs [16], was first introduced by Feige and Shamir [14]. A proof system is said to be witness indistinguishable if the view of any malicious verifier is computationally independent of the witness that the prover uses. Witness indistinguishable protocols have many applications in design of cryptographic protocols. For example, the well-known FLS technique [13] and the closure under concurrent composition [10, 27] make witness indistinguishable protocols become a quite popular tool in constructing zero knowledge proofs [1, 15, 19, 22, 24, 27].

---

* This work is supported by NSFC (61070172, 61003276, 60803128) and the National 973 Program (2007CB311201).

C.-K. Wu, M. Yung, and D. Lin (Eds.): Inscrypt 2011, LNCS 7537, pp. 363–378, 2012.

In some settings, the most basic security guarantees of cryptographic protocols are not sufficient. Especially in an asynchronous network environment, protocols susceptible to man-in-the-middle attacks may give rise to devastating results (e.g. contract bidding implemented by a commitment scheme [11]). In order to address the above concerns, Dolev et al. brought out the concept of non-malleability and demonstrated how to achieve non-malleability with respect to encryption schemes, signature schemes, commitments, zero knowledge proofs etc. [9]. Since its introduction, the notion of non-malleability has received a lot of attentions and many constructions of non-malleable zero knowledge (NMZK) [15, 19, 22, 24, 28, 29] and non-malleable commitments [2, 5–7, 12, 17, 23, 25] have been worked out.

1.1 Related Results on NMWI and SNMWI

The notion of *non-malleable witness indistinguishability* was firstly considered by Ostrovsky, Persiano and Visconti [21] (see also [22]). For a man-in-the-middle adversary who attacks the *stand-alone* execution of a WI protocol (P, V), on one hand, he acts as a malicious verifier to interact with P on common input x in the left (called left interaction). On the other hand, in the right he plays the role of a prover to try to convince V the membership of a statement x' adaptively chosen by himself (right interaction). Informally speaking, NMWI requires that the witness encoded in the right interaction is computationally independent of the witness uses by prover P in the left. Concurrent NMWI is a security notion defined with respect to a stronger man-in-the-middle adversary who has the power of starting up any polynomial number of sessions in the left and in the right and scheduling these sessions in an interleaving way. In [22], Ostrovsky et al. gave a separation between NMWI and NMZK and proposed a constant-round concurrent NMWI argument. However, because their construction was built by using a non-black-box NMZK [24, 25] as sub-protocol, it was non-black-box and based on claw-free permutation.

In STOC 2009, Lin et al. defined the concept of *strongly non-malleable witness-indistinguishability* (SNMWI) only for a language $L \in \mathbf{NP}$ which has unique witnesses (that is, every instance in L has a unique witness) [18]. Different from NMWI, SNMWI for a language with unique witnesses requires the indistinguishability of the witnesses extracted from the right interactions, whenever the tuples containing a statement proved in the left and an auxiliary input to the man-in-the-middle adversary are indistinguishable. Then, they extended the concept of SNMWI to general $\mathbf{NP}$ languages and presented a $\mathcal{O}(1)^{log^*(n)}$-round (almost constant-round)SNMWI argument based on one-way function. There, the proof of security of their SNMWI construction depends on black-box techniques.

1.2 Our Results

In this paper, we firstly discuss the relation of NMWI and SNMWI, and show that these two notions are incomparable. That is, there exists a SNMWI argument which is not NMWI, and vice versa. Furthermore, it is pointed out that the SNMWI construction in [18] is not NMWI, which implies that the following problem left in [22] is still open:

Does there exist a concurrent NMWI argument for **NP** *languages based on the minimal assumption whose security relies on black-box techniques?*

Then, we give an affirmative answer to the above question by presenting a variant of LPV08 scheme [17] and showing that this variant is concurrent NMWI. The main results in this paper are the following

Theorem 1. *There exists a SNMWI argument that is not NMWI for language $L \in$ **NP** which has infinite instances with at least two witnesses.*

Theorme 2. *There exists a NMWI argument that is not SNMWI for language $L \in$ **NP**.*

Theorme 3. *If one-way functions exist, there exists a NMWI argument for $L \in$ **NP** which can be shown secure relying on black-box techniques.*

It is organized as follows: In section 2, some notations and definitions are given. Then, in section 3, we give two constructions to show the separation between NMWI and SNMWI. At last, We present the concurrent NMWI argument in section 4.

2 Preliminaries

For any **NP** language L, there is a natural witness relation R_L that determines L. R_L consists of pairs (x, w), where w is a witness for the membership of $x \in L$. Let $W_L(x)$ denote the set of witnesses for $x \in L$. A function $f(n)$ is said to be *negligible* if for every positive polynomial $q(n)$, there exists a positive integer N such that for all integers $n \geq N$, $f(n) \leq 1/q(n)$. For a string x, let $|x|$ denote the length of x. A *probability ensemble* is a sequence $X = \{X_i\}_{i \in I}$ of random variables X_i over $\{0,1\}^{p(|i|)}$, where I is a countable index set and $p(\cdot)$ is a polynomial.

Two ensembles $X = \{X_i\}_{i \in I}$ and $Y = \{Y_i\}_{i \in I}$ are *computationally indistinguishable* if no probabilistic polynomial time (PPT) algorithm can distinguish them with more than negligible probability. That is, for any PPT algorithm D, for any positive polynomial $p(\cdot)$, for sufficiently long i, we have $|Pr[D(i, X_i) = 1] - Pr[D(i, Y_i) = 1]| < \frac{1}{p(|i|)}$.

For a pair of interactive machines (P, V), $< P(y), V(z) > (x)$ denotes the output of V when interacting with P on common input x, y and z are auxiliary inputs of P and V respectively.

2.1 Witness Indistinguishability

In this paper, we consider witness indistinguishable arguments.

Definition 1 (Interactive Proof (Argument)). *A pair of PPT interactive machines (P, V) is said to be an interactive proof (argument) for language $L \in$ **NP** if the following conditions hold*

- Completeness: *When $x \in L$, for every $y \in W_L(x)$, $z \in \{0,1\}^*$, we have that $Pr[< P(y), V(z) > (x) = 1] = 1$.*
- Soundness: *When $x \notin L$, for any (computatoinally-bounded) machine P^*, for any $y, z \in \{0,1\}^*$, $Pr[< P^*(y), V(z) > (x) = 1]$ is a negligible function in $|x|$.*

Definition 2 (Witness Indistinguishable Argument). *An interactive argument (P, V) for language $L \in NP$ is witness indistinguishable if for every (expected) PPT verifier V^*, for two sequences $\{w_x^1\}_{x \in L}$ and $\{w_x^2\}_{x \in L}$ such that $w_x^1, w_x^2 \in W_L(x)$, the following two ensembles are computationally indistinguishable:*

- $\{< P(w_x^1), V^*(z) > (x)\}_{x \in L, z \in \{0,1\}^*}$
- $\{< P(w_x^2), V^*(z) > (x)\}_{x \in L, z \in \{0,1\}^*}$

That is, for every PPT algorithm D, for every positive polynomial $p(\cdot)$, for sufficiently long $x \in L$, for every $z \in \{0,1\}^*$, we have

$$|Pr[D(x, z, < P(w_x^1), V^*(z) > (x)) = 1] - Pr[D(x, z, < P(w_x^2), V^*(z) > (x))$$
$$= 1] < \frac{1}{p(|x|)}.$$

Special-Sound WI Proofs [4, 8]: A 3-round public-coin WI proof for language $L \in \mathbf{NP}$ with witness relation R_L is called *special-sound*, if for any two accepting transcripts (α, β, γ) and $(\alpha, \beta', \gamma')$ where $\beta \neq \beta'$, a witness $w \in W_L(x)$ can be computed efficiently.

Special-sound WI proof for any **NP** language can be constructed based on one-way function. More precisely, in [3], Blum proposed a special-sound WI proof for Hamiltonian Graphs [3]. When the commitment used in [3] is replaced by Naor's commitment [20], we get a 4-round special-sound WI proof for Hamiltonian Graphs based on one-way function. Therefore, based on one-way function, any language $L \in \mathbf{NP}$ has a 4-round special-sound WI proof. For simplicity, we use a 3-round special-sound WI proof in this paper, though our proof also works with a 4-round special-sound WI proof.

2.2   Commitment Scheme

In this paper, we consider statistically binding commitment schemes.

A commitment scheme enables a party, called the *committer* to commit itself to a secret value while keeping it secret from the *receiver*(hiding property). Furthermore, in a latter stage when the commitment is revealed, it is required that the opening can yield only a single value determined in the commit phase (binding property). The formal definition is described as follows

Commitment Scheme: A pair of PPT interactive machines (C, R) is said to be a statistically binding commitment scheme if the following two properties hold:

– Computational Hiding: For every PPT machine R^*, the two following ensembles are computationally indistinguishable

  (a) $\{sta^{R^*}_{(C,R)}(v_1, z)\}_{v_1 \in \{0,1\}^n, n \in \mathbb{N}, z \in \{0,1\}^*}$

  (b) $\{sta^{R^*}_{(C,R)}(v_2, z)\}_{v_2 \in \{0,1\}^n, n \in \mathbb{N}, z \in \{0,1\}^*}$

  where $sta^{R^*}_{(C,R)}(v, z)$ denotes the random variable describing the output of R^* after receiving a commitment to v using (C, R).

– Statistical Binding: For any computationally unbounded committer C^*, the probability that he succeeds in opening a given commitment in two different ways is only negligible.

2.3 NMWI

As stated in [22], we formalize the concept of NMWI for language $L \in \mathbf{NP}$ with respect to a special kind of argument —*commit-and-prove argument*, where on common input x the prover firstly commits to a witness $w \in W_L(x)$ by using a statistically binding commitment scheme and then he proves that the committed value w is actually a witness for $x \in L$.

Suppose (P_s, V_s) is a tag-based commit-and-prove argument for language $L \in \mathbf{NP}$, where the prover and verifier receive a "tag" as an additional common input, besides a statement x. For a PPT man-in-the-middle adversary $\mathcal{A}$ with auxiliary input z, he simultaneously participates in one left interaction and one right interaction: In the left interaction, on common input (x, t), he acts as a verifier to interact with P_s who has a private input $w \in W_L(x)$ to get a proof of statement x, using tag t. In the right interaction, he adaptively chooses $(\tilde{x}, \tilde{t})$ and attempts to convince V_s the statement $\tilde{x}$ using tag $\tilde{t}$. Define $wmim^{\mathcal{A}}(tag, x, w, z)$ as follows: $wmim^{\mathcal{A}}(tag, x, w, z)$ is a random variable describing the witness extracted from the right interaction, if the right interaction is accepting and $\tilde{t} \neq t$; Otherwise, $wmim^{\mathcal{A}}(tag, x, w, z)$ is set to $\perp$.

Definition 3 (Tag-Based NMWI Argument [22]). *A family of commit-and-prove arguments* $\{(P_s, V_s)\}_s$ *for language* $L \in NP$ *is a tag-based non-malleable witness indistinguishable argument with tags of length* ℓ *if, for all PPT man-in-the-middle adversary* $\mathcal{A}$, *for all PPT algorithm* D, *there exists a negligible function* v *such that for* $x \in L$, *for all tags* $t \in \{0,1\}^\ell$, *for two witnesses* $w, w' \in W_L(x)$, *for all auxiliary input* $z \in \{0,1\}^*$, *it holds that*

$$|Pr[D(x, w, w', wmim^{\mathcal{A}}(t, x, w, z), z) = 1] - Pr[D(x, w, w', wmim^{\mathcal{A}}(t, x, w', z), z) = 1]| < v(|x|)$$

For a PPT *concurrent* man-in-the-middle adversary $\mathcal{A}$ with auxiliary input z who opens up $m = poly(k)$ left and right interactions (k is the security parameter), on common inputs $X = (x_1, \cdots, x_m)$ and $T = (t_1, \cdots, t_m)$, $\mathcal{A}$ simultaneously participants in m left interactions and m right interactions and controls the schedules of these left (right) interactions in an interleaving way: In the left, $\mathcal{A}$ gets a proof of statement x_i by interacting with P_s who has a private input $w_i \in W_L(x_i)$, using tag t_i. In the right, $\mathcal{A}$ selects $\tilde{x}_j, \tilde{t}_j$ and tries to prove each statement $\widetilde{x}_j$ using tags $\widetilde{t}_j$, for $j = 1, 2, \cdots, m$. Let $W = (w_1, \cdots, w_m)$, define $wmim^{\mathcal{A}}(T, X, W, z) = (y_{1_1} \cdots, y_m)$ as follows: for $j = 1, 2, \cdots, m$, if the proof of $\widetilde{x}_j$ is accepting and tag $\widetilde{t}_j$ is not contained in T, let y_j be the random variable describing the witness extracted from this interaction; Otherwise, set y_j to $\bot$.

Definition 4 (Concurrent NMWI Argument [22]). *A family of commit-and-prove arguments* $\{(P_s, V_s)\}_s$ *for language* $L \in NP$ *is a tag-based concurrent non-malleable witness-indistinguishable argument with tags of length* ℓ *if, for any PPT concurrent man-in-the-middle adversary* $\mathcal{A}$, *for all any positive polynomial* $m = poly(k), n = poly(k)$, *for all PPT algorithm* D, *there exists a negligible function* v *such that for all sequences* $X = (x_1, \cdots, x_m)$ *where each* $x_i \in L \cap \{0,1\}^n$, *for all sequences* T *of tags of length* ℓ, *for all sequences* W *and* W' *of witnesses for* X, *for any* $z \in \{0,1\}^*$, *it holds that*

$$|Pr[D(X, W, W', wmim^{\mathcal{A}}(T, X, W, z), z) = 1] - Pr[D(X, W, W',$$
$$wmim^{\mathcal{A}}(T, X, W', z), z) = 1]| < v(k)$$

2.4   SNMWI

In [18], in order to make the witness extracted from the right interaction well-defined, Lin et al. firstly formalized the notion of SNMWI for language $L \in$ **NP** with *unique* witnesses, and then extended this notion to general **NP** languages. Here, we present the extended definition of SNMWI.

Consider a tag-based argument (P_s, V_s) for **NP** language L: For a man-in-the-middle adversary $\mathcal{A}$ with auxiliary input z, on one hand, he participates in the left interaction to get a proof of statement x from P_s on private input $w \in W_L(x)$, using tag t; On the other hand, he adaptively chooses $\widetilde{x}, \widetilde{t}$ and plays the role of prover to prove statement $\widetilde{x}$ using tag $\widetilde{t}$. Let $\widetilde{w}$ denote the random variable describing the witness extracted from the right interaction, if this right interaction is accepting and $\widetilde{t} \neq t$ and $\widetilde{x}$ has only one witness; Otherwise, set $\widetilde{w} = \bot$. Define $mim^{\mathcal{A}}(x, w, z, t)$ to be a random variable describing $\widetilde{w}$ and the view of $\mathcal{A}$ in the above man-in-the-middle execution.

Definition 5 (SNMWI Argument [18]). *A family of tag-based arguments* $\{(P_s, V_s)\}_s$ *for language* $L \in$ **NP** *with witness relation* R_L *is strongly non-malleable witness indistinguishable, if for every non-uniform PPT man-in-the-middle adversary* $\mathcal{A}$, *for every* $t \in \{0,1\}^*$ *and every two sequences of input distributions* $\{D_n^1\}_{n \in N}$ *and* $\{D_n^2\}_{n \in N}$, *the following holds: if the ensembles* $\{(x, w, z) \leftarrow D_n^1 : (x, z)\}_{n \in N}$ *and* $\{(x, w, z) \leftarrow D_n^2 : (x, z)\}_{n \in N}$ *are computationally indistinguishable, so are the following ensembles*

- $\{(x, w, z) \leftarrow D_n^1 : mim^{\mathcal{A}}(x, w, z, t)\}_{n \in N, t \in \{0,1\}^*}$
- $\{(x, w, z) \leftarrow D_n^2 : mim^{\mathcal{A}}(x, w, z, t)\}_{n \in N, t \in \{0,1\}^*}$

2.5   Security for Signature Schemes

Security for Signature Schemes: A signature scheme is a tuple $(Gen, Sign, Ver)$, where Gen is a probabilistic key generator, $Sign$ is a probabilistic signature algorithm and Ver is a deterministic verification algorithm. On input 1^k, Gen outputs a random signature-key sk and the corresponding verification-key vk. To sign a message m, $Sign$ is run on input (m, sk) to generate a signature s. Given pk, m, s, Ver outputs 1 if s is a valid signature for the message m.

A signature scheme is *existentially unforgeable against chosen-message attacks* if any PPT adversary, upon seeing polynomial number of signatures on the messages adaptively chosen by himself, cannot forge a valid signature on a new message. Based on one-way functions, signature schemes existentially unforgeable against chosen-message attacks do exist [26].

3   Separation of SNMWI and NMWI

In this section, we present two constructions: The first one is SNMWI but not NMWI; The second one is NMWI but not SNMWI.

3.1   A SNMWI Argument that is not NMWI

Our construction of SNMWI argument that is not NMWI comes from the following observations: SNMWI *only* requires the indistinguishability of the witnesses used in the right with respect to *well-behaved* man-in-the-middle adversaries, when the inputs in the left are computationally indistinguishable. Here "well-behaved" means that, except with negligible probability, the man-in-the-middle adversary only chooses a statement with unique witness in the right. Thus, a SNMWI argument for $L \in$ **NP** with unique witnesses must be NMWI. However, the concept of NMWI is motivated by considering the malleability of WI arguments against *all* man-in-the-middle adversaries, including those who are not well-behaved.

We use the technique used in constructing a NMZK that is not NMWI [22]. For a general **NP** language L with witness relation R_L and a statistically binding commitment scheme Com, define language L_1 as: $L_1 = \{(x, c) : \exists w, r, s.t. c = Com(w, r) \wedge (x, w) \in R\}$. From [23], we know that every language in **NP** has a SNMWI argument, then suppose $\Pi = \{(\mathcal{P}_t, \mathcal{V}_t)\}_t$ is a SNMWI argument for L_1. The construction of protocol $\Gamma = \{(P_{t_0, t_1}, V_{t_0, t_1})\}_{t_0, t_1}$ for L is described in *Figure 1*.

Lemma 1. *Protocol Γ is a SNMWI argument for language L.*

Proof: From the completeness and soundness of $\Pi_{t_0 \circ 0}$ and $\Pi_{t_1 \circ 1}$, it follows that Γ is an argument for L. Next, we prove the SNMWI property. For any man-in-the-middle adversary $\mathcal{A}$, for two sequences of input distributions $\{D_n^1\}_{n \in N}$ and $\{D_n^2\}_{n \in N}$, if $\{(x_1, w_1, z_1) \leftarrow D_n^1 : (x_1, z_1)\}_{n \in N}$ and $\{(x_2, w_2, z_2) \leftarrow D_n^2 : (x_2, z_2)\}_{n \in N}$ are computationally indistinguishable, what we need is to prove the indistinguishability of the following two ensembles

- $\{mim^{\mathcal{A}}(x_1, w_1, z_1, (t_0, t_1))\}_{n \in N, t_0, t_1 \in \{0,1\}^*}$
- $\{mim^{\mathcal{A}}(x_2, w_2, z_2, (t_0, t_1))\}_{n \in N, t_0, t_1 \in \{0,1\}^*}.$

Tag: (t_0, t_1);
Common Input: x;
Private input to prover: witness w for $x \in L$;
1. P_{t_0,t_1} computes $(com_0, dec_0) \leftarrow Com(w)$ and sends com_0 to V_{t_0,t_1};
2. P_{t_0,t_1} computes $(com_1, dec_1) \leftarrow Com(w)$ and sends com_1 to V_{t_0,t_1};
3. On common input (x, com_0), run the SNMWI protocol $\Pi_{t_0 \circ 0}$ in which P_{t_0,t_1} runs algorithm $\mathcal{P}_{t_0 \circ 0}$ with private input (w, dec_0) and V_{t_0,t_1} runs algorithm $\mathcal{V}_{t_0 \circ 0}$ to prove statement (x, com_0). Let $trans_0$ be the transcript;
4. On common input (x, com_1), run the SNMWI protocol $\Pi_{t_1 \circ 1}$ in which P_{t_0,t_1} runs algorithm $\mathcal{P}_{t_1 \circ 1}$ with private input (w, dec_1) and V_{t_0,t_1} runs algorithm $\mathcal{V}_{t_1 \circ 1}$ to prove statement (x, com_1). Let $trans_1$ be the transcript;
5. V_{t_0,t_1} outputs 1 iff $trans_0$ and $trans_1$ are both accepting transcripts.

Fig. 1. The description of protocol Γ

we use the *hybrid argument* technique to prove the above indistinguishability. For a fixed tag (t_0, t_1) used in the left, for $i, j, k = 1, 2$, define the hybrid experiment $mim^{\mathcal{A}}_{ijk}$ as follows: In the left, the prover firstly computes $c_0 = Com(w_j, r_j)$ and $c_1 = Com(w_k, r_k)$ and sends c_0, c_1 to adversary $\mathcal{A}$ whose auxiliary input is z_i, where r_j, r_k are random strings used in generating commitments c_0, c_1. Then, the prover runs sub-protocol $\Pi_{t_0 \circ 0}$ on common input (x_j, c_0) and sub-protocol $\Pi_{t_1 \circ 1}$ on common input (x_k, c_1) sequentially with $\mathcal{A}$ in which $\mathcal{A}$ acts as a verifier. In the right, $\mathcal{A}$ adaptively chooses a statement $\widetilde{x}$ and tag $(\widetilde{t_0}, \widetilde{t_1})$ and proves $\widetilde{x} \in L$ using the tag $(\widetilde{t_0}, \widetilde{t_1})$. If this right interaction is accepting and $(\widetilde{t_0}, \widetilde{t_1}) \neq (t_0, t_1)$ and $\widetilde{x}$ has only one witness, $mim^{\mathcal{A}}_{ijk}$ outputs the view of $\mathcal{A}$ and the witness of $\widetilde{x}$; Otherwise, he outputs $\bot$.

From the definition of $mim^{\mathcal{A}}_{ijk}$, we get $mim^{\mathcal{A}}_{111} = mim^{\mathcal{A}}(x_1, w_1, z_1, (t_0, t_1))$ and $mim^{\mathcal{A}}_{222} = mim^{\mathcal{A}}(x_2, w_2, z_2, (t_0, t_1))$. Thus, the desired indistinguishability of $mim^{\mathcal{A}}_{111}$ and $mim^{\mathcal{A}}_{222}$ can be obtained from the following

1. $mim^{\mathcal{A}}_{111}$ and $mim^{\mathcal{A}}_{211}$: The indistinguishability of these two experiments is reduced to the indistinguishability of z_1 and z_2. Specifically, assume that there exists a PPT algorithm D that distinguishes $mim^{\mathcal{A}}_{111}$ and $mim^{\mathcal{A}}_{211}$, then we can construct a PPT non-uniform algorithm D' to distinguish z_1 and z_2: On input z_i and $z' = x_1 \circ w_1 \circ t_0 \circ t_1$, D' firstly performs in the same way as experiment $mim^{\mathcal{A}}_{i11}$. Then, he invokes algorithm D and outputs what D outputs.

2. $mim^{\mathcal{A}}_{211}$ and $mim^{\mathcal{A}}_{212}$: The indistinguishability of these two experiments is reduced to the SNMWI property of the sub-protocol used in step 4. Assume that $mim^{\mathcal{A}}_{211}$ and $mim^{\mathcal{A}}_{212}$ are distinguishable, we can construct a man-in-the-middle adversary $\mathcal{A}'$ for protocol $\Pi_{t_1 \circ 1}$ as follows: The auxiliary input to $\mathcal{A}'$ is $z' = x_1 \circ w_1 \circ t_0 \circ t_1 \circ z_2$. On common input $(x_i, c_{1i} = Com(w_i, r_{1i}))$ where r_{1i} is a random string in committing to w_i, $\mathcal{A}'$ invokes $\mathcal{A}$ and acts in the following way:
   - $\mathcal{A}'$ computes a commitment c_0 to w_1 and feeds $\mathcal{A}$ with c_0, c_{1i};
   - On common input (x_1, c_0), $\mathcal{A}'$ interacts internally with $\mathcal{A}$ to finish the left and right interactions of sub-protocol $\Pi_{t_0 \circ 0}$: In the left, $\mathcal{A}'$ runs

algorithm $\mathcal{P}_{t_0 \circ 0}(x_1, c_0)$ to answer $\mathcal{A}$'s challenges; In the right, $\mathcal{A}'$ acts as an honest verifier $\mathcal{V}_{\widetilde{t}_0 \circ 0}$.

- On common input (x_i, c_{1i}), $\mathcal{A}'$ simultaneously interacts with an honest prover $\mathcal{P}_{t_1 \circ 1}$ and an honest verifier $\mathcal{V}_{\widetilde{t}_1 \circ 1}$: He feeds $\mathcal{A}$ with what he receives in the left and right interactions and forwards $\mathcal{A}$'s messages to $\mathcal{P}_{t_1 \circ 1}$ and $\mathcal{V}_{\widetilde{t}_1 \circ 1}$ respectively.

From the construction of $\mathcal{A}'$, it can be concluded that $\mathcal{A}'$ has the power of distinguishing $mim^{\mathcal{A}'}((x_1, c_{11}), (w_1, r_1), z_2, t_1 \circ 1)$ and $mim^{\mathcal{A}'}((x_2, c_{12}), (w_2, r_2),$ $z_2, t_1 \circ 1)$, a contradiction with the SNMWI property of the sub-protocol in step 4.

3. $mim_{212}^{\mathcal{A}}$ and $mim_{222}^{\mathcal{A}}$: These two experiments are indistinguishable. By a similar way as used above, we can reduce the indistinguishability between them to the SNMWI property of the sub-protocol used in step 3.

Theorem 1. *There exists a SNMWI but not NMWI argument for $L \in$* **NP** *which has infinite instances with at least two witnesses.*

Proof: It is sufficient to show that Γ is not NMWI for $L \in$ **NP** which has infinite instances with at least two witnesses. A man-in-the-middle adversary $\mathcal{A}$ can be constructed as follows: Suppose x is a statement with at least two witnesses. In the left, the common input is $(x, (t_0, t_1))$ and the private input to the honest prover is $w \in W_L(x)$. $\mathcal{A}$ chooses the statement x and a tag $(t_0, \widetilde{t}_1)$ in the right, where $\widetilde{t}_1 \neq t_1$. On auxiliary input $w \in W_L(x)$, $\mathcal{A}$ starts the malleable attacks in the following way

- $\mathcal{A}$ copies and forwards what he receives in step 1 of the left interaction to the verifier.
- In step 2 of the right interaction, $\mathcal{A}$ computes a commitment c_1 to w and sends c_1 to the verifier.
- By simply forwarding what the verifier asks for to the prover and copying the prover's answers, $\mathcal{A}$ completes step 3 of the right interaction.
- At last, $\mathcal{A}$ completes step 4 of the right interaction by using the witness w.

From above construction, it is clear that the witness extracted from $\mathcal{A}$'s accepting proof with tag $(t_0, \widetilde{t}_1)$ is dependent on the witness used in the left. Thus, Γ is not NMWI.

Remark: For the SNMWI scheme given in [18], a similar man-in-the-middle adversary can be constructed to break the NMWI property. Thus, the SNMWI scheme proposed in [18] is not NMWI.

3.2 A NMWI Argument That Is Not SNMWI

Suppose $f : \{0,1\}^n \to \{0,1\}^n$ is a one-way permutation and $b : \{0,1\}^* \to \{0,1\}$ is its hard-core predicate. Define relation R to be $R = \{(f(y), y) : y \in \{0,1\}^*\}$, then the language L_R that R determines is in **NP**. From [22], we know that there exists a NMWI argument $\Pi = \{(\mathcal{P}_t, \mathcal{V}_t)\}_t$ for L_R.

Next, we construct a man-in-the-middle adversary $\mathcal{A}$ for Π in the following way: Suppose the statement and the tag in the left are $f(y)$ and t. $\mathcal{A}$ chooses $f(y)$ and $\tilde{t} \neq t$ in the right. On auxiliary input the witness y, $\mathcal{A}$ can prove the statement $f(y)$ in the right using the tag $\tilde{t}$. Consider the random variable X_n^i that is randomly distributed on $\{f(y) : y \in \{0,1\}^* \wedge b(y) = i\}$, $i = 0, 1$. For $\{(X_n^0, y_n^0, y_n^0)\}_{n \in N}$ and $\{(X_n^1, y_n^1, y_n^1)\}_{n \in N}$, $\{(X_n^0, y_n^0)\}_{n \in N}$ and $\{(X_n^1, y_n^1)\}$ are computationally indistinguishable, where y_n^i is the witness of $X_n^i \in L_R$. However, the following two ensembles are distinguishable

- $\{mim^{\mathcal{A}}(X_n^0, y_n^0, y_n^0, t)\}_{n \in N, t \in \{0,1\}^*}$;
- $\{mim^{\mathcal{A}}(X_n^1, y_n^1, y_n^1, t)\}_{n \in N, t \in \{0,1\}^*}$;

The reason is that: for an accepting right interaction generated by $\mathcal{A}$, since $\tilde{t} \neq t$ and X_n^i has unique witness, the witness extracted from this right interaction is exactly y_n^i satisfying $X_n^i = f(y_n^i)$ and $b(y_n^i) = i$. Thus, by only computing $b(y_n^i)$, we can distinguish the above two ensembles.

Theorem 2. *There exists a NMWI argument which is not SNMWI.*

4   Construction of Concurrent NMWI Argument

In this section, we show that a variant of LPV08 scheme [17] is concurrent NMWI argument for language $L \in NP$.

4.1   The Message Scheduling Sub-protocol

Our concurrent NMWI construction is mainly built from the tag-based *message-scheduling protocol* $(\mathcal{P}_t, \mathcal{V}_t)$ depicted in *Figure 2*, which is used in [17]

Common Input: an instance x of length n;
Tag: t;
For i=1 to t
   $\mathcal{P}_t$ executes $design_{t_i}$ with $\mathcal{V}_t$ to prove the statement x;
   $\mathcal{P}_t$ executes $design_{1-t_i}$ with $\mathcal{V}_t$ to prove the statement x;

Fig. 2. Protocol $(\mathcal{P}_t, \mathcal{V}_t)$ for language L'

where $design_0$ and $design_1$ contain two executions $(\alpha_1, \beta_1, \gamma_1)$ and $(\alpha_2, \beta_2, \gamma_2)$ of a special-sound WI proof for L' which are scheduled in the way as in *Figure 3*.

Related to the message-scheduling sub-protocols, there is a notion called *safe-point* from which we can extract the witness used in the right proof *safely* (e.g., without rewinding the left).

Definition 6 (Safe-Point [17]). *A prefix ρ of a transcript Δ is called safe-point, if there exists an accepting proof $(\alpha_r, \beta_r, \gamma_r)$ in the right, such that*

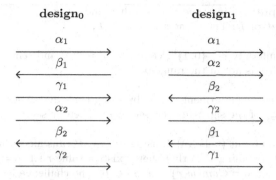

Fig. 3. The description of protocol $design_0$ and $design_1$

1. α_r occurs in ρ but not β_r and γ_r;
2. For any proof $(\alpha_\ell, \beta_\ell, \gamma_\ell)$ in the left, if only α_ℓ occurs in ρ, then β_ℓ occurs after γ_r.

In [17], it has been proved that

Lemma 2 (Safe-Point Lemma [17]). *In any one-many concurrent man-in-the-middle execution of $(\mathcal{P}_t, \mathcal{V}_t)$, for any accepting right interaction with a tag different from the left, there exists a safe-point for this right interaction.*

4.2   Construction of Concurrent NMWI

Suppose f be a one-way function with efficiently recognizable range, Com is a statistically binding commitment scheme, $Sign = (Gen, Sig, Ver)$ is a signature scheme existentially unforgeable against adaptive chosen message attacks. Let R be the polynomial-time relation that determines L. The concurrent NMWI argument (P, V) is described in *Figure 4*.

For $x \in L$, from the completeness of $(\mathcal{P}_{pk}, \mathcal{V}_{pk})$, we can get the completeness of (P, V). For $x \notin L$, if there exists a malicious prover who succeeds in convincing V the false statement with a non-negligible probability, this implies that the prover can invert f with non-negligible probability, a contradiction with the one-wayness of f. Thus, (P, V) is an argument for language L. In addition, (P, V) is in commit-and-prove style. Therefore, we have

Lemma 3. *The construction (P, V) is a commit-and-prove argument for language L with the witness relation R.*

As in [17], the NMWI property stems from the message scheduling technique. More precisely, for an accepting right interaction that the man-in-the-middle adversary generates (provided that its tag is different from the left), there exists a right proof in this right interaction which the adversary can not answer correctly by only mauling the left interaction. The proof of security of (P, V) is similar to that of LPV08 scheme [17], with the *difference* that here we reduce the NMWI

Common Input: An instance x of length n and a tag t.
Private Input of P: The witness w for $x \in L$.
Stage 1:
- V picks uniformly $r \in \{0,1\}^n$, computes $u = f(r)$ and sends u to P.
- P aborts if u is not in the range of f.

Stage 2:
- P computes a commitment c to w by using Com and generates a pair of (sk, pk)keys of the signature scheme $Sign$. Then he sends (c, pk) to V.

Stage 3:
- On common input $(u, (x, c)), t$, using tag pk, P runs algorithm $\mathcal{P}_{pk}$ to prove to V (running $\mathcal{V}_{pk}$) that there exists a value r s.t. u=f(r) or there exist w, r, s.t. $c = Com(w, r) \wedge (x, w) \in R$. The challenge length of the verifier is $2n$. Let $trans$ be the transcript of this interaction.
- P signs $t \circ trans$ to produce a signature s.

Fig. 4. The construction of concurrent NMWI argument (P, V)

property to the witness-indistinguishability of some WI argument, instead of the computationally hiding property of some commitment scheme.

In [22], it was shown that a *one-many* concurrent NMWI argument is *fully* concurrent NMWI. Therefore, it is sufficient to prove that (P, V) satisfies one-many concurrent non-malleable witness indistinguishability. In the proof, the following notations will be used later: For a PPT one-many concurrent man-in-the-middle adversary $\mathcal{A}$ with auxiliary input z, suppose $\mathcal{A}$ interacts with P on common inputs x and t in the left. In the right, $\mathcal{A}$ opens up $m = poly(k)$ sessions with honest verifier V and in the j-th right interaction the statement proved by A is x^j. Let pk be the public key used in the left, pk^j be the public key in the j-th right interaction, and $|pk| = |pk^j| = \ell$.

Lemma 4. *For any $j \in \{1, 2, \cdots, m\}$, if the j-th right interaction is accepting and its tag $t^j \neq t$, then except with negligible probability, $pk^j \neq pk$.*

Proof: If there exists a $j \in \{1, 2, \cdots, m\}$ such that the j-th right interaction is accepting and its tag $t^j \neq t$ and $pk^j = pk$, then we can construct a PPT algorithm B to break the security of $Sign$. On input a public key pk and the auxiliary input $z' = x \circ w \circ z$, B incorporates $\mathcal{A}$ and simulates the left and right interactions internally. Specifically, in the left interaction, B does what an honest prover does except that he gets a signature on $t \circ trans$ by querying the signature oracle. In the right interaction, B runs the honest verifier algorithm to interact with $\mathcal{A}$. At last, B outputs the signature in the j-th right interaction. Therefore, B gets a signature on a new message, which contradicts with the security of $Sign$.

Let $\Gamma(\mathcal{A}, z)$ denote the distribution of all joint view τ of $\mathcal{A}$ and honest verifiers in the right, such that $\mathcal{A}$ starts the right interaction directly after receiving the messages in τ. Let $Z(z, \tau) = z \circ \tau \circ x_1 \circ w_1 \circ \cdots \circ x_q \circ w_q$, where each (x_i, w_i) is a statement-witness pair proved by $\mathcal{A}(z)$ in τ, $q \in \{1, 2, \cdots, m\}$.

Lemma 5. *For the argument (P, V) constructed above, for any man-in-the-middle adversary $\mathcal{A}$, there exists a witness indistinguishable argument $(\hat{P}, \hat{V})$ and an expected PPT malicious verifier $\hat{V}^*$ for $(\hat{P}, \hat{V})$ such that the following two ensembles are computationally indistinguishable*

(a) $\{\tau \leftarrow \Gamma(\mathcal{A}, z), z' \leftarrow Z(z, \tau) :< \hat{P}(w), \hat{V}^*(z') > (x, t)\}_{x \in L, z \in \{0,1\}^*}$

(b) $\{wmim^{\mathcal{A}}(x, w, t, z)\}_{x \in L, z \in \{0,1\}^*}$

Proof: The protocol $(\hat{P}, \hat{V})$ can be constructed as follows: $(\hat{P}, \hat{V})$ works in the same way as (P, V) except that in stage 2 *design* is executed an arbitrary number of rounds and in each round the verifier picks $i \in \{0, 1\}$ to ask the prover to run $design_i$. By the completeness, soundness and the witness indistinguishability of Π, $(\hat{P}, \hat{V})$ is an argument with witness indistinguishability.

The malicious verifier $\hat{V}^*$ can be constructed in the following way: On common input x, a tag t, auxiliary input $z' = z \circ \tau \circ x_1 \circ w_1 \circ \cdots \circ x_q \circ w_q$, $\hat{V}^*$ interacts with $\hat{P}(x, w, t)$ to emulate the one-many man-in-the-middle of $P, \mathcal{A}, V$ in the following way:

- $\hat{V}^*$ incorporates $\mathcal{A}(z, t)$ and externally interacts with $\hat{P}$ to emulate the left interaction of $(P, \mathcal{A})$ by requesting the appropriate *design* expected by $\mathcal{A}(z, t)$.
- $\hat{V}^*$ performs the right interactions of $(\mathcal{A}, V)$ internally.
- For right interaction $j \in \{q+1, \cdots, m\}$ which is not accepting or the tag $t^j = t$, set $w^j = \perp$. By *safe-point lemma*, for right interaction $j \in \{q+1, \cdots, m\}$ which is accepting and has a tag $t^j \neq t$, $\hat{V}^*$ rewinds interaction j from the first safe-point to extract the witness w^j, without rewinding any left interaction. At last, $\hat{V}^*$ outputs $(w^1, \cdots, w^q, w^{q+1}, \cdots, w^m)$.

It can be seen that the running time of $\hat{V}^*$ is expected polynomial time and what $\hat{V}^*(z')$ outputs is indistinguishable from $wmim^{\mathcal{A}}(x, w, t, z)$.

Lemma 6. (P, V) *is a one-many concurrent non-malleable witness indistinguishable argument.*

Proof: From the witness indistinguishability of $(\hat{P}, \hat{V})$, for the expected PPT $\hat{V}^*$ constructed as above, for the witnesses $w, w' \in W_L(x)$, it holds that the following two ensembles are computationally indistinguishable

- $\{< \hat{P}(w), \hat{V}^*(z') > (x, t)\}_{x \in L, z' \in \{0,1\}^*}$
- $\{< \hat{P}(w'), \hat{V}^*(z') > (x, t)\}_{x \in L, z' \in \{0,1\}^*}$

which implies the indistinguishability of the following two ensembles

- $\{\tau \leftarrow \Gamma(\mathcal{A}, z), z' \leftarrow Z(z, \tau) :< \hat{P}(w), \hat{V}^*(z') > (x, t)\}_{x \in L, z \in \{0,1\}^*}$
- $\{\tau \leftarrow \Gamma(\mathcal{A}, z), z' \leftarrow Z(z, \tau) :< \hat{P}(w'), \hat{V}^*(z') > (x, t))\}_{x \in L, z \in \{0,1\}^*}$

By lemma 5, the ensembles listed below are computationally indistinguishable

- $\{\tau \leftarrow \Gamma(\mathcal{A}, z), z' \leftarrow Z(z, \tau) :< \hat{P}(w), \hat{V}^*(z') > (x, t)\}_{x \in L, z \in \{0,1\}^*}$
- $\{wmim^{\mathcal{A}}(x, w, t, z)\}_{x \in L, z \in \{0,1\}^*}$

Therefore, we get the computational indistinguishability of the following two ensembles

- $\{wmim^{\mathcal{A}}(x, w, t, z)\}_{x \in L, z \in \{0,1\}^*}$
- $\{wmim^{\mathcal{A}}(x, w', t, z)\}_{x \in L, z \in \{0,1\}^*}$

which concludes the proof of the following theorem.

Theorem 3. *If one-way functions exist, then every language $L \in NP$ has a concurrent NMWI argument which can be shown secure relying on black-box techniques.*

On the Complexity Assumption: For simplicity of exposition, the above description of (P, V) relies on the existence of one-way functions with efficiently recognizable range. In fact, our protocol can be modified to work with any arbitrary one-way function by simply providing a witness-hiding proof that an element is in the range of the one-way function.

5   Conclusion

Non-Malleability is an important property that guarantees the security of cryptographic protocols against man-in-the-middle attacks. Many non-malleable constructions such as non-malleable zero knowledge and non-malleable commitments have been worked out. Witness indistinguishability, as one of the most basic cryptographic protocols, its non-malleability is much of interest.

In this paper, we firstly give a separation between NMWI and SNMW and point out that the SNMWI scheme based on one-way function given in [18] is not NMWI. Then, we show that a variant of LPV08 scheme [17] is concurrent NMWI. Compared with the NMWI construction of [22] which was built from a non-black-box claw-free permutation based NMZK argument, our scheme relies on black-box techniques and is based on the existence of one-way functions.

Acknowledgments. We thank anonymous referees for their helpful suggestions to improve this paper.

References

1. Barak, B.: How to Go Beyond the Black-Box Barrier. In: 42nd Annual Symposium on Foundations of Computer Science (FOCS 2001), pp. 106–115. IEEE Computer Society Press, Washington (2001)
2. Barak, B.: Constant-Round Coin-Tossing or Realizing the Shared random String Model. In: 43rd Annual Symposium on Foundations of Computer Science (FOCS 2002), pp. 345–355. IEEE Computer Society Press, Washington (2002)
3. Blum, M.: How to Prove a Theorem So No One Else Can Claim It. In: International Congress of Mahematicians (ICM 1986), pp. 1444–1451 (1986)
4. Cramer, R., Damgård, I., Schoenmakers, B.: Proof of Partial Knowledge and Simplified Design of Witness Hiding Protocols. In: Desmedt, Y.G. (ed.) CRYPTO 1994. LNCS, vol. 839, pp. 174–187. Springer, Heidelberg (1994)

5. Di Crescenzo, G., Ishai, Y., Ostrovsky, R.: Non-Interactive and Non-Malleable Commitments. In: Vitter, J.S. (ed.) 30th Annual ACM Symposium on Theory of Computing (STOC 1998), pp. 141–150. ACM Press, New York (1998)

6. Di Crescenzo, G., Katz, J., Ostrovsky, R., Smith, A.: Efficient and Non-interactive Non-malleable Commitment. In: Pfitzmann, B. (ed.) EUROCRYPT 2001. LNCS, vol. 2045, pp. 40–59. Springer, Heidelberg (2001)

7. Damgård, I., Groth, J.: Non-Interactive and Reusable Non-Malleable Commitment Schemes. In: Larmore, L.L., Goemans, M.X. (eds.) 35th Annual ACM Symposium on Theory of Computing (STOC 2003), pp. 426–437. ACM Press, New York (2003)

8. Damgård, I.: On Σ-Protocols, http://www.daimi.au.dk/~ivan/CPT.html

9. Dolev, D., Dwork, C., Naor, M.: Non-Malleable Cryptography. SIAM Journal on Computing 30(2), 391–437 (2000)

10. Dork, C., Naor, M., Sahai, A.: Concurrent Zero Knowledge. In: Vitter, J.S. (ed.) 30th Annual ACM Symposium on Theory of Computing (STOC 1998), pp. 141–150. ACM Press, New York (1998)

11. Even, S., Goldreich, O., Lempel, A.: A Randomized Protocol for Signing Contracts. Communications of the ACM 28(6), 637–647 (1985)

12. Fischlin, M., Fischlin, R.: Efficient Non-Malleable Commitment Schemes. In: Bellare, M. (ed.) CRYPTO 2000. LNCS, vol. 1880, pp. 413–431. Springer, Heidelberg (2000)

13. Feige, U., Lapidot, D., Shamir, A.: Multiple Non-Interactive Zero Knowledge Proofs Under General Assumptions. SIAM Journal on Computing 29(1), 1–28 (1999)

14. Feige, U., Shamir, A.: Witness Indistinguishable and Witness Hiding Protocols. In: Ortiz, H. (ed.) 22nd Annual Symposium on Theory of Computing (STOC 1990), pp. 416–426. ACM Press, New York (1990)

15. Garay, J.A., Mackenzie, P., Yang, K.: Strengthening Zero Knowledge Protocols Using Signatures. Journal of Cryptology 19(2), 169–209 (2006)

16. Goldwasser, S., Micali, S., Rackoff, C.: The Knowledge Complexity of Interactive Proof Systems. SIAM Journal on Computing 18(1), 186–208 (1989)

17. Lin, H., Pass, R., Venkitasubramaniam, M.: Concurrent Non-malleable Commitments from Any One-Way Function. In: Canetti, R. (ed.) TCC 2008. LNCS, vol. 4948, pp. 571–588. Springer, Heidelberg (2008)

18. Lin, H., Pass, R., Venkitasubramaniam, M.: A Unified Framework for Concrrent Security: Universal Composability from Stand-Alone Non-Malleability. In: Mitzenmacher, M. (ed.) 41st Annual ACM Symposium on Theory of Computing (STOC 2009), pp. 179–188. ACM Press, New York (2009)

19. Lin, H., Pass, R., Tseng, W.-L.D., Venkitasubramaniam, M.: Concurrent Non-Malleable Zero Knowledge Proofs. In: Rabin, T. (ed.) CRYPTO 2010. LNCS, vol. 6223, pp. 429–446. Springer, Heidelberg (2010)

20. Naor, M.: Bit Commitment Using Pseudo-Randomness. Journal of Crypto. 4(2), 151–158 (1991)

21. Ostrovsky, R., Persiano, G., Visconti, I.: Concurrent Non-Malleable Witness Indistinguishability and Its Applications. Electronic Colloquium on Computational Complexity (ECCC), Report (2006)

22. Ostrovsky, R., Persiano, G., Visconti, I.: Constant-Round Concurrent Non-malleable Zero Knowledge in the Bare Public-Key Model. In: Aceto, L., Damgård, I., Goldberg, L.A., Halldórsson, M.M., Ingólfsdóttir, A., Walukiewicz, I. (eds.) ICALP 2008, Part II. LNCS, vol. 5126, pp. 548–559. Springer, Heidelberg (2008)

23. Ostrovsky, R., Persiano, G., Visconti, I.: Simulation-Based Concurrent Non-Malleable Commitments and Decommitments. In: Reingold, O. (ed.) TCC 2009. LNCS, vol. 5444, pp. 91–108. Springer, Heidelberg (2009)

24. Pass, R., Rosen, A.: New and Improved Constructions of Non-Malleable Cryptographic Protocols. In: Gabow, H.N., Fagin, R. (eds.) 37th Annual ACM Symposium on Theory of Computing (STOC 2005), pp. 533–542. ACM Press, New York (2005)

25. Pass, R., Rosen, A.: Concurrent Non-Malleable Commitments. In: 46th Annual Symposium on Foundations of Computer Science (FOCS 2005), pp. 563–572. IEEE Computer Society Press, Washington (2005)

26. Rompel, J.: One-Way Function are Necessary and Sufficient for Secure Signatures. In: Ortiz, H. (ed.) 22nd Annual ACM Symposium on Theory of Computing (STOC 1990), pp. 387–394. ACM Press, New York (1990)

27. Richardson, R., Kilian, J.: On the Concurrent Composition of Zero-Knowledge Proofs. In: Stern, J. (ed.) EUROCRYPT 1999. LNCS, vol. 1592, pp. 415–431. Springer, Heidelberg (1999)

28. Sahai, A.: Non-Malleable Non-Interactive Zero Knowledge and Adaptive Chosen Cipher-Text Security. In: 40th Annual Symposium on Foundations of Computer Science (FOCS 1999), pp. 543–553. IEEE Computer Society Press, Washington (1999)

29. De Santis, A., Di Crescenzo, G., Ostrovsky, R., Persiano, G., Sahai, A.: Robust Non-interactive Zero Knowledge. In: Kilian, J. (ed.) CRYPTO 2001. LNCS, vol. 2139, pp. 566–598. Springer, Heidelberg (2001)

Pseudorandom Generators Based on Subcovers for Finite Groups*

Chenggen Song, Maozhi Xu, and Chunming Tang

Laboratory of Mathematics and Applied Mathematics, School of Mathematical
Sciences, Peking University, Beijing 100871, P.R. China
{cgsong,mzxu,cmtang}@pku.edu.cn

Abstract. In this article, we describe a new approach for constructing pseudorandom generator using subcovers for large finite groups. The
Gennaro generator (J Cryptol 15:91-110, 2005) and Farashahi et al. generator (PKC LNCS 4450: 426-441, 2007) can be specific instances of the
new approach. We focus, in particular, on the class of symmetric group
S_n and construct the first pseudorandom generator based on non-abelian
group whose security can be proven. We successfully carry out a test of
the generator based on non-abelian group by using the NIST Statistical
Test Suite.

Keywords: Pseudorandom generator, Subcover, Finite group.

1 Introduction

Many (if not all) cryptographic algorithms rely on the availability of some form
of randomness. However, perfect randomness is a scare resource. Fortunately, for
almost all cryptographic applications, it is sufficient to use pseudorandom bits.

The concept of cryptographically strong pseudorandom bit generator was introduced in papers by Blum and Micali [2] and Yao [28]. In 1989, Goldreich
[10] stated the computational indistinguishability, and Håstad et al. [7] showed
how to construct a pseudorandom generator from any one-way function. Several
generator based on hard assumption have been presented [1, 4, 9, 21, 23, 26].
However, their hard assumptions (RSA,DLP,DDH) lie in the intractability of
the mathematical problems closer to number theory than group theory. Number
theory deals mostly with abelian groups.

Unfortunately, Shor's quantum algorithm [24] showed that the integer factoring and solving the DLP seem not hard. Some papers payed their attention to
the non-abelian group, and gave some cryptosystem based on non-abelian group
[12–17].

In 1984, Magliveras et al. [13] showed a new random number generator from
permutation groups. Marquarde et al. [18] generalized this approach to general
finite groups. However, their can not give a more rigorously mathematical proof
of the randomness of the generators, rather than statistical test.

---

* This work is supported by NSFC Grant No.10990011

C.-K. Wu, M. Yung, and D. Lin (Eds.): Inscrypt 2011, LNCS 7537, pp. 379–392, 2012.

1.1 Our Contributions

We show that it is possible to construct an efficient non-abelian-group-based pseudorandom generator whose security can be proven.

We generalize the DDH problem to decision subcover membership problem. On this basis, we modify and generalize the Gennaro generator [9] and Farashahi et al. [4] generator such that the modified version is provable secure under the decision subcover membership problem. Actually, we describe a new approach for constructing pseudorandom generator using subcovers for large finite groups.

We present three specific instances of the new pseudorandom generator.

The first two instances are similar to the genreators in [4, 9]. In the last instance, we give the fist pseudorandom generator based on non-abelian group whose security can be proven. We focus, in particular, on the class of symmetric group S_n. We successfully carry out a test of the generator by using the NIST Statistical Test Suite[22].

1.2 Organization

The paper is organized as follows. In Section 2 we summarize notations, definitions and prior work. Section 3 presents the main contribution of our paper, the new approach for constructing pseudorandom generator and its security proof. In Section 4, we give three instances of our new generator and present the statistical test result of the third instance. At last, in Section 5, we draw some conclusions.

2 Preliminaries

In this section we summarize notations, definitions and prior work which is relevant to our result.

2.1 Pseudorandom Generators

In this subsection, we recall basic definitions about pseudorandom generators. More details can be found in [11].

Let X and Y be random variables taking on values in a finite set $\mathcal{S}$. The statistical distance between X and Y is defined as

$$\triangle(X, Y) = \frac{1}{2} \sum_{\gamma \in \mathcal{S}} |Pr[X = \gamma] - Pr[Y = \gamma]|.$$

We say that algorithm D distinguishes X and Y with advantage ϵ if and only if

$$|Pr[D(X) = 1] - Pr[D(Y) = 1]| \geq \epsilon.$$

If the statistical distance between X and Y is less than ϵ then no algorithm distinguishes X and Y with advantage ϵ (see, e.g., [11]).

Throughout, we let U_M denote a random variable uniformly distributed on $\mathbb{Z}_M$. And, we say that an algorithm is T-time if it halts in time at most T.

Consider a deterministic algorithm $PRG : \{0,1\}^n \mapsto \{0,1\}^m$, where $m > n$. Loosely speaking, PRG is called a pseudorandom generator if it maps uniformly distributed input into an output which is computationally indistinguishable from uniform. The input is called the seed and the output is called the pseudorandom sequence. The precise definition is given as follows.

A T-time algorithm $D : \{0,1\}^m \mapsto \{0,1\}$ is said to be a (T,ϵ)-distinguisher for PRG if

$$|Pr[D(PRG(U_{2^n})) = 1] - Pr[D(U_{2^m}) = 1]| \geq \epsilon$$

Definition 1. *(Pseudorandom generator) Algorithm PRG is called a (T,ϵ)- secure pseudorandom generator if no (T,ϵ)-distinguisher exists for PRG.*

A (T, ϵ)-secure pseudorandom generator is said to be secure if time T is bounded by the polynomial in n and ϵ is negligible ($\epsilon < \frac{1}{p(n)}$, for any positive polynomial $p(\cdot)$).

2.2   Subcovers for Finite Groups

In this section we briefly present notations, definitions and some facts about logarithmic signature, covers, subcovers for finite group, and their induced mappings. For more details, the reader is referred to [12–17].

Let $\mathcal{G}$ be a finite abstract group, we define the width of $\mathcal{G}$ as the positive integer $w_{\mathcal{G}} = \lceil \log |\mathcal{G}| \rceil$. Denote by $\mathcal{G}^{[\mathbb{Z}]}$ the collection of all finite sequences of elements in $\mathcal{G}$.

Suppose that $\alpha = [A_1, A_2, \cdots, A_s]$ is a sequence of $A_i \in \mathcal{G}^{[\mathbb{Z}]}$ such that $\sum_{i=1}^{s} |A_i|$ is bounded by a polynomial in $w_{\mathcal{G}}$. Let $\mathcal{S}$ be a subset of $\mathcal{G}$. We call α a cover for $\mathcal{S}$ if each element $h \in \mathcal{S}$ can be expressed in at least one way as a product of the from

$$h = g_1 \cdot g_2 \cdots g_{s-1} \cdot g_s \tag{1}$$

for $g_i \in A_i$.

In particular, if each $h \in \mathcal{S}$ can be expressed in exactly one way by Eq.(1), α is called a logarithmic signature for $\mathcal{S}$. If the elements in each set $A_i, i = 1, \cdots, s$, are chosen at random from the elements in $\mathcal{G}$, we refer to α as a random cover. If $\mathcal{S} = \mathcal{G}$, α is called a cover for $\mathcal{G}$.

The A_i are called the blocks, and the vector $(r_1, \cdots, r_s)$ with $r_i = |A_i|$ the type of α. We say that α is nontrivial if $s \geq 2$ and $r_i \geq 2$ for $1 \leq i \leq s$, otherwise α is said to be trivial.

We define the order of α as the positive integer $|\alpha| = \prod_{i=1}^{s} r_i$ and the width of α as the positive integer $w_\alpha = \lceil \log |\alpha| \rceil$. Actually, the widths of $\mathcal{G}$ and α play important roles in the construction of the pseudorandom generator. We extend the definition of covers to subcovers.

Definition 2. *Let $\mathcal{G}$, α, $w_{\mathcal{G}}$ and w_α be as above. We say that α is a subcover of $\mathcal{G}$ if $w_{\mathcal{G}} > w_\alpha$. Denote the subset $\mathcal{S}_\alpha$ of $\mathcal{G}$ as*

$$\mathcal{S}_\alpha = \{ h \mid \exists \; g_i \in A_i, \; s.t. \; h = g_1 \cdot g_2 \cdots g_{s-1} \cdot g_s \} \tag{2}$$

Notice that $|\mathcal{S}_\alpha| \leq |\alpha|$.

Let $\alpha = [A_1, A_2, \cdots, A_s]$ is a cover (subcover) of type $(r_1, r_2, \cdots, r_s)$ for a group $\mathcal{G}$ with $A_i = [a_{i,1}, a_{i,2}, \cdots, a_{i,r_i}]$. Let $m_1 = 1$ and $m_i = \prod_{j=1}^{i-1} r_j$ for $i = 2, \cdots, s$. Let τ denote the canonical bijection from $\mathbb{Z}_{r_1} \oplus \mathbb{Z}_{r_2} \oplus \cdots \oplus \mathbb{Z}_{r_s}$ on $\mathbb{Z}_{|\alpha|}$, i.e.,

$$\tau : \mathbb{Z}_{r_1} \oplus \mathbb{Z}_{r_2} \oplus \cdots \oplus \mathbb{Z}_{r_s} \to \mathbb{Z}_{|\alpha|},$$

$$\tau(j_1, j_2, \cdots, j_s) := \sum_{i=1}^{s} j_i m_i.$$

Using τ, we now define the surjective mapping $\breve{\alpha}$ induce by α:

$$\breve{\alpha} : \mathbb{Z}_{|\alpha|} \to \mathcal{S}_\alpha,$$

$$\breve{\alpha}(x) := a_{1,j_1} a_{2,j_2} \cdots a_{s,j_s}.$$

where $(j_1, j_2, \cdots, j_s) = \tau^{-1}(x)$. Since τ and τ^{-1} are efficiently computable, the mapping $\breve{\alpha}$ is efficiently computable.

2.3   Decision Subcover Membership Problem

In general, the problem of finding a factorization as in Eq.(1) with respect to a cover is presumed intractable. For finite groups, there are instances where the problem is believed to be hard. For example, let q be a prime power for which the discrete logarithm problem in the multiplicative group of the finite field $\mathbb{F}_q$ is believed to be hard. Suppose that $2^{l-1} < q - 1 \leq 2^l$, and let $\mathcal{G}_l$ be the multiplicative group $\mathbb{F}_q^*$ just mentioned. let g be a generator of $\mathcal{G}_l$. If $\alpha_l = [A_1, A_2, \cdots, A_l]$, where $A_i = [1, g^{2^{i-1}}]$, than α_l is a cover of $\mathcal{G}_l$, and factorization problem with respect to α_l amounts to solving the discrete logarithm problem (DLP) in $\mathcal{G}_l$.

If we consider the group $\mathcal{G}_l \times \mathcal{G}_l$ and $\alpha_l' = [B_1, B_2, \cdots, B_l]$ where $B_i = [(1,1), (g^{2^{i-1}}, g'^{2^{i-1}})]$, we get the DDH problem. Actually, we could consider the DDH problem as a subgroup membership problem.

There are several papers discuss the public key cryptosystem based on the subgroup membership problem [8, 19, 20, 27]. However, their problem assumption is limited on abelian groups. In this paper, we extend the problem to general groups.

If α is a subcover for $\mathcal{G}$, we always consider the membership problem respect to α, that is

Definition 3. *(Decision Subcover Membership Problem) Let α is a subcover for $\mathcal{G}$. Let $X \in \mathbb{Z}_{|\alpha|}$ be a random variable uniformly distributed on $\mathbb{Z}_{|\alpha|}$ and $Y \in \mathcal{G}$*

be a random variable uniformly distributed on $\mathcal{G}$. Algorithm D is said to solve the decision subcover membership problem respect to α in $\mathcal{G}$ with advantage ϵ if it distinguishes the random variables $\breve{\alpha}(X)$ and Y with advantage ϵ, that is,

$$|Pr[D(\breve{\alpha}(X), 1^{w_{\mathcal{G}}})] = 1] - Pr[D(Y, 1^{w_{\mathcal{G}}}) = 1]| \geq \epsilon$$

We say that the DSM (decision subcover membership) problem is hard in $\mathcal{G}$ if there is no efficient algorithm to solve the DSM problem in time T with advantage ϵ where T is bounded by the polynomial in $w_{\mathcal{G}}$ and ϵ is negligible.

3   DSM Generator

In this section, our main result is presented. We propose a new provably secure pseudorandom generator. We call it the DSM generator, since the security of this generator relies on the intractability of the decision subcover membership problem in the corresponding group. In contrast with the Gennaro's generator[9] and the DDH generator[4], the DSM generator can be based on any group, no matter abelian or not.

3.1   Construction of the Generator

Let $\mathcal{G}$ be a finite group with width $w_{\mathcal{G}}$ and α be a subcover of $\mathcal{G}$ with width w_{α}. We assume that there is a bijective mapping $Fun : \mathcal{G} \mapsto \mathbb{Z}_{|\mathcal{G}|}$, which efficiently identify elements of $\mathcal{G}$ with numbers in $\mathbb{Z}_{|\mathcal{G}|}$. Thus, on uniformly distributed input, function Fun produces uniformly distributed output.

For given $|\mathcal{G}|$ and $|\alpha|$, let $M = \lceil \frac{|\mathcal{G}|}{|\alpha|} \rceil$. We denote $ODE_{|\mathcal{G}|,|\alpha|}$ as the function with input $x \in_R \mathbb{Z}_{\mathcal{G}}$ and output unique (a, b) satisfy $x = a * M + b$, $0 \leq a < |\alpha|$ and $0 \leq b < M$.

We present our generator in Algorithm 1. The seed of the DSM generator is $s_0 \in \mathbb{Z}_{|\alpha|}$. The DSM generator transforms the seed into the sequence of k pseudorandom numbers from $\mathbb{Z}_M$.

Algorithm 1. DSM Generator

INPUT: $s_0 \in \mathbb{Z}_{|\alpha|}$, $k > 0$
OUTPUT: k pseudorandom integers from $\mathbb{Z}_M$.
    for i from 1 to k **do**
        Set $(a, b) = ODE_{|\mathcal{G}|,|\alpha|}(Fun(\breve{\alpha}(s_{i-1})))$
        Set $s_i = a$
        Set $output_i = b$
    end for
Return$(output_1, \cdots, output_k)$

Note that the subcover α is not part of the seed. The subcover is system parameters that is not necessarily kept secret. This is different from the RPGM generator based on permutation groups[14]. In the security analysis of the generator we assume that α is known to the distinguisher.

3.2 Security Analysis

Actually, if the DSM problem is hard in $\mathcal{G}$, we can consider the function $\breve{\alpha}$ as a pseudorandom generator with expansion factor $l(w_\alpha) = w_\mathcal{G}$ for the reason $w_\alpha < w_\mathcal{G}$.

The following theorem implies that under the DSM problem for group $\mathcal{G}$ an output sequence of the DSM generator is indistinguishable from a sequence of uniformly random numbers in $\mathbb{Z}_M$. We modify the proof in [4] to satisfy our theorem.

Theorem 1. *Suppose these exists a T-time algorithm that distinguishes the output of DSM generator from the sequence of independent uniformly distributed random numbers in $\mathbb{Z}_M$ with advantage ϵ. The the DSM problem in $\mathcal{G}$ can be solved in time T with advantage ϵ/k.*

Proof. Suppose there exists a T-time algorithm D that distinguishes the output of the DSM generator from a sequence of independent uniformly distributed random numbers in $\mathbb{Z}_M$ with advantage ϵ, that is ,

$$|Pr[D(output_1, \cdots , output_k) = 1] - Pr[D(U) = 1]| \geq \epsilon,$$

where $U = (u_1, \cdots , u_k)$, $u_i \in_R \mathbb{Z}_M$, $i = 1, \cdots , k$. Let $j \in_R 1, 2, \cdots , k$. Due to the classical hybrid argument (see, e.g., [11]Section 3.2.3),

$$|Pr[D(Z_j) = 1] - Pr[D(Z_{j+1})] = 1| \geq \epsilon/k,$$

where

$$Z_j = (u_1, \cdots , u_{j-1}, output_1, \cdots , output_{k-j+1}),$$

the probability is taken not only over internal coin flips of D but also over the choice of j. Now, we show how to solve the DSM problem in $\mathcal{G}$ using the distinguisher D as a building block. Let $h \in \mathcal{G}$. A solver for the DSM problem decide if $h \in \mathcal{S}_\alpha$ or h are uniformly distributed random elements of $\mathcal{G}$ as follows.

Select $j \leftarrow_R 1, 2, \cdots , k$
Select $r_1, \cdots , r_{j-1} \leftarrow_R \mathbb{Z}_M$
Select $(a, b) = ODE_{|\mathcal{G}|, |\alpha|}(Fun(h))$
Set $s_1 = a$
Set $r_j = b$
for $i = 2$ to $k - j$ do
    Set $(a, b) = ODE_{|\mathcal{G}|, |\alpha|}(Fun(\breve{\alpha}(s_{i-1})))$
    Set $s_i = a$
    Set $r_{i+j-1} = b$
end for
Set $Z \leftarrow (r_1, \cdots , r_k)$
Return $D(Z)$

If $h \in \mathcal{S}_\alpha$ then r_j is distributed as the first output of the DSM generator respectively, so Z is distributed as Z_j.

Otherwise, if h is a uniformly distributed random elements of $\mathcal{G}$ then r_{j+1} is distributed as the first output of DSM generator while r_j is uniformly distributed over $\mathbb{Z}_M$ and independent of r_{j+1}, so Z is distributed as Z_{j+1}.

Therefore, the above algorithm solves the DSM problem in $\mathcal{G}$ in time at most T with advantage ϵ/k. $\qquad\square$

Our generator outputs numbers in $\mathbb{Z}_M$ rather than bits. However, converting random numbers into random bits is a relatively easy problem. For instance, one can use Algorithm Q_2 from [6].

For the sake of simplicity, throughout this paper, we assume that M is close to a power of 2, that is $0 \leq (2^n - M)/2^n \leq \delta$ for a small δ and a positive integer n. So, the uniform element $U_M \in_R \mathbb{Z}_M$ is statistically close to n uniformly random bits.

The following simple lemma is a well-known result

Lemma 1. *Under the condition that $0 \leq (2^n - M)/2^n \leq \delta$, the statistical distance between U_M and U_{2^n} is bounded above by δ*

Proof. The proof can be found in [3] $\qquad\square$

The next statement implies that if M is close to a power of 2, the DSM generator is a cryptographically secure pseudorandom generator under the condition the DSM problem is hard in $\mathcal{G}$.

Corollary 1. *Let $0 \leq (2^n - M)/2^n \leq \delta$. Suppose the DSM generator is not (T, ϵ)-secure. Then there exists an algorithm that solves the DSM problem in $\mathcal{G}$ in time at most T with advantage $\epsilon/k - \delta$.*

Proof. Suppose there exists a distinguisher $D : \{0,1\}^{kn} \mapsto \{0,1\}$ that runs in time at most T and

$$|Pr[D(output_1, \cdots, output_k) = 1] - Pr[D(U_{2^{kn}}) = 1]| \geq \epsilon.$$

Let $u_i \in_R \mathbb{Z}_M$, $i = 1, \cdots, k$ and $U = (u_1, \cdots, u_k)$. Lemma 1 implies that the statistical distance $\triangle(U, U_{2^{kn}}) \leq k\delta$. Thus,

$$|Pr[D(output_1, \cdots, output_k) = 1] - Pr[D(U) = 1]| \geq \epsilon - k\delta$$

Now, the statement follows from Theorem 1. $\qquad\square$

4   Specific Instances of the DSM Generator

To implement the DSM generator, one has to choose the finite group $\mathcal{G}$ and function Fun that enumerates the group elements. One can construct applicable subcover α so that $M = \lceil \frac{|\mathcal{G}|}{|\alpha|} \rceil$ is close to a power of 2, that is, $0 \leq (2^n - M)/2^n \leq \delta$ for a small δ and a positive integer n. We like to emphasize that this assumption is made for the sake of simplicity only.

In this section, we propose three specific instances of the DSM generator. Actually, the first two instances are presented in formerly papers [4, 9] in different models and the two instances can be evidences of the security of our DSM generator. In the last instance, we propose the first pseudorandom generator based on non-abelian group whose security can be proven.

4.1   DSM Generators Based on the c-DLSE Assumption

To present the first instance of DSM generator, we modify the idea of [9] to our generator.

Let p be a safe prime, $p = 2q+1$, where q is prime. Let $\mathcal{G}_1$ be the multiplicative group modulo p, thus $\mathcal{G}_1 = \mathbb{F}_p^*$. The bijection mapping Fun_1 is the natural mapping. Let $g \in \mathcal{G}_1$ be a generator of $\mathcal{G}_1$. For a parameter $c \in \mathbb{Z}$, $c < w_{\mathcal{G}_1}$ we set the subcover α_1 as $\alpha_1 = [A_0, A_1, A_2, \cdots, A_c]$ where $A_0 = [1, g]$ and $A_i = [1, g^{2^{|w_{\mathcal{G}_1}|+i-c-1}}]$, $i = 1, 2, \cdots, c$.

Let $s_0 \in_R \mathbb{Z}_{2^c+1}$ be the seed. Generator $DSMG_1$ is a deterministic algorithm that transforms the seed into the sequence of $k(w_{\mathcal{G}_1} - c - 1)$ pseudorandom bits.

Algorithm 2. $DSMG_1$

INPUT: $s_0 \in \mathbb{Z}_{2^c+1}$, $k > 0$
OUTPUT: k **pseudorandom integers from** $\mathbb{Z}_{2^{w_{\mathcal{G}_1}-c-1}}$.
    for i **from** 1 **to** k **do**
        Set $(a, b) = ODE_{2^{w_{\mathcal{G}_1}}, 2^c+1}(Fun_1(\check{\alpha}_1(s_{i-1})))$
        Set $s_i = a$
        Set $output_i = b$
    end for
Return($output_1, \cdots, output_k$**)**

Actually, the generator $DSMG_1$ is the same as the $IRG_{n,c}$ presented in [9].

Theorem 2. *[9] Under the c-DLSE Assumption, $IRG_{n,c}$ is a secure pseudo-random number genreator.*

In [9], Gennaro suggested the parameters $w_{\mathcal{G}_1} = 3000$ and $c = 225$.

4.2   DSM Generators Based on the DDH Assumption

In this section, wo modify the idea in [4].

Let p be a safe prime, $p = 2q + 1$, where q is prime. We assume that $0 \le (2^n - q)/2^n \le \delta$ for a small δ and some integer n. Let $\mathbb{G}_2$ be a group of nonzero quadratic residues modulo p. The order of $\mathbb{G}_2$ equals q. Consider the following function $f : \mathbb{G}_2 \mapsto \mathbb{Z}_q$,

$$f(x) = \begin{cases} x & 1 \le x \le q; \\ p - x & q + 2 \le x \le p; \\ 0 & \text{otherwise.} \end{cases}$$

Let $\mathcal{G}_2 = \mathbb{G}_2 \times \mathbb{G}_2$ and $(u, v) \in \mathcal{G}_2$, $u, v \in \mathbb{G}_2$. Thus, we can construction the bijection function Fun_2 as $Fun_2((u, v)) = f(u) * q + f(v)$.

We set the subcover α_2 as $\alpha_2 = [B_1, B_2, \cdots, B_n]$ where $B_i = [(1, 1), (x^{2^{i-1}}, y^{2^{i-1}})]$, $i = 1, 2, \cdots, n$, and $x, y \in \mathbb{G}_2$.

Algorithm 3. $DSMG_2$

INPUT: $s_0 \in \mathbb{Z}_{2^n}$, $k > 0$
OUTPUT: k **pseudorandom integers from** $\mathbb{Z}_{2^n}$.
   for i **from** 1 **to** k **do**
      Set $(a, b) = ODE_{q^2,2^n}(Fun_2(\breve{\alpha}_2(s_{i-1})))$
      Set $s_i = a$
      Set $output_i = b$
   end for
Return($output_1, \cdots, output_k$**)**

Let $s_0 \in \mathbb{Z}_{2^n}$ be the seed. Generator $DSMG_2$ is a deterministic algorithm that transforms the seed into the sequence of kn pseudorandom bits.

Actually, the generator $DSMG_2$ is similar to the PRG_1 in [4].

Proposition 1. *[4] Suppose pseudorandom generator PRG_1 is not (T, ϵ)-secure. Then there exists an algorithm that solves the DDH problem in $\mathbb{G}_2$ in time at most T with advantage $\epsilon/k - \delta$.*

In [4], Farashahi et al. suggested that $n = 1600$. If we consider the group $\mathbb{G}_2 \times \mathbb{G}_2 \times \cdots \times \mathbb{G}_2$, we can get a more efficient pseudorandom generator as the generator NG_p presented in [23].

4.3 DSM Generators Based on Non-Abelian Groups

In this subsection, we propose the first pseudorandom generator based on non-abelian groups whose security can be proven.

Let $\mathcal{G}_3 = S_l$ be the full symmetric group on $\{1, 2, \cdots, l\}$. Let $\alpha_3 = [C_1, C_2, \cdots, C_s]$ be a subcover of type $(r_1, r_2, \cdots, r_s)$ for $\mathcal{G}_3$.

It is known that if $\mathcal{S}_{\alpha_3}$ is a subgroup of $\mathcal{G}_3$, then the (subcover) membership problem can be tested in polynomial time in the width and the number of the generators of the subgroup [5]. If we assume that for every $i = 1, 2, \cdots, s$, $1_{\mathcal{G}_3} \in C_i$, then we have the following proposition,

Proposition 2. *Let $\mathcal{G}_3$ and α_3 be defined as above, and for every $i = 1, 2, \cdots, s$, $1_{\mathcal{G}_3} \in C_i$. If $\mathcal{S}_{\alpha_3}$ is a subgroup, then it equals to the group generated by $C_1 \cup C_2 \cup \cdots \cup C_s$.*

Proof. Because that for every $i = 1, 2, \cdots, s$, $1_{\mathcal{G}_3} \in C_i$, we have that for every $a \in C_i$, $i = 1, 2, \cdots, s$, $a \in \mathcal{S}_{\alpha_3}$. If $\mathcal{S}_{\alpha_3}$ is a subgroup, we have that $a^{-1} \in \mathcal{S}_{\alpha_3}$ too. Thus, $\mathcal{S}_{\alpha_3} = < C_1 \cup C_2 \cup \cdots \cup C_s >$. $\qquad\square$

If $\mathcal{S}_{\alpha_3}$ is a subgroup, we can use the $Schreier - Sims$ [25] or similar algorithm to build "strong generators" for $\mathcal{S}_{\alpha_3}$ using $C_1 \cup C_2 \cup \cdots \cup C_s$.

Proposition 3. *Let C be a subset of $\mathcal{G}_3$, $1_{\mathcal{G}_3} \in C$. If there exists $a_1, a_2 \in \mathcal{G}_3$, so that $a_1 C a_2$ is a subgroup of $\mathcal{G}_3$, then C is a subgroup too.*

Proof. If $a_1 C a_2$ is a subgroup of $\mathcal{G}_3$, then for every $x \in C$, there exists a unique y so that $a_1 x a_2 a_1 y a_2 = 1_{\mathcal{G}_3}$. That is $a_2 a_1 x a_2 a_1 y = 1_{\mathcal{G}_3}$, so we have the $a_2 a_1 C$ is a subgroup. So C is a coset of $a_2 a_1 C$. However, $1_{\mathcal{G}_3} \in C$, so C is a subgroup of $\mathcal{G}_3$. □

We always assume that for every $i = 1, 2, \cdots, s$, $1_{\mathcal{G}_3} \in C_i$. In any case, to our knowledge, there is no efficient algorithm to solve the decision subcover membership problem respect to β if $\mathcal{S}_\beta$ is not contained in any subgroup. In this case, the group generated by $C_1 \cup C_2 \cup \cdots \cup C_s$ is equal to S_l.

We consider the bijection mapping Fun_3 as a iterative algorithm, that is if we can "enumerate" the symmetric group S_{l-1} then we can "enumerate" the symmetric group S_l. Let $(k_1, k_2, \cdots, k_l) \in S_l$, we construct the bijection mapping Fun_3 on S_l as,

---

Algorithm 4. bijection mapping Fun_3

INPUT: $(k_1, k_2, \cdots, k_l) \in S_l$, l
OUTPUT: a number in $\{1, 2, \cdots, l!\}$.
    If $l = 1$ **Return** 1.
    Set $tmp = (k_1 - 1) * (l - 1)!$.
    Set $(m_1, m_2, \cdots, m_{l-1}) = (k_2, k_3, \cdots, k_l)$.
    If $m_i > k_1$ **Set** $m_i = m_i - 1$, for $i = 1, 2, \cdots, l - 1$.
    Set $tmp = tmp + Fun_3((m_1, m_2, \cdots, m_{l-1}), l - 1)$.
    Return tmp.

Let $s_0 \in \mathbb{Z}_{|\alpha_3|}$ be the seed. Generator $DSMG_3$ is a deterministic algorithm that transforms the seed into the sequence of $k(w_{\mathcal{G}_3} - w_{\alpha_3})$ pseudorandom bits. Let $M = \lceil \frac{|\mathcal{G}_3|}{|\alpha_3|} \rceil$, and assume that $0 \le (2^n - M)/2^n \le \delta$ for a small δ and a positive integer n.

Algorithm 5. $DSMG_3$

INPUT: $s_0 \in \mathbb{Z}_{|\alpha_3|}$, $k > 0$
OUTPUT: k pseudorandom integers from $\mathbb{Z}_M$.
    for i from 1 to k **do**
        Set $(a, b) = ODE_{|\mathcal{G}_3|, |\alpha_3|}(Fun_3(\check{\alpha}_3(s_{i-1})))$
        Set $s_i = a$
        Set $output_i = b$
    end for
Return$(output_1, \cdots, output_k)$

The next statement follows from Corollary 1.

Proposition 4. *Suppose pseudorandom generator $DSMG_3$ is not (T, ϵ)-secure. Then there exists an algorithm that solves the DSM problem in $\mathcal{G}_3$ in time at most T with advantage $\epsilon/k - \delta$.*

Table 1. NIST test results on DSM_3

Test	P-value	Protortion	P-value	Propotion	P-value	Propotion
NonOverlapping	0.603841	0.9870	0.614226	0.9890	0.471146	0.9850
Template	0.628790	0.9900	0.612147	0.9920	0.104993	0.9910
	0.933472	0.9860	0.984415	0.9900	0.129620	0.9870
	0.886162	0.9890	0.632955	0.9870	0.668321	0.9930
	0.846338	0.9920	0.082010	0.9870	0.263572	0.9870
	0.856359	0.9920	0.624627	0.9940	0.864494	0.9930
	0.725829	0.9870	0.877083	0.9900	0.820143	0.9900
	0.834308	0.9840	0.950247	0.9900	0.059734	0.9880
	0.915317	0.9880	0.192724	0.9930	0.248014	0.9900
	0.560545	0.9880	0.983453	0.9870	0.664168	0.9910
	0.755819	0.9940	0.867692	0.9870	0.111389	0.9870
	0.846338	0.9910	0.388990	0.9860	0.858002	0.9900
	0.380407	0.9920	0.026410	0.9910	0.044508	0.9990
	0.254411	0.9900	0.277082	0.9920	0.104993	0.9930
	0.012562	0.9890	0.227180	0.9910	0.562591	0.9880
	0.366918	0.9910	0.954930	0.9950	0.488534	0.9910
	0.075719	0.9870	0.169981	0.9900	0.277082	0.9910
	0.371941	0.9860	0.900569	0.9910	0.979788	0.9830
	0.786830	0.9880	0.314544	0.9880	0.846338	0.9910
	0.965860	0.9910	0.068999	0.9870	0.099513	0.9930
	0.794391	0.9860	0.524101	0.9940	0.954015	0.9870
	0.264901	0.9890	0.478839	0.9900	0.894918	0.9910
	0.583145	0.9920	0.864494	0.9900	0.682823	0.9870
	0.798139	0.9910	0.361938	0.9970	0.892036	0.9960
	0.786830	0.9940	0.639202	0.9930	0.616305	0.9870
	0.486588	0.9870	0.745908	0.9910	0.717714	0.9870
	0.096000	0.9870	0.562591	0.9870	0.610070	0.9900
	0.717714	0.9880	0.936823	0.9890	0.968863	0.9880
	0.788728	0.9960	0.323668	0.9890	0.674543	0.9940
	0.267573	0.9890	0.375313	0.9910	0.783019	0.9920
	0.520102	0.9980	0.310049	0.9920	0.520102	0.9880
	0.221317	0.9910	0.721777	0.9930	0.131122	0.9920
	0.039329	0.9940	0.955835	0.9940	0.655854	0.9910
	0.021262	0.9930	0.904708	0.9920	0.560545	0.9940
	0.344048	0.9950	0.893482	0.9900	0.986227	0.9920
	0.610070	0.9930	0.574903	0.9920	0.292519	0.9860
	0.329850	0.9900	0.676615	0.9910	0.947308	0.9910
	0.827279	0.9860	0.957612	0.9940	0.382115	0.9890
	0.599693	0.9870	0.512137	0.9880	0.289667	0.9940
	0.769527	0.9890	0.229559	0.9890	0.165340	0.9850
	0.115387	0.9910	0.277082	0.9910	0.729870	0.9900
	0.927677	0.9920	0.771469	0.9950	0.329850	0.9900
	0.969588	0.9920	0.138069	0.9920	0.013664	0.9910
	0.597620	0.9940	0.189625	0.9890	0.556460	0.9900
	0.208837	0.9930	0.965083	0.9860	0.062821	0.9890
	0.689019	0.9930	0.735908	0.9890	0.765632	0.9940
	0.624627	0.9860	0.715679	0.9840	0.117432	0.9870
	0.442831	0.9870	0.353733	0.9900	0.769527	0.9900
	0.610070	0.9860	0.536163	0.9910	0.717714	0.9920
	0.649612	0.9930				

Table 1. *(continued)*

Test	P-value	Protortion	P-value	Propotion	P-value	Propotion
Frequency	0.589341	0.9870				
BlockFrequency	0.908760	0.9890				
CumulativeSums	0.484646	0.9820	0.721777	0.9880		
Runs	0.431754	0.9890				
LongestRun	0.222480	0.9920				
Rank	0.807412	0.9910				
FFT	0.142872	0.9880				
OverlappingTemplate	0.568739	0.9900				
Universal	0.896345	0.9880				
ApproximateEntropy	0.192724	0.9910				
RandomExcursions	0.609831	0.9821	0.916724	0.9918	0.081494	0.9853
	0.741558	0.9967	0.346518	0.9902	0.522624	0.9951
	0.073678	0.9918	0.837157	0.9902		
RandomExcursions Variant	0.376284	0.9918	0.792601	0.9902	0.894495	0.9886
	0.851109	0.9869	0.626879	0.9935	0.579291	0.9918
	0.275709	0.9918	0.535799	0.9902	0.522624	0.9918
	0.579291	0.9951	0.256024	0.9837	0.142912	0.9869
	0.801804	0.9853	0.721743	0.9902	0.991206	0.9918
	0.021803	0.9902	0.519349	0.9918	0.519349	0.9918
	0.519349	0.9918	0.061921	0.9935		
Serial	0.988677	0.9930	0.686955	0.9920		
LinearComplexity	0.729870	0.9870				

One can set that $|C_i|$ equals to 4 or a prime, $i = 1, 2, \cdots, s$, to get the minimum storage requirements. In particularly, we choose $l = 200$, so $w_{S_{200}} = 1246$. We set the type of α_3 as the sequence of all the 315 prime factors (repeated) of $|S_{200}|$ except 2. So, $w_{\alpha_3} = 1049$ and $M = 2^{197}$. For every block C_i, we set $1_{S_{200}} \in C_i$ and $(1, 2) \in C_{2k}$, $(1, 2, \cdots, 100) \in C_{2k+1}$. At last, we construct the rest part of α_3 by randomly choosing elements in S_{200}. Then we get $w_{\mathcal{G}_3} - w_{\alpha_3} = 197$ bits per 315 multiplications in symmetric group. We know that the multiplication in symmetric group can be implemented very fast.

The NIST Statistical Test Suite consists of fifteen core tests that, by reason of different parameter inputs, can be considered as 188 statistical tests. We generate 1000 sample sequences of 10^6 bits by the generator DSM_3. The significance level σ was chosen to be the default of 0.01 (99% confidence), so a test has passed if the additional P-values ≥ 0.01, and the proportion of binary sequences passing the statistical test should lie above 0.9805607. The range of acceptable proportions is determined using the confidence interval defined as, $(1 - \sigma) \pm 3 \times \sqrt{\frac{\sigma(1-\sigma)}{m}}$, where m is is the sample size. It can be seen that the DSM_3 passes the NIST Statistical Test suite. The details can be found in Table 1.

For more discussion about covers (subcovers) on symmetric group, readers are referred to [13–17].

5   Conclusion

In this paper, we generalize the DDH problem to decision subcover membership problem. On this basis, we modify and generalize the Gennaro generator [9] and Farashahi et al. [4] generator such that the modified version is provable secure under the decision subcover problem. Actually, we describe a new approach for constructing pseudorandom generator using subcovers for large finite groups.

We present three specific instances of the new pseudorandom generator.

The first two instances are similar to the genreators in [4, 9]. These two instances can be evidences of the security of our new approach.

In the last instance, we give the fist pseudorandom generator based on non-abelian group whose security can be proven. We successfully carry out a test of the generator by using the NIST Statistical Test Suite.

References

1. Alexi, W., Chor, B., Goldreich, O., Schnorr, C.: RSA and Rabin functions: certain parts are as hard as the whole. SIAM J. Comput. 17(2), 194–209 (1988)
2. Blum, M., Micali, S.: How to generator cryptographically strong sequences of the pseudo-random bits. SIAM J. Comput. 13(4), 850–864 (1984)
3. Chevassut, O., Fouque, P., Gaudry, P., Pointcheval, D.: The Twist-AUgmented Technique for Key Exchange. In: Yung, M., Dodis, Y., Kiayias, A., Malkin, T. (eds.) PKC 2006. LNCS, vol. 3958, pp. 410–426. Springer, Heidelberg (2006)
4. Farashahi, R.R., Schoenmakers, B., Sidorenko, A.: Efficient Pseudorandom Generators Based on the DDH Assumption. In: Okamoto, T., Wang, X. (eds.) PKC 2007. LNCS, vol. 4450, pp. 426–441. Springer, Heidelberg (2007)
5. Furst, M., Hopcroft, J., Luks, E.: Polynomial-time algorithms for permutations groups. In: Proceeding of the 21st IEEE Symposium and Foundation of Camputation Sciense, pp. 36–41 (1980)
6. Juels, A., Jakobsson, M., Shriver, E., Hillyer, B.K.: How to turn loaded dice into fair coins. IEEE Transactions on Information Theory 46(3), 911–921 (2000)
7. Håstad, J., Impagliazzo, R., Levin, L., Luby, M.: A Pseudorandom generator from any one-way function. In: Proc. 21st ACM Symp. on Theory of Computing (1989)
8. Gjøsteen, K.: Symmetric Subgroup Membership Problems. In: Vaudenay, S. (ed.) PKC 2005. LNCS, vol. 3386, pp. 104–119. Springer, Heidelberg (2005)
9. Gennaro, R.: An improved pseudo-random genreator based on the discrete logarithm problem. J. Cryptol. 18(2), 91–110 (2005)
10. Goldreich, O.: A note on computational indistinguishability. Infor. Proc. Letters 34, 277–281 (1990)
11. Goldreich, O.: Foundations of cryptography, basis tools. Cambridge University Press (2001)
12. Lempken, W., Magliveras, S.S., van Trung, T., Wei, W.: A public key cryptosystem based on non-abelian finite groups. J. Cryptol. 22, 62–74 (2009)
13. Magliveras, S.S., Oberg, B.A., Surkan, A.J.: A new random number generator from permutation groups. Rend. del Sem. Matemat. e Fis. di Milano 54, 203–223 (1984)
14. Magliveras, S.S.: A cryptosystem from logarithmic signatures of finite groups. In: Proceedings of the 29th Midwest Symposium on Circuits and Systems, pp. 972–975. Elsevier, Amsterdam (1986)

15. Magliveras, S.S., Memon, N.D.: Random Permutations from Logarithmic Signatures. In: Sherwani, N.A., Kapenga, J.A., de Doncker, E. (eds.) Great Lakes CS Conference 1989. LNCS, vol. 507, pp. 199–205. Springer, Heidelberg (1991)
16. Magliveras, S.S., Memon, N.D.: Algebraic properties of cryptosystem PGM. J. Cryptol. 5, 167–183 (1992)
17. Magliveras, S.S., Stinson, D.R., van Trung, T.: New approaches to designing public key cryptosystems using one-way functions and trapdoors in finite groups. J. Cryptol. 15, 285–297 (2002)
18. Marquardt, P., Svaba, P., van Trung, T.: Pseudorandom number generators based on random convers for finite groups. Des. Codes Cryptogr. (2011)
19. González Nieto, J.M., Boyd, C., Dawson, E.: A Public Key Cryptosystem Based on the Subgroup Membership Problem. In: Qing, S., Okamoto, T., Zhou, J. (eds.) ICICS 2001. LNCS, vol. 2229, pp. 352–363. Springer, Heidelberg (2001)
20. Nieto, J.M.G., Boyd, C., Dawson, E.: A public key cryptosystem based on the subgroup membership problem. Des. Codes Cryptogr. 36, 301–316 (2005)
21. Patel, S., Sundaram, G.S.: An Efficient Discrete Log Pseudo Random Generator. In: Krawczyk, H. (ed.) CRYPTO 1998. LNCS, vol. 1462, pp. 304–317. Springer, Heidelberg (1998)
22. Rukhin, A., et al.: Statistical test suite for random and pseudorandom number generators for cryptographic applications. NIST Special Publication 800-22, Revised April 2010, National Institute of Standards and Technology (2010), http://csrc.nist.gov/rng
23. Shi, H., Jiang, S., Qin, Z.: More efficient DDH pseudo-random generators. Des. Codes Cryptogr. 55, 45–64 (2010)
24. Shor, P.: Polynomial time algorithms for prime factorization and discrete logarithms on quantum computers. SIAM J. Comput. 26(5), 1484–1509 (1997)
25. Sims, C.C.: Some group-theoretic algorithms. In: Newman, M.F. (ed.) Topics in Algebra. Lecture Notes in Math., vol. 697, pp. 108–124. Springer (1978)
26. Steinfeld, R., Pieprzyk, J., Wang, H.: On the Provable Security of an Efficient RSA-Based Pseudorandom Generator. In: Lai, X., Chen, K. (eds.) ASIACRYPT 2006. LNCS, vol. 4284, pp. 194–209. Springer, Heidelberg (2006)
27. Yamamura, A., Saito, T.: Private Information Retrieval Based on the Subgroup Membership Problem. In: Varadharajan, V., Mu, Y. (eds.) ACISP 2001. LNCS, vol. 2119, pp. 206–220. Springer, Heidelberg (2001)
28. Yao, A.: Theory and Applications of Trapdoor Functions. In: Proc. IEEE FOCS, pp. 80–91 (1982)

Author Index

Adhikari, Avishek   341

Bringas, Pablo G.   24

Cao, Jianyu   93
Cao, Zhengjun   77
Chen, Shan   210
Chen, Shao-zhen   227
Chen, Xiaofeng   142

Dai, Yi-bin   227
Dou, Yunqi   102

Fan, Xiao   77
Fan, Xiubin   160
Feng, Dengguo   113, 160

Gao, Neng   309
Gu, Dawu   57
Guo, Teng   86

Hu, Lei   363
Huang, Guifang   363
Huang, Wei   113

Jiang, Zhengtao   142
Jing, Jiwu   251

Kato, Ryo   289
Kiribuchi, Naoto   289

Li, Bao   131
Li, Nan   179
Li, Yajun   93
Li, Yanjun   237
Libert, Benoît   1
Lin, Dongdai   210
Liu, Feng   86
Liu, Yamin   131
Liu, Yining   93
Liu, Zongbin   251
Lu, Xianhui   131

Ma, Chuangui   102
Mei, Qixiang   131

Mouha, Nicky   57
Mu, Yi   179

Nguyen, Phong Q.   22
Nishide, Takashi   289, 341

Pan, Wuqiong   251
Preneel, Bart   57

Qiao, TongXu   44

Rhee, Kyung-Hyune   341

Sakurai, Kouichi   341
Santos, Igor   24
Sekar, Gautham   269
Sha, Qian   77
Shen, Bing   44
Sheng, Rennong   113
Song, Chenggen   379
Song, Haixin   160
Sun, Peiyong   93
Susilo, Willy   179

Tang, Chunming   379
Tian, Haibo   142

Ugarte-Pedrero, Xabier   24

Wang, Lin   44
Wang, Qingju   57
Weng, Jiang   102
Wu, Chuankun   86, 160
Wu, Wenling   237

Xia, Luning   251
Xiang, Ji   309
Xie, Xiang   195
Xu, Maozhi   379

Yan, Jihong   93
Yoshiura, Hiroshi   289
Yu, Meng   251
Yu, Xiaoli   237
Yung, Moti   1

Zhang, Jiang   195, 324
Zhang, Lei   237

Zhang, Rui   195
Zhang, Xusheng   210
Zhang, Zhenfeng   195, 324

Zhao, Liang   341
Zhao, Xianfeng   113
Zhou, Jian   309